A HANDBOOK FOR PANCHAYATI RAJ ADMINISTRATION (TAMIL NADU)

By Prof. G. Palanithurai:

Building Skill and Capability among Gram Panchayat
Capacity Building for Local Body Leaders
Dyanamics of New Panchayati Raj Systems in India (in 15 volumes series)
Emerging Dimensions in Decentralisation
Ethnic Identity and National Loyalty of Ethnic Group (A case study of Tamil Nadu)
Grassroot Democracy in Indian Society
New Panchayati Raj System at Work: An Evaluation
New Panchayati Raj in Tamil Nadu (with Act in Original)
Process and Performance of Gram Panchayat Women and Dalit Presidents
(with 38 case studies of Tamil Nadu Panchayats)
Rural Transformation and People's Entitlements
New Public Management: A Case Analysis of District Administration

---

About the Authors

Ganpathy Palanithurai, is a Professor in Rajiv Gandhi Chair, Gandhgram Rural Institute heading the Department of Political Science and Development Administration. He has been associated himself with State Planning Commission of Tamil Nadu, Population Foundation of India, Rajiv Gandhi Foundation, CAPART, Ministry of Rural Areas and Employment and DANIDA (Danish-Indo Development Agency) in specific areas of activities in connection with empowerment of people. He has to his credit twenty-four books, seventy-five articles in reputed journals, ten working papers, seven monographs, seven monographs, seven review articles on three major areas, namely, Legislative Behaviour, Ethnicity and Panchayati Raj System. He was a recipient of Fellowship from Sastri Indo-Canadian Institute, New Delhi and World Academy of Art and Science, USA. He was a visiting fellow in the MiGill University, Canada in 1989. He is a member of the Expert Committee constituted by the Government of Tamil Nadu, to monitor the training programme for local body leaders.

K. Vallinayagam is a graduate in law and retired after 36 years of service in the Rural Department of the Tamil Nadu Government. He was a member of the Committee constituted to frame Rules under the Tamil Nadu Panchayats Act, 1994. He is now practising as an advocate in the Madras High Court and actively involved in the training of Panchayat Raj functionaries in collaboration with the Rajiv Gandhi Chair for Panchayati Raj Studies of the Gandhigram Rural Institute (Deemed University).

N.S. Chidambaram worked in the Rural Development Department for more than 36 years and retired as Additional Director of Rural Development. Also, he worked as Principal of Rural Extension Training Centre for more than four years and took active part in imparting training to the officers and staff of the Rural Development Department. He was a member of the Committee constituted to frame Rules under the Tamil Nadu Panchayats Act. Currently he is actively involved in imparting training to the Panchayati Raj functionaries.

K. Subramanian retired as Additional Director of Rural Development Department after 37 years of service. He was also involved actively in the formulation of Rules under the Tamil Nadu Panchayats Act, 1994.

Also, he was involved in the training of Panchayati Raj functionaries sponsored by the Rajiv Gandhi Chair for Panchayati Raj Studies of Gandhigram Rural Institute (Deemed University), for nearly 4000 village Panchayat Presidents for both men and women.

A HANDBOOK FOR PANCHAYATI RAJ ADMINISTRATION (TAMIL NADU)

G. PALANITHURAI
K. VALLINAYAGAM
N. S. CHIDAMBARAM
K. SUBRAMANIAM

CONCEPT PUBLISHING COMPANY, NEW DELHI-110059

Cataloging in Publication Data—DK
Courtesy: D.K. Agencies (P) Ltd. <docinfo@dkagencies.com>

A Handbook for panchayati raj administration (Tamil Nadu) / G. Palanithurai ... [et al.].
p. cm.
Includes index.
ISBN 8180693406

1. Panchayat—India—Tamil Nadu. 2. Local government—Law and legislation—India—Tamil Nadu. I. Palanithurai, G. (Ganapathy), 1953-

DDC 320.840 954 82 22

ISBN 81-8069-340-6

First Published 2007

Published and Printed by
Ashok Kumar Mittal
Concept Publishing Company
A/15-16, Commercial Block, Mohan Garden
New Delhi-110059 (INDIA)

Phones : 25351460, 25351794
Fax : 091-11-25357103
Email : publishing@conceptpub.com

FOREWORD

Panchayati Raj Institutions have come to stay in India. They are now an integral part of our federal structure as per the Constitution of India. All the Indian States have enacted confirmatory legislations almost a decade ago. The elected Panchayats are now in position throughout the country. As all of us know, occupying the chair is very different from exercising the powers or discharging the duties. In how many States have the Panchayats been empowered to discharge their legitimate duties? Even in the States where Panchayats have substantial powers, have they adopted systems and procedures not only to guide the elected representatives but also to ensure transparency? Have these rules and regulations been widely disseminated so that the elected representatives always remain accountable to their electorate?

Historically, Tamil Nadu has been one State where the Village Panchayats have been very effective. With the advent of the community development programmes, the village panchayats and the panchayat unions in Tamil Nadu did become mere development agencies of the State, carrying out the schemes assigned to them by the Central and State Governments. The Constitution (Seventy-Third Amendment) attempts however to alter this position and enhance the prestige of the Panchayats by truly making them organs of governance in our federal set up. This handbook therefore rightly starts with the contents of the Constitution amendment and follows it up with the Tamil Nadu Panchayats Act, 1994, which carries out the mandate of the Constitution in concrete terms.

As a State that is well known for its administrative capabilities, Tamil Nadu has framed several rules and regulations, dealing with the nuts and bolts of the Panchayat administration during the last ten years. The number and size of these regulations are so vast that an ordinary citizen, as also an elected representative, has to wade through voluminous literature, before locating the rules required to be followed to meet an immediate requirement. This handbook is an excellent effort by Dr. G. Palanithurai and his colleagues to make this task simpler. I must compliment them for their painstaking efforts, first to collect the required rules, notifications and government instructions and then to present them in an orderly fashion so that an average reader can lay his hands on the rules and procedures he or she is looking for, without much difficulty.

This handbook, to start with, reproduces the rules and instructions common to all the three tiers of Panchayats in Chapter III and then proceeds to single out the regulations relating to individual tiers including the Grama Sabha. Reproduction of the Right to Information Act as well as the Tamil Nadu Transparency in Tenders Act which are the inseparable ingredients to ensure transparency at the Panchayat level makes this handbook complete. By quoting the relevant rules, notifications and instructions verbatim, this volume eliminates possible errors of interpretation.

Dr. G. Palanithurai and his colleagues deserve our appreciation for bringing out this excellent compilation. However, rules and regulations can provide only the skeleton for decentralized governance. The flesh and blood will have to come from the way in which we make use of these rules and regulations for the welfare of the people, particularly the poor and the weaker sections of the society at the village level. Let us hope that the efforts of Prof. Palanithurai and his friends are effectively put to use and this handbook is followed both in letter and spirit so that decentralized governance in Tamil Nadu becomes a model for other States in India.

Bangalore **Dr. S.S. Meenakshi Sundaram**

ACKNOWLEDGEMENTS

Even after eleven years of development administration carried out at the grassroots, one cannot find an administrative manual for Panchayat administration at the three levels. The 73rd Amendment to the Constitution of India and the subsequent State Conformity Act of Tamil Nadu 1994 established the Panchayat system as an institution of governance for development on a sustainable basis. There are different stakeholders with different roles and responsibilities in Panchayat administration. All those responsibilities are to be carried out by different individuals well within the established framework of administration. To guide the administration meticulously we need to have an administrative manual.

We had a manual for Panchayat administration as per the Tamil Nadu Panchayats Act of 1958. But after the introduction of the New Panchayati Raj System through the 73rd Amendment to the Constitution of India and the state conformity legislation, there is no such administrative manual to guide the Panchayat administration. In the absence of a Panchayat manual both officials and elected representatives find it very difficult to run the administration. Moreover a number of problems are being faced by both elected representatives and non-elected officials in the Panchayat system at all the three levels as there is no standardized format. In many places mere adhocism prevails and the observations and rulings of officials are the final word. Administrative actions are not uniform. They vary from district to district.

Against this background, we have taken the initiative to bring out a manual as in other states. We took earnest efforts to collect the needed information. It took a year to complete this work. We have done a thorough work. We requested Dr. S.S. Meenakshi Sundaram, Former Secretary to the Government of India, Department of Rural Development, to give a foreword to this manual. He went through the manual and offered constructive suggestions. All his suggestions have been well taken and incorporated. We express our gratitude to the Ford Foundation and PRIA, New Delhi for their support in helping us to bring out this manual.

We express our sincere thanks to all officials who extended their help in the form of needed material. We record our sincere thanks to Dr. S.S. Meenakshi Sundaram for his foreword to this manual. Finally, we express our thanks to our Project Staff for their excellent co-operation in completing this task. Mr. Ashok Mittal of Concept Publishing Company has to be complimented and thanked for his devoted attention to Panchayat work. In the present context he brought out this volume within a short span of time.

Gandhigram

G. Palanithurai
K. Vallinayagam
N. S. Chidambaram
K. Subramaniam

CONTENTS

PART VI
RULES RELATING TO PANCHAYAT UNION COUNCIL

PART VIII
RULES AND INSTRUCTIONS RELATING TO DISTRICT PLANNING COMMITTEE

PART IX
RIGHT TO INFORMATION ACT

PART X
TAMIL NADU TRANSPARENCY IN TENDERS ACT, 1998

PART I

THE CONSTITUTION (SEVENTY-THIRD AMENDMENT) ACT, 1992

1.1. THE CONSTITUTION (SEVENTY-THIRD AMENDMENT) ACT, 1992

An Act further to amend the Constitution of India

Be it enacted by Parliament in the Forty-Third year of the Republic of India as follows:

1. Short Title and Commencement—(1) This Act may be called the Constitution (Seventy-third Amendment) Act, 1992.

(2) It shall come into force on such date as the Central Government may, by notification in the official Gazette, appoint.

2. Insertion of New Part IX—After Part VIII of the Constitution, the following Part shall be inserted, namely:

'PART IX THE PANCHAYATS'

Definition (243)—In this Part, Unless the Context, Otherwise Requires:

(a) "District" means a district in a State;
(b) "Grama Sabha" means a body consisting of persons registered in the electoral rolls relating to a village comprised within the area of a Panchayat at the village level;
(c) "intermediate level" means a level between the village and district levels specified by the Governor of a State by public notification to be the intermediate level for the purpose of this Part;
(d) "Panchayat" means an institution (by whatever name called) of self-government constituted under Article 243B, for the rural areas;
(e) "Panchayat area" means the territorial area of a Panchayat;
(f) "Population" means the population as ascertained at the last preceding census of which the relevant figures have been published;
(g) "Village" means a village specified by the Governor by public notification to be a village for the purposes of this Part and includes a group of villages so specified.

Grama Sabha (243A)—A Grama Sabha may exercise such powers and perform such functions at the village level as the Legislature of a State may, by law, provide.

Constitution of Panchayats (243B)—(1) There shall be constituted in every State, Panchayats at the Village, intermediate and district levels in accordance with the provision of this Part.

(2) Notwithstanding anything in clause (1), Panchayats at the intermediate level may not be constituted in a State having a population not exceeding twenty lakhs.

Composition of Panchayats (243C)— (1) Subject to the provisions of this Part, the Legislature of a State may, by law, make provisions with respect to the composition of Panchayats:

Provided that the ratio between the population of the territorial area of a Panchayat at any level and the number of seats in such Panchayat to be filled by election shall, so far as practicable, be the same throughout the State.

(2) All the seats in a Panchayat shall be filled by persons chosen by direct election from territorial constituencies in the Panchayat area and, for this purpose, each Panchayat area shall be divided into territorial constituencies in such manner that the ratio between the population of each constituency and the number of seats allotted to it shall, so far as practicable, be the same throughout the Panchayat area.

(3) The Legislature of a State may, by law, provide for the representation:

(a) Of the Chairpersons of the Panchayats at the village level, in the Panchayats at the intermediate level or, in the case of a State not having Panchayats at the intermediate level, in the Panchayats at the district level;
(b) Of the Chairpersons of the Panchayats at the intermediate level, in the Panchayats at the district level;
(c) Of the members of the House of the People and the members of the Legislative Assembly of the State representing constituencies which

comprise wholly or partly a Panchayat area at a level other than the village level, in such Panchayat;

(d) Of the members of the Council of States and the members of the Legislative Council of the State, where they are registered as electors within:

(i) A Panchayat area at the intermediate level, in Panchayat at the intermediate level;

(ii) A Panchayat area at the district level, in Panchayat at the district level.

(4) The Chairperson of a Panchayat and other members of a Panchayat whether or not chosen by direct election from territorial constituencies in the Panchayat area shall have the right to vote in the meetings of the Panchayats.

(5) The Chairperson of—(a) a Panchayat at the village level shall be elected in such manner as the Legislature of a State may, by law, provide, and

(b) a Panchayat at the intermediate level or district level shall be elected by, and from amongst, the elected members thereof.

Reservation of Seats (243 D)—(1) Seats shall be reserved for:

(a) the Scheduled Castes; and

(b) the Scheduled Tribes, in every Panchayat and the number of seats so reserved shall bear, as nearly as may be, the same proportion to the total number of seats to be filled by direct election in that Panchayat as the population of the Scheduled Castes in that Panchayat areas or of the Scheduled Tribes in that Panchayat area bears to the total population of that area and such seats may be allotted by rotation to different constituencies in a Panchayat.

(2) Not less one-third of the total number of seats reserved under clause (1) shall be reserved for women belonging to the Scheduled Castes or, as the case may be, the Scheduled Tribes.

(3) Not less than one-third (including the number of seats reserved for women belonging to the Scheduled Castes and the Scheduled Tribes) of the total number of seats to be filled by direct election in every Panchayat shall be reserved for women and such seats may be allotted by rotation to different constituencies in a Panchayat.

(4) The offices of the Chairpersons in the Panchayats at the village or any other level shall be reserved for the Scheduled Castes, the Scheduled Tribes and women in such manner as the Legislature of a State may, by law, provide:

Provided that the number of offices of Chairpersons reserved for the Scheduled Castes and the Scheduled Tribes in the Panchayats at each level in any State shall bear, as nearly as may be, the same proportion to the total number of such offices in the Panchayats at each level, as the population of the Scheduled Castes in the State or of the Scheduled Tribes in the State bears to the total population of the State:

Provided further that not less than one-third of the total number of offices of Chairpersons in the Panchayats at each level shall be reserved for women:

Provided also that the number of offices reserved under this clause shall be allotted by rotation to different Panchayats at each level.

(5) The reservation of seats under clauses (1) and (2) and the reservation of offices of Chairpersons (other than the reservation for women) under clause (4) shall cease to have effect on the expiration of the period specified in Article 334.

(6) Nothing in this Part shall prevent the Legislature of a State from making any provision for reservation of seats in any Panchayat or offices of Chairperson in the Panchayats at any level in favour of backward class of citizens.

Duration of Panchayats etc. (243 E)—(1) Every Panchayat, unless sooner dissolved under any law for the time being in force, shall continue for five years from the date appointed for its first meeting and no longer.

(2) No amendment of any law for the time being in force shall have the effect of causing dissolution of a Panchayat at any level, which is functioning immediately before such amendment, till the expiration of its duration specified in clause (1).

(3) An election to constitute a Panchayat shall be completed:

(a) before the expiry of its duration specified in clause (1);

(b) before the expiration of a period of six months from the date of its dissolution:

Provided that where the remainder of the period for which the dissolved Panchayat would have continued is less than six months, it shall not be necessary to hold any election under this clause for constituting the Panchayat for such period.

(4) A Panchayat constituted upon the dissolution of a Panchayat before the expiration of its duration

shall continue only for the remainder of the period for which the dissolved Panchayat would have continued under clause (1) had it not been so dissolved.

Disqualification for Membership (243 F)—(1) A person shall be disqualified for being chosen as, and for being, a member of a Panchayat:

(a) if he is so disqualified by or under any law for the time being in force for the purposes of elections to the Legislature of the State concerned:

Provided that no person shall be disqualified on the ground that he is less than twenty five years of age, if he has attained the age of twenty-one years.

(b) if he is so disqualified by or under any law made by the Legislature of the State.

(2) If any question arises as to whether a member of a Panchayat has become subject to any of the disqualifications mentioned in clause (1), the question shall be referred for the decision of such authority and in such manner as the Legislature of a State may, by law, provide.

Powers, Authority and Responsibilities of Panchayats (243 G)—Subject to the provisions of this Constitution, the Legislature of a State may, by law, endow the Panchayats with such powers and authority as may be necessary to enable them to function as institutions of self-government and such law may contain provisions for the devolution of powers and responsibilities upon Panchayats at the appropriate level, subject to such conditions as may be specified therein, with respect to:

(a) the preparation of plans for economic development and social justice,

(b) the implementation of schemes for economic development and social justice as may be entrusted to them including those in relation to the matters listed in the Eleventh Schedule.

Power to Impose Taxes by, and Funds of, the Panchayats (243 H)—The Legislature of a State may, by law:

(a) authorize a Panchayat to levy, collect and appropriate such taxes, duties, tolls and fees in accordance with such procedure and subject to such limits;

(b) assign to a Panchayat such taxes, duties, tolls and fees levied and collected by the State Government for such purposes and subject to such conditions and limits;

(c) provide for making such grants-in-aid to the Panchayats from the Consolidated Fund of the State; and

(d) provide for constitution of such Funds for crediting all moneys received respectively, by or on behalf of the Panchayats and also for the withdrawal of such moneys therefrom, as may be specified in the law.

Constitution of Finance Commission to Review Financial Position (243I)—(1) The Governor of a State shall, as soon as may be within one year from the commencement of the Constitution (Seventy-third Amendment) Act, 1992, and thereafter at the expiration of every fifth year, constitute a Finance Commission to review the financial position of the Panchayats and to make recommendations to the Governor as to—

(a) The principles which should govern—

(i) the distribution between the State and the Panchayats of the net proceeds of the taxes, duties, tolls and fees leviable by the State, which may be divided between them under this Part and the allocation between the Panchayats at all levels of their respective shares of such proceeds;

(ii) the determination of the taxes, duties, tolls and fees which may be assigned to, or appropriated by the Panchayats;

(iii) the grants-in-aid to the Panchayats from the Consolidated Fund of the State;

(b) the measures needed to improve the financial position of the Panchayats;

(c) any other matter referred to the Finance Commission by the Governor in the interests of sound finance of the Panchayats.

(2) The Legislature of a State may, by law, provide for the composition of the Commission, the qualifications which shall be requisite for appointment as members thereof and the manner in which they shall be selected.

(3) The Commission shall determine the procedure and shall have such powers in the performance of their functions as the Legislature of the State may, by law, confer on them.

(4) The Governor shall cause every recommendation made by the Commission under this article together with an explanatory memorandum as to the action taken thereon to be laid before the legislature of the State.

Audit of Accounts of Panchayats (243 J)—The Legislature of a State may, by law, make provisions with respect to the maintenance of accounts by the Panchayats and the auditing of such accounts.

Elections to the Panchayats (243 K)—(1) The superintendence, direction and control of the preparation of electoral rolls for, and the conduct of, all elections to the Panchayats shall be vested in a State Election Commission consisting of a State Election Commissioner to be appointed by the Governor.

(2) Subject to the provisions of any law made by the Legislature of a State, the conditions of service and tenure of office of the State Election Commissioner shall be such as the Governor may by rule determine:

Provided that the State Election Commissioner shall not be removed from his office except in like manner and on the like grounds as a Judge of a High Court and the conditions of service of the State Election Commissioner shall not be varied to his disadvantage after his appointment.

(3) The Governor of a State shall, when so requested by the State Election Commission, make available to the State Election Commission such staff as may be necessary for the discharge of the functions conferred on the State Election Commission by clause (1).

(4) Subject to the provisions of this Constitution, the Legislature of a State may, by law, make provisions with respect to all matters relating to or in connection with, elections to the Panchayats.

Application to Union Territories (243 L)—The provision of this Part shall apply to the Union Territories and shall, in their application to a Union Territory, have effect as if the references to the Governor of a State were references to the Administrator of the Union Territory, appointed under Article 239 and references to the Legislature or the Legislative Assembly of a State were references, in relation to a Union Territory having a Legislative Assembly, to that Legislative Assembly:

Provided that the President may, by public notification, direct that the provisions of this Part shall apply to any Union Territory or part thereof subject to such exceptions and modifications as he may specify in the notification.

Part not to Apply to Certain Areas (243 M)—(1) Nothing in this Part shall apply to the Scheduled Areas referred to in clause (1), and the Tribal areas referred to in clause (2), of Article 244.

(2) Nothing in this Part shall apply to—

(a) the State of Nagaland, Meghalaya and Mizoram;

(b) the hill areas in the State of Manipur for which District Councils exist under any law for the time being in force.

(3) Nothing in this Part—

(a) relating to Panchayats at the district level shall apply to the hill areas of the District of Darjeeling in the State of West Bengal for which Darjeeling Gorkha Hill Council exists under any law for the time being in force;

(b) shall be construed to affect the functions and powers of the Darjeeling Hill Council constituted under such law.

(4) Notwithstanding anything in this Constitution—

(a) the legislature of a State referred to in sub-clause (a) of clause (2) may, by law, extend this Part to that State, except the areas, if any, referred to in clause (1) if the Legislative Assembly of that State passes a resolution to that effect by a majority of the total membership of that House and by a majority of not less than two-thirds of the members of that House present and voting;

(b) Parliament may, by law, extend the provisions of this Part to the Scheduled Areas and the Tribal areas referred to in clause (1) subject to such exceptions and modifications as may be specified in such law and no such law shall be deemed to be an amendment of this Constitution for the purposes of Article 368.

Continuance of Existing Laws and Panchayats (243 N)—Notwithstanding anything in this Part, any provision of any law relating to Panchayats in force in a State immediately before the commencement of the Constitution (Seventy-third Amendment) Act, 1992, which is inconsistent with the provisions of this Part, shall continue to be in force until amended or repealed by a competent legislature or other competent authority or until the expiration of one year from such commencement, whichever is earlier:

Provided that all the Panchayats existing immediately before such commencement shall continue till the expiration of their duration, unless sooner dissolved by a resolution passed to that effect by the Legislative Assembly of that State or, in the case of a State having a Legislative Council, by each House of the Legislature of that State.

Bar to Interference by Courts in Electoral Matters (243 O)—Notwithstanding anything in this Constitution—

(a) the validity of any law relating to the delimitation of constituencies or the allotment of seats to such constituencies made or purporting to be made under Article 243K, shall not be called in question in any court;

(b) no election to any Panchayat shall be called in question except by an election petition presented to such authority and in such manner as is provided for by or under any law made by the Legislature of a State.

3. Amendment of Article (280)—In clause (3) of Article 280 of the Constitution, after sub-clause (b), the following sub-clause shall be inserted, namely:

"(bb) the measures needed to augment the Consolidated Fund of a State to supplement the resources of the Panchayats in the State on the basis of the recommendations made by the Finance Commission of the State".

4. Addition of Eleventh Schedule—After the Tenth Schedule to the Constitution, the following Schedule shall be added, namely:

ELEVENTH SCHEDULE (Article 243 G)

(a) Agriculture, including agricultural extension.
(b) Land improvement, implementation of land reforms, land consolidation and soil conservation.
(c) Minor irrigation, water management and watershed development.
(d) Animal husbandry, dairying and poultry.
(e) Fisheries.
(f) Social forestry and farm forestry.
(g) Minor forest produce.
(h) Small scale industries, including food processing industries.
(i) Khadi, village and cottage industries.
(j) Rural housing.
(k) Drinking water.
(l) Fuel and fodder.
(m) Roads, culverts, bridges, ferries, water ways and others means of communication.
(n) Rural electrification, including distribution of electricity.
(o) Non-conventional energy sources.
(p) Poverty alleviation programme.
(q) Education including primary and secondary schools.
(r) Technical training and vocational education.
(s) Adult and non-formal education.
(t) Libraries.
(u) Cultural activities.
(v) Markets and fairs.
(w) Health and sanitation, including hospitals, primary health centres and dispensaries.
(x) Family welfare.
(y) Women and child development.
(z) Social welfare, including welfare of the handicapped and mentally retarded.
(aa) Welfare of the weaker sections, and in particular, of the Scheduled Castes and Scheduled Tribes.
(bb) Public distribution system.
(cc) Maintenance of community assets."

1.2. THE CONSTITUTION (SEVENTY-FOURTH AMENDMENT) ACT, 1992 – ARTICLE 243ZD

243ZD. Committee for district planning—(1) There shall be constituted in every State at the district level a District Planning Committee to consolidate the plans prepared by the Panchayats and the Municipalities in the district and to prepare a draft development plan for the district as a whole.

(2) The Legislature of a State may, by law, make provision with respect to:

(a) the composition of the District Planning Committees;

(b) the manner in which the seats in such Committees shall be filled:

Provided that not less than four-fifths of the total number of members of such Committee shall be elected by, and from amongst, the elected members of the Panchayat at the district level and of the Municipalities in the district in proportion to the ratio between the population of the rural areas and of the urban areas in the district.

(c) the functions relating to district planning which may be assigned to such Committees;

(d) the manner in which the Chairpersons of such Committees shall be chosen.

(3) Every District Planning Committee shall, in preparing the draft development plan,—

(a) have regard to—

(i) matters of common interest between the Panchayat and the Municipalities including spatial planning, sharing of water and other physical and natural resources, the integrated development of infrastructure and environmental conservation;

(ii) the extent and type of available resources whether financial or otherwise;

(b) consult such institutions and organizations as the Governor may, by order, specify.

(4) The Chairperson of every District Planning Committee shall forward the development plan, as recommended by such Committee, to the Government of the State.

1.3 DISTRICT PLANNING COMMITTEE—SECTION 241 OF TAMIL NADU PANCHAYATS ACT, 1994

(1) The Government shall constitute in every district a District Planning Committee (hereinafter in this section referred to as the Committee) to consolidate the plans prepared by the district Panchayats, Panchayat union councils, village Panchayats. [2][Town Panchayat] Municipal councils and municipal corporations in the district and to prepare a draft development plan for the district as a whole.

[3]["(2) (a) The Committee shall consists of,—

(i) The Chairman of the district Panchayat;

(ii) the Mayor of the City Municipal Corporation in the district;

(iii) the Collector of the district;

(iv) such number of persons, not less than four-fifth of the total number of members of the Committee as may be specified by the Government, elected in the prescribed manner from amongst the members of the district Panchayats, town Panchayats and councillors of the municipal corporations and the municipal councils in the district, in proportion to the ratio between the population of the rural areas and of the urban areas in the district.

(b) The following persons shall be permanent special invitees of the Committee—

(i) Members of the House of the people who represent the whole or part of the district;

(ii) Members of the Council of States who are registered as electors in the district;

(iii) Members of the Tamil Nadu State Legislative Assembly whose constituencies lie within the district;

(iv) All the Chairmen of the Panchayat union councils in the district;

(v) All the Chairmen of the municipal councils in the district;

(vi) All the Chairmen of the town panchayats in the district.

(c) The permanent special invitees referred to in clause (b) shall be entitled to take part in the proceedings in the meetings of the Committee.

(3) The Secretary of the District Panchayat shall be the Secretary to the Committee.

[4][(4) The Chairman of the District Panchayat shall be the Chairperson of the Committee and the Collector of the District shall be the Vice-Chairman of the Committee.]

(5) The Committee shall meet at such place, at such interval and at such time and observe such rules of procedure in regard to transaction of business at its meetings (including the quorum at its meetings) as may be prescribed.

(6) The Committee shall consolidate the plans prepared by the district panchayat, panchayat union councils, village panchayats, town panchayats, municipal councils and the municipal corporation in the district and prepare a draft development plan for the district as a whole.

(7) Every Committee shall, in preparing the draft development plan:

(a) have regard to:

(i) the matters of common interest between the district panchayats, panchayat union councils, village panchayats, town panchayats, municipal corporations and municipal councils in the district including spatial planning, sharing of water and other physical and natural resources, the integrated development of infrastructures and environmental conservation;

(ii) The extent and type of available resources whether financial or otherwise.

(b) consult such institutions and organisations as the Governor may, by order, specify.

(8) The Chairperson of every committee shall forward the development plan, as recommended by such Committee to the Government.

(9) The committee shall allocate funds to various schemes to the panchayats unions and shall monitor the implementations of the schemes.

Explanation. For the purposes of this section "town panchayat" and "municipal council", shall mean the town panchayat and the municipal council constituted under the Tamil Nadu District Municipalities Act, 1920, and "municipal corporation" means the corporations constituted under the Madurai City Municipal

Corporation Act, 1971 or the Coimbatore City Municipal Corporation Act, 1981 or the Tiruchirappalli City Municipal Corporation Act, 1994 or the Tirunelveli City Municipal Corporation Act, 1994 or the Salem City Municipal Corporation Act, 1994 or any other municipal corporation that may be constituted under any law for the time being in force as the case may be"].

NOTES

1. The whole section 241 has been substituted for the existing section by Act 37/1997.
2. Inserted by Act 55/1997.
3. Sub-section (2) has been substituted by Act 30/2000 for the sub-section (2) which was substituted by Act 37/1997.
4. Substituted by Act 24/2000.

PART II

TAMIL NADU PANCHAYATS ACT, 1994

2.1 TAMIL NADU PANCHAYATS ACT, 1994
CONTENTS

The following Act of the Tamil Nadu Legislative Assembly Received the Assent of the Governor on the 22nd April 1994 and is hereby Published for General Information:

2.2 ACT NO. 21 OF 1994 [CORRECTED UPTO JANUARY, 2005]

An Act to repeal and re-enact the Tamil Nadu Panchayats Act, 1958

WHEREAS it is expedient to repeal and re-enact the Tamil Nadu Panchayats Act, 1958, for establishing a three-tier panchayat raj system in the State to the elected bodies at the village, intermediate and district level in keeping with the Constitution (Seventy-third Amendment) Act, 1992, relating to panchayats for greater participation of the people so as to make them institutions of self-government and for more effective implementation of rural development programmes;

Be it enacted by the Legislative Assembly of the State of Tamil Nadu in the Forty-fifth Year of the Republic of India as follows:

CHAPTER I
PRELIMINARY

1. Short Title, Extent and Commencement—(1) This Act may be called the Tamil Nadu Panchayats Act, 1994.

(2) It extends to the whole of the State of Tamil Nadu except—

(i) the City of Chennai;

(ii) the City of Madurai constituted under the Madurai City Municipal Corporation Act, 1971; (Tamil Nadu Act 15 of 1971)

(iii) the City of Coimbatore constituted under the Coimbatore City Municipal Corporation Act, 1981; (Tamil Nadu Act 25 of 1981)

(iv) the municipalities, town panchayats and industrial townships constituted under the Tamil Nadu District Municipalities Act, 1920 (Tamil Nadu Act V of 1920); and

(v) the cantonments constituted under the Cantonments Act, 1924 (Central Act II of 1924)

(3) It shall come into force on such date as the Government may, by notification, appoint.

2. Definitions—In this Act, unless the context otherwise requires—

[2][(1) Deleted]

[3][(1A) 'building' includes a house, out-house, tent, stable, latrine, shed, hut, wall (other than a boundary wall not exceeding 2.5 metres in height) and any other such structure, whether of masonry, bricks, wood, mud, metal or any other material whatsoever;]

(2) 'casual vacancy' means a vacancy occurring otherwise than by efflux of time and 'casual election' means an election held to fill a casual vacancy;

(3) 'Chairman' means the chairman of a panchayat union council or a district panchayat, as the case may be;

[4][(4) omitted]

(5) 'Collector' means the Collector of a revenue district;

(6) 'Commissioner' means the Commissioner of a panchayat union;

(7) 'Company' means a company as defined in the Companies Act, 1956 (Central Act 1 of 1956) and includes a foreign company within the meaning of section 591 of that Act;

(8) 'District' means a revenue district;

(9) 'District Panchayat' means the district panchayat constituted under sub-section (1) of section 24;

(10) 'Drain' means a rain or storm water drain and water tables, chutes and the side drain exclusively meant to drain away the rain water falling on the surface of any street, bridge or causeway, but does not include a drain or sewer within the meaning of the Chennai Metropolitan Water Supply and Sewerage Act, 1978; (Tamil Nadu Act 28 of 1978)

[5][(11) 'executive authority' means a person notified as such by the Government under section 83"];

(12) 'Government' means the State Government;

(13) 'Grama Sabha' means a body consisting of persons registered in the electoral rolls relating to a Panchayat village comprised within the area of village panchayat concerned;

(14) 'house' means a building fit for human occupation, whether as a residence or otherwise, having a separate principal entrance from the common way, and includes any shop, workshop or warehouse or any building used for garaging or parking buses or as bus stand.

(15) 'hut' means any building which is constructed principally of wood, mud, leaves, grass or thatch and includes any temporary structure of whatever size or any small building of whatever material made, which the panchayat may declare to be a hut for the purposes of this Act;

(16) 'Inspector' means any officer not below the rank of a Collector appointed by the Government

to exercise or perform any of the powers or duties of the Inspector under this Act;

(17) 'latrine' includes privy, water-closet and urinal;

(18) 'member' means a member of the village panchayat, the panchayat union council or the district panchayat, as the case may be;

(19) 'ordinary vacancy' means a vacancy occurring by efflux of time and 'ordinary election' means an election held to fill an ordinary vacancy;

(20) 'owner' includes—

(a) the person for the time being receiving or entitled to receive whether on his own account or on behalf of another person as agent, trustee, guardian, manager or receiver or for any religious or charitable purpose, the rents or profits of the property in connection with which the word is used; and

(b) the person for the time being in charge of the animal or vehicle in connection with which the word is used;

(21) 'panchayat' means a village panchayat, a panchayat union council or a district panchayat constituted under this Act;

(22) 'panchayat development block' means the area declared by the Government from time-to-time to be a panchayat development block for the purpose of this Act;

(23) 'panchayat union' means any local area which is declared to be a panchayat union under this Act;

(24) 'panchayat union council' means the body constituted for the administration of a panchayat union under this Act;

(25) 'panchayat village' means any local area over which a village panchayat has jurisdiction;

(26) 'president' means the president of a village panchayat;

(27) 'private road' means any street, road, square, court, alley, passage, cart-track, foot-path or riding-path which is not a 'public road' but does not include a path-way made by the owner of premises on his own land to secure, access to, or the convenient use of, such premises;

(28) 'public road' means any street, road, square, court, alley, passage, cart-track, foot-path or riding-path, over which the public have a right of way, whether a thoroughfare or not, and includes—

(a) the roadway over any public bridge or causeway;

(b) the footway attached to any such road, public bridge or causeway; and

(c) the drains attached to any such road, public bridge or causeway, and the land, whether covered or not by any pavement, verandha, or other structure, which lies on either side of the roadway the boundaries of the adjacent property, whether that property is private property or property belonging to the State or Central Government;

(29) a person is deemed to have his residence or to 'reside' in any house if he sometimes uses any portion thereof as a sleeping apartment, and a person is not deemed to cease to reside in any such house merely because he is absent from it or has elsewhere another dwelling in which he resides, if he is at liberty to return to such house at any time and has not abandoned his intention of returning;

(30) 'revenue district' means any local area which for the purposes of revenue administration is under the charge of a Collector, after excluding there from all areas included in—

(a) the City of Chennai;

(b) the City of Madurai constituted under the Madurai City Municipal Corporation Act, 1971; (Tamil Nadu Act 15 of 1971)

(c) the City of Coimbatore constituted under the Coimbatore City Municipal Corporation Act, 1981; (Tamil Nadu Act 25 of 1981)

(d) the municipalities, town panchayats and industrial townships constituted under the Tamil Nadu District Municipalities Act, 1920 (Tamil Nadu Act V of 1920); and

(e) the cantonments constituted under the Cantonments Act, 1924; (Central Act II of 1924)

(31) 'Scheduled Castes' shall have the same meaning as in the Constitution;

(32) 'Scheduled Tribes' shall have the same meaning as in the Constitution;

[6][(32-a) 'Secretary' means the Secretary of a District Panchayat];

[142][(32-b) "Special village panchayat" means the special village panchayat referred to in sub-section (4) of Section 6];

[7][(33) 'Tamil Nadu State Election Commission'] means the Tamil Nadu State Election Commission referred to in section 239;

[8][(34)'Tamil Nadu State Election Commissioner'] means the Tamil Nadu State Election Commissioner referred to in section 239;

(35) 'unreserved forest' means a forest not notified under section 4 of the Tamil Nadu Forest Act, 1882 (Tamil Nadu Act V of 1882) and includes unreserved land at the disposal of the Government;

(36) 'village' means any local area which is declared to be a panchayat village under sub-section (1) of section 4, and 'revenue village' means any local area which is recognised as a village in the revenue accounts of Government after excluding therefrom the areas, if any, included in—

(a) the City of Chennai;
(b) the City of Madurai constituted under the Madurai City Municipal Corporation Act, 1971; (Tamil Nadu Act 15 of 1971)
(c) the City of Coimbatore constituted under the Coimbatore City Municipal Corporation Act, 1981; (Tamil Nadu Act 25 of 1981)
(d) the municipalities, town panchayats and industrial townships constituted under the Tamil Nadu District Municipalities Act, 1920; (Tamil Nadu Act V of 1920) and
(e) the cantonments constituted under the Cantonments Act, 1924; (Central Act of II/1924);

(37) 'village panchayat' means a panchayat constituted as a village panchayat under sub-section (1) of section 6; and includes a special village panchayat;

(38) "water-course" includes any river, stream or channel, whether natural or artificial;

(39) 'year' means the financial year.

CHAPTER II
GRAMA SABHA

3. Grama Sabha—(1) There shall be a Grama Sabha for every village panchayat consisting of persons registered in the electoral roll relating to the panchayat village, comprised within the area of the said village panchayat.

[9]["(2) Subject to the general orders of the Government, the Grama Sabha shall meet at least twice in a year but six months shall not intervene between any two meetings.

(2A) Every meeting of the Grama Sabha shall be convened by the president of the village panchayat. If the president fails to convene the meeting of the Grama Sabha, the Inspector shall convene the meeting".]

(3) (a) The Grama Sabha shall—

(i) approve the village plan;
(ii) approve the village budget for the year; [10][.] [11]["(ii-a) approve the audit report on the village panchayat accounts of the previous year; and"]
(iii) review the progress of the implementation of all schemes entrusted to the village panchayat;

(b) The Government may by notification, entrust to the Grama Sabha such other functions as may be specified.

(4) The village panchayat shall give due consideration to the recommendations and suggestions of the Grama Sabha.

(5) The quorum for a meeting [...[12]] and the procedure for convening and conducting such meetings of the Grama Sabha shall be such as may be prescribed.

(6) Every meeting of the Grama Sabha shall be presided over by the president and in his absence, by the vice-president and in the absence of both the president and vice-president, by a member chosen by the members present at the meeting.

CHAPTER III
FORMATION AND CONSTITUTION OF VILLAGE PANCHAYATS, PANCHAYAT UNION COUNCILS AND DISTRICT PANCHAYATS

Village Panchayats

4. Formation of Panchayat Villages—(1) The Inspector

(a) shall, by notification, classify and declare every local area comprising a revenue village or villages or any portion of a revenue village or contiguous portions of two or more revenue villages with a population estimated at not less than five hundred as a panchayat village for the purposes of this Act; and
(b) shall, by notification, specify the name of such panchayat village.

(2) (a) The Inspector may, by notification, exclude from a panchayat village any area comprised therein, provided that the population of the panchayat village after such exclusion, is not less than five hundred.

(b) In regard to any area excluded under clause (a), the Inspector shall by notification under sub-section (1) declare it to be a panchayat village if it has a population of not less than five hundred or if its population is less than five hundred, include it in any contiguous panchayat village under clause (c) (i).

(c) The Inspector may, by notification,—

(i) include in a panchayat village any local area contiguous thereto; or

(ii) cancel or modify a notification issued under sub-section (1); or

(iii) alter the name of any panchayat village specified under sub-section (1).

(d) Before issuing a notification under clause (a) or under clause (b) read with sub-section (1) or under clause (c), the Inspector shall give the village panchayat or village panchayats which will be affected by the issue of such notification, a reasonable opportunity of showing cause against the proposal and shall consider the explanations and objections, if any, of such village panchayat or village panchayats.

(3) Any rate-payer or inhabitant of such areas or any village panchayat concerned, may, if he or it objects to any notification under sub-section (1) or sub-section (2), appeal to the government within such period as may be prescribed.

(4) The Inspector may pass such orders as he may deem fit:

(a) as to the disposal of any part of the property vested in a village panchayat which has ceased to exist, and the discharge of its liabilities;

(b) as to the disposal of any part of the property vested in a village panchayat which has ceased to exercise jurisdiction over any local area, and the discharge of the liabilities of the village panchayat relating to such property or arising from such local area.

(5) An order made under sub-section (4) may contain such supplemental, incidental and consequential provisions as the Inspector may deem necessary and in particular may direct:

(i) that any tax, fee or other sum due to the village panchayat or where a village panchayat has ceased to exercise jurisdiction over any local area, such tax, fee or other sum due to the village panchayat as relates to that area shall be payable to such authorities as may be specified in the order;

(ii) that appeals, petitions, or other applications with reference to any such tax, fee or sum which are pending on the date on which the village panchayat ceased to exist or, as the case may be, on the date on which the village panchayat cease to exercise jurisdiction over the local area, shall be disposed of by such authorities as may be specified in the order.

[13]["**4-A. Special Provision Relating to Town Panchayat Constituted as Village Panchayat**

(1) Notwithstanding anything contained in this Act—

(a) the Chairman and members of a town panchayat holding office as such immediately before the date of constitution of such town panchayat as village panchayat under this Act consequent on the cancellation or modification of the notification declaring it as town panchayat under section 3-B of the Tamil Nadu District Municipalities Act, 1920 (Tamil Nadu Act V of 1920), shall be deemed to be the elected president and members of such village panchayat under this Act and such president and members shall continue to hold office upto such date as the Government may, by notification, fix in this behalf or in case no such date is fixed, upto the date on which their term of office would expire under the Tamil Nadu District Municipalities Act, 1920 (Tamil Nadu Act V of 1920) if they had been elected as Chairman or members of the town panchayat and such president and members shall exercise all powers and perform all duties conferred on the president and members by or under the provisions of this Act:

Provided that such village panchayat shall have no representation in the panchayat union council or the district panchayat, as the case may be, till such president and members of the village panchayat continue to hold office as such president and members under this sub-section;

(b) all the employees, other than the provincialised employees, of the town panchayat immediately before its constitution as village panchayat shall be the employees of such village panchayat under this Act. The provincialised employees shall continue to serve under the village panchayat and they shall be transferred by the Director of Town Panchayats within three months from the date on which such village panchayat is constituted under this Act.

(2) Subject to the provisions of sub-section (1), the provisions of this Act and the rules made there under shall apply to the village panchayat referred to in sub-section (1)."]

5. Extension of Provisions of Tamil Nadu District Municipalities Act, 1920 or of Any Rules Made Thereunder—(1) The Inspector may, whether at the request of the village panchayat or otherwise, by notification, declare that any of the provisions of the Tamil Nadu District Municipalities Act, 1920 or of any rules made thereunder, shall be extended to, and be in force in, the panchayat village or any specified area therein. (Tamil Nadu Act V of 1920)

(2) The provisions so notified shall be construed with such alterations (not affecting the substance) as may be necessary or proper for the purpose of adapting them to the panchayat village or specified area therein.

(3) Without prejudice to the generality of the foregoing provision, all references in the provisions so notified to a municipal council or the chairman or the executive authority thereof shall be construed as references to the village panchayat or the president or the executive authority of the village panchayat and all references to any officer or servant of a municipal council as references to the corresponding officer or servant of the village panchayat, and all references to the municipal limits as references to the limits of the panchayat village or specified area therein, as the case may be.

6. Constitution of Village Panchayats and Their Incorporation—(1) A village panchayat shall be constituted for each panchayat village consisting of such number of elected members, with effect from such date as may be specified in the notification issued in that behalf by the Inspector.

(2) Subject to the provisions of this Act, the administration of the panchayat village shall vest in the village panchayat but the village panchayat shall not be entitled to exercise functions expressly assigned by or under this Act or any other law to its president or to any panchayat union council or the district panchayat or other authority.

(3) Every village panchayat shall be body corporate by the name of the panchayat village specified in the notification issued under section 4, shall have perpetual succession and a common seal, and subject to any restriction or qualification imposed by or under this Act or any other law, shall be vested with the capacity of suing or being sued in its corporate name, of acquiring, holding and transferring property, movable or immovable, of entering into contracts, and of doing all things necessary, proper or expedient for the purposes for which it is constituted.

Amendment of Section 6—(3) In section 6 of the Principal Act, for sub-section (4), the following sub-sections shall be substituted, namely:–

*(4) The village panchayats constituted as such under section 4 on the 14th day of June 2004 consequent on the cancellation of the notification declaring them as town panchayats under section 3-B of the Tamil Nadu District Municipalities Act, 1920 (Tamil Nadu Act V of 1920) shall be called as special village panchayats and the rest of the village panchayats constituted under this Act shall be called as village panchayats.

(5) The Government may, by notification, classify the special village panchayats referred to in sub-section (4) and village panchayats into various grades for the purpose of effective administration of the said village panchayats in accordance with such norms as may be prescribed".

7. Alteration of Classification of Panchayat Villages—(1) The Government may alter any classification notified under sub-section (1) of section 4, if in their opinion the panchayat village satisfies or ceases to satisfy the conditions referred to in that sub-section.

(2) Any decision made by the Government under this section shall not be questioned in a court of law.

8. Strength of a Village Panchayat—(1) Notwithstanding anything contained in section 12 or any other provisions of this Act, the total number of members of a village panchayat (exclusive of its president) shall be notified by the Inspector in accordance with such scale as may be prescribed with reference to population of the panchayat village concerned, as ascertained at the last preceding census of which the relevant figures have been published.

(2) The Inspector may, from time-to-time, by notification alter the total number of members of a village panchayat notified under sub-section (1).

(3) The number notified under sub-section (1) or the number as altered by notification under sub-section (2) shall not be less than five or more than twenty-one.

9. Duration of Village Panchayats—(1) Every village panchayat unless sooner dissolved, shall continue for five years from the date appointed for its first meeting after each ordinary election and no longer.

(2) Where a village panchayat is dissolved before the expiration of the said period of five years,

election to constitute such village panchayat shall be completed in accordance with the provisions of section 214 as soon as may be, and in any case before the expiration of a period of six months from the date of such dissolution:

Provided that where a village panchayat is dissolved, within six months before the expiration of the said period of five years, it shall not be necessary to hold any election to such village panchayat.

[15]["9-A. **Appointment of Special Officers in Certain Circumstances**—(1) Notwithstanding anything contained in this Act, or in any other law for the time being in force, in respect of village panchayats specified in Schedule – VI, which could not be constituted even after resorting to election process, the Government may, by notification, appoint special officers to exercise the powers and discharge the functions of the village panchayats, until the day on which the first meeting of the village panchayats are held after elections to the said village panchayats.

(2) The special officer appointed under sub-section (1) shall hold office only for [16][one year] from the date of his appointment or for such shorter period as the Government may, by notification, specify in this behalf".]

10. Election of Members of Village Panchayat—The members of the village panchayat shall be elected in such manner as may be prescribed:

[17] [Provided that no person shall be eligible to be elected as a member of more than one ward in the same village panchayat or as a member of more than one village panchayat].

[18]["Provided further that a person who stands for election as a member of a village panchayat shall not be eligible to stand for election as president of a village panchayat, a member of a panchayat union council or a member of a district panchayat"].

[19]["Provided also that no member of a village panchayat shall be eligible to stand for election as president of a village panchayat, a member of a panchayat union council or a member of a district panchayat"].

11. Reservation of Seats—(1) Seats shall be reserved for the persons belonging to the Scheduled Castes and the Scheduled Tribes in every Village Panchayats and the number of seats so reserved shall bear as nearly as may be, the same proportion to the total number of seats to be filled by direct election in that Village Panchayat as the population of the Scheduled Castes in that Village Panchayat area or of the Scheduled Tribes in that Village Panchayat area bears to the total population of that area:

Provided that for the first election for the Village Panchayat to be held immediately after the commencement of this Act, the provisional population figures of the Panchayat Village as published in relation to 1991 census shall be deemed to be the population of the Panchayat Village.

(2) Seats shall be reserved for women belonging to the Scheduled Castes and the Scheduled Tribes from among the seats reserved for the persons belonging to the Scheduled Castes and the Scheduled Tribes which shall not be less than one-third of the total number of seats reserved for the persons belonging to Scheduled Castes and the Scheduled Tribes.

[20][(2-A)]

[21][(2-B)]

[(3) Seats shall be reserved for women in the Village Panchayat and the number of seats reserved for women shall be, as nearly as may be, one-third (including the number of seats reserved for women belonging to the Scheduled Castes and the Scheduled Tribes) of the total number of seats in the Village Panchayat:][22]

Provided that such seats reserved for women shall be allotted by rotation to different wards in such a manner as the Inspector may, by notification, direct.

(4) The reservation of seats under sub-sections (1) and (2) shall cease to have effect on the expiration of the period specified in Article 334 of the Constitution.

12. Division of Panchayat Village into Wards—For the purpose of election of members to a village Panchayat, the Inspector may, after consulting the Village Panchayat, by notification, divide the Panchayat Village into wards and determine the number of members to be returned by each ward in accordance with such scale as may be prescribed.

13. Term of Office of Members—(1) The term of office of the members of every Village Panchayat, who are elected at ordinary elections, shall, save as otherwise expressly provided, be five years from the date appointed for the first meeting of such Village Panchayat after ordinary election.

(2) Ordinary vacancies in the office of an elected member of the Village Panchayat shall be filled at

ordinary elections which shall be fixed by the Tamil Nadu State Election Commissioner to take place on such day or days within six months before the occurrence of the ordinary vacancies, as he thinks fit.

(3) The member of a Village Panchayat elected in a casual vacancy shall enter upon office forthwith, but shall hold office only so long as the member in whose place he is elected would have been entitled to hold office if the vacancy had not occurred.

14. Electoral Roll for Village Panchayats— (1) Subject to the provisions of sub-section (2) the electoral roll of the panchayat union council for the time being in force in a Village Panchayat shall be deemed to be the electoral roll for such Village Panchayat.

(2) No amendment, transposition or deletion of any entry in the electoral roll of the panchayat union council made after the last date of making nominations for an election in any Village Panchayat ward and before the notification of the result of such election, shall form part of the electoral roll for such election for the purpose of this section.

(3) The executive authority of the Village Panchayat shall maintain in the prescribed manner, an electoral roll for each ward of the Panchayat Village.

PANCHAYAT UNION COUNCILS

15. Formation of Panchayat Union Council— (1) The Government may, from time-to-time, publish a notification of their intention:

(a) to declare any local area forming a development block for the purposes of the National Extension Service Scheme or Community Development, to be a panchayat development block; and
(b) to constitute for every such panchayat development block a panchayat union.

(2) Any inhabitant of a local area in respect of which any such notification has been published may submit his objection in writing to anything contained in the notification to the Government within six weeks from the publication of the notification and the Government shall take all such objections into consideration.

(3) After the expiry of six weeks from the publication of the notification and after considering the objections, if any, which have been submitted, the Government may, by notifications–

(a) declare the local area to be a panchayat development block;
(b) declare the said panchayat development block to be a panchayat union; and
(c) specify the name of the panchayat union.

(4) The Government may, by notification—

(i) exclude from a panchayat development block any area or village comprised therein, or
(ii) include in a panchayat development block any area contiguous to it, or
(iii) cancel or modify a notification issued under sub-section (3), or
(iv) alter the name of a panchayat union.

(5) Before issuing a notification under sub-section (4), the Government shall consult the district panchayat concerned and give the panchayat union council or panchayat union councils and the village panchayat or village panchayats which will be affected by the issue of such notification, a reasonable opportunity for showing cause against the proposal and shall consider their explanations and objections, if any.

(6) The Government may pass such orders as they may deem fit:

(a) for the disposal of the assets of, or institutions belonging to, the panchayat union council which has ceased to exist, and for the discharge of the liabilities, if any, of such panchayat union council relating to such assets or institutions, or
(b) for the disposal of any part of the assets of, or institutions belonging to a panchayat union council which has ceased to exercise jurisdiction over any panchayat development block and for the discharge of the liabilities, if any, of the panchayat union council relating to such assets or institutions.

(7) An order made under sub-section (6) may contain such supplemental, incidental and consequential provisions as the Government may deem necessary, and in particular may direct:

(i) that any tax, fee or other sum due to the panchayat union council or where a panchayat union council has ceased to exercise jurisdiction over any Panchayat development block, such tax, fee or other sum due to the panchayat union council as relates to that block shall be payable to such authorities as may be specified in the order;
(ii) that appeals, petitions or other applications with reference to any such tax, fee or sum which are pending on the date on which the panchayat union council ceased to exist, or as the case may be, on the date on which the

panchayat union council ceased to exercise jurisdiction over the panchayat development block, shall be disposed of by such authorities as may be specified in the order.

16. Constitution of Panchayat Union Councils and Their Incorporation—(1) A panchayat union council shall be constituted for each panchayat union with effect from such date as may be specified in the notification issued in that behalf by the Government.

(2) Subject to the provisions of this Act, the administration of the panchayat union shall vest in the panchayat union council but the panchayat union council shall not be entitled to exercise functions expressly assigned by or under this Act or any other law to its chairman or the Commissioner or to the Village Panchayat or District Panchayat or any other authority:

Provided that if and so long as there is no Village Panchayat in any part of a panchayat union, the panchayat union council shall exercise all the powers including the power of taxation, discharge the duties, perform the functions and be credited with the receipts and debited with the charges of the Village Panchayat, and the chairman and the Commissioner of the panchayat union council shall exercise the powers, discharge the duties and perform the functions of the president and the executive authority, respectively in such part of the Panchayat development block.

(3) Every panchayat union council shall be a body corporate by the name of the panchayat union specified in the notification issued under section 15, shall have perpetual succession and a common seal, and subject to any restriction or qualification imposed by or under this Act or any other law, shall be vested with the capacity of suing or being sued in its corporate name, of acquiring, holding and transferring property, movable or immovable, of entering into contracts, and of doing all things necessary, proper or expedient for the purposes for which it is constituted.

[23]["**17. Composition and Strength of Panchayat Union Council**—A panchayat union council constituted for any panchayat union, shall consist of the elected members as notified under section 19."]

18. Duration of Panchayat Union Council—(1) Every panchayat union council unless sooner dissolved shall continue for five years from the date appointed for its first meeting after each ordinary election and no longer.

(2) Where a panchayat union council is dissolved before the expiration of the said period of five years, election to reconstitute such panchayat union council shall be completed in accordance with the provisions of section 215 as soon as may be, and in any case, before the expiration of a period of six months from the date of such dissolution:

Provided that where a panchayat union council is dissolved within six months before the expiration of the said period of five years it shall not be necessary to hold any election to such panchayat union council.

[24]["**19. Election of Members of Panchayat Union Council**—Every panchayat union council shall consist of persons elected from the wards in the panchayat union, as may be notified from time to time by the Government at the rate of one member, as nearly as may be, for every five thousand population of the panchayat union area as ascertained in the last preceding census of which the relevant figures have been published. Such a ward of the panchayat union area may either comprise a full ward or one or more wards of the village panchayats:

Provided that no person shall be eligible to be elected as a member of more than one ward in the same panchayat union or as a member of more than one panchayat union council under this Act:

Provided further that a person who stands for election as a member of a panchayat union council shall not be eligible to stand for election as a member of a village panchayat, president of a village panchayat or a member of a district panchayat:

Provided also that no member of a panchayat union council shall be eligible to stand for election as a member of a village panchayat, president of a village panchayat, or a member of a district panchayat."]

20. Reservation of Seats—(1) Seats shall be reserved for the persons belonging to the Scheduled Castes and the Scheduled Tribes in every panchayat union council and the number of seats so reserved shall bear as nearly as may be, the same proportion to the total number of seats to be filled by direct election in that panchayat union council as the population of the Scheduled Castes in that panchayat union area or of the Scheduled Tribes in that panchayat union area bears to the total population of that area:

Provided that for the first election for the panchayat union council to be held immediately after the commencement of this Act, the provisional population figures of the panchayat union as published in relation to 1991 census shall be deemed to be the population of that panchayat union.

(2) Seats shall be reserved for women belonging to the Scheduled Castes and the Scheduled Tribes from among the seats reserved for the persons belonging to the Scheduled Castes and the Scheduled Tribes which shall not be less than one-third of the total number of seats reserved for the persons belonging to the Scheduled Castes and the Scheduled Tribes.

[25][(2-A) Omitted]

[26][(2-B) Omitted]

[27][(3) Seats shall be reserved for women in the panchayat union council and the number of seats reserved for women shall not be less than one-third including the number of seats reserved for women belonging to the Scheduled Castes and Scheduled Tribes of the total number of seats in the panchayat union council]:

Provided that such seats reserved for women shall be allotted by rotation to different wards in such manner as the Inspector may, by notification, direct.

(4) The reservation of seats under sub-sections (1) and (2) shall cease to have effect on the expiration of the period specified in Article 334 of the Constitution.

21. Division of Panchayat Union into Wards—(1) For the purpose of election of members to the panchayat union council, the Inspector shall, after consulting the panchayat union council, by notification, divide the panchayat union area into wards and determine the number of members to be elected in accordance with such scale as may be prescribed.

(2) Only one member shall be elected from each ward.

22. Term of Office of Members—(1) Except as otherwise provided in this Act, members of the panchayat union council elected at an ordinary election, shall hold office for a term of five years.

(2) The term of office of the members elected at an ordinary election shall commence on the date appointed for the first meeting of the panchayat union council after ordinary election.

(3) The member of a panchayat union council elected in a casual vacancy, shall enter upon office forthwith but shall hold office only so long as the member in whose place he is elected would have been entitled to hold office if the vacancy had not occurred.

23. Electoral Roll for the Panchayat Union Council—(1) Subject to the provision of sub-section (2), the electoral roll of the district panchayat for the time being in force for such part of the panchayat union shall be deemed to be the electoral roll for such panchayat union council.

(2) No amendment, transposition or deletion of any entry in the electoral roll of the district panchayat made after last date for making nominations for an election in any panchayat union council ward and before the notification of the result of such election, shall form part of the electoral roll for such election, for the purpose of this section.

(3) The Commissioner of panchayat union council shall maintain in the prescribed manner, electoral roll for each ward in the panchayat union.

DISTRICT PANCHAYATS

24. Formation and Incorporation of District Panchayat—(1) The Government may, by notification, constitute for each district with effect from such date as may be prescribed in the said notification, a district panchayat having jurisdiction over the entire district excluding such portions of the district as are included in a municipality or town panchayat or industrial township or under the authority of a municipal corporation or a cantonment.

(2) Every district panchayat shall be a body corporate by the name of the district, shall have perpetual succession and a common seal and subject to such restrictions as are imposed by or under this or any other enactment, shall be vested with the capacity of suing or being sued in its corporate name, of acquiring, holding and transferring property, movable or immovable, whether without or within the limits of the area over which it has authority, of entering into contracts and of doing all things, necessary, proper or expedient for the purpose for which it is constituted.

[28]["**25. Constitution of District Panchayat**—(1) The district panchayat shall consist of:

(a) all the elected members as determined under section 27;

(b) the members of the House of People and the members of the State Legislative Assembly representing a part or whole of the district whose constituencies lie within the district;

(c) the member of the Council of States who is registered as elector within the district.

(2) Members of the house of people, the State Legislative Assembly and the Council of the States, referred to in clauses (b) and (c) of sub-section (1),

shall be entitled to take part in the proceedings [29][and vote at the meeting of the district panchayat]].

26. Election of Members—The number of elected members of a district panchayat shall consist of persons elected from the wards in the district panchayat, as may be notified from time to time by the Government based on the population of the district as ascertained at the last preceding census:

[30]["Provided that no person shall be eligible to be elected as a member of more than one ward in the same district panchayat or as a member of more than one district panchayat"]:

[31]["Provided further that a person who stands for election as a member of a district panchayat shall not be eligible to stand for election as a member of a village panchayat, president of a village panchayat or a member of panchayat union council"]:

[32]["Provided also that no member of district panchayat shall be eligible to stand for election as a member of a village panchayat, president of a village panchayat or a member of a panchayat union council"].

27. Determination of Elected Members after Census—Upon the publication of the figures for each census, the number of elected members of a district panchayat shall be determined in accordance with such scale as may be prescribed on the basis of the population of the district as ascertained at the last preceding census:

Provided further that for the first election to the district panchayat to be held immediately after the commencement of this Act, the provisional population figures of the district panchayat as published in relation to 1991 census, shall be deemed to be the population of the district panchayat as ascertained in that census:

Provided that the determination of the members as aforesaid, shall not affect the then composition of the district panchayat until the expiry of the term of office of the elected members then in office.

28. Delimitation of Territorial Wards—The Government shall, by notification:

(a) divide the area, within the jurisdiction of every district panchayat, for the purpose of election to such district panchayat into as many single member territorial wards as the number of members required to be elected under section 26;

(b) determine the extent of each territorial ward which shall be a panchayat village or panchayat union or part of a panchayat village or panchayat union; and

[33][(c) determine the territorial ward or wards in which seats are reserved for the Scheduled Castes, Scheduled Tribes and women].

29. Term of Office of Members—(1) Except as otherwise provided in this Act, members of a district panchayat elected at an ordinary election, shall hold office for a term of five years.

(2) The term of office of the members elected at an ordinary election shall commence on the date appointed for the first meeting of the district panchayat after ordinary election.

(3) The member of a district panchayat elected in a casual vacancy, shall enter upon the office forthwith but shall hold office only so long as the member in whose place he is elected would have been entitled to hold office, if the vacancy had not occurred.

30. Electoral Roll for District Panchayat—(1) The electoral roll of a district panchayat shall be the same as the electoral roll of the Tamil Nadu Legislative Assembly prepared and revised in accordance with the provision of the law for the time being in force in the district and as revised, modified, updated and published in accordance with the provisions of sub-section (2).

(2) Subject to the superintendence, direction and control of the Tamil Nadu State Election Commission, the electoral roll shall be revised, modified, up-dated and published by such officer as may be designated by the Tamil Nadu State Election Commission in this behalf in the prescribed manner.

(3) No amendment, transposition or deletion of any entry in the electoral roll of the Tamil Nadu Legislative Assembly made after the last date for making nomination for election in any district panchayat territorial ward and before the notification of the result of such election, shall form part of the electoral roll for such election, for the purpose of this section.

31. Duration of District Panchayat—(1) Every district panchayat constituted under this Act unless sooner dissolved, shall continue for five years from the date appointed for its first meeting after each ordinary election and no longer.

(2) Where a district panchayat is dissolved before the expiration of the said period of five years, election to reconstitute such district panchayat shall be completed as soon as may be and in any case, before the expiration of a period of six months from the date of such dissolution.

Provided that where a district panchayat is dissolved within six months before the expiration of the said period of five years, it shall not be necessary to hold any election to such district panchayat.

32. Reservation of Seats—(1) Seats shall be reserved for the persons belonging to the Scheduled Castes and the Scheduled Tribes in every district panchayat and the number of seats so reserved shall bear as nearly as may be, the same proportion to the total number of seats to be filled by direct election in that district panchayat as the population of the Scheduled Castes in that district panchayat area or of the Scheduled Tribes in that district panchayat area bears to the total population of that area:

Provided that for the first election for the district panchayat to be held immediately after the commencement of this Act, the provisional population figures of the district panchayat area as published in relation to 1991 census, shall be deemed to be the population of that district panchayat area.

(2) Seats shall be reserved for women belonging to the Scheduled Castes and the Scheduled Tribes from among the seats reserved for the persons belonging to the Scheduled Castes and the Scheduled Tribes which shall not be less than one-third of the total number of seats reserved for the persons belonging to the Scheduled Castes and the Scheduled Tribes.

[34][(2-A) Omitted]

[35][(2-B) Omitted]

[36][(3) Seats shall be reserved for women in the district panchayat and number of seats reserved for women shall not be less than one-third (including the number of seats reserved for women belonging to the Scheduled Castes and the Scheduled Tribes) of the total number of seats in the district panchayat]:

Provided that such seats reserved for women shall be allotted by rotation to different territorial wards in such manner as the Government may, by notification, direct.

(4) The reservation of seats under sub-sections (1) and (2) shall cease to have effect on the expiration of the period specified in Article 334 of the Constitution.

(5) Reservation of seats under this section, section 11 and section 20, shall be made by the Government or by any officer authorised by the Government in this behalf.

(6) While determining the number of seats in village panchayats, panchayat union councils and district panchayats under this section, section 11, and section 20 for the purpose of reservation, any fraction thereof shall be disregarded.

QUALIFICATION, DISQUALIFICATION, ETC., OF MEMBERS

33. Qualification of Candidates—No person shall be qualified for election as a member or president [37][***] of a panchayat unless—

(i) his name appears on the electoral roll of the concerned panchayat; and

(ii) he has completed his twenty-first year of age.

34. Disqualification of Officers and Servants of Government and Local Bodies etc.—(1) No Village Administrative Officer, or village servant and no other officer or servant of the State or Central Government or of a village panchayat, panchayat union council, district panchayat, municipal council or the municipal corporation of Madras, or of Madurai or of Coimbatore or of any other municipal corporation that may be constituted under any law for the time being in force or of any industrial township or of cantonment or of anybody corporate, owned or controlled by the State or Central Government, shall be qualified for election as a member or for holding office as a member.

(2) If any question arises either before or after an election whether any person is or is not disqualified under this section, the question shall be referred to the Government whose decision shall be final.

(3) Before taking any decision on any such question, the Government shall obtain the opinion of the Tamil Nadu State Election Commission and shall act according to such opinion.

35. Disqualification of Persons Convicted of Election Offences—Every person convicted of an offence punishable under sections 58 to 71 of this Act or under Chapter IX-A of the Indian Penal Code, or is so disqualified by or under any law for the time being in force for the purposes of election to the Legislative Assembly of the State or is disqualified by or under any law for the time being in force, shall be disqualified from voting or from being elected in any election to which this Act applies or from holding the office of president or member of a village panchayat or of the office of chairman or member of a panchayat union council or a district panchayat, for a period of five years from the date of his conviction.

36. Disqualification of Voters—No person who is of unsound mind and declared so by a competent court and no person who is disqualified under section 35 shall be qualified to vote so long as the disqualification subsists.

37. Disqualification of Candidates—(1) A person who has been sentenced by a criminal court to imprisonment for any offence involving moral delinquency (such sentence not having been reversed) shall be disqualified for election as a member [38][while the sentence is in force] and for [39][six years] from the date of the expiration thereof.

(2) A person convicted of an offence punishable under the Protection of Civil Rights Act, 1955, shall be disqualified for election as a member for a period of [40][six years] from the date of such conviction.

(3) A person shall be disqualified for election as a member if, at the last date for filing of nomination or at the date of election he is—

(a) of unsound mind, or a deaf-mute;

(b) an applicant to be adjudicated as an insolvent or an undischarged insolvent;

(c) interested in a subsisting contract made with or any work being done for, any panchayat except as a share holder (other than a director) in a company;

(d) employed as paid legal practitioner on behalf of the panchayat or as legal practitioner against the panchayat:

[41]["(dd) found that he does not belong to Scheduled Caste or Scheduled Tribe for contesting any seat reserved for Scheduled Caste or Scheduled Tribe in a Panchayat"].

(e) already a member of a panchayat, whose term of office will not expire before his fresh election can take effect or has already been elected as a member of a panchayat whose term of office has not yet commenced; or

(f) in arrears of any kind due by him (otherwise than in a fiduciary capacity) to a panchayat upto and inclusive of the previous year.

[42]["(4) If the Tamil Nadu State Election Commission is satisfied that a person:

(a) has failed to lodge an account of election expenses within the time and in the manner required by or under this Act, and

(b) has no good reason or justification for the failure, the Tamil Nadu State Election Commission shall, by order published in the Tamil Nadu Government Gazette, declare him to be disqualified for being chosen as, and for being, a member or president, as the case may be, and any such person shall be disqualified for a period of three years from the date of the order"].

38. Disqualification of Members—Subject to the provision of section 41, a member shall cease to hold office as such, if he:

(a) is sentenced by a criminal court to such punishment and for such offence as is described in sub-section (1) of section 37;

(b) is convicted of an offence punishable under the Protection of Civil Rights Act, 1955; (Central Act XXII of 1955);

(c) becomes of unsound mind or of deaf-mute;

(d) applies to be adjudicated, or is adjudicated, as an insolvent;

(e) acquires any interest in any subsisting contract made with or work being done for any panchayat except as a shareholder (other than a director) in a company or except as permitted by rules made under this Act;

(f) is employed as paid legal practitioner on behalf of any panchayat or accepts employment as legal practitioner against any panchayat;

[43]["(ff) is found that he does not belong to Scheduled Caste or Scheduled Tribe, but has been elected from the seat reserved for Scheduled Caste or Scheduled Tribe"];

(g) is appointed as an officer or servant under this Act;

(h) ceases to reside in the village, the panchayat union or the district, as the case may be;

(i) fails to pay arrears of any kind due by him (otherwise than in a fiduciary capacity) to any panchayat within three months after such arrears became due; or

(j) absents himself from the meetings of the panchayat for a period of three consecutive months reckoned from the date of the commencement of his term of office, or of the last meeting which he attended, or of his restoration to office as member under sub-section (1) of section 39, as the case may be, or if within the said period, less than three meetings have been held, absents himself from the three consecutive meetings held after the said date:

Provided that no meeting from which a member absented himself shall be counted against him under this clause if:

(i) due notice of that meeting was not given to him; or

(ii) the meeting was held after giving shorter notice than that prescribed for an ordinary meeting; or

(iii) the meeting was held on a requisition of members.

[44][38-A. **Disqualification for President, Vice-president, Chairman, Vice-chairman and Member**—Notwithstanding anything contained in this Act, no person shall be qualified for being elected as, and for being, a president, vice-president or member of a village panchayat or a chairman, vice-chairman or member of a panchayat union council or of a district panchayat if he is a member of the Legislative Assembly of the State or a member of either House of Parliament"].

39. Restoration of Members to Office—(1) Where a person ceases to be a member under section 35 or clause (a) or clause (b) of section 38, such person shall be restored to office for such portion of the period for which such person was elected, as may remain unexpired at the date of such restoration, if and when the conviction or sentence is annulled on appeal or revision; and any person elected to fill the vacancy in the interim, shall on such restoration, vacate office.

(2) Where a person ceases to be a member under clause (j) of section 38 the executive authority or the Commissioner or the Secretary as the case may be, shall, at once intimate the fact in writing to such person and report the same to the panchayat concerned at its next meeting. If such person applies for restoration *suo moto* to the panchayat concerned on or before the date of its next meeting or within fifteen days of the receipt by him of such intimation, such panchayat may at the meeting next after the receipt of such application restore him to his office of member:

Provided that a member shall not be restored more than twice during his term of office.

40. Oath or Affirmation to be Made by Members—(1) Notwithstanding anything contained in the Oaths Act, 1969, (Central Act X of 1969), every person who is elected to be a member or who becomes a member shall, before taking his seat, make at a meeting of the panchayat an oath or affirmation in the following form, namely—

"I, A.B. having been elected a member—having become a member of this village panchayat/ panchayat union council—district panchayat do swear in the name of God/solemnly affirm that I will bear true faith and allegiance to the Constitution of India as by law established, that I will uphold the sovereignty and integrity of India and that I will faithfully discharge the duty upon which I am about to enter".

(2) Any person who, having been elected to be a member or who, having become a member, fails to make within three months of the date on which his term of office commences or at one of the first three meetings held after the said date whichever is later, the oath or affirmation laid down in sub-section (1), shall cease to hold his office and his seat shall be deemed to have become vacant.

(3) Any person who has been elected to be a member or who has become a member shall not take his seat at a meeting of the panchayat or do any act as such member unless he has made the oath or affirmation as laid down in sub-section (1).

(4) Notwithstanding anything contained in sub-section (3), the president or the chairman of a panchayat or the member of a committee constituted under this Act, who has not made the oath or affirmation as a member, shall be entitled to act as such president, chairman or member provided he makes the oath or affirmation and takes his seat at the first meeting of the panchayat which he attends within two months after he is elected or appointed as, or becomes entitled to exercise the functions of, the president, chairman or member, as the case may be.

Explanation. For the purposes of this section:

(i) 'President' includes a vice-president exercising the functions of the president under sub-section (1) or sub-section (2) of section 47 and the temporary president appointed under sub-section (3) of that section; and

(ii) 'Chairman' includes vice-chairman exercising the functions of the chairman under sub-section (1) or sub-section (5) of section 54 or a revenue divisional officer who is *ex-officio* chairman under sub-section (2) of that section.

41. Authority to Decide the Questions of Disqualification of Members—(1) Whenever it is alleged that any person who has been elected as a member of a panchayat or who becomes a member of a panchayat is not qualified or has become disqualified under sections 33, 35, 37, 38 and 40 the executive authority or the Commissioner or the Secretary as the case may be, shall, by notice in writing inform such member of the allegation and place the matter at the next meeting of the panchayat concerned. If before the date of the expiry of two months from the date of receipt of such notice, such member does not apply to the prescribed judicial authority under sub-section (2), he shall become not qualified or disqualified from such date of expiry of the said two months.

(2) The executive authority or the Commissioner or the Secretary, as the case may be, if so directed by the panchayat or by the Tamil Nadu State Election

Commissioner, shall, or any such member or any other member may apply to the prescribed judicial authority whose decision on such allegation shall be final.

(3) Where an application has been made under sub-section (2), the member shall, pending decision on such application be entitled to act as if he is qualified or was not disqualified.

(4) Nothing contained in this section shall be deemed to affect the provisions of section 39.

PRESIDENT AND VICE-PRESIDENT OF VILLAGE PANCHAYAT

42. President and Vice-president of Village Panchayat—There shall be a president and a vice-president for every village panchayat.

43. Election of President—(1) (a) The president shall be elected by the persons whose names appear in the electoral roll for the village panchayat from among themselves in accordance with such procedure as may be prescribed.

(b) If at an ordinary or casual election, no president is elected, a fresh election shall be held:

[45]["Provided that a person who stands for election as president shall not be eligible to stand for election as a member of village panchayat, a member of panchayat union council or a member of district panchayat:

Provided further no president shall be eligible to stand for election as a member of village panchayat, a member of panchayat union council or a member of district panchayat"];

(2) The election of the president may be held ordinarily at the same times and in the same places as the ordinary elections of the members of the village panchayat.

(3) The term of office of the president who is elected at an ordinary election shall, save as otherwise expressly provided in, be five years beginning at noon on the day on which the ordinary vacancy occurs.

(4) Any casual vacancy in the office of the president shall be filled by a fresh election and a person elected as president in any such vacancy shall enter upon office forthwith and hold office only so long as the person in whose place he is elected would have been entitled to hold office, if the vacancy had not occurred.

(5) Unless the Tamil Nadu State Election Commissioner otherwise directs, no casual vacancy in the office of the president shall be filled within six months before the date on which the ordinary election of the president under sub-section (1) is due.

(6) The provisions of sections 34 to 41 (both inclusive), shall, as far as may be, apply in relation to the office of the president as they apply in relation to the office of an elected member of the panchayat.

(7) The president shall be an *ex-officio* member of the village panchayat and shall have all the rights and privileges of an elected member of the village panchayat.

44. Election of Vice-President—(1) The vice-president shall be elected by the village panchayat from among its elected members in accordance with such procedure as may be prescribed.

(2) If at an election held under sub-section (1), no vice-president is elected, a fresh election shall be held for electing a vice-president.

45. Cessation of Office as President and Vice-President—The president or vice-president shall cease to hold office as such:

(a) in the case of the president, on his becoming disqualified for holding the office or on his removal from office or on the expiry of his term of office or on his otherwise ceasing to be a president;

(b) in the case of the vice-president, [46]["on his becoming disqualified for holding the office or on his removal from office or"] on the expiry of his term of office as a member or on his otherwise ceasing to be a member.

46. Functions of President—(1) The president shall:

[47]["(a) convene the meetings of the village panchayat and of the Grama Sabha"];

(b) have full access to the records of the village panchayat;

(c) discharge all the duties specifically imposed and exercise all the powers conferred on the president by this Act.

(2) No official correspondence between the village panchayat and the Government shall be conducted except through the president. The president shall be bound to transmit communications addressed through him by the executive authority to the Government or by the Government to the executive authority.

47. Devolution of [48][**] President's Functions and Filling up of Vacancies in the Office of President—(1) When the office of president is vacant, the vice-president shall exercise the functions of the president until a new president is declared elected and assumes office.

(2) If the president has been continuously absent from jurisdiction for more than thirty days or is

incapacitated, his functions during such absence or incapacity shall, except in such circumstances as may be prescribed, devolve on the vice-president.

(3) When the office of president is vacant or the president has been continuously absent from jurisdiction for more than thirty days or is incapacitated and there is either a vacancy in the office of vice-president or the vice-president has been continuously absent from jurisdiction for more than thirty days or is incapacitated, the functions of the president shall devolve on a member of the village panchayat appointed by the Inspector in this behalf, and if no member of the village panchayat is available for such appointment, on such person as may be appointed by the Inspector in this behalf.

The member of the village panchayat or the person so appointed (who shall be called as the temporary president) shall perform the functions of the president subject to such restrictions and conditions as may be prescribed, until a new president or vice-president is declared elected and assumes office, or either the president or the vice-president returns to jurisdiction or recovers from his incapacity, as the case may be.

(4) Any vacancy in the office of president shall be reported to the Tamil Nadu State Election Commissioner by such person and within such time as may be prescribed and the Tamil Nadu State Election Commissioner shall arrange for the election of the president.

(5) The president shall have power to control and revise the exercise or discharge of any functions devolving on the vice-president under sub-section (2).

48. Delegation of Functions of President—Subject to such restrictions and control as may be prescribed, the president may by an order in writing delegate any of his functions as such to the vice-president and in the absence of the vice-president to any other member, provided that the exercise or discharge of any functions so delegated shall be subject to such further restrictions and conditions as may be laid down by the president and shall also be subject to his control and revision:

Provided that he shall not delegate any functions which the village panchayat expressly prohibits him to delegate.

CHAIRMAN AND VICE-CHAIRMAN

49. Chairman and Vice-Chairman of Panchayat Union Council—There shall be a chairman and a vice-chairman for every panchayat union council.

50. Election of Chairman of Panchayat Union Council—(1) The chairman shall be elected by the panchayat union council from among its elected members in accordance with such procedure as may be prescribed.

(2) If at an election held under sub-section (1), no chairman is elected, a fresh election shall be held for electing a chairman.

51. Election of Vice-Chairman of Panchayat Union Council—(1) The vice-chairman shall be elected by the panchayat union council from among its elected members in accordance with such procedure as may be prescribed.

(2) If at an election held under sub-section (1), no vice-chairman is elected, a fresh election shall be held for electing a vice-chairman.

52. Functions of Chairman—(1) The chairman shall—

(a) convene the meetings of the panchayat union council, and

(b) discharge all the duties specifically imposed and exercise all the powers conferred on the chairman by this Act and the rules made thereunder.

(2) The chairman shall have full access to all the records of the panchayat union council and no official correspondence between the council and the Government shall be conducted except through the chairman. The chairman shall be bound to transmit communications addressed through him by the commissioner to the Government or by the Government to the commissioner.

53. Cessation of Office of Chairman and Vice-Chairman of a Panchayat Union Council—The chairman and vice-chairman shall cease to hold office as such:

(a) in the case of the chairman of a panchayat union council on his becoming disqualified for holding the office or on his removal from office or on the expiry of his term of office or on his otherwise ceasing to be chairman or member of the panchayat union council;

(b) in the case of the vice-chairman [49]["on his becoming disqualified for holding the office or on his removal from office or"] on the expiry of his term of office as a member of the panchayat union council or on his otherwise ceasing to be a member of the panchayat union council.

54. Devolution and Delegation of Chairman's Functions and Filling up of Vacancies in the Office of Chairman—(1) When the office of chairman is vacant, the vice-chairman shall exercise the functions of the chairman until a new chairman assumes office.

(2) When the office of chairman is vacant and there is either a vacancy in the office of vice-chairman, or the vice-chairman has been continuously absent from jurisdiction for more than thirty days or is incapacitated and until a new chairman or vice-chairman is elected and assumes office, or the vice-chairman returns to jurisdiction or recovers from his incapacity, as the case may be, the revenue divisional officer shall, notwithstanding anything contained in this Act, or in the rules or notifications issued thereunder, be *ex-officio* member and chairman of the panchayat union council.

(3) An out-going chairman or vice-chairman is eligible for re-election.

(4) The chairman may, by an order in writing, delegate any of his functions to the vice-chairman:

Provided that he shall not delegate any functions which the panchayat union council expressly forbids him to delegate.

(5) If the chairman has been continuously absent from jurisdiction for more than thirty days or is incapacitated, his functions during such absence or incapacity shall, except in such circumstances as may be prescribed, devolve on the vice-chairman.

(6) If the vice-chairman also has been continuously absent from jurisdiction for more than thirty days or is incapacitated or if the office of vice-chairman is vacant, the chairman may, by an order in writing, delegate any of his functions to any member of the panchayat union council who shall be called "chairman delegate" during the period of delegation:

Provided that:

(i) when an order of delegation made under this sub-section is in force, no further order of delegation of any function shall be made in favour of any member other than the member in whose favour the order in force was made;

(ii) no delegation under this sub-section shall be made for any period exceeding in the aggregate ninety days in any year without the special sanction of the panchayat union council; and

(iii) every order made under this sub-section shall be communicated to the panchayat union council at its next meeting.

(7) The exercise or discharge of any functions delegated under this section shall be subject to such restrictions, limitations and conditions as may be laid down by the chairman.

55. Chairman and Vice-Chairman of District Panchayat—There shall be a chairman and a vice-chairman for every district panchayat.

56. Election of Chairman and Vice-Chairman of District Panchayat—(1) The elected members of the district panchayat shall as soon as may be elect two members from among themselves, to be respectively the chairman and vice-chairman.

(2) The provisions of [50]["sub-section (2) of section 50, sub-section (2) of section 51 and sections 52, 53 and 54"] shall as far as may be, apply in relation to the office of the chairman and vice-chairman of district panchayat, as they apply in relation to the office of the chairman and vice-chairman of panchayat union council and any reference to panchayat union council or Commissioner in the said sections shall be deemed to be a reference to the district panchayat or Secretary as the case may be, in so far as it applies to the office of chairman and vice-chairman of district panchayat.

57. Reservation of Seats in the Office of President, Chairman etc.—(1) Office of the presidents of village panchayats, chairmen of panchayat union councils and chairmen of district panchayats, shall be reserved for the persons belonging to the Scheduled Castes and the Scheduled Tribes and the number of seats so reserved shall bear as nearly as may be, the same proportion to the total number of offices in the State as the population of the Scheduled Castes in the State or the Scheduled Tribes in the State bear to the total population of the State:

[51][**]

[52]["(1-A). Offices of the presidents of village panchayats, chairmen of panchayat union councils and chairmen of district panchayats shall be reserved for women belonging to the Scheduled Castes and the Scheduled Tribes from among the offices reserved for the persons belonging to the Scheduled Castes and the Scheduled Tribes which shall not be less than one-third of the total number of offices reserved for the persons belonging to the Scheduled Castes and the Scheduled Tribes"].

[53][(1-B) (omitted)]

[54][(1-C) (omitted)]

[55]["(1-D). Offices of the presidents of village panchayats, chairmen of panchayat union councils and chairmen of district panchayats in the State shall

be reserved for women which shall not be less than one-third (including the number of offices reserved for women belonging to the Scheduled Castes, the Scheduled Tribes of the total number of such offices in the State"]:

[56]["Provided that the offices reserved under this section, shall be allotted to different panchayats at each level in such manner, as may be prescribed"].

(2) Reservation of the offices of the presidents of village panchayats, chairmen of panchayat union councils and chairmen of district panchayats, shall be made by the Government or by any officer authorised by the Government in this behalf.

(3) The reservation of the offices of presidents of the village panchayats, chairmen of the panchayat union councils and chairmen of the district panchayats made under sub-section (1) in respect of the persons belonging to the Scheduled Castes and the Scheduled Tribes shall cease to have effect on the expiration of the period specified in Article 334 of the Constitution.

(4) While determining the number of offices of presidents of village panchayats, chairmen of panchayat union councils and chairmen of district panchayats, under sub-section (1) for the purpose of reservation, any fraction thereof shall be disregarded [57][any fraction which is less than half shall be disregarded and half and more than half shall be regarded as one].

CHAPTER IV
OFFENCES RELATING TO ELECTIONS

58. Infringement of Secrecy of Election—Every officer, clerk, agent or other person performing any duty in connection with the recording or counting of votes at an election who, except for some purpose authorised by law, communicates to any person any information showing directly or indirectly for which candidate any voter has voted, and every person who by any improper means, procures any such information, shall be punished with imprisonment which may extend to six months or with fine, or with both.

59. Minimum Penalty for Personation at an Election—Notwithstanding anything contained in section 171-F of the Indian Penal Code (Central Act XLV/1860), any person who in connection with an election under this Act commits an offence of personation punishable under that section shall be punishable with imprisonment for a term which shall not be less than six months and not more than two years and with fine.

60. Promoting Enmity between Classes in Connection with Election—Any person who in connection with an election under this Act promotes or attempts to promote on grounds of religion, race, caste, community or language, feelings of enmity or hatred between different classes of the citizens of India shall be punishable with imprisonment for a term which may extend to three years or with fine, or with both.

61. Prohibition of Public Meetings on the Day Preceding the Election Day and on the Election Day—(1) No person shall convene, hold or attend any public meeting in any local area comprised in a panchayat within forty-eight hours before the date of termination of the poll or on the date or dates on which a poll is taken for an election in that panchayat.

(2) Any person who contravenes the provisions of sub-section (1) shall be punishable with fine which may extend to two hundred and fifty rupees.

62. Disturbances at Election Meeting—(1) Any person who at a public meeting to which this section applies acts or incites others to act, in a disorderly manner for the purpose of preventing the transaction of the business for which the meeting was called shall be punishable with fine which may extend to two hundred and fifty rupees.

(2) This section applies to any public meeting of a political character held in any local area comprised in a panchayat between the earliest date for making nomination of candidates for an election and the date in which such election is held.

(3) If any police officer reasonably suspects any person of committing an offence under sub-section (1), he may, if requested so to do by the chairman of the meeting, require that person to declare to him immediately his name and address and, if that person refuses or fails so to declare his name and address, or if the police officer reasonably suspects him of giving a false name or address, the police officer may arrest him without warrant.

63. Restrictions on Printing of Pamphlets, Posters, etc.—(1) No person shall print or publish or cause to be printed or published, any election pamphlet or poster which does not bear on its face the names and address of the printer and the publisher thereof.

(2) No person shall print or cause to be printed any election pamphlet or poster:

(a) unless a declaration as to the identity of the publisher thereof signed by him and attested by two persons to whom he is personally known, is delivered by him to the printer in duplicate; and

(b) unless, within a reasonable time, after the printing of the document, one copy of the declaration is sent by the printer together with one copy of the document to the executive authority or Commissioner or the Secretary, as the case may be.

(3) For the purposes of this section:

(a) any process for multiplying copies of a document, other than copying it by hand, shall be deemed to be printing and the expression 'printer' shall be construed accordingly; and

(b) "election pamphlet or poster" means any printed pamphlet, hand-bill or other document distributed for the purpose of promoting or prejudicing the election of a candidate or group of candidates or any placard or poster having reference to an election, but does not include any hand-bill, placard or poster merely announcing the date, time, place and other particulars of an election meeting or routine instructions to election agents or workers.

(4) Any person who contravenes any of the provisions of sub-section (1) or sub-section (2) shall be punishable with imprisonment for a term which may extend to six months, or with fine which may extend to two thousand rupees, or with both.

64. Officers, etc., at Elections not to Act for Candidates or to Influence Voting—(1) No person who is a returning officer, or an assistant returning officer or a presiding or polling officer at an election, or an officer or clerk appointed by the returning officer or the presiding officer to perform any duty in connection with an election shall in the conduct or the management of the election do any act (other than the giving of vote) for the furtherance of the prospects of the election of a candidate.

(2) No such person as aforesaid, and no member of the police force, shall endeavour—

(a) to persuade any person to give his vote at an election, or

(b) to dissuade any person from giving his vote at an election, or

(c) to influence the voting of any person at an election in any manner.

(3) Any person who contravenes the provisions of sub-section (1) or sub-section (2) shall be punishable with imprisonment for a term which may extend to six months or with fine, or with both.

65. Prohibition of Canvassing in or near Polling Stations—(1) No person shall, on the date or dates on which a poll is taken at any polling station, commit any of the following acts within the polling station or in any public or private place within a distance of one hundred metres of the polling station, namely:

(a) canvassing for votes; or

(b) soliciting the vote of any elector; or

(c) persuading any elector not to vote for any particular candidate; or

(d) persuading any elector not to vote at the election; or

(e) exhibiting any notice or sign (other than an official notice) relating to the election.

(2) Any person who contravenes the provisions of sub-section (1) shall be punishable with fine which may extend to two hundred and fifty rupees.

(3) An offence punishable under this section shall be cognizable.

66. Penalty for Disorderly Conduct in or near Polling Stations—(1) No person shall, on the date or dates on which a poll is taken at any polling station:

(a) use or operate within or at the entrance of the polling station, or in any public or private place in the neighbourhood thereof, any apparatus for amplifying or reproducing the human voice, such as a megaphone or a loudspeaker, or

(b) shout, or otherwise act in a disorderly manner within or at the entrance of the polling station or in any public or private place in the neighbourhood thereof, so as to cause annoyance to any person visiting the polling station for the poll, or so as to interfere with the work of the officers and other persons on duty at the polling station.

(2) Any person who contravenes, or willfully aids or abets the contravention of the provisions of sub-section (1) shall be punishable with imprisonment for a term which may extend to three months or with fine, or with both.

(3) If the polling officer of a polling station has reason to believe that any person is committing or has committed an offence punishable under this section, he may direct any police officer to arrest such person, and thereupon the police officer shall arrest him.

(4) Any police officer may take such steps and use such force, as may be reasonably necessary for preventing any contravention of the provisions of sub-section (1) and may seize any apparatus used for such contravention.

Explanation. In this section, the expression "polling officer" means the polling officer of a polling station or if there is a presiding officer at the polling station, such presiding officer.

67. Penalty for mis-conduct at the Polling Station—(1) Any person who during the hours fixed for the poll at any polling station misconducts himself or fails to obey the lawful directions of the polling officer may be removed from the polling station by the polling officer or by any police officer on duty or by any person authorised in this behalf by such polling officer.

(2) The powers conferred by sub-section (1) shall not be exercised so as to prevent any elector who is otherwise entitled to vote at a polling station from having opportunity of voting at that polling station.

(3) If any person who has been so removed from a polling station re-enters the polling station without the permission of the polling officer, he shall be punishable with imprisonment for a term which may extend to three months or with fine, or with both.

(4) An offence punishable under sub-section (3) shall be cognizable.

Explanation. In this section, the expression "polling officer" has the same meaning as in section 66.

68. Penalty for Illegal Hiring or Procuring of Conveyance at Elections—(1) No candidate or his agent or any other person with the consent of a candidate or his agent shall hire or procure whether on payment or otherwise any vehicle or vessel for the conveyance of any elector (other than the candidate himself, the members of his family or his agent) to or from any polling station:

Provided that nothing in this sub-section shall apply to:

(a) the hiring of a vehicle or vessel by an elector or several electors at their joint cost for the purpose of conveying him or them to or from the polling station, if the vehicle or vessel so hired is a vehicle or vessel not propelled by mechanical power; and

(b) the use of any public transport vehicle or vessel or any railway carriage by any elector at his own cost for the purpose of going to or coming from the polling station.

Explanation. In this sub-section, the expression "vehicle" means any vehicle used or capable of being used for the purpose of road transport whether propelled by mechanical power or otherwise and whether used for drawing other vehicles or otherwise.

(2) Any person who contravenes the provisions of sub-section (1) at or in connection with an election shall be punishable with fine which may extend to two hundred and fifty rupees.

69. Breaches of Official Duty in Connection with Election—(1) If any person to whom this section applies is without reasonable cause guilty of any act or omission in breach of his official duty, he shall be punishable with fine which may extend to five hundred rupees.

(2) No suit or other legal proceedings shall lie against any such person for damages in respect of any such act or omission as aforesaid.

(3) The persons to whom this section applies are the returning officers, assistant returning officers, presiding officers, polling officers and any other person appointed to perform any duty in connection with the receipt of nomination or withdrawal of candidatures, or the recording or counting of votes at an election; and the expression "official duty" shall for the purpose of this section be construed accordingly, but shall not include duties imposed otherwise than by or under this Act.

70. Removal of Ballot Papers from Polling Stations to be an Offence—(1) Any person who at any election fraudulently takes or attempts to take a ballot paper out of the polling station, or wilfully aids or abets the doing of any such act, shall be punishable with imprisonment for a term which may extend to one year or with fine which may extend to five hundred rupees, or with both.

(2) If the presiding officer of a polling station has reason to believe that any person is committing or has committed an offence punishable under sub-section (1), such officer may before such person leaves the polling station arrest or direct a police officer to arrest such person and may search such person or cause him to be searched by a police officer:

Provided that when it is necessary to cause a woman to be searched, the search shall be made by another woman with strict regard to decency.

(3) Any ballot paper found upon the person arrested on search shall be made over for safe custody to a police officer by the presiding officer or when the search is made by a police officer, shall be kept by such officer in safe custody.

(4) An offence punishable under sub-section (1) shall be cognisable.

71. Other Offences and Penalties Therefor—(1) No person at an election shall:

(a) fraudulently deface or fraudulently destroy any nomination paper; or
(b) fraudulently deface, destroy or remove any list, notice or other document affixed by or under the authority of a returning officer; or
(c) fraudulently deface or fraudulently destroy any ballot paper or the official mark on any ballot paper; or
(d) without due authority supply any ballot paper to any person or receive any ballot paper from any person or be in possession of any ballot paper; or
(e) fraudulently put into any ballot box anything other than the ballot paper which he is authorised by law to put in; or
(f) without due authority destroy, take, open or otherwise interfere with any ballot box or ballot paper then in use for the purpose of the election; or
(g) fraudulently or without due authority, as the case may be, attempt to do any of the foregoing acts or wilfully aid or abet the doing of any such acts.

(2) Any person who contravenes the provisions of sub-section (1) shall:
(a) if he is a returning officer or an assistant returning officer or a presiding officer at a polling station or any other officer or clerk employed on official duty in connection with the election, be punishable with imprisonment for a term which may extend to two years or with fine, or with both;
(b) if he is any other person be punishable with imprisonment for a term which may extend to six months or with fine, or with both.

(3) For the purpose of this section, a person shall be deemed to be on official duty if his duty is to take part in the conduct of an election or part of an election including the counting of votes or to be responsible after an election for the used ballot papers and other documents in connection with such election, but the expression "official duty" shall not include any duty imposed otherwise than by or under this Act.

(4) An offence punishable under clause (b) of sub-section (2) shall be cognizable.

72. Cognizance of Certain Election Offences—No court shall take cognizance of any offence punishable under section 64 or under section 69 or under clause (a) of sub-section (2) of section 71 except on complaint in writing made by order of, or under authority from the Government.

REQUISITIONING OF PROPERTY FOR ELECTION PURPOSES

73. Requisitioning of Premises, Vehicles etc., for Election Purposes—(1) If it appears to the Government, that in connection with an election under this Act:
(a) any premises other than residential building actually occupied are needed or likely to be needed for the purpose of being used as a polling station or for the storage of ballot boxes after a poll has been taken, or
(b) any vehicle, vessel or animal is needed or is likely to be needed for the purpose of transport of ballot boxes to or from any polling station, or transport of members of the police force for maintaining order during the conduct of such election or transport of any officer or other person for performance of any duty in connection with such election, the Government may, by order in writing, requisition such premises, or such vehicle, vessel or animal, as the case may be and may make such further orders as may appear to them to be necessary or expedient in connection with the requisitioning:

Provided that no vehicle, vessel or animal which is being lawfully used by a candidate or his agent for any purpose connected with the election of such candidate shall be requisitioned under this sub-section until the completion of the poll at such election.

(2) The requisition shall be effected by an order in writing addressed to the person deemed by the Government to be the owner or person in possession of the property, and such order shall be served on the person to whom it is addressed.

(3) Whenever any property is requisitioned under sub-section (1), the period of such requisition shall not extend beyond the period for which such property is required for any of the purposes mentioned in that sub-section.

(4) In this section:
(a) 'premises' means any land, building or part of a building and includes a hut, shed or other structure or any part thereof;
(b) 'vehicle' means any vehicle used or capable of being used for the purpose of road transport, whether propelled by mechanical power or otherwise.

74. Payment of Amount—(1) Whenever in pursuance of section 73, the Government requisition any premises, the persons interested, shall be paid by the Government, an amount which shall be determined by the Government by taking into consideration the following, namely—

(i) the rent payable in respect of the premises or if no rent is so payable the rent payable for similar premises in the locality:

Provided that the rent payable in respect of the premises to which the provisions of the Tamil Nadu Buildings (Lease and Rent Control) Act, 1960 (Tamil Nadu Act 18 of 1960) apply shall be the fair rent payable for the premises under the Act.

(ii) If in consequence of the requisition of the premises, the person interested is compelled to change his residence or place of business, the reasonable expenses if any, incidental to such change:

Provided that where any person interested, being aggrieved by the amount so determined makes an application to the Government within one month from the date of service of the order determining the amount, for referring the matter to an arbitrator, the amount to be paid shall be such as the arbitrator appointed by the Government may determine:

Provided further that where there is any dispute as to the title to receive the amount or as to the apportionment of the amount it shall be referred by the Government to an arbitrator appointed in this behalf by the Government for determination and shall be determined in accordance with the decision of such arbitrator.

Explanation. In this sub-section, the expression "person interested" means the person who was in actual possession of the premises requisitioned under section 73 immediately before the requisition, or where no person was in such actual possession, the owner of such premises.

(2) Whenever in pursuance of section 73, the Government requisition any vehicle; vessel or animal, there shall be paid by the Government to the owner thereof an amount which shall be determined by the Government on the basis of the fares or rates prevailing in the locality for the hire of such vehicle, vessel or animal:

Provided that where the owner of such vehicle, vessel or animal being aggrieved by the amount so determined makes an application to the Government within one month from the date of service of the order determining the amount for referring the matter to an arbitrator, the amount to be paid shall be such sum as the arbitrator appointed in this behalf by the Government may determine:

Provided further that where immediately before the requisitioning, the vehicle or vessel was by virtue of a hire purchase agreement in the possession of a person other than the owner, the total amount determined under this sub-section payable in respect of the requisition shall be apportioned between that person and the owner in such manner as they may agree upon, and in default of agreement, in such manner as an arbitrator appointed by the Government in this behalf may decide.

75. Power to Obtain Information—The Government may, with a view to requisitioning any property under section 73 or determining the amount payable under section 74, by order, require any person to furnish to such authority as may be specified in the order such information in his possession relating to such property as may be so specified.

76. Power of Entry into and Inspection of Premises etc.—(1) Any person authorised in this behalf by the Government may enter into any premises and inspect such premises and any vehicle, vessel or animal therein for the purpose of determining whether and if so in what manner, an order under section 73 should be made in relation to such premises, vehicle, vessel or animal or with a view to securing compliance with any order made under that section.

(2) In this section, the expression "premises" and "vehicle" shall have the same meaning as in section 73.

77. Eviction from Requisitioned Premises—(1) Any person remaining in possession of any requisitioned premises in contravention of any order made under section 73 may be summarily evicted from the premises by any officer empowered by the Government in this behalf.

(2) Any officer so empowered may, after giving to any woman not appearing in public, reasonable warning and facility to withdraw, remove or open any lock or bolt or break open any door of any building or do any other act necessary for effecting such eviction.

78. Release of Premises from Requisition—(1) When any premises requisitioned under section 73 are to be released from requisition, the possession thereof shall be delivered to the person from whom possession was taken at the time when the premises were requisitioned, or if there were no such person to the person deemed by the Government to be the owner of such premises and such delivery of possession shall be a full discharge of the Government from all liabilities in respect of such delivery, but shall not prejudice any rights in respect of the premises which any other person may be entitled by due process of law to enforce against the person to whom possession of the premises is so delivered.

(2) Where the person to whom possession of any premises requisition of under Section 73 is to be given under sub-section (1), cannot be found or is not readily ascetainable, or has no agent or any other person empowered to accept delivery on his behalf, the Government shall cause a notice declaring that such premises are released from requisition to be affixed on some conspicuous part of such premises and publish the notice in the District Gazette concerned.

(3) When a notice referred to in sub-section (2) is published in the District Gazette, the premises specified in such notice shall cease to be, subject to requisition on and from the date of such publication and be deemed to have been delivered to the person entitled to possession thereof, and the Government shall not be liable for any claim in respect of such premises for any period after the said date.

79. Delegation of Function of the Government with Regard to Requisitioning—The Government may, by notification, direct that any power conferred or any duty imposed on the Government by any of the provisions of sections 73 to 78 shall, under such conditions, if any, as may be specified in the direction, be exercised or discharged by such officer or class of officers as may be so specified.

80. Penalty for Contravention of Any Order of Requisitioning—If any person contravenes any order made under section 73 or section 75, he shall be punishable with imprisonment for a term which may extend to one year or with fine, or with both.

MEMBERS

81. Rights of Individual Member—(1) Any member may call the attention of the executive authority or the commissioner or the Secretary, as the case may be, to any neglect in the execution of panchayat work, to any waste of panchayat property or to the wants of any locality, and may suggest any improvement which may appear desirable.

(2) Every member shall have the right to move resolutions and to interpolate the president or chairman on matters connected with the administration of the panchayat, subject to such rules as may be prescribed.

(3) Every member shall have access during office hours to the records of the panchayat after giving due notice to the executive authority or the Commissioner or the Secretary, provided that the executive authority or Commissioner or the Secretary may, for reasons recorded in writing, forbid such access.

82. No President, Vice-President, Chairman, Vice-Chairman or Member to Receive Remuneration—No president, vice-president, chairman, vice-chairman or member shall receive, or be paid from the funds at the disposal of or under the control of the panchayat, [58]["any salary or other remuneration except travelling allowance, fixed monthly travelling allowance, daily allowance and sitting fees as may be fixed by the Government from time-to-time"] for services rendered by him whether in his capacity as such or in any other capacity.

82A. President, Vice-President, Chairman, Vice-Chairman or member to obtain permission to undertake trip to foreign country—No person holding the office of President, Vice-President or member of a village panchayat or chairman, vice-chairman or member of a panchayat union council or of a District Panchyat shall undertake any trip to any foreign country in his official capacity as such, except with the permission in writing of the government.

CHAPTER V
POWERS AND DUTIES OF THE EXECUTIVE AUTHORITY

83. Executive Authority of Village Panchayat.—[59]["The Government may by notification, appoint any person, who shall, subject to such rules as may be prescribed, exercise the powers and perform the functions of the executive authority of a village panchayat:"] [143][and different persons may be appointed to different classes of village panchayats].

84. Functions of Executive Authority—The executive authority shall—

(a) carry into effect the resolutions of the village panchayat:

Provided that where the [60]["executive authority"] considers that a resolution has not been legally passed or is in excess of the powers conferred by this Act or that, if carried out, it is likely to endanger human life or health or the public safety, the executive authority shall refer the matter to the Government for orders and their decision shall be final;

(b) control all the officers and servants of the village panchayat;

(c) discharge all the duties specifically imposed and exercise all the powers conferred on the executive authority and subject to all restrictions and conditions imposed, by or under this Act, exercise the executive power for the purpose of carrying out the provisions of this Act and be directly responsible for the due fulfilment of the purposes thereof.

COMMISSIONER

85. Commissioner—(1) A commissioner shall be appointed by the Government in the case of each panchayat union council. Such Commissioner shall ordinarily be the Development Officer appointed in pursuance of the National Extension Service Scheme of Community Development for the panchayat development block.

(2) No recovery shall be made from the panchayat union council towards the salary and allowances paid to any Commissioner or towards his leave allowances, pension and provident fund.

(3) The Government shall have power to regulate the method of recruitment, conditions of service, pay and allowances and discipline and conduct of the Commissioner appointed under sub-section (1).

(4) The Commissioner shall—

(a) have the right to attend the meetings of the panchayat union council or of any committee thereof and take part in the discussions thereat, but without the right to move any resolution or to vote;

(b) attend any meeting of the panchayat union council or of any committee thereof if required to do so by the chairman;

(c) carry into effect the resolutions of the panchayat union council;

(d) furnish to the panchayat union council such periodical reports regarding the progress made in carrying out the resolutions of that body and in the collection of taxes as the council may direct;

(e) control all the officers and servants of the panchayat union council;

(f) perform all the duties specifically imposed and exercise all the powers conferred on the Commissioner by this Act and subject, whenever it is hereinafter expressly so provided, to the sanction of the panchayat union council and subject also to all other restrictions, limitations and conditions hereinafter imposed, exercise the executive power for the purpose of carrying out the provisions of this Act and be directly responsible for the fulfilment of the purposes of this Act.

(5) Notwithstanding anything contained in sub-section (2) of section 16 and subject to all other provisions of this Act and the rules made thereunder the panchayat union council shall have power to issue such specific directions as it may think fit regarding the performance by the Commissioner of any of the functions assigned to him under this Act:

Provided that where such directions relate to any National Extension Service Scheme of Community Development or any other scheme specially entrusted by the Government to the panchayat union council, the directions issued by the council shall be in conformity with the terms and conditions of such entrustment.

(6) Subject to any directions given or restrictions imposed by the Government or the panchayat union council, the Commissioner may, by an order in writing, delegate any of his functions to any officer or servant of the panchayat union council or to any servant of the Government. The exercise or discharge of any functions so delegated shall be subject to such restrictions, limitations and conditions as may be laid down by the Commissioner and shall also be subject to his control and revision.

86. Emergency Power of Executive Authority and Commissioner—The executive authority or the Commissioner may in cases of emergency direct the execution of any work or the doing of any act which requires the sanction of the village panchayat or the panchayat union council, as the case may be, and the immediate execution or doing of which is, in his opinion, necessary for the health or safety of the public and may direct that the expenses of executing such work or doing such act shall be paid from the Village Panchayat Fund or the Panchayat Union Fund, as the case may be:

Provided that:

(a) he shall not act under this section in contravention of any order of the village panchayat or the panchayat union council prohibiting the execution of any particular work or the doing of any particular act, and

(b) he shall report the action taken under this section and the reasons therefore to the village panchayat or the panchayat union council at its next meeting.

SECRETARY

87. Secretary—(1) The Government shall appoint an officer not below the rank of [61]["Divisional Development Officer in the Tamil Nadu Panchayat Development Service"] as Secretary of the district panchayat.

(2) The Government shall have power to regulate the method of recruitment and conditions of service, pay and allowances and discipline and conduct of the Secretary appointed under sub-section (1).

88. Functions, Powers and Duties of Secretary—(1) The Secretary shall—

(a) exercise all the powers specially imposed or conferred upon him by or under this Act or under any other law for the time being in force;

(b) supervise and control the execution of all works of the district panchayat, and have the right to attend meetings of the district panchayat or any committee thereof and take part in the discussions thereat, but without the right to move any resolution or to vote;

(c) attend any meeting of the district panchayat or any committee thereof if required to do so by the chairman;

(d) carryout the resolutions of the district panchayat;

(e) furnish to the district panchayat such periodical reports regarding the progress made in carrying out the resolutions of that body and in the collection of taxes as the council may direct;

(f) control the officers and servants of the district panchayat; and

(g) exercise such other powers and discharge such other functions as may be prescribed.

(2) Notwithstanding anything contained in sub-section (1), the district panchayat shall have power to issue such specific direction as it may think fit regarding the performance by the Secretary of any of the functions assigned to him under this Act.

(3) Subject to any directions given or restrictions imposed by the Government or the district panchayat, the Secretary may, by an order in writing, delegate any of his functions to any officer or servant of the district panchayat or to any servant of the Government. The exercise or discharge of any function so delegated shall be subject to such restrictions, limitations and conditions as may be laid down by the Secretary and shall also be subject to his control and revision.

(4) The Secretary shall within fifteen days from the date of the meeting of the district panchayat or of any of its committee, submit to the Government every resolution of the district panchayat or any of its committee which in his opinion is inconsistent with the provisions of this Act or other law and it shall not implement such resolution otherwise than as decided by the Government.

CHAPTER VI
PROCEDURE

89. Presidency at Meetings of Panchayat—(1) Every meeting of a panchayat shall be presided over by the president or the chairman, as the case may be, and in the absence of the president, chairman, vice-president, vice-chairman, by a member chosen by the members present at the meeting to preside for the occasion.

(2) The president or the chairman, as the case may be, shall preserve order and decide all points of order arising at or in connection with meetings. There shall be no discussion on any point of order and the decision of the president or chairman, as the case may be, on any point of order shall be final.

(3) A vice-president, a vice-chairman or member presiding for the occasion shall, for that meeting and during the period he presides over it, have all the powers of the president or chairman, as the case may be.

90. Meetings of Panchayat—Every panchayat shall meet at such times and places and shall, subject to the provisions of section 89, observe such rules of procedure in regard to transaction of business at its meetings (including the quorum at meetings) as may be prescribed:

Provided that not more than sixty days shall elapse between any two meetings of the panchayat.

91. Members when to Abstain from Taking Part in Discussion and Voting—(1) No member shall vote on, or take part in the discussion of, any question coming up for consideration at a meeting of the panchayat or any committee if the question is one in which, apart from its general application to the public he has any direct or indirect pecuniary interest by himself or his partner.

(2) The president or chairman, as the case may be, may prohibit any member from voting or taking part in the discussion of any matter in which he believes such member to take such interest, or he may require such member to absent himself during the discussion.

(3) Such member may challenge the decision of the president or chairman, who shall thereupon put the question to the meeting. The decision of the meeting shall be final.

(4) If the president or chairman is believed by any member present at the meeting to have any such pecuniary interest in any matter under discussion, he may, if a motion to that effect is carried, be required to absent himself from the meeting during such discussion.

(5) The member concerned shall not be entitled to vote on the question referred to in sub-section (3) and the president or chairman concerned shall not be entitled to vote on the motion referred to in sub-section (4).

Explanation. The terms "president" and "chairman" in this section include a vice-president, vice-chairman or member presiding for the occasion.

92. Minutes of Proceeding—A copy of the minutes of the proceedings of every meeting of a panchayat as well as of all minutes of dissent in respect of such proceedings received from any member present at the meeting, within forty-eight hours of the close thereof, shall be submitted by the president or chairman, as the case may be, within three days of the date of the meeting to the Inspector:

Provided that the Inspector may direct that such minutes shall be submitted either generally or in any specified classes of cases to any officer empowered by him in this behalf.

93. Power of Panchayat to Call for Records—A panchayat may require the executive authority or the Commissioner or the Secretary as the case may be, to produce any document which is in his custody and he shall, subject to such rules as may be prescribed comply with every such requisition.

94. Proceedings of Panchayat and Committees—(1) The proceedings of every panchayat, and of all committees thereof shall be governed by such rules as may be prescribed and by regulations, not inconsistent with such rules or the provisions of this Act, made by the panchayat with the approval of the Inspector.

(2) The Inspector may remit for reconsideration and re-submission any regulation or part thereof to the panchayat:

Provided that it shall be competent for the Inspector to add to, omit or alter any regulation which contravenes the provisions of this Act or the rules made thereunder.

95. Appointment of Joint Committees—(1) A panchayat may, and if so required by the Inspector, shall, join with one, or more than one, other local authority in constituting a joint committee for any purpose for which they are jointly responsible.

(2) The constitution, powers and procedure of a joint committee and the method of settling differences of opinion arising in connection with the committee between the local authorities concerned shall be in accordance with such rules as may be prescribed.

96. Committees—(1) (a) There shall be an Appointment Committee for every panchayat union, which shall be composed of the chairman of the panchayat union council, the Commissioner and one member elected annually by the panchayat union council. The chairman of the panchayat union council shall be the chairman of the committee. Subject to the provisions of section 102 and to such rules as may be made by the Government in this behalf, appointments to all posts under the panchayat union council, the pay of which is debitable to the funds of the panchayat union council shall be made with the prior approval of the committee.

(b) (i) There shall be an Agricultural Production Committee for every panchayat union, which shall be composed of the chairman of the panchayat union council who shall be the chairman of that committee, the Commissioner and three persons nominated by the panchayat union council.

(ii) No person shall be nominated under sub-clause (i), if

(A) he is not a member of the panchayat union council; or

(B) in the opinion of the panchayat union council, he does not possess adequate knowledge of and experience in, agriculture.

(c) There shall be an Education Committee and a General Purposes Committee in every panchayat union. The panchayat union council may, and if so required by the Government, shall appoint such other committees as may be necessary for the efficient performance of its duties and functions under this Act. Each of the committee constituted under this clause shall consist of such number of members as may be specified by the council and shall include the chairman *ex-officio*. The members of each committee constituted under this clause, other than the chairman, shall be elected by the panchayat union council from among its elected members.

(2) Subject to such rules, as may be made by the Government in this behalf, the panchayat union council shall have power, by regulations made from time-to-time, to determine the powers and duties of every committee constituted under sub-section (1).

97. Standing Committees—(1) (a) For the purpose of assisting the district panchayat in exercising such of its powers, discharging such of its duties and performing such of its functions specified under this Act, a district panchayat may constitute standing committees for dealing with—

(i) food and agriculture;
(ii) industries and labour;
(iii) public works;
(iv) education;
(v) health and welfare including prohibition;

(b) a district panchayat may constitute additional standing committees for such purposes as it thinks fit.

(2) Each standing committee shall consist of such number of persons not exceeding five including the chairman as specified by the district panchayat and elected by the district panchayat from among its elected members.

(3) The chairman of the district panchayat shall be the *ex-officio* member in all the standing committees constituted by the district panchayat.

(4) Each standing committee shall elect its own chairman from among its members who are elected members of the district panchayat.

(5) No member of the district panchayat shall be eligible to serve on more than two standing committees.

(6) The Secretary shall nominate one of the officers under his control as *ex-officio* secretary for each of the standing committees. The Secretary shall be entitled to attend the meetings of all the standing committees.

ADMINISTRATION REPORT

98. Administration Report of Village Panchayats—(1) Every village panchayat shall submit to the panchayat union council a report on its administration for each year as soon as may be after the close of such year and not later than the prescribed date, in such form, with such details and through such authority as may be prescribed.

(2) The report shall be prepared by the executive authority and the village panchayat shall consider it and forward the same to the panchayat union council with its resolution thereon.

99. Administration Report of Panchayat Union Councils and District Panchayats—(1) Every panchayat union council shall submit to the district panchayat a consolidated report on its administration and on the administration of all village panchayats in the panchayat union for each year as soon as may be after the close of such year and not later than the prescribed date, in such form, with such details and through such authority as may be prescribed.

(2) The report shall be prepared by the Commissioner and the panchayat union council shall consider it and forward the same to the district panchayat with its resolution thereon.

(3) The district panchayat shall prepare a general report on the administration of panchayat union councils and village panchayats in the district and submit the same to the Government before such date as may be prescribed. The district panchayat shall also send a copy of the report to the Inspector.

(4) The report and resolution thereon shall be published in such manner as the Government may direct.

100. Acts of Village Panchayat, Panchayat Union Council and District Panchayat, etc. not to be Invalidated by any Infirmity, Vacancy, etc.—No act of a village panchayat or of a panchayat union council or of a district panchayat or of a committee thereof or of any person acting as president, vice-president, chairman, vice-chairman or member of such village panchayat or panchayat union council or district panchayat or committee, shall be deemed to be invalid by reason only of a defect in the establishment of such panchayat or committee, as the case may be, or on the ground that the president, vice-president, chairman, vice-chairman or member of such village panchayat or panchayat union council or district panchayat or chairman or member of a committee was not entitled to hold or continue in such office by reason of any disqualification or by reason of any irregularity or illegality in his election or by reason of such act having been done during the period of any vacancy in the office of president, vice-president, chairman, vice-chairman or member of such village panchayat, panchayat union council or district panchayat or committee.

"CHAPTER VI-A

100-A. Certain modifications of provisions of this Act.—Notwithstanding anything contained in this Act, in respect of special village panchayats:

(a) the executive officer of the special village panchayat shall be the executive authority;

(b) the provisions of the Tamil Nadu District Municipalities Act, 1920 (Tamil Nadu Act V of 1920) and the rules made thereunder shall apply,–

(i) in respect of the regulation or restriction of building and the use of sites for building;

(ii) in respect of levy of property tax;

(c) all cheques for payment from panchayat fund or other funds shall be signed by the executive officer of the special village panchayat."

CHAPTER VII
ESTABLISHMENT, POWERS AND FUNCTIONS OF PANCHAYATS

101. Establishment of Panchayats—(1) The sanction of the panchayat shall be obtained for all proposals for fixing or altering the number, designations and grades of its officers and servants and the salaries, fees and allowances payable to them.

(2) Such proposals shall be taken into consideration by the panchayat, only at the instance of the executive authority or the Commissioner or the Secretary, as the case may be, and the panchayat may sanction the proposal with or without modifications:

Provided that no proposal adversely affecting any officer or servant of a panchayat who has been in the permanent service of such panchayat for more than five years and is drawing a salary of not less than five hundred rupees per mensem shall be considered except at a special meeting convened for the purpose and no such proposal shall be given effect to unless assented to by at least one-half of the members then in the panchayat.

(3) Notwithstanding anything contained in sub-sections (1) and (2), the Government in the case of panchayat union councils and district panchayats and the Inspector in the case of village panchayats shall have power to fix or alter the number, designations and grades of, and the salaries, fees and allowances payable to the officers and servants of any village panchayat or panchayat union council or the district panchayat or any class of such officers and servants and it shall not be open to the village panchayat or panchayat union council or the district panchayat to vary the number, designations, grades, salaries, fees or allowances as so fixed or altered except with the previous sanction of the Government in the case of panchayat union councils and district panchayats and of the Inspector in the case of village panchayats.

[62]["Provided that the Inspector shall observe any guidelines issued by the Government in this regard"].

102. Conditions of Service of Officers and Servants of Panchayats–(1) The Government shall have power to make rules regarding the authorities who may appoint the officers and servants of panchayats, other than the Commissioners and the Secretaries and the classification, method of recruitment, pay and allowances, discipline and conduct and conditions of service of such officers and servants.

Such rule may provide for the constitution of any class of officers or servants of village panchayats, panchayat union councils and the district panchayats, as the case may be, other than the Commissioners and the Secretaries, into a separate service for the whole or any part of the State.

(2) Subject to the provisions of this Act and any rules which the Government may make in this behalf, the panchayat union council or the district panchayat, as the case may be, may frame regulations in respect of the officers and servants on the staff of the panchayat union council or the district panchayat:

(a) fixing the amount and nature of the security to be furnished;

(b) prescribing educational and other qualifications;

(c) regulating the grant of leave, leave allowances, acting allowances and travelling allowances;

(d) regulating the grant of pensions and gratuities;

(e) establishing and maintaining provident funds and making contributions thereto compulsory;

(f) regulating conduct; and

(g) generally prescribing conditions of service.

Provided:

(i) that the grant of any leave, leave allowances, pension or gratuity provided for in such regulations shall in no case, without the special sanction of the Government exceed what would be admissible in the case of Government servants of similar standing and status;

(ii) that the conditions under which such allowances are granted or any leave, superannuation or retirement is sanctioned shall not without similar sanction, be more favourable than those for the time being prescribed for such Government servants.

(3) A rule may be made under sub-section (1) in so far as it relates to officers and servants of village panchayats and panchayat union councils, so as to have retrospective effect on and from a date not earlier than the date of commencement of this Act.

103. Appointment of Common Officers—Two or more village panchayats or two or more panchayat union councils may, subject to such rules as may be prescribed, and shall if so required by any authority empowered in this behalf by rules, appoint the same officer or servant to exercise or discharge any powers or duties of a similar nature for both or all of them.

104. Transfer of Officers and Servants of Village Panchayats and Panchayat Union Councils—(1) Any officer or servant of a village panchayat may be transferred to the service of any panchayat union council or any other village panchayat by the Inspector:

Provided that no officer or servant shall be so transferred except after consulting the Commissioner or the executive authority concerned:

Provided further that in making a transfer under this sub-section, the Inspector may issue such general or special directions as may in his opinion be necessary for the purpose of giving due effect to such transfer.

(2) Notwithstanding anything contained in this Act or the Tamil Nadu District Municipalities Act, 1920, any officer or servant of a panchayat union council (including the Commissioner) may be transferred by the Government to the services of any other panchayat union council or any municipality constituted under the Tamil Nadu District Municipalities Act, 1920: (Tamil Nadu Act, V of 1920)

Provided that no officer or servant (other than the Commissioner) shall be so transferred except after consulting the panchayat union councils or municipal councils concerned:

Provided further that the Government while making a transfer under this sub-section may issue such general or special directions as may in their opinion be necessary for the purpose of giving due effect to such transfer.

105. Power of Government to Transfer Officers and Servants of District Panchayats—(1) Notwithstanding anything contained in this Act or in the Tamil Nadu District Municipalities Act, 1920 (Tamil Nadu Act V of 1920), the Government shall have power:

(a) to transfer any officer or servant of the district panchayat (including the Secretary) to the service of any other district panchayat or to any municipality constituted under the Tamil Nadu District Municipalities Act, 1920.

(b) to issue general or special direction as they may think necessary for the purpose of giving due effect to any transfer made under clause (a).

106. Power to Punish Officers and Servants of Panchayats—Subject to such control as may be prescribed, the executive authority, the Commissioner or the Secretary may censure, fine, withhold increments or promotion from, or reduce to a lower rank in the seniority list, or to a lower post or time-scale or to a lower stage in a time-scale, suspend, remove or dismiss any officer or servant in the service of village panchayat or panchayat union or the district panchayat, as the case may be, for any breach of departmental rules or discipline, or for carelessness, unfitness, neglect of duty or other misconduct.

107. Applicability of Certain Directions to Public Against Health Establishment—Subject to the provisions of section 109, the provisions of sections 101 to 106 shall also apply to the public health establishments of panchayats, notwithstanding anything contained in the Tamil Nadu Public Health Act, 1939.

108. Teachers Including Headmaster and Basic Servants in the Panchayat Union Schools to be Government Servants—(1) Notwithstanding anything contained in this Act or in any other law for the time being in force, on and from the 1st June 1981, all teachers (including headmasters) and basic servants in the panchayat union schools in the State of Tamil Nadu shall become whole-time Government servants.

(2) Notwithstanding anything contained in sub-section (1) of section 96 or in any other provisions of this Act and subject to the provisions of Article 311 of the Constitution, the Government may make

rules regulating the conditions of service of the teachers (including headmasters) and basic servants in the panchayat union schools.

109. Health Assistants, Auxiliary Nurses, Mid-wives and Maternity Assistants in Public Health Establishments of Panchayat Union Councils to be Government Servants—(1) Notwithstanding anything contained in this Act or in any other law for the time being in force, on and from the 1st October 1982, all health assistants, auxiliary nurses, mid-wives and maternity assistants in the public health establishments of panchayat union councils, in the State shall become whole-time Government servants.

(2) Notwithstanding anything contained in sub-section (1) of section 96 or in any other provisions of this Act and subject to the provisions of Article 311 of the Constitution, the Government may make rules regulating the conditions, of service of the health assistants, the auxiliary nurses, mid-wives and maternity assistants in the public health establishments of panchayat union councils.

CHAPTER VIII
FUNCTIONS, POWERS AND PROPERTY OF VILLAGE PANCHAYATS, PANCHAYAT UNION COUNCILS AND DISTRICT PANCHAYATS

110. Duty of Village Panchayat to Provide for Certain Matters—Subject to provisions of this Act and the rules made thereunder, it shall be the duty of village panchayat, within the limits of its funds, to make reasonable provision for carrying out the requirements of the panchayat village in respect of the following matters, namely:

(a) the construction, repair and maintenance of all village roads, that is to say, all public roads in the village (other than those classified as National Highways, State Highways, major district roads and panchayat union roads) and of all bridges, culverts, road-dams and causeways on such roads:

[63] "[(aa) The extension of village sites and the regulation of building;"]

(b) the lighting of public roads and public places in built-up areas;

(c) the construction of drains and the disposal of drainage water and sullage not including sewage;

(d) the cleaning of streets, the removal of rubbish heaps, jungle growth and prickly pear, the filling in of disused wells, in sanitary ponds, pools, ditches pits or hollows and other improvement of the sanitary condition of the village;

(e) the provision of public latrines and arrangements to cleanse latrines whether public or private;

(f) the opening and maintenance of burial and burning grounds;

(g) the sinking and repairing of wells, the excavation, repair and maintenance of ponds or tanks and the construction and maintenance of water-works [64]["for the supply of water for drinking, washing"] and bathing purposes; and

(h) such other duties as the Government may, by notification, impose.

111. Power of Village Panchayat to Provide for Certain Other Matters—Subject to the provisions of this Act and the rules made thereunder a village panchayat may also make such provisions as it thinks fit for carrying out the requirements of the village in respect of the following matters, namely:

(a) the planting and preservation of trees on the sides of all public roads in the village subject to mutually agreed terms and conditions between the village panchayat and the authority which maintains the road in case the road is not maintained by the village panchayat itself;

(b) the lighting of public roads and public places in areas other than built-up areas;

(c) the opening and maintenance of public markets other than markets which are classified as panchayat union markets;

(d) the control of fairs and festivals other than those classified as panchayat union fairs and festivals;

(e) the opening and maintenance of public landing places, halting places and cart-stands and of public cattle-sheds;

(f) the opening and maintenance of public slaughter-houses;

(g) the opening and maintenance of reading rooms;

(h) the establishment and maintenance of wireless receiving sets [65]["television sets"] playgrounds, parks, sports clubs and centres of physical culture;

(i) the opening and maintenance of literacy centres and centres for imparting social education; and

(j) the construction of works of public utility and the provisions of other facilities for the safety, health, convenience, culture or recreation of the inhabitants of the village;

[66][**] – omitted

112. Duty of Panchayat Union Council to Provide for Certain Matters—Subject to the provisions of this Act and the rules made thereunder, it shall be the duty of a panchayat union council, within the limits of its funds, to make reasonable provision for carrying out the requirements of the panchayat union in respect of the following matters, namely:

(a) the construction, repair and maintenance of all public roads in the panchayat union which are classified as panchayat union roads and of all bridges, culverts, road dams and cause ways on such roads;

[67]"(aa) the construction of water works for the supply of water for drinking, washing and bathing purpose";

[68]["(aaa) the construction and maintenance of comprehensive water supply schemes for the supply of protected drinking water covering one or more village panchayats as may be notified by the Government"];

(b) the establishment and maintenance of dispensaries and the payments of subsidies to rural medical practitioners;

(c) the establishment and maintenance of maternity and child welfare centres, including the maintenance of a that service and offering advice and assistance to mothers in family planning;

(d) The construction and maintenance of poor houses, orphanages, shops, stalls, plinths, the training and employment of vaccinators, the removal of congestion of population and the provision of house-sites;

(e) the opening and maintenance and expansion or improvement of elementary schools, including the payment of grants to private managements in respect of elementary schools;

(f) preventive and remedial measures connected with any epidemic or with malaria;

(g) the control of fairs and festivals classified by the panchayat union council as those reserved for control by it;

(h) veterinary relief;

(i) [69][***]

(j) opening and maintenance of public markets which are classified as Panchayat Union Market;

(k) the maintenance of statistics relating to births and deaths;

(l) the establishment and maintenance of choultries;

(m) improvements of agriculture, agricultural stock and the holding of agricultural shows;

(n) the promotion and encouragement of cottage industries; and

(o) such other duties as the Government may, by notification, impose.

113. Entrustment of Execution of National Extension Service Scheme of Community Development to Panchayat Union Councils—The Government shall as soon as may be after the constitution of a panchayat union council for a panchayat development block under this Act entrust to the panchayat union council subject to such conditions and restrictions as may be specified by the Government, the execution in the panchayat development block of the National Extension Service Scheme of Community Development, including in particular, all measures relating to the development of agriculture, animal husbandry and village industries organised on an individual or co-operative basis.

114. Entrustment of Certain Schemes to Panchayat Union Councils—(1) Save as otherwise provided in section 113, the Government may, subject to such conditions and restrictions as may be specified, entrust all or any of the schemes, programmes and activities for economic development, whether such schemes, programmes and activities are to be executed as implemented either by the Government or by any statutory body or other agency to the panchayat union council for its execution or implementation.

(2) The panchayat union council may, if so notified by the Government, review the schemes, programmes and other activities executed by the Government or by any statutory body or other agency within the panchayat union.

115. Power of Panchayat Union Council to Provide for Certain other Matters.—Subject to the provisions of this Act and the rules made thereunder, a panchayat union council may, within the limits of its funds, make such provisions as it thinks fit for carrying out the requirements of the panchayat union in respect of measure of public utility other than those specified in section 112, calculated to promote the safety, health, comfort or convenience of the inhabitants of the panchayat union:

[70][Proviso] – omitted

116. Common Burial and Burning Grounds, etc.—Subject to the provisions of this Act and the rules made thereunder, two or more village panchayats:

(i) may construct and maintain water-works [71]["for the supply of water for drinking, washing and bathing purposes"] from a common source and may also provide a common burial and burning ground, and

(ii) may entrust to the panchayat union council with its consent and on such terms as may be agreed upon, the management of any institution or the execution or maintenance of any work.

117. Lighting of Public Roads and Public Places—Notwithstanding anything contained in clause (b) of section 111, the Government may, by general or special order, direct any village panchayat or panchayat union council [72]["or district panchayat"] to provide for the lighting of public roads and public places within its jurisdiction and it shall be the duty of the village panchayat or panchayat union council [73]["or district panchayat"] to provide for such light:

Provided that where such a direction is given, the Government shall make such provision for the cost of lighting as they may consider reasonable and the decision of the Government shall be final.

118. Maintenance of Common Dispensaries, Child Welfare Centres, etc.—Subject to the provisions of this Act and the rules made thereunder, two or more panchayat union councils may establish and maintain common dispensaries, child welfare centres, and institutions of such other kind as may be prescribed.

119. Transfer of Immovable Property, Management of Institutions, Execution or Maintenance of Works, etc. to a Village Panchayat—(1) The panchayat union council may, subject to such control as may be prescribed, by notification declare that any immovable property vested in itself shall vest in any village panchayat in the same panchayat union and such property shall, from the date specified in the said notification, vest accordingly.

(2) Subject to such rules as may be prescribed, [74]["the Government, Director of Rural Development or any other Head of Department or the Collector,"] the district panchayat, the panchayat union council or the Secretary, the Commissioner, or any person or body of persons, may transfer to the village panchayat, with its consent and subject to such conditions as may be agreed upon, the management of any institution, or the execution or maintenance of any work, or the exercise of any power or the discharge of any duty, whether within or without the village and whether provided for in this Act or not.

120. Transfer to Village Panchayat of Unreserved Forests—(1) (a) All unreserved forests in the village at the commencement of this Act shall vest in the village panchayat and be administered by it for the benefit of such village.

(b) In respect of every forest so vested, the village panchayat shall, if so required by the Collector, pay to the Government such rent as the Collector may, from time-to-time, subject to the control of the Commissioner of Land Administration, fix in this behalf.

(2)(a) If the Revenue Divisional Officer is of opinion that a village panchayat is not administering properly a forest vested in it under sub-section (1), he may by order, withdraw such forest from the control of the village panchayat for such period as may be specified in the order, not exceeding the period if any, prescribed in this behalf. He may in respect of such forest direct that it be vested in the panchayat union council and be administered by it.

(b) The Revenue Divisional Officer may, from time-to-time, by order, extend the period specified in any order issued under clause (a) subject to the period prescribed in this behalf.

(c) Before issuing an order under clause (a) or (b) a reasonable opportunity shall be given to the village panchayat to show cause against such issue.

(d) When an order is issued under clause (a) or (b), the village panchayat concerned may, within three months of the service of the order, appeal against it to the Collector and the Collector may confirm, modify or reverse the order.

(3) The Commissioner of Land Administration may, at any time, either *suo moto* or on application, call for and examine the record or any order issued by the Revenue Divisional Officer or the Collector under sub-section (2) for the purpose of satisfying himself as to the legality or propriety of such order, and may pass such order in reference thereto as he thinks fit.

121. Power of Government to Resume Possession of Unreserved Forest Vested in a Village Panchayat and Payment of Compensation etc.—(1) If in the opinion of the Government any unreserved forest vested in a village panchayat under section 120 is required for any public purpose, they may, by notification, resume the possession and administration of such unreserved forest and upon such resumption by the Government, all rights and interest created in or over such unreserved forest before such resumption shall as against the Government cease and determine.

(2) Whenever the possession and administration of such unreserved forest is resumed by the Government under sub-section (1), there shall be paid to the village panchayat concerned compensation for any improvement made by such village panchayat in such unreserved forest, as determined in the manner hereinafter provided by the Collector within whose jurisdiction such unreserved forest is situated.

Explanation. For the purposes of this sub-section, 'improvement' means any work or product of a work which adds to the value of the unreserved forest or is suitable to it and consistent with the purpose for which it was vested in the village panchayat and shall include the following works or the products of such works:

(a) the erection of buildings or any other structure, the construction of tanks, wells, channels, dams and other works for the storage or supply of water for agricultural or domestic purposes;

(b) the preparation of land for irrigation;

(c) the reclamation, clearance, enclosure or permanent improvement of land for agricultural purposes;

(d) the renewal or reconstruction of any of the foregoing works or alterations therein or addition thereto;

(e) the planting or protection and maintenance of fruit trees, timber-trees and other useful trees and plants.

(3) The compensation payable in respect of the improvement referred to in clauses (a) to (d) of the Explanation to sub-section (2) shall be the actual value of such improvements as on the date of resumption of the unreserved forest by the Government which shall include actual cost of the labour, supervision thereof, and of the materials, together with other expenditure, if any, which would be required to make such improvements, less a reasonable deduction on account of the deterioration, if any, which may have taken place from age or other cause. The compensation payable in respect of improvement referred to in clause (c) of the Explanation to sub-section (2) shall be such sum which the trees or plants might reasonably be expected to realise if sold by public auction to be cut and carried away at the time of resumption of the unreserved forest by the Government:

Provided that in computing the actual value of such improvements the value of the unreserved forest to which such improvements have been made shall not be taken into account:

Provided further that if any grant for the purpose of making such improvements has been paid by the Government to the village panchayat concerned then, the amount of such grant paid shall be deducted from the amount of compensation payable in respect of such improvements:

Provided also that in the case of trees and plants in the unreserved forest which are of spontaneous growth, the compensation payable in respect of such trees and plants shall be the proper cost of protection and maintenance of such trees and plants.

(4) The amount of compensation referred to in sub-section (2) shall be given to every village panchayat, at its option—

(a) in cash in such annual instalments with interest at such rates as may be prescribed, or

(b) in saleable or otherwise transferable promissory notes or other securities or stock certificates of the Government, or

(c) partly in cash or partly in such securities specified in clause (b), as may be required by the village panchayats.

(5) The option of the village panchayat referred to in sub-section (4) shall be exercised by such village panchayat before the expiry of a period of three months from the date of resumption of the possession and administration of the unreserved forest by the Government and the option so exercised shall be final and shall not be altered or rescinded after it has been exercised. Any village panchayat which omits or fails to exercise the option referred to in sub-section (4) within the time specified above shall be deemed to have opted for payment in securities and stock certificates referred to in clause (b) of sub-section (4). The amount of compensation payable in instalments shall be paid, and the securities and stock certificates referred to in clause (b) of sub-section (4) shall be issued, within sixty days from the date of receipt by the Government of the option referred to above or where no such option has been exercised from the date before which such option ought to have been exercised.

(6) Any village panchayat aggrieved by an order relating to compensation under this section may

appeal to the Commissioner of Land Administration within such period and in such manner as may be prescribed. The order of the Commissioner of Land Administration on such appeal and where no appeal is preferred, the order which has not been appealed against, shall be final and shall not be called in question in any court of law.

122. Power of Commissioner of Land Administration to Transfer or Resume Control of Endowments and Inams—(1) (a) Subject to the control of the Government, the Commissioner of Land Administration may, by notification, make over to a panchayat union council, with its consent, the management and superintendence of any charitable endowment in respect of which powers and duties attached to the Commissioner of Land Administration under the provisions of the Tamil Nadu Endowments and Estates Regulation, 1817; (Tamil Nadu Regulation VII of 1817) and thereupon all powers and duties attached to the Commissioner of Land Administration in respect thereof shall attach to the panchayat union council as if it had been specially named in the said Regulation, and the panchayat union council shall manage and superintend such endowment.

(b) The Commissioner of Land Administration may, of his own motion and shall on a direction from the Government, by notification resume the management and superintendence of any endowment made over to a panchayat union council under clause (a) and duties attached to the panchayat union council in respect of the endowment shall cease and determine.

(2) The Government may assign to a panchayat union council with its consent, a charitable inam, resumed by the Government or any other authority, provided that the net income from such inam can be applied exclusively to any purpose to which the funds of such panchayat union council may be applied; and may revoke any assignment so made.

(3) The management and superintendence of any charitable endowment which immediately before the constitution of a panchayat union council for any panchayat development block under this Act was vested in a district board under the Tamil Nadu District Boards Act, 1920 (Tamil Nadu Act XIV of 1920) shall, on such constitution, vest in the panchayat union council exercising jurisdiction over the place where the endowment is situated.

123. Government's Power to Add to Function of Panchayat Union Councils—Subject to such rules as may be prescribed, [75]["the Government, the Director of Rural Development or any other Head of Department or the Collector"] or any person or body of persons may transfer to the panchayat union council with its consent and on such terms as may be agreed upon, the management of any institution or the execution or maintenance of any work, or the exercise of any power or the discharge of any duty whether within or without the panchayat union and whether provided for in this Act or not.

124. Limitation of Power to Accept Donations and Trusts—A panchayat may accept donations for, or trusts relating exclusively to, the furtherance of any purpose to which its funds may be applied.

125. Vesting of Public Roads in Village Panchayat—(1) All public roads in any village (other than roads which are classified by the Government as National Highways or State highways or as major district roads or as panchayat union roads) shall vest in the village panchayat together with all pavements, stones, and other materials thereof, all works, materials and other things provided therefor, all drains, drainage works, tunnel and culverts whether made at the cost of the village panchayat or otherwise, in, alongside or under such roads, and all works, materials and things appertaining thereto.

(2) The Government may, by notification, exclude from the operation of this Act any such public road, drain, drainage work, tunnel or culvert and may also modify or cancel such notification.

126. Vesting of Public Roads in Panchayat Union Councils—(1) All public roads in any panchayat union which are classified as panchayat union roads shall vest in the panchayat union council together with all pavements, stones and other materials, thereof, all works, materials and other things provided therefore, all drains, drainage works, tunnels and culverts, whether made at the cost of the panchayat union council or otherwise, in, alongside or under such roads, and all works, materials, and things appertaining thereto.

(2) The Government may, by notification, exclude from the operation of this Act any panchayat union road, drain, drainage work, tunnel or culvert and may also modify or cancel such notification.

127. Duty of Village Panchayat in Respect of Public Roads Excluded from the Operation of the Act—Where any public road has been excluded from the operation of this Act under sub-section (2) of section 125 or sub-section (2) of section 126 and placed under the control of the Highways Department of Government (hereinafter referred to as the Highways Department), the village panchayat may and if so required by the Government shall make provision—

(a) for the watering and maintenance of the drainage of such road;

(b) for the provision, maintenance and repair of the drains in, alongside or under such road;

(c) for the provision, maintenance and repair of foot-ways attached to such road:

Provided that where in carrying out of the above provisions it is necessary for the village panchayat to open and break up the soil or pavement of any such road, the village panchayat shall obtain the previous consent of such officer of the Highways Department as the Government may, by general or special order, specify:

Provided further that in cases of emergency the village panchayat may, without such consent, open and break up the soil or pavement of any such street, but shall, as far as practicable restore such soil or pavement to the condition in which it was immediately before it was opened and broken up; and a report of the action so taken and the reasons therefore shall be sent forthwith to the officer specified under the foregoing proviso:

Provided also that where the execution of any work is required by the Government, the Government shall make provision for the cost thereof.

128. Precautions in Case of Dangerous Structures—(1) If any structure adjoining a public road vested in a panchayat union council or a village panchayat appears to the Commissioner or the executive authority, as the case may be, to be in a ruinous state and dangerous to the passers by, the Commissioner or executive authority may, by notice require the owner of the said tree to secure, lop or cut down the said tree so as to prevent any danger there from.

(2) If immediate action is necessary, the Commissioner or executive authority shall himself, before giving such notice or before the period of such notice expires, fence off, take down, secure or repair such structure or fence off a part of any road or take such temporary measures as he may think fit to prevent danger, and the cost of doing so shall be recoverable from the owner or occupier in the manner hereinafter provided.

129. Precautions in Case of Dangerous Trees—(1) If any tree or any branch of a tree standing on land adjoining a public road vested in a panchayat union council or village panchayat appears to the Commissioner or executive authority to be likely to fall and thereby endanger any person using, or any structure on such road, the Commissioner or executive authority may, by notice, require the owner of the said tree to secure, lop or cut down the said tree so as to prevent any danger there from.

(2) If immediate action is necessary, the Commissioner or executive authority shall himself, before giving such notice or before the period of such notice expires, secure, lop or cut down the said tree or fence off a part of the public road or take such other temporary measures as he thinks fit to prevent danger and the cost of so doing shall be recoverable from the owner of the tree in the manner hereinafter provided.

130. Fencing of Building or Lands and Pruning of Hedges and Trees—Where a public road is vested in a panchayat union council or village panchayat, the Commissioner or executive authority may, by public notice, require the owner or occupier of any building or land near such road to:

(a) fence the same to the satisfaction of the Commissioner or executive authority;

(b) trim or prune any hedges bordering on such road so that they may not exceed such height from the level of the adjoining roadway as the Commissioner or executive authority may determine; or

(c) cut and trim any hedges or trees overhanging such road and obstructing it or the view of traffic or causing it damage; or

(d) lower an enclosing wall or fence which, by reasons of its height and situation, obstructs the view of traffic so as to cause danger.

131. Prohibition against Obstructions in or Over Public Roads, etc.—(1) No person shall, except as permitted by rules made under this Act and except in accordance with the conditions imposed by any licence made requisite by such rules:

(a) build any wall or erect any fence or other obstruction or projection or make any encroachment whatsoever, whether permanent or temporary, [76]["in or over any public road or any property vested in or belonging to or regulated or owned by, a village panchayat or panchayat union council"];

(b) make any hole or deposit any matter [77]["in or upon any public road or any property vested in or belonging to or regulated or owned by, a village panchayat or panchayat union council"];

(c) work a quarry in or remove stone, earth or other material from any place within twenty metres of a public road or of other immovable property vesting in or belonging to a village panchayat or a panchayat union council, provided that nothing in this clause shall be deemed to apply to any work which, in the opinion of the Inspector, is done in connection with a *bona fide* agricultural operation;

(d) erect any building over any drain or any part thereof;

(e) plant any tree on any public road or other property vesting in or belonging to a village panchayat or a panchayat union council; or

(f) fell, remove, destroy, lop or strip bark, leaves, or fruits from or otherwise damage, any tree which is growing on any such public road or other property or on any poramboke land, the use of which is regulated by a village panchayat under section 134 or section 135 and the right to which has not been established by such person as vesting in or belonging to him.

(2) It shall be the duty of the Village Administrative Officer of every revenue village to report on encroachments on properties vested in village panchayats or panchayat union councils to the executive authority or the Commissioner concerned and to the officer of the Revenue Department, and [78]["it shall be the duty of the executive authority or the Commissioner concerned either *suo moto* or on obtaining a report from the Village Administrative Officer in this regard"] to institute proceedings under this Act and secure the removal of the encroachments within such time as may be specified by the Government by general or special order. If the removal of the encroachments has not been secured within the period specified in such order, the officers of the Revenue Department shall institute proceedings under the Tamil Nadu Land Encroachment Act, 1905 (Tamil Nadu Act III of 1905) and secure such removal.

[79]["**131-A. Prohibition of Erection of Certain Hoardings**—Notwithstanding anything contained in this Act or in any other law for the time being in force:

(a) (i) On or after the date of the commencement of the Tamil Nadu Panchayats (Third Amendment) Act, 2000 (hereafter in this section referred to as the amendment Act), no person shall erect any hoarding (other than traffic sign and road sign) visible to the traffic on the road and which is hazardous and disturbance to safe traffic movement so as to adversely affect free and safe flow of traffic;

(ii) where any hoarding is erected in contravention of sub-clause (i), it shall be confiscated and removed by the executive authority without any notice;

(b) (i) where any hoarding (other than traffic sign and road sign) visible to the traffic on the road is hazardous and disturbance to safe traffic movement so as to adversely affect free and safe flow of traffic and which is in existence immediately before the date of the commencement of the amendment Act, the executive authority shall, by notice in writing, require the owner or any person in possession of such hoarding, to remove such hoarding within such time as may be specified in the notice:

Provided that such time shall not exceed fifteen days from the date of issue of such notice;

(ii) where the hoarding referred to in sub-clause (i) is not removed within the time specified in the notice, the executive authority shall, without further notice, remove such hoarding and recover the expenditure for such removal as an arrear of land revenue.

Explanation. For the purpose of this section, "hoarding" means any screen of boards at any place whether public or private used or intended to be used for exhibiting advertisement including the framework or other support, erected, wholly or in part upon or over any land, building wall or structure visible to public wholly or partly"][80].

132. Vesting of Communal Property or Income in Village Panchayat—Any property or income including any fishery right which by custom belongs to, or has been administered for the common benefit of the inhabitants of the village or of the holders in common of village land generally or of the holders of lands of a particular description or of the holders of lands under particular source of irrigation shall, if so declared by the Government, vest in the village panchayat and be administered by it for the benefit of the inhabitants or holders aforesaid.

133. Maintenance of Irrigation Works, Execution of Kudimaramat, etc.—(1) Subject to such conditions and control as may be prescribed, the Government may transfer to any village panchayat or to any panchayat union council the protection and maintenance of any irrigation work, the management of turns of irrigation, or the regulation of distribution of water from any irrigation work to the fields depending on it.

(2) The village panchayat or the panchayat union council shall have power, subject to such restrictions and control as may be prescribed, to execute Kudimaramat in respect of any irrigation source in the village and to levy such fee and on such basis for the purposes thereof as may be prescribed:

Provided that nothing contained in this section shall be deemed to relieve the village community or any of its members of its or his liability under the Tamil Nadu Compulsory Labour Act, 1858, (Central Act I of 1858) in respect of any irrigation source in the village in case the village panchayat makes default in executing the Kudimaramat in respect of that irrigation source.

(3) Where the maintenance of any irrigation work, is transferred under this section, the fishery rights of Government in such work shall be transferred to and be vested in the village panchayat or the panchayat union council, as the case may be, subject to such terms and conditions including terms and conditions regarding the utilisation of the income, as may be specified by the Government.

134. Village Panchayat to Regulate the Use of Certain Porambokes in Ryotwari Tracts—(1) The provisions of this section shall apply only in ryotwari tracts.

(2) The following porambokes, namely, grazing grounds, threshing floors, burning and burial-grounds, cattle-stands, cart-stands and topes shall vest in the village panchayat, and the village panchayat shall have power, subject to such restrictions and control as may be prescribed to regulate the use of such porombokes, provided the porambokes are at the disposal of the Government.

(3) The Collector, after consulting the village panchayat, may, by notification, exclude from the operation of this Act, any poramboke referred to in sub-section (2), and may also modify or cancel such notification.

(4) The village panchayat shall also have power, subject to such restrictions and control as may be prescribed, to regulate the use of any other poramboke which is at the disposal of the Government, if the village panchayat is authorised in that behalf by an order of the Government.

(5) The village panchayat may, subject to such restrictions and control as may be prescribed, plant trees on any poramboke, the use of which is regulated by it under sub-section (2) or sub-section (4).

135. Village Panchayat to Regulate the Use of Certain Communal Lands in Estates Governed by the Tamil Nadu Estates Land Act, 1908—(1) In estates governed by the Tamil Nadu Estates Land Act, 1908 (Tamil Nadu Act I of 1908) not withstanding anything contained in that Act, the village panchayat shall have power subject to such restrictions and control as may be prescribed:

(a) to regulate the use of lands which are set apart for any of the purposes referred to in item (b) of clause (16) of section 3 of the said Act, namely, threshing floors, cattle-stand, village-sites and other lands situated in the village which are set apart for the common use of the inhabitants of such village;

(b) to exercise the powers vested in the Collector by section 20-A of the said Act, namely to direct that any land referred to in clause (a) which is no longer required for its original purpose shall be used for any other specified communal purpose, provided that the sanction of the Collector is obtained therefore; and

(c) to plant trees on any land the use of which is regulated by the village panchayat under clause (a):

Provided that nothing contained in clause (b) shall be deemed to affect in any way the operation of the proviso to sub-section (1) of the said section 20-A.

(2) After an estate ceases to be governed by the Tamil Nadu Estates Land Act, 1908 (Tamil Nadu Act I of 1908) the provisions of sub-section (1) shall apply to the lands referred to in that sub-section, to such extent and with such modifications, as may be prescribed.

136. Collected Rubbish etc., to Belong to Village Panchayat—All rubbish, filth and other matter collected by a village panchayat under this Act shall belong to it.

137. Immovable Property Required by Village Panchayats and Panchayat Union Councils may be Acquired under the Land Acquisition Act, 1894—Any immovable property which any village panchayat or panchayat union council is authorised by this Act or any rules made thereunder may be acquired under the provisions of the Land Acquisition Act, 1894 (Central Act I of 1894) and on payment of the compensation awarded under the said Act, in respect of such property and of any other charges incurred in acquiring it, the said property shall vest in the village panchayat or panchayat union council, as the case may be.

138. Contributions from Persons having Control Over Places of Pilgrimage, etc.—Where a mosque, temple, mutt or any place of religious worship or institution or any place which is used for holding fair or festivals or for other like purposes is situated within the limits of a village or in the neighbourhood thereof and attracts either throughout the year or on particular occasions a large number of persons, any special arrangement necessary for public health, safety or convenience, whether permanent or temporary, shall be made by the village panchayat; but the Government may after consulting the trustee or other person having control over such place require him to make such recurring or non-recurring contribution to the funds of the village panchayat as they may determine.

139. Power to Order Closure of Places of Public Entertainment—In the event of the prevalence of any dangerous disease within a panchayat development block or a village, the Commissioner may by notice require the owner or occupier of any building, booth or tent used for purposes of public entertainment to close the same for such period as they may fix.

140. Minor Suffering from Dangerous Disease not to Attend Schools—No person being the parent or having the care or charge of a minor who is or has been suffering from dangerous disease or has been exposed to infection there from shall, after a notice from the Commissioner or any person duly appointed by such Commissioner in this behalf that the minor is not to be sent to school or college permit such minor to attend school or college without having procured from the Commissioner or such person or a registered medical practitioner a certificate that in his opinion such minor may attend without risk of communicating such disease to others.

Explanation. In this section and in section 139 "dangerous disease" means an infectious disease within the meaning of section 52 of the Tamil Nadu Public Health Act, 1939 (Tamil Nadu Act III of 1939) which is notified as a dangerous disease by the Government.

141. Compulsory Vaccination—The panchayat union council shall enforce vaccination throughout the panchayat union and it may enforce revaccination throughout the panchayat union or in any part thereof, in respect of such persons, to such extent, and in such manner, as may be prescribed.

142. Obligation to Give Information of Small-pox or Cholera—Where an inmate of any dwelling place is suffering from smallpox or cholera the head of the family to which the inmate belongs and in default the occupier or person in charge of such place, shall give intimation of the fact to the Commissioner or the Village Administrative Officer with the least possible delay.

143. Precautions in Case of Dangerous Tanks, Wells, Holes, etc.—(1) If any tank, pond, well, hole, stream, dam, bank or other place appears to him to be, for want of sufficient repair, protection or enclosure, dangerous to the public health or safety, the Commissioner or executive authority may with the approval of the panchayat union council or village panchayat, as the case may be, by notice require the owner to fill in, remove, repair, protect or enclose the same so as to prevent any danger there from.

(2) If immediate action is necessary, he shall, before giving such notice or before the period of notice expires, himself take such temporary measures as he thinks fit to prevent danger, and the cost of doing so shall be recoverable from the owner in the manner hereinafter provided.

144. Removal of Filth or Noxious Vegetation from Lands and Buildings—(1) The Commissioner or executive authority may by notice require the owner or occupier of any building or land which appears to him to be in a filthy or unwholesome state or overgrown with any thick obnoxious vegetation, trees or undergrowth injurious to health or dangerous to the public or offensive to the neighbourhood, or otherwise a source of nuisance, to clear, cleanse or otherwise put the building or land in proper state or to clear away and remove such vegetation, trees or under growth or to take such other action as may be deemed by the Commissioner or executive authority necessary to remove such nuisance within such period and in such manner as may be specified in the notice.

(2) If it appears to the Commissioner or executive authority necessary for sanitary purposes so to do, he may by notice require the owner or occupier of any building or land to cleanse or lime-wash the same in the manner and within a period to be specified in the notice.

145. Power of Commissioner or Executive Authority to Use or Sell Materials of Dangerous Structure Taken Down, etc.—(1) When the Commissioner or executive authority takes down any structure or part thereof or cuts down any tree or hedge or shrub or part thereof in virtue of his powers under this chapter, the Commissioner or executive authority may sell the materials or things taken down, cut down or remove and apply the proceeds in, or towards payment of the expenses incurred.

(2) If after a reasonable enquiry it appears to the Commissioner or executive authority that there is no owner or occupier to whom notice can be given under any section in this chapter, he may himself take such order with the property mentioned in such section as may appear to him to be necessary and may recover the expenses incurred by the sale of such property (not being immovable property) or of any portion thereof.

146. Limitation of Compensation—No person shall be entitled, save as otherwise expressly provided, to compensation for any damages sustained by reason of any action taken by the authorities of a panchayat union council or a village panchayat in pursuance of their powers under this chapter.

147. Public Markets—(1) The panchayat union council may, after obtaining the previous written permission of the Inspector, provide places for use as public markets and, with the sanction of the Inspector, close any such market or part thereof.

(2) Subject to such rules as may be prescribed, the village panchayat or panchayat union council may after obtaining the previous written permission of the Inspector, levy any one or more of the following fees in any public market at such rates, not exceeding the maximum rates, if any, prescribed in that behalf as the panchayat union council or village panchayat may think fit:

(a) fees for the use of, or for the right to expose goods for sale in such market;

(b) fees for the use of shops, stalls, pens or stands in such market;

(c) fees on vehicles including motor vehicles as defined in the Motor Vehicles Act, 1988 (Central Act 59 of 1988) or pack animals bringing, or on persons taking into such market any goods for sale;

(d) fees on animals brought for sale into or sold in such market;

(e) licence fees on brokers, commission agents, weighmen and measures practising their calling in such market.

148. Licensing of Private Markets—(1) No person shall open a new private market or continue to keep open a private market unless he has obtained a licence from the village panchayat or panchayat union council, as the case may be, to do so. Such licence shall be renewed every year.

(2) (a) The village panchayat or panchayat union council, as the case may be, shall grant the licence applied for subject to such conditions as it may think fit as to supervision and inspection, sanitation, weights and measures to be used, rents and fees to be charged and such other matters as may be prescribed.

(b) The village panchayat or panchayat union council as the case may be, may, modify the conditions of licence to take effect from a specified date.

(c) The village panchayat or panchayat union council, as the case may be, may at any time, suspend or cancel any licence granted under clause (a) for breach of the conditions thereof.

(d) Any person aggrieved by an order of the village panchayat or panchayat union council under clauses (a), (b) or (c) may appeal against such order to the Inspector who may, if he thinks fit, suspend the execution of the order pending the disposal of the appeal.

(3) (a) Any person claiming to levy in a private market lawfully established prior to the coming into force of the Madras Local Boards Act, 1884 (Madras Act V of 1884) fees of the nature specified in sub-section (2) of section 147, shall apply to the Inspector for a certificate recognizing his right in that behalf; and the Inspector shall pass order on such application after giving due notice to the village panchayat or panchayat union council, as the case may be, and considering any representations made by it.

(b) Any person aggrieved by an order of the Inspector refusing to grant a certificate under clause (a) may, within six months from the date of communication of such order, institute a suit to establish the right claimed by him, and subject to the result of such suit, the Inspector's order shall be final.

(4) When a licence granted under sub-section (2) does not permit the levy of any fee, it shall be granted free of charges; but when such permission is given, a fee not exceeding fifteen per cent of the gross income of the owner from the market in the preceding year shall be charged by the village panchayat or panchayat union council, as the case may be, for such licence.

(5) The village panchayat or panchayat union council as the case may be, or any officer duly

authorised by it may, close a private market which is unlicensed or the licence for which has been suspended or cancelled, or which is held or kept open contrary to the provisions of this Act

149. Decision of Disputes as to Whether Places are Markets—If any question arises as to whether any place is a market or not, the village panchayat or panchayat union council, as the case may be, shall make a reference thereon to the Government and their decision shall be final.

150. Prohibition of Sale in Unlicensed Private Markets—No person shall sell or expose for sale any animal or article:

(a) in any public or licensed private market without the permission of the executive authority or Commissioner or licensee, as the case may be, or of any person authorised by him, or

(b) in any unlicensed private market.

151. Prohibition Against Sale in Public Roads—The executive authority or Commissioner may, with the sanction of the village panchayat or panchayat union council as the case may be, prohibit by public notice or licence or regulate the sale or exposure for sale of any animal or article in or upon any public road or place or part thereof.

152. Classification of Markets—The Government shall have power to classify public and private markets situated in a panchayat development block as panchayat union markets and village panchayat market, and provide for the control of any such market, and for the apportionment of the income derived therefrom between the panchayat union council and the village panchayat or the payment of a contribution in respect thereof to the village panchayat or the panchayat union, as the case may be. It shall be open to the Government to revise from time-to-time the apportionment of income ordered or the contribution directed to be paid under this section if such revision is recommended by the district panchayat.

153. Acquisition of Right of Persons to Hold Private Market—(1) A panchayat union council may acquire the rights of any person to hold a private market in any place in a panchayat development block and to levy fee therein. The acquisition shall be made under the Land Acquisition Act, 1894 (Central Act I of 1894) and such rights shall be deemed to be land for the purposes of that Act.

(2) On payment by the panchayat union council of the compensation awarded under the said Act in respect of such property and any other charges incurred in acquiring it, the rights of such person to hold a private market and to levy fees therein shall vest in the panchayat union council.

154. Public Landing Places and Cart-stands, etc.—Subject to such rules as may be prescribed, the village panchayat may:

(a) provide public landing places, halting places and cart-stands (which last expression includes stands for animals and vehicles of any description including motor vehicles) and levy fees for their use; and

(b) where any such place or stand has been provided, prohibit the use for the same purpose by any person, within such distance thereof of any public place or the sides of any public road as the village panchayat may, subject to the control of the Inspector, specify.

155. Private Cart-stand—(1) No person shall open a new private cart-stand or continue to keep open a private cart-stand unless he obtains from the village panchayat a licence to do so. Such licence shall be renewed every year.

(2) The village panchayat shall, as regards private cart-stands already lawfully established, and may at its discretion as regards new private cart-stands grant the licence applied for, subject to such conditions as the village panchayat may think fit as to supervision and inspection, conservancy and such other matters as may be prescribed; or the village panchayat may refuse to grant such licence for any new cart-stand.

(3) The village panchayat may modify the conditions of the licence to take effect from a specified date.

(4) The village panchayat may at any time suspend or cancel any licence granted under sub-section (2) for breach of the conditions thereof.

(5) The village panchayat may levy on every grant or renewal of a licence under this section, a fee not exceeding two hundred rupees.

156. Public Slaughter-houses—A village panchayat may provide places for use as public slaughter-houses and charge rents and fees for their use.

157. Prohibition or Regulation of the Use of Places for Slaughtering Animals and the Licensing of Slaughterers—The Government shall have power to make rules for:

(a) prohibiting or regulating the slaughter, cutting up or skinning of animals specified in the rules on all occasions not excepted therein, at places other than public slaughter-houses;

(b) licensing persons to slaughter animals specified in the rules for purposes of sale to the public; and

(c) the infection of slaughter houses and of the meat there in and the payment of remuneration to the officers employed for such inspection.

158. Numbering or Naming of Building, etc.—(1) In any area to which this Act applies, such authority as may be prescribed in this behalf, may cause a number to be affixed to the side or outer door of any building or to some place at the entrance of the premises.

(2) With the approval of the Government, the village panchayat or the panchayat union council shall give name to new village road or panchayat union road, as the case may be, and shall also give name to park, playground, bus-stand, arch or new property belonging to, or vesting in, village panchayat or panchayat union council and may, subject to the approval of the Government, alter the name of any such road, park, playground, bus-stand, arch or property.

(3) No person shall, without lawful authority, destroy, pull down or deface any such number.

(4) When a number has been affixed under sub-section (1), the owner of the building shall be bound to maintain such number and to replace it if removed or defaced; and if he fails to do so, the authority referred to in sub-section (1) may by notice require him to replace it.

159. Purposes for which Places may not be Used without a Licence—(1) The Government may, by notification, specify the purposes which in their opinion, are likely to be offensive or dangerous to human life or health or property.

[81]["(2) The village panchayat may, with the previous approval of the prescribed authority, notify that no place within the limits of the panchayat village shall be used for any of the purposes specified in the notification issued under sub-section (1) without a licence and except in accordance with the conditions specified in such licence"].

(3) No notification issued under sub-section (1) or sub-section (2) shall take effect until sixty days from the date of its publication.

[82]["(4) The village panchayat shall be the authority competent to grant the licence or to refuse to grant it.]

160. Permission for Construction of Factories and the Installation of Machinery—No person shall, without the permission of the panchayat union council in panchayat villages and except in accordance with the conditions specified in such permission:

(a) construct or establish any factory, workshop or workplace in which it is proposed to employ steam power, water power or other mechanical power or electrical power, or

(b) install in any premises any machinery or manufacturing plant driven by any power as aforesaid not being machinery or manufacturing plant exempted by the rules.

161. Power of Government to Make Rules in Respect of the Grant and Renewal of Licences and Permissions—(1) The Government may make rules:

(a) prohibiting or regulating the grant or renewal of licences under section 159 and the period for which such licences shall be valid;

(b) as to the time within which applications for such licences or renewals thereof shall be made; and

(c) prohibiting or regulating the grant of permissions under section 160.

(2) Rules made under clause (c) of sub-section (1) may empower the panchayat union council in panchayat villages and panchayat unions to set apart specified areas for industrial purposes and provide for the refusal of permissions under section 160 in respect of any factory, workshop, workplace or premises outside such areas and also, subject to the sanction of the prescribed authority for the removal to such areas, of any factory, workshop or work place which has been already established at any place or any machinery which has already been installed in any premises, situated outside such areas:

Provided that no such rule shall authorise the removal of any factory, workshop or workplace or machinery installed in any premises, in the occupation or under the control of the Central or the State Government or of a market committee established under the Tamil Nadu Agricultural Produce Marketing (Regulation) Act, 1987. (Tamil Nadu Act 27 of 1989)

(3) The Government may either generally or in any particular case, make such order or give such directions as they deem fit in respect of any action taken or omitted to be taken under section 159 or section 160.

(4) The income derived from fees on licences under section 159 and on permission under section 160 shall, if received by the panchayat union council, credited to the funds of the village panchayat concerned.

162. Modification of the Tamil Nadu Places of Public Resort Act, 1888 (Tamil Nadu Act II of 1888)—Notwithstanding anything contained in the Tamil Nadu Places of Public Resort Act, 1888, when the Government extend that Act to any village, or part thereof—

(a) the authority to whom application shall be made for a licence under the Act in respect of any place or building to be used exclusively for purposes other than the holding of cinematograph exhibitions, and who may grant or refuse such licence, shall be the Commissioner in the case of panchayat villages;

(b) the appeal from the order of the Commissioner granting, refusing, revoking or suspending a licence, shall lie to the panchayat union council;

(c) the income derived from fees on licences under this section shall, if received by the panchayat union council be credited to the funds of the village panchayats concerned.

163. Functions of District Panchayat—(1) The district panchayat shall advise the Government on all matters concerning the activities of village panchayats, panchayat union councils in the district as well as on all matters relating to the development of the economic resources of the district and the services maintained therein for promoting the culture and welfare of the inhabitants of the district.

(2) In particular, it shall be the duty of the district panchayat to perform the following functions, namely:

(a) advising the Government on all matters relating to the services maintained by and all development schemes undertaken by all village panchayats and panchayat union councils in the district as well as those agencies in the district, which are under the administrative control of the Government;

(b) watching the progress of the measure undertaken by the Government, village panchayats, panchayat union councils and departmental agencies in respect of the services and development schemes aforesaid;

(c) advising the Government on matters concerning the implementation of any provision of law or any order specifically referred to by the Government to the district panchayat such as:

(i) classification of markets as village panchayat markets and panchayat union markets and fixing rates of contribution payable by one authority to the other;

(ii) classification of fairs and festivals as village panchayat fairs, village panchayat festivals and panchayat union fairs and panchayat union festivals;

(iii) classification of public roads (other than roads classified by the Government as National Highways, State Highways and major district roads) as panchayat union roads and panchayat village roads;

(d) advising the Government on all matters relating to development of road transport.

164. General Powers of District Panchayat—For the purpose of efficiently performing its functions under this Act, every district panchayat may, within the limits of its jurisdiction—

(a) undertake such measures as it deems necessary;

(b) collect such data as it deems necessary;

(c) publish statistics or other information relating to the various aspects of the regulation or development of the activities of panchayat union councils and village panchayats in the district;

(d) require any panchayat union council or village panchayat to furnish such information as may be required by it in relation of the measures undertaken by that panchayat union council or village panchayat for the regulation or development of its activities and such other matters as may be prescribed.

165. Annual Report of District Panchayat—(1) The district panchayat shall prepare in such form and at such time each year as may be prescribed, an annual report giving a true and full account of its activities during the previous year and copies thereof shall be forwarded to the Government.

(2) The Government shall lay on the table of the Legislative Assembly all such reports together with their comments thereon.

166. Returns and Reports of District Panchayat—Every district panchayat shall furnish to the Government such returns, reports, statistics and other informations with respect to its activities as the Government may from time-to-time require.

CHAPTER IX
TAXATION AND FINANCE

167. Local Cess—(1) There shall be levied in every panchayat development block, a local cess at the rate of one rupee on every rupee of land revenue payable to the Government in respect of any land for every fasli.

Explanation. In this section and in section 168, 'land revenue' means public revenue due on land and includes water cess payable to the Government for water supplied or used for the irrigation of land, royalty, lease amount or other sum payable to the Government in respect of land held direct from the Government on lease or licence, but does not include any other cess or the surcharge payable under section 168, provided that land revenue remitted shall not be deemed to be land revenue payable for the purpose of this section.

(2) The local cess payable under sub-section (1) shall be deemed to be public revenue due on all the lands in respect of which a person is liable to pay local cess and all the said lands, the buildings upon the said lands and their products shall be regarded as security for the local cess.

(3) The provisions of the Tamil Nadu Revenue Recovery Act, 1864 (Tamil Nadu Act II of 1864) shall apply to the payment and recovery of the local cess payable under this Act just as they apply to the payment and recovery of the revenue due upon the lands in respect of which the local cess under this Act is payable.

[83][“(4) The local cess so collected in every panchayat development block shall be credited to the village panchayat fund concerned”].

(5)......(*Deleted by Act 30/1999*)

168. Local Cess Surcharge—Every panchayat union council may levy on every person liable to pay land revenue to the Government in respect of any land in the panchayat union, a local cess surcharge at such rate as may be considered suitable as an addition to the local cess levied in the panchayat development block under section 167 provided that the rate of local cess surcharge so levied shall not be less than five rupees and not more than ten rupees on every rupee of land revenue payable in respect of such land.

169. Rules Regarding Collection of Local Cess—The Government may make rules not inconsistent with this Act for regulating the collection of the local cess, the payment thereof to the village panchayats [84][***] and the deduction of any expenses incurred by the Government in the collection thereof.

170. Land Revenue Assignment—The Government shall pay to each panchayat union council a sum representing one rupee for each individual of the population of the panchayat development block concerned from out of the total land revenue (including water-cess) collected in the State during that year. The sum thus credited to the panchayat union council shall be referred to as the Land Revenue Assignment of that Block.

171. Taxes Leviable by Village Panchayats—(1) Every village panchayat shall levy in the panchayat village a house-tax [85][*****].

(2) A duty shall also be levied in every panchayat village on certain transfers of property in accordance with the provisions of section 175.

(3) Subject to such rules as may be prescribed and with the sanction of the Inspector and subject to such restrictions and conditions, if any, as may be imposed by him either at the time of granting sanction or later, the village panchayat may also levy in the village a tax on agricultural land for a specific purpose.

172. House-tax—(1) The house-tax shall be levied on all houses in every panchayat village on the basis on which such tax was levied in the local area concerned immediately before the commencement of this Act or on the basis of classified plinth area at the rates specified in Schedule I, as the village panchayat may adopt subject to the provisions of sub-section (3).

(2) The house-tax shall, subject to the prior payment of the land revenue, if any, due to the Government in respect of the site of the house, be a first charge upon the house and upon the movable property, if any, found within or upon the same and belonging to the person liable to such tax.

(3) The Government shall, by notification, determine in regard to any panchayat village or any class of panchayat villages whether the house-tax shall be levied every half-year or year and in so doing have regard to the following matters, namely:

(a) the classification of the local areas under section 4;

(b) the annual receipts of the village panchayat;

(c) the population of the panchayat village and the predominant occupation of such population; and

(d) such other matters as may be prescribed.

(4) The Government may make rules providing for:

(a) the persons who shall be liable to pay the tax and the giving of notices of transfer of houses;

(b) the grant of vacancy and other remissions;

(c) the circumstances in which, and the conditions subject to which, houses constructed, reconstructed or demolished, or situated in areas included in, or excluded from the panchayat village during any half-year or year, shall be liable or cease to be liable to the whole or any portion of the tax.

(5) If the occupier of a house pays the house-tax on behalf of the owner thereof, such occupier shall be entitled to recover the same from the owner and may deduct the same from the rent then or thereafter due by him to the owner.

[86]["**172-A. Levy and Collection of Advertisement Tax**—Every person who erects, exhibits fixes or retains upon or over any land, building, wall, hoarding or structure any advertisement, or who displays any advertisement to public view in any manner whatsoever in any place whether public or private, in the panchayat village shall pay on every advertisement which is so erected, exhibited, fixed retained or displayed to public view, a tax calculated at such rates and in such manner as the village panchayat may, determine in accordance with such rule as may be prescribed:

Provided that the rates shall be subject to the rates that may be prescribed by the Government and different rates may be prescribed for different village panchayats taking into consideration the location, the size of the advertisement board, the period and the types of advertisements:

Provided further that no tax shall be levied under this section on any advertisement or a notice:

(a) of a public meeting; or

[87]["(b) of an election to the Parliament, Legislative Assembly, or a Panchayat; or"]

(c) of a candidature in respect of such an election:

Provided also that no such tax shall be levied on advertisement which is not a sky-sign and which:

(a) is exhibited within the windows of any building; or

(b) relates to the trade or business carried on, within the land or building upon or over which such advertisement is exhibited, or to any sale or letting of such land or building or any effects therein or to any sale, entertainment or meeting to be held upon or in the same; or

(c) relates to the name of the land or building upon or over which the advertisement is exhibited, or to the name of the owner or occupier of such land or building; or

(d) relates to the business of any railway administration; or

(e) is exhibited within any railway station or upon any wall or other property of a railway administration except any portion of the surface of such wall or property fronting any street.

Explanation. For the purpose of this section:

(i) the expression "structure" shall include any movable board on wheels used as an advertisement medium;

(ii) the expression "sky-sign" means any advertisement supported on or attached to any post, pole, standard, framework or other support wholly or in part upon or over any land, building, wall or structure which, or any part of sky-sign which shall be visible against the sky from some point in any public place and includes all and every part of any such post, pole, standard, framework or other support. The expression "sky-sign" shall also include any balloon, parachute or other similar device employed wholly or in part or the purposes of any advertisement upon or over any land, building or structure or upon or over any public place but shall not include:

(a) any flag staff, pole vane or weather-cock, unless adopted or used wholly or in part for the purpose of any advertisement; or

(b) any sign, or any board, frame or other contrivance securely fixed to or on the top of the wall or parapet of any building or on the cornice or blocking of any wall, or to the ridge of a roof:

Provided that such board, frame or other contrivance shall be of one continuous face and not open work, and does not extend in height more than one metre above any part of the wall, or parapet, or ridge to, against or on, which it is fixed or supported; or

(c) any advertisement relating to the name of the land or building, upon or over which the advertisement is exhibited, or to the name of the owner or occupier of such land or building; or

(d) any advertisement relating exclusively to the business of a railway administration and placed wholly upon or over any railway, railway yard station platform or station approach belonging to a railway administration and so placed that cannot fall in any street or public; or

(e) any notice of land or building to be sold, or let placed upon such land or building:

(iii) the expression "public place" means any place which is open to the use and enjoyment of the public whether it is actually used or enjoyed by the public or not;

(iv) the expression "advertisement" shall not include any advertisement published in any newspaper]."

172-B. Prohibition of Advertisements—No advertisement shall after the levy of tax under section 172-A as determined by the Village Panchayat be erected, exhibited, fixed or retained upon or over any land, building, wall, hoarding or structure within the panchayat village, or shall be displayed in any manner whatsoever in any place except in accordance with the rules made under this Act:

Provided that the Village Panchayat shall regulate the height of the advertisement in the Panchayat Village and shall remove such objectionable advertisement in such manner as may be prescribed:

Provided further that the Government may, by notification, prohibit advertisements in any place within any panchayat village".][89]

[90][**173. Vehicle Tax**—[****] (Omitted)]

174. Appeal Against Assessments—An appeal shall lie to such authority and within such time, as may be prescribed against any assessment of tax made in pursuance of [91]["Sections 171, 172 and 172-A"].

175. Duty on Transfer of Property—(1) The duty on transfer of property shall be levied:

(a) in the form of a surcharge on the duty imposed by the Indian Stamp Act, 1899 (Central Act II of 1899), as in force for the time being in the State of Tamil Nadu, on every instrument of the description specified below, which relates to immovable property situated in the area under the jurisdiction of a village panchayat; and

(b) at such rate, as may be fixed by the Government, not exceeding five per cent on the amount specified below against each instrument:

(i) Sale of immovable property—The market value of the property as set forth in the instrument, and in a case where the market value is finally determined by any authority under section 47-A of the Indian Stamp Act, 1899, the market value as so determined by such authority.

(ii) Exchange of immovable property—The market value of the property of the greater value as set forth in the instrument and in a case where the market value is finally determined by any authority under section 47-A of the Indian Stamp Act, 1899, (Central Act II of 1899) the market value as so determined by such authority.

(iii) Gift of immovable property—The market value of the property as set forth in the instrument, and in a case where the market value is finally determined by any authority under section 47-A of the Indian Stamp Act, 1899 (Central Act II of 1899) the market value as so determined by such authority.

(iv) Mortgage with possession of immovable property—The amount secured by the mortgage as set forth in the instrument.

(v) Lease in perpetuity of immovable property—An amount equal to one-sixth of the whole amount or value of the rents which would be paid or delivered in respect of the first fifty years of the lease, as set forth in the instrument.

(2) On the introduction of the duty aforesaid:

(a) section 27 of the said Indian Stamp Act shall be read as if it specifically require the particulars to be set forth separately in respect of property situated outside such on the area under the jurisdiction of the village panchayat and in respect of property situated area;

(b) section 64 of the said Act shall be read as if it referred to the village panchayat as well as the Government.

(3) The amount collected in the panchayat village in the panchayat development block as surcharge on the duty on transfers of property under this section shall be pooled every year for the entire block and distributed among all the village panchayats in the block in proportion to the land revenue of the panchayat village.

(4) The Government may make rules not inconsistent with this Act for regulating the collection of the duty, the payment thereof to the village panchayat and the deduction of any expenses incurred by the Government in the collection thereof.

176. Exemption—No exemption from the payment of any surcharge or tax specified in section 168 or 171 shall be granted by the village panchayat or the panchayat union council except in accordance with such rules as may be prescribed:

Provided that in any particular case, such exemption may be granted with the previous sanction of the Government.

177. Power to Require Land Revenue Staff to Collect Taxes and Fees Due to Village Panchayat—Subject to such rules as may be prescribed, the executive authority or the Commissioner shall have power to require the staff of the Land Revenue Department to prepare at quinquinnial intervals a House-tax Assessment Register in such form as may be prescribed and to collect any tax or fee due to the village panchayat or panchayat union council on payment of such remuneration not exceeding 6¼ per cent of the gross sum collected as the Collector may, by general or special order, determine.

178. Write-off of Irrecoverable Amounts—Subject to such restrictions and control as may be prescribed, a village panchayat or panchayat union council may write-off any tax, fee or other amount whatsoever due to it, whether under a contract or otherwise, or any sum payable in connection therewith, if in its opinion such tax, fee, amount or sum is irrecoverable:

Provided that where the Collector or any of his subordinates is responsible for the collection of any tax, fee or other amount due to a village panchayat or panchayat union council the power to write-off such tax, fee or amount or any sum payable in connection therewith, on the ground of its being irrecoverable, shall be exercised by the Commissioner of Land Administration or subject to his control, by the Collector or any officer authorised by him.

179. Local Education Grant—The Government shall pay annually to every panchayat union council a Local Education Grant the amount of which shall be calculated as follows:

The total amount of expenditure approved by the Government for being debited to the Panchayat Union (Education) Fund shall be divided into slabs in the manner specified below:

So much of the expenditure as may be equal to the land revenue assignment of the block referred to in section 170 shall constitute the first slab.

So much of the expenditure as may be in excess of the first slab subject to a maximum of 250 paise for each individual of the population of the panchayat development block concerned shall constitute the second slab.

To each panchayat union council, the Government shall make a Local Education Grant which shall be a proportion of the second slab not less than fifty per cent and not more than eighty per cent as may be specified by the Government in respect of that block.

[92][**180. Local Cess Surcharge Matching Grant**—[***] Omitted].

181. Classification of Panchayat Development Blocks—For the purpose of sanctioning grants to panchayat union councils, the Government may classify panchayat development blocks in such manner as they may deem fit once in every five years and it shall be open to the Government to sanction grants at varying rates for the different classes of panchayat development blocks. It shall also be open to the Government to revise the classification of panchayat development blocks once in every five years.

[93]["**181-A. Deposit of Fund of Panchayat**—Any panchayat having surplus fund shall, with the prior approval of the Inspector, deposit such surplus fund in any of the financial institutions specified by the Government:

Provided that no such deposit shall be made when there is need to utilize this fund for administration or development work during the next twelve months.

181-B. Grant or Loan for Scheme or Project—(1) The Government may make grant or loan to a panchayat for the execution of specific scheme, project, programme or plan relating to any of the matters administered by such panchayat subject to such terms and conditions as may be prescribed.

(2) Such panchayats shall utilize such grant or loan only for the purpose for which such grant or loan is given.

(3) The provisions of the Local Authorities Loans Act, 1914 (Central Act IX of 1914) shall apply in respect of the loan given by the Government under this section.

181-C. Raising of Loan by Panchayat—Every panchayat shall be competent to raise loan in full or in part from any financial institution or agency or bank for any of the following purposes, subject to the conditions imposed by the Government in this behalf, namely:

(a) to carry out any of the works connected with the improvement and development of infrastructure in panchayat areas;

(b) to carry out relief works at the time of natural calamities;

(c) to undertake any measure in connection with, or ancillary to, the above purposes; and

(d) to carry out any of its other statutory functions.

181-D. Procedure for Inter-panchayats Lending—(1) Any panchayat may raise loan from any other panchayat and any panchayat may sanction loan to another panchayat to carry out any of its functions for the creation of capital assets or income generating assets, with the prior sanction of the Inspector.

(2) The procedure for the receipt, utilization and repayment of the loan under this section and section 181-C shall be subject to such terms and conditions, as may be agreed upon by the financial institution or agency or bank or lending panchayat, as the case may be, and the borrowing panchayat. Every panchayat shall maintain in respect of the loan, such books of accounts, as may be prescribed.

(3) Every panchayat shall utilize the loans only for the purposes for which such loans are borrowed"][95].

[96][**182. Local Roads Grant**—****] Omitted.

[97][**183. Village House-tax Matching Grant**—****] Omitted.

[98][**184. Deduction from Grant in Certain Cases**—****] Omitted.

185. Constitution of Panchayat Union Fund and Village Panchayat Fund—There shall be constituted:

(a) for each panchayat union, a Panchayat Union (General) Fund and a Panchayat Union (Education) Fund;

(b) for each village panchayat, a village panchayat fund.

186. Panchayat Union (General) Fund—The receipts which shall be credited to the Panchayat Union (General) Fund shall include—

[99][(a) [****] Omitted].

(b) the local cess surcharge collected in the panchayat development block under section 168;

[100][(c) [****] Omitted]

[101][(d) [****] Omitted]

(e) fees on licences issued and permissions given by the panchayat union councils;

(f) fees levied in public markets classified as panchayat union markets after deducting the contribution, if any, paid by the panchayat union council to the village panchayat on the scale fixed by the Government;

(g) the contribution paid to the panchayat union council by village panchayats in respect of markets classified as village panchayat markets;

(h) fees for the temporary occupation of roads or road margins;

(i) fees for the use of choultries;

(j) receipts from dispensaries maintained by the panchayat union council;

(k) income from endowments and trusts under the management of the panchayat union council;

(l) the proportionate share of the proceeds of the entertainments tax received by the panchayat union council under section 13 of the Tamil Nadu Entertainments Tax Act, 1939 (Tamil Nadu Act X of 1939);

(m) contributions from Government other panchayat union councils, municipalities, other local authorities and persons in aid of every institution or service maintained or financed from panchayat union funds or managed by the panchayat union council;

(n) sale-proceeds of tools and plants, stores and materials and of trees and avenue produce appertaining to panchayat union roads;

(o) income from panchayat union ferries and fisheries;

(p) interest on loans and securities;

(q) interest on arrears of revenue;

(r) income from and sale-proceeds of, buildings, lands and other property belonging to the panchayat union council;

(s) unclaimed deposits and other forfeitures;

(t) fines and penalties levied under this Act by the panchayat union council or at its instance or on its behalf;

(u) all sums other than those enumerated above or in section 187 which arise out of or are received in aid of, or for expenditure on, any institutions or services maintained or financed from the panchayat union funds or managed by the panchayat union council;

(v) all other moneys received by the panchayat union council.

187. Panchayat Union (Education) Fund—The receipt which shall be credited to the Panchayat Union (Education) Fund shall include—

[102][(a) [****] Omitted]

(b) the land revenue assignment paid by the Government under section 170;

(c) the Local Education Grant paid by the Government;

(d) such contribution from the Panchayat Union (General) Fund as the Government may decide to be necessary in any year in order to balance the budget of the fund for that year;

(e) all fines and penalties levied within the jurisdiction of the panchayat union council under the provisions of the Tamil Nadu Elementary Education Act, 1920 (Tamil Nadu Act, VIII of 1920);

(f) all income derived from any endowments or other property owned or managed by the panchayat union council for the benefit of elementary education;

(g) all other sums which may be contributed or received by the panchayat union council for the purposes of elementary education.

188. Village Panchayat Fund—[103][(1)] The receipts which shall be credited to the village panchayat fund shall include:

[104]["(a) the house-tax and any other tax or any cess or fee, levied under sections 171 and 172"];

[105]["(b) The profession tax levied by village panchayat under Chapter IX-A"];

(c) the proceeds of the duty on transfers of property levied under section 175;

[106][(d) [****] the local cess under section 167];

[107][(e) [****] (Omitted)]

(f) the taxes and tolls levied in the village under sections 117 and 118 of the Tamil Nadu Public Health Act, 1939 (Tamil Nadu Act, VIII of 1939);

(g) fees levied in public markets classified as village panchayat markets after deducting the contributions, if any, paid by the village panchayat to the panchayat union council on the scale fixed by the Government;

(h) the contribution paid to the village panchayat by panchayat union councils in respect of markets classified as panchayat union markets;

(i) fees for the temporary occupation of village sites, roads and other similar public places or parts thereof in the panchayat village;

(j) fees levied by the village panchayat in pursuance of any provision of this Act or any rule or order made thereunder;

(k) income from endowments and trusts under the management of the village panchayat;

(l) the net assessment on service inams which are resumed by the Government;

(m) the proportionate share of the proceeds of the entertainment tax received by the village panchayat under section 13 of the Tamil Nadu Entertainments Tax Act, 1939 (Tamil Nadu Act X of 1939);

(n) income derived from panchayat village fisheries;

(o) income derived from ferries under the management of the village panchayat;

(p) unclaimed deposits and other forfeitures;

(q) a sum equivalent to the seigniorage fees collected by the Government every year from persons permitted to quarry for road material in the panchayat village;

(r) all income derived from porambokes the use of which is vested in the village panchayat;

(s) where the panchayat village is in a ryotwari tract, all income derived from trees standing on porombokes although the use of the porambokes is not vested in the village panchayat;

(t) income from leases of Government property obtained by the village panchayat;

(u) fines and penalties levied under this Act by the village panchayat or at the instance or on behalf of the village panchayat;

(v) all sums other than those enumerated above which arise out of, or are received in aid of or for expenditure on any institutions or services maintained or financed from the village panchayat fund or managed by the village panchayat;

(w) all other moneys received by the village panchayat].

[108]["(2) Notwithstanding anything contained in sub-section (1), the Government may direct any village panchayat to constitute separate funds to which shall be credited such receipt as may be specified and such funds shall be applied and disposed of in such manner as may be prescribed.

(3) Subject to such general control as the village panchayat may exercise from time-to-time, all cheques for payment from village panchayat fund or other funds constituted under sub-section (2) shall be signed jointly by the President and Vice-President and in the absence of the President or Vice-President, as the case may be, by the Vice-President or the President and another member authorised by the Village Panchayat at a meeting in this behalf"].

189. District Panchayat (General) Fund—(1) There shall be constituted for each district panchayat, a District Panchayat (General) Fund and the following shall form part of, or be paid into, the District Panchayat (General) Fund, namely:

(a) The amount transferred to the District Panchayat (General) Fund by appropriation from out of the Consolidated Fund of the State;

(b) all grants, assignments, loans and contributions made by the Government;

(c) all rents from lands or other property of the district panchayat;

(d) all interest, profits and other moneys accruing by gift, grants, assignments or transfer from private individual or institutions;
(e) all proceeds of land, security and other properties sold by the district panchayat;
(f) all fees and penalties paid to or levied by or on behalf of the district panchayat under this Act;
(g) all sums received by or on behalf of the district panchayat by virtue of this Act.

(2) The Government shall make a grant to every District Panchayat (General) Fund, to cover the expenses of establishment at such scale as may be determined by it.

EXPENDITURE

190. Application of Moneys Received and Expenditure from Funds—All moneys received by the panchayat union council and the village panchayat shall be applied and disposed of in accordance with the provisions of this Act and other laws:

Provided that the panchayat union council or the village panchayat shall have power subject to such rules as may be prescribed to direct that the proceeds of any tax or additional tax levied under this Act shall be earmarked for the purpose of financing any specific public improvement. A separate account shall be kept of the receipts from every such tax or additional tax and the expenditure thereof.

191. Expenditure from Village Panchayat Fund and Panchayat Union Fund—(1) The purposes to which the funds of the panchayat union council or of the village panchayat may be applied include all objects expressly declared obligatory or discretionary by this Act or any rules made thereunder or by any other laws or rules and the funds shall be applicable thereto within the panchayat development block or the panchayat village, as the case may be, subject to such rules or special orders as the Government may prescribe or issue and shall, subject as aforesaid be applicable to such purposes outside the panchayat development block or panchayat village if the expenditure is authorised by this Act or specially sanctioned by the Inspector.

(2) It shall be the duty of every panchayat union council and village panchayat to provide for the payment of:

(a) any amount falling due on any loans contracted by it;
(b) the salaries and allowances and the pensions, pensionary contributions and provident fund contributions of its officers and servants;
(c) sums due under any decree or order of a court; and
(d) Any other expenses rendered obligatory by or under this act or any other law.

(3) A panchayat union council or village panchayat may, with the sanction of the Government, contribute to any fund for the defence of India.

(4) A panchayat union council or village panchayat may, with the sanction of the Inspector also:

(a) contribute towards the expenses of any public exhibition, ceremony or entertainment in the panchayat development block or panchayat village;
(b) contribute to any charitable fund, or to the funds of any institution for the relief of the poor or the treatment of disease or infirmity or the reception of indisposed or infirm persons or the investigation of the causes of disease; and
(c) defray any other extraordinary charges.

192. Preparation and Sanction of Budgets—(1) The executive authority of the village panchayat and the Commissioner, shall in each year frame and place before the village panchayat or the panchayat union council, as the case may be, a budget showing the probable receipts and expenditure during the following year.

(2) The budget of a village panchayat or panchayat union council shall after preparation by the executive authority or the Commissioner, be submitted on or before such date and to such officer as may be prescribed, and if the prescribed officer is satisfied that adequate provision has not been made therein for the performance of any necessary service or services, he shall have power to return the budget for modification in such manner as may be necessary to secure such provision.

(3) The village panchayat or the panchayat union council as the case may the, shall sanction the budget with such modification as it thinks fit. If there is a difference of opinion between the officer referred to in sub-section (2) and the village panchayat and the panchayat union council, as the case may be, the budget shall be referred to the Inspector in the case of village panchayat and the Government in the case of the panchayat union council. The Inspector or the Government as the case may be,

shall have power to modify the budget in such manner as he or they may consider necessary.

(4) If in the course of a year, a village panchayat or panchayat union council finds it necessary to alter the figures shown in the budget with regard to its receipts or to the distribution of the amounts to be expended on the different services undertaken by it, a supplemental or revised budget may be framed, sanctioned, submitted and modified in the manner provided in sub-sections (1) and (2), provided that no such alteration shall be given effect to except with the consent of the prescribed officer.

(5) On or before such date in each year as may be prescribed, every Commissioner shall submit to the Government through such officer and in such forms as may be prescribed a budget for the ensuing financial year showing the income and expenditure relating to the Panchayat Union (Education) Fund.

(6) The Government may pass such orders as they think fit in respect of the budget referred to in sub-section (5) and the panchayat union council concerned shall be bound to carry out all such orders.

(7) The accounts of the Panchayat Union (Education) Fund shall, be examined and audited by an auditor appointed by the Government under section 193, and the panchayat union council concerned shall carry out any instruction which the Government may issue on the audit report.

193. Appointment of Auditors—(1) The Government shall appoint auditors for the accounts of the receipts and expenditure of the funds of the panchayat. Such auditors shall be deemed to be "public servants" within the meaning of section 21 (Central Act XLV of 1860) of the Indian Penal Code.

[109]["(2) No contribution shall be recovered by the Government from the panchayat towards the pay and allowances of such auditors or towards any other expenditure involved in the audit of the accounts of the panchayat"].

194. Contribution to Expenditure by other Local Authorities—If the expenditure incurred by the Government or by any panchayat union council or by any village panchayat or by any other local authority in the State for any purpose authorised by or under this Act, is such as to benefit the inhabitants of the panchayat union or panchayat village, the panchayat union council or the village panchayat, as the case may be, may, with the sanction of the Inspector, and shall, if so directed by him, make a contribution towards such expenditure.

195. Recovery of Loans and Advances Made by Government—(1) Notwithstanding anything contained in the Local Authorities Loans Act, 1914 (Central Act IX of 1914) the Government may:

(a) by order direct any person having custody of the funds of the panchayat union council or the village panchayat to pay to them in priority to any other charges against such fund, except charges for the service of authorised loans, any loan or advance made by them to the panchayat union council or the village panchayat for any purpose to which its funds may be applied under this Act;

(b) Recover any such loan or advance by suit.

(2) The person to whom the order referred to in clause (a) of sub-section (1) is addressed shall be bound to comply with such order.

196. Application of Certain Sections of this Act to District Panchayat—The provisions of sections 190, 191, 192, 194 and 195 (both inclusive) shall, in as far as may be, apply in relation to the district panchayat as they apply in relation to village panchayat and panchayat union council.

197. Certain Powers and Functions of District Panchayat to be Notified by the Government—(1) It shall be lawful for the Government from time-to-time to direct by notification that—

(a) any of the powers and functions of the village panchayat or panchayat union council or of the Government; or

(b) any road, bridge, channel, building or other property movable, or immovable which is vested in the village panchayat or the panchayat union council or the Government and which is situated in the district, shall with the consent of the district panchayat and subject to such exemption and conditions as the Government may make and impose, be exercised or placed under the control and administration of the district panchayat for the purposes of this Act and thereupon such powers and functions and such road, bridge, channel, building or other property, shall be under the control and administration of the district panchayat, subject to all exceptions and to all charges and liabilities affecting the same.

(2) It shall be competent for the Government by notification, to resume any of the powers and functions or property, placed under the control of the district panchayat under sub-section (1) on such terms as the Government may determine.

198. Finance Commission—(1) The Governor shall as soon as may be, after the commencement of this Act, but not later than 24th April 1994 and thereafter at the expiration of every fifth year, constitute a Finance Commission referred to in Article 243-I of the Constitution to review the financial position of the panchayats, and to make recommendations to the Governor as to

(a) the principles which should govern:

(i) the distribution between the State and panchayats of the net proceeds of the taxes, duties, tolls and fees leviable by the Government which may be divided between them and allocation between the district panchayats, panchayat union councils and village panchayats of their respective shares of such proceeds;

(ii) the determination of the taxes, duties, tolls and fees which may be assigned to or appropriated by the panchayats;

(iii) the grants-in-aid to the panchayats, from the Consolidated Fund of the State;

(b) the measures needed to improve the financial position of the panchayats;

(c) any other matter referred to the Finance Commission by the Governor in the interest of sound finance of the Panchayats.

(2) The Finance Commission shall consist of a chairman and four other members.

(3) The chairman and members of Finance Commission shall possess such qualifications and shall be appointed in such manner as may be prescribed.

(4) The Finance Commission shall determine their procedure.

(5) The chairman or a member of the Finance Commission may resign his office by writing under his hand and addressed to the Finance Secretary to the Government, but he shall continue in office until his resignation is accepted by the Governor.

(6) The casual vacancy created by the resignation of the member or chairman under sub-section (5) or for any other reasons may be filled by fresh appointment and a member or chairman so appointed, shall hold office for the remaining period for which the member or chairman in whose place he was appointed would have held office.

(7) The Finance Commission shall have the following powers in the performance of its functions, namely:

(a) to call for any record from any officer or authority;

(b) to summon any person to give evidence or produce records; and

(c) such other powers as may be prescribed.

(8) The Finance Commission shall prepare a report on the activities of he Commission and submit the same to the Government at the end of each financial year.

(9) The Governor shall cause every recommendation made by the Finance Commission under this section together with an explanatory memorandum as to the action taken thereon to be placed in the table of the Legislative Assembly.

[110]"CHAPTER IX-A
TAX ON PROFESSION, TRADE, CALLING AND EMPLOYMENT

198-A. Definitions—For the purposes of this Chapter:

(a) "employee" means a person employed on salary and includes:

(i) a Government servant receiving pay from the revenue of the Central Government or any State Government;

(ii) a person in the service of a body whether incorporated or not, which is owned or controlled by the Central Government or any State Government where such body operates within the panchayat village even though its headquarters may be outside that panchayat village; and

(iii) a person engaged in any employment by an employer, not covered by sub-clauses (i) and (ii);

(b) "employer" in relation to an employee earning any salary on a regular basis under him means, the person or the officer who is responsible for disbursement of such salary and includes the head of the office or any establishment as well as the Manager or Agent of the employer;

(c) "half year" shall be from the 1st day of April to the 30th day of September and from the 1st day of October to the 31st day of March of a year;

(d) "month" means a calendar month;

(e) "person" means any person who is engaged actively or otherwise in any profession, trade, calling or employment in the State of Tamil Nadu and includes a Hindu Undivided Family, firm, company, corporation or other corporate body, any society, club, body of persons or association, so engaged, but does not include any person employed on a casual basis;

(f) "tax" means the tax on profession, trade, calling and employment levied under this chapter.

198-B. Levy of Profession Tax—(1) There shall be levied by the village panchayat a tax on profession, trade, calling and employment.

(2) Every company which transacts business and every person, who is engaged actively or otherwise in any profession, trade, calling or employment within the Panchayat Village on the first day of the half year for which return is filed, shall pay half yearly tax at the rates specified in the Table below in such manner as may be prescribed:

Table

Sl. No.	*Average Half-Yearly Income*		*Half-Yearly Tax*
	From	*To*	
(1)	*(2)*	*(3)*	*(4)*
1.	Upto Rs. 21,000		Nil
2.	Rs. 21,001	Rs. 30,000	Rs. 60
3.	Rs. 30,001	Rs. 45,000	Rs. 150
4.	Rs. 45,001	Rs. 60,000	Rs. 300
5.	Rs. 60,001	Rs. 75,000	Rs. 450
6.	Rs. 75,001	and above	Rs. 600

(3) The rate of Tax payable under sub-section (2) shall be published by the Inspector in such manner as may be prescribed.

(4) Where a company or person proves that it or he has paid the sum due on account of the tax levied under this Chapter or any tax of the nature of a profession tax imposed under the Cantonments Act, 1924 (Central Act II of 1924) for the same half year to any local authority or containment authority in the State of Tamil Nadu, such company or person shall not be liable, by reason, merely of change of place of business, exercise of profession, trade, calling or employment, or residence, to pay the tax to any other local authority or cantonment authority.

(5) The tax leviable from a firm, association or Hindu Undivided Family may be levied on any adult member of the firm, association or family.

(6) Where a person doing the same business in the same name in one or more places within the Panchayat Village, the income of such business in all places within the Panchayat Village shall be computed for the purpose of levy of tax and such person shall pay the tax in accordance with the provisions of this Chapter.

(7) Where any company, corporate body, society, firm, body of persons or association pays the tax under this Chapter, any director, partner or member, as the case may be, of such company, corporate body, society, firm, body of persons or association shall not be liable to pay tax under this Chapter for the income derived by such director, partner or member from such company, corporate body, society, firm, body of persons or association:

Provided that such director, partner or member shall be liable to pay tax under this Chapter for the income derived from other sources.

(8) Every person who is liable to pay tax, other than a person earning salary or wage shall furnish to the executive authority a return in such form for such period and within such date and in such manner as may be prescribed:

Provided that subject to the provisions of sub-sections (10) and (11), such person may make a self-assessment on the basis of average half yearly income of the previous financial year and the return filed by him shall be accepted without calling for the accounts and without any inspection.

(9) Every such return shall accompany with the proof of payment of the full amount of tax due according to the return and a return without such proof of payment shall not be deemed to have been duly filed.

(10) Notwithstanding anything contained in the proviso to sub-section (8), the executive authority may select ten per cent of the total number of such assessment in such manner as may be prescribed for the purpose of detailed scrutiny regarding the correctness of the return submitted by a person in this connection and in such cases final assessment order shall be passed in accordance with the provisions of this Chapter.

(11) If no return is submitted by any person under sub-section (8) within the prescribed period or if the return submitted by him appears to the executive authority to be incomplete or incorrect, the executive authority shall, after making such enquiry as he may consider necessary, assess such person to the best of his judgement:

Provided that before taking action under this sub-section, the person shall be given a reasonable opportunity of proving the correctness or completeness of any return submitted by him.

(12) Every person who is liable to pay tax under this section, other than a person earning salary or wage:

(a) shall be issued with a pass book containing such details relating to such payment of tax as may be prescribed and if the pass book is lost or accidentally destroyed, the executive authority may, on an application made by the person accompanied by such fees as may be fixed by the village panchayat issue to such person a duplicate of the pass book;

(b) shall be allotted a permanent account number and such person shall:

(i) quote such number in all his returns to or correspondence with the Executive Authority;

(ii) quote such number in all chalans for the payment of any sum due under this Chapter.

(13) The rate of tax specified under sub-section (2) shall be revised by the village panchayat once in every five years and such revision of tax shall be increased not less than twenty-five per cent and not more than thirty-five per cent of the tax levied immediately before the date of revision.

198-C. Employers Liability to Deduct and Pay Tax on Behalf of the Employees—The tax payable by any person earning a salary or wage shall be deducted by his employer from the salary payable to such person, before such salary or wage is paid to him in such manner as may be prescribed and such employer shall irrespective of whether such deduction has been made or not when the salary or wage is paid to such person be liable to pay tax on behalf of such person:

Provided that if the employer is an officer of the State or Central Government, the Government may, notwithstanding anything contained in this Chapter prescribe the manner in which such employer shall discharge the said liability.

198-D. Filing of Returns by Employer—(1) Every employer liable to pay tax under this Chapter shall file a return to the executive authority, in such form, for such period and by such date as may be prescribed, showing therein the salaries paid by him to the employees and the amount of tax deducted by him in respect of such employees.

(2) Every such return shall accompany with the proof of payment of the full amount of tax due according to the return and a return without such proof of payment shall not be deemed to have been duly filed.

198-E. Assessment of the Employer—(1) The executive authority, if satisfied that any return filed by any employer under sub-section (1) of section 198-D is correct and complete, shall accept the return;

(2) Where an employer has failed to file any return under sub-section (1) of section 198-D within the time or if the return filed by him appears to the executive authority to be incorrect or incomplete, the executive authority shall, after making such enquiry as he considers necessary, determine the tax due and assess the employer to the best of his judgement and issue a notice of demand for the tax so assessed:

Provided that before assessing the tax due, the executive authority shall give the employer a reasonable opportunity of being heard.

198-F. Penalty and Interest— (1) In addition to the tax assessed under sub-section (11) of section 198-B or sub-section (2) of section 198-E, the executive authority shall direct the person or employer to pay by way of penalty a sum, which shall be, in the case of submission of incorrect or incomplete return, one hundred per cent of the difference of the tax assessed and the tax paid as per return:

Provided that no penalty under this sub-section shall be imposed after the period of three years from the date of the order of the assessment under this Chapter and unless the person affected has had a reasonable opportunity of showing cause against such imposition.

(2) On any amount remaining unpaid after the date specified for its payment, the person or employer shall pay, in addition to the amount due, interest at such rate not exceeding one per cent per mensem of such amount for the entire period of default, as may be prescribed.

198-G. Appeal—(1) Any person or employer aggrieved by any order or decision of the executive authority in relation to the payment of tax (including penalty, fee and interest) may, within such time as may be prescribed, appeal to the authority prescribed under section 174.

(2) The decision of the authority referred to in sub-section (1) shall be final and shall not be questioned in any court of law:

Provided that no such decision shall be made except after giving the person affected a reasonable opportunity of being heard.

198-H. Exemptions—Nothing contained in this Chapter shall apply to:

(a) the members of the Armed Forces of the Union serving in any part of this State, to whom the provisions of the Army Act, 1950 (Central Act XLVI of 1950), the Air Force Act, 1950 (Central Act XLV of 1950) or the Navy Act, 1957 (Central Act 62 of 1957) applies:

(b) the members of the Central Reserve Police Force to whom the Central Reserve Police Force Act, 1949 (Central Act XLVI of 1949) applies and serving in any part of this State;

(c) physically disabled persons with total disability in one or both the hands or legs, spastics, totally dumb or deaf persons or totally blind persons:

Provided that such physical disability shall be duly certified by a Registered Medical Practitioner in the service of the Government not below the rank of a Civil Surgeon.

198-I. Repeal and Savings—(1) The Tamil Nadu Tax on Professions, Trades, Callings and Employments Act, 1992 (Tamil Nadu Act 24 of 1992) (hereafter in this section referred to as the 1992 Act), in its application to the Village Panchayat is hereby repealed.

(2) The repeal of the 1992 Act under sub-section (1) shall not affect:

(i) the previous operation of the said Act or anything done or duly suffered thereunder; or

(ii) any right, privileges, obligations or liabilities acquired, accrued or incurred under the said Act; or

(iii) any penalty, forfeiture or punishment incurred in respect of any offence committed.

(3) Notwithstanding the repeal of the 1992 Act, the rates of tax of professions, trades, callings and employments specified in the Schedule to the said Act shall continue to apply for period commencing on the 1st day of April 1992 and ending with the 30th day of September 1998 for the levy and collection of such tax for the said period where the taxes due under that Act has not been paid for the said period.

(4) The provisions of this Chapter, other than the rates of tax specified in sub-section (2) of section 198-B and the provisions relating to penalty and interest, shall *mutatis mutandis* apply to the levy and collection of tax for the period mentioned in sub-section (3).

(5) The arrears of tax under the 1992 Act shall be paid in six equal half-yearly instalments in such manner and within such period as may be prescribed]."

CHAPTER X
CONTROLLING AUTHORITIES

199. Appointment of Officers to Supervise Panchayats—(1) The Government may appoint such officers as may be required for the purpose of inspecting or superintending the operations of all or any of the panchayats constituted under this Act.

(2) The Government shall have power to regulate by rules made under this Act, the classifications, methods of recruitment, conditions of service, pay and allowances and discipline and conduct of the officers referred to in sub-section (1) and of the members of their establishments.

200. Powers of Inspecting Officers—(1) The Inspector or the Collector or any officer appointed under section 199 or any other officer or person whom the Government or the Inspector or the Collector may empower in this behalf, may:

(a) enter on and inspect any immovable property, or any work in progress, under the control of any panchayat or any executive authority or Commissioner or Secretary;

(b) enter any school, dispensary, vaccination station or choultry maintained by or under the control of any panchayat or any other institution maintained by or under the control of any panchayat and inspect any records, registers or other documents kept in any such institution;

(c) enter the office of any panchayat and inspect any records, registers or other documents kept therein.

(2) Village panchayats and their presidents, executive authorities, panchayat union councils and their chairmen, Commissioners, district panchayats and their chairmen, Secretaries and the officers and servants of panchayats shall be bound to afford to the officers and persons aforesaid, such access, at all reasonable times, to panchayat property or premises and to all documents as may, in the opinion of such officer or persons, subject to such rules as may be prescribed, be necessary to enable them to discharge their duties under this section.

201. Powers of Officers for Purpose of Control—The Inspector or any officer or person whom the Government or the Inspector, may empower in this behalf may:

(a) direct the village panchayat or panchayat union council or the district panchayat to make provision for and to execute or provide any public work or amenity, or service of the description referred to in sections 110, 112 and 163;

(b) call for any record, register or other document in the possession, or under the control, of any panchayat or executive authority, or Commissioner or Secretary;

(c) require any panchayat or executive authority or Commissioner or the Secretary to furnish any return, plan, estimate, statement, account or statistics;

(d) require any panchayat or executive authority or Commissioner or the Secretary to furnish any information or report on any matter connected with such panchayat;

(e) require any panchayat or executive authority or the Commissioner or the Secretary to obtain his previous sanction before giving up claim or closing down any institution which is a source of income;

(f) record in writing for the consideration of any panchayat or executive authority or Commissioner or the Secretary, any observations in regard to its or his proceedings or duties.

202. Power to Suspend or Cancel Resolution, etc. under the Act—(1) The Inspector may, by order in writings:

(i) suspend or cancel any resolution passed, order issued, or licence or permission granted, or

(ii) prohibit the doing of any act which is about to be done or is being done, in pursuance or under colour of this Act, if in his opinion:

 (a) such resolution, order, licence, permission or act has not been legally passed, issued, granted or authorised, or

 (b) such resolution, order, licence, permission or act is in excess of the powers conferred by this Act or any other law or an abuse of such powers or is considered by the Inspector to be otherwise undesirable, or

 (c) the execution of such resolution or order, or the continuance in force of such licence or permission or the doing of such act is likely to cause danger to human life, health or safety, or is likely to lead to a riot or an affray:

Provided that nothing in this sub-section shall enable the Inspector to set aside any election which has been held.

(2) The Inspector shall, before taking action on any of the grounds, referred to in clauses (a) and (b) of sub-section (1), give the authority or person concerned an opportunity for explanation.

(3) The power conferred on the Inspector under clause (c) of sub-section (1) may be exercised by the Collector in accordance with the provisions of that clause.

203. Emergency Powers of Collector and Inspector—Subject to such control as may be prescribed, the Inspector or the Collector may, in cases of emergency, direct or provide for the execution of any, work, or the doing of any act which a panchayat or executive authority or Commissioner or Secretary is empowered to execute or do, and the immediate execution or doing of which is in his opinion necessary for the safety of the public, and may direct that the expenses of executing such work or doing such act shall be paid by the person having the custody of the Village Panchayat Fund or the Panchayat Union (General) Fund or the District Panchayat (General) Fund in priority to any other charges against such Fund except charges for the service of authorised loans.

204. Power to Take Action in Default of a Village Panchayat, President or Executive Authority, etc.—(1) If any time it appears to the Inspector that a village panchayat, president or executive authority or that a panchayat union council or its chairman or Commissioner or a district panchayat or its chairman or Secretary, has made default in performing any duty imposed by or under this or any other Act, he may, by order in writing, fix a period for the performance of such duty.

(2) If such duty is not performed within the period so fixed, the Inspector may appoint some person to perform it, and may direct that the expense of performing it shall be paid by the person having the custody of the Village Panchayat Fund or the Panchayat Union Fund or the District Panchayat (General) Fund as the case may be, in priority to any other charges against such Fund except charges for the service of authorised loans.

(3) If on a representation in writing made by the president, the Inspector is satisfied that due to the non-cooperation of the members with the president, the village panchayat is not able to function, the Inspector may, by notification, authorise the president to perform, subject to the control of the Inspector, such of the duties imposed upon the village panchayat by law and for such period not exceeding six months as may be specified in such notification. During the period for which the president is so authorised, there shall be no meeting of the village panchayat.

(4) If on a representation in writing made by the chairman, the Government are satisfied that due to the non-cooperation of the members with the chairman, the panchayat union council or the district panchayat, as the case may be, is not able to function, the Government may, by notification, authorise the chairman to perform, subject to the control of the Government or any officer authorised by the Government in this behalf, such of the duties imposed upon the panchayat union council or the district panchayat, as the case may be, by law and for such period not exceeding six months as may be specified in such notification. During the period for which the chairman is so authorised, there shall be no meeting of the panchayat union council or the district panchayat.

205. Removal of President—(1) The Inspector:

(a) of his own motion, or

(b) on a representation in writing signed by not less than two-thirds of the sanctioned strength of the village panchayat containing a statement of charges against the president and presented in person to the Inspector by any two of the members of the village panchayat, is satisfied that the president wilfully omits or refuses to carry out or disobeys any provision of this Act, or any rule, by-law, regulation, or lawful order made or issued under this Act or abuses any power vested in him, the Inspector shall, by notice in writing, require the president to offer within a specified date, his explanation with respect to his acts of omission or commission mentioned in the notice.

(2) If the explanation is received within the specified date and the Inspector considers that the explanation is satisfactory, he may drop further action with respect to the notice. If no explanation is received within the specified date or if the explanation received is in his opinion not satisfactory, he shall forward to the Tehsildar of the taluk a copy of the notice referred to in sub-section (1) and the explanation of the president if received within the specified date with a proposal for the removal of the president for ascertaining the views of the village panchayat.

(3) The Tehsildar shall then convene a meeting for the consideration of the notice and the explanation, if any, and the proposal for the removal of the president, at the office of the village panchayat at a time appointed by the Tehsildar.

(4) A copy of the notice of the meeting shall be caused to be delivered to the president and to all the members of the village panchayat by the Tehsildar at least seven days before the date of the meeting.

(5) The Tehsildar shall preside at the meeting convened under this section and no other person shall preside thereat. If, within half an hour appointed for the meeting, the Tehsildar is not present to preside at the meeting, the meeting shall stand adjourned to a time to be appointed and notified to the members and the president by the Tehsildar under sub-section (6).

(6) If the Tehsildar is unable to preside at the meeting, he may, after recording his reasons in writing, adjourn the meeting to such other time as he may appoint. The date so appointed shall be not later than thirty days from the date so appointed for the meeting under sub-section (3), Notice of not less than seven clear days shall be given to the members and president of the time appointed for the adjourned meeting.

(7) Save as provided in sub-sections (5) and (6), a meeting convened for the purpose of considering the notice and the explanation, if any, and the proposal for the removal of the president under this section shall not for any reason, be adjourned.

(8) As soon as the meeting convened under this section is commenced, the Tehsildar, shall read to the village panchayat the notice of the Inspector and the explanation, if any, of the president [116]["and the proposal for the removal of the president"] for the consideration of which it has been convened.

[117]["(8A) There shall be no debate in any meeting under this section"].

(9) The Tehsildar shall not speak on the merits of the notice or explanation nor shall be entitled to vote at the meeting.

(10) The views of the village panchayat shall be duly recorded in the minutes of the meeting and a copy of the minutes shall forthwith on the termination of the meeting be forwarded by the Tehsildar to the Inspector.

(11) The Inspector may, after considering the views of the village panchayat in this regard, in his discretion either remove the president from office by notification with effect from a date to be specified therein or drop further action.

(12) The Government shall have power to cancel any notification issued under sub-section (11) and may, pending a decision on such cancellation, postpone the date specified in such notification.

(13) Any person in respect of whom a notification has been issued under sub-section (11) removing him from the office of president shall, unless the notification is cancelled under sub-section (12), be ineligible for election as president until the date on which notice of the next ordinary elections to the village panchayat is published in the prescribed manner, or the expiry of one year from the date specified in such notification as postponed by the order, if any, issued under sub-section (12) whichever is earlier.

206. Removal of Vice-president—(1) If in the opinion of the Inspector, the vice-president wilfully omits or refuses to carry out or disobeys any provisions of this Act, or any rule, bye-law, regulation, or lawful order made or issued under this Act or abuses any power vested in him, the Inspector shall by notice in writing, require the vice-president to offer within a specified date, his explanation with respect to his cases of omission or commission mentioned in the notice.

(2) The provisions of sub-sections (2) to (13) (both inclusive) of section 205 shall, as far as may be, apply in relation to the removal of the vice-president as they apply in relation to the removal of the president by the Inspector on his own motion.

207. Removal of Chairman of Panchayat Union Council—(1) If the Government:

(a) of their own motion, or

(b) on a representation in writing signed by not less than two-thirds of the strength of the panchayat union council containing a statement of charges against the chairman of the panchayat union council and presented in person to any officer appointed by the Government in this behalf by any two of the members of the panchayat union council, are satisfied that the chairman wilfully omits or refuses to carry out or disobeys the provisions of this Act, or any rules, bye-laws, regulations or lawful orders issued thereunder or abuses the powers vested in him, the Government shall, by notice in writing, require the chairman to offer within a specified date, his explanation with respect to his acts of omission or commission mentioned in the notice.

(2) If the explanation is received within the specified date and the Government consider that the explanation is satisfactory, the Government may drop further action with respect to the notice. If no explanation is received within the specified date or if the explanation received is in their opinion not satisfactory, the Government shall forward to the Revenue Divisional Officer of the division concerned, a copy of the notice referred to in sub-section (1) and the explanation of the chairman with a proposal for the removal of the chairman from office for ascertaining the views of the panchayat union council.

(3) The Revenue Divisional Officer shall then convene a meeting for the consideration of the notice and the explanation, if any, and the proposal for the removal of the chairman at the office of the panchayat union council at a time appointed by the Revenue Divisional Officer.

(4) A copy of the notice of the meeting shall be caused to be delivered to the concerned chairman and to all the members of the panchayat union council by the Revenue Divisional Officer at least seven days before the date of the meeting.

(5) The Revenue Divisional Officer shall preside at the meeting convened under this section and no other person shall preside thereat. If within half an hour appointed for the meeting, the Revenue Divisional Officer is not present to preside at the meeting, the meeting shall stand adjourned to a time to be appointed and notified to the members by the Revenue Divisional Officer, under sub-section (6).

(6) If the Revenue Divisional Officer is unable to preside at the meeting, he may, after recording his reasons in writing, adjourn the meeting to such other time as he may appoint. The date so appointed shall be not later than thirty days from the date appointed for the meeting under sub-section (3). Notice of not less than seven clear days shall be given to the members of the time appointed for the adjourned meeting.

(7) Save as provided in sub-sections (5) and (6) a meeting convened for the purpose of considering the notice and the explanation, if any, and the proposal for the removal of the chairman under this section shall not, for any reason, be adjourned.

(8) As soon as the meeting convened under this section is commenced, the Revenue Divisional Officer shall read to the panchayat union council the notice of the Government and the explanation, if any, of the chairman [118][and the proposal for the removal of the chairman] for the consideration of which it has been convened.

(9) There shall be no debate in any meeting under this section.

(10) The Revenue Divisional Officer shall not speak on the merits of the notice or explanation nor shall he be entitled to vote at the meeting.

(11) The views of the panchayat union council shall be duly recorded in the minutes of the meeting and a copy of the minutes shall forthwith on the termination of the meeting be forwarded by the Revenue Divisional Officer to the Government.

(12) The Government may, after considering the views of the panchayat union council in this regard in their discretion either remove the chairman from office by notification with effect from a date to be specified therein or drop further action.

(13) Any person in respect of whom a notification has been issued under sub-section (12) removing him from the office of chairman shall be ineligible for election as chairman and for holding any of those offices until the date on which notice of the next ordinary elections to the panchayat union council is published in the prescribed manner or the expiry of one year from the date specified in the notification whichever is earlier.

208. Removal of Vice-chairman of Panchayat Union Council—(1) If, in the opinion of the Government, the vice-chairman of the panchayat union council wilfully omits or refuses to carry out or disobeys any provisions of this Act, or any rules, bye-laws, regulations or lawful orders issued thereunder or abuses any power vested in him, the Government shall, by notice in writing, require the vice-chairman to offer within a specified date, his explanation with respect to his acts of omission or commission mentioned in the notice.

(2) The provisions of sub-sections (2) to (13) (both inclusive) of section 207 shall, as far as may be, apply in relation to the removal of the vice-chairman as they apply in relation to the removal of the chairman of the panchayat union council by the Government on their own motion.

209. Removal of Chairman of District Panchayat—(1) If the Government:

(a) of their own motion, or

(b) on a representation in writing signed by not less than two-thirds of the strength of the district panchayat containing a statement of charges against the chairman of the district panchayat and presented in person to any officer appointed by the Government in this behalf, by any two of the members of the district Panchayat, are satisfied that the chairman wilfully omits or refuses to carry out or disobeys the provisions of this Act, or any rules, bye-laws, regulations or lawful orders issued thereunder or abuses the powers vested in him, the Government shall, by notice in writing, require the chairman to offer within a specified date, his explanation with respect to his acts of omission or commission mentioned in the notice.

(2) The provisions of sub-sections (2) to (13) (both inclusive) of section 207 shall, as far as may be, apply in relation to the removal of the chairman of district panchayat as they apply in relation to the removal of the chairman of panchayat union council by the Government on their own motion.

210. Removal of Vice-chairman of District Panchayat—(1) If, in the opinion of the Government, the vice-chairman of district panchayat, wilfully omits or refuses to carry out or disobeys any provisions of this Act, or any rules, bye-laws, regulations or lawful orders issued thereunder or abuses any power vested in him, the Government shall, by notice in writing, require the vice-chairman of district panchayat to offer within a specified date, his explanation with respect to his acts of omission or commission mentioned in the notice.

(2) The provisions of sub-sections (2) to (13) (both inclusive) of section 207 shall, as far as may be, apply in relation to the removal of the vice-chairman of district panchayat, as they apply in relation to the removal of the chairman of panchayat union council, by the Government on their own motion.

[143][**210A. Removal of President, Vice-President, Chairman, Vice-Chairman or member convicted under Section 246A**—(1) Notwithstanding anything contained in this Act, the government may, by notification, remove any president, vice-president or member of a village panchayat or chairman, vice-chairman or member of a panchayat union council or of a District Panchayat who is convicted twice of an offence punishable under Section 246A.

(2) The government shall, when they propose to take action under sub-section (1), give the president, vice-president, chairman, vice-chairman or member concerned an opportunity to explain and the notification issued under the said sub-section shall contain a statement of the reasons of the government for the action taken.

(3) Any person removed under sub-section (1) from the office of president, vice-president, chairman, vice-chairman or member, as the case may

be, shall not be eligible for election to the said office until the date on which notice of the next ordinary election to the village panchayat, panchayat union council or district panchayat as the case may be is punished in the prescribed manner or the expiry or one year from the date specified in such notification, whichever is earlier.]

211. Motion of No Confidence in Vice-president of Panchayat—(1) Subject to the provisions of this section, a motion expressing want of confidence in the vice-president of a village panchayat may be made in accordance with the procedure laid down herein.

(2) Written notice of intention to make the motion, signed by members of the village panchayat not less in number than one-half of the sanctioned strength of the village panchayat, together with a copy of the motion which is proposed to be made, and a written statement of the charges against the vice-president, shall be delivered in person to the Tehsildar of the taluk by any two of the members of the village panchayat signing the notice.

(3) A copy of the statement of charges along with the notice of the meeting shall be caused to be delivered to the vice-president concerned by the Tehsildar, and the vice-president shall be required to give a statement in reply to the charges within a week of the receipt of the notice by the vice-president.

(4) The Tehsildar shall, after the expiry of the period of the notice issued under sub-section (3) convene a meeting for the consideration of the motion, at the office of the village panchayat at a time appointed by him.

(5) The Tehsildar shall give to the members notice of not less than fifteen clear days of such meeting and of the time appointed therefor.

(6) The Tehsildar shall preside at the meeting convened under this section, and no other person shall preside thereat. If within half an hour after the time appointed for the meeting, the Tehsildar is not present to preside at the meeting, the meeting shall stand adjourned to a time to be appointed and notified to the members by the Tehsildar under sub-section (7).

(7) If the Tehsildar is unable to preside at the meeting, he may, after recording his reasons in writing, adjourn the meeting to such other time as he may appoint. The date so appointed shall not be later than thirty days from the date appointed for the meeting under sub-section (4). Notice of not less than seven clear days shall be given to the members, of the time appointed for the adjourned meeting.

(8) Save as provided in sub-sections (6) and (7), a meeting convened for the purpose of considering a motion under this section shall not for any reason be adjourned.

(9) As soon as the meeting convened under this section has commenced, the Tehsildar shall read to the village panchayat, the motion for the consideration of which it has been convened, the statement of charges and the written statement, if any, of the vice-president in reply to the said charges.

(10) There shall be no debate on any motion under this section.

(11) The Tehsildar shall not speak on the merits of the motion, nor shall he be entitled to vote thereon.

(12) A copy of the minutes of the meeting together with a copy of the motion and the result of the voting thereon shall forthwith on the termination of the meeting be forwarded by the Tehsildar to the Inspector.

(13) If the motion is carried with the support of not less than two-thirds of the sanctioned strength of the village panchayat, the Inspector shall, by notification, remove the vice-president of the village panchayat.

(14) If the motion is not carried by such a majority as aforesaid, or if the meeting cannot be held for want of the quorum referred to in sub-section (13), no notice of any subsequent motion expressing want of confidence in the same vice-president shall be received until after the expiry of six months from the date of the meeting.

(15) No notice of a motion under this section shall be received within six months of the assumption of office by the vice-president.

212. Motion of No Confidence in [119]["Chairman or Vice-chairman"] of Panchayat Union Council—(1) Subject to the provisions of this section, a motion expressing want of confidence in the [120]["Chairman or vice-chairman"] of a panchayat union council may be made in accordance with the procedure laid down herein.

(2) Written notice of intention to make the motion, signed by members of the panchayat union council not less in number than one-half of the sanctioned strength of the panchayat union council, together with a copy of the motion which is proposed to be made and a written statement of the charges against the [121]["Chairman or vice-chairman"] shall be

delivered in person to the Revenue Divisional Officer of the division by any two of the members of the panchayat union council signing the notice.

(3) A copy of the a statement of charges along with the motion shall be caused to be delivered to the concerned [122]["Chairman or vice-chairman"] by the Revenue Divisional Office and the [123]["Chairman or vice-chairman"] shall be required to give a statement in reply to the charges within a week of the receipt of the motion by the chairman or vice-chairman.

(4) The Revenue Divisional Officer shall then convene a meeting for the consideration of the motion at the office of the panchayat union council at a time appointed by him.

(5) The Revenue Divisional Officer shall give to the members notice of not less than fifteen clear days of the meeting and of the time appointed therefor.

(6) The Revenue Divisional Officer shall preside at the meeting convened under this section, and no other person shall preside thereat. If within half an hour after the time appointed for the meeting, the Revenue Divisional Officer is not present to preside at the meeting, the meeting shall stand adjourned to a time to be appointed and notified to the members by the Revenue Divisional Officer under sub-section (7).

(7) If the Revenue Divisional Officer is unable to preside at the meeting, he may, after recording his reasons in writing adjourn the meeting to such other time as he may appoint. The date so appointed shall not be later than thirty days from the date appointed for the meeting under sub-section (4). Notice of not less than seven clear days shall be given to the members of the time appointed for the adjourned meeting.

(8) Save as otherwise provided in sub-sections (6), (7) a meeting convened for the purpose of considering a motion under this section shall not for any reason be adjourned.

(9) As soon as the meeting convened under this section has commenced, the Revenue Divisional Officer shall read to the panchayat union council, the motion for the consideration of which it has been convened, the statement of charges and the written statement, if any, of the [124]["chairman or the vice-chairman"] in reply to the said charges.

(10) There shall be no debate on any motion under this section.

(11) The Revenue Divisional Officer shall not speak on the merits of the motion, nor shall he be entitled to vote thereon.

(12) A copy of the minutes of the meeting together with a copy of the motion and the result of the voting thereon shall forthwith on the termination of the meeting be forwarded by the Revenue Divisional Officer to the Government.

(13) If the motion is carried with the support of not less than two-thirds of the sanctioned strength of the panchayat union council, the Government shall, by notification, remove the [125]["chairman or vice-chairman"] of the panchayat union council.

(14) If the motion is not carried by such a majority as aforesaid, or if the meeting cannot be held for want of the quorum referred to in sub-section (13), no notice of any subsequent motion expressing want of confidence in the same [126]["chairman or vice-chairman"] shall be received until after the expiry of [127]["one year"] from the date of the meeting.

(15) No notice of a motion under this section shall be received within [128]["one year"] of the assumption of office by [129]["chairman or the vice-chairman"].

213. Motion of No Confidence in [130]["Chairman or Vice-chairman"] of District Panchayat—A motion expressing want of confidence in the [131]["chairman or vice-chairman"] of a district panchayat may be made in accordance with the procedure specified in sub-sections (2) to (15) (both inclusive) of section 212, subject to the modification that the reference to Revenue Divisional Officer in the said sub-sections shall be construed as a reference to Collector.

214. Dissolution of Village Panchayat—(1) If, in the opinion of the Government, a village panchayat is not competent to perform or persistently makes default in performing the duties imposed on it by law, or exceeds or abuses its powers, they may, by notification, direct that the village panchayat be dissolved with effect from a specified date and reconstituted with effect from a specified date which shall be within a period of six months from the date of such dissolution.

(2) Before publishing a notification under sub-section (1), the Government shall communicate to the village panchayat, the grounds on which they propose to do so, fix a reasonable period for the village panchayat to show cause against the proposal and consider its explanations and objections, if any.

(3) On the date fixed for the dissolution of a village panchayat under sub-section (1) all its members as well as its president and vice-president shall forthwith be deemed to have vacated their

offices as such and thereupon the provisions contained in the proviso to sub-section (2) of section 16 shall apply.

(4) In case the president of a village panchayat which is dissolved under this section is a member of a panchayat union council, he shall, with effect on and from the date of the dissolution, be deemed to have vacated his office as such member notwithstanding anything contained in section 22.

(5) On the reconstitution of the village panchayat after the dissolution, the Government may pass such orders as they deem fit as to the transfer to the village panchayat from the panchayat union council during the period of dissolution on behalf of the village panchayat and as to the discharge of the liabilities if any, of such village panchayat relating to such assets or institutions.

(6) In the case of a village panchayat reconstituted after dissolution, the elected member including the president shall enter upon their offices on the date fixed for its reconstitution and shall hold their offices only for the remainder of the period for which the dissolved village panchayat would have continued under sub-section (1) of section 9, had it not been dissolved.

215. Dissolution of Panchayat Union Council—(1) If, in the opinion of the Government a panchayat union council is not competent to perform or persistently makes default in performing the duties imposed on it by law or exceeds or abuses its powers, they may, by notification:

(a) dissolve the panchayat union council from a specified date; and

(b) direct that the panchayat union council be reconstituted with effect from a date which shall not be later than six months from the date of dissolution.

(2) Before publishing a notification under sub section (1), the Government shall communicate to the panchayat union council the grounds on which they propose to do so, fix a reasonable period for the panchayat union council to show cause against the proposal and consider its explanations and objections, if any.

(3) On the date fixed for the dissolution of a panchayat union council under sub-section (1) all its members as well as its chairman and vice-chairman shall forthwith be deemed to have vacated their offices as such.

(4) During the interval between the dissolution and the reconstitution of a panchayat union council, the Inspector may appoint a person to exercise the powers and discharge the duties of the panchayat union council and of its chairman:

Provided that any person to be appointed under the provisions of this sub-section shall be a person in the service of the Government not below the rank of a Tehsildar or a Commissioner.

(5) The Government may direct that the panchayat union council be reconstituted before the date fixed for its reconstitution under clause (b) of sub-section (1).

(6) The members as well as the chairman and vice-chairman of a reconstituted panchayat union council shall enter upon their offices on the date fixed for its reconstitution and they shall hold their offices only for the remainder of the period for which the dissolved panchayat union council would have continued under sub-section (1) of section 18, had it not been dissolved.

(7) When a panchayat union council is dissolved under this section, the Government until the date of the reconstitution of the panchayat union council and the reconstituted panchayat union council thereafter shall be entitled to all the assets and be subject to all the liabilities of the panchayat union council as on the date of the reconstitution respectively.

216. Dissolution of District Panchayat—(1) If, in the opinion of the Government, a district panchayat is not competent to perform or persistently makes default in performing the duties imposed on it by law or exceeds or abuses its powers, they may, by notification:

(a) dissolve the district panchayat from a specified date; and

(b) direct that the district panchayat be reconstituted with effect from the date, which shall not be later than six months from the date of dissolution.

(2) The provisions of sub-sections (2) to (7) (both inclusive) of section 215 shall, as far as may be apply in relation to the dissolution of a district panchayat as they apply in relation to the dissolution of a panchayat union council.

217. Powers of Officers Acting on Behalf of Panchayat and Liability for Payment of Compensation—The Government, the Inspector or any other person lawfully taking action on behalf, or in default, of a panchayat under this Act, shall have such powers as are necessary for the purpose and shall be entitled to the same protection under this Act as the panchayat or its officers or servants whose powers are exercised; and compensation shall be recoverable from the Village Panchayat Fund or the Panchayat Union Fund or the District Panchayat (General) Fund by any person suffering damage from the exercise of such powers to the same extent, as if the action had been taken by the panchayat or their officers or servants.

218. Delegation of Powers—(1) The Government may, by notification, authorize any authority or officer not below the rank of a Collector to exercise in regard to any panchayat or any class of panchayats in any area or all panchayats in any area, any of the powers vested in them by this Act except the power to make rules and may in like manner withdraw such authority.

(2) The Inspector or the Collector may by notification authorise any officer not below the rank of a Revenue Divisional Officer to exercise in respect of any panchayat union council or all panchayat union councils in the area under the jurisdiction of such officer, any of the powers vested by this Act on the Inspector or the Collector as the case may be and may in like manner withdraw such authority.

(3) The Inspector or the Collector may, by notification, authorise any officer not below the rank of a Commissioner to exercise in respect of any village panchayat or any class of village panchayats or all village panchayats in the panchayat development block any of the powers vested by this Act on the Inspector or the Collector as the case may be and may in like manner withdraw such authority.

(4) The exercise of any power delegated under sub-sections (1) to (3) shall be subject to such restrictions and conditions as may be prescribed or as may be specified in the notification and also to control and revision by the delegating authority, or where such authority is the Government by such officer as may be empowered by the Government in this behalf. The Government shall also have power to control and revise the acts or proceedings of any officer so empowered.

(5) The exercise of any power conferred on the Inspector or the Collector by any of the provisions of this Act including sub-sections (2) to (4) of this section shall whether such power is exercised by the Inspector or the Collector himself or by any officer to whom it has been delegated under sub-section (2) or (3) be subject to such restrictions and conditions as may be prescribed and also controlled by the Government or by such officer as may be empowered by them in this behalf. The Government shall also have power to control the acts or proceedings of any officer so empowered.

219. Revision—(1) The Government may, after consulting the Inspector, Collector or such other officer or authority as they may deem fit, at any time, either *suo moto* or on application, call for and examine the record of any order passed or proceeding recorded under the provisions of this Act by:

(a) the Inspector or the Collector or any officer authorised by the Inspector or the Collector under sub-section (2) or (3) of section 218; or
(b) any officer authorised by the Government under sub-section (1) of that section or any officer empowered by them under sub-section (4) of that section; or
(c) any other authority or officer;

for the purpose of satisfying themselves as the legality or propriety of such order, or as to the regularity of such proceeding and pass such order in reference thereto as they think fit.

(2) The powers of the nature referred to in sub-section (1) may also be exercised by such authority or officer as may be empowered in this behalf by the Government.

CHAPTER XI
GENERAL AND MISCELLANEOUS LICENCES AND PERMISSIONS

220. General Provisions Regarding Licence and Permission—(1) Save as otherwise expressly provided in or may be prescribed under this Act, every application for any licence or permission under this Act or any rule, bye-law or regulation made thereunder, or for the renewal thereof, shall be made not less than thirty and not more than ninety days before the earliest date with effect from which, or the commencement of the period (being a year or such less period as is mentioned in the application) for which the licence or permission is required.

(2) Save as aforesaid, for every such licence or permission, fees may be charged on such units and at such rates as may be fixed by the panchayat, provided that the rates shall not exceed the maximum, if any, prescribed.

(3) Save as aforesaid, if orders on an application for any such licence or permission are not communicated to the applicant within thirty days or such longer period as may be prescribed in any class of cases after the receipt of the application by the executive authority of the village panchayat or the Commissioner or the Secretary. The application shall be deemed to have been allowed for the period,

if any, for which it would have been ordinarily allowed and subject to the law, rules, bye-laws and regulations and all conditions ordinarily imposed.

(4) The acceptance of the pre-payment of the fee for any such licence or permission shall not entitle the person making such pre-payment to the licence or permission, but only to a refund of the fee in case of refusal of the licence or permission.

(5) If an act, for which any such licence or permission is necessary, is done without such licence or permission, or in a manner inconsistent with the terms of the licence or permission obtained, then:

(a) the executive authority of the village panchayat or the Commissioner or the Secretary may by notice require the person so doing such act to alter, remove, or as far as practicable restore to its original state, the whole, or any part of any property, movable or immovable, public or private affected thereby, within a time to be specified in the notice; and further,

(b) if no penalty has been specially provided in this Act for so doing such act the person so doing it shall be punishable with fine not exceeding fifty rupees for such offence.

(6) Whenever any person is convicted of an offence in respect of the failure to obtain any such licence or permission, the Magistrate shall, in addition to any fine which may be imposed, recover summarily and pay over to the panchayat the amount of the fee chargeable for the licence or permission, and may, in his discretion, also recover summarily and pay over to the panchayat such amount, if any as he may fix as the costs of the prosecution.

Explanation. The recovery of the fee for a licence or permission under this sub section shall not entitle the person convicted to the licence or permission.

221. Government and Market Committees not to Obtain Licence and Permission—Nothing in this Act or in any rule, bye-law or regulation made thereunder shall be construed as requiring the taking out of any licence or the obtaining of any permission under this Act or any such rule, bye-law or regulation in respect of any place in the occupation or under the control of the Central or the State Government or of a market committee established under the Tamil Nadu Agricultural Produce Marketing (Regulation) Act, 1987 (Tamil Nadu Act 27 of 1989) or in respect of any property of the Central or the State Government or of any property belonging to such market committee.

POWER TO ENFORCE NOTICES, ORDERS, ETC.

222. Time for Complying with Notice, Order, etc. and Power to Enforce in Default—(1) Whenever by any notice, requisition or order under this Act, or under any rule, bye-law or regulation made thereunder, any person is required to execute any work to take any measures or to do anything, a reasonable time shall be named in such notice, requisition or order within which the work shall be executed, the measure taken or the thing done.

(2) If such notice, requisition or order is not complied with within the time so named:

(a) the executive authority of the village panchayat or the Commissioner or the Secretary, as the case may be, may cause such work to be executed, or may take any measure or do anything which may, in his opinion, be necessary for giving due effect to the notice, requisition or order; and

(b) if no penalty has been specially provided in this Act for failure to comply with such notice, requisition or order, the said person shall be punishable with fine not exceeding fifty rupees for every such offence.

POWER OF ENTRY AND INSPECTION

223. Power of Entry and Inspection—(1) Subject to such restrictions and conditions as may be prescribed, the executive authority or the Commissioner or the Secretary or any person authorised by him may enter on or into any place, building or land, with or without assistants or workmen in order

(a) to make any enquiry, inspection, test, examination, survey, measurement or valuation or to execute any other work, which is authorised by the provisions of this Act or of any rule, bye-law, regulation or order made under it or which it is necessary to make or execute for any of the purposes of this Act or in pursuance of any of the said provisions, or

(b) to satisfy himself that nothing is being done in such place, building or land for which a licence or permission is required under any of the said provisions, without such licence or permission or otherwise than in conformity with the terms of the licence or permission obtained.

(2) No claim shall lie against any person for any damage or inconvenience necessarily caused by the exercise of powers under sub-section (1) or the use of any force necessary for effecting an entrance under that sub-section.

224. Testing of Weights and Measures—The executive authority or the Commissioner or the Secretary or any person authorised by him, may examine and test the weights and measures used in the markets and shops in the panchayat village or the panchayat union or the district panchayat area as the case may be, with a view to the prevention and punishment of offences relating to such weights and measures under Chapter XIII of the Indian Penal Code (Central Act XLV of 1860).

225. Power to Call for Information from Village Administrative Officer—(1) The executive authority or the Commissioner or the Secretary may, by an order in writing, require the Village Administrative Officer of any revenue village comprised within the jurisdiction of the village panchayat or panchayat union council or district panchayat to furnish him with information on any matter falling within such categories as may be prescribed in respect of such village or any part thereof or any person or property therein.

(2) The order shall specify the period within which it may be complied with but the executive authority or the Commissioner or the Secretary, may, from time-to-time, extend such period.

LIMITATION

226. Limitation for Recovery of Dues—No distraint shall be made, no suit shall be instituted and no prosecution shall be commenced in respect of any tax or other sum due to a panchayat under this Act or any rule, bye-law, regulation or order made under it after the expiration of a period of six years from the date on which distraint might first have been made, a suit might first have been instituted or prosecution might first have been commenced, as the case may be, in respect of such tax or sum.

PROSECUTIONS, SUITS, ETC.

227. Persons Empowered to Prosecute—Save as otherwise expressly provided in this Act (Central Act 2 of 1974), no person shall be tried for any offence against this Act or any rule or bye-law made thereunder unless complaint is made within three months of the commission of the offence by the police, [132]["the village panchayat"], the executive authority, the panchayat union council, the Commissioner, the district panchayat, the Secretary or a person expressly authorised in this behalf by the village panchayat, panchayat union council, district panchayat, executive authority or Commissioner or the Secretary but nothing herein shall affect the provisions of the Code of Criminal Procedure, 1973 (Central Act II of 1974) in regard to the power of certain Magistrates to take cognizance of offence upon information received or upon their own knowledge or suspicion:

Provided that failure to take out a licence or obtain permission under this Act shall, for the purposes of this section, be deemed to be a continuing offence until the expiration of the period, if any, for which the licence or permission is required and if no period is specified, complaint may be made at any time within twelve months from the commencement of the offence.

228. Composition of Offences—The executive authority or the Commissioner or the Secretary may, subject to such restrictions and control, as may be prescribed, compound any offence against this Act or any rule or bye-law made thereunder, which may by rules, be declared compoundable.

229. Prosecutions and Compositions to be Reported to Village Panchayat, Panchayat Union Council or District Panchayat—Every prosecution instituted or offence compounded by the executive authority or the Commissioner or the Secretary shall be reported by him to the village panchayat or panchayat union council or the district panchayat, as the case may be, at its next meeting.

230. Sanction of Prosecution—(1) When the president or the executive authority or the chairman or vice-chairman of a panchayat union council or district panchayat or the Commissioner or the Secretary or any member is accused of any offence alleged to have been committed by him while acting or purporting to act in the discharge of his official duty, no court shall take cognizance of such offence except with the previous sanction of the Government.

(2) When according previous sanction under sub-section (1), it shall be open to the Government to direct by order that the president, executive authority, chairman, vice-chairman or Commissioner or the Secretary, as the case may be, shall not discharge his duties as such until the disposal of the case.

231. Notice of Action Against Village Panchayat, etc.—(1) Subject to the provisions of section 232, no suit or other legal proceeding shall be brought against any village panchayat or its president or executive authority or any panchayat union council or its chairman or the Commissioner or the district panchayat or its chairman or the Secretary or any member, officer or servant thereof or against any person acting under the direction of such village panchayat, president, panchayat union council or its chairman, district panchayat or its chairman, executive authority, Commissioner, Secretary, member, officer or servant, in respect of any act done or purporting to be done under this Act, or in respect of any alleged neglect or default in the execution of this Act or any rule, bye-law, regulation or order made under it until the expiration of two months next after notice in writing, stating the cause of action, the nature of the relief sought, the amount of compensation claimed and the name and place of residence of the intended plaintiff has been left at the office of the village panchayat or panchayat union council and if the proceeding is intended to be brought against any such president, executive authority, chairman, Commissioner, chairman of district panchayat, Secretary, member, officer servant or person, also delivered to him or left at his place of residence.

(2) Every such proceeding shall, unless it is a proceeding for the recovery of immovable property or for a declaration of title thereto, be commenced within six months after the date on which the cause of action arose or in case of a continuing injury or damage, during such continuance or within six months after the ceasing thereof.

(3) If any village panchayat, panchayat union council or district panchayat or person to whom notice is given under sub-section (1), tenders amount to the plaintiff before the proceeding is commenced and if the plaintiff does not in such proceeding recover more than the amount so tendered, he shall not recover any costs incurred by him after such tender and the plaintiff shall also pay all costs incurred by the defendant after such tender.

232. Protection of Chairman, President and Officers Acting in Good Faith—No suit or other legal proceeding shall be brought against the chairman, Commissioner, president, executive authority, Secretary or any member, officer or servant of a panchayat or any person acting under the direction of a panchayat or of such chairman, Commissioner, president, executive authority, Secretary, member, officer or servant in respect of any act done or purporting to be done under this Act or in respect of any alleged neglect or default on his part in the execution of any act under this Act, or any rule, bye-law regulation or order made under it, if such act was done, or such neglect or default occurred in good faith; but any such proceeding shall, so far as it is maintainable in a court, be brought against the panchayat except in the case of suits brought under section 234.

233. Injunction not to be Granted in Election Proceedings—Notwithstanding anything contained in the Code of Civil Procedure, 1908, (Central Act V of 1908) or in any other law for the time being in force, no court shall grant any permanent or temporary injunction or make any interim order restraining any proceeding which is being or about to be taken under this Act for the preparation or publication of any electoral roll for the conduct of any election.

234. Liability of the President, Executive Authority and Members, etc. for Loss, Waste or Misapplication of Property—(1) The president, executive authority and every member of a village panchayat and the chairman, Commissioner and every member of a panchayat union council and the chairman, Secretary and every member of a district panchayat shall be liable for the loss, waste or misapplication of any money or other property owned by or vested in the village panchayat or panchayat union council or the district panchayat if such loss, waste or misapplication is a direct consequence of his neglect or misconduct; and a suit for compensation may be instituted against him in any court of competent jurisdiction by the panchayat or panchayat union council or the district panchayat with the previous sanction of the Inspector.

(2) Every such suit shall be commenced within three years after the date on which the cause of action arose.

235. Assessment etc. not to be Impeached—(1) No assessment or demand made, and no charge imposed under the authority of this Act shall be impeached or affected by reason of any clerical error or by reason of any mistake (a) in respect of the name, residence, place of business or occupation of any person; or (b) in the description of any property or thing; or (c) in respect of the amount assessed, demanded or charged, provided that the provisions of this Act have in substance and effect been complied with and no proceedings under this Act shall, merely for defect in form, be quashed or set aside by any court of law.

(2) No suit shall be brought in any court to recover any sum of money collected under the authority of this Act or to recover damages on account of assessment or collection of money made under the said authority:

Provided that the provisions of this Act have in substance and effect been complied with.

(3) No distraint or sale under this Act shall be deemed unlawful, nor shall any person making the same be deemed a tress-passer, on account of any error, defect, or want of form in the bill, notice, schedule, form, summon, notice of demand, warrant of distraint, inventory, or other proceeding relating thereto, if the provisions of this Act, and of the rules and bye-laws made thereunder have in substance and effect been complied with:

Provided that every person aggrieved by any irregularity may recover satisfaction for any special damage sustained by him.

236. Public Roads, Markets, Wells, Tanks etc. to be Open to All—All roads, markets, wells, tanks, reservoirs and waterways vested in or maintained by a panchayat shall be open to the use and enjoyment of all persons, irrespective of their caste or creed.

237. Power to Farm Out Fees—A panchayat shall have power to farm out the collection of any fees due to it under this Act or any rule, bye-law or regulation made thereunder for any period not exceeding three years at a time, on such conditions as it thinks fit.

238. Adjudication of Disputes Between Local Authorities—(1) When a dispute exists between a village panchayat or a panchayat union council or a district panchayat and one or more other local authorities in regard to any matter arising under the provisions of this or any other Act and the Government are of opinion that the village panchayat or the panchayat union council or the district panchayat and the other local authorities concerned are unable to settle it amicably among themselves, the Government may take cognizance of the dispute, and

(a) decide it themselves, or

(b) refer it for inquiry and report, to an arbitrator or a board of arbitrators or to a joint committee constituted for the purpose.

(2) The report referred to in clause (b) of sub-section (1) shall be submitted to the Government who shall decide the dispute in such manner, as they deem fit.

(3) Any decision given under clause (a) of sub-section (1) or under sub-section (2) may be modified from time-to-time by the Government in such manner as they deem fit, and any such decision with the modifications, if any made therein under this sub-section may be cancelled at any time by the Government:

Provided that any such decision or any modification therein or cancellation thereof shall be binding on the village panchayat, the panchayat union council, the district panchayat and each of the other local authorities concerned and shall not be liable to be questioned in any court of law.

(4) Where one of the local authorities concerned is a cantonment authority or the port authority of a major port, the powers of the Government under this section shall be exercisable only with the concurrence of the Central Government.

239. Tamil Nadu State Election Commission—(1) The superintendence, direction and control of the preparation of electoral rolls for, and the conduct of all elections to the village panchayats, panchayat union councils and district panchayats shall be vested in the Tamil Nadu State Election Commission consisting of a Tamil Nadu State Election Commissioner to be appointed by the Governor under Article 243-K of the Constitution.

(2) (a) No person shall be qualified for appointment as Tamil Nadu State Election Commissioner unless he is or has been an officer of the Government not below the rank of Secretary to the Government.

(b) The Tamil Nadu State Election Commissioner shall hold office for a term of two years and shall be eligible for re-appointment for two successive terms:

Provided that no person shall hold the office of the Tamil Nadu State Election Commissioner for more than six years in the aggregate:

Provided further that a person appointed as Tamil Nadu State Election Commissioner shall retire from office if he completes the age of sixty-two years during the term of his office.

(3) Subject to the provisions of sub-section (2), the conditions of service and tenure of office of the Tamil Nadu State Election Commissioner shall be such as the Governor may by rules determine:

Provided that the Tamil Nadu State Election Commissioner shall not be removed from his office except in like manner and on the like grounds as a

Judge of a High Court and conditions of service of the Tamil Nadu State Election Commissioner shall not be varied to his disadvantage after his appointment.

(4) The Governor shall, when so requested by the Tamil Nadu State Election Commission make available to the Tamil Nadu State Election Commission such staff as may be necessary for the discharge of the functions conferred on the Tamil Nadu State Election Commission by sub-section (1).

240. Preparation of Development Plan—(1) Every village panchayat shall prepare every year a development plan for the panchayat village and submit it to the panchayat union council before such date and in such form as may be prescribed.

(2) Every panchayat union council shall prepare every year a development plan for the panchayat union after including the development plans of the village panchayats and submit it to the district panchayat before such date and in such form as may be prescribed.

(3) Every district panchayat shall prepare every year a development plan for the district after including the development plans of the panchayat union councils and submit it to the District Planning Committee constituted under section 241.

[133][**"241. District Planning Committee**–(1) The Government shall constitute in every district a District Planning Committee (hereinafter in this section referred to as the Committee) to consolidate the plans prepared by the district panchayats, panchayat union councils, village panchayats. [2][Town Panchayat] Municipal councils and municipal corporations in the district and to prepare a draft development plan for the district as a whole

[133]["(2) (a) The Committee shall consist of:

(i) The Chairman of the district panchayat;

(ii) the Mayor of the City Municipal Corporation in the district;

(iii) the Collector of the district;

(iv) such number of persons, not less than four-fifth of the total number of members of the Committee as may be specified by the Government, elected in the prescribed manner from amongst the members of the district panchayats, town panchayats and councillors of the municipal corporations and the municipal councils in the district, in proportion to the ratio between the population of the rural areas and of the urban areas in the district.

(b) The following persons shall be permanent special invitees of the Committee:

(v) Members of the House of the people who represent the whole or part of the district;

(vi) Members of the Council of States who are registered as electors in the district;

(vii) Members of the Tamil Nadu State Legislative Assembly whose constituencies lie within the district;

(viii) All the Chairmen of the panchayat union councils in the district;

(ix) All the Chairmen of the municipal councils in the district;

(x) All the Chairmen of the town panchayats in the district.

(c) The permanent special invitees referred to in clause (b) shall be entitled to take part in the proceedings in the meetings of the Committee.

(3) The Secretary of the District Panchayat shall be the Secretary to the Committee.

[134][(4) The Chairman of the District Panchayat shall be the Chairperson of the Committee and the Collector of the District shall be the vice-chairman of the Committee].

(5) The Committee shall meet at such place, at such interval and at such time and observe such rules of procedure in regard to transaction of business at its meetings (including the quorum at its meetings) as may be prescribed.

(6) The Committee shall consolidate the plans prepared by the district panchayat, panchayat union councils, village panchayats, town panchayats, municipal councils and the municipal corporation in the district and prepare a draft development plan for the district as a whole.

(7) Every Committee shall, in preparing the draft development plan:

(a) have regard to:

(i) the matters of common interest between the district panchayats, panchayat union councils, village panchayats, town panchayats, municipal corporations and municipal councils in the district including spatial planning, sharing of water and other physical and natural resources, the integrated development of infrastructures and environmental conservation;

(ii) the extent and type of available resources whether financial or otherwise.

(b) consult such institutions and organisations as the Governor may, by order, specify.

(8) The chairperson of every committee shall forward the development plan, as recommended by such Committee to the Government.

(9) The committee shall allocate funds to various schemes to the panchayats unions and shall monitor the implementations of the schemes.

Explanation. For the purposes of this section "town panchayat" and "municipal council", shall mean the town panchayat and the municipal council constituted under the Tamil Nadu District Municipalities Act, 1920, and "municipal corporation" means the corporations constituted under the Madurai City Municipal Corporation Act, 1971 or the Coimbatore City Municipal Corporation Act, 1981 or the Tiruchirappalli City Municipal Corporation Act, 1994 or the Tirunelveli City Municipal Corporation Act, 1994 or the Salem City Municipal Corporation Act, 1994 or any other municipal corporation that may be constituted under any law for the time being in force as the case may be"].

RULES

242. Power of Government to Make Rules—(1) The Government shall in addition to the rule making powers conferred on them by any other provision contained in this Act, have power to make rules generally to carry out the purposes of this Act.

[135]["(1-A) A rule under section 188 may be made so as to have retrospective effect on and from a date not earlier than the 26th day of March 1997"].

(2) In particular, and without prejudice to the generality of the foregoing power, the Government may make rules:

(i) as to the principles to be followed in regard to the exclusion of any local area from or the inclusion of any local area in a village under sub-section (2) of section 4;

(ii) providing for:

[136][(a) the adjudication of disputes arising out of election by the district judge having jurisdiction];

(b) all matters relating to electoral rolls or elections, not expressly provided for in this Act, including deposits to be made by candidates standing for election and the conditions under which such deposits may be forfeited, and the conduct of inquiries and the decision of disputes relating to electoral rolls;

(iii) as to the determination of the population for the purposes of this Act;

(iv) as to the resignations of chairman, vice-chairman and members of panchayat union councils and district panchayats and of the presidents, vice-presidents and members of village panchayats and the date on which such resignations shall take effect;

(v) as to the interpellation of the chairman and vice-chairman by the members of a panchayat union council or the district panchayat and of the president of a village panchayat by the members of the village panchayat, and the moving of resolutions at meetings;

(vi) as to the constitution of committees of the panchayat and the inclusion of outsiders therein and the delegation of functions to such committees;

(vii) providing for the procedure to be followed at meetings of the panchayats and at committees thereof and for the conduct of business and the number of members which shall form a quorum at any meeting;

(viii) providing for the classification of resolutions of panchayats as those involving financial implications or otherwise and for laying down the proportion of the sanctioned strength of panchayats with whose support such resolution shall be carried;

(ix) as to the powers of the panchayat union council and district panchayats, its chairman and committees thereof with respect to the incurring of expenditure and the powers and duties of the Commissioner and Secretary.

(x) providing for the travelling and other allowances of the chairman, vice-chairman and other members of the panchayat union council, district panchayat and of members of the committees of the panchayat union council and district panchayat;

(xi) as to the delegation of any function of a panchayat to the president, chairman, member, any officer of the panchayat or any servant of the Central or State Government;

(xii) for the lodging and investment of the moneys of the panchayats and for the manner in which such moneys may be drawn upon;

(xiii) as to the transfer of allotments entered in the sanctioned budget of a panchayat from one head to another;

(xiv) as to the estimates of receipts and expenditure, returns, statements and reports to be submitted by panchayat;

(xv) as to the preparation of plans and estimates for works and the power of panchayat and of servants of the Central or State Government to accord professional or administrative sanction to estimates;

(xvi) as to the accounts to be kept by panchayat, the audit and publication of such accounts and the conditions under which rate-payers may appear before auditors, inspect books and accounts, and take exception to items entered or omitted;

(xvii) as to the powers of auditors to disallow and surcharge items, appeals against orders of disallowance or surcharge and recovery of sums disallowed or surcharged;

(xviii) as to the powers of auditors, inspecting and superintending officers and officers authorised to hold inquiries, to summon and examine witness and to compel the production of documents, and all other matters connected with audit, inspection and superintendence;

(xix) as to the conditions on which property may be acquired by a panchayat or on which property vested in or belonging to a panchayat may be transferred by sale, mortgage, lease, exchange or otherwise;

(xx) as to the conditions on which and the mode in which contracts may be made or on behalf of panchayat;

(xxi) as to the assessment of taxes under this Act and the revision of assessments;

(xxii) as to the acceptance in lieu of any tax due under this Act of any service by way of labour, cartage or otherwise;

(xxiii) as to the realisation of any tax or other sum due to a panchayat under this Act or any other law or any rules or bye-laws, whether by distraint and sale of movable property, by prosecution before a Magistrate, by a suit, or otherwise;

(xxiv) as to the realisation of fees due in respect of the use of cart-stands and the like, whether by the seizure and sale of the vehicle or animal concerned or any part of its burden or otherwise;

(xxv) as to the form and contents of licences, permissions and notices granted or issued under this Act, the manner of their issue or the method of their service, and the modification, suspension or cancellation thereof;

(xxvi) as to the powers of executive authorities, Commissioners, Secretaries to call for information on any matter, to summon and examine witness, and to compel the production of documents;

(xxvii) For the use of the facsimiles of the signatures of the executive authorities, Commissioners, Secretaries and officers of panchayat;

(xxviii) as to the grant to the public of copies of any proceeding or record of the panchayat not relating to any matter classified as confidential by the Government or any authority empowered by them, and the fees to be levied for the grant of such copies;

(xxix) as to the opening, maintenance, management and supervision of elementary schools;

(xxx) regulating contracts between the panchayat and the owners or occupiers of private premises for the removal there from of rubbish or filth, or any kind of rubbish or filth;

(xxxi) as to the provision of burial and burning grounds; the licensing of private burial and burning grounds; the regulation of the use of all grounds so provided or licensed; the closing of any such grounds; and the prohibition of the disposal of corpses except in such grounds or other permitted places;

(xxxii) as to the licensing of pigs and dogs and the destruction of unlicensed pigs and dogs;

(xxxiii) as to the regulation or restriction of building and the use of sites for building;

(xxxiv) for the removal of encroachments of any description from public roads vesting in panchayat and the repair of any damage caused to such roads by the person causing the damage or at his expense;

(xxxv) for the determination of any claim to trees growing on public roads or other property vesting in or belonging to panchayat or on porambokes or on lands the use of which is regulated by them under section 134 or 135; and for the presumptions to be drawn as regards the ownership of such trees;

(xxxvi) as to the imposition and recovery of penalties for the unauthorised occupation of public roads or other land vesting in or belonging to panchayat and the assessment and recovery of compensation for, and damage caused by, such occupation;

(xxxvii) as to the powers which may be exercised by the panchayat or the executive authority or the Commissioner or the Secretary in respect of any public or private market or the user thereof, and the enforcement of any order issued in pursuance of such powers;

(xxxviii) for compelling owners of cattle to stall them in cattle-sheds provided by the panchayat and the fees leviable in respect thereof;

(xxxix) as to the disposal of household and farmyard waste in the village, the acquisition of land by the panchayat or laying out plots for digging pits in which such waste may be thrown, the assignment of those plots to persons in the village, and the conditions subject to which such assignment may be make, including the rent to be charged;

(xl) as to the duties to be discharged by officers in relation to panchayats and their executive authorities their chairmen, Commissioners and Secretaries;

(xli) as to appeals against orders (including orders granting or refusing licences or permissions) passed under this Act, and the time within which appeals whether allowed by this Act or by rules or otherwise should be presented;

(xlii) as to the classification of public roads and fairs and festivals as appertaining to the panchayat;

(xliii) for regulating the sharing between local authorities in the State of the proceeds of any tax or income levied or obtained under this or any other Act;

(xliv) for decision of disputes between two or more local authorities of which one is a panchayat;

(xlv) regulating the principles in accordance with which grant and contribution may be paid by the Government to the panchayat;

(xlvi) as to the accounts to be kept by owners, occupiers and farmers of private markets and the audit and inspection of such accounts;

(xlvii) as to the manner of publication of notifications or notices to the public under this Act.

CHAPTER XII
PENALTIES

243. Penalties for Breach of Rules—In making any rule under this Act, the Government may provide that a breach thereof shall be punishable with fine which may extend to one hundred rupees, or in case of a continuing breach, with fine not exceeding fifteen rupees for everyday during which the breach continues after conviction for the first breach.

244. Bye-Laws and Penalties for Their Breach—(1) Subject to the provisions of this Act and of any other law and to such rules as may be prescribed, a panchayat may, with the approval of the Inspector, make bye-laws for carrying out any of the purposes for which it is constituted.

(2) In making a bye-law, the panchayat may provide that any person who commits a breach thereof shall be liable to pay by way of penalty such sum as may be fixed by the panchayat not exceeding fifteen rupees or, in case of a continuing breach, not exceeding five rupees for everyday during which the breach continues after a penalty has been levied for the first breach.

(3) The Government shall have power to make rules regarding the procedure for the making of bye-laws, the publication thereof, and the date on which they shall come into effect.

245. General Provisions Regarding Penalties Specified in the Schedules—(1) Whoever:

(a) contravenes any of the provisions of this Act specified in the first and second columns of Schedule II; or

(b) contravenes any rule or order made under any of the provisions so specified; or

(c) fails to comply with any directions lawfully given to him, or any requisition lawfully made upon him under or in pursuance of any of the said provisions shall be punishable with fine which may extend to the amount mentioned in that behalf in the fourth column of the said Schedule.

(2) Whoever after having been convicted of:

(a) contravening any of the provisions of this Act specified in the first and second columns of Schedule III, or

(b) contravening any rule or order made under any of the provisions so specified; or

(c) failing to comply with any direction lawfully given to him or any requisition lawfully made upon him under or in pursuance of any of the said provisions, or continues to contravene the said provision or the said rule or order fail to comply with the said direction or requisition,

shall be punishable for each day after the previous date conviction during which he continues so to offend, with fine which may extend to the amount mentioned in that behalf in the fourth column of the said Schedule.

Explanation. The entries in the third column of Schedules II and III headed "subject" are not intended as definitions of the offences described in the provisions specified in the first and second columns thereof, or even as abstracts of those provisions, but are intended merely as references to the subject dealt with therein.

246. Penalty for Acting as Member President or Vice-president of a Village Panchayat or as Member Chairman or Vice-chairman of a Panchayat Union Council or District Panchayat when Disqualified—(1) Whoever acts as a member of a panchayat or panchayat union council or district Panchayat knowing that, under this Act or the rules made thereunder, he is not entitled or has ceased to be entitled to hold office as such, shall be punishable with fine not exceeding two hundred rupees for every such offence.

(2) Whoever acts as the president, temporary president or vice-president of a village panchayat, or exercises any of his functions including where he is also the executive authority, any of his functions as such and whoever acts as the chairman, temporary chairman or vice-chairman of a panchayat union council or district panchayat or as Commissioner or Secretary or exercise any of his functions as such knowing that, under this Act or the rules made thereunder, he is not entitled or has ceased to be entitled to hold office as such, or to exercise such functions, shall be punishable with fine not exceeding one thousand rupees for every such offence.

(3) Any person who having been the president, temporary president or vice-president of a village panchayat, or the chairman, temporary chairman or vice-chairman of a panchayat union council or district panchayat fails to hand over any documents of, or any moneys or other properties vested in or belonging to the village panchayat or panchayat union council or district panchayat which are in or have come into his possession or control, to his successor in office or other prescribed authority:

(a) in every case as soon as his term of office as such president, temporary president or vice-chairman or as such chairman, temporary chairman or vice-chairman expires;

(b) in the case of a person who was the vice-president also on demand by the president; and

(c) in the case of a person who was the vice-chairman also on demand by the chairman

shall be punishable with fine not exceeding one thousand rupees for every such offence.

[144][**246-A. Penalty for failure to obtain permission of government for foreign trip**—Whoever undertakes a trip to any foreign country in violation of Section 82-A shall on conviction be punished with fine which may extend to fifty thousand rupees.]

247. Penalty for Acquisition by an Officer or Servant of Interest in Contract Work—If any officer or servant of a panchayat knowingly acquires, directly or indirectly by himself or by a partner, employer or servant, any personal share or interest in any contract or employment with, by or on behalf of, the panchayat, he shall be deemed to have committed an offence under section 168 of the Indian Penal Code (Central Act XLV of 1860):

Provided that no person shall, by reason of being a shareholder in, or member of, any company, be held to be interested in any contract entered into between such company and the panchayat unless he is a director of such company.

248. Wrongful Restraint of Executive Authority or Commissioner or Secretary or his Delegates

Any person who prevents the executive authority or the Commissioner or the Secretary or any person to whom the executive authority or the Commissioner or the Secretary has lawfully delegated his powers of entering on or into any place, building or land from exercising his lawful power of entering thereon or there into shall be deemed to have committed an offence under section 341 of the Indian Penal Code. (Central Act XLV of 1860)

249. Prohibition Against Obstruction of Panchayat—Any person obstructing or molesting the president, or the executive authority or the chairman or the Secretary or a member of the panchayat, or any person employed by the panchayat or any person with whom a contract has been entered into by or on behalf of the panchayat in the discharge of their duty or of anything which they are empowered or required to do by virtue or in consequence of this Act or of any rule, bye-law, regulation or order made thereunder, shall be punished with fine which may extend to fifty rupees.

250. Prohibition against Removal of Obliteration of Notice—Any person who, without authority in that behalf removes, destroys, defaces or otherwise obliterates any notice exhibited or any sign or mark erected by, or under the orders of, a panchayat or its executive authority, or by the Commissioner or by the Secretary shall be punishable with fine which may extend to fifty rupees.

251. Penalty for not Giving Information or Giving False Information—Any person required by this Act or by any notice or other proceedings issued thereunder to furnish any information, who omits to furnish such information, or knowingly furnishes false information, shall be punishable with fine not exceeding one hundred rupees.

CHAPTER XIII
MISCELLANEOUS

252. Construction or Reference to a Panchayat etc.—In the application of any law, rule, bye-law, regulation, notification, scheme, form or order to any area, in the absence of an intention to the contrary appearing in this Act and unless the Government otherwise direct, any reference to a "Panchayat" or a "Union Council" or a "Panchayat Village" or a "Panchayat Union" shall be deemed to include also a reference to the village panchayat or a panchayat union council or a district panchayat or a panchayat village or a panchayat union constituted under this Act.

253. Special Provisions Relating to Newly Constituted Panchayat—(1) The provisions of this section shall apply when a panchayat is constituted for the first time under this Act.

(2) When a panchayat is newly constituted under this section, the Tamil Nadu State Election Commissioner shall make arrangements for the election of members and of the president or the chairman, as the case may be, so that the member and the president or the chairman, may come into office on the date specified in the notification issued for the constitution of such panchayat.

(3) When a panchayat is constituted under this section, the Government may appoint a special Officer not below the rank of a Tehsildar, for such period not exceeding six months as the Government may, by order, specify, to exercise the powers, discharge the duties perform the functions of the panchayat, its president or chairman as the case may be (Tamil Nadu Act 44 of 1999).

[137]["(3A) Notwithstanding anything contained in sub-section (3), the special officers appointed under that sub-section in respect of the village panchayats and panchayat union specified in Schedule IV-A shall hold office upto the 31st day of March, 2000 or such shorter period as the Government may by notification, specify in this behalf."].

(4) The special officer shall exercise the powers, discharge the duties and perform the functions of the panchayat, its president or chairman, until the members of the panchayat have come into office and a president or chairman has been elected.

254. Construction or Reference to "Local Boards" Madras Local Boards Act, 1920 etc.–In the application of any law, rule, bye-law, regulation, notification, scheme form or order to any panchayat after the constitution of a panchayat under this Act, in the absence of an intention to the contrary appearing in this Act and unless the Government otherwise direct:

(i) any reference to a village or local area shall be deemed to be reference to a panchayat village, panchayat development block or a panchayat union or panchayat district as the circumstances may require; Tamil Nadu Act XIV of 1920, Tamil Nadu Act X of 1950, Tamil Nadu XXXV of 1958.

(ii) any reference to local boards shall be deemed to be a reference to district panchayats, panchayat union councils or village panchayats as the case may be.

(iii) any reference to the Madras Local Boards Act, 1920 shall be deemed to be a reference to the Tamil Nadu District Boards Act, 1920 (Tamil Nadu Act XIV of 1920), the Tamil Nadu Village Panchayats Act, 1950 (Tamil Nadu Act X of 1950), the Tamil Nadu Panchayats Act, 1958 (Tamil Nadu Act

XXXV of 1958) and the Tamil Nadu Panchayats Act, 1994.

(iv) any reference to the Tamil Nadu District Boards Act, 1920 (Tamil Nadu Act XIV of 1920) or the Tamil Nadu Village Panchayats Act, 1950 (Tamil Nadu Act X of 1950) or the Tamil Nadu Panchayats Act, 1958 (Tamil Nadu Act XXXV of 1958), shall be deemed to be a reference to the Tamil Nadu Panchayats Act, 1994.

(v) any reference to district boards or its president shall be deemed to be a reference to the panchayat union council having jurisdiction or its chairman, as the case may be.

255. Repeal and Savings—(1) The Tamil Nadu Panchayats Act, 1958 (Tamil Nadu Act XXXV of 1958), (hereinafter referred to in this section as the said Act) is hereby repealed.

(2) The repeal, by sub-section (1) of the said Act shall not affect:

(a) the previous operation of the said Act or anything done or duly suffered thereunder, or

(b) any right, privilege, obligation or liability acquired, accrued or incurred under the said Act; or

(c) any penalty, forfeiture, or punishment incurred in respect of any offences committed against the said Act; or

(d) any investigation, legal proceedings or remedy in respect of any such right, privilege, obligation, liability, penalty, forfeiture or punishment as aforesaid and any such investigation, legal proceedings or remedy may be instituted, continued or enforced and any such penalty, forfeiture or punishment may be imposed as if this Act had not been passed.

(3) Subject to the provisions of sub-section (2) anything done or any action taken, including any appointment, or delegation made, notification, order, instruction or direction issued, or any rule, regulation or form framed, certificate granted or registration effected, under the said Act shall be deemed to have been done or taken under this Act and shall continue to have effect accordingly, unless and until superseded by anything done or any action taken under this Act.

256. Power to Remove Difficulties—(1) If any difficulty arises in giving effect to the provisions of this Act, the Government may, by order published in the Tamil Nadu Government Gazette, make such provisions, not inconsistent with the provisions of this Act and to be in conformity with the provisions of the Constitution (Seventy-third Amendment) Act 1992 as appear to it to be necessary or expedient for removing the difficulty:

Provided that no such order shall be made after the expiry of a period of two years from the date of commencement of this Act.

(2) Every order made under this section, shall, as soon as may be, after it is made, be placed on the table of the Legislative Assembly.

257. Power, Authority and Responsibilities of Panchayats—Save as otherwise provided in this Act, the Government may, by notification and subject to such conditions and restrictions as may be specified therein, entrust to a panchayat or any other committee constituted under this Act with such powers and responsibilities with respect to the preparation of plans for economic development and social justice and also with such powers and authority as may be necessary to enable them to carry out the responsibilities conferred upon them including those in relation to the matters listed in Schedule IV.

[145][**257-A. Provision of Rain Water Harvesting Structure**—(1) In every building owned or occupied by the government or a statutory body or a company or an institution owned or controlled by the government, rain water harvesting structure shall be provided by the government or by such statutory body or company or other institution, as the case may be, in such manner and within such time as may be prescribed.

(2) Subject to the provisions of sub-section, every owner or occupier of a building shall provide rain water harvesting structure in the building in such manner and within such period as may be prescribed.

Explanation. Where a building is owned or occupied by more than one person, every such person shall be liable under this sub-section.

(3) Where the rain water harvesting structure is not provided as required under sub-section (2) the executive authority or any person authorized by him in this behalf may, after giving notice to the owner or occupier of the building, cause rain water harvesting structure to be provided in such building and recover the cost of such provision along with the incidental expense thereof in the same manner as property tax.

(4) Notwithstanding any action taken under sub-section (3), where the owner or occupier of the building fails to provide the rain water harvesting structure in the building before the date as may be prescribed, the water supply connection provided for such building shall be disconnected till rain water harvesting structure is provided.]

DISPUTES REGARDING ELECTIONS

258. Election Petitions—(1) No election of a president or a chairman or a member shall be called in question except by an election petition presented to the district judge of the district in which the panchayat is situated, within [138]["forty five days"] from the date of the publication of the result of the election under this Act.

(2) An election petition calling in question any such election may be presented on one or more of the grounds specified in section 259 by any candidate at such election, by any elector of the ward concerned or by any member.

(3) A petitioner shall join as respondents to his petition all the candidates at the election.

(4) an election petition:

(a) shall contain a concise statement of the material facts on which the petitioner relies;

(b) shall, with sufficient particulars, set forth the ground or grounds on which the election is called in question; and

(c) shall be signed by the petitioner and verified in the manner laid down in the Code of Civil Procedure, 1908 (Central Act V of 1908) for the verification pleadings.

[139]["(5) The trial of an election petition shall, so far as is practicable consistently with the interest of justice in respect of the trial, be continued from day-to-day until its conclusion, unless the district judge finds the adjournment of the trial beyond the following day to be necessary for reasons to be recorded.

(6) Every election petition shall be tried as expeditiously as possible and endeavour shall be made to conclude the trial within six months from the date on which the election petition is presented to the district judge for trial"].

259. Grounds for Declaring Election to be Void—(1) Subject to the provisions of sub-section (2), if the District Judge is of opinion:

(a) that on the date of his election returned candidate was not qualified or was qualified, to be chosen as a member under this Act, or

(b) that any corrupt practice has been committed by a returned candidate or his agent or by any other person with the consent of a returned candidate or his agent, or

(c) that any nomination paper has been improperly rejected, or

(d) that the result of the election in so far as it concerns a returned candidate has been materially affected:

(i) by the improper acceptance of any nomination, or

(ii) by any corrupt practice committed in the interests of the returned candidate by a person other than that candidate or his agent or a person acting with the consent of such candidate or agent, or

(iii) by the improper acceptance or refusal of any vote or reception of any vote which is void; or

(iv) by the non-compliance with the provisions of this Act or of any rules or orders made thereunder, the court shall declare the election of the returned candidate to void.

(2) If in the opinion of the Court, a returned candidate has been guilty by an agent of any corrupt practice, but the court is satisfied:

(a) that no such corrupt practice was committed at the election by the candidate, and every such corrupt practice was committed contrary to the orders, and without the consent of the candidate;

(b) that the candidate took all reasonable means for preventing the commission of corrupt practice at the election; and

(c) that in all other respects the election was free from any corrupt practice on the part of the candidate or any of his agents, then, the court may decide that the election of the returned candidate is not void.

260. Corrupt Practices—The following shall be deemed to be corrupt practice for the purposes of this Act:

(1) Bribery as defined in clause (1) of section 123 of the Representation of the People Act, 1951. (Central Act XLIII of 1951)

(2) Undue influence as defined in clause (2) of the said section.

(3) The systematic appeal by a candidate or his agent or by any other person to vote or refrain from voting on grounds of caste, race, community or religion or the use of or appeal to, religious symbols,

or, the use of or appeal to, national symbols such as the national flag or the national emblem, for the furtherance of the prospects of the candidate's election.

(4) The publication by a candidate or his agent or by any other person of any statement of fact which is false, and which he either believes to be false or does not believe to be true, in relation to the personal character or conduct of any candidate, or in relation to the candidate, or withdrawal from [140]["contest"] of any candidate, or statement reasonably calculated to prejudice the prospects of that candidate's election.

(5) The hiring or procuring whether on payment otherwise of any vehicle or vessel by a candidate or his agent or by any other person for conveyance of any elector (other than the candidate himself, and the members of his family or his agent) to or from any polling station provided in accordance with the rules made under this Act:

Provided that the hiring of a vehicle or vessel by an elector or by several electors at their joint costs for the purpose of conveying him or them to or from any such polling station shall not be deemed to be a corrupt practice under this clause if the vehicle or vessel so hired is a vehicle or vessel not propelled by mechanical power:

Provided further that the use of any public transport vehicle or vessel or any tram, car or railway carriage by an elector at his own cost for the purpose of going to or coming from any such polling station shall not be deemed to be corrupt practice under this clause.

Explanation. In this clause the expression "vehicle" means any vehicle used or capable of being used for the purpose of road transport whether propelled by mechanical power or otherwise and whether used for drawing other vehicles or otherwise.

(6) The holding of any meeting in which intoxicating liquors are served.

(7) The issuing of any circular, play-card or poster having a reference to election which does not bear the name and address of the printer and publisher thereof.

(8) Any other practice which the Government may by rules, specify to be corrupt practice.

261. Transitory Provision—(1) Notwithstanding anything contained in this Act, or in any other law for the time being in force, the Government may, by notification, if necessary, appoint special officers to exercise the powers and discharge the functions of the village panchayats, the panchayat union councils, or the district panchayats, as the case may be, until the day on which the first meetings of the village panchayats, panchayat union councils, or the district Panchayats as the case may be, are held after ordinary elections to the said panchayats after commencement of this Act.

[141]["(2) The special officers appointed under sub-section (1) in respect of the village panchayats and panchayat union councils specified in Schedule V shall hold office upto 24th day of October, 2002 or for such shorter period as a Government may by notification specify in this behalf"].

262. Rules, Notifications and Orders to be Placed Before the Legislative Assembly—(1) All rules, notifications and orders made or issued under this Act except the notifications issued under sections 3, 5, 7 read with sections 4, 11, 12, 20, 21 and 32 shall be published in the Tamil Nadu Government Gazette and unless they are expressed to come into force on a particular day, shall come into force on the day on which they are so published.

(2) All notifications issued under sections 3, 5, 7 read with sections 4, 11, 12, 20, 21 and 32 shall be published in the District Gazette concerned and unless they are expressed to come into force on a particular day, shall come into force on the day on which they are so published.

(3) Every rule, notification or order made or issued by the Government under this Act shall, as soon as possible after it is made or issued, be placed on the table of the Legislative Assembly, and if before the expiry of the session in which it is so placed or the next session, the Legislative Assembly agrees in making any modification in any such rule, notification or order, or legislative assembly agrees that the rule notification or order should not be made or issued, the rule, notification or order shall, thereafter have effect only in such modified form or be of no effect, as the case may be, so, however, that any such modification or annulment shall be without prejudice to the validity of anything previously done under that rule, notification or order.

Explanation I. In respect of buildings which are partly concrete, terraced, tiled or thatched, the rates applicable to the respective categories as above shall be applicable for the portions covered by each kind:

Provided that in respect of buildings the plinth area of which does not exceed 18.58 square metres and which are fully concrete, terraced or tiled, or partly concrete, terraced or tiled, house-tax shall be levied at a flat rate of rupees twenty per half year.

SCHEDULE I

[See Section 172(1)]

Sl. No.	*Classification* (1)	*If the tax is levied every half year* (2) *Minimum rate per half year* (i) Rs. Ps		*Maximum rate per half year* (ii) Rs. Ps		*If the tax is levied every year* (3) *Minimum rate per year* (iii) Rs. Ps		*Maximum rate per year* (iv) Rs. Ps	
(i)	Concrete houses, Madras terraced houses storied houses	0.25	Per 9.29 square decimetres of the plinth area	0.50	Per 9.29 square decimetres of the plinth area	0.50	Per 9.29 square decimetres of the plinth area	1.00	Per 9.29 square decimetres of the plinth area
(ii)	Tiled houses	0.15	Per 9.29 square decimetres of the plinth area	0.30	Per 9.29 square decimetres of the plinth area	0.50	Per 9.29 square decimetres of the plinth area	0.60	Per 9.29 square decimetres of the plinth area
(iii)	Thatched houses 20 square metres and above	1.10	Per 9.29 square decimetres of the plinth area	0.20	Per 9.29 square decimetres of the plinth area	0.20	Per 9.29 square decimetres of the plinth area	0.40	Per 9.29 square decimetres of the plinth area
(iv)	Thatched houses below 20 square metres	0.20	For every 9.29 square metres or part thereof plinth area	0.50	For every 9.29 square metres or part thereof plinth area	0.40	For every 9.29 square metres or part thereof plinth area	1.00	For every 9.29 square metres or part thereof plinth area

Explanation I. In respect of buildings which are partly concrete, terraced, tiled, or thatched, the rates applicable to the respective categories as above shall be applicable for the portions covered by each kind:

Provided that in respect of buildings the plinth area of which does not exceed 18.58 square metres and which are fully concrete, terraced or tiled, or partly concrete, terraced or tiled, house tax shall be levied at a flat rate of rupees twenty per half year.

Explanation II. The use of the building may be classified and surcharge shall be levied on the levy of house-tax at the rates specified below:

	Class of Usage		Rate of Surcharge
(i)	Purely residential	Village Panchayats	Nil
(ii)	Simple commercial like petty shops and other small commercial establishments	Village Panchayats	20%
(iii)	Largely commercial, industrial and business establishments, Cinema theatres, Hostels, Lodges etc.	Village Panchayats	60%

Provided that in respect of buildings used partly as residential and partly as commercial, industrial, etc., purposes, the rate of surcharge applicable to the respective categories as above shall be applicable for the portions covered by each class of usage:

Provided further that Educational institutions (not commercial in nature) exempted from levy of house tax immediately before the commencement of this Act shall continue to be exempted under this Act.

SCHEDULE II
ORDINARY PENALTIES

[See Section 245 (I)]

Section (1)	*Sub-section or clause (2)*	*Subject (3)*	*Fine which may be imposed (4)*
128	(1)	Failure to obey requisition to fence off, take down, secure or repair dangerous structure.	Five hundred rupees
129	(1)	Failure to obey requisition to secure, lop or cut down dangerous trees.	Fifty rupees
130		Failure to obey requisition to fence building or land or trim, prune or cut hedges and trees or lower an enclosing wall.	Fifty rupees
131	(1) (a)	Unlawful building of wall or erecting of fence, etc., in or over public road.	One hundred rupees
131	(1)(b)	Unlawful making of hole or depositing of matter in or upon public road.	Fifty rupees
131	(1) (c)	Unlawful quarrying in any place near public road etc.	Fifty rupees
131	(1) (d)	Unlawful erection of building over drain.	Two hundred rupees
131	(1) (e)	Planting of trees without permission on any public road or other property vested in a Panchayat or Panchayat Union Council.	Two hundred rupees
131	(1) (f)	Felling, etc. without permission of trees growing on public road or other property vested in a Panchayat or on poramboke or land the use of which is regulated by it under section 134 or section 135.	Two hundred rupees
139		Failure to close place of public entertainment.	Two hundred rupees
140		Sending infected child to school.	Fifty rupees
142		Failure to give information of smallpox.	Fifty rupees
143	(1)	Failure to obey requisition to fill in, etc. tank or other place dangerous to public health or safety	Fifty rupees
144	(1)	Failure to obey requisition to clear or cleanse etc. building or land in filthy state or overgrown with noxious vegetation.	Fifty rupees
148	(1)	Opening a new private market or continuing to keep open a private market without licence or contrary to licence.	Five hundred rupees
148	(3)	Levy of fees in private market without a Certificate.	One hundred rupees
150		Sale or exposure for sale in public or private market of any animal or article without permission.	Twenty rupees
151		Sale, etc. of articles in public roads or places after prohibition or without licence or contrary to regulations.	Ten rupees
154	(b)	Using any public place or road side as a landing or halting place or as a cart-stand without prohibited distance.	Fifty rupees
155	(1)	Opening a private cart-stand or continuing to keep open a private cart-stand without licence or contrary licence.	Two hundred rupees
157	(a)	Slaughtering, cutting up or skinning etc. of animals outside public slaughter-houses in contravention of rules.	Two hundred rupees

(Contd.)

Section (1)	*Sub-section or clause (2)*	*Subject (3)*	*Fine which may be imposed (4)*
157	(b)	Slaughtering animals for purposes of sale without licence or contrary to licence.	Twenty rupees
158	(3)	Unlawful destruction etc. of number affixed of buildings	Five rupees
158	(4)	Failure to replace number when required to do so	Twenty rupees
159		Using a place for offensive or dangerous trade without licence or contrary to licence.	Five hundred rupees
160		Unlawful erection of factory, workshop etc.	One thousand rupees.
236		Obstructing a person in the use or enjoyment of a public road market, well, tank etc.	Five hundred rupees

SCHEDULE III
PENALTIES FOR CONTINUING BREACHES

[See Section 245 (2)]

Section (1)	*Sub-section or clause (2)*	*Subject (3)*	*Fine which may be imposed (4)*
128	(1)	Failure to obey requisition to fence off, take down, secure or repair dangerous structure.	Fifty rupees
129	(1)	Failure to obey requisition to secure, lop or cut down dangerous trees.	Ten rupees
130		Failure to obey requisition to fence building or land or trim, prune or cut hedges and trees or lower an enclosing wall.	Ten rupees
131	(1) (a)	Unlawful building of wall or erecting of fence, etc. in or over public road.	Twenty rupees
131	(1) (b)	Unlawful making of hole or depositing of matter in or upon public road.	Ten rupees
131	(1) (c)	Unlawful quarrying in any place near public road etc.	Ten rupees
131	(1) (d)	Unlawful erection of building over drain	Fifty rupees
139		Failure to close place of public entertainment	One hundred rupees
143	(1)	Failure to obey requisition to fill in, etc. tank or other place dangerous to public health or safety.	Ten rupees
144	(1)	Failure to obey requisition to clear or cleanse etc. building or land in filthy state or overgrown with noxious vegetation	Ten rupees
148	(1)	Keeping open a private market without licence or contrary to licence.	One hundred rupees
148	(3)	Levy of fees in private market without a certificate.	Fifty rupees
150		Sale or exposure for sale in public or private market of any animal or article without permission.	Ten rupees
155	(1)	Keeping open a private cart-stand without licence or contrary to licence.	Twenty rupees
159		Using a place for offensive or dangerous trade without licence or contrary to licence.	Twenty rupees
160		Unlawful erection of factory, workshop etc.	One hundred rupees

SCHEDULE IV

(See Section 257)

1. Agriculture, including agricultural extension
2. Land improvement, implementation of land reforms, land consolidation and soil conservation
3. Minor irrigation, water management and watershed development
4. Animal husbandry, dairying and poultry
5. Fisheries
6. Social forestry and farm forestry
7. Minor forest produce
8. Small scale industries, including food processing industries
9. Khadi, village and cottage industries
10. Rural housing
11. Drinking water
12. Fuel and fodder
13. Roads, culverts, bridges, waterways and other means of communication
14. Rural electrification, including distribution of electricity
15. Non-conventional energy sources
16. Poverty alleviation programme
17. Education, including primary and secondary schools
18. Technical training and vocational education
19. Adult and non-formal education
20. Libraries
21. Cultural activities
22. Market and fairs
23. Health and sanitation, including hospitals, primary health centres and dispensaries
24. Family welfare
25. Women and child development
26. Social welfare, including welfare of the handicapped and mentally retarded
27. Welfare of the weaker sections, and in particular, of the Scheduled Castes and Scheduled Tribes
28. Public distribution system
29. Maintenance of community assets

SCHEDULE IV-A

[See Section 253 (3-A)]

PART – A

Serial Number	*Name of the Village Panchayats*	*Serial Number*	*Name of the Village Panchayats*
(1)	(2)	(1)	(2)
1.	Yercaud	6.	Semmanatham
2.	Manjakuttai	7.	Valavanthi
3.	Vellakkadai	8.	Thalaisholai
4.	Velur	9.	Maramangalam
5.	Nagalur		

PART – B

Yercaud Panchayat Union".

SCHEDULE V

[See Section 261 (2)]

Serial Number	*Name of the Village Panchayats*
1.	Keeripatti
2.	Pappapatti

Inserted by Act 46 of 1999 and Act 42 fo 2003.

Schedule V was added by Act 10/1997 containing six village panchayats namely: 1. S. Malayandipattinam, 2. Kottakatchiyendal, 3. Keeripatti, 4. Pappapatti, 5. Marudhangudi and 6. Thandanur. The village panchayat, namely Maruthangudi was deleted in Act 46/1999 and the village panchayats S. Malayandipattinam, Kottakatchiyendal, and Thandanur were deleted by Act 53/1998 leaving only two village panchayats, namely Keeripatti and Pappapatti in the schedule now.

SCHEDULE VI
[(See Section 9-A (1)]

Serial Number	*Name of the Village Panchayats*
1.	Kottkatchiyendal
2.	Nattarmangalam

Schedule VI was originally added by Act 3/2002 containing three village panchayats, namely Kottakatchiyendal, Melasathambur and Nattarmangalam and was later substituted by Act 8/2002 by deleting the village panchayat Melasathambur from the original list of village panchayats mentioned in the schedule added by Act 3/2002, leaving only two village panchayats mentioned above.

AMENDMENTS TO TAMIL NADU PANCHAYATS ACT, 1994

(T.N. Act 21 of 1994)

1. Tamil Nadu Panchayats (Amendment) Act, 1994 (T.N. Act No.51 of 1994).
2. Tamil Nadu Panchayats (Amendment) Act, 1995 (T.N. Act No.29 of 1995).
3. Tamil Nadu Panchayats (Second Amendment) Act, 1995 (T.N. Act No.30 of 1995)
4. Tamil Nadu Panchayats (Third Amendment) Act, 1995 (T.N. Act No.45 of 1995).
5. Tamil Nadu Panchayats (Amendment) Act, 1996 (T.N. Act No.14 of 1996).
6. Tamil Nadu Panchayats (second Amendment) Act, 1996 (T.N. Act No.15 of 1996)
7. Tamil Nadu Panchayats (Third Amendment) Act, 1996 (T.N. Act No.21 of 1996)
8. Tamil Nadu Panchayats (Amendment) Act, 1997 (T.N. Act No.10 of 1997).
9. Tamil Nadu Panchayats (Second Amendment) Act, 1997 (T.N. Act No.37 of 1997).
10. Tamil Nadu Panchayats (Third Amendment) Act, 1997 (T.N. Act No.54 of 1997)
11. Tamil Nadu Panchayats (Fourth Amendment) Act, 1997 (T.N. Act No.55 of 1997)
12. Tamil Nadu Panchayats (Amendment) Act, 1998 (T.N. Act No.4 of 1998)
13. Tamil Nadu Panchayats (Second Amendment) Act, 1998 (T.N. Act No.5 of 1998)
14. Tamil Nadu Panchayats (Third Amendment) Act, 1998 (T.N. Act No.28 of 1998)
15. Tamil Nadu Panchayats (Fourth Amendment) Act, 1998 (T.N. Act No.29 of 1998)
16. Tamil Nadu Panchayats (Fifth Amendment) Act, 1998 (T.N. Act No.53 of 1998)
17. Tamil Nadu Panchayats (Sixth Amendment) Act, 1998 (T.N. Act No.54 of 1998)
18. Tamil Nadu Panchayats (Seventh Amendment) Act, 1998 (T.N. Act No.55 of 1998)
19. Tamil Nadu Panchayats (Amendment) Act, 1999 (T.N. Act No.2 of 1999).
20. Tamil Nadu Panchayats (Second Amendment) Act, 1999 (T.N. Act No.19 of 1999)
21. Tamil Nadu Panchayats (Third Amendment) Act, 1999 (T.N. Act No.29 of 1999)
22. Tamil Nadu Panchayats (Fourth Amendment) Act, 1999 (T.N. Act No.30 of 1999.
23. Tamil Nadu Panchayats (Fifth Amendment) Act, 1999 (T.N. Act No. 31 of 1999).
24. Tamil Nadu Panchayats (Sixth Amendment) Act, 1999 (T.N. Act No.32 of 1999)
25. Tamil Nadu Panchayats (Seventh Amendment) Act, 1999 (T.N. Act No.44 of 1999)
26. Tamil Nadu Panchayats (Eighth Amendment) Act, 1999 (T.N. Act No.46 of1999)
27. Tamil Nadu Panchayats (Amendment) Act, 2000 (T.N. Act No.5 of 2000)
28. Tamil Nadu Panchayats (Second Amendment) Act, 2000 (T.N. Act No.23 of 2000)
29. Tamil Nadu Panchayats (Fifth Amendment) Act, 2000 (T.N. Act No.24 of 2000).
30. Tamil Nadu Panchayats (Third Amendment) Act, 2000 (T.N. Act No.27 of 2000)
31. Tamil Nadu Panchayats (Sixth Amendment) Act, 2000 (T.N. Act No.30 of 2000)
32. Tamil Nadu Panchayats (Fourth Amendment) Act, 2000 (T.N. Act No.1 of 2001)
33. Tamil Nadu Panchayats (Amendment) Act, 2001 (T.N. Act No.18 of 2001)
34. Tamil Nadu Panchayats (Second Amendment) Act, 2001 (T.N. Act No.19 of 2001)
35. Tamil Nadu Panchayats (Amendment) Act, 2002 (T.N. Act No.3 of 2002)
36. Tamil Nadu Panchayats (Third Amendment) Act, 2002 (T.N. Act No.8 of 2002)
37. Tamil Nadu Panchayats (Second Amendment) Act, 2002 (T.N. Act No.28 of 2002).
38. Tamil Nadu Panchayats Amendment Act 5 of 2002.

39. Tamil Nadu Panchayats Amendment Act 54 of 2002.
40. Tamil Nadu Panchayats Amendment Act 34 of 2003.
41. Tamil Nadu Panchayats Amendment Act 39 of 2004.

NOTES

1. This Act has been brought into force with effort from 22.4.1994 in G.O.MS.No.84 R.D. (C1 dated 22.4.1994).
2. Inserted by Act No.30/1995 but deleted by Act 15/1996.
3. Re-numbered by Act 30/1995.
4. Omitted the wage "Chief Executive Officer" by Act 28/1999.
5. Substituted by Act 21/1996.
6. Inserted by Act 28/1998. [The word 'secretary' is substituted for the words "Chief Executive Officer" wherever they occurred in this Act].
7. Substituted by Act 28/1998. [The words "Tamil Nadu" have been added wherever the expression "State Election Commission or State Election Commissioner" occurs in this Act].
8. *Ibid.*
9. Substituted by Act 28/1998.
10. Omitted by Act 28/1998.
11. Inserted by Act 28/1998.
12. Omitted by Act 28/1998.
13. Inserted by Act 29/1998.
14. Added by Act 29/1998.
15. Inserted by Act 3/2002.
16. Substituted by Act 8/2002.
17. Substituted by Act 21/1996.
18. Added by Act 30/1995.
19. Added by Act 30/1995.
20. Inserted by Act 30/1995, but omitted by Act 15/1996.
21. *Ibid.*
22. Amended by Acts 30/1995 and 15/1996 (the expression 'Backward classes of citizens' was inserted by Act 30/1995, but omitted by Act 15/1996).
23. Substituted by Act 21/1996.
24. Two additional provisos were added by Act 30/1995 to the original section with had only one proviso. But the whole section has been substituted by Act 21/1996.
25. Substituted by Act 30/1995 but omitted by Act 15/1996.
26. *Ibid.*
27. The expression 'Backward classes of citizens' was inserted by Act 30/1995, but was omitted by Act 15/1996.
28. Whole section substituted by Act 21/1996.
29. Substituted by Act 37/1997.
30. Existing proviso substituted in Act 21/1996.
31. New provisos added by Act 30/1995.
32. *Ibid.*
33. The expression 'Backward classes of citizens' was inserted by Act 30/1995, but was omitted by Act 15/1996.
34. Substituted by Act 30/1995, but omitted by Act 15/1996.
35. *Ibid.*
36. *Ibid.*
37. The words "or chairman" omitted by Act 21/1996.
38. Substituted for words "while undergoing the sentence" by Act 1/2001.
39. Substituted for words "five years" by Act 1/2001.
40. *Ibid.*
41. Inserted in by Act 2/1999.
42. Added by Act 54/1998.
43. Inserted by Act 2/1999.
44. Inserted by Act 28/2002.
45. Substituted by Act 30/1995 for 3 existing provisos.
46. Inserted by Act 29/1999.
47. Substituted by Act 29/1999.
48. The words "and delegation" omitted by Act 29/1999.
49. Inserted by Act 29/1999.
50. Substituted by Act 29/1999.
51. Proviso omitted by Act 30/1995.
52. Inserted by Act 30/1995.
53. Inserted by Act 30/1995, but omitted by Act 15/1996.
54. *Ibid.*
55. Inserted by Act 30/1995.
56. Inserted by Act 15/1996.
57. Substituted by Act 29/1999.
58. Substituted by Act 28/1998.
59. Substituted by Act 21/1996.
60. Substituted by Act 2/1999.
61. Substituted by Act 29/1998.
62. Added by Act 28/1998.
63. Inserted by Act 37/1997.
64. Substituted by Act 28/1998.
65. Inserted by Act 29/1999.
66. Existing proviso was omitted by Act 29/1999.
67. Inserted by Act 28/1998.
68. Inserted by Act 29/1999.
69. Omitted by Act 37/1997.
70. Omitted by Act 29/1999.
71. Substituted by Act 29/1999.
72. *Ibid.*
73. *Ibid.*
74. *Ibid.*
75. *Ibid.*
76. *Ibid.*
77. *Ibid.*
78. *Ibid.*
79. Inserted by Act 27/2000.
80. *Ibid.*

81. Substituted by Act 19/1999.
82. *Ibid.*
83. Sub-sections (4) & (5) have been substituted with one sub-section, namely sub-section (4) by Act 30/1999.
84. The words "panchayat union councils and district panchayats" have been omitted by Act 30/1999.
85. The words "and a vehicle tax" have been omitted by Act 29/1995.
86. Sections 172-A and 172-B have been inserted by Act 32/1999.
87. Substituted by Act 1/2001.
88. Inserted by Act 32/1999.
89. *Ibid.*
90. Omitted by Act 29/1995.
91. Substituted by Act 29/1995 for the expression "sections 171 and 172".
92. Omitted by Act 30/1999.
93. Sections 181-A to 181-D have been inserted by Act 23/2000.
94. Sections 181-A to 181-D have been inserted by Act 23/2000.
95. Inserted by Act 23/2000.
96. Omitted by Act 30/1999.
97. *Ibid.*
98. *Ibid.*
99. *Ibid.*
100. *Ibid.*
101. *Ibid.*
102. *Ibid.*
103. The whole section 188 has been renumbered as sub-section (1) of that section by Act 54/1997.
104. Substituted by Act 29/1995.
105. Substituted by Act 30/1999.
106. The expression "the share of" has been omitted by Act 30/1999.
107. Omitted by Act 30/1999.
108. Added by Act 54/1997.
109. Substituted by Act 19/2001.
110. New sections 198-A to 198-I have been inserted by Act 55/1998.
111. *Ibid.*
112. *Ibid.*
113. *Ibid.*
114. *Ibid.*
115. *Ibid.*
116. Inserted by Act 2/1999.
117. *Ibid.*
118. Inserted by Act 2/1999.
119. Substituted by Act 31/1999 for the expression "vice-chairman".
120. *Ibid.*
121. *Ibid.*
122. *Ibid.*
123. *Ibid.*
124 Substituted by Act 31/1999 for the expression "vice-chairman".
125. *Ibid.*
126. *Ibid.*
127. Substituted by Act 31/1999 for the expression "six months".
128. *Ibid.*
129. Substituted by Act 31/1999 for the expression "vice-chairman".
130. *Ibid.*
131. *Ibid.*
132. Inserted by Act 2/1999.
133. Sub-section (2) has been substituted by Act 30/2000 for the sub-section (2) which was substituted by Act 37/1997.
134. Substituted by Act 24/2000.
135. Inserted by Act 54/1997.
136. Substituted by Act 21/1996.
137. Inserted by Act 44/1999.
138. Substituted by Act 18/2001 for the expression "fifteen days".
139. Added by Act 1/2001.
140. Substituted by Act 2/1999 for the word "contact".
141. The original sub-section (2) in the parent Act, 21/1994 contained a period of nine months from the date of commencement of the parent Act 21/1994 (viz., 22.4.1994). This date was extended to 31.12.1995 in Act 51/1994, to 30.06.1996 in Act 45/1995 and to 31.12.1996 in Act 14/1996. Then the whole sub-section (2) was substituted by Act 10/1997 in the present form given above the except the period mentioned therein, viz., upto 30.6.1997. This sub-section (2) was periodically substituted by Act 55/1997, Act 5/1998, Act 53/1998, Act 46/1999, and Act 5/2000, extending the dates suitably and lastly by Act 8/2002 prescribing the date as mentioned above.
142. Inserted by Act 39 of 2004.
143. Inserted by Act 39 of 2004.
144. Inserted by Act 52 of 2002.
145. Inserted by Act 34 of 2003.
146. Inserted by Act 5 of 2002.

2.2 ADOPTATION OF THE ACT

2.2.1 Date of Coming into force of the Tamil Nadu Panchayats Act, 1994

Repealing the Tamil Nadu Panchayats Act, 1958, and in consonance with the Constitution (73rd Amendment) Act, 1992—Tamil Nadu Panchayats Act, 1994 was brought into force with effect from the 22nd April 1994.

(Notification issued vide G.O. Ms. No.84, Rural Development Department, dated 22nd April, 1994).

PART III

RULES AND INSTRUCTIONS COMMON TO THE THREE TIERS OF PANCHAYAT

3.1 FORMATION AND CONSTITUTION OF PANCHAYATS

3.1.1 Determination of Population

For the first election to be held immediately after the commencement of the Act the provisional population figures as published in relation to 1991 census shall be deemed to be the population. For subsequent elections the population figures as published in the preceding census will be adopted.

[G.O.Ms.No.130, Rural Development (C4) Department, dated 18th July 1995]

3.1.2 Fixation of Strength of Members, Division of Wards of Village Panchayats, Panchayat Union Councils and District Panchayats

1. Short title—These rules may be called the Tamil Nadu Panchayats (Fixation of Strength of Members and Division of Wards) Rules, 1995.

2. Definitions—In these rules unless the context otherwise requires:

(1) "Act" means the Tamil Nadu Panchayats Act, 1994 (Tamil Nadu Act 21 of 1994); and

(2) All other words and expressions used in these rules but not defined therein shall have the meanings respectively assigned to them in the Act.

3. Fixation of strength of members of panchayats

(1) *Village Panchayats*—The number of members to be elected from the wards in every village panchayat shall be fixed with reference to the population of such panchayat village as per the scale given below:

Population (1)	*Number of Members* (2)
500 and above upto and inclusive of 2000	6
Over 2000 and upto and inclusive of 6000	9
Over 6000 and upto and inclusive of 10000	12
Over 10000	15

(2) *Panchayat Union Councils*—The number of members to be elected from the wards in every panchayat union council shall be fixed, at the rate of one member, as far as practicable for every five thousand population of that panchayat union area.

(3) *District Panchayat*—The number of members to be elected from the territorial wards of every district panchayat shall be fixed at the rate of one member, as far as practicable for every fifty thousand population of that district panchayat area.

4. Division of Wards and Allocation of Seats

1. Village panchayat—(1) For the purpose of the elections of the members of village panchayats, area of every panchayat village shall be divided into convenient number of territorial constituencies known as wards depending upon the number of inhabited areas in the panchayat village, their population and their geographical locations.

(2) The number of wards in every panchayat village shall not be less than two or more than five.

(3) Every ward so divided under sub-rule (1) shall be compact, contiguous and of easily recognizable areas like localities, colonies, habitations hamlets etc., and also comprised in as far as practicable full house numbering blocks.

(4) The number of members determined for village panchayat shall be allocated among the wards so divided in such manner that the ratio between the population of each ward and the number of members allocated to it for purposes of election shall, as far as practicable, be the same throughout the panchayat village area:

Provided that where uniform ratios between the population of a ward and the number of members allocated to it could not be ensured due to practical difficulties like unequal distribution of population or peculiar geographical location of inhabited areas and as such it has become necessary to deviate from the aforesaid ratio in respect of any particular ward or wards, such deviation shall not exceed twenty-five per cent either way:

Provided further that the number of members that may be allocated to a ward shall not exceed three.

Explanation. Where the population figures in relation to any census are not available in respect of any ward of a panchayat village, the Inspector may determine the population of such area with reference to the voting strength of the area as per the relevant portion of the current electoral roll of the Tamil Nadu Legislative Assembly Constituency.

2. **Panchayat union council**—For the purposes of election of members, area of every panchayat union shall be divided into as many territorial constituencies, known as ward as the total number of members to be elected to the panchayat union council in such manner:

(a) that every ward of a panchayat union shall, as far as practicable, have equal population; and

(b) that every ward of panchayat union shall as far as practicable, be contiguous, compact, and comprise one or more panchayat village generally. Where it is not practically possible to secure such contiguous and compact area with the required population in one or more panchayat villages, the panchayat union ward may comprise portion or portions of panchayat villages, which are full ward or wards, of such panchayat village.

3. **District panchayat**—For the purpose of election of members, areas of every district panchayat shall be divided into as many territorial constituencies known as "territorial wards"' as the total number of members to be elected to that district panchayat in such manner:

(a) that each territorial ward, as far as practicable has equal population;

(b) that each territorial ward as far as practicable be contiguous, compact and comprised of one or more full panchayat union wards; and

(c) that no panchayat village in any such union ward shall lie in the jurisdiction of more than one such territorial ward.

[G.O.Ms No.139, Rural Development (C2) Department, dated 18.7.1995]

3.1.3 Reservation of Seats and Rotation of Reserved Seats

1. **Short title**—These rules may be called the Tamil Nadu Panchayats (Reservation of Seats and Rotation of Reserved Seats) Rules, 1995.

2. **Definition**—(1) In these rules, unless the context otherwise require "Act" means Tamil Nadu Panchayats Act, 1994 (Tamil Nadu Act 21 of 1994).

(2) All other words and expressions used in these rules, but not defined in these rules, shall have the meanings respectively assigned to them in the Act.

3. **Reservation of seats for the members of Scheduled Castes and Scheduled Tribes**—(1) In every village panchayat, panchayat union council and district panchayat, the number of seats reserved for the persons belonging to the Scheduled Castes and Scheduled Tribes out of the total number of seats fixed under Rule 3 of the Tamil Nadu Panchayats (Fixation of Strength of Members and Division of Wards) Rules, 1995 in the village panchayat, panchayat union council or district panchayat, as the case may be, shall bear as nearly as may be the same proportion to the total number of seats to be filled by direct election in that village panchayat, panchayat union council or district panchayat as the case may be, as the population of the Scheduled Castes or the Scheduled Tribes in that village panchayat area, panchayat union council area or district panchayat area, as the case may be, bears to the total population of that area.

(2) While determining the number of seats to be reserved in favour of Scheduled Castes or Scheduled Tribes any fraction shall be ignored.

(3) Among the seats reserved for Scheduled Castes or Scheduled Tribes not less than one-third shall be reserved for women belonging to Scheduled Castes/Scheduled Tribes:

Provided that if the number of seats reserved for Scheduled Castes/Scheduled Tribes is not more than one, it would not be necessary to reserve any seat for women belonging to SCs/STs.

4. **Deleted**

5. **Reservation of seats for women**—In every village panchayat, panchayat union council and district panchayat council not less than one-third shall be reserved for women including the number of seats reserved for women belonging to Scheduled Castes and Scheduled Tribes out of the total number of seats fixed under Rule 3 of the Tamil Nadu Panchayats (Fixation of Strength of Members and Division of Wards) Rules, 1995.

6. **Reservations in respect of offices of presidents of village panchayat and chairmen of panchayat union councils and district panchayats**—(1) Seats shall be reserved in the offices of presidents of village panchayats, chairman of panchayat union councils and

chairmen of district panchayats for persons belonging to Scheduled Castes and Scheduled Tribes. The total number of seats in the offices so reserved shall bear as nearly as may be, the same proportion to the total number of offices in the panchayats at each level in the State as the population of Scheduled Castes and Scheduled Tribes in the State bears to the total population of the State:

Provided that not less than one-third of such offices shall be reserved for women belonging to the Scheduled Castes and Scheduled Tribes.

(1A) The office of the Chairman of District Panchayats referred under sub-rule (1) shall be allotted to districts taking into consideration the population of the SC and ST in every district in such a manner that the total number of offices so allotted does not exceed the total number of offices reserved under sub-rule (1),

(1B) The offices of the chairman of panchayat union council (reserved) under sub-rule (1) shall be allotted to every district, taking into consideration the population of the SC and ST in every such district in such a manner that the total number of offices so allotted to the panchayat union councils in all districts does not exceed the total number of offices reserved under sub-rule (1).

(1C) The offices of the presidents of village panchayats reserved under sub-rule (1) shall be allotted to every panchayat union, taking into consideration the population of the Scheduled Castes and Scheduled Tribes in every such panchayat union in such a manner that the total number of offices so allotted to the village panchayats in all panchayat union does not exceed the total number of offices reserved under sub-rule (1).

(1D) Of the total number of offices of presidents of village panchayats, chairman of panchayat union councils and chairman of district panchayats not less than one-third shall be reserved for women including the offices reserved for women belonging to SC and ST.

7. Rotation of reserved seats and offices— Reservation of seats, or offices under Rules 3, 5, and 6 shall be made as far as practicable in the ward or territorial ward or panchayat where the population of the Scheduled Castes, Scheduled Tribes, or women, as the case may be is comparatively large to the total population of the ward or territorial ward or the panchayat; By adopting a list of wards of panchayats arranged in the descending order of the percentage of SC, ST and women:

Provided that such seats reserved for women in wards of village panchayats or panchayat unions or territorial wards of district panchayats and such seats reserved for Scheduled Castes, Scheduled Tribes, and for women in the offices of presidents of village panchayats, chairpersons of panchayat union councils and chairpersons of district panchayats, shall be allotted by rotation (at the expiry of every ten years) and re-allotted to other wards or territorial wards or panchayats where the percentage of population of women or Scheduled Castes, Scheduled Tribes, as the case may be, is next larger to the total population of that ward, territorial ward or panchayat, by adopting a list of wards or panchayats arranged in the descending order of the percentage of Scheduled Castes, Scheduled Tribes and women.

[G.O.Ms.No.142, Rural Development Department, dated 7th August 1995]

[G.O.Ms.No. 178, Rural Development Department, dated 4th October 1995]

[G.O.Ms.No. 162, Rural Development Department (PE), dated 7th August 1996]

[G.O.Ms.No. 189, Rural Development Department, dated 11th October 1996]

[G.O.Ms.No. 179, Rural Development Department (PE), dated 29th August 1996]

[G.O.Ms.No. 157, Rural Development Department (C1), dated 14th June 2001].

3.1.4 Converted Scheduled Caste not Eligible to Contest in Reserved Seats

Under Sections 11, 20 and 32 of the Tamil Nadu Panchayats Act, 1994, provision has been made for reservation of seats to ward members of village panchayats, panchayat union councils and district panchayats. During conduct of elections instances may occur that the Scheduled Castes who are converted to Christianity may claim, to contest in reserved wards allotted to Scheduled Caste.

In this regard Government reiterates the following clarification already issued by the Government:

Persons belonging to Scheduled Castes after their conversion to Christianity are not eligible to contest for election or to hold office to seats reserved for Scheduled Caste.

(Govt. Memo No.152118/53-2-1, Local Administration, dated 9th April 1953)

(Govt. Lr. No. 9835/C4/2001-2, Rural Development Department, dated 9th April 2001)

3.1.5 Delegation of Powers to the Collector for Reservation of Seats

(a) To exercise the powers of the Government under clauses (a) and (b) of Section 28 of the Tamil Nadu Panchayats Act, 1994, relating to the division of the area within the jurisdiction of every District Panchayat, into as many single member territorial wards as the number of members required to be elected under Section 26 of the said Act, and to determine the extent of each territorial ward which shall be a panchayat village or panchayat union or part of a panchayat village or panchayat union; and

(b) to exercise the powers of the Government under sub-section (5) of Section 32 of the said Act, relating to the reservation of seats for election of members of a village panchayat under Section 11 of the said Act.

[Notification issued vide G.O.Ms.No.156, Rural Development (C-I) Department dated 9th August 1995]

3.1.6 Term of Office of Elected Representatives

The Government ordered that the term of office for elected representatives of all three tiers of Panchayat shall be notified by the Tamil Nadu State Election Commission. No other date need be taken into account for the purpose.

(G.O. Ms. No.29, Rural Development Department, dated 8th February 1999)

3.1.7 First Meeting of Panchayats—Taking Oath of Affirmation

The Government issued the following orders on the first meeting of the panchayats, for taking of oath of affirmation and for electing chairman, vice-chairman, vice-president after the conduct of election to the panchayats.

1. **First meeting**—The first meeting of the elected members shall be held in the respective Panchayats on 25.10.96. On the same day, Oath of affirmation, election of chairman and vice-chairman of district panchayats and panchayat union council and election of vice-president in village panchayats shall be conducted.

2. **Oath of affirmation**—(a) The Collectors will be convening the meeting for conduct Election of chairman of district panchayats and the Returning Officers appointed by the Tamil Nadu State Election Commission shall be convening the meeting for the election of chairmen of panchayat union councils.

According to Section 40 of Tamil Nadu Panchayats Act, 1994, each elected member of panchayat shall take oath of affirmation. The Returning Officer shall invite the senior member from among the elected members to preside over the meeting. The member so invited shall first take the oath of affirmation in the prescribed form.

Afterwards, he shall make all other members to take oath of affirmation in the prescribed form. The fact of taking of oath of affirmation shall be recorded in the minutes of the meeting of the Panchayats.

Similarly, the first meeting of village panchayat for the election of vice-president shall be convened by the Returning Officer appointed by the State Election Commission. In the meeting, the panchayat president directly elected by the people shall take oath of affirmation in the prescribed form. He shall make all the members to take oath of affirmation subsequently. In case, while the village panchayat president is not elected the senior elected member shall be invited by the Returning Officer to take oath of affirmation, first. Then he will be asked to make the other members to take oath of affirmation. The fact of taking of oath of affirmation by all the members shall be recorded in the Minutes of the Meeting.

(b) Those members who could not take of oath of affirmation in the first meeting of the village panchayats shall take oath of affirmation within 3 months from the date of commencement of office or in any one of three meetings conducted after the date, according to sub-section 2 of Section 40 of Tamil Nadu Panchayats Act, 1994. Similarly, the village panchayat president or chairman of district panchayat or panchayat union or member or president of panchayat union committee who have not taken oath of affirmation as a member of the panchayat shall take oath of affirmation according to sub-section 40 within 2 months after his assumption of office.

(c) Those who failed to take oath of affirmation shall be disqualified to hold Office as such.

[G.O.Ms.No.211, Rural Development (Panchayat Election) Department, dated 11th October 1996]

3.1.8 Change of Territory of Village Panchayat—Formation of District Level Committee—Orders

1. Several representations have been received by the Government that the areas of certain panchayats and

panchayat unions are bigger and unwieldy and as such it is very difficult to improve the administration and execute planned development programmes. It is also necessary to amalgamate or bifurcate these panchayats and proposals towards these have been received by the Government. The Government therefore have decided, in consultation with Director of Rural Development, on the requests for bifurcation of village panchayat and panchayat unions, that exclusion or inclusion of area, can come into effect only after, next panchayat general election. There will be no changes in the existing members of village panchayats or panchayat union, because of the above decision. But ward division and fixing of strength for each ward have to be decided before conduct of next general election. Hence the proposals for bifurcation of village panchayats or panchayat union, inclusion or exclusion of areas may be considered by a committee constituted in each district under the Chairmanship of the District Collector and the decisions on the proposals will be taken on the recommendation of the committee and after getting views of the concerned local body. The Government orders that a committee shall be formed in each district consisting of following members for the purpose.

District Collector	-	Chairman
Project Officer, DRDA	-	Member Secretary
All the MPs in the District	-	Member
All the MLAs in the District	-	Member
District Panchayat Chairman	-	Member
Five Panchayat Union Ward Members nominated by the District Collector	-	Member
One Village Panchayat President from each Panchayat Union nominated by the District Collector	-	Member
Assistant Director (Panchayats)	-	Member

From among the members to be selected from local bodies, due representation for women, Scheduled Castes and Schedules Tribes shall be given. The District Level Committee shall be considered as class I Committee.

2. The Collectors are requested to issue proceedings constituting the District Level Committee before 15th July, 1999. The Committee shall subject to the following conditions, examine the following subjects and furnish report to the Government within a period of 3 months.

Bifurcation or amalgamation of village panchayats.

Inclusion of a portion of the village panchayat in another village panchayat or exclusion thereof.

Bifurcation of panchayat unions or inclusion or exclusion of certain areas.

While recommending for constitution of new village panchayats or panchayat unions, the committee shall satisfy, that adequate financial resources are available for functioning of village panchayat or panchayat unions. Opinion of the public as well as the resolution of the concerned local body shall be obtained.

The additional expenditure involved due to bifurcation shall be examined and remarks given. The boundaries and population of the recommended newly constituted village panchayat or panchayat unions shall confirm to those fixed as per Tamil Nadu Panchayats Act, 1994. The committee shall submit final report within three months from the date of issue of this order.

3. The Travelling Allowance of the MPs and MLAs included in the committee shall be met from the Head of Account of Development Section of the Collectorate. The T.A. of other members may be met from their respective local body.

(G.O.Ms.No.113, Rural Development (C1) Department, Dated 29.6.99)

3.2 ELECTED REPRESENTATIVES OF PANCHAYATS

3.2.1 Devolution and Delegation of the Functions of Chairman of Panchayat Union Council or District Panchayat

1. **Short title**—These rules may be called the Tamil Nadu Panchayats (Devolution and Delegation of the Functions of Chairman of Panchayat Union Council or District Panchayat).

2. **Restriction**—Where the absence from jurisdiction of the chairman of panchayat union council or district panchayat is within the State of Tamil Nadu and is on business connected with the functions, of the panchayat union council or district panchayat as the case may be, his functions except to the extent, if any, to which they have been delegated to the vice-chairman of panchayat union council or district panchayat, as the case may be, shall not devolve on the said vice-chairman.

[G.O. Ms. No.140, Rural Development (C-4) Department, dated 21st July 1999]

3.2.2 Resignation of Elected Representatives

1. Short title—These rules may be called the Tamil Nadu Panchayats (Resignation of Chairman, Vice-chairman and Members of District Panchayat, Chairman, Vice-chairman and Members of Panchayat Union Council and the Presidents, Vice-Presidents and Members of Village Panchayat) Rules, 1999.

2. Procedure for resignation of chairman and president of panchayat—A chairman of a district panchayat or a panchayat union council, or a president of a village panchayat may resign his office by giving notice in writing addressed to the Inspector and deliver it in person or by post under acknowledgement.

3. Placing of the resignation of chairman and president before the panchayat—The Inspector shall convene a special meeting of the district panchayat or panchayat union council or village panchayat, as the case may be, and place the resignation notice for information within fifteen days from the date of receipt of resignation notice before the district panchayat or panchayat union council or village panchayat as the case may be. If the concerned chairman or president does not contest the validity of his resignation, his resignation shall be deemed to have come into effect from the date of the meeting. The Secretary in the case of district panchayat, the Commissioner in the case of panchayat union and president-in-charge of village panchayat shall send a report to the Inspector and Tamil Nadu State Election Commission intimating the vacancy.

*Provided that whenever only the President of a village panchayat is elected and the village panchayat could not be constituted, the resignation of such presidents shall be accepted by the Inspector.

*Amended by SRO A-54/2004. (G.O.(Ms.) No.167, Rural Development (C-4), 1st Nov, 2004).

4. Resignation of members, vice-chairman and vice-president of panchayat—Any member or vice-chairman of a district panchayat or of a panchayat union council or any member or vice-president of village panchayat may resign his office by giving notice in writing addressed to the chairman of the district panchayat or panchayat union council or the president of village panchayat, as the case may be, and deliver it in person or by post under acknowledgement with a copy marked to the Inspector.

5. Placing of resignation of members, vice-chairman and vice-president of panchayat—It shall be the duty of the chairman of the district panchayat, the chairman of panchayat union council, the president of village panchayat, as the case may be, to place the resignation notice at a special meeting of the district panchayat or panchayat union council or village panchayat as the case may be, for its information, within fifteen days of the receipt of notice of resignation. If the chairman of district panchayat or panchayat union council or president of village panchayat does not for any reason, convene the special meeting, then the Inspector shall convene the same immediately. The notice for such meeting shall also be served on the person who tendered the resignation. If the member concerned or vice-chairman or vice-president does not contest the validity of his resignation or does not raise any objection at such a meeting, his resignation shall be deemed to have come into effect from the date of the meeting. The chairman of district panchayat or panchayat union council or the president of village panchayat, as the case may be, shall send a copy of minutes of such meeting to the Inspector and Tamil Nadu State Election Commissioner along with a report intimating the vacancy.

(G.O.Ms.No.35, Rural Development (C-4) Department, 22nd February 1999)

3.2.3 Transfer of Charge of Chairman of Panchayat Union Council and District Panchayat

1. Short title—These rules may be called the Tamil Nadu Panchayat Union Councils and District Panchayats (Transfer of Charge of the Office of Chairman) Rules, 2001.

2. Definition—In these rules, unless the context otherwise requires, "Act" means the Tamil Nadu Panchayats Act, 1994 (Tamil Nadu Act 21 of 1994).

3. Transfer of charge on expiry of term—(1) In case the term of the office of chairman of the panchayat union council or district panchayat, as the case may be, expires by efflux of time, the outgoing chairman shall hand over the charge immediately to the Revenue Divisional Officer concerned. As soon as a chairman is elected by the members of the newly constituted panchayat union council, or district panchayat, as the case may be, the Revenue Divisional Officer shall hand over charge to the newly elected chairman.

(2) In case no person is elected as chairman; or the election of chairman is stayed by an order of a competent Court, the Officer specified in sub-rule (1) shall hand over charge to the person elected as the vice-chairman of the panchayat union council or district panchayat, as the case may be. The vice-chairman concerned shall, in turn hand over charge to the chairman as soon as he is elected.

4. Transfer of charge on resignation, disqualification, removal, etc.—(1) In case of resignation of chairman; or otherwise ceasing to hold office consequent on his incurring any disqualification, or on removal from office, the chairman shall immediately hand over charge to the vice-chairman. The vice-chairman, in turn, shall hand over charge to the newly elected chairman.

(2) If the office of the vice-chairman is vacant, the chairman shall hand over charge to the Officer specified in sub-rule (1) of Rule 3 who, in turn, shall hand over charge to the person elected as chairman in the casual election or if no person is elected as chairman in the casual election, then to the person elected as vice-chairman. The vice-chairman shall hand over charge to the newly elected chairman.

(3) In case the chairman is disqualified to continue in office by an order of a competent Court, the vice-chairman shall take over charge of the office of chairman with effect from the date of order and he shall hand over charge to the newly elected chairman:

Provided that in case the office of vice-chairman is vacant, the Officer specified in sub-rule (1) of Rule 3 shall assume charge as chairman.

(4) In the case of chairman removed from office under Section 207 of the Act in the case of panchayat union council and under Section 209 of the Act in the case of district panchayat, the vice-chairman shall take over charge of the office of the chairman and he shall hand over charge to the newly elected chairman:

Provided that in the case of the office of the vice-chairman is vacant, the Officer specified in sub-rule (1) of Rule 3 shall assume charge as chairman and he shall hand over charge to the newly elected chairman and in case the chairman is not elected, to the newly elected vice-chairman.

5. Transfer of charge on dissolution—In the case of dissolution of the panchayat union council under Section 215 or district panchayat under Section 216 of the Act, the outgoing chairman of the panchayat union council or district panchayat, as the case may be, shall hand over charge to the person appointed by the Inspector to exercise the powers and discharge the duties of the panchayat union council or district panchayat and of its chairman, as the case may be. The person or officer shall, in turn hand over charge to the newly elected chairman on the reconstitution of the panchayat union council or district panchayat, as the case may be:

Provided that in case no person is elected as chairman on the reconstitution of the panchayat union council or district panchayat, as the case may be, the person or officer shall hand over charge to the Officer specified in sub-rule (1) of Rule 3 who in turn, shall hand over charge to the chairman as soon as he is elected.

6. Transfer of charge on the vice-chairman vacating office—If before filling up of the casual vacancy in the office of the chairman or the vice-chairman has to vacate his office due to resignation, disqualification or of his otherwise ceasing to be a member of the panchayat union council or district panchayat, as the case may be, the vice-chairman shall immediately hand over charge to the officer specified in sub-rule (1) of Rule 3 and he shall in turn, hand over charge to the newly elected chairman or vice-chairman, as the case may be.

7. Assumption of charge by the vice-chairman on the demise of chairman—(1) In case of death of the chairman while in office, the vice-chairman shall immediately take over charge of the office of chairman and he shall in turn hand over charge to the person elected as chairman in the casual election.

(2) If the office of the vice-chairman is vacant, the officer specified in sub-rule (1) of Rule 3, shall take over charge of the office of chairman, who shall hand over charge to the person elected as chairman or vice-chairman, as the case may be.

8. Procedure in cases of failure or refusal of chairman to hand over charge—(1) In case the chairman, of the panchayat union council or district panchayat, as the case may be, on ceasing to hold office, fails or refuses to hand over charge within twenty-four hours of his ceasing to be the chairman, to the vice-chairman or the officer specified in sub-rule (1) of Rule 3, as the case may be, the vice-chairman or the officer specified in sub-rule (1) of Rule 3, as the case may be, shall take over charge of the office of the chairman in the form specified below, and send a report to the Inspector. The vice-chairman or the officer specified in sub-rule (1) of Rule 3, as the case may be, shall hand over charge to the person elected as the chairman in the Casual/Ordinary election.

THE FORM

Certificate of taking over the charge of the office of the chairman of the ...... panchayat union council/district panchayat.

Certified that Thiru .... who ceased to hold the office as chairman of the .... panchayat union council/district panchayat consequent on ....(reason) refused/failed to hand over charge of the office of the chairman of .... panchayat union council/district panchayat and that I .... (name), the vice-chairman/Revenue Divisional Officer .... have taken over charge of the office of the chairman of the said panchayat union council/district panchayat on this .... day of .... month of .... year of.

Signature

*(Strike out whichever is not applicable)

(2) As soon as the report mentioned in sub-rule (1) above is received, the Inspector shall take action to secure the documents, records etc., left with the outgoing chairman and also, if found necessary, to prosecute him for his failure or refusal to hand over charge of the office of the chairman of the panchayat union council or district panchayat, as the case may be, under sub-section (3) of Section 246 of the Act.

9. Certificate on transfer of charges—The certificate of transfer of charge of the office of chairman shall be in the form specified below:

THE FORM

Certificate of transfer of charge of the office of the chairman of the ...... panchayat union council/district panchayat.

Certified that I have handed over the charge of the office of the chairman .... panchayat union council/district panchayat together with records etc. mentioned in the annexure to Thiru .... vice-chairman/Revenue Divisional Officer* of this .... day of ...... month of ....year.

Signature

Certified that I have taken over the charge of the office of the chairman of .... panchayat union council, district panchayat together with records etc. mentioned in the annexure, from Thiru .... the outgoing chairman/vice-chairman/Revenue Divisional Officer * on this .... day of .... month of .... year.

Signature

*(Strike out whichever is not applicable)

10. Intimation of transfer of charge—Intimation regarding the handing over and taking over charge of the office of the chairman of the panchayat union council or district panchayat, as the case may be, should be sent to the Director of Rural Development and the Inspector. It shall be the duty of the Commissioner of the panchayat union council and or the Secretary of the district panchayat to bring immediately to the notice of the Tamil Nadu State Election Commission and the Inspector, any vacancy arising in the office of the chairman or vice-chairman.

(G.O. Ms. No. 65, Rural Development (C-4) Department, dated 12th March 2001)

3.2.4 Judicial Authority to Decide Questions of Disqualification of Members

1. Short title—These rules may be called the Tamil Nadu Panchayats (Judicial Authority to Decide Questions of Disqualification of Members) Rules, 1999.

2. The prescribed judicial authority—The Judicial Authority to whom applications under sub-section (1) of Section 41 of the Tamil Nadu Panchayats Act, 1994 (Tamil Nadu Act 21 of 1994) may be made, shall be the District Munsif having territorial jurisdiction over the place in which the office of the village panchayat or panchayat union council or district panchayat concerned is situated or if there is more than one such District Munisif, the Principal District Munisif.

(G.O.Ms.No.159, Rural Development (C-4) Department, dated 22nd August 1999)

3.3. POWERS AND FUNCTIONS OF PANCHAYATS AND EXECUTIVES

3.3.1 Power to Call for Information on any Matter

1. Short title—These rules may be called the Tamil Nadu Panchayats (Power to Call for Information on Any Matter) Rules, 1999.

2. Definition—In these rules, unless the context otherwise requires, "Act" means the Tamil Nadu Panchayats Act, 1994 (Tamil Nadu Act 21 of 1994).

3. Power to call for information—(1) The Executive Authority, Commissioner or Secretary, as the case may be of a panchayat may summon any person to appear before him and to give evidence or produce documents, as the case may be, in respect of any question relating to taxation or inspection or to the grant of any licence or permission under the provisions of the Act.

(2) Whoever fails to obey the summons issued by the Executive Authority, Commissioner or Secretary, as the case may be, under this rule shall be punishable with fine which may extend to one hundred rupees.

(G.O.Ms.No.188, Rural Development (C-4) Department, dated 14th September 1999)

3.3.2 Grant of Copies of Proceedings or Records

1. Short title—These rules may be called the Tamil Nadu Panchayats (Grant of Copies of Proceedings or Records) Rules, 1999

2. Application for grant of copies of proceedings or records—(1) A person requiring copies or extracts of the proceedings or records of a panchayat shall submit an application giving his full name and address and accurate description of the proceedings or records as far as possible to the Executive Authority or Commissioner or Secretary, as the case may be. When the proceedings or records of which the copies or extracts are applied for belong to any year prior to the calendar year in which the application is made, a search fee according to the scale specified below shall be remitted to the panchayat as soon as the application has been admitted:

(a) for searching records of any one year for a single document or entry, Ten rupees.

(b) for searching the records of every additional year, Five rupees.

Explanation. (1) For the purpose of these rules, the term person includes a member, vice-president or president of the village panchayat, vice-chairman or chairman of a panchayat union or district panchayat as the case may be.

(2) Separate application need not be presented in respect of each proceeding or record of which a copy or extract is required.

(3) Enclosures or annexures to letters, accounts or other documents form part of the documents to which they appertain and shall not be reckoned for the purpose of search as separate documents.

3. Rejection of application—If the Executive Authority or Commissioner or Secretary, as the case may be considers that the grant of the copy or extracts of any proceeding or records is objectionable, he shall reject the application by an endorsement stating briefly the reasons for doing so.

4. Issue of certificate for proceedings or records not found—If the record is not found, the fee paid shall not be refunded to the applicant. He shall be furnished with a certificate stating that the document applied for cannot be found.

5. Receipt for search fee or copying fees—(1) If the record is found and the Executive Authority or Commissioner or Secretary, as the case may be, decides to grant copies or extracts thereof, the applicant shall deposit in cash, a fee to be fixed by the Panchayat which shall not be less than five rupees for every page or part thereof.

(2) In the case of maps or plans a reasonable fee shall be fixed by the Executive Authority or Commissioner or Secretary as the case may be, in consultation with the engineering staff-in-charge of Panchayat works and in any case the fee shall not be less than twenty five rupees per copy of a map or plan, as the case may be. A receipt signed by the Executive Authority or Commissioner or Secretary as the case may be or any person empowered by him in this behalf shall be furnished to the person depositing search fees or copying fees.

6. Fees chargeable for copy of extracts—The Executive Authority or Commissioner or Secretary as the case may be shall intimate to the applicant the fees chargeable for the copy or extract from the proceeding or record. On receipt of the fee he shall have the copies, extracts or tracing prepared. Typed or photo copy of such proceeding or record shall be permissible. The copies or extracts shall then, be certified by him as true copy, after scrutiny and furnished to the applicant if he appears in person to receive them, or sent by post if the applicant has deposited necessary postage stamps for the purpose.

(G.O.Ms.No.190, Rural Development (C-4) Department, dated 14th September 1999)

3.3.3 Time Limit for Communication of Orders on Application for Licences and Permissions

1. Short title—These rules may be called the Tamil Nadu Panchayats (Time Limit for Communication of Orders on Application for Licences and Permission) Rules, 1999.

2. Definition—In these rules unless the context others-wise requires, "Act" means the Tamil

Nadu. Panchayats Act, 1994 (Tamil Nadu Act 21 of 1994).

3. Time limit

(i) In case where a panchayat does not need to consult any outside authority before passing orders on an application for any licence or permission or renewal thereof made under the Act or any rule or bye-law or regulation made thereunder, orders in respect of such application shall be communicated within 30 days from the date of receipt of applications by the Executive Authority or Commissioner or Secretary, as the case may be.

(ii) In cases where any outside authority, such as the Deputy Director of Public Health and Preventive Medicine or the Inspector of Factories or Officer of Town and Country Planning or any other officer has to be consulted before passing orders on an application for any licence or permission or renewal thereof, made under, the Act or any rule, bye-law or regulation made thereunder orders in respect of such application shall be communicated to the applicant within sixty days after the receipt of the application by the executive authority of the village panchayat or Commissioner of the panchayat union council or Secretary of district panchayat, as the case may be.

(iii) In cases where the Executive Authority or Commissioner or Secretary, as the case may be has sought clarification or details on such application coming under sub-rules (1) and (2) of Rule 3 above, the time limit of thirty days or sixty days, as the case may be, shall apply from the date of receipt of clarification or details from the applicant concerned.

(G.O.Ms.No.138, Rural Development (C-4) Department, dated 21st July 1999)

3.3.4 Calling for Information from Village Administrative Officer

1. Short title—These rules may be called the Tamil Nadu Panchayats [Calling for Information from Village Administrative Officers] Rules, 1999.

2. Particulars to be furnished by the Village Administrative Officer—The Executive Authority of a village panchayat or Commissioner of a panchayat union council or Secretary of a district panchayat, as the case may be, may, by an order in writing, require the Village Administrative Officer of any revenue village comprised within the jurisdiction of the panchayat concerned to furnish him with information on any matter falling within the following categories in respect of such village or any part thereof or any person or property therein:

(a) Particulars of survey number, sub-division, classification, description such as whether the land is dry or wet, extent, assessment and name of the registered holder or occupier of any land within the limits of the village panchayat, panchayat union council or district panchayat available in the village records.

(b) Particulars of roads vested with village panchayat or panchayat union and particulars of encroachment if any, thereon.

(c) Particulars of encroachments on poramboke lands vested and regulated by the village panchayat.

(d) Details of births and deaths within the limit of the village panchayat concerned.

(e) Any other particulars available in the registers and accounts maintained by Village Administrative Officer for the purpose of administration of the village panchayat and also for the effective conduct of Grama Sabha.

(f) Details about cultivating tenants and agricultural labourers.

(g) Details of the crops cultivated in the village panchayat area concerned.

(G.O. Ms.No.220, Rural Development (C-4) Department, dated 20th October 1999)

3.3.5 Production of Documents by Executive Authority, Commissioner, or Secretary

1. Short title—These rules may be called the Tamil Nadu Panchayats (Production of Documents by Executive Authority, Commissioner, or Secretary) Rules, 1999.

2. Production of documents—The Executive Authority or Commissioner or Secretary, as the case may be, shall comply with every requisition of the panchayat, to produce any document which is in his custody, unless in his opinion that, immediate compliance therewith would be prejudicial to the interest of the panchayat or of the public, in which case he shall make a declaration in writing to that effect and shall, if required by the panchayat, refer the question to the Inspector or any Officer empowered by him in this behalf and the decision of such Inspector or empowered officer, as the case may be, shall be final.

(G.O.Ms.No.118, Rural Development (C-4) Department, dated 5th July 1999)

3.3.6 Classification of Fairs and Festivals

1. **Short title**—These rules may be called the Tamil Nadu Village Panchayats (Classification of Fairs and Festivals) Rules, 1999.

2. **Definition**—In these rules unless the context otherwise requires, "Act" means the Tamil Nadu Panchayats Act, 1994 (Tamil Nadu Act 21 of 1994)

3. **Classification of fairs and festivals**—The classification of fairs and festivals in any village panchayat area as appertaining to the panchayat union council or the village panchayat shall be ordered by the Inspector in consultation with the secretary of district panchayat and Joint Director of Public Health and Preventive Medicine of the district concerned. The Government may notify any fair or festival in a district as district fair and festival, which shall be organised by the district panchayat and district Collector.

4. **Consultation with the district panchayat, panchayat union council and the village panchayat**—Before any classification is ordered under Rule 3, the district panchayat, panchayat union council and the village panchayat concerned shall be given a reasonable opportunity for expressing their opinion.

5. **Maintenance of list of fairs and festivals**—Every panchayat shall maintain a list of fairs and festivals taking place in its jurisdiction. The district panchayat shall maintain a master list of village panchayat, and panchayat union wise classified fairs and festival. The master list shall indicate the place, purpose, objective, importance, period, day of each fair and festival taking place in the district concerned.

6. **Revision of classification**—The Government in respect of classification ordered by the Inspector under Rule 3 may revise the classification. The advice of the district panchayat under Section 163 (2) (c) (ii) of the Act shall be obtained before deciding any such revision of classification. The district panchayat may furnish annually in the month of March, its suggestion for any revision in classification.

(G.O.Ms.No.145, Rural Development (C-4) Department, dated 21st July 1999)

3.3.7 Classification of Public Roads

1. **Short title**—These rules may be called the Tamil Nadu Panchayats (Classification of Public Roads) Rules, 1999.

2. **Village panchayat roads**—Every public road in village panchayat area other than those classified as National Highways road, State Highways road, Major District road and panchayat union road shall be the village panchayat road.

3. **Panchayat union road**—Every public road in a panchayat union area, other than those classified as National Highways road, State Highways road, Major District road and village panchayat road shall be the panchayat union road.

4. **Classification of public roads**—(1) The Inspector shall by notification in the District Gazette classify all the public roads vested with the village panchayat and panchayat union as village panchayat road and panchayat union road, as the case may be.

(2) Before ordering such classification under sub-rule (1), the Inspector shall obtain the resolution of the respective village panchayat or panchayat union council, as the case may be.

(3) While offering such classification the Inspector shall obtain technical opinion of the Executive Engineer (Rural Development) and also the views of the Divisional Engineer (Highways) of the district concerned.

5. **Re-classification of public roads**—(1) The Inspector may by notification in the District Gazette, order reclassification of village panchayat road as panchayat union road and *vice versa* either *suo motto* or on the basis of the resolution of the respective village panchayat or panchayat union council, as the case may be:

Provided that the village and the panchayat union council concerned shall be consulted prior to the publication of the notification under sub-rule (1).

(2) The Inspector may send proposal to the Government for upgradation of any of the public roads vested with the local bodies, as State Highways road or National Highways roads or Major District road on the basis of the resolution passed by the village panchayat and panchayat union council. On receipt of the proposal from the Inspector or on their own accord the State Government may order such upgradation.

(3) While ordering such classification or re-classification of the roads, intensity of traffic, connectivity of towns and village shall also be taken into account.

(4) Notwithstanding anything contained in these rules, such re-classification shall be ordered, only

in consultation with the district panchayat concerned.

6. Revision of classification or re-classification of public roads—Not with standing anything contained in these rules, the Government may revise *suo motto* or on application the classification or re-classification of roads proposed by the Inspector.

7. Register of roads—Every village panchayat and panchayat union shall maintain a register of roads in the Form appended to these rules.

(G.O.Ms.No.200, Rural Development (P-1) Department, dated 27th September 1999)

APPENDIX

FORM

(See Rule 7)

Register Showing the Details of Roads of Village Panchayat and Panchayat Union

Sl. No.	*Name of the Road*	*Nature of Road (Sand Road/Red Sand Metal Black Topping)*	*Length*	*Breadth*	*In case of Length Developed Nature of Road Sand Red Sand Metal Black Topping*	*Length*	*Breadth*	*Expenditure*	*Name of the Place of the construction of culverts in the road and the nature of culvert Bed Tank Culvert Wooden Culvert Concrete Culvert Metal Culvert*	*Signature*
(1)	(2)	(3)	(4)	(5)	(6)	(7)	(8)	(9)	(10)	(11)

3.3.8 Prohibition Against Obstructions in or Over Public Roads, Removal of Encroachments etc.

1. Short title—These rules may be called the Tamil Nadu Panchayat (Prohibition Against Obstruction in or Over Public Roads, Removal of Encroachments, etc.) Rules, 2000.

2. Definition—Unless the context otherwise requires "Act" means the Tamil Nadu Panchayats Act, 1994 (Tamil Nadu Act 21 of 1994).

3. Restriction on quarrying in or over public roads—(1) The village panchayat or panchayat union council may grant a licence for any work referred to in clause (c) of sub-section (1) of Section 131 of the Act on such terms and conditions and subject to such restrictions as it may determine and where it refuses to grant such licence it shall communicate to the person or persons concerned its reasons for the refusal.

(2) If in the opinion of the village panchayat or panchayat union council, the working of any quarry or the removal of stone, earth or other material from any place is dangerous to person residing in or having legal access to the neighbourhood thereof, or creates or is likely to create a nuisance, the village panchayat, panchayat union council may, by order, require the owner or person having control of the said quarry or place to discontinue working the same or to discontinue removing stone, earth or other material from such place or to take such other action on the quarry or place as it shall deem necessary for the purpose of preventing danger or of abating the nuisance arising or likely to arise therefrom.

4. Restriction on fixing of door etc. appertaining to public road—(1) No door, window gate, bar in ground and other floors shall be hung or placed so as to open outwards upon any public road vested in the village panchayat or panchayat union council without a licence from the Executive Authority or Commissioner as the case may be.

(2) The Executive Authority or Commissioner may, by notice, require the owner of such door, gate bar or window to alter it so that no part thereof, when open, shall project over the public road.

5. Issue of notice for removal of obstructions, etc.—The Executive Authority or the Commissioner may, by notice require the owner or occupier of any premises, to remove or alter any projection, encroachment, or obstruction situated against or in front of such premises and in or over any public road vesting in the village panchayat or panchayat union council.

6. Licence for putting up of temporary sunshades etc.—(1) The Executive Authority or the Commissioner may with the approval of the village panchayat or panchayat union council grant a licence, subject to such conditions and restrictions as he may think fit, to the owner or occupier of any premises to put up temporary sunshades, weather frames and the like to project over a public road vested in the village panchayat or panchayat union council, or to construct any step or drain cover necessary or access to the premises.

(2) Every application for a licence under sub-rule (1) shall furnish information in Form 1 appended in these rules as to the material of which it is proposed to construct the structure and the period for which a licence is required.

(3) The licence may be granted or renewed in Form 2 appended in these rules by the village panchayat or panchayat union council, if the structure is of temporary material, such as palmyra or coconut leaves, bamboo or other matting or gunny cloth or other similar materials, or is of such a nature as to be movable easily, and if the period of the licence does not exceed twelve months.

(4) No licence for a structure not in accordance with the description given in sub-rule (3) or for a period exceeding twelve months, shall be granted by a village panchayat or panchayat union council except with the previous approval of the Inspector, who, in granting approval may lay down such conditions, as he may consider necessary subject to which the licence may be granted by the village panchayat or panchayat union council. The village panchayat or panchayat union council shall embody such conditions in the licence before it is granted. In the case of licence granted under this rule, the approval of the Inspector shall not be necessary for renewal, if such renewal does not extend the duration of the licence for a period exceeding three years.

7. Licence for the construction of steps etc.—Licence for the construction of steps or drain cover, necessary for giving access to premises, shall be granted, subject to the following further conditions, which should be specified in the licence:

(i) The steps or slabs over drains shall not project into the road beyond the retaining wall of the drain. The step or slab over the drain leading to a premise directly abetting the road shall not be more than one metre long in the case of domestic premises and 1.5 metres long in the case of shops or business premises but in the case of shops or business premises, which have a frontage of less than six metres in length, only one flight of step shall be allowed. In the case of premises having compound in front into which vehicular traffic is likely to pass over the drain the Executive Authority or Commissioner shall fix the length of the covering.

(ii) Coverings over the drains shall be fixed with the top of the retaining walls of the drains, provided that the depth of the drain below the coverings is considered sufficient by the village panchayat or panchayat union council to carry the storm water flow. A covering slab may be laid on the top of the retaining walls, in rare cases where it may be necessary to do so in order that the water way of the drain may not be restricted, or in cases where the licensing authority has no objections. Provided that the previous sanction of the Inspector is obtained and that a suitable cement concrete ramp is constructed on the road side of the raised slab leading from the level of the top of the slab on the road.

(iii) The drain covering in the case of premises abutting on the road shall be five to ten centimetres in thickness for drains fifteen to ninety centimetres wide. In the case of premises with a compound in front where heavy vehicular traffic is likely to pass over the drain, the covering may be of granite or reinforced concrete slab of the following thickness.

Width of Over drain (in centimetres)	*Thickness of reinforced concrete slabs (in centimetres)*	*Thickness of Granite slabs (each 45 centimetres width) (in centimetres)*
(1)	(2)	(3)
15-30	10	12
31-60	15	18
61-90	18	24

In the case of larger drains, the thickness and materials of the covering shall be such as may be decided by the Executive Authority or Commissioner in each case to suit:

(a) the class of stone or other covering materials used;

(b) the width of individual slab members carrying the load;

(c) the load concentration expected; and

(d) the depth of fill, if any, over the slab;

Provided that the above condition may be relaxed in exceptional cases with the previous approval of the Inspector.

(iv) They shall be liable to be removed at the cost of the licensee, whenever necessary in order that the drain may be inspected or repaired.

(v) The Executive Authority or Commissioner may, whenever he thinks fit by order in writing direct, the removal of the step or drain coverings altogether without payment of compensation:

Provided that the order aforesaid shall specify the reasons for the action proposed and shall not be issued without notice to the persons concerned.

(vi) The top of the drain covering shall not be used as part of a shop or be otherwise encroached upon.

8. Power of Inspector for cancellation of licence—The Inspector shall have power to cancel any licence granted under sub-rule (3) or (4) of Rule 6 or Rule 7, if, in his opinion; the projection, erection or structure, which has been licensed, has become objectionable or if he considers it necessary in the public interest that the projection, erection or structure should be removed and upon such order, the village panchayat or panchayat union council shall have the projection, erection or structure removed.

9. Conditions for issue of licence—It shall be condition of every licence granted under sub-rule (3) or (4) of Rule 6 or Rule 7:

(i) that it shall be liable to be cancelled at any time in the circumstances referred to in those Rules; and

(ii) that an annual fee shall, if levied, be paid to the village panchayat or panchayat union council in advance so long as the licence is in force and that in default of payment of such fee, the licence to be cancelled.

10. Licence for pandal etc.—The Executive Authority or Commissioner may grant a licence, subject to such conditions and restrictions as he may think fit, for the temporary erection of pandals and other structures in a public road vested in the village panchayat or panchayat union council.

11. Powers of Government for restrictions—The Government may, by notification, restrict any place under such control as they may think fit, the exercise by any village panchayat or panchayat union council of the powers under Rules 6 and 8.

12. Removal of construction on expiry of lease period—On the expiry of any period for which a licence has been granted under Rules 6 and 8 the Executive Authority or Commissioner, may without notice, cause any projection or construction put up under the said rules, be removed and the cost of so doing shall be recoverable from the person to whom the licence was granted.

13. Construction over drain—No building shall be erected without the written permission of the Executive Authority or Commissioner, over any sewer or drain or any part of sewer or drain or upon any ground vested in the village panchayat or panchayat union council which has been covered, raised or leveled wholly, or in part, by road sweepings or other rubbish.

(2) The Executive Authority or Commissioner may, by notice require any person, who has erected a building without such permission or in a manner contrary to, or inconsistent with the terms of such permission to demolish the same.

14. Notice for removal of obnoxious vegetation etc.—The Executive Authority or Commissioner, may by notice, require the owner or occupier of any land adjoining a public road or adjoining other land or water source vested in the village panchayat or panchayat union council to clear away prickly pear, wattle, lantana or other obnoxious vegetation where it encroaches on such property and so far as it has spread from such land on to such property.

15. Restriction on making hole etc., on road—(1) The village panchayat or panchayat union council shall earmark certain places with readymade holes for erecting poles in any public road vested with them.

(2) No person shall make a hole, or cause any obstruction in any public road other than those places specified in sub-rule (1) unless he previously obtains the permission of the Executive Authority or Commissioner and complies with such conditions as the Executive Authority or Commissioner may impose.

(3) When such permission is granted, such person shall, at his own expense, cause such hole or obstruction to be sufficiently fenced and enclosed until the hole or obstruction is filled up or removed and shall cause such hole or obstruction to be sufficiently lighted during the night.

(4) If any person contravenes the provisions of this rule, the Executive Authority or Commissioner shall fill up the hole or remove the obstruction or cause the hole or obstruction to be lighted as the case may be, and may recover the cost of so doing from such person.

16. Penalty and compensation—(1) The Executive Authority or Commissioner shall have power to permit a person to plant any tree on any public road or other property vesting in or belonging to the village panchayat or panchayat union council on such conditions as the Executive Authority or Commissioner may impose.

(2) The Executive Authority or Commissioner shall have power to permit a person to fell, remove destroy, lop or strip bark or leaves from or otherwise damage any tree referred to in clause (f) of sub-section (1) of Section 131 of the Act, on such condition as the Executive Authority or Commissioner may impose.

FORM 1

Application for Licence/Renewal of Licence
[See Rule 6 (2)]

To
The Executive Authority/Commissioner
....Village Panchayat/Panchayat Union
.... District

1. Name of person/firm:
2. Father's name:
3. Address

House No.	Street:
Village:	Post:
District:	Pin Code:

4. Purpose for which licence is applied;
5. Type and description of temporary structure proposal.
6. This is to certify that .... Dimension of temporary structure will be erected by me on the road at.................(Place) and I am to inform that all these temporary structures will be removed by me as and when informed by you and request to issue of licence for the temporary structure. I certify that the said temporary structure will not be obstructing normal road traffic. I have paid Rs. ....towards the licence/renewal of licence in the .... village Panchayat/Panchayat Union Office vide Receipt No.............. dated................ I shall abide by all the terms and conditions of the licence.

Date: **Signature of the Applicant.**

Place:

FORM 2

[See Rule 6 (3)]
Licence/Renewal of Licence for Temporary Structure on Roads

........................Village Panchayat
..............................Panchayat Union
...............................District

Licence is issued in favour of Thiru/Tmt...............Address...........for erecting temporary structure on the road located at............... (place) coming under the jurisdiction of this Village Panchayat/Panchayat Union. The licence is valid for............... days (not exceeding 365 days). The applicant has paid licence fee of Rs............/- (Rupees............................ vide........... this Village Panchayat/Panchayat Union Receipt No...........dated............

Signature of the Executive Authority and Date

Office Seal:

Commissioner
Designation:
Original to the licence
Counterfoil-Office copy

TERMS AND CONDITIONS OF LICENCE

1. Erection of temporary structures shall be done as per the laws and rule in force.
2. Temporary structures will be of the dimensions and quality as indicated in this licence and as per rule.
3. This licence is liable for cancellation in case the licensee violates any of the conditions of the licence.
(G.O. Ms. No. 311 Rural Development (C-4), 29th November 2000)

3.3.9 Prohibition and Regulation of the Use of Public or Private Springs, Tanks, Wells

1. Short title—These rules may be called the Tamil Nadu Panchayats (Prohibition and Regulation of the Use of Public or Private Springs, Tanks, Wells) Rules, 1999.

2. Power of the village panchayat to regulate spring, tank, well—The village panchayat may, in the interest of public health by an order, regulate or prohibit the washing of animals or clothes or other articles or fishing, in any public spring or tank or well or any public water-course or part thereof and may set apart any such place for drinking or for bathing or for washing animals or clothes or for any other specified purpose. Panchayat union council or district panchayat by specific resolution may, if deem fit, request a village panchayat to exercise this power.

3. Consent of the owner—The power conferred by Rule 2, in the case of any private spring, tank, well or water-course, be exercised by the village panchayat, with the consent of the owner of such place.

4. Right to take water for drinking purpose—The village panchayat may, in the interest of public health, by an order, regulate or prohibit the washing of animals or clothes or other articles or fishing in any private spring, tank, well or water-course from which the public have a right to take water for drinking purpose

5. Notice as to prohibition for use of water—The Executive Authority of a village panchayat, on receipt of a certificate from any medical officer in the employment of the Government, or village panchayat, panchayat union and district panchayat stating that the water in any tank, well, spring or other source of water supply to which the public have access in the village is likely to endanger or cause the spread of any dangerous disease may, by public notice, prohibit the use of such water. Such notice shall be served by affixing a copy of it near the source of water supply or by beat of drum, stating the number of days during which such prohibition shall last. The Executive Authority may extend or modify the notice without the production of a further certificate.

6. Restriction for a place set apart for drinking purpose—No person shall:

(a) bathe in or defile the water in any place set apart for drinking purpose;
(b) deposit any offensive or deleterious matter in foreshore and the foreshore dry-bed of any place and water sources set apart as aforesaid for drinking purpose; or
(c) wash clothing in any place set apart as aforesaid for drinking purpose or for bathing; or
(d) wash any animal or any cooking utensil or wool, skin or other foul or offensive substance or deposit any offensive or deleterious matter in any place set apart as aforesaid for drinking purpose or for bathing or for washing clothes; or
(e) allow the water from a sink, sewer, drain, engine or boiler or any other offensive matter or effluent belonging to him or flowing from any building or land or factory belonging to or occupied by him, to pass into any place set apart as aforesaid for drinking purpose or for bathing, or for washing clothes.

7. Penalty for contravention of these rules—Whosoever contravenes any order issued under any of the provisions of Rules 2 to 4 a notice under Rule 5 or any of the provision of Rule 6 or fails to comply with any direction lawfully given to him or any requisition lawfully made upon him under any of these rules shall be punishable with fine which may extend to one hundred rupees and in case of a continuing breach with fine not exceeding fifteen rupees for everyday during which the breach continues after conviction for the first breach. The village panchayat issuing an order or notice under these rules, shall give the person, whosoever contravenes any order or notice issued under these rules, adequate opportunity to furnish the written defence and accord necessary hearing before passing orders of punishment.

(G.O.Ms.No.158, Rural Development (C-4) Department, dated 2nd February 1999)

3.3.10 Lease and Licensing of Fishery Rights in Water Sources Vested and Regulated by Village Panchayats and Panchayat Union Councils

1. Short title—These rules may be called the Tamil Nadu Panchayats (Lease and Licensing of Fishery Rights in Water Sources Vested and Regulated by Village Panchayats and Panchayat Union Councils) Rules, 1999.

2. Prohibition of fishing without lease or licence in water sources under the control of village panchayat or panchayat union council—No person shall take any fish from the water sources specified in Appendix I of these rules except under a lease or licence granted by the village panchayat or the panchayat union council, as the case may be, or by such authority as may be authorised by them with such condition as may be specified in the lease or licence, as the case may be, which may be suitably modified or amended from time-to-time.

3. Penalty—Whoever commits a breach of the provisions of Rule 2 shall be publishable with fine which may extend to five hundred rupees and when the breach is a continuing one, with a further fine which may extend to fifty rupees for everyday after the date of commission of first offence, during which the breach is proved to have been persisted in.

4. Forfeiture—A Magistrate may, on the imposition of the penalty specified in Rule 3 on any person for the breach of these rules, order the seizure, forfeiture and removal of the engines fixed and erected or used or not used in contravention of these rules, and also order the forfeiture of any fish taken by means of any such fixed, engine or net.

5. Proof of possession of fish within the jurisdiction—A licensee or his authorised agent found in possession of fish within two hundred metres of the licensed area shall be liable to prove to the satisfaction of the Executive Authority of the village panchayat or the Commissioner of the panchayat union as to how he came into possession of the fish, failing which the fish shall be forfeited to the village panchayat or the panchayat union council concerned, as the case may be.

6. Production of licence on demand—The licence issued under these rules shall be produced on demand to the Executive Authority of the village panchayat or the panchayat union Commissioner or any person authorised by them.

7. Transfer of licence—The licence shall not be transferable. But in the event of the death of the licensee or in case he becomes incapable or physically disqualified for fishing, it may be transferred in the name of his legal heir on an application to the village panchayat or panchayat union council, as the case may be.

8. Issue of duplicate licence—If a licence is lost and cannot be recovered or mutilated, a duplicate licence shall be issued on payment of five rupees.

9. Conditions and form of licence—The licence shall be in the form appended to these rules. The conditions of the licence shall be as specified in the said form in Appendix II.

10. Cancellation of licence—The Executive Authority of the village panchayat or the panchayat union Commissioner may cancel any licence, if the licensee fails to conform to any of the conditions prescribed in the licence after giving a reasonable opportunity to the licensee.

11. Lease of fishery rights—The lease of fishery rights in the water sources vested in the village panchayats or the panchayat union council shall be given after conducting public auction by the respective village panchayat or panchayat union council, as the case may be. Such lease shall be for a period of five years. Lease amount shall be raised every year at the rate of 10 per cent over the lease amount of the previous year.

Upset lease amount shall be fixed by the village panchayat and the panchayat union council concerned in consultation with the Inspector of Fisheries of the respective area.

12. Authority competent to conduct auction of fishery rights—(1) The Executive Authority of village panchayat concerned shall be competent to conduct public auction of fishery rights in its respective water sources specified in items (3) of Appendix I. The Commissioner of panchayat union concerned shall be competent to conduct public auction of fishery rights in the water sources specified in items (1) and (2) of Appendix I. Such auction of fishery rights shall be conducted after giving sufficient notice and publicity. When the auction for the fishery rights takes place, if any Fisheries Co-operative Society participating in the auction comes forward to match the highest bid, preference shall be given to such Fisheries Co-operative Society. In case of more than one Fisheries Co-operative Society participating in the auction, the highest bid of the Co-operative Society shall be finalised.

(2) The fisheries co-operative society not participating in the auction shall have no right to

claim for fishery right by offering to match the highest bid amount.

(3) For the purpose of participating in the auction, earnest money deposit amount shall be fixed at the rate of 5 per cent of upset lease amount.

13. Authority competent to confirm the auction—The Inspector of panchayats shall confirm the auction. In case the lease or auction amount is less than the previous year it shall be referred to the Inspector for disposal.

14. Termination of lease—The leaser shall remit 25 per cent of the lease amount at the time to the lease and the balance of 75 per cent shall be remitted within seven days from the date of confirmation of the auction as provided in Rule 13. In case of default, the lease shall be terminated without assigning any reason. The village panchayats or panchayat union council concerned shall have the right to re-lease.

15. Appeal—Any person aggrieved by the orders of the village panchayat or panchayat union council in accepting the bid under Rule 13 may prefer an appeal to the Inspector within thirty days from the date of confirmation of the auction. The decision of the Inspector in the matter shall be final.

16. Revisionary powers—Any person aggrieved by the orders of the Inspector may prefer a revision application within thirty days from the date of the receipt of the orders by the Inspector to the Director of Rural Development.

(G.O. Ms. No.169, Rural Development (P3) Department, dated 16th August 1999)

APPENDIX I

(See Rules 2 and 12)

(1) Irrigation sources which are entrusted to panchayat union council under Section 133 (1) of the Tamil Nadu Panchayat Act, 1994 and maintained by them and non-provincialised water sources of the Public Works Department and maintained by them.

(2) Irrigation sources which are entrusted to panchayat union council under Section 133 (1) of the Tamil Nadu Panchayat Act, 1994, but maintained by village panchayats.

(3) All public water sources vested with village panchayats.

APPENDIX II

Form of Licence

(See Rule 9)

District *Village Panchayat/* *Panchayat Union Council*	*District* *Village Panchayat/* *Panchayat Union Council*
Fishing Permit Licence issued for Fishing In .... tank Location details with S.No. and Revenue Village Name of the Licensee Address of the Licensee Mode of fishing Amount paid Period Signature and date Designation (Counterfoil-office copy)	Fishing Permit Licence issued for Fishing In .... tank Location details with S.No. and Revenue Village Name of the Licensee Address of the Licensee Mode of fishing Amount paid Period Signature and date Designation (Original to the Licensee)

Conditions

(i) ...... Kind .... Size .... quantity of species alone shall be caught.
(ii) No fishing is allowed between .... period.
(iii) .... Tank .... Hours .... Days is allowed for fishing.
(iv) The licensee shall maintain and surrender the licence when called for.
(v) The Licensee shall produce the fish .... at .... for inspection and weighment and for calculation of drayage.
(vi) The licensee shall abide by any other condition that may be stipulated by the competent authority, from time-to-time.

3.3.11 Composition of Offences

1. Short title—(1) These rules may be called the Tamil Nadu Panchayats (Composition of Offences) Rules, 2000.

The offences punishable under the sections of the Tamil Nadu Panchayats Act, 1994 (Tamil Nadu Act 21 of 1994) specified in column (1) of the Table below shall be declared as compoundable by the executive authority or the Commissioner or the Secretary as the case may be, for the amount specified in the corresponding entries in column (2) and with the permission of the Court before which any prosecution for such offence is pending, wherever such permission is necessary as specified in the corresponding entries in column (3) thereof.

Table

Sl. No.	*Offence and the corresponding section of the Act (1)*		*Amount (2)*	*Whether compoundable with the permission of the Court (3)*
1.	Unlawful building over drain	131(1)(d)	Two thousand rupees	Compoundable with the permission of the Court
2.	Sale, etc. of articles in public roads or places after prohibition or without licence or contrary to regulation	151	One hundred rupees	do
3.	Using any public place or roadside as a landing or halting place or as a cart-stand within prohibited distance	154(b)	Five hundred rupees	do
4.	Opening a private cart-stand or continuing to keep open a private cart-stand without licence or contrary to licence in a village panchayat	155(1)	Two thousand rupees	do
5.	Slaughtering, cutting up or skinning, etc. of animals outside public slaughter-houses in contravention of rules	157(a)	Two thousand rupees	do
6.	Slaughtering animals for purposes of sale without licence or contrary to licence	157(b)	Two hundred rupees	do
7.	Unlawful destruction, etc., of number affixed on buildings	158(3)	Fifty rupees	do
8.	Unlawful building of wall or erecting of fence, etc., in or over public road	131(1)(a)	One thousand rupees	Compoundable
9.	Unlawful quarrying in any place near public road	131(1)(c)	Five hundred rupees	do
10.	Planting of trees without permission on any public road or other property vested in a village panchayat or panchayat union council	131(1)(e)	Two thousand rupees	do

(Contd.)

Sl. No.	*Offence and the corresponding section of the Act* (1)		*Amount* (2)	*Whether compoundable with the permission of the Court* (3)
11.	Felling, etc., without permission of trees growing on public road or other property vested in a village panchayat on a poramboke or land the use of which is regulated by it under Section 134 or 135	131(1)(f)	Two thousand rupees	Compoundable
12.	Opening a new private market or continuing to keep open a private market without licence from the village panchayat or panchayat union council or contrary to licence	148(1)	Five thousand rupees	do
13.	Levy of fees in private market without a certificate	148(3)	One thousand rupees	do
14.	Sale or exposure for sale in public or private market of any animal or article without permission	150	Two thousand rupees	do
15.	Failure to replace number assigned to buildings when required to do so	158(4)	Two hundred rupees	do
16.	Using a place for an offensive or dangerous trade without licence from the village panchayat or contrary to licence	159(2)	One thousand rupees	do

(G.O. Ms. No. 205, Rural Development (C4) Department, dated 17th August 2000)

3.3.12 Restriction, Control and Power of Entry and Inspection

1. Short title—These rules may be called the Tamil Nadu Panchayats (Restriction Control and Powers of Entry and Inspection) Rules, 1999.

2. Condition for entry—For the purposes of clause (a) of sub-section (1) of Section 223:

(a) no entry shall be made by the Executive Authority or Commissioner or Secretary, as the case may be, or any person authorised by him between sunset and sunrise.

(b) no dwelling house, or any part of a public building used as a dwelling place, shall be entered into by the Executive Authority or Commissioner, or Secretary, as the case may be or any person authorised by him, with out the consent of the occupier thereof, unless the said occupier has received at least six hours' previous notice of the intention to make such entry.

(c) Sufficient notice shall be given by the Executive Authority or Commissioner, or Secretary, as the case may be, or any person authorised by him, in every case even when any premises may otherwise be entered without notice under clause (2) of Rule 2 to enable the inmates of any apartment appropriated to women to move to some part of the premises where their privacy may be preserved.

(d) Due regard shall be given by the Executive Authority or Commissioner or Secretary, as the case may be or any person authorised by him, so far as may be compatible with the exigencies of the purpose of the entry to the social and religious usage of the occupants of the premises.

3. Inspection of building or place or land for which licence or permission is required—For the purposes of clause (b) of sub-section (1) of Section 223:

(1) The Executive Authority or Commissioner or Secretary, as the case may be or any person authorised by him may enter any premises between sunrise and sunset and also between sunset and sunrise if it is open to the public, or any industry is being carried in it, at the time.

(2) If there is reason to believe that any premises is being used for any of the purposes mentioned below without a licence or permission, where the same is required by or under the Act or anything is

being done in such premises otherwise than in conformity with the conditions of such licence or permission, the Executive Authority or Commissioner or Secretary, as the case may be, or any person authorised by him may at any time, by day or night without notice enter such premises for the purpose of satisfying himself whether any provision of law, rules, bye-laws or regulations, any condition of a licence or permission or any lawful direction or prohibition is being contravened:

(a) Tanning hides or skins;
(b) Manufacturing storing or selling of gunpowder or fire works;
(c) Brewing beer, manufacturing arrack or other spirit containing alcohol (whether denatured or not) by distillation; and
(d) Storing any explosive or combustible materials.

(G.O. Ms.No.148, Rural Development (C4) Department, dated 21st July 1999)

3.3.13 Grant of Remission of Rent to Lessees and Contractors

1. **Short title**—These rules may be called the Tamil Nadu Panchayats (Grant of Remission of Rent to Lessees and Contractors) Rules, 1999.

2. **Adherence of terms and conditions by the lessees**—All leassees of village panchayat and all persons who have entered into contracts with village panchayat shall be held strictly the terms and conditions of their leases or contracts and no remission of lease rent shall be granted to them except in accordance with the provision of Rules 3 and 4.

3. **Restrictions and control**—The grant of remission of lease rent to lessees and contractors shall be subject to the following restrictions and control, namely:

(a) Remission of lease rent shall be granted only in cases in which the lessee or contractor is prevented from carrying out his part of the lease or contract by reason on the occurrence of some extraordinary extrinsic cause which could not reasonably be anticipated. For example the compulsory closing on account of the outbreak of an epidemic or the act of God like heavy flood or storm, of a market or the site or any work spot which has been washed out or where the work could not be carried out;
(b) The amount of remission of lease rent granted shall not exceed the proportionate amount payable under the lease or contract for the period for which the lessee or contractor was prevented from carrying out his part of the lease or contract on account of such extraordinary cause as referred to in clause (a); and
(c) When the amount remitted exceeds five hundred rupees, the previous sanction of the Inspector shall be obtained.

4. **Penalties**—Penalties provided in the lease or contract shall be strictly enforced in accordance with the terms of the lease or contract. Penalties for the last payment of the amount due to the village panchayat under the lease or contract shall not be remitted except in cases where the payments of instalments of the amount due are in the opinion of the village panchayat fairly regular and the whole amount due to the village panchayat under the lease or contract is paid before the end of the period to which the lease or contract relates:

Provided that when the amount remitted exceeds Rs. 500 in each case, the previous sanction of the Inspector shall be obtained.

(G.O. Ms. No. 204, Rural Development (C4) Department, dated 28th September 1999)

3.3.14 Power to Write-off Irrecoverable Taxes, Fees, etc.

1. **Short title**—These rules may be called the Tamil Nadu Village Panchayats (Recovery of Sums and Power to Write-off Irrecoverable Taxes, Fees etc. Restrictions and Control), Rules 1999.

2. **Definition**—In these rules, unless the context otherwise requires, "Act" means the Tamil Nadu Panchayats Act, 1994 (Tamil Nadu Act 21 of 1994).

3. **Recovery of sums due to the village panchayats**—Where there is no provision in the Act or the rules made thereunder for the recovery of any amount due to a village panchayat such amount shall be demanded by raising bills which shall be served on the person (or) persons concerned and recovered in the same manner provided in the rules for the collection of taxes under the Act.

4. **Approval of the village panchayat for write-off the amount due to the village panchayat**—Amounts found irrecoverable shall be reported by the panchayat assistant/part-time clerk or any other officer of the Revenue Department when he is entrusted with the work of collection of taxes or fees under Section 177 of the Act, with reasons therefor,

which shall be verified by the Executive Authority. A list of all such amounts shall be prepared once a quarter and submitted to the village panchayat at its next meeting for approval with the reasons and recommendations of the Executive Authority for writing-off the same. The Executive Authority shall ensure that the defaulter has no attachable property and that all means of recovery have been tried and found unsuccessful, before recommending the proposal to write-off of the amount payable to the village panchayat.

5. Maintenance of Registers—(1) A register for recording the amount written-off shall be maintained in the form specified in the Appendix.

(2) When a village panchayat approves that any amount be written-off, particulars as to the nature of the tax, fee or other amount assessment number, in the case of items relating to tax, the amount written-off and the period to which it relates shall be given in detail in the minutes book.

(3) The demand notice and warrants (both foil and counterfoil) for the taxes, fees or other amounts written-off, shall, as soon as possible after approval for writing-off is given by the village panchayat, be stamped with inscription "Written-off" and necessary entries shall be made in the demand register.

6. Limit for the Executive Authority for writing-off—When any single item of tax, fee or other amount found to be irrecoverable exceeds one hundred rupees, the Executive Authority shall obtain the approval of the Collector.

(G.O. Ms. No. 244, Rural Development (C4) Department, dated 2nd December 1999)

APPENDIX

Register to Write-off Tax, Fee etc.

(See Rule 5)

Sl. No.	*Name of the applicant and date on which application for write-off is made*	*Details*	*Period to which it relates*	*Demand Rs.*	*Reasons for write-off of the demand*	*Amount written-off Rs.*	*Number and date of the resolution of village panchayat*
(1)	(2)	(3)	(4)	(5)	(6)	(7)	(8)

3.3.15 Transfer of Irrigation Function to Panchayats

1. Short title—These Rules may be called the Tamil Nadu Panchayats (Transfer of Irrigation Function to Village Panchayats and Panchayat Union Councils) Rules, 1999.

2. Definition—In these rules, unless the context otherwise requires, "Act" means the Tamil Nadu Panchayats Act, 1994 (Tamil Nadu Act 21 of 1994).

3. Restrictions and conditions relating to transfer—The transfer of maintenance in respect of irrigation work specified in sub-section (1) of Section 133 to any village panchayat or panchayat union council shall be restricted to any minor irrigation source, which is situated within such village panchayat or panchayat union council if such source does not form part of a river irrigation system:

Provided that tank under the control of the Public Works Department shall not be transferred even if it is unconnected with a river irrigation system.

4. Arrangement for discharge of functions—A village panchayat or panchayat union council as the case may be shall with effect from the date on which the functions in respect of any village irrigation work are transferred to it makes its own arrangements for the discharge thereof and shall if necessary employ its own staff, in the exercise, of such functions. The village panchayat or union council, as the case may be, shall also have general control over work charged labourers, if any employed by the Government. The Rural Development Department shall have the power of appointment, punishment, dismissal and payment of salary and other allowances to them if they were in service at the time of transfer of such minor irritation sources.

5. Power to regulate supply of water, etc.—The village panchayat or panchayat union council as the case may be shall have the power to regulate the manner and order in which the lands in the village under the irrigation work shall be irrigated, the time at which the supply of water shall commence, the period during which the supply of water shall continue and the total quantity of water to be supplied. But, the village panchayat or panchayat union council, as the case may be, shall so exercise its power of regulation so as not to interfere with any established customary right to preferential or proportional supply.

6. Regulation of turns of irrigation—(1) The village panchayat or panchayat union council, as the case may be, shall be responsible as a body to decide on all details regarding the regulation of turns of irrigation. The actual operation of the shutters shall be the responsibility of the village administrative officer only, subject to the general control of the village panchayat or panchayat union council as the case may be.

(2) The village panchayat or panchayat union council, as the case may be, may empower the committee appointed by it under clause (b) of sub-section (1) of Section 96 of the Act for the efficient performance of its duties and functions under sub-section (1) of Section 133 of the Act, to regulate the turns of irrigation.

7. Alteration in sluices, etc.—The village panchayat or panchayat union council, as the case may be, shall not effect any alteration in the sluices of the irrigation work or interfere with the standard and specification laid down in the Tank Restoration Scheme Memoirs in respect of such work, or raise lower or extend the weirs of calingulas, or make any material alteration in or interfere with the head works, if any, of the channels without the prior approval of the Collector.

8. Watch over bunds—The village panchayat or panchayat union council, as the case may be, shall be responsible for keeping watch over the bund of the respective irrigation work during the rainy season.

9. Damage to sluices, weirs, etc.—The village panchayat or panchayat union council, as the case may be, shall make good any damage to the sluices, weirs, calingulas, channels, head works, bund or other works forming part of or connected with the irrigation work resulting from its misfeasance or non-feasance. The decision of the collector as to whether any particular item of damage was the result of any misfeasance or non-feasance on the part of the village panchayat or panchayat union council, as the case may be, shall be final.

10. Prohibition of excavation of earth—The village panchayat or panchayat union council, as the case may be shall not excavate or allow any person to excavate earth at any time for any purpose within ten metres or five times the height of the bund whichever is more or either toe of the bund of the irrigation work.

11. Power of Government to resume works—Any function in respect of a village irrigation work, transferred to village panchayat or panchayat union council, as the case may be, may at any time, be resumed without assigning any reason, by the Government or the authority to whom powers may be delegated under Section 218 of the Act.

12. Controlling and supervision—The maintenance of all irrigation works transferred to the village panchayat or panchayat union council, as the case may be, shall be under the control and supervision of the Assistant Engineer, Rural Development or Union Engineer and shall be subject to inspection by the Inspector or any authority authorized by him.

(G.O. Ms. No. 222, Rural Development (C4) Department, dated 20th October 1999)

3.3.16 Opening and Maintenance of Markets

1. Short title—These rules may be called the Tamil Nadu Panchayats (Opening and Maintenance of Markets) Rules, 2001.

2. Definition—In these rules unless the context otherwise requires:

(a) Act means the Tamil Nadu Panchayats Act 1994 (Tamil Nadu Act 21 of 1994);

(b) "Form" means a Form appended to these rules;

(c) "Market" means a place used by the public for buying and selling goods and includes shandy or any other name by which, the place is called by the local public;

(d) "Public market" means a market opened and maintained either by the village panchayat or the panchayat union;

(e) "Private market" means a market run by a private person under licence either from the village panchayat or the panchayat union council as per the conditions laid down in sub-section (1) of Section 148 of the Act;

(f) "Panchayat union market" means the public market opened and maintained by the panchayat union council;

(g) "Schedule" means a Schedule appended to these rules;

(h) "Village panchayat market" means the public

market opened and maintained by the village panchayat.

3. Opening and maintenance of public market by panchayat union—(1) Panchayat union council shall apply to the Inspector for permission to open and maintain public market in the land owned by or leased to it. Such application shall indicate the rates of fees to be levied which shall not be lower than the fees prescribed by the Government, from time-to-time.

(2) The Inspector shall examine the proposals of the panchayat union with reference to the following:

(a) commercial viability of the proposed market *vis-à-vis* the existing panchayat union or the village panchayat market or private market within a radius of 10 kilometres.

(b) accessibility of the proposed market by the public and the traders.

(c) health and sanitation aspect specified by the Deputy Director of Public Health and Preventive Medicine.

4. Opening and maintenance of public market by the village panchayat—(1) Village panchayat shall apply to the Inspector for permission to open and maintain public market in the land owned by or leased to it. Such application shall indicate the rates of fees to be levied and which shall not be lower than the fees prescribed by the Government from time-to-time.

(2) The Inspector shall examine the proposals of the village panchayat with reference to the following:

(a) commercial viability of the proposed market *vis-à-vis* the existing nearby panchayat union and the village panchayat market or private market within a radius of 5 kilometres,

(b) accessibility of the proposed market by the public and the traders,

(c) Health and sanitation aspect specified by the Deputy Director of Public Health and Preventive Medicine.

(3) Notwithstanding anything contained in these rules no new market shall be permitted if it will affect the commercial viability of the already existing market either private or public situated within 5 kilometres radius from the proposed place.

5. Classification of public and private market as the panchayat union or the village panchayat market—(1) In consultation with the district panchayat, the Government shall classify public and private market and to classify whether public market is a panchayat union market or a village panchayat market and also fix the ratio of the apportionment of income between the panchayat union council and the village panchayat concerned. The rates of apportionment shall be revised from time-to-time by the Government after consulting the district panchayat.

(2) Notwithstanding anything contained in these rules, all the existing public markets opened and maintained by the panchayat union councils or the village panchayat before the commencement of these rules, shall continue as such. A list of such markets shall be compiled by each village panchayat and panchayat union council as the case may be and transmit the list to district panchayat. At the district level, the district panchayat shall maintain a master list and register of all such markets in the district and update the same once in every year in the first week of April.

6. Auctioning of public market—(1) The Executive Authority or the Commissioner, as the case may be, may lease out by public auction the right to collect various fees at rates not exceeding the rates fixed by the village panchayat or the panchayat union council, as the case may be, for the markets maintained by them respectively.

(2) The lease by auction shall come into effect only after the confirmation of the village panchayat or the panchayat union council, as the case may be.

(3) The lessee shall follow all conditions and maintain all records and registers as laid down in Rules 13, 14 and 15 of these rules.

7. Licence for private market—(1) No person shall open and maintain a private market without obtaining a licence from the village panchayat. Such licence shall be renewed every year.

(2) A person or a firm or a co-operative society as the case may be, intending to open a private market, shall apply to the Executive Authority of the village panchayat or the Commissioner of the panchayat union council, as the case may be, seeking its licence, duly furnishing the details and informations specified below:

(a) records showing the title of the applicant to the proposed site or land or a lease deed for renting a site with a sketch;

(b) Provisions made or to be made for the drainage or storm water disposal system;

(c) Provisions made or to be made for sanitary facilities for the use of the visiting public;

(d) Provisions made or to be made for proper and adequate access to the proposed market site from a public road or street.

(e) the rates of fees or rents proposed to be charged for keeping articles or goods for sale to the public;

(f) details as to whether it is a weekly market or a daily market and the day or days of assembly in a week;

(g) arrangements made or to be made for the disposal of sweepings, garbage, cattle dung or market waste;

(h) arrangements made or to be made for providing adequate water including drinking water to the visiting public and toilet facilities; and

(i) such other details or information's as may be found necessary and required by the Executive Authority or the Commissioner, as the case may be, in respect of a particular site or application.

(3) In case the village panchayat or the panchayat union council agrees to approve the proposal, the Executive Authority or the Commissioner, as the case may be, shall send the proposal to the Deputy Director of Public Health and Preventive Medicine of the district concerned for his opinion as to the suitability of the site on public health point of view. Within thirty days of the receipt of the proposal from the Executive Authority, or the Commissioner, as the case may be. The Deputy Director of Public Health and Preventive Medicine shall communicate his remarks, failing which, the approval sought for shall be deemed to have been granted.

(4) The village panchayat or the panchayat union council may by notice require the owner/occupier of any private market to

(a) construct approaches, entrances, passages, gates, drains and cesspits, soak pit, garbage, bins, for such market and provide it with toilets of such description and in such position and number as the village panchayat or the panchayat union council may think fit;

(b) roof and pave the whole or any portion of it, or pave any portion of the floor with such material as will in the opinion of the panchayat secure imperviousness and ready cleaning;

(c) Ventilate it properly and provide it with supply of water;

(d) Provide passages of sufficient width between the stalls and make such alterations in the stalls, passages, shops, doors or other parts of the market as the panchayat may direct;

(e) keep in a clean and proper state, remove all filth and refuse and dispose of them at such place and in such manner as the panchayat may direct;

(f) make such other sanitary arrangements as the panchayat may consider necessary;

(g) to display prominently in Tamil the rates of fees as fixed by the village panchayat or the panchayat union council, as the case may be, to be collected from the sellers;

(h) The Executive Authority or the Commissioner, as the case may be shall conduct periodical inspection of the Private Market and the licensee shall be bound to rectify and carry out suggestion pointed out;

(i) to use only weights and measures certified by the competent authority of the Labour Department; and

(j) To put-up display boards in Tamil and English.

8. Grant or refuse of licence—(1) The Executive Authority or the Commissioner, as the case may be on receipt of an application in a complete shape in all respects after scrutinizing the application shall inspect the site and after satisfying himself about its possibilities of not affecting any public market of the village panchayat or the panchayat union council, if any functioning within a reasonable radius of 10 kilometres shall place the proposal before the village panchayat or the panchayat union council within ten days of its receipt, along with his remarks for a decision on the proposal. If the village panchayat or the panchayat union council does not agree the proposal, it may reject it, after giving the applicant reasonable opportunity to make his representation. The Executive Authority or the Commissioner, as the case may be shall communicate the decision of rejection of the proposal in writing to the applicant.

(2) Any person aggrieved by the decision may file an appeal to the Inspector within thirty days of receipt of the communication from the Executive Authority or the Commissioner, as the case may be, and the decision of the Inspector thereon shall be final.

(3) After receipt of the opinion of the Deputy Director of Public Health and Preventive Medicine or on the expiry of thirty days of sending the proposal to him the Executive Authority or the Commissioner, as the case may be shall issue a notice in writing asking him to carryout measures on the suggestions, or to fulfil the conditions prescribed, if any, by the Deputy Director of Public Health and Preventive Medicine.

(4) The Executive Authority or the Commissioner, as the case may be, shall within forty five days of receipt of application from the applicant, place the subject before the village panchayat or the panchayat union council as the case may be for granting licence to the applicant for opening a private market and approval to the proposed rates of fees and rents to be collected by the applicant in such market premises.

(5) On the sanction by the village panchayat or the panchayat union council, as the case may be for issuing the licence applied for, and approval of rate fee with or without modifications of the rates of fees and rents proposed by the applicant, the licence shall be granted in Form-I by the Executive Authority or the Commissioner, as the case may be after requiring the applicant to carryout preliminary arrangements as contemplated in the conditions for such a licence.

(6) The Executive Authority or the Commissioner, as the case may be, shall also arrange to publish a notification in the *District Gazette*, at the expenses of the licensee, showing the nature of market, the day of assembly in the case of weekly market, the details of location of the market site and the rates of fees leviable for various purposes.

9. Powers of the Executive Authority—(1) The Executive Authority or the Commissioner, as the case may be, may expel, any person who or whose servant has been convicted of any offence for having violated any of the provisions of these rules at the time in force from such market, and may prevent such person from further carrying on, by himself or his servants or agents, any trade or business in such market, or occupying any shop, stall or other place therein and may determine any lease or tenure which such person may possess in any such shop, stall or place.

(2) The Executive Authority or the Commissioner, as the case may be, on the basis of the decision of the village panchayat or the panchayat union council, as the case may be, may issue a notice and requiring the owner or lessee of any private market to:

(a) construct approaches, entrances, passages, gates, drains, cesspits, soak pits, and garbage bins for such market and provide it with toilets of such description and in such position and number as the village panchayat or the panchayat union council, as the case may be, think fit;

(b) roof and pave the whole or any portion of it, or pave any portion of the floor with such materials as will in the opinion of the village panchayat or panchayat union council, as the case may be, imperviousness and ready cleaning;

(c) ventilate it properly and provide it with supply of water;

(d) provide passages of sufficient width between the stalls and make such alterations in the stalls, passages shops, doors or other parts of the market as the village panchayat or the panchayat union council, as the case may be, may direct;

(e) keep in a clean and proper state remove all filth and refuse and dispose of them at such place and in such manner as the village panchayat or the panchayat union council, as the case may be may direct; and

(f) make such other sanitary arrangements as the village panchayat or the panchayat union council, as the case may be, consider necessary.

(3) If any person, after receipt of such notice, fails within the period and in the manner laid down in the said notice to carry out any work specified in sub-rule (2) the village panchayat or the panchayat union council, as the case may be, may suspend the licence of the said person, until such works have been completed.

(4) It shall not be lawful for any person to keep open any private market during such period of suspension or until the licence is renewed.

(5) No owner, lessee, agent or manager in charge of any private market, or of any shop, stall, shed or other place therein, shall keep the same so to cause any nuisance or fail to remove or alter anything which is or which may cause a nuisance to a place to be specified by the village panchayat or the panchayat union council, as the case may be.

(6) (a) Whoever fails to comply with the terms of a notice under this rule or contravenes the provisions of any of the other rules specified in the second column of Schedule-I shall be punishable with fine which may extend to the amount mentioned in that behalf in the third column of the said Schedule-I.

(b) Whoever after having been convicted of any of the offences referred to in sub-clause (a) above continues to commit such offence shall be punishable, for each day after the previous date of conviction during which he continues so to offend, with fine which may extend to the amount mentioned in that behalf in the third column of Schedule-II.

(7) The Executive Authority, or the Commissioner, as the case may be, shall have power to order closure of any market, during the prevalence of cholera or other epidemic diseases and such directions shall be complied with immediately.

(8) The Executive Authority or the Commissioner, as the case may be, may after receipt of the written request of the licensee or leassee, prohibit the sales of articles on market day in any public place within the limits of the villages where the private market is located.

(9) No person shall or no licensee shall permit any person to conduct auction of any articles brought inside the market without obtaining a licence from the Executive Authority, or the Commissioner as the case may be, which may be granted subject to such terms and conditions and subject to payment of such fees as may be specified by the village panchayat or the panchayat union council as the case may be in this behalf.

(10) No compensation is payable to the licensee or to any person on account of any action taken or omitted to be taken by the Executive Authority of the village panchayat or the Commissioner as the case may be or any of the inspecting or controlling authorities of the village panchayat either in pursuance of those rules or the Act.

10. Payment of licence fee— (1) A licensee shall pay at least thirty days before the date of expiry of the validity thereof to the village panchayat or the panchayat union council, as the case may be, the license fees every year at such rate as may be fixed by the village panchayat or the panchayat union council as the case may be, from time-to-time which shall not be less than fifteen per cent of the gross income of the licensee in the preceding year.

(2) When a market is opened for the first time, the license fees may be paid at a sum as the village panchayat or the panchayat union council, as the case may fix provisionally or at the rate fixed on the anticipated receipts as per the statement of the licensee subject to the conditions that any amount found surplus or deficit of the amount due, may be adjusted in the subsequent year or years towards the fee due for that year or any amount found short is collected in the next year along with the fees due for that year.

(3) In the case of renewal of licence, the fee shall be paid in advance along with application of renewal at one hundred and twenty five per cent of the previous years licence fee paid subject to the adjustment of excess or deficit after finalising the gross income for the previous year.

11. Renewal of licence—The licensee shall apply for the renewal of licence at least thirty days prior to the date of expiry of the existing licence period with pre payment of one hundred and twenty five per cent of the previous year licence fees subject to the finalisation of actual licence fees to be collected after finalising the accounts of the private market for the previous year for ascertaining the correct income and either refunding excess fees collected or collect the shortfall fees from the licensee.

12. Accounts of private markets—(1) The licensee shall issue tickets for collections made daily and receipts for collections made periodically.

(2) The receipts and ticket books shall be printed as in Forms II and III and each receipt shall bear the office seal of the village panchayat or the panchayat union council, as the case may be.

(3) The ticket books shall be printed separately for each rate of fees charged.

(4) The licensee of the said market shall keep true and complete accounts of the receipts from the markets and expenditure incurred on their maintenance and shall produce them whenever required for inspection, check or audit by the Executive Authority or the Commissioner or such other person as may be authorised by the Executive Authority of the village panchayat or the panchayat union council as the case may be.

(5) A register of collections and disbursements shall be maintained in Form IV and V respectively given in the appendix. The registers, tickets and receipt books shall be checked by the Executive Authority or the Commissioner of panchayat union council, as the case may be, or such other person as may be authorised by the Executive Authority of the village panchayat or the panchayat union council, as the case may be not less than once in every month and such remarks as are called for recorded therein. If the accounts have been found to be kept correctly, a certificate to that effect shall be recorded in the said registers.

13. Verification of records and registers—The Executive Authority or the Commissioner, as the case may be, shall specify fixed date or dates every month requiring the licensee to produce such records and registers and also to file reports prescribed above duly signed by the licensee. He shall preserve all the reports and accounts submitted by the licensee, and such records in his office safely for a period of one year after the audit of the village panchayat or the panchayat union council, as the case may be, is over or till the audit objection, if any, raised on this item is settled whichever is later.

14. Tickets and receipt books—As and when the tickets and receipt books are produced, by the licensee, the Executive Authority or the Commissioner, as the case may be shall affix rubber stamps showing office seal with date of the village panchayat or the panchayat union council as the case may be and the facsimile of his full signature on the front side of the leaves of the books and also note the date of affix of office seal and facsimiles. Licensee shall not use any tickets and receipt books which are not authenticated by the Executive Authority, or the Commissioner as the case may be.

15. Running of private markets on lease—When a licensee desires to let the running of the private markets on lease, he shall do so, only after getting the prior approval of the village panchayat or the panchayat union council, as the case may be, in writing to that effect. In such an event, the terms and conditions prescribed for the licensee shall apply to the lessee.

(G.O. Ms. No.3, Rural Development (C4) Department, dated 4th January 2001)

3.3.17 Framing of Bye-Laws by the Panchayats

1. Short title—These rules may be called the Tamil Nadu Panchayats (Framing of Bye-Laws) Rules, 1999.

2. Definition—In these rules, unless the context otherwise requires, "Act" means the Tamil Nadu Panchayats Act, 1994 (Tamil Nadu Act 21 of 1994).

3. Power of the panchayat to frame bye-law—A panchayat may frame bye-laws not inconsistent with the Act or rules made thereunder on matters enumerated below and also on such other matters required for implementing the provisions of the Act or any other law, to provide, for

(a) all matters expressly required or allowed by the Act to be provided in bye-law;
(b) the regulation of the time and mode of collection of taxes under this Act;
(c) use of public tanks, wells, conduits and other places or works for drinking water supply;
(d) the protection of avenues, trees, grass and other appurtenances of public street;
(e) planting of trees by private persons in public lands on which the village panchayats has powers of control, protection and management and granting licences for the same;
(f) the inspection of public and private markets and stall and other places therein, including the regulation of their use and the control of their sanitary conditions;
(g) licensing and controlling brokers, commission agents, weigh men and measure practicing their calling in markets, other than markets coming under regulated market committee;
(h) prescribing the method of sale of articles whether by measure, weight, bale or piece;
(i) the enumeration of inhabitants of the village panchayat area;
(j) letting out of public place and buildings like Kalyana Mandapam, Community hall, for public use;
(k) procedure for getting temporary licences for encroachment made for putting up temporary structure during the times of fairs, ceremonies and seasonal covering and other purposes;
(l) conditions to be prescribed while calling for tender for executing works or for supply of goods, materials and other than those prescribed under the rules; and
(m) terms and conditions to be laid down while auctioning leases of rights of enjoyment of panchayat properties and collection of fees for various purposes.

4. Publication and deposit of bye-law—Any bye-law or cancellation or alteration thereof when it has been duly confirmed shall, if it is not in Tamil, be translated into Tamil and also in any other language or languages in which the electoral roll of the village panchayat is published and deposited in the office of the village panchayat and a copy thereof shall also be exhibited on the notice board of the said office and at such places as the village panchayat or panchayat union council or district panchayat may direct. A public proclamation by beat of drum or otherwise that such copy has been so exhibited and that the original is open to inspection at the office if the village panchayat or panchayat union council or district panchayat. The period for receipt of objections or suggestions if any, shall not be less than thirty days from the date of publication of such bye-law.

5. Manner of cancellation or alteration of bye-law—No bye-law or cancellation or alteration thereof made by a village panchayat shall have effect, until the same has been approved and confirmed by the Inspector or any other officer authorized by him except those relating to drinking water supply and drainage works and by the Superintending Engineer, Tamil Nadu Water Supply and Drainage Board or any other technical officer notified by the Government from time-to-time in this regard in respect of those relating to drinking water supply and drainage works.

6. Effect of any bye-law—Any bye-law or cancellation or alteration thereof shall come into force on the expiry of three months from the date on which it was deposited in the office of the village panchayat or panchayat union or district panchayat, as the case may be.

(G.O.Ms.No.177, Rural Development (C4) Department, dated 30th August 1999)

3.4 PROPERTIES OF PANCHAYATS

3.4.1 Acquisition and Transfer of Immovable Property

1. Short title—These rules may be called Tamil Nadu Panchayat (Acquisition and Transfer of Immovable Property) Rules, 2000.

2. Definitions—In these rules, unless the context otherwise requires. "Form" and "Schedule" shall mean the Forms and Schedules appended to these rules.

3. Condition for acquisition of immovable property—(1) Every panchayat shall acquire any immovable property subject to the conditions that

(a) the property, if intended for any purpose other than roads, bridges, culverts or quarries, is approved by the Deputy Director of Public Health and Preventive Medicine of the district concerned or any person authorised by him as suitable from the Public Health and sanitary point of view for the purpose for which it is intended;

(b) the property is also approved by the Engineer of the Government department specified by the Government, from time to time, as suitable for the purpose for which it is intended in cases when the estimated cost exceeds ten thousand rupees;

(c) the property, if the value exceeds ten thousand rupees and if it is intended for educational purposes, is also approved by the Chief Educational Officer of the district;

(d) the property, if its value exceeds ten thousand rupees and if it is intended for dispensaries, is approved by the Joint Director of Medical Services of the district concerned also;

(e) the property, shall not be acquired otherwise than under the Land Acquisition Act, 1894 (Central Act 1 of 1894), unless the previous approval of the Collector has been obtained therefor;

(f) In the case of lands acquired otherwise than under the said Act a valuation certificate is obtained from the Revenue Department and that no amount in excess of such valuation shall be paid without obtaining the specific approval of the Collector in that behalf;

(g) In the case of buildings, a valuation certificate and a certificate of structural stability are obtained from the Engineer of the government department as prescribed by the Government and that no amount in excess of such valuation shall be paid without obtaining the specific approval of the Collector in that behalf; and

(h) In every case where the consideration for the property is not less than two thousand rupees, an encumbrance certificate is obtained from the Registration Office in respect of such property and examined by the legal adviser of the panchayat concerned unless the nature of the transaction is such as will.

(2) The deed transferring the property to the panchayat shall be in the appropriate forms in Schedule I, with such variations as circumstances may require.

(3) The provisions of sub-rules (1) and (2) shall not apply to a case where the panchayat has to purchase immovable property brought to sale in the execution of a court decree obtained by it.

4. Transfer otherwise than by lease of immovable property vesting in but not belonging to a panchayat—(1) Immovable property vesting in but not belonging to a panchayat shall not be transferred or charged in contravention of the conditions subject to which such property became vested in the panchayat.

(2) The deed of transfer shall be in the appropriate Form in Schedule II, with such variations as circumstances may require.

5. Transfer otherwise than by lease of immovable property belonging to a village panchayat or panchayat union council—(1) A panchayat shall not, without the previous sanction of the Inspector make or sanction any transfer, except by way of lease, of any immovable property belonging to it, or create or sanction the creation of any charge upon any such property. If the value of the property to be transferred or the amount for which the charge to be created exceeds fifty thousand rupees, the previous sanction of the Government shall also be obtained for such transaction.

(2) The deed of transfer shall be in the appropriate Form in Schedule II with such variations as circumstances may require.

6. Transfer by lease of immovable property belonging to a panchayat—(1) A panchayat may lease out any immovable property belonging to it:

Provided that no such lease shall be valid in case the period of the lease exceeds three years or where the lessee is permitted to put up any building or structure whether of masonry, bricks, wood, mud or any other material unless the sanction of the Collector has been obtained therefor.

(2) The lease-deed shall be in Form-III (a) in Schedule III with such variations as circumstances may require.

7. Transfer by lease of immovable property vested in but not belonging to a panchayat—(1) A panchayat may lease out any property vested in but not belonging to the panchayat other than road sides and street margins:

Provided that no lease shall be granted:

(a) in contravention of the conditions subject to which such property became vested in the panchayat; or

(b) for a period exceeding twelve months without the previous sanction of the Collector:

Provided further that no such lease shall be valid if the lessee is permitted to put up any building or structure whether of masonry, bricks, wood, mud or any other material, unless the sanction of the Collector has been obtained therefor.

(2) The lease-deed shall be in the Form-III (a) in Schedule III with such variations as circumstances may require.

8. Lease of road sides and street margins—(1) Leases of road sides and street margins vested in a panchayat shall be subject to the following certificates and control:

(i) Every panchayat shall require that every application for a lease shall furnish information as to the use to which the land will be put and the period for which a lease is required. If any structure is proposed to be constructed thereon, information as to the materials to be used in the construction shall also be furnished.

(ii) The lease may be granted by the panchayat if the structure is to be constructed of temporary materials such as palmyrah or coconut leaves, bamboo or other matting or gunny cloth or other similar materials or which are of such a nature as to be movable daily, and if the period of lease does not exceed twelve months. A fee shall be levied and collected in advance for every lease.

(iii) No lease for a structure made of materials other than those maintained in item (ii) or for a period exceeding twelve months, shall be granted by a panchayat except with the previous approval of the Collector who in granting approval may lay down such conditions as he may consider necessary subject to which the lease may be granted by the panchayat. The panchayat shall embody such conditions in the lease before it is granted. It must be expressly provided in every case that amount of the lease shall be paid to the panchayat in advance so long as the lease is in force and that in default of payment of such amount the lease is liable to be cancelled.

(iv) No lease shall be granted ordinarily for a period exceeding three years at a time. The approval of the Collector shall not be necessary for a renewal of a lease granted under this rule.

(v) Every lease under item (ii) or (iii) shall expressly provide that the lease is liable to be terminated at any time within the period of the lease without payment of compensation to the lessee if, in the opinion of the panchayat or of the Collector, it is necessary in the public interest to remove any structure erected on the land.

(vi) No road margin shall be leased out for cultivation.

(2) The lease-deed shall be in Form-III (b) in Schedule III with such variations as circumstances may require.

9. Publication of proposed transfers and leases—(1)(a) In every case of transfer falling under Rule 4, 5, 6, or 7, the panchayat shall publish a notice of the proposed transfer, giving full particulars of the property to be transferred, the name of the proposed transferee or lessee and the consideration for the transfer or the rent reserved under the lease in the District Gazette, if the consideration for the transfer exceeds ten thousand rupees; and

(b) by affixture in a conspicuous place in the village where the property lies:

(i) at the offices of the village panchayat, panchayat union council, district panchayat and of the Collector;

(ii) at the village chavadi of the village in which the property is situated, and

(iii) on the property to be transferred.

(2) In every case where such transfer is to be made by public auction, a notice with full particulars of the property to be transferred shall be published:

(a) in the District Gazette and in one or two prominent local Tamil newspapers, circulated within the jurisdiction of the village panchayat if the consideration for the transfer exceeds ten thousand rupees;

(b) in the manner specified in clause (b) of sub-rule (1); and

(c) by tom-tom in suitable places.

10. Transfer and leases to be subject to condition of transferees or lessees paying assessment ground-rent, peshkash or quit-rent to government—(1) Except in cases falling under sub-rule (3), no transfer of any immovable property made by the village panchayat shall be valid unless it be a condition thereof that the transferee shall be liable to pay to the Government such assessment, ground-rent, peshkash or quit-rent, as the Collector may determine to be payable in respect of the property and that the said assessment, ground-rent, peshkash or quit-rent, is subject to revision, from time-to-time, in accordance with the rules in force at the time of such revision except in respect of quit-rent on enfranchised inam lands and peshkash on lands in proprietary village acquired by the panchayat by private negotiation.

(2) Nothing contained in this rule shall affect the right of the Government to recover from the panchayat the assessment, ground-rent, peshkash or quit-rent leviable on lands not transferred by sale or exchange or otherwise permanently alienated.

(3) In cases where the assessment, ground-rent, peshkash or quit-rent leviable on the land after transfer is already being paid by the panchayat and the land is not transferred by sale or exchange leased in perpetuity or otherwise permanently alienated, the village panchayat shall continue to pay such assessment, ground, rent peshkash or quit-rent and the liability shall not be imposed on the transferee.

(G.O. Ms. No. 209, Rural Development (C4) Department, dated 17th August 2000)

SCHEDULE-I

[See Rule 3(2)]

Form-I (a)

Transfer by Sale to a Village Panchayat or Panchayat Union Council or District Panchayat by a Private Person

This indenture made the ____________day of ____________year of __________ between ________________ son of ______________________________Residing at____ (hereinafter called the "vendor" which expression shall where the context so admits include his heirs, executors administrators, legal representatives and assigns) of the ONE PART AND the village panchayat/panchayat union council, district panchayat of _________________________ Constituted under the Tamil Nadu Panchayats Act, 1994 (Tamil Nadu Act 21 of 1994) (hereinafter called the "Purchaser" which expression shall where the context so admits include its successors and assigns) of the OTHER PART;

WHEREAS, the vendor is well and sufficiently entitled to the land and premises described in the schedule hereunder;

AND WHEREAS, the purchaser in exercise of its powers, has agreed with the vendor to purchase the said land and premises intended to be hereby granted, conveyed and assigned subject to the quit-rent (if any), payable in respect of the same but otherwise free from encumbrances at the prices of rupees;

NOW THIS INDENTURE WITNESSES that in pursuance of the said agreement and in consideration of the sum of rupees ________________________________ paid to the vendor by the purchaser on or before the execution of these presents (the receipt whereof the vendor doth hereby acknowledge) he, the vendor doth hereby grant, convey and assign unto the purchaser all that piece or parcel of land situated in ________________and more particularly described in the schedule hereunder written and which together with the message or tenement erected thereon is commonly called or known as ______________________________ together with all buildings, godowns, tress, commons, hedges, ditches, fences, ways, waters, water-courses, liberties, privileges, easements, advantages and appurtenances whatsoever to the said piece or parcel of land message and premises or any of them in anywise appertaining or heretofore occupied or enjoyed therewith AND all the estate right, title, interest property claim and demand whatsoever of the vendor into and upon the same premises TO HAVE AND TO HOLD the said piece or parcel of land message and premises hereby granted, conveyed and assigned unto the purchaser for ever AND the vendor doth hereby covenant with the purchaser that he the vendor now hath good right to grant, convey and assign the premises hereby granted, conveyed and assigned unto the purchaser in manner aforesaid and that the purchaser shall and may at all times hereafter peaceably and quietly possess and enjoy the said premise free from all encumbrances whatsoever and receive the rents and profits thereof without any lawful eviction, interruption, claim or demand whatsoever from or by the vendor or any other person or persons AND further that he, the vendor and all persons having lawfully or equitably claiming any estate or interest in the said premises or any of them or any part thereof from under or in trust for the vendor or from or under any of his ancestors shall and will, from time-to-time and at all times hereafter at the request and cost of the purchaser do execute and register or cause to be done, executed and registered all such acts, deeds and things whatsoever for further and more perfectly assuring the said premises and every part thereof unto the purchaser in manner aforesaid as shall or may be reasonably required.

The Schedule above referred to

All that piece or parcel of land and premises situated in the village/town of ____________________ in the registration sub-district of__________on the south by____________in the registrations district of ________and bounded on the north by__________on the east by ______________and on the west by__________________bearing Re-survey No____________and Old Survey No ______________and containing on the whole by measurement __________(be the same more or less).

Signed, sealed and delivered by the above named in the presence of

IN WITNESS whereof the vendor hath hereunto set his hand and seal the day and year first above written.

Form I-(b)
Transfer by Lease to a Panchayat by a Private Person

THE INDENTURE MADE THE ________________ day of ____________Year of ______________ Between son of __________________Residing______________at____________________and carrying on business at (hereinafter called the "lessor" which expression where the context admit shall include his heirs, executors, administrators, legal representatives and assigns) of the ONE PART AND the village panchayat/panchayat union council/district panchayat of ____________________constituted under the Tamil Nadu Panchayats Act, 1994 (Tamil Nadu Act 21 of 1994) (hereinafter called "the lessee" which expression where the context admits shall include its successors in office and assigns) of the OTHER PART; WITNESSETH AS FOLLOWS:-

1. Inconsideration of the rent hereby reserved and of the covenants by the lessee (herein contained the lessor demises unto the lessee ALL that piece or parcel of land together with the building and premises known as __________________situate in the registration sub-district of____________________In the registration district of __________________Bearing S. No_______________and more particularly described in the schedule hereunder for the term of___________Years from the________day of_______________PAYING therefor in advance the monthly rent of Rs______________clear of all deductions the first of such payments to be made on the _____________day of _______________
2. The lessee covenants with the lessor as follows:
   (a) To pay the reserved rent on or before the first day of each month in advance and in manner aforesaid.
   (b) To bear, pay and discharge all existing and future taxes, charges, assessments and outgoings payable in respect of the said premises.
   (c) To keep the exterior and interior of the demised premises and all additions thereto, the boundary wall and fences thereof, the drains, soil and other pipes sanitary and water apparatus, electric fittings and fixtures thereof in good and tenantable repair and condition.
   (d) Not to make or permit to be made under any circumstances any alterations in or additions to the demised building without the previous consent in writing of the lessor PROVIDED ALWAYS that if the lessee is permitted to make any alterations, by the lessor, the lessee shall not be entitled to any compensation therefor.
   (e) To permit the lessor with or without workmen or others at all reasonable times on giving one day's previous notice to enter upon the demised premises and to view the condition thereof and upon notice being given by the lessor to repair within one month from the service of the notice in accordance therewith.
   (f) Not to assign underlet or part with the possession of the demised premises or any part thereof without first obtaining the written consent of the lessor.
   (g) To yield up the demised premises with all fixtures and additions thereto at the determination of the tenancy in good and tenantable repair and condition in accordance with the covenants herein contained.
3. The lessor covenants with the lessee as follows:
   (i) That the lesser paying the rent hereby reserved and observing and performing the several covenants and

stipulations herein on its part contained shall peacefully hold and enjoy the demised premises during the said term without any interruption by the lessor or any person right-fully claiming under or in trust for him.

(ii) To carry out all repairs to main wall roof and foundations due to fair wear and tear, the decision of the Executive Engineer for the time being of______division as to the necessity for such repairs being final.

4. PROVIDED ALWAYS and it is hereby expressly agreed by and between the parties hereto as follows:

(a) If the rent hereby reserved or any part thereof shall be unpaid for fourteen days after becoming payable (whether formally demanded or not) or if any covenant on the lessee's part herein contained shall not be performed or observed then and in any of the said cases it shall be lawful for the lessor at any time thereafter to re-enter upon the demised premises or any part thereof in the name of the whole and thereupon this demise shall absolutely determine but without prejudice to the right of action of the lessor in respect of the breach of any of the lessee's covenants herein contained.

(b) If the lessee shall desire to determine the present demise and shall give to the lessor three calendar month's previous notice in writing of such desire then immediately on the expiration of the three calendar months the present demise and everything herein contained shall cease and be void but without prejudice to the remedies of either party against the other in respect of any antecedent claim or breach of covenant.

(c) That the lessor will on the written request of the lessee made within three calendar months before the expiration of the term hereby granted grant to the lessee a lease of the demised premises for the further term of________years and containing the like covenants and provisos as are herein contained except the including a covenant for renewal.

The Schedule above referred to

ALL THAT piece or parcel of land and premises situated in the village/town of ________________________in the registration sub-district of __________________________in the registration district of__________________________and bounded on the north by_______________on the south by_______________on the east by __________________and on the west by__________________________bearing Re-survey No__________________________and Old Survey No____________________and containing on the whole by admeasurement __________________(be the same more or less).

Signed, sealed and delivered by the above names in the presence of.

Signed by the Executive Authority/Commissioner/Secretary of the village panchayat/panchayat union council/ district panchayat________________________In the presence of__________________The common seal of the village panchayat/panchayat union/district panchayat was hereunto affixed in the presence of ___________________

IN WITNESS whereof __________________________The lessor hath hereunto set his hand and seal and the common seal of the village panchayat/panchayat union council/district panchayat of____________________The lessee was hereunto affixed the day and year first above written.

Form I-(c)
Transfer by Mortgage to a Panchayat by a Private Person

THIS INDENTURE made the____day of __________________________year of____between____son of____residing at (hereinafter called "the mortgagor" which expression shall where the context so admits include his heirs, executors, administrators, legal representatives and assigns) of the ONE PART AND the village panchayat/panchayat union council/district panchayat of____constituted under the Tamil Nadu Panchayats Act, 1994 (Tamil Nadu Act 21 of 1994) (hereinafter called "the mortgagee" which expression shall where the context so admits include its successors and assigns) of the OTHER PART;

WHEREAS the mortgagor is well and truly entitled to and possessed of the piece or parcel of land and premises described in the Schedule hereunder;

AND WHEREAS, the mortgagee has agreed to lend the mortgagor the sum of Rs___________________________On having the repayment thereof in the manner hereinafter appearing;

NOW THIS INDENTURE WITNESSETH that in consideration of the sum of Rs________________on or before the execution of these presents paid to the mortgagor by the mortgagee (the receipt whereof the mortgagor doth hereby acknowledge) he, the mortgagor doth hereby give, grant and assign unto the mortgagee an usufructuary mortgage of ALL THAT piece or parcel of land situate in__________________________And more particularly described in the schedule hereunder written and which together with the message or tenement erected therein is commonly called or known as ___________________________TOGETHER with all buildings, godowns, trees, commons, hedges, ditches, fences, ways, waters, water courses, liberties, privileges, easements, advantages and appurtenances whatsoever to the said piece or parcel of land message and premises or any of them in anywise appertaining or heretofore or hereafter to be occupied or enjoyed therewith AND all the estate right, title, interest, property, claim and demand whatsoever of the mortgagor into and upon the same premises TO HAVE AND to HOLD the said piece or parcel of land message and premises hereby granted, convéyed and assigned or expressed so to be unto the mortgagee for ever subject to the proviso for redemption hereinafter contained. The mortgagor hereby declares that he has put the mortgages, in possession of the mortgaged property and that the mortgagee shall continue in such possession of the property until the said sum of Rs__________Is repaid to the mortgagee and that the mortgagee shall appropriate the rents and profits accruing from the property in lieu of the interest due in respect of the mortgage money. AND the mortgagor doth hereby covenant and the mortgagor doth hereby covenant with the mortgagee that he, the mortgagor will as long as any money shall remain due on the security of these presents keep all the messages and buildings now existing or hereafter to be erected on the said premises herein before expressed to be hereby granted, conveyed and assigned in good and substantial repair and insured against loss or damage by fire in the sum of Rs____________________________at the least in some office or offices approved by and in the name of the mortgagee and will duly and punctually pay all premiums and sums of money necessary for such purpose and for keeping such insurance on foot and also all quit-rent assessment rates, taxes and other outgoings for the time being payable in respect of or charged upon the said premises or any of them and bill forthwith deliver to the mortgagee the policy or policies of insurance and the receipt for every sum payable as aforesaid and that if default be made in keeping the said buildings so repaired or in effecting or keeping on foot such insurance or in payment of any such quit-rent, assessment rates, taxes and other outgoings as a foresaid or in so delivering any policy or policies or receipt as aforesaid it shall be lawful for but not incumbent upon the mortgagee to put the said premises in proper and substantial repair or (as the case may be) to insure and keep insured the said buildings in any sum not exceeding the amount aforesaid and to pay the premiums and all expenses incurred in so doing or (as the case may be) any such quit-rent, assessment, rates, taxes, of other outgoings as aforesaid AND further that the mortgagor will forthwith repay to the mortgagee all such premiums expenses and other moneys with interest thereon at the rate of ______per cent per annum from the time of each payment and that until repayment the premises hereby mortgaged shall stand charged with the amount to be repaid and interest thereon at the rate aforesaid and that all moneys received in respect of any insurance shall at the option of the mortgagee be applied either in reinstating or restoring the buildings insured or in or towards payment of the moneys for the time-being on the security on these presents AND the mortgagor doth hereby covenant with the mortgagee that he, the mortgagor now path power to give and grant this usufructuary mortgage unto the mortgagee AND it is hereby expressly agreed and declared that on payment at any time by the mortgagor to the mortgagee of the said sum of Rs__________and all other moneys, if any, due under these presents the mortgagee shall at the request and cost of the mortgagor recover and reassign unto the mortgagor or as he may direct all and singular the plot or piece of land and premises hereby expressed to be granted, conveyed or assigned.

The Schedule above referred to

ALL THAT piece or parcel of land and premises situated in the village/town of ___________in the registration sub-district of____________________in the registration district of______________________and bounded on the north by____________on the south by _________________on the east by_________________________and on the west by ________________________bearing Re-survey No______________________and Old Survey No____________and containing on the whole by admeasurement__________________(be the same more or less).

Signed, sealed and delivered by the above names in the presence of.

IN WITNESS WHERE OF MORTGAGOR hath hereunto set his hand seal the day and year first above written.

Form-I (d)
Transfer of Gift a Panchayat by a Private Person

THIS INDENTURE made the ___________________day of__________________year of _______________between ___________________son of __________________residing at (hereinafter called the "Donor" which expression shall where the context so admits include his heirs, executors, administrators, legal representatives and assigns) of the ONE PART AND the village panchayat/panchayat union council/district panchayat of _________________constituted under the Tamil Nadu Panchayats Act, 1994 (Tamil Nadu Act 21 of 1994) (hereinafter called "the done" which expression shall where these context admits include its successors and assigns) of the OTHER PART;

WHEREAS, the donor is well and sufficiently entitled free from encumbrances to the piece or parcel of land and premises hereinafter described and intended to be hereby granted, conveyed and assigned;

AND WHEREAS, the donor has agreed to transfer the said piece or parcel of land and premises to the donee as a gift subject to the payment by the donee of all existing and future taxes, charges, assessments and ground rent in respect of the same and the donee has agreed to accept the same subject to the such conditions;

AND WHEREAS, the said piece or parcel of land and premises is of the value of Rs_____________________for the purpose of stamp duty;

NOW THIS INDENTURE WITNESSETH that the donor doth hereby give, grant, convey and assign unto the donee who hereby accepts the same ALL THAT piece or parcel of land bearing Survey No_____________, situated in the village of_____________In the registration sub-district of_____________in the registration district ___________And more particularly described in the Schedule hereunder written TOGETHER with all buildings, trees commons, liberties, privileges, easements, advantages and appurtenances whatsoever to the said piece or parcel of land, buildings and premises or any of them in anywise appertaining or heretofore occupied or enjoyed therewith AND all the estate right, title, interest, property, claim and demand whatsoever of the donor into and upon the same premises TO HAVE TO HOLD the said piece or parcel of land and premises hereby granted, conveyed and assigned unto the donee for ever AND the donor doth hereby covenant with the donee that the donor now hath good right to grant, convey and assign the premises hereby granted, conveyed and assigned unto the donee in the manner aforesaid AND that the donee shall and may at all times hereafter peaceably and quietly possess and enjoy the said premises free from all encumbrances whatsoever without any lawful eviction, interruption, claim or demand whatsoever from or by the donor or any person claiming under or in trust for him AND further that the donor and all persons having or lawfully or equitable claiming any estate or interest in the said premises or any part thereof from under or in trust for the donor or form or under any of his ancestors shall and will from time to time and at all times hereafter at the request and cost of the donee do execute and register or cause to be executed and registered all such acts, deeds and things whatsoever for further and more perfectly assuring, the said premises and every part thereof unto the donee in the manner aforesaid or as shall or may be reasonably required.

The Schedule above referred to

ALL THAT piece or parcel of land and premises situated in the village/town of ___________________in the registration sub-district of____________________in the registration district of______________________and bounded on the north by___________on the south by_______________________on the east by_______________________and on the west by_________________________bearing Re-survey No________________and Old Survey No_______________and containing on the whole by admeasurement be the same more or less).

Signed, sealed and delivered by the above names in the presence of.

Signed by the Executive Authority/Commissioner/Secretary of________________the village panchayat/panchayat union council/district panchayat in the presence of.

The common seal of the village panchayat/panchayat union council/district panchayat was hereunto affixed in the presence of_______________

IN WITNESS whereof the Donor hath hereunto set his hand and seal and the common seal of the village panchayat/panchayat union council/district panchayat of .... the donee was hereunto affixed the day and year first above written.

SCHEDULE-II

[See Rules-4 (2) and 5 (2)]

Form-II (a)

Transfer by Sale by a Panchayat to a Private Person

THIS INDENTURE made the______________________day of________________________year of between the Village Panchayat/Panchayat Union Council/District Panchayat of_______________________constituted under Tamil Nadu Panchayats Act, 1994 (Tamil Nadu Act 21 of 1994) (hereinafter called the vendor which expression shall where the contexts admits include its successors and assigns) of the one part and____________son of________________residing at_________________(hereinafter called which expression shall where the context admits include his heirs, executors, administrators, legal representatives and assigns) of the other part.

WHEREAS, the vendor is possessed of and entitled to and the piece or parcel of land and premises described in the schedule hereto and has agreed with the purchaser for sale to him of the same subject to the quit-rent (if any) payable in respect of the same but otherwise free from encumbrances, for the sum of Rs_____________,

AND WHEREAS, the Collector of_______________district by an order No___________, dated the _____________has sanctioned the sale of the property hereinafter contained;

AND WHEREAS, the Government of Tamil Nadu have also by an order No________________________dated the ______________________sanctioned the sale of the property hereinafter contained;

AND WHEREAS, due notice of the sale of the property hereinafter contained has been given in accordance with the provisions of the rules relating thereto;

NOW THIS INDENTURE WITNESSETH that in pursuance of the said agreement and in consideration of the sum of Rs___________paid to the vendor by the purchaser on or before the execution of these presents (the receipt whereof the vendor doth hereby acknowledge) the vendor as beneficial owner and in pursuance of every statutory and other authority hereunto enabling it doth hereby grant, convey and assign unto the purchaser ALL THAT piece or parcel of land situated in and more particularly described in the schedule hereunder written and which together with the message or tenement erected thereon is commonly called or known as _______________TOGETHER with all buildings, godowns, trees commons, hedges, ditches, fences, ways, waters, watercourses, liberties, privileges, easements, advantages and appurtenances whatsoever to the said piece or parcel of land message and premises or any of them in anywise appertaining or heretofore occupied or enjoyed therewith AND all the estate right, title interest, property-claim and demand whatsoever of the vendor into and upon the same premises TO HAVE AND TO HOLD the said piece or parcel of land message and premises hereby granted, conveyed and assigned and to the purchaser for ever AND the Vendor doth hereby covenant with the purchaser that the vendor now hath good right to grant, convey and assign the premises hereby granted, conveyed and assigned unto the purchaser in manner aforesaid AND that the purchaser shall and may at all times hereafter peaceably and quietly possess and enjoy the said premises free from all encumbrances whatsoever and receive the rents and profits thereof without any lawful eviction, interruption, claim or demand whatsoever from or by the vendor or any other person or persons AND further that the vendor and all persons having or lawfully or equitable claiming any estate or interest in the said premises or any of them or any part thereof from under or in trust for the vendor shall and will from time-to-time and at all times hereafter at the request and cost of the purchaser do execute and register or cause to be executed and registered all such acts, deeds and things whatsoever for further and more perfectly assuring, the said premises and every part thereof unto the purchaser in the manner aforesaid as shall or may be reasonably required AND the purchaser doth hereby covenant with the vendor that he the purchaser as aforesaid will at all times hereafter pay all assessments and taxes that may be reasonably required AND the purchaser doth hereby upon the said premises hereby conveyed by the Government of Tamil Nadu under any rules that are now or may hereafter be in force for the levy of assessments and taxes on lands and premises of a like nature.

The Schedule above referred to

ALL THAT piece or parcel of land and premises situated in the village/town of__________________in the registration sub-district of__________________in the registration district of bearing Re-survey No.______________and Old Survey No.________________and bounded on the north by__________on the south by______________________on the east by__________________and on the west by_________________________and containing admeasurement _______________________or there about.

Signed by the Executive Authority/Commissioner/Secretary of the village panchayat/panchayat union council/ district panchayat_______________in the presence of.

The common seal of the village panchayat/panchayat union council/district panchayat was hereunto affixed in the presence of_____________

Signed, sealed and delivered by the above names in the presence of.

IN WITNESS whereof common seal of the village panchayat/panchayat union council/district panchayat of _______________________was hereunto affixed and__________________has herewith affixed his hand and seal the day and year first above written.

Form-II (b)

Transfer by Exchange by a Village Panchayat/Panchayat Union Council/ District Panchayat to a Private Person

THIS INDENTURE made the____________________day of______________Year of__________________BETWEEN the village panchayat/panchayat union council/district panchayat of_______________________Constituted under the Tamil Nadu Panchayats Act, 1994 (Tamil Nadu Act 21 of 1994) hereinafter called village "the panchayats" which expression shall where the contest admits include its successors and assigns) of the ONE PART and____________________, son of ______________________residing at_________________(hereinafter called "the party" which expression shall where the context admits include his heirs, executors, administrators, legal representative and assigns) of the OTHER PART;

WHEREAS, the panchayat is well and truly entitled to and possessed of the piece or parcel of land more particularly described in the first schedule hereunder together with the buildings thereon free from encumbrances and the party is also well and truly entitled to and possessed of the piece of parcel of land more particularly described in the second schedule hereunder together with the building thereon free from encumbrances.

AND WHEREAS, the panchayat and the party hereto have agree to effect such exchange as is hereinafter contained of the said pieces or parcels of land more particularly described in the first and second schedules hereunder respective;

AND WHEREAS, the Collector of____________________district by an order No._______________, dated the ________________has sanctioned the exchange of the properties in the manner hereinafter contained;

AND WHEREAS, the Government of Tamil Nada have also by an order No.________dated the ________sanctioned the exchange of the properties in the manner hereinafter contained;

AND WHEREAS, due notice of the exchange in the manner hereinafter contained has been given in accordance with the provisions of the rules relating thereto;

NOW THAT INDENTURE WITNESSETH that in consideration of the conveyance by the party hereinafter contained the panchayat in pursuance of every statutory and other authority hereunto enabling it doth hereby grant, convey and assign unto the party all that piece or parcel of land of the value of Rs.________________or thereabouts situated in _________________and more particularly described in the first schedule hereunder written and coloured on the map or plan marked A hereunto annexed TOGETHER with all buildings, trees, commons, hedges, ditches, fences, ways, waters, water-courses, liberties, privileges, easements, advantages and appurtenances whatsoever to the said piece or parcel of land and premises or any of them in anywise appertaining or heretofore occupied or enjoyed therewith AND all the estate, right, title, interest, property claim and demand whatsoever of the panchayat into and upon the same premises to HAVE AND TO HOLD the said piece or parcel of land and premises hereby granted and assigned or expressed so to be unto the party for ever and the party doth hereby covenant with the panchayat that he, the party, will at all times hereafter pay the assessment or ground rent of___________________or such other amount as the Collector of ____________________may, from time-to-time, determine and any other ground-rent assessment and taxes that are or may from time-to-time be levied upon the said piece or parcel of land or premises by the Central Government or the Government of Tamil Nadu or by any local or other authority AND THIS INDENTURE FURTHER WITNESSETH that in consideration of the conveyance by the panchayat herein before contained the party doth hereby grant, convey and assign unto the panchayat all that piece or parcel of land of the value of ____________rupees or thereabouts situated in_________and being more particularly described in the second schedule hereunder written and coloured on the map or plan marked B hereto annexed TOGETHER with all buildings, trees, commons, hedges, ditches, fences, ways, waters, water courses, liberties, privileges, easements, advantages and appurtenances whatsoever to the said piece or parcel of land and premises or any of them in anywise appertaining or heretofore occupied or enjoyed therewith AND all the estate, right, title, interest, property-claim and demand whatsoever of the party into and upon such last-mentioned premises TO HAVE AND TO HOLD the said piece or parcel of land and premises lastly herein before expressed to be hereby granted, conveyed and assigned unto the panchayat for ever and the panchayat doth hereby covenant with the party that the panchayat will at all times, hereafter pay the assessments and taxes that are or may, from time-to-time be levied upon the said piece or parcel of land or premises by the Central Government or the Government of Tamil Nadu or by any local or other authority AND THE PARTIES HERETO MUTUALLY COVENANT AND AGREE EACH WITH OTHER OF THEM that notwithstanding any act deed or thing done or executed or knowingly suffered to the contrary they now have good right to grant, convey and assign, respectively, the said premises expressed to be hereby granted, conveyed and assigned in manner aforesaid and that either party shall and may at all times hereafter peacefully and quietly possess and enjoy such last-mentioned premises and receive the rents and profits thereof without any lawful eviction, interruption, claim or demand whatsoever from or by the other party or any person or persons lawfully or equitably claiming from under or in trust for the said party and that free from all encumbrances whatsoever made or suffered by either party or any person or persons lawfully or equitably claiming as aforesaid AND FURTHER, that the parties and all person having or lawfully or equitably claiming any estate or interest in the said premises or any part thereof from under or in trust for any of the parties shall and will, from time-to-time and at all times hereafter at the request and cost of the other party do execute and register or cause to be executed and registered all such acts, deeds and things whatsoever for further and more perfectly assuring such last-mentioned premises and every part thereof unto the other party in manner aforesaid as shall or may be reasonably required

The First Schedule above referred to

All that piece or parcel of land and premises coloured_________In the plan marked A attached hereto and situate in the village of ____________________In the registration sub-district of_______________in the registration district of___________bearing Re-survey No.______________and Old Survey No. _______________bounded on the north by Re-survey No.________________, on the east by Re-survey No______________, on the south by____________and on the west by___________and containing by admeasurements__________or thereabouts.

The common seal of the panchayat of________________was hereunto affixed in the presence of:

Signed by the Executive Authority/Commissioner/Secretary of__________________village panchayat/panchayat union council/district panchayat in the presence of.

Signed sealed and delivered by the above named in the presence of____________________________

IN WITNESS WHEREOF, the common seal of the village panchayat/panchayat union council/district panchayat was hereunto affixed and hath hereunto set his hand and seal the day and year first above written.

The Second Schedule above referred to

ALL that piece or parcel of land and premises coloured ____________in the plan marked B attached hereto and situate in the village of____________In the registration sub-district of ____________in the registration district of ________and bounded on the north by.__________, on the south by_________on the east by ___________and on the west by__________, bearing Survey No.__________and containing on the whole_____________by admeasurements __________or thereabouts.

Signed by the Executives Authority/Commissioner/Secretary of the village panchayat/panchayat union council/ district panchayat of ____________In the presence of ___________

The common seal of the panchayat/panchayat union council/district panchayat was hereunto affixed in the presence of:

IN WITNESS WHEREOF, the common seal of the village panchayat/panchayat union council/district panchayat of _____________the donor was hereunto affixed and the donee hath hereunto set his hand and seal the day and year first above written.

Form-II (c)
Transfer by Mortgage by Village Panchayat/Panchayat Union Council/ District Panchayat to a Private Person

THIS INDENTURE made the____________day of_______year of between the village panchayat/panchayat union council/district panchayat of ___________constituted under the Tamil Nadu Panchayats Act, 1994 (Tamil Nadu Act 21 of 1994) (hereafter called "the mortgager" which expression shall where the context so admits include its successors and assigns) of the ONE PART AND son of_____________Residing at__________(hereinafter called "the Mortgagee" which expression shall where the context so admits include his heirs, executors, administrators, legal representatives and assigns) of the other part.

WHEREAS, the mortgager is well and truly entitled to and possessed of the piece or parcel of land and premises described in the schedule hereunder;

AND WHEREAS, the mortgagee has agreed to lend the mortgager the sum of Rs.___________on having the repayment thereof with interest at the rate hereinafter mentioned secured in manner hereinafter appearing;

AND WHEREAS, the Collector of______________district by an order No.___________dated the ______________has sanctioned the mortgage of the properties in manner hereinafter contained;

AND WHEREAS, the Government of Tamil Nadu have also by an order No.______________,dated the __________sanctioned the mortgage of the properties in the manner hereinafter contained;

AND WHEREAS, due notice of the mortgage in manner hereinafter contained has been given in accordance with the provisions of the rules relating thereto;

NOW THIS INDENTURE WITNESSETH that in consideration of the sum of Rs._______on or before the execution of these presents paid to the mortgager by the mortgage (the receipt where of the mortgager doth hereby acknowledge) the mortgager doth here by covenant with the mortgage that the mortgager will on demand pay to the mortgagee the sum of Rs.__________with interest thereon at the rate of Rs.__________per cent per annum;

AND THIS INDENTURE ALSO WITNESSETH that for the same consideration the mortgage doth hereby give and grant unto the mortgage a simple mortgagee of ALL THAT piece or parcel of land situated in ____________and more particularly described in the schedule hereunder written and which together with the message or tenement erected thereon is commonly called or known as ____________________TOGETHER with all buildings, godowns, trees, commons, hedges, ditches, fences, ways, waters, water-courses, liberties, privileges, easements, advantages and appurtenances whatsoever to the said piece or parcel of land message and premises or any of them in anywise appertaining heretofore or hereafter to be occupied or enjoyed therewith AND all the estate, right, title, interest, property-claim and demand whatsoever of the mortgager into and upon the same premises AND the mortgager doth hereby covenant with the mortgagee that the mortgager will so long as any money shall remain due on the security of these present keep all the messages and buildings now existing or hereafter to be erected on the said premises hereinbefore expressed to be hereby granted, conveyed and assigned in good and substantial repair and insured against loss or damage by fire in the sum of Rs.__________at the least in some office or offices approved by and in the name or names of the mortgagee and will duly and punctually pay all premiums and sums of money necessary for such purpose and for keeping such insurance on foot and also all quit-rent assessment rates taxes and other out-goings for the time being payable in respect of or charged upon the said premises or any of them and forthwith deliver to the mortgage the policy or policies of insurance and the receipt for every sum payable as aforesaid or in so delivering any policy or policies or receipt as aforesaid it shall be lawful for but not incumbent upon the mortgagee to enter into and upon the said premises and put the same into proper and substantial repair or (as the case may be) to insure and keep insured the said buildings in any sum not exceeding the amount aforesaid and to pay the premiums and all expenses incurred in so doing or (as the case may be) any such quit-rent assessment rates taxes or other out-goings as aforesaid AND further that the mortgager will forthwith repay to the mortgagee all such premiums, expenses and other moneys with interest thereon at the rate aforesaid from the time of each payment and that until repayment the hereby mortgaged premises shall stand charged with the amount to be repaid and interest thereon at the rate aforesaid and that all moneys received in respect of any insurance shall at the option of the mortgagee be applied either in reinstating or restoring the buildings insured or in or towards payment of the moneys for the time being owing on the security of these presents and the mortgager doth hereby covenant with the mortgagee that the mortgager now hath power to give and grant a simple mortgage unto the mortgagee AND it is hereby expressly agreed and declared that should the properties described in the schedule hereunder prove insufficient when sold to satisfy the amount due under this mortgagee the mortgager will be personally liable for the amount for the time being due and owing under this mortgage.

The Schedule above referred to

ALL THAT piece or parcel of land and premises situated in the village of .... in the registration sub-district of .... in the registration district of .... and bounded on the north by .... on the south by ...., on the east by .... and on the west by bearing Re-survey No........................ and Old Survey No................. and containing on the whole by admeasurements .... (be the same more or less).

Signed by the Executive Authority/Commissioner/Secretary of the village panchayat/panchayat union council/ district panchayat of .... in the presence of.

The common seal of the village panchayat/panchayat union council/district panchayat...................... was hereunto affixed in the presence of............

IN WITNESS whereof the common seal of the mortgager hath hereunto been affixed the day and year first above written.

Form-II (d)

Transfer by Gift by a Village Panchayat/Panchayat Union Council/ District Panchayat to a Private Person

THIS INDENTURE made the __________________Day of ______________Year of ________________BETWEEN the village panchayat/panchayat union council/district panchayat of ____________________ constituted under the Tamil Nadu Panchayats Act, 1994 (Tamil Nadu Act 21 of 1994) (hereinafter called "the donor" which expression shall where the context so admits include its successor and assigns) of the ONE PART and ______________________ son of ________________________, residing at ____ (hereinafter called "the donee" which expression shall where the context so admits include his heirs, executors, administrators and legal representatives and assigns) of the OTHER PART;

WHEREAS, the donor is well and sufficiently entitled free from encumbrances to the piece of land and premises hereinafter described and intended to be hereby granted, conveyed and assigned;

AND WHEREAS, the donor has agreed to transfer the said piece of land premises to the donee as a gift to be used for the purposes of ______________________Subject to the payment by the donee of all existing and future taxes, charges, assessments and ground-rent in respect of the same and the donee has agreed to accept the said piece of land and premises subject to the said conditions.

AND WHEREAS, the said piece of land and premises is of the value of Rs. _____________ for the purpose of stamp duty;

AND WHEREAS, the Collector of __________________ district by an order No._______dated the _______________ has sanctioned the gift of the property hereinafter contained.

AND WHEREAS, due notice of the gift in manner hereinafter contained has been given in accordance with the provisions of the rules relating thereto;

AND WHEHREAS, the Government of Tamil Nadu have also by an order No.__________dated the _______________ have sanctioned the gift of the property hereinafter contained.

NOW THIS INDENTURE WITNESSETH that the donor doth hereby give grant, convey and assign unto the donee who hereby accepts the same ALL THAT piece or parcel of land bearing Survey No.________________In the registration sub-district of _________________________in the registration district of ______________ and more particularly described in the schedule hereunder written TOGETHER with all buildings, trees, commons, hedges, ditches, fences, ways, waters, water courses, liberties, privileges, easements advantages and appurtenances whatsoever to the said piece or parcel of land, buildings and premises or any of them in any wise appertaining or hereto force occupied or enjoyed therewith. And all the estate, right, title, interest, property claim and demand whatsoever of the donor into and upon the same premises TO HAVE AND TO HOLD the said piece or parcel of land and premises hereby granted, conveyed and assigned unto the donee for ever AND the donor doth hereby covenant with the donee that the donor now hath good right to grant, convey and assign the premises hereby granted, conveyed and assigned unto the donee in the manner aforesaid AND that the donee shall and may at all times hereafter peaceably and quietly possess and enjoy the said premises free from all encumbrances whatsoever without any lawful eviction, interruption, claim or demand whatsoever from or by the donor AND further that the donor and all person having or lawfully or equitably claiming any estate or interest in the said premises or any part thereof from under or in trust for the donor shall and will from time-to-time, and at all times hereafter at the request and cost of the donee do execute and register or cause to be executed and registered all such acts, deeds and things whatsoever for further and more perfectly assuring the said premises and every part thereof unto the donee in manner aforesaid or as shall or may be reasonably required and the donee doth hereby covenant with the donor that he will at all times hereafter hear, pay and discharge all existing and future taxes or charges assessments payable in respect of the aforesaid land and premises inclusive of the ground rent or assessment of Rs. ______________________ of any other sum that may, from time-to-time, be levied as such upon the piece or parcel of land by the Collector of the district on behalf of the Central Government or the Government of Tamil Nadu.

The Schedule above referred to

ALL THAT piece or parcel of land and premises situated in the Village of ____________ in the registration sub-district of ________________in the registration district of _____________ and bounded on the north by ___________on the south by ______________on the east by ________________ and on the west by _________________ Bearing Survey No. ________and containing on the whole ______________ by admeasurements__________________ or thereabouts.

Signed by the Executive Authority/Commissioner/Secretary of the village panchayat/panchayat union council/ district panchayat of ________________in the presence of __________________

Signed sealed and delivered by the above named in the presence of __________________

The common seal of the village panchayat/panchayat union council/district panchayat was hereunto affixed in the presence of:

IN WITNESS whereof the common seal of the village panchayat/panchayat union council/district panchayat of ____________the donor was hereunto affixed and the donee hath hereunto set his hand and seal the day and year first above written.

SCHEDULE-III

[See Rules 6(2), 7(2) and 8(2)]

Form-III (a)

[See Rules 6(2) 7(2)]

Transfer by Lease of Own Lands to Private Person by Village Panchayat/ Panchayat Union Council/District Panchayat

THIS INDENTURE made the ___________________ day of ____________ Between the village panchayat/panchayat union council/district panchayat of ________________ constituted under the Tamil Nadu Panchayats Act, 1994 (Tamil Nadu Act 21 of 1994) (hereinafter called the lesser which expression where the context admits shall include its successors and assigns) of the One part and _____________ son of _____________ residing at _____________________ and carrying on business as ______________ (hereinafter called the lessee which expression where the context admits shall include his heirs, executors and administrators, legal representatives, and permitted assigns) of the other part. Whereas, the lessee has applied to the lessor for a lease of the property more particularly described in the first schedule hereunder for the period and at the rate of rent and subject to the terms and conditions hereinafter contained.
And Whereas the lessor has agreed to grant a lease of the said property in a manner hereinafter contained.
And Whereas the Collector __________________ by an order No. ___________ dated _______________________ has sanctioned the lease of the property on and subject to the special conditions contained in the second schedule hereunder.
And Whereas the Government of Tamil Nadu have also by an order No.________________dated the________________ sanctioned the transfer by lease of the properties in the manner hereinafter contained.

And Whereas due to notice of the lease of the property has been given in accordance with the provisions of the rules relating thereto.

NOW THIS INDENTURE WITNESSETH

1. That is consideration of the rent hereby and of the covenants by the lessee herein contained the lessor demises

unto the lessee. All the piece or parcel of land together with the building and premises known as ____________ situate in the registration sub-district of ________________ in the registration district of _________ bearing Survey No. __________________ for the term of __________________ year from the ______________ paying thereof in advance the monthly rent to Rs. ________________ clear of all deductions the first of such payments to be made on the ________________

The lease covenants with the lessor as follows:

2. To pay the reserved rent on or before the first day of each month in advance and in manner aforesaid.
   (a) To bear, pay and discharge all existing and future charges assessments and out goings payable in respect of the said premises inclusive of the ground rent of Rs. ______________ or any other sum that may, from time-to-time, be levied as such upon the piece or parcel of land by the Collector of the ____________ district on behalf of the Central Government or the Government of Tamil Nadu.
   (b) To keep the exterior and the interior of the demised premises and all additions thereto and the boundary walls and fences thereof and the rains soil and other pipes and sanitary and water apparatus and electric fittings and fixtures thereof in good and tenantable repair and condition.
   (c) Not to make or permit to be made under any circumstances any alterations in or additions to the demised buildings without the previous consent in writing of the lessor or its duly authorized officers provided always that if the lessee is permitted to make any alterations by the lessor or its duly authorized officers the lessee shall not be entitled to any compensation therefor.
   (d) To permit the lessor and its authorized officers, agents with or without workmen or others at all reasonable times on giving on days previous notice to enter upon the demised premises and to view the condition thereof and upon notice being given by the lessor or his authorized officers to repair within one month from the service of the notice in accordance therewith.
   (e) To observe and fulfil the terms and conditions prescribed by the Inspector and contained in the second schedule hereunder.
   (f) Not to assign, underlet or part with the possession of the demised premises or any part thereof without first obtaining the written consent of the lessor or its authorized officers.
   (g) To yield up the demised premises with all fixtures and additions thereto at the determination of the tenancy in good tenantable repair and condition in accordance with the covenants herein contained.
3. The lessor covenants with the lessee as follows:
   (i) The lessee paying the rent hereby reserved and observing and performing the several covenants and stipulations herein on his part contained shall peaceably hold, enjoy the demised premises during the said term without any interruption by the lessor or any person right fully claiming under or in trust for him.
   (ii) To carry out all repairs to main walls, roof and foundations due to fair reasonable wear and tear, the decision of the Executive Engineer for the time being of ______________ division as to the necessity for such repairs being final.
4. Provided always and it is hereby expressly agreed by and between the parties hereto as follows:
   (i) If the rent hereby reserved or any part thereof shall be unpaid for fourteen days after becoming payable (whether formally demanded or not) or if any covenant on the lessees part herein contained shall not be performed or observed or if the lessee or other person in whom for the time being the term hereby created shall be vested shall become insolvent then and in any of the said cases it shall be lawful for the lessor or its authorized officers at any time thereafter to re enter upon the demised premises or any part there of in the name of whole and thereupon this demise shall absolutely determine but without prejudice to the right of action of the lessor in respect of the breach of any of the lessees covenants herein contained.
   (ii) If at any time it appears to the Collector or the lessor (whose decision shall be final) that it is necessary in the public interest to determine the lease it shall be lawful for the said Collector or the lessor forthwith to cancel this lease by notice in writing addressed to the lessee at his last known place of residence and thereupon this demise shall absolutely determine and the lessee shall not be entitled to any compensation whatsoever in respect of such determination except a proportionate abatement of any rent that may have been paid by the lessee in advance.

The First Schedule above referred to

All that piece or parcel of land and premises situated in the village/town of ____________in the registration sub-district of ____________________ in the registration district of __________________ and bounded on the north by ______________ on the south by ________________ on the west by __________________ and on the east by ____________________bearing Survey No.________________ and Door No. and containing on the whole by admeasurement ________________ be the same more or less.

The Second Schedule above referred to

Conditions imposed by the Collector __________________ of the district _______________signed by the Executive Authority/Commissioner/Secretary of ______________________ panchayat/panchayat union council/district panchayat of the presence of _______________.

The common seal of the village panchayat/panchayat union council/district panchayat of _______________ was herewith affixed in the presence of _______________

Signed sealed and delivered by the above named in the presence of _______________

IN WITNESS whereof the common seal of the village panchayat/panchayat union/district panchayat of _____________the lessor was hereunto affixed and the issued hath hereunto set his hand and seal the day and year first above written.

Form-III (b)

[See Rule 8(2)]

Transfer by Lease of Vested Lands to the Private Person by the Village Panchayat/ Panchayat Union Council/District Panchayat

THIS INDENTURE made the ________________ day of _____________between the village panchayat/panchayat union council/district panchayat of __________________ constituted under the Tamil Nadu Panchayats Acts, 1994 (Tamil Nadu Act 21 of 1994) (hereinafter called the lessor which expression where the context admits shall include its successors and assigns) of the One part and ___________son of ____________(hereinafter called the lessee which expression where the context admits shall include his heirs executors, administrators, legal representative and permitted assigns) of the Other part.

WHEREAS, the lessee has applied to the lessor for a lease of the property more particularly described, in the first schedule hereunder for the period and at the rate of rent and subject to the terms and conditions hereinafter contained.

And Whereas, the lessor has agreed to grant a lease of the said property in manner hereinafter contained.

And Whereas the Collector of ________________ district by an order No. _________________dated ____________ has sanctioned the lease of the property on and subject to the special conditions contained in the second schedule hereunder (retain if necessary).

And Whereas the Government of Tamil Nadu have also by an order No._________dated the ________________ sanctioned the transfer by lease of the property in the manner hereinafter contained.

And Whereas due notice of the lease of the property has been given in accordance with the provisions of the rules relating thereto;

Now this Indenture Witnesseth as follows:

(1) in consideration of the rent hereby reserved and of the covenants by the lessee herein contained the lessor demises unto the lessee all that piece of land forming part of the road side/street margin and more particularly described in the schedule attached hereto for a term of ________________ years from the _______________ paying therefor in advance the rent of Rs. _________________ for each year clear of all deductions the first of such payments to be made on the day of ___________________________.

(2) The lessee covenants with the lessor as follows:

  (a) To pay the reserved rent on before the 1st day of each year in advance and in the manner aforesaid.

  (b) To bear, pay and discharge all existing and future taxes, charges, assessments and outgoing payable in respect of the demised land (inclusive of the ground rent of Rs. ________________________ or any other sum that may, from time-to-time, be levied as such upon the piece or parcel of land by the Collector of the _______________district on behalf of the Central Government or the Government of Tamil Nadu).

  (c) To keep the demised land in good condition.

  (d) Not to make or permit to be made under any circumstances any alterations in or additions to the demised land without the previous consent to writing of the lessor or its duly authorized officers provided always that if the lessee is permitted to make any alternatives by the lessor or its duly authorised officer the lessee shall not be entitled to any compensation therefor.

  (e) To permit the lessor and its authorized officers or agents with or without workmen at all reasonable times on giving one days previous notice to enter upon the demised land and to view the condition thereof.

  (f) To use the demised land only for the purposes for which it is leased.

  (g) Not to assign or under let or part with the possession of the demised land or any part thereof without first obtaining the written consent of the lessor or its authorized officers.

  (h) To yield up the demised land in good condition in accordance with the covenants herein contained.

3. The lessor covenants with the lessee that the lessee paying the rent hereby reserved and observing and

performing the several covenants and stipulations herein on his part contained shall peaceably hold and enjoy the demised land during the said term without any interruption by the lessor or any person rightly claiming under or in trust for the lessor.

4. The lease is liable to be terminated at any time within the period of the lease without payment of any compensation to the lessee, if in the opinion of the lessor or of the District Collector, it is necessary in the public interest to remove any structure erected on the demised land.
5. If the rent hereby reserved or any part thereof is not paid, whether formally demanded or not, in accordance with the stipulation herein contained or if any covenants on the lessee part herein contained shall not be performed or observed or if the lessee or other persons in whom for the time being the term hereby erected shall be vested shall become insolvent, then and in any of the said cases, if shall be lawful for the lessor or its authorized officers at any time thereafter to re-enter upon the demised land or any part thereof in the name of the whole and thereupon this demised shall absolutely determine but without prejudice to the right of action of the lessor in respect of the breach of any of the lessees covenants herein contained.
6. If either party shall desire to determine the present demise and shall give to the other party three calendar months previous notice in writing of such desire then immediately on the expiration of the three calendar months the present demise and everything herein contained shall cease and be void but without prejudice of the remedies of either party against the other in respect of any antecedent claim or breach of covenant.
7. On the expiry of the period for which the lease is granted unless the lease is renewed by the lessor or when the lease is terminated under clause 4 the lessee is bound to remove all the structures existing on the demised land. If the lessee fails to remove the structure within three months from the date on which the lease expired or within three months from the date of the receipt of a notice under clause 4 whichever is earlier the lessor shall be at liberty to cause the same to be removed without notice to the lessee and the lessee hereby makes himself liable for the cost of such removal and the lessee shall not claim any compensation for the structure so removal or for any damage or loss caused by such removals.

The First Schedule above referred to

ALL THAT piece or parcel of land and premises situated in the village of_____in the registration sub-district of_________in the registration district of___and bounded on the north by_________on the south by________on the west by_________and on the east by_____bearing Survey No.____and Door No.______and containing on the whole by admeasurement be the same more or less.

The Second Schedule above referred to

Conditions imposed by the Collector of_______district.

Signed by the Executive Authority/Commissioner/Secretary to_______village panchayat/panchayat union council/ district panchayat in the presence of_______

The common seal of the village panchayat/panchayat union council/district panchayat was hereunto affixed in the presence of

Signed, sealed and delivered by the above named in the presence of_________

In witness whereof the common seal of the village panchayat/panchayat union council/district panchayat of the lessor was hereunto affixed and the lessee hereunto set his hand and seal the day and year first above written.

3.4.2 Instructions Regarding Maintenance of Unreserved Forests

1. **Grazing**—(a) The unreserved forest in panchayat areas should be mainly used for the grazing of village cattle under cover of permits issued by the panchayat.

(b) Goat browsing in the forest should not be allowed.

(c) The forest areas should be closed to all grazing for two or three months every year. If it is not convenient to close the entire forest, it should be divided into three convenient blocks and each block closed in turn, one after the other.

2. **Felling or sale by auction**—(1) The panchayat should not cut and remove or sell by auction, live trees in unreserved forest without the previous sanction of the Collector. In order to meet the legitimate needs of the villagers, coupes should be laid out and they should be worked under the simple coppice system. The firewood, thorns and small timber for agricultural requirements should be made available only from the coupe of the year.

Note: Simple coppice system is the method of regeneration, under which the trees are cut flush with the ground with a view to its regeneration from coppice shoots springing from the stumps. Such clear felled areas should be closed to grazing for a period of about five years so that the tender coppice shoots springing from the stumps are not damaged by cattle.

Under any circumstances felling should not be allowed in slopes which are steeper than one in three.

If there are any sandal trees in the area, the panchayat will not be entitled to extract them or to receive the revenue from the sandal wood. The panchayat will be held responsible for the proper protection of these trees.

3. **Minor forest produce**—The right to collect minor forest produce in the forest may be sold in auction by the panchayat. The sale will be subject to confirmation by the Collector.

4. **Miscellaneous**—Subject to the previous approval of the Collector the panchayat may allow the removal of sand, metal, etc. at the rates fixed by the Collector.

5. **Regeneration**—Steps should be taken to regenerate, the blank areas by growing trees of fast-growing species like Prosephis, Sissoo, Eucalyptus, Rostrata, etc.

6. **Protection**—The panchayat should employ a watchman whose duty will be to protect the unreserved forest and maintain their boundaries. In cases which do not warrant the appointment of a full-time watchman, the panchayat may depute its sweeper to keep watch over the unreserved forest on payment of some additional remuneration to him.

7. **General**—The Tehsildar or the Deputy Tehsildar and the Revenue Divisional Officer should inspect the areas as often as practicable.

8. **Accounts**—Correct accounts of revenue and expenditure should be maintained by the panchayat as detailed below:

(i) Lease of the right of collection of minor forest produce sold in auction and sale of firewood, thorns and small timber for agricultural requirements through coppice system should be entered in the Miscellaneous Demand Register in a separate set of pages.

(ii) Other miscellaneous items such as removal of sand, metal, etc., should be entered in the Miscellaneous Sales Register.

(iii) The receipt from the unreserved forests maintained by a panchayat should be shown in the account under "Receipts—Ordinary-VI Remunerative Enterprises" opening a new head "Unreserved Forests—Receipts".

(iv) The expenditure on pay of establishment employed for the maintenance of forests and for growing trees in blank areas, and on payment of rent under Section 120 (1) (b) of the Tamil Nadu Panchayats Act, 1994 should be exhibited in the account under "Expenditure—Ordinary-V Remunerative Enterprises" against a separate head "Maintenance of Unreserved Forests—(i) Pay of establishments; (ii) Contingencies".

(G.O. Ms. No. 91, Local Administration Department, dated 20th January 1955)

3.5 ADMINISTRATION

3.5.1 Use of Minority Languages for Official Purpose by the Panchayat

1. G.O. Ms. No. 2223, Rural Development and Local Administration, dated 22.9.1966
2. From the Director of Rural Development, Chennai, Lr. Roc. No. 88788/2000/PCA-4, dated 14.3.2001
3. G.O. Ms. No. 83, Backward and Most Backward Classes Department, dated 29.12.1993

(1) In supersession of the orders issued in the G.O. first cited the Government directs that the local areas for the purpose of use of minority languages for official purposes in Tamil Nadu is shown in the Annexure to the order.

(2) The Government also directs that the following steps shall be taken in regard to use of minority language or languages in the said local areas, besides the use of the official language:

(i) All important notices, electoral rolls, etc., should be published in the official language as well as in the minority language or languages.

(ii) Forms, etc. to be used by the public should be printed both in the official language and in the minority language or languages.

(iii) Correspondence with Government offices can be permitted in the minority language also.

(iv) Arrangement should be made for translating important regulations and bye-laws in the mother-tongue of linguistic minority groups.

(G.O. Ms. No.128, Rural Development (C-4) Department, dated 23rd April 2001)

ANNEXURE

Sl. No.	Name of the District	Name of Taluk	Name of Non-Municipal/Town Panchayat areas of the Taluk	Name/Names of minority language/languages
1.	Thiruvallur	Tiruttani	Tiruttani	Telugu
		Thiruvallur	Thiruvallur	Telugu
		Ponneri	Ponneri	Telugu
		Gummidipoondi	Gummidipoondi	Telugu
		Uthukottai	Uthukottai	Telugu
		Pallipattu	Pallipattu	Telugu
2.	Vellore	Gudiyatham	Gudiyatham	Telugu
3.	Dharmapuri	Hosur	Hosur	Telugu & Kannada
		Denkanikotta	Denkanikotta	Telugu & Kannada
		Krishnagiri	Krishnagiri	Telugu
4.	Erode	Gobichettipalayam	Gobichettipalayam	Telugu
		Perundurai	Perundurai	Telugu
		Sathyamangalam	Sathayamangalam	Telugu & Kannada
5.	Coimbatore	Coimbatore	Coimbatore	Telugu
		Udamapet	Udumalpet	Telugu
		Palladam	Palladam	Telugu
		Avinasi	Avinasi	Telugu
		Pollachi	Pollachi	Telugu
		Mettupalayam	Mettupalayam	Telugu & Kannada
6.	Nilgris	Udhagamandalam	Udhagamandalam	Kannada
		Coonoor	Coonoor	Kannada
		Kothagiri	Kothagiri	Kannada
		Gudalur	Gudalur	Malayalam
7.	Dindigul	Kodaikanal	Kodaikanal	Telugu
		Palani	Palani	Telugu
8.	Madurai	Periyakulam	Periyakulam	Telugu
		Thirumangalam	Thirumangalam	Telugu
9.	Virudhunagar	Virudhunagar	Virudhunagar	Telugu
		Sathoor	Sathoor	Telugu
		Aruppukkottai	Aruppukkottai	Telugu
10.	Kanyakumari	Vilavankode	Vilavankode	Malayalam

3.5.2 Adoption of Tamil as Official Language

1. G.O. Ms. No. 1748, Rural Development and Local Administration, dated 2.8.1962
2. Govt. Memo No. 52210/C2/63-7, dated 24.12.1963
3. From the Director of Rural Development, Chennai, Lr. Roc.No.88788/2000/PCA-4, dated 14.3.2001

In supersession of the orders should in the G.O. first cited and Government Memo second cited, the Government direct that Tamil shall be the official language of the panchayats and that all communications from that panchayats shall be in Tamil. The Government also direct that English shall be used for the following proposals only:

(i) communications to be addressed to the Accountant General, Chennai;
(ii) in all correspondence addressed to Courts and Central Government Offices; and
(iii) in all statutory orders which are subject to appeal to or revision, to any authority in respect of whose office a notification under Section 4 of the Tamil Nadu Official Language Act, 1956 (Madras Act XXXIX of 1956) has not been issued by the State Government.

(G.O. Ms. No. 127, Rural Development (C-4) Department, dated 23rd April 2001)

3.5.3 Grant of Holidays by Panchayats to its Institutions

1. **Short title**—These rules may be called the Tamil Nadu Panchayats (Grant of Holidays by Panchayats to Institutions Under its Control) Rules, 1999.

2. **Holidays to institutions under the control of panchayat**—(1) The offices and institutions under the control of a panchayat shall be permitted to observe only such public and special local holidays as may be sanctioned by the Government or respective District Collector, from time-to-time in respect of Government offices and institutions.

(2) No panchayat shall grant to offices and institutions under its control holidays other than those sanctioned to Government offices and institutions, without the previous permission of the Inspector.

(G.O. Ms. No.124, Rural Development (C4) Department, dated 7th July 1999)

3.5.4 Travelling Allowance and Other Allowances Payable to Elected Representatives of Panchayats

1. **Short title**—These rules may be called the Tamil Nadu Panchayats (Travelling Allowance and Other Allowances Payable to the Presidents, Chairman and Members of Panchayats and their Committee) Rules, 1999.

2. **Definition**—In these rules, unless the context otherwise requires, "functionary" means the president, vice-president or member of a village panchayat or chairman, vice-chairman or member of a panchayat union council or district panchayat.

3. **Fixed monthly travelling allowance for the journey performed within the jurisdiction**—(1) Every president of the village panchayat, chairman and member of the panchayat union council and district panchayat shall be paid fixed monthly travelling allowance from the funds of the panchayat concerned at the rate fixed by the Government from time-to-time.

(2) They shall not claim any other travelling allowance other than the fixed travelling allowance for any journey made within their jurisdiction.

4. **Daily or travelling allowance for journey performed out side the jurisdiction**—The rates of daily allowance and travelling allowance admissible to a functionary of a panchayat for attending to official work outside his jurisdiction shall be as determined by the Government, from time-to-time:

Provided that travelling allowance shall not be admissible for a journey undertaken within eight kilometres from his headquarters:

Provided further that when a journey is performed to, and from, Chennai, the rate of daily allowance shall be increased by one hundred per cent on the rate specified above.

5. **Admissibility of daily allowance**—(1) The daily allowance shall be admissible to a functionary for a block of twenty-four hours absence from his headquarters for the journey exceeding eight kilometres for attending to official work. The following percentage of daily allowance is admissible for a journey undertaken by him for more than eight kilometres from his headquarters:

(a)	Daily allowance for not more than six hours	30 per cent
(b)	Daily allowance for more than six hours but less than twelve hours	70 per cent
(c)	Daily allowance for more than twelve hours	100 per cent

6. **Place of headquarters**—Where a functionary resides within the jurisdiction of the village panchayat or panchayat union council or district panchayat concerned, but at a place different from where the office of village panchayat or panchayat union or district panchayat concerned is situated, such place of residence shall be treated as head quarters for the purpose of calculating travelling allowance.

7. **Requirement of panchayat resolution**—Where a functionary has to perform journey outside his jurisdiction for attending to official work and claim travelling allowance for such journey, it shall be sanctioned by a resolution of the panchayat concerned:

Provided that the prior sanction of the Inspector shall be obtained for a journey to be undertaken by a functionary outside the district.

8. **Sitting fees for attending panchayat meeting**—(1) Every functionary who attends the meeting of the panchayat concerned shall be paid sitting fees at the rates as determined by the Government from time-to-time.

(2) The expenditure for travelling allowance and sitting fees shall be met from the funds of the panchayat concerned.

9. **Power of the Government to restrict the travelling allowance**—Notwithstanding anything contained in these rules, the Government shall have power to restrict the amount of travelling allowance payable for a month or a year to any of the functionaries.

(G.O.Ms.No.258, Rural Development Department (C4), 14th December 1999)

3.5.5 Travelling Allowance – Daily Allowance – Sitting Fee for Elected Representatives

The Government fix the following rates for fixed monthly travelling allowance, daily allowance and sitting fees to the chairman and members of district panchayat, chairman and members of panchayat union council and president and members of village panchayats.

(1) Fixed Travelling allowance for undertaking tours with in the panchayat area for attending to the work of the panchayat.

Village Panchayat President	Rs. 300/-
Chairman Panchayat Union Council	Rs. 500/-
Panchayat Union Ward Members	Rs. 200/-
District Panchayat Chairman	Rs. 1000/-
Members of District Panchayat	Rs. 300/-

(2) Travelling and Daily allowance for tours made on Official work outside the area of the panchayat and outside district.

(a) Table

Sl. No.	*Post*	*Train*	*Eligibility of Daily Allowance*	*Bus Fare*
1.	Chairman and Members of District Panchayat	I Class	Rs. 50/-	Actual Bus fare
2.	Chairman Panchayat Union	I Class	Rs. 30/-	Actual Bus fare
3.	Panchayat Council Members	II Class	Rs. 30-/	Actual Bus fare
4.	Village Panchayat President	I Class	Rs. 20/-	Actual Bus fare
5.	Village Panchayat Members	II Class		Actual Bus fare

(b) No Travelling allowance will be paid for journeys undertaken within 8 kms of Head-quarters.

(c) For Journeys exceeding 8 kms travelling allowance shall be paid as follows:
   (1) Journeys not exceeding 6 hours: 30 per cent D.A.
   (2) Journeys not exceeding 6 to 12 hours: 70 per cent D.A.
   (3) Journeys exceeding 12 hours : 100 per cent D.A.

(d) To claim daily and travelling allowance by the members of panchayat for journeys undertaken outside the jurisdiction of the panchayat, resolution of the concerned panchayat shall be obtained.

(e) If journey is to be undertaken outside the district, prior sanction of the Inspector (District Collector) shall be obtained.

Sitting fees for attending meetings of panchayat:

Sl. No.	*Name of the Post*	*Sitting Fees*
1.	District Panchayat Chairman and Members	Rs. 100/- (Allowed only for two meetings in a month)
2.	(a) Chairman, Panchayat Union Council	Rs. 75/- (Allowed only for two meetings in a month)
	(b) Members of Panchayat Union Council	Rs. 50/- (Allowed only for two meetings in a month)
	(c) Village Panchayat Presidents	Rs. 50/- (Allowed only for two meetings in a month)
	(d) Village Panchayat Members	Rs. 25/- (Allowed only for two meetings in a month)
3.	The expenditure to be sanctioned for the above purposes shall be incurred from the funds of district panchayats/panchayat unions/village panchayat	

(G.O. Ms. No. 362, Rural Development (C1) Department, dated 20th December 1997)

3.5.6 Revision of Fixed Travelling Allowance to Elected Representatives of Panchayats

The fixed travelling allowance sanctioned to elected representatives of three tier local bodies are as follows:

(a) Village Panchayat President	:	Rs. 330/-
(b) Chairman Panchayat Union	:	Rs. 550/-
(c) Members of Panchayat Union	:	Rs. 220/-
(d) District Panchayat President	:	Rs. 1,100/-
(e) District Panchayat Members	:	Rs. 330/-

(G.O. Ms. No. 226, Rural Development (C1) Department, dated 25th October 1999)

3.5.7 Manner of Publication of Notification or Notice and Service of Documents to the Public

1. Short title—These rules may be called the Tamil Nadu Panchayats (Manner of Publication of Notification or Notice and Manner of Service of Documents to the Public) Rules, 2000.

2. Definition—In these rules, unless the context otherwise requires, "Act" means the Tamil Nadu Panchayats Act, 1994 (Tamil Nadu Act 21 of 1994).

3. Publication in Gazette—Save as otherwise expressly provided in the Act or in the rules made thereunder every notification under the Act, other than one issued by the Government or the Inspector shall be published in the Official Gazette of the district to which such notification applies both in English and in Tamil:

Provided that the Government shall have power to direct that any such notification:

(a) shall be published in the said gazette in English and in Tamil if necessary;

(b) shall, instead of being published in the said gazette, be published in any other manner specified by them; or

(c) shall, in addition to being published in the said gazette, be published in such manner as may be specified by them.

4. Manner of publication of document, order or notice other than meeting notice—(1) Whenever a village panchayat or a panchayat union council or a district panchayat sets apart any place for any purpose or prohibits the doing of anything in any place, the Executive Authority or the Commissioner or the Secretary, as the case may be, shall cause to be put up in such place a notice in Tamil and also in a language other than Tamil in which the electoral roll is published in such place, specifying the purpose for which such place has been set apart or the doing of any act is prohibited in such place.

(2) Save as otherwise expressly provided in the Act or in the rules made thereunder, every notice, other than a notice of the meeting to the public under the Act shall be published:

(a) by affixing a copy thereof in some conspicuous place in the panchayat village;

(b) by affixing a copy thereof in the office of the village panchayat or panchayat union council or district panchayat, as the case may be;

(c) by affixing a copy thereof in the chavadi or chavadies, if any, in the village to which such notice relates to; and

(d) by beat of drum in the village or villages to which such notice relates to.

5. Notwithstanding anything contained in the above rules, any notification issued under Section 4, 8, 11, 20 or 32 of the Act

(a) shall be published in the Tamil Nadu Government Gazette and a copy of the notification in Tamil shall be affixed in some conspicuous place by the Executive Authority or the Commissioner or the Secretary as the case may be in the office of the village panchayat or panchayat union council or district panchayat concerned and in the chavadi or chavadies, if any, in the village; and

(b) shall be published in the District Gazette both in English and in Tamil.

6. Manner of service of document or notice other than a notice of the meeting—(1) When any document or notice other than a notice of the meeting is required by the Act of any rules or bye-law or regulation or order made thereunder to be served on or sent to any person the service or sending thereof shall be effected in the manner specified below and a record of service maintained in the office of the village panchayat or panchayat union council or district panchayat, as the case may be:

(a) by giving or tendering the document or notice in person to the person concerned.

(b) if such person is not found, which shall be recorded by the person deputed for effecting the service, by giving or tending the same to an adult member or servant of his family; or by leaving such document or notice securely at a conspicuous place, at his last known place of abode or business, which shall be specified in the record of service; or

(c) if such person is reported to be not residing in the village and his address elsewhere is known to the Executive Authority or the Commissioner or Secretary, as the case may be, by sending the same by registered post with acknowledgement due; or

(d) if none of the means aforesaid is available, by affixing the same in some conspicuous part of such place of abode or business.

(2) The manner of service specified above shall be tried one after another in the above order and not in any other order.

7. Name of the owner or occupier—When only one person is the owner or occupier of any building or land, it shall not be necessary to name the owner or occupier in the notice and in the case of joint names or occupiers, it shall be sufficient to serve it on or sent it to one of such owners or occupiers.

8. Calculation of period of service of notice or bill or document or form—Whenever in any bill, notice, form or other document served or sent under the Act, a period is fixed within which any tax or other sum is to be paid or any work executed, or anything provided, such period shall, in the absence of any distinct provision to the contrary in the Act or the rules framed thereunder, be calculated from the date of such service or sending.

(G.O.Ms.No.208, Rural Development (C4) Department, 17th August 2000)

3.5.8 Use of Facsimile of Signatures of the Executive Authority, Commissioner and Secretary of Panchayats

1. Short title—These rules may be called the Tamil Nadu Panchayats (Use of Facsimile of Signatures of the Executive Authority, Commissioner, and Secretary of Panchayats) Rules, 1999.

2. Use of facsimile—(1) Every licence, permission, notice, bill, schedule, summons or other document which is required by the Tamil Nadu Panchayats Act, 1994 (Tamil Nadu Act 21 of 1994), or by any rule, by law or regulation made thereunder to bear the signature of the Executive Authority or Commissioner or Secretary or any Officer of a Panchayat, as the case may be, it shall be deemed to be properly signed if it bears a facsimile of the signature of the Executive Authority or Commissioner or Secretary or such Officer, as the case may be.

(2) Nothing in Rule 2 shall be deemed to apply to a cheque drawn upon a panchayat or to any deed of contract entered into by a panchayat.

(G.O. Ms. No.117, Rural Development (C4) Department, dated 5th July 1999)

3.5.9 Communication of Tour Programme of Ministers and Senior Officers to Local Bodies

1. Government Memo No. 225991-A/C.2/62-1 dated 1.12.62

2. From the Director of Rural Development, Chennai, Lr. Roc. No.88788/2000/PCA-4, dated 14.3.2001

In supersession of the orders already issued in the Government Memo first cited, the Government direct that the chairmen and the presidents of the panchayats of such of those panchayats which fall in the route of march of the Ministers or Officers who are on tour should be informed in advance about the tour programme of the Ministers or the officer concerned. The Government also direct that the Personal Assistant (Panchayat Development) are responsible to see that the copies of the tour programme received by the Collector are communicated promptly to the chairmen and the presidents of the concerned panchayats.

(G.O. Ms. No. 129, Rural Development (C-4) Department, dated 23rd April 2001)

3.5.10 Auction and Lease Rules

The Tamil Nadu Panchayats (Procedure for Conducting Public Auction of Lease and Sales in Panchayats) Rules, 2001.

1. Short title—These rules may be called the Tamil Nadu Panchayats (Procedure for Conducting Public Auction of Leases and Sales in the Panchayats) Rules, 2001.

2. Definition—In these rules, unless the context otherwise requires, "Act" means the Tamil Nadu Panchayats Act, 1994 (Tamil Nadu Act 21 of 1994).

3. Properties and rights to be auctioned—(1) The panchayat shall lease out or sell, in public auction in an open and transparent manner, the right to enjoyment of properties of a panchayat or right to the collection of fees for the use of public places in the panchayat for commercial and other purposes, specified in sub-rule (2). The panchayat shall also sell in public auction any unusable or unserviceable articles as specified in clause (xi) in sub-rule (2) whose estimated value is more than Rs. 100 (Rupees Hundred only).

(2) The list of item that may be leased out are:

(i) Own lands and other immovable properties of the panchayat;

(ii) Vested or regulated poramboke lands under the control of the panchayat;

(iii) Buildings consisting of shop rooms, rest sheds, carriages, market stalls, canteens, hotels, lodging houses and other permanent buildings for which rent is payable monthly or for a longer period;

(iv) Cutting of grass (vizhal for laying roof for huts) grown in irrigation tanks and other places under the control of panchayat;

(v) Usufructs of trees on the panchayat roads, topes and on roads belonging to the Highways and Rural Work Department. Trees on Public Works Department lands over which the panchayats have been given control and other panchayat properties;

(vi) Right to collect the fees in the public market, cart stand, public landing or halting places, bus stand, slaughter houses, fish markets of ferry places under the control of the panchayat;

(vii) Collection of minor forest produce as defined in Section 130-A of the Tamil Nadu Forest Code collected in the unreserved forest of the panchayat and other panchayat properties;

(viii) Use of road margins under the control of the panchayat and street margins for sale of articles;

(ix) Use of public places for erecting advertisement boards etc.;

(x) Any other items of which right of enjoyment or collection offers can be leased out;

(xi) The sale of unusable or unserviceable articles are:

(i) Wind fallen and withered trees;

(ii) Sweepings in the panchayat properties;

(iii) Unserviceable and worn out machinery tools, plants and electrical fittings;

(iv) Old stores materials and furniture;

(v) Old news papers, journals and obsolete records after tearing out them; and

(vi) In the case of stalls or banks or other structures or buildings constructed by the government from their funds for rehabilitation of the repatriates from other countries, if any handed over to the village panchayat or the panchayat union council as the case may be, for maintenance they shall be leased out only to such persons according to the instruction of the government in force at the time of auction.

4. Lease of land and immovable property belonging to a panchayat—The panchayat shall have power to lease out its own land or any other immovable property belonging to it as referred to in Rule 3 above:

Provided that no such lease shall be valid in case the period of lease exceeds three years or where the lessee is permitted to put up any building or structure whether of masonry, brick, wood, mud or any materials unless the sanction of the Inspector has been obtained therefor.

5. Lease of Government poramboke vested with the panchayat—The panchayat shall have power to lease out any property vested in it but not belonging to it other than road sides and street margins referred to in Rule 3 above:

Provided that no lease shall be granted

(a) in contravention of the conditions, subject to which such property became vested in the panchayat.

(b) for a period exceeding twelve months without the previous sanction of the Inspector. Provided further that no such lease shall be valid if the lessee is permitted to put up any building or structure whether of masonry, brick, wood, mud or any other materials unless prior sanction of the Inspector has been obtained.

6. Lease of roadside and street margins, the panchayat shall have power to lease out road margins under the control of the panchayat and street margins subject to the following restrictions and control—

(i) The panchayat shall require each intending bidder to furnish information as to the use to which the land will be put and the period for which lease is required which shall not exceed one year at a time. If the intending bidder desires to construct any temporary structure, information to the materials to be used for the construction shall be furnished;

(ii) For a lease period not exceeding twelve months materials like prefabricated structures or palmyrah or coconut leaves, bamboos jute or gunny cloth or similar other materials which may be removed easily shall be permitted for the structures. Necessary fees if any, leviable for such temporary structure shall also be collected before permitting such construction. Such a temporary structure is liable for removal by the panchayat, if the panchayat or the Inspector considers so in public interest during the middle of the lease period and lessee shall have no right to claim any compensation for the same;

(iii) No lease for a structure made of materials other than those mentioned in items (i) and (ii) above or for a period exceeding twelve months shall be granted without the previous approval of the Inspector, who while granting approval may lay down such conditions as may be considered necessary, subject to which the lease may be granted by the panchayat. The panchayat shall embody such conditions in the lease notice and the lease deed before granting orders to entry into the property;

(iv) No road margins shall be leased out for cultivations; and

(v) Every lease under item (ii) or item (iii) shall expressly provide that the lease is liable to be terminated at any time within the period of the lease without payment of compensation to the lessee, if in the opinion of the panchayat or the Inspector it is necessary in the public interest to remove any structure erected in the land.

7. Collection of ground rent assessment, peshkash or quit-rent and payable to Government—(1) Whenever any vested property of the panchayat is leased out, the lessee shall pay to the Government such assessment of ground rent, peshkash or quit-rent as the Inspector may determine from time-to-time and the same is subject to revision, from time-to-time, in accordance with the rules in force at the time of revision except in respect of quit-rent on enfranchised Inam lands and peshkash on lands in proprietary villages acquired by the panchayat by private negotiation. Such assessment of quit-rent shall be an addition to the lease amount and the lessee shall be liable to pay the amount in addition to the lease amount.

(2) Nothing contained in this rule shall affect the right of the Government to recover from the panchayat the assessment, ground rent, peshkash or quit-rent leviable on lands not transferred by sale or exchange or other wise permanently alienated.

8. Leasing out of public places for erecting advertisement boards and hoardings for advertisement—(1) The panchayat may set apart places in the lands owned by it or in the premises of its buildings or in the vested porambokes and lease out such places for erecting up advertisement boards or hoardings.

(2) The panchayat may also erect advertisement boards and hoardings at its own cost and lease out such structures for the exhibition of advertisements.

9. Authority to conduct auction and sale—The Executive Authority or the Commissioner or the Secretary as the case may be shall conduct auction of lease or sale of articles belonging to panchayat.

10. Time to conduct auction—(1) The auction of lease shall be conducted sufficiently in advance of period or date from which the lease period is due to commence, taking into consideration the extra period that may become necessary for conducting re-auction on account of any compelling circumstances. Action may be taken to complete well in advance the preliminary steps like preparing auction notices, publication in proper manner, conducting of auction, getting approval of the panchayat and execution of lease deed.

(2) So far as the sale of article in an outright manner is concerned, such article may be got condemned by the panchayat well in advance, wherever necessary, and then sold out in public auction without undue delay, thereby avoiding theft, pilferage, natural loss, damage or wearing out, rendering their sale difficult or infructuous. In case where technical opinion or advice is considered essential or have been prescribed by the Inspector for condemning any article by the panchayat such as radio, television set, electric motor pump set, electrical fittings, vehicles, etc., such technical advice or opinion in respect of that materials shall also be obtained.

11. Period of lease—The panchayat shall in respect of property other than the property vested with it, fix the period of lease of right to enjoy the property, and the period of lease of properties as specified in table below, subject to conditions prescribed under this rule:

Table

	Nature of Property *(1)*	*Maximum lease period at a time* *(2)*
(1)	Own lands	Three years initially and renewal for a further period of three years.
(2)	Own buildings used as shops, rooms carriage canteen, hotels, lodging, houses, rest sheds.	Three years initially and renewal for a further period of three years.
(3)	Government poramboke land vested with or regulated by the village panchayat or the panchayat union council as the case may be excluding road and street margins.	One Year
(4)	Rights to cut grasses in minor and major irrigation tanks and other water sources.	One Year
(5)	Usufructs of avenue trees in the village panchayat or the panchayat union council roads trees as the case may be in Public Works Department lands and Highways and Rural Works Department roads and trees in topes.	One Year
(6)	Minor forest produces as defined in Section 130-A of the Tamil Nadu Forest Code.	One Year
(7)	Right to collect fees for the use of public places like markets/fairs, during festivals, landing and halting places, bus stand, car stand, slaughter house, fish market, fishing in water supply sources under the control or vested with the village panchayat or the panchayat union council as the case may be, ferry.	One Year
(8)	Sale on road margins and street margins and public places in the villages.	One Year
(9)	Right to enjoy fishery rights in water sources under the control of the village panchayat or the panchayat union council as the case may be. The Tamil Nadu Panchayats (Lease and Licensing of Fishery Rights in Water Sources Vested and Regulated by the Village Panchayats and the Panchayat Union Councils) Rules, 1999, will apply for the auction procedures.	Five Years

12. Fixing of number and amount of instalments—(1) The panchayat shall fix the number of instalments for the payment of lease amount by the lessee as follows:

(a) Where the lease period does not exceed one year the lease amount may be permitted to be paid in not exceeding two instalments, to be decided by the panchayat in respect of every lease:

Provided that the last instalment shall be paid before six months of expiry of the period of lease:

Provided further that in case the lease amount does not exceed Rs. 5,000 (Rupees five thousand only), it shall be paid in one lump sum within five days of execution of lease deed:

Provided also that in the case of lease of usufructs of avenue trees, the lease amount shall be paid in one lump sum before the execution of lease deed.

(b) Where the lease period exceeds one year, the lease amount may be permitted to be paid in not more than two instalments for every year of lease, the last instalment being payable at least one year before the period of expiry of the period of lease or in the beginning of the lease period, whichever is earlier.

(2) The panchayat shall take action to terminate the lease in case a lessee fails to remit the instalment within seven days after the expiry of due date besides initiating action to realise the balance as per the lease deed from the lessee.

(3) The panchayat shall fix the amount of the security deposit for each item of lease, so that he may not retreat from the lease after the final bid. This amount shall be retained till the expiry of the lease period as a security against the violation of lease condition. In case where the estimated lease amount exceeds Rs. 10,000 (Rupees ten thousand only), the bidder shall be required to produce suitable solvency certificate for an amount to be specified in the auction notice.

(4) Every successful bidder in an auction shall be required to remit, soon after the bidding is over for an item, and before starting the bid for the next item an initial amount, excluding the recently deposited amount, calculated at not less than ten per cent of the bid amount which, together with early paid amount, would constitute the first instalment of the amount in the case of lease not exceeding one year and fifteen per cent of the bid amount in cases where the lease period exceeds more than a year, equal to two instalments of amount.

13. Place of auction—Ordinarily, every auction or sale shall be conducted in the office of the panchayat. In special cases, the Executive Authority or the Commissioner or the Secretary, as the case may be shall decide the place of auction of the lease or sale depending upon the nature of lease or sale and the place where the properties or articles lie. However the auction of usufructs of the trees, wind fallen and withered trees may be conducted at the site itself. In case of avenue trees the entire road length may be divided into convenient reaches, that is, say two hundred or four hundred metres and may be auctioned reach by reach individually.

14. Issue of auction notice—(1) The notice of auction of lease or sale may be issued not less than ten days and not more than twenty one days prior to the date of auction or sale. The panchayat shall approve the terms and conditions and for each kind or type of lease, before they are included in the auction notice. If new conditions or terms are to be included or existing conditions or terms to be amended, the prior approval of the panchayat shall be necessary. The notice may contain *inter alia*, terms and conditions on the following matters subject to which the lease shall be granted:

(i) place of auction or sale, date and time of auction;

(ii) period of lease;

(iii) details of property to be sold or rights to be auctioned. In the case of avenue trees, the details of reach or the road and other cases the location of the property may be specified clearly;

(iv) security deposit payable for each item;

(v) number of instalments of lease amount permitted for each item;

(vi) initial amount payable at the time of auction or sale by the successful bidder;

(vii) details of solvency certificate to be produced where it is considered necessary;

(viii) prohibition of defaulters in the payment of past leases from participating in the auction or sale;

(ix) confirmation of auction or sale being subject to the approval of the panchayat;

(x) rate of interest chargeable for belated payment of instalment;

(xi) need for and mode of execution of lease or sale deed;

(xii) details of payment of assessment, ground rent, peshkash or quit-rent fixed by the Inspector from time-to-time which will be in addition to the lease amount;

(xiii) schedule of payment of the lease or sale amount;

(xiv) in case where the rent of own lands, poramboke lands and own building of the panchayats, proposed to be leased out, the rent, lease amount, may be reckoned in terms of monthly rent for the entire lease period. This information may be specified in the auction notice also for the information of the intending bidders; and

(xv) power of the administration to reserve any right either to postpone the sale or auction of any lease and also to cancel any lease in public interest with or without showing any reasons therefor in the middle of the lease period for which the lessee has no right to claim any compensation.

15. Publication of auction notice—(1) The auction notice for the lease of property or right to collect fees or sale of articles shall be published in the manner specified below. Due publicity shall be given by publishing a notice containing full particulars of the property to be transferred or leased or sold and the fees to be collected.

(i) in the notice board of the concerned panchayat;

(ii) in the notice board of the panchayat union or the district panchayat in which the village panchayat or panchayat union council, as the case may be is situated;

(iii) in the notice board of the adjacent panchayat lying within five kilometres radius of the village panchayat or the panchayat union council as the case may be in which the property lies;

(iv) in important places in the panchayat village area or panchayat union council, as the case may be, like chavadi, post office, fair price shops, temples etc;

(v) by beat of tom tom in the panchayat village or the panchayat union council, as the case may be, where the property or places lies, on the day of auction three hour before the time fixed for auction;

(vi) a record of publication of auction notice shall be prepared and kept in the relevant file;

(vii) by sending copy of notice to the prospective traders, dealers or agents in the district who are dealing with the property of the nature mentioned in the auction;

(viii) on the property to be leased out or place where the fees are to be collected;

(ix) any other method the panchayat may consider necessary.

(2) The auction notice shall be caused to be published

(i) in the District Gazette at least seven days in advance of the date of auction, in case the lease amount is expected not to exceed Rs. 10,000 (Rupees ten thousand only);

(ii) by inserting brief advertisement, in a Tamil daily newspaper having wide daily circulation in the panchayat area, at least three days ahead of the date of auction in case the lease is expected to exceed Rs. 10,000 (Rupees ten thousand only).

(3) The Executive Authority or the Commissioner or the Secretary, as the case may be, shall estimate and decide whether a lease or sale of article would fetch an amount below or above Rs. 2,000 (Rupees two thousand only), as the case may be, and record his decision in the relevant file quoting reasons therefor.

(4) The panchayat may dispense with the publication of auction notice in the District Gazette or in the newspapers in the case of re-auction during the middle of the lease period arising out of termination of the lease for non-fulfilment lease conditions.

16. Auction procedure—(1) In the case of auction conducted by the panchayat, a committee comprising of three members for supervising the conduct of auction, of lease or sale may be constituted by the concerned panchayat for ensuring greater transparency. In case of a village panchayat such Committee may include besides the Executive Authority or the vice-president and the members from the ward where the property to be leased or sold lies. The Executive Authority or the Commissioner or the Secretary, as the case may be shall inform the Committee members in writing atleast three days in advance for making themselves present at the place of auction or sale.

(2) The Executive Authority or the Commissioner or the Secretary, as the case may be, or the person authorized to conduct the auction shall be present sixty minutes ahead of the time fixed for auction at the appointed place. If more number of items are to be auctioned, auction shall be conducted one after another. The highest bid amount shall be either recovered along with necessary security deposit or the first instalment of total bid are collected before commencing the next item of auction. The deposit of all unsuccessful bidders may be refunded to them on the spot after all the auctions under the question are over with due acknowledgement.

(3) No person shall be eligible to participate in the auction if he was irregular in paying instalment amounts in respect of any previous auction held in that panchayat or if he has failed to comply with any of the terms or conditions of a previous auction, resulting in the damage to the lease property.

(4) A suitable upset price may be fixed at the commencement of auction which may be based on the last auction the prevailing market prices and the prospect at the present auction. If the situation warrants, reasons for which shall be recorded in writing amount may be lowered to a further reasonable level from which the bid be increased by the bidders.

(5) As soon as the auction is over, the security deposit amount and the lease amount realised in full or in parts shall be remitted into the concerned panchayat fund account and printed receipts issued to the payees by the Executive Authority or the Commissioner or the Secretary, as the case may be.

17. Procedure for lease cancellation in the middle of lease period—(1) If it is found that a lessee has violated any of the lease conditions, which is considered by the panchayat as a serious irregularity, like failure to remit the instalment of the dues on or before the due date or cause serious damages to the leased property and failed to restore the damages to the original position, the Executive Authority or the Commissioner or the Secretary, as the case may be shall issue a show cause notice to the lessee as to why the lease should not be terminated on account of the violation of lease conditions which shall be specified in the show cause notice and require him to submit his reply within seven days. This notice shall be served on him as per the provisions of the Tamil Nadu Panchayats (Manner of Publication and Notification or Notice and Manner of Service of Documents to the Public) Rules, 2000.

(2) After the expiry of the period specified in the show cause notice, the Executive Authority or the Commissioner of the Secretary, as the case may be, shall decide on the merit of the case after taking into consideration the explanation of the lessee, if any, received and after obtaining the resolution of the panchayat for termination of lease, issue suitable orders to the lessee. If the lease is terminated such order shall also be served on the lessee as per the provisions of the Tamil Nadu Panchayats (Manner of Notification or Notice and Manner of Service of Documents to the Public) Rules, 2000. The orders of termination shall include the consequences of termination in accordance with the conditions of lease deed, the important among them being that the lessee shall be liable to pay any loss to the panchayat arising out of the termination of lease and re-auctioning or by departmental management of the lease property or right.

18. Circumstances and procedures to conduct re-auction—(1) Re-auction of lease may be conducted in the following circumstances:

(a) When the lease was cancelled due to violation of lease condition by the lessee;

(b) When another person comes forward to bid for higher amount by remitting an amount higher, by one and half times more than the bid amount;

(c) When the Inspector or any other authority empowered by him cancels the auction on account of proven irregularities committed in the auction held already; and

(d) When the panchayat itself resolves to conduct re-auction on the ground that the bid amount is too low to be considered as a reasonable bid, compared to the last auction or taking into consideration of the prevailing circumstances.

(2) In the event of re-auction, the procedure laid down for conducting auction in these rules shall be observed all over again, starting from the issue or re-auction notice onwards. Before commencing re-auction proceedings a written order cancelling the previous auction shall be issued by the Executive Authority or the Commissioner or the Secretary as the case may be based on the resolution of the panchayat or the order of the Inspector.

(3) The Executive Authority or the Commissioner or the Secretary, as the case may be shall be competent to cancel the auction in the event of a situation specified in clause (b) in sub-rule (1) and issue orders before seeking permission of the panchayat for conducting a re-auction.

(4) When re-auction is ordered, the publication of a notice in the District Gazette and the newspapers may be dispensed with, if the Executive Authority or the Commissioner or the Secretary, as the case may be considers that the bid amount at the re-auction may not be at a level, warranting such publication and accordingly notice for shorter duration may be given.

19. Confirmation of auction—The Executive Authority or the Commissioner or the Secretary, as the case may be shall as soon as possible or within a week of conduct of auction, during which period a request for auction for a higher amount is likely to be expected, place before the panchayat, the records of auction of lease or sale with his remarks in writing on the acceptability or otherwise of one or all the bids. The panchayat shall decide as to which of the bids shall be accepted and record its reasons where the bid accepted is not the highest or for rejecting a bid or bids higher than the one is accepted. In case the panchayat decides to reject all the bids and resolve to conduct re-auction, it shall record the reasons for ordering such re-auction. If the Executive Authority or the Commissioner or the Secretary, as the case may be is not satisfied with the decision of the panchayat, he may bring it to the notice of the Inspector. The decision of the Inspector thereon shall be final.

20. Execution of lease deed—(1) Soon after the approval of the auction of a lease by the panchayat the Executive Authority or the Commissioner or the Secretary as the case may be shall confirm the auction in writing to the successful bidder.

If the lease amount exceeds Rs. 10,000 (Rupees ten thousand only) the bidder shall be directed to execute a lease deed within five days of the confirmation of the auction on a stamped paper of suitable value and register it. If the bidder fails to execute the lease deed, the auction shall be cancelled forfeiting the security deposit and the initial amount paid on the day of auction and also the re-auction of lease shall be ordered. The successful bidder shall not enter into the lease property before executing lease deed and obtaining permission for such entry from the Executive Authority or the Commissioner or the Secretary as the case may be initial amount paid on the day of auction and also the re-auction of lease shall be ordered.

(2) The lease deed shall specify the terms and conditions, *inter alia*, or the following matters in addition to the other condition specified in the auction notice:

(a) duration of the lease.

(b) amount of each instalment of the lease amount and the due date before which it is payable.

(c) lease liable for cancellation in case the instalment of the lease amount is not paid within seven days of the expiry of the due date or such larger period or as the Executive Authority or the Commissioner or the Secretary as the case may be, may fix and not exceeding thirty days from the due date, at any rate.

(d) liability of the lessee to make good, the loss if any, caused to the panchayat on re-auction, departmental management of the property, or right of re-auction, owing to the default on the part of the lessee to fulfil the terms of his contract.

(e) the rate of fees leviable by the lessee in respect of public markets, landing places, halting places, cart stands, slaughter houses, fisheries and ferries under the control of the panchayat.

(f) restrictions and controls to be imposed for preventing damages to the lease property in any way as would affect the revenue yielding capacity of the property and should it happen, the lessee shall restore the property to its original position or state, failing which the damage shall be restored at his cost which shall be recoverable from him besides cancellation of the lease.

(g) prohibition against indiscriminate cutting of any branch of a tree or palmyrah or coconut leaves for a better yield.

(h) liability of the lessee to pay assessment, ground rent, peshkash or quit-rent at such rate as the Inspector may fix from time-to-time.

(i) right to enjoy the lease is subject to the satisfactory compliance with all the terms and conditions in the auction notice, as well as that of the lease deed.

(j) any other conditions or terms which may be found necessary in the case of a different type or particular kind of lease.

(3) The lease deed shall be executed in the prescribed form depending upon the property leased out for enjoyment or right of collecting fees for using public places belonging to or vested with or regulated by the panchayat.

(4) No person shall be allowed to exercise his right under the lease until he has executed the lease deed.

(5) In case any lessee fails to pay the instalment of the lease amount, as agreed upon within thirty days of due date of payment, the Executive Authority or the Commissioner or the Secretary, as the case may be, shall forthwith report the matter to the concerned panchayat which shall have power to terminate the lease and order its management departmentally at the risk of the lessee till it is leased out in re-auction.

(6) No sale deed is necessary in the case of sale of articles and for which the sale amount has been realized in full, but when confirming the auction for sale, the Executive Authority or the Commissioner or the Secretary, as the case may be, shall specify the date before which the property sold may be removed from the spot or taken possession of. Any balance amount due from the bidder shall be collected with due sales tax and surcharge if any, before permitting the removal of the property from the spot or taking possession of the property.

21. Procedure for sealed tenders—(1) The panchayat shall have power to invite tenders in an open and transparent manner for the enjoyment of lease of a property or right to collect fees covering the salient formalities and legal aspects of (i) if, the panchayat has reason to believe that due to collision among the bidders or due to any other reason like either there was no bid at least on two occasions, or (ii) the bid was kept at a very low level whereby the interest of the panchayat was deliberately defeated. The terms and conditions which are normally prescribed in the auction notice for lease may be adopted with such modifications as are necessary when calling for tenders.

(2) When tenders are invited for letting out the lease of a property or right to collect fees the panchayat shall have power to accept either the highest tender or a tender which is not the highest but the next higher, after recording the reasons for the same in writing.

22. Auction-cum-tender procedure—(1) If the panchayat considers and decides it advantageous to adopt the auction-cum-tender procedure, it shall have power to adopt such procedure in the sale of property or leasing out the right to enjoy property or to collect fees for the use of public places, if it has reason to believe that due to collusion amount the intending bidders or due to threat or habitual participants, to the new entrants in the bidding, either there is a low bid or no bid at all, at least on two occasions, it shall record the fact in the minutes of the meeting and opt for adopting auction-cum-tender procedure in respect of lease of sale of any item which it proposes to conduct.

(2) When the panchayat decides to adopt the auction-cum-tender procedure the Executive Authority or the Commissioner or the Secretary as the case may be, shall issue auction-cum-tender notice with appropriate terms and conditions covering the salient formalities and legal aspects of each of the system in the same notice fixing, a suitable time for conducting the auction and some other time on the same day following the completion of auction proceedings, for opening the tenders for the same items of leases or sales. Under any circumstances the time appointed for the receipt of tenders shall not exceed the time appointed for the conduct of auction, and any tender received after the commencement of the auction shall be straight away rejected without opening. Security deposits shall be specified separately for auction and tender. The time, place and the last day for the receipt of tender and the time, place and last day for the sale of tender documents and payment of tender deposits shall also be specified in the notice. A tenderer can send his tender by registered post sufficiently in advance so as to reach the office of the tender before the appointed date and time and the official who receives the postal cover upto the time on the last day fixed for the receipt of tenders shall deposit it into tender box prepared and kept for that purpose.

(3) On the day and time fixed for the conduct of auction strictly observing all the formalities and subject to the terms conditions mentioned to take auction current order notice the Executive Authority or the Commissioner or the Secretary, as the case may be, shall commence the auction proceedings, conduct and complete the auction or sale of each item one by one and simultaneously completing the records of auction or sale and obtain necessary initial amount from the successful bidders at the time appointed for the opening of the tenders. The tenders received upto the prescribed time and date shall be opened and the amount quoted therein in respect of each item, shall be read openly at the meeting of bidders and tenders. The tender details may be entered in the register of tenders maintained for that purpose. After completing all the formalities, Executive Authority or the Commissioner or the Secretary as the case may be shall place before the concerned panchayat the records of auction and of tenders for approval. The panchayat shall have power either to decide the higher bid in an auction or one quoted in tender or any suitable bid or tender amount which is next to the higher amount. In case, it accepts a lower amount than the highest tender or the auction amount the reasons for the same shall be specifically recorded in the minutes of the meeting.

23. Renewal of lease—(1) The panchayat shall have power to renew the lease or right of enjoyment of shops, rooms, garages, public markets, canteen, hotels or lodging houses belonging to it and for which rent is payable on a monthly basis or for a longer period in favour of the existing lessee if the lessee agrees to the renewal of the lease for a higher amount to be decided by the panchayat supported by not less than one half of the members then holding office which shall not be less than fifteen per cent for every year on the previous years lease or of rent fixed:

Provided that such extension of renewal of lease shall be done only upto a maximum of three years.

(2) The existing lessees, if he desires to continue the lease for a further period he may apply to the Executive Authority or the Commissioner or the Secretary, as the case may be, requesting the renewal of the lease in his favour atleast three months before the expiry of the lease period. On receipt of such a request the Executive Authority or the Commissioner or the Secretary, as the case may be, shall place the matter or the Commissioner or the Secretary, as the case may be, shall place the matter before the respective panchayats to fix provisionally a sum at which the lease can be renewed, taking into consideration the following factors:

(a) the increase in the market value of the building subsequent to the letting out of the present lease;
(b) the appreciation in the increase of rental value of the building and other similar buildings in the locality;
(c) consideration of growth and business of the locality in which the building is situated;
(d) other factors such as the location of the property in close proximity to railway station, bus stand, business area and other factors

which may have effect in the promotion of business.

(3) The Executive Authority or the Commissioner or the Secretary, as the case may be, may fix the lease amount at fifteen per cent, if the annual rise in prices is less then fifteen per cent, over the existing lease amount for the fourth year of lease and this rate of interest may be fixed at more than fifteen per cent for the fifth year and sixth year of the lease period as may be decided by the panchayat.

(4) The Executive Authority or the Commissioner or the Secretary, as the case may be, shall place before the panchayat, within two weeks of the receipt of the request from the lessee, the request for renewal together with his recommendation regarding the probable amount of lease or rent to be fixed for ensuing lease period.

(5) The panchayat shall be at liberty to accept the offer of the lessee and fix up the rent for each of the next three years at a progressive rate of increase so as to derive not less than forty-five per cent of the total amount for the next term of three years over the previous term of lease. If the panchayat decides, not to accept the request of the lessee, the Executive Authority or the Commissioner or the Secretary, as the case may be, shall take further action to conduct auction of the lease for that particular item of lease in the usual manner, by observing the procedures prescribed under these rules.

(6) In case the panchayat decides to accept the offer at a meeting where not less than fifty per cent of members then on the panchayat is present, it shall fix lease rent for each year for the next three years period and the Executive Authority or the Commissioner or the Secretary, as the case may be, shall intimate the lessee the decision of the panchayat before six weeks to the expiry of the lease period with the condition to indicate his willingness to accept the offer within a week of the date of receipt of intimation from the Executive Authority or the Commissioner or the Secretary, as the case may be. On receipt of the intimation from the Executive Authority or the Commissioner or the Secretary, as the case may be, the lessee may express his willingness to accept the offer consisting of graded increase of lease amount for any year of the renewal at an amount indicated by the panchayat or unwillingness to accept the offer. In which case the Executive Authority or the Commissioner or the Secretary as the case may be, shall take action to conduct the auction of the lease before the expiry of the period of lease after getting the approval of the panchayat. In case the lessee expresses his willingness in writing the Executive Authority or the Commissioner or the Secretary, as the case may be, to accept the offer of the panchayat, the Executive Authority or Commissioner or the Secretary as the case may be, shall get fresh lease deed executed and registered by the lessee. The lease deed shall contain all the conditions normally stipulated for such a lease with a specific reference for the acceptance of increase of lease amount during cash year of the three years period in a graded manner. If the lessee fails to execute the lease deed within the period mentioned above, the offer of the panchayat shall stand withdrawn and the Executive Authority, or the Commissioner or the Secretary, as the case may be, shall report the matter to the panchayat immediately, obtain its permission to let the property on auction.

(7) The panchayat is competent to renew the lease of the property only for a period of three years to an existing lessee and shall not renew for the second time even if the lessee is willing to pay higher rent. The Executive Authority or the Commissioner or the Secretary, as the case may be, shall put on such lease of property on auction after the sixth year when the existing lessee will be free to compete in auction and knock out the lease at any amount as he may desire.

(8) Where the lessee fails to pay the rent specified in the lease deed or where he fails to pay the revised rent, he shall be evicted in accordance with the conditions of the deed and a fresh lease of the property shall be effected in public auction in the manner specified in these rules.

24. Direct management by the panchayat— (1) The panchayat shall have power to manage itself the affairs of letting on lease, the enjoyment or right of a property or collection of fees, for the use of public places, like public market, bus stands, vehicles stand etc., in one or more of the following circumstances. However the panchayat may resort to the management by itself only for a short period till the lease of such property is let out.

(a) When the lease is terminated for the violation of conditions of lease deed by the lessee and the lease property or right has to be necessarily managed by the panchayat at the risk of the lessee till the lease for the remaining period is auctioned and a fresh lease deed is executed for its management.

(b) When the process of leasing could not be finalized due to extraordinary, unforeseen circumstances or administrative reasons, before the period of commencement of lease.

(c) In case of collection of fees during an annual festival of a temple, lasting for a very short period, when there is no bid at the first auction of a lease or when the lease amount is comparatively low due to collusion or other unhealthy means and the panchayat does not see reason to accept such a low lease amount.

(2) When a panchayat decides to take up the management by itself of a lease of enjoyment or right of a property, the Executive Authority or the Commissioner or the Secretary, as the case may be, may utilize the service of its employees for the collection work. In exceptional cases, where it is essential to engage temporary staff for collection, it shall also decide regarding the appointment of temporary staff, their daily wages not exceeding the rates fixed by the Inspector for such period of panchayat management mode of selection of person for appointment, the amount of security deposit to be collected from the temporary staff, expenditure on the printing of tickets or receipt books and other contingent expenditure. The panchayat shall be competent to incur expenditure for the departmental management not exceeding thirty per cent of the anticipated receipt without outside sanction and for any expenditure exceeding this limit the previous permission of the Inspector shall be obtained.

(3) The Executive Authority or the Commissioner or the Secretary, as the case may be, shall decide the colour of ticket for different denominations for different rates of fees, the design and size of ticket leaves, the number of series of ticket books for different rates of fees, the actual letter of series (such as "A, B, C") of ticket books for different rates of fees, the number of ticket leaves to be provided for each denomination, the details to be provided in the ticket leaf, the size of the leaf. The number for tickets to be printed in each series in each denomination etc., the details of ticket leaf may be similar to those approved by the panchayat already when the lease for a particular purpose was auctioned last. Each ticket book shall contain one hundred leaves having printed serial number on the leaves. Depending upon the number of series of ticket book to be printed and number of books to be prefixed in each series the first letter of each series may be printed to serial number of leaf. By this way the leaves of same denomination can be identified on the basis of letter of series prefixed of such serial numbers. The ticket book in each denomination in each series shall be serially numbered. The receipt for the printing of ticket books shall show details, names of series of ticket books printed in each denomination, the total number of leaves in each book and the total number of ticket leaves printed in each series in each denomination.

(4) A stock register of ticket books shall be maintained in two parts. In the part one of the register, the details of ticket books printed and brought to stock shall be entered and the details of issues of ticket book to the collecting staff, who are appointed with a separate set of serially numbered for all ticket books under each denomination, the ticket books serially numbered in a separate series for each denomination, the total number of leaves serially numbered under each denomination is serial number of leaves bound in a ticket book being printed on the ticket book. The leaves in the tickets shall bear the fascimile of the signature of the Executive Authority or the Commissioner or the Secretary, as the case may be, and signature of the collecting staff in ink. Part two of this register shall be treated as a personal ledger for each collecting staff, showing the details of ticket books issued to each collecting person under each denomination together with total number or leaves and total value ticket books supplied. Whenever ticket books are issued the dated signature of the collecting person shall be obtained in the register as a token of his acknowledgement. The details of amount daily collected and remitted into the panchayat shall be noted in this part of the register denomination-wise and date-wise under the dated signature of the collecting person. In this way the balance amount to be remitted by each collecting person can be ascertained on any date and the responsibility and accountability of the collecting person can be ensured and fixed.

(5) The Executive Authority or the Commissioner or the Secretary as the case may be, shall issue a set of directions to the collecting staff on all matters enumerated below relating to the collection work.

(a) Area or zone allotted for each collecting person.

(b) Rate of fees to be collected for different articles purposes or person etc.

(c) Remittance of daily collection at the panchayat office in the evening of everyday with details of the collection work for the day and surrender the counterfoil books.

(d) Authorized persons for receiving the collections and counterfoil books from the collecting staff and give acknowledgement in the register or note book maintained by him for this record.

(e) Any other pertinent matter which may arise in a particular case.

(f) The person receiving the cash daily at the panchayat must verify the number of counterfoils and assess the amount which should have been collected, and total it with the cash actually received. If any discrepancy is noticed in the verification, then he should take up the matter to the notice of the Executive Authority or the Commissioner or the Secretary, as the case may be, for suitable further action.

(6) The Executive Authority or the Commissioner or the Secretary, as the case may be, shall keep strict watch over the collection work of the staff. He shall undertake the following measures in this regard. He shall take immediate and effective action in case he notices any irregularity or misappropriation during his check.

(a) Verify with vendors or other persons who have to pay fees, whether they receive tickets for the amount they pay to the collecting person, whether they were demanded to pay or give more amount than that specified in the ticket or mentioned in the notice board installed on the site of collection.

(b) Verify whether the collecting persons are collecting fees from all persons/vendors or they omit to collect fee from some persons vendors or whether they collect money but omit to give receipts.

(c) Whether the tickets available with the vendors are genuine or spurious.

(d) Any other kind of check as he may consider necessary or essential.

(e) If he thinks desirable or necessary he can authorize the vice-president to undertake the measures he is taking on days on which he could not undertake them, due to his pre-occupation with any other official business.

(f) Surprise verification of stock of tickets and cash on hand with the collecting person at frequent intervals.

(7) Each and every collecting person shall maintain a separate account in two parts for his record in respect of ticket entrusted to him and collections made and remitted into the panchayat. Details of collections made and remitted into panchayat shall be entered daily in the register.

(8) The Executive Authority or the Commissioner or the Secretary, as the case may be, shall verify the number of ticket books used, cash on hand with every collecting person and append a certificate of verification in the stock register of the collecting persons with a view to keeping strict vigil to prevent misappropriation and defalcation. Any irregularity noticed during such verification should be given due serious consideration and follow up action taken. The Executive Authority or the Commissioner or the Secretary, as the case may be, shall arrange to issue a receipt for the cash remitted into the panchayat office daily to the collecting person when they remit money and receive used ticket book. The miscellaneous register shall also indicate the serial number of tickets from which fees were collected and the serial number of used ticket books received by the office.

(9) After the period of management by the panchayat is over, the Executive Authority or the Commissioner or the Secretary, as the case may be, shall review the over all position with reference to the number of tickets/books printed, number issued, amount collected, and remitted and the net savings accrued and report the matter to the concerned panchayat at its next meeting.

25. Collection of lease and sale amount—(1) After completing the execution of lease deed, necessary entries shall be made in the register of miscellaneous demand under the attestation of the Executive Authority or the Commissioner or the Secretary, as the case may be.

(2) The Executive Authority or the Commissioner or the Secretary, as the case may be shall make necessary posting regarding the total amount, initial payment when the deed is executed, watch the amount to be recovered in instalments at the beginning of each month, scrutinize this register, note down the due date of instalments of lease amount, and issue advance reminder to the lessee for remitting the dues. If they fail to remit the instalments due even after a reasonable period, the Executive Authority or the Commissioner or the Secretary, as the case may be, shall take action to terminate the lease besides taking appropriate action to realize the dues with interest.

(G.O.Ms. No. 277, Rural Development (C-4), 22nd November 2001).

3.6 ESTABLISHMENT

3.6.1 Panchayat Employees' Conduct Rules

1. Short title and application—(1) These rules may be called the Tamil Nadu Panchayats Employees' Conduct Rules, 2001.

(2) They apply to all person appointed to panchayat services and posts in connection with the affairs of all panchayat institutions whether on duty or on leave.

Unless otherwise provided these rules shall not apply to the Commissioner of the panchayat union and the Secretary of the district panchayat and the Government servants working in panchayats.

The powers of the panchayats under these rules shall be exercisable even when the employee is outside India, whether on duty, leave or foreign service.

2. Definition—In these rules, unless the context otherwise requires,

(i) "Act" means the Tamil Nadu Panchayats Act, 1994 (Tamil Nadu Act 21 of 1994);

(ii) "Close Relation", in relating to a panchayat employee includes,—father, step-father, mother, step-mother, husband, wife, son, adopted son, daughter, adopted daughter, brother, step-brother, sister, step-sister, wife's father, wife's mother, husband's father, husband's mother, brother's wife, sister's husband, daughter's husband and son's wife. All other expression used in these rules shall have the same meaning as in the Act.

(iii) "Members of the Family", in relation to a panchayat employee includes—

(a) the wife or husband as the case may be, of the panchayat employee whether residing with the panchayat employee or not but does not include a wife or husband, as the case may be, separated from the panchayat employee by a decree or order of a competent court;

(b) son or daughter or step-son or step-daughter of the panchayat unemployed and wholly dependent on him, but does not include a child or step child who is no longer in any way dependent on the panchayat employee or of whose custody the panchayat employee has been deprived by or under any law;

(c) any other person related, whether by blood or marriage, to the panchayat employee or to the panchayat employee's wife or husband and wholly dependent on the panchayat employee;

(iv) "Panchayat employee" means any person appointed by the panchayat in connection with the affairs of the panchayat, who may be officer or servant.

3. Gifts—(1) A panchayat employee shall avoid accepting lavish hospitality or frequent hospitality from any individual having official dealings with him or from industrial or commercial firms, organisation, etc.

(2) Save as otherwise provided in these rules, no panchayat employee shall except with the previous sanction of the respective panchayat, accept or permit his wife, or any other member of his family to accept from any person any gift:

Provided that the sanction of panchayat shall not be necessary for the acceptance of:

(a) Gifts from a personal friend of a value not exceeding one thousand rupees on special occasions such as weddings, anniversaries, funerals and religious functions when the giving or receiving of such gifts is in conformity with the prevailing religious or social customs;

(b) Gifts from close relations of a value not exceeding five thousand rupees on special occasions, such as weddings, anniversaries, funerals and religious functions when the making or receiving of such gifts is in conformity with the prevailing religious or social customs:

Provided that a report shall be made to the respective panchayat if the value of any such gift exceeds rupees one thousand or five thousand, as the case may be, within one month of the acceptance of such "gift".

Explanation. (1) The expression "gift" shall include free transport, boarding, lodging other service or any other pecuniary advantage when provided by any person other than close relations or personal friend having no official dealings with the panchayat employee. A casual meal, lift or other social hospitality shall not be deemed to be a gift.

(2) If any question arises whether any gift is one which can be accepted without the permission of the panchayat or if a panchayat employee is in any doubt whether a gift offered to him is one which can be accepted without the permission of the panchayat, a reference shall be made to the

panchayat by such panchayat employee and the decision of the panchayat thereon shall be final.

(3) No panchayat employee shall enter into any transaction with any private person or firm or company engaged in any business or profession, for the purchase of costly second hand goods such as vehicles for conveyance, furniture and electrical domestic appliances at a favourable price, which may tend to result in favouritism or patronage being shown to the panchayat employee or which may render such panchayat employee under an obligation to such private person or firm or company and which may be construed as a subtle form of corruption.

Explanation. Nothing in this sub-rule shall prevent any panchayat employee from entering into any transaction with any person or firm or company for the purchase of second hand articles at the normal or prevailing market rate of such second hand article.

4. Dowry—No panchayat employee shall—

(i) give or take, abet the giving or taking of dowry; or

(ii) demand, directly or indirectly, from the parents or guardian of a bride or bridegroom, as the case may be, any dowry.

Explanation. For the purposes of this rule, dowry has the same meaning as in the Dowry Prohibition Act, 1961 (Central Act 28 of 1961).

5. Public demonstrations in honour of panchayat employee—No panchayat employee shall except with the previous sanction of the panchayat, receive any complimentary or valedictory address or accept any testimonial or attend any meeting or entertainment held in his honour, or in the honour of any other panchayat employee or Government employee:

Provided that nothing in this rule shall apply to:

(i) a farewell entertainment of a substantially private and informal character held in honour of a panchayat employee or any other panchayat employee on the occasion of his retirement or transfer or any person who has recently quitted the service of any panchayat; or

(ii) the acceptance of simple and inexpensive entertainments arranged by public bodies or institutions; or

(iii) the sitting for or acceptance of a copy of a group photograph of the employee of his office on the occasion of his transfer or retirement.

6. Subscriptions—(1) (a) Save as provided in sub-rule (3), no panchayat employee, shall, except with the previous sanction of the panchayat, ask for or accept contributions to or otherwise associate himself with the raising of any fund or other collections in cash or in kind in pursuance of any object whatsoever.

(b) Where, however, a service association applies for previous sanction of the panchayat, the association shall specify the particular person(s) who will collect funds, if such sanction is granted.

(2) Permission may, after due consideration, be accorded in all cases where the panchayat support the institution concerned by way of grants or otherwise.

(3) In the case of Flag Day collections and any other collections authorised by the Government, panchayat employee may participate on a voluntary basis.

7. Investments, lending and borrowing—(1) No panchayat employee shall, speculate in any stock, share or other investment.

Explanation. (1) The habitual purchase or sale or both of shares, securities or other investments shall be deemed to be speculation within the meaning of this sub-rule.

(2) No panchayat employee shall make, or permit any member of his family or any person acting on his behalf to make, any investment which is likely to embarrass or influence him in the discharge of his official duties.

(3) If any question arises as to whether any transaction is of the nature referred to in sub-rule (1) or sub-rule (2), the decision of the concerned panchayat thereon shall be final.

(4) (a) No panchayat employee, shall save in the ordinary course of business with a bank, a firm or a Public Limited Company of standing, duly authorized to conduct banking business either himself or through any member of his family or any other person acting on his behalf—

(i) lend or borrow money, as principal or agent, to or from any person within the local limit of his authority or with whom he is likely to have official dealings, or otherwise place himself under any pecuniary obligation to such person; or

(ii) lend money to any person at interest or in a manner whereby return in money or in kind is charged or paid:

Provided that a panchayat employee may, give to or accept from, a relative or personal friend, a purely temporary loan of a small amount free of interest, or operate a credit account with a bonafide tradesman or make an advance of pay to his private employee:

Provided further that nothing in this sub-rule shall apply in respect of any transaction entered into by a panchayat employee with the previous sanction of the concerned panchayat;

(iii) No panchayat employee shall, either himself or through any member of his family any other person acting on his behalf, except with the previous sanction of the panchayat, lend or borrow money to or from any private individual any amount exceeding Rs. 10,000/- (Rupees ten thousand only);

(iv) When a panchayat employee is appointed or transferred to a post of such nature as would involve him in the breach of any of the provisions of sub-rule (2) or sub-rule (4), he shall forthwith report the circumstances to the Executive Authority, Commissioner or Secretary, as the case may be, and shall thereafter act in accordance with such order, as may be made by the panchayat.

(5) Panchayat employee may become members of and make deposits in non-agricultural co-operative societies including the Tamil Nadu State Co-operative Bank Limited, other Central Co-operative Banks and Urban Co-operative Banks.

(6) Panchayat employee may place deposits in, and purchase debentures and bonds, of Institutions and Companies who float such bonds and debentures for public offer.

8. Movable, immovable and valuable property—(1) No panchayat employee shall, except after notice to the concerned panchayat acquire or dispose of any immovable property by lease, mortgage, purchase, sale, gift, exchange or otherwise either in his own name or in the name of any dependent member of his family.

Such a notice will be necessary even where any immovable property is acquired by any member of the family of the panchayat employee out of the resources of the panchayat employee:

Provided that the previous sanction of the concerned panchayat shall be obtained in any such transaction with person having official dealings with the panchayat employee:

Provided further that the previous sanction of the panchayat shall not be necessary for the acquisition of immovable property in respect of house-site assigned by the Government to the panchayat servant.

Explanation. (1) A panchayat employee is not required to give notice to the concerned panchayat or seek prior permission from the concerned panchayat for acquisition or disposal of immovable properties by the members of his family under sub-rule (1), if the immovable property in question is not acquired from the resources of the panchayat employee concerned.

(2) Every panchayat employee, for the construction or extension or acquisition of a house, shall report to the concerned panchayat in the following manner:

(i) before starting the construction or extension or entering into transaction for acquisition of a house either from out of loan or part-final withdrawal from the Provident Fund, he shall obtain previous sanction of the panchayat in Form I or II, as the case may be;

(ii) after completing the construction or extension, he shall report to the concerned panchayat;

(iii) Every panchayat employee, shall, if he is a member of the Hindu undivided family and the share of the panchayat employee in the cost of repairs made to the undivided property of the joint family, out of the joint fund exceeds Rs. 10,000/- (Rupees ten thousand only) intimate the fact to the concerned panchayat as and when such repairs are brought to his notice.

(3) No panchayat employee shall encroach upon the panchayat lands or Government lands.

(4) A panchayat employee who enters into any transaction concerning any movable property exceeding Rs. 15,000/- (Rupees fifteen thousand only) in value (whether by way of purchase or sale) shall report to the concerned panchayat within one month from the date of every such transaction:

Provided that the previous sanction of the concerned panchayat shall be obtained if any such transaction is with a person having official dealings with the panchayat employee:

Provided further that a panchayat employee who is about to quit the local limits of his official authority may, without reference to the concerned panchayat dispose of any of his movable property by circulating lists of it among the public generally or by causing it to be sold by public auction.

Explanation. For the purpose of this sub-rule the expression "movable property" include the following property, namely:

(a) Jewellery, Insurance Policies, Shares and services and debentures;

(b) Motor cars, Motor cycles, or any other means of conveyance; and

(c) Refrigerators, Colour Television, Video Cassette Recorder, Computer.

(5) The concerned panchayat shall dispose of the application seeking the sanction/permission referred to in sub-rules (1) and (2) and within a period of two months from the date of receipt of such application from the panchayat employee. If any clarifications or particulars are sought for from the panchayat employee, the said period of two months shall be reckoned from the date of receipt such clarifications or particulars. Where no order according such sanction or granting such permission is issued within the said period of two months, it shall be deemed that the concerned panchayat has accorded the sanction or granted the permission on the expiry of the said period of two months and the panchayat employee can acquire or dispose the immovable property; purchase or sale the movable property or commence the construction/extension of the house.

(6) Every panchayat employee shall submit a return of his assets and liabilities as on the 31st December before the 31st March every year and thereafter at an interval of five years on or before the 31st day of March of the year immediately following the year to which the return relates giving the full particulars in the format specified in Form III appended to these rules:

Provided that every panchayat employee shall within three months of his first appointment to service or post, submit his return of assets and liabilities as on his entry into service in the form specified in Form IV:

Explanation. In all returns, the value of immovable property worth less than Rs. 10,000/- (Rupees ten thousand only) may be added and shown as lump sum. The value of the articles of daily use such as clothes, utensils, crockery, books, etc. need not be included in such return. The movable or immovable properties acquired by the members of the family of a panchayat employee solely with their own resources need not be included in such returns.

(7) The return mentioned in sub-rule (6) shall be handled as a secret document and the provision of Rule 11, shall as far as may be, apply to the said return also.

(8) The panchayat which maintains the personal files and Record Sheets shall maintain registers group-wise in respect of all panchayat employees working under its administrative control showing all immovable properties held by each of them and shall revise them with reference to the particulars furnished by the panchayat employee in subsequent returns as prescribed in sub-rule (6).

(9) Any attempt to mislead and any failure to give full and correct information shall render the panchayat employee concerned liable to severe disciplinary action.

(10) Sanction shall, on no account be accorded for the purchase of land for any commercial purpose in any part of India, by a person employed, or concerned, in the collection of revenue.

(11) The restrictions on the acquisition and possession of immovable property shall apply in the acquisition and possession of any personal interest in such property and to the acquisition and possession of such property by a panchayat employee in the name of any other person, but not to the acquisition or possession of an interest as trustee, executor or administrator only.

(12) Except in accordance with the procedure laid down by the Government, no panchayat land shall be sold or granted on lease to any panchayat employee, whether in permanent or temporary employment.

(13) A panchayat employee shall not be allowed to acquire land, except house site or ready built house, for any other purpose within the revenue district in which he is serving.

9. Private trade or employment—(1) No panchayat employee shall, except with the previous sanction of the panchayat, engage himself directly or indirectly in any trade or business or undertake any employment:

Provided that a panchayat employee may, without such sanction, undertake honorary work of a social or charitable nature or occasional work of literary, artistic of scientific character, participate in sports activities subject to the condition that his official duties do not thereby suffer, but he shall not undertake, or shall discontinue such work if so directed by the panchayat.

(2) Notwithstanding anything contained in sub-rule (1), no panchayat employee shall undertake any part-time employment.

(3) Every panchayat employee shall, if any member of his family is engaged in a trade or business or owns or manages an insurance agency or commission agency, report the fact to the concerned panchayat:

Provided that, if it is found that the trade or business is of such a nature that the association of a member of the panchayat employees family in that trade or business can embarrass either the panchayat employee concerned or the concerned panchayat the panchayat employee shall not permit the said member of his family to continue his association with the trade or business in question.

Explanation. Canvassing by a panchayat employee in support of any trade, business, insurance agency or commission agency engaged in, owned or managed by any member of his family shall, be deemed to be a breach of this sub-rule.

(4) No panchayat employee shall, except with the previous sanction of the panchayat take part in the registration, promotion or management of any bank or company registered under the Banking Regulation Act, 1949, (Central Act X of 1949) or the Companies Act, 1956 (Central Act I of 1956), or any other law for the time being in force.

(5) No panchayat employee shall accept a paid employment in any company, mutual benefit society or co-operative society or act as an agent, whether paid by salary or commission to any insurance company or society.

(6) Panchayat employee shall be at liberty to take part in the promotion of co-operative societies, but no panchayat employee shall, except with the sanction of the panchayat hold office in any co-operative society or serve on any committee appointed for the management of its affairs, unless the society is composed wholly of panchayat employees or partly of panchayat employees and partly of employees of other local bodies and his official duties shall not thereby suffer and he shall, within a period of one month of his taking part in such activities, report to the panchayat giving details of the nature of his participation.

(7) No panchayat employee shall engage himself in the activities of a 'tout'.

Explanation. In the said sub-rule 'tout' shall have the same meaning as in Section 3 of the Legal Practioners Act, 1879 (Central Act XVIII of 1879).

10. Insolvency and habitual indebtedness—A panchayat employee shall endeavour to avoid habitual indebtedness or insolvency. If a panchayat employee is adjudged or declared insolvent or has incurred debts aggregating a sum which in ordinary circumstances he could not repay within a period of two years or if a part of his salary is frequently attached for debt, has been continuously so attached for a period of two years, or is attached for a sum which in ordinary circumstances he could not repay within a period of two years, he shall be presumed to have contravened this rule. But he shall not be so deemed, if he proves that the insolvency or indebtedness is the result of circumstances which with the exercise of ordinary diligence he could not have foreseen or over which he had no control and had not preceded from extravagant or dissipated habits. A panchayat employee who becomes the subject of legal proceedings for insolvency shall forthwith report the full facts to the panchayat in which he is employed.

11. Unauthorised communication of information—No panchayat employee shall, except in accordance with any general or special order of the panchayat or in the performance in good faith of the duties assigned to him, communicate directly or indirectly any official document or any part thereof or information to any other panchayat employee or any other person to whom he is not authorised to communicate such document or information.

12. Connection with press, television or radio—(1) No panchayat employee shall, except with the previous sanction of the panchayat, own wholly or in part or conduct or participate in the editing or managing of any newspaper or other periodical publication.

(2) No panchayat employee shall, except with the previous sanction of the panchayat or in the *bona fide* discharge of his duties contribute any article or write any letter either unanimously or in his own name or in the name of any other person to any newspaper or other periodical publications:

Provided that no such sanction shall be required if such contribution or writing is of a purely literary, artistic or scientific character.

(3) No panchayat employee shall except with the previous sanction of the panchayat, participate in a television programme or radio broadcast:

Provided that no such sanction shall be required if such television programme or radio broadcast, is of a purely literary, artistic or scientific character.

(4) A panchayat employee who is invited or who wished to participate in a television programme or to deliver a radio broadcast talk and has to obtain the previous sanction under sub-rule (3) shall intimate the panchayat the particulars relating to the television programme or the subject of the radio broadcast talk and if so required shall submit the full material relating to the television programme or the full text of the radio broadcast talk for their

approval before participating in the television programme or before the radio broadcast talk is delivered.

(5) The provisions of sub-rules (3) and (4) shall apply *mutadis mutandis* to the playing of prepared 'recitals' or gramophone records.

(6) In respect of television programme or radio broadcasts, the powers of the panchayat shall be exercised by the Executive Authority of the village panchayat or Commissioner of the panchayat union council or Secretary of the district panchayat, as the case may be.

13. Criticism of panchayat and Government—(1) No panchayat employee shall in any radio broadcast or in any document published anonymously or in his own name or in the name of any other person or in any communication to the press or in any public utterance, make any statement of fact or opinion:

(i) which has the effect of an adverse criticism of any current or recent policy or action of the Central Government or a State Government, or a panchayat; or

(ii) which is capable of embarrassing the relations between the State Government and any other Government; or panchayat; or

(iii) which is capable of embarrassing the relations between the Central Government and the Government of any foreign State:

Provided that in the case of any panchayat employee nothing contained in this rule apply to *bona fide* expression of views by him as an office bearer of any recognised association of panchayat employees for the purpose of safeguarding the conditions of service of panchayat employees or for securing an improvement thereof.

(2) A panchayat employee shall not, except in the discharge of his official duties, preside over or take part in the organization of or occupy a prominent position at or address, any non-official meeting or conference at which it is likely that speeches may be made or resolutions may be proposed or passed criticising the action of the Government and panchayat or requesting the Government and panchayat to take certain action other than to make grants admissible under the Government/ panchayat rules or orders in support of educational or similar institutions.

(3) A panchayat employee who intends to publish any document or to make any communication to the press or to deliver any public utterance containing statements in respect of which any doubt as to the application of the restrictions imposed by this rule may arise, shall submit to the panchayat a copy of draft of the documents which he intends to publish or of the utterance which he intends to deliver and shall thereafter act in accordance with such orders as may be passed by the panchayat.

14. Evidence before committee or any other authority—(1) Save as provided in sub-rule (3), no panchayat employee shall, except with the previous sanction of the panchayat, give evidence in connection with any enquiry conducted by any person, committee or authority.

(2) Where any sanction has been accorded under sub-rule (1), no panchayat employee giving such evidence shall criticise the policy or any action of the Central Government or of a State Government or any local body institutions.

(3) Nothing contained in this rule apply to evidence given in any judicial enquiry or evidence given at any department enquiry.

15. Taking part in politics and elections and position of panchayat employees in relation to elections—(1) No panchayat employee shall be a member of or be otherwise associated with any political party or any organisation in respect of which there is reason to believe that the organisation has a political aspect, nor shall he take part in, subscribe in aid of, or assist in any other manner any political movement or activities. He shall also not only maintain political neutrality but shall also appear to do so. He shall also avoid giving room for any suspicion that he is favouring any political party or any candidate in elections.

(2) It shall be the duty of every panchayat employee to endeavour to prevent any member of his family from taking part in subscribing, in aid of or assisting in any other manner, any movement or activity which is, or tends directly or indirectly to be, subversive of any Government or local body as established, and where a panchayat employee is unable to prevent a member of his family taking part in, or subscribing in aid of or assisting in any other manner, any such movement or activity, he shall make a report to that effect to the concerned panchayat.

(3) If any question arises whether a party is a political party or whether any organisation takes part in politics or whether any movement or activity falls within the scope of this rule, the decision of the Inspector thereon shall be final.

(4) No panchayat employee shall canvass or otherwise interfere or use his influence in connection

with or take part in, an election to any legislature or local authority:

Provided that:

(i) a panchayat employee qualified to vote at such election may exercise his right to vote but where he does so, he shall, give no indication of any manner in which he proposes to vote or voted.

(ii) a panchayat employee shall not be deemed to have contravened the provisions of this rule by reason only that he assists in the conduct of an election in due performance of a duty imposed on him by or under any law for the time being in force.

Explanation. (1) Nothing contained in this sub-rule shall be deemed to prohibit the wife/husband of panchayat employee or any other member of his family living with or in any way dependent on him from standing for election to any legislature or to any local authority and from canvassing for other candidates.

(2) The display by a panchayat employee on his person, vehicle or residence of any electoral symbol shall amount to using his influence in connection with an election within the meaning of this rule.

(3) Seditious propaganda or the expressing of disloyal sentiments by a panchayat employee shall be regarded as sufficient ground for dispensing with his services.

(4) A panchayat employee proposing or seconding the nomination of candidate at an election or acting as a polling agent shall be deemed to have committed a breach of this rule.

16. Prohibition of membership of any communal organisation etc.—(1) No panchayat employee shall be a member of or be otherwise associated with any organization,

(a) which promotes or attempts to promote on grounds of religion, race, place of birth, residence, language, caste or community or any other ground whatsoever disharmony or feelings of enmity hatred or ill will between different religious, racial, language or regional groups or castes or communities; or

(b) whose activities are prejudicial to the maintenance of harmony between different religious, racial, language or regional groups or castes or communities and which disturbs or is likely to disturb the public tranquillity; or

(c) which organises any exercise, movement, drill or other similar activity intending that the participants in such activity shall use or be trained to use criminal force or violence or knowing it to be likely that the participants in such activity will use or be trained to use criminal force or violence against any religious, racial, language or regional group or caste or community and such activity for any reason whatsoever causes or is likely to cause fear or alarm or a feeling of insecurity amongst members of such religious, racial, language or regional group or caste or community.

(2) If any question arises whether any organisation falls under sub-rule (1) the decision of the Inspector thereon shall be final.

17. Vindication of acts and character of panchayat employee—(1) No panchayat employee shall, except with the previous sanction of the concerned panchayat have recourse to the press for the vindication of any official act which has been the subject matter of adverse criticism or an attack of defamatory character.

Explanation. (1) Nothing in this rule shall be deemed to prohibit a panchayat employee from vindicating his private character or any act done by him in his private capacity and where any action for vindicating his private character or any act done by him in private capacity the panchayat employee shall submit a report to the panchayat regarding such action.

(2) No panchayat employee shall, except with the previous sanction of the panchayat accept from any person or body of persons compensation of any kind for any malicious prosecution brought against him or for any defamatory attack made on his public acts or character unless such compensation has been awarded by a competent court.

18. Membership of service association—No panchayat employee shall be a member, representative or office bearer of any association representing or purporting to represent, panchayat employees unless such association satisfies the following conditions, namely:

(a) Membership of the association shall be confined to a distinct class of panchayat employees and shall be open to all panchayat employees of that class;

(b) The association shall not, in any way, be connected with any political party or organisation or engage in any political activity;

(c) The association shall not, in any way, be connected with, or affiliated to;

(i) any association which does not; or

(ii) any federation of association, which do not satisfy conditions (a) and (b).

(d) The association shall not—

(i) issue or maintain any periodical publication except in accordance with any general or special order of the Government,

(ii) except with the previous sanction of the panchayat, publish any representation on behalf of its members, whether in the press or otherwise;

(iii) in respect of any election to a legislative body whether in India or elsewhere, or to a local authority or body—

(A) pay or contribute towards any expenses incurred in connection with his candidature by a candidate for such election;

(B) by any means support the candidature of any person for such election; or

(C) undertake or assist in the registration of election or the selection of a candidate for such election;

(iv) maintain or contribute towards the maintenance of any member of legislative body whether in India or elsewhere or of any member of a local authority or body;

(v) pay, or contribute towards the expenses of any trade union which has constituted a fund under Section 16 of the India Trade Unions Act, 1926 (Central Act XVI of 1926).

19. Employment under or with near relatives in service and employment of relatives in firms enjoying panchayat patronage—(1) No panchayat employee shall in the discharge of his official duties deal with any matter or give or sanction any contract to any undertaking or any other person if any member of his family or close relation is employed in that undertaking or under that person or if he or any member of his family or close relation is interested in such matter or contract in any other manner and the panchayat employee shall refer every such matter or contract shall thereafter be disposed of according to the instructions of the authority to whom the reference is made.

20. Canvassing of non-official or other outside influence—No panchayat employee shall bring or attempt to bring any political or other outside influence to bear upon any superior authority to further his interests in respect of matters pertaining to his service under the panchayats.

21. Bigamous marriage—(1) (i) No panchayat employee shall enter into or contract, a marriage with a person having a spouse living; and

(ii) No panchayat employee having a spouse living shall enter into or contract a marriage with any person:

Provided that the panchayat may permit a panchayat employee to enter into or contract, any such marriage as is referred to in clause (i) or clause (ii) if they are satisfied that:

(a) such marriage is permissible under the personal law applicable to such panchayat employee and the other party to the marriage; and

(b) there are other grounds for so doing.

(2) No panchayat employee involve himself in any act involving moral turpitude on his part including any unlawful act, which may cause embarrassment or which may bring discredit to Government or local body.

22. Integrity and devotion to duty—(1) Every panchayat employee shall at all times maintain absolute integrity and devotion to duty and shall do nothing which is unbecoming of an employee of a panchayat.

(2) Every panchayat employee shall take all possible steps to ensure integrity and devotion to duty by all panchayat employees for the time being under his control and authority.

(3) (i) No panchayat employee shall in the performance of his official duties or in the exercise of powers conferred on him, act otherwise that in his best judgement, except when he is acting under the direction of his official superior.

(ii) The direction of the official superior shall ordinarily be in writing. Oral directions to subordinates shall be avoided. Where the issue of oral direction becomes unavoidable the official superior shall confirm it in writing immediately thereafter.

(iii) A panchayat employee who has received oral directions from his official superior shall seek confirmation of the same in writing as early as possible, where upon it shall be the duty of the official superior to confirm the direction in writing.

(iv) No panchayat employee shall, in the performance of his official duties or in the exercise of powers conferred on him evade the responsibility devolving legitimately on him and seek instruction from or approval of a superior authority when such instruction or approval is not necessary as the scheme of distribution of powers and responsibilities.

Explanation. A panchayat employee who habitually fails to perform a task assigned to him within the time set for the purpose and with the quality of performance expected of him shall be deemed to be lacking in devotion to duty within the meaning of sub-rule (1).

23. Panchayat servant not to be found drunk while attending office—A panchayat employee:

(a) shall strictly abide by any law relating to consumption of liquor or intoxicating drugs in force in any area in which he may happen to be for the time being;

(b) shall not be found drunk or under the influence of liquor while attending office or appearing in a public place.

24. Strikes—No panchayat employee shall engage himself in strike or in incitements thereto or in similar activities.

Explanation. For the purpose of this rule the expression 'similar activities' shall be deemed to include the absence from work or neglect of duties without permission and with the object of compelling something to be done by his superior officers or the panchayat or any demonstrative fast usually called "hunger strike" for similar purposes.

25. Procession and meetings—No panchayat employee shall conduct any procession or hold or address any meeting in any part of any open ground adjoining any local body office or inside any office premises—

(a) during office hours on any working day; and

(b) outside office hours or on holidays, save with the prior permission of the Executive Authority or Commissioner or Secretary, as the case may be.

26. Anti-secular or social disharmony activity and demonstration—No panchayat employee shall engage himself or participate in any activity which is anti-secular or which tends to create disharmony in society or in any demonstration which is prejudicial to the interest of the sovereignty and integrity of India, the security of the State, public order, decency or morality or which involves contempt of court, defamation or incitement to an offence.

27. Joining of associations by panchayat employees—No panchayat employee shall be or continue to be a member of an association the objects or activities of which are prejudicial to the interest of the sovereignty and integrity of India or public order of morality.

28. Obtaining of No Objections Certificate before applying for passport or undertaking any foreign trip—No panchayat employee shall, except after obtaining No Objection Certificate from the concerned Inspector, apply for grant or renewal of passport or undertake trip to a foreign country. While applying for such No Objection Certificate information regarding the purpose of the visit, the duration of stay and the names of Countries proposed to be visited shall be furnished.

29. Interpretation—If any question arises relating to the interpretation of these rules it shall be referred to the Government whose decision thereon shall be final.

(G.O. Ms. No. 51, Rural Development (C-4) Department, dated 15th February 2001)

APPENDIX

Form I

[See Rule 8(2)(1)]

Form of Report/Application for Permission of the Panchayats for the Building of or Addition to a House

Sir,

This is to report you that I propose to build a house or to make an addition to my house. This is to request that permission may be granted to me for the building of the house or making addition to my house. The estimated cost of land and materials for the construction or extension of the house is given below:

LAND:

(1) Location (Survey numbers, Villages, districts, State)
(2) Area
(3) Cost

BUILDING MATERIALS, ETC.

(1) Bricks (Rate/quantity/cost)
(2) Cement (Rate/quantity/cost)
(3) Iron and Steel (Rate/quantity/cost)
(4) Timber (Rate/quantity/cost)
(5) Sanitary Fitting (cost)
(6) Electrical fitting (cost)
(7) Any other special fittings (cost)
(8) Labour charges
(9) Other charges, if any

TOTAL COST OF LAND AND BUILDINGS:

2. The construction will be supervised by myself. The construction will be done by ....* I do not have any official dealings with him in the past. I have/had official dealings with the Contractor and the nature of my dealings with him is/was as under:
3. The cost of the proposed construction will be met as under:

Amount

(i) Own savings
(ii) Loans/Advances with full details
(iii) Other sources with details.

Yours faithfully,

Strike out portion not applicable.

*Enter the name and place of business of the Contractor.

Form II

[See Rule 8(2)(i)]

Form of Report/Application for Permission for Acquisition of House

To

....

Sir,

This is to report you that I propose to acquire a ready built house at .... This is to request that permission may be granted to me for the acquisition of the house. The particulars of the house to be acquired and its estimated cost are given below:

(1) Location of the house (Plot No., Survey No., Village, Taluk, District and State)
(2) Area ....
(3) Name of the seller ....
(4) Address and occupation of the seller ....
(5) Cost of the house ....
(6) The cost of the house will be met as under

Amount.

(i) Personal savings.......... ....
(ii) Loans/Advances with full details ....
(iii) Other sources with full details ....

Yours faithfully,

VALUATION REPORT

I/We hereby certify that I/We have valued house .... of that .... to be purchased by Thiru/ Thirumathi .... and I/We give below the value at which we estimate the cost of the house under the following headings:

Heading

Cost

1. Approximate value of plot ....
2. Area and approximate value of building ....
3. Approximate value of Electrical, Sanitary and other fittings and fixtures ....

Total cost of the buildings ....
Date:

Signature of the Valuation Authority.

Form III
[See Rule 8(6)]
Statement of Immovable Property held by Panchayat Employee
(e.g. Lands, House, Shops, Other Buildings, etc.)

Serial Number	Description of property	Precise location (Name of District, Taluk and village in) which the property is situated and also its distinctive number etc.	Area of Land (in case of land and buildings) (square metre/Ha)	Nature of land (in case of landed property)	Extent of interest	If not in own name, state in whose name held and his/her relationship, if any to the panchayat	Date of acquisition
(1)	(2)	(3)	(4)	(5)	(6)	(7)	(8)
How acquired (whether by purchase mortgage lease inheritance, gift or otherwise) and name with details of persons from whom acquired (address and connection of the panchayat, if any, with the person/persons concerned (please see Note 1 below)	Value of the property (See Note 2 below)	Sources of Income	Details of payments	Particulars of sanction of prescribed authority, if any	Total income from the property	Remarks	
(9)	(10)	(11)	(12)	(13)	(14)	(15)	

Date Signature

Notes:

1. For purpose of column (9) the term "lease" would mean a lease of immovable property from year to year or for any term exceeding one year or reserving a yearly rent. Where, however the lease of immovable property is obtained from a person having official dealings with the panchayat employee, such a lease should be shown in this column irrespective of the term of the lease, whether it is short-term or long-term, and the periodicity of the panchayat of rent.
2. In column (10) should be shown:
   (a) Where the property has been acquired by purchase, mortgage or lease, the price or premium paid for such acquisition;
   (b) Where it has been acquired by lease, the total annual rent thereof also; and
   (c) Where the acquisition is by inheritance, gift or exchange the approximate value of the property so acquired.

Form IV
[See Rule 8(6)]
Return of Assets and Liabilities held by Panchayat Employee

(1) Name of Panchayat Employee in full (in block letters) :
(2) Service to which he belongs :
(3) Total length of service up-to-date :
(4) Present post held :
(5) Total annual income from all sources during the calendar year immediately preceding the 1st day of January 200—
(6) Declaration :

I hereby declare that the return enclosed, are complete, true and correct as on .... to the best of my knowledge and belief, in respect of information due to be furnished by me under the provisions of Rule 8 of the Tamil Nadu Panchayat Employees Conduct Rules, 2000.

Date:

Signature:

Note: This return shall contain particulars of all assets and liabilities of the panchayat employee either in his own name or in the name of any other person.

3.6.2 Payment of Arrear Claim of Panchayat Employees

1. Short title—These Rules may be called the Tamil Nadu Panchayats (Payment of Arrears Claims of Officers and Employees of Panchayats) Rules, 1999.

2. Claim of arrears of pay, allowance or increments—(1) Every claim of an officer or servant of a panchayat for arrears of pay, allowance or increment of pay which has been allowed to remain in abeyance shall, before payment, be investigated by the Executive Authority or the Commissioner or the Chief Executive Officer, as the case may be

(i) with the sanction of the concerned panchayat in the case of the claims relating to a period with in two years.

(ii) with the sanction of the panchayat concerned and of the Assistant Director (Panchayats) in the case of village panchayat and panchayat union, and the Inspector in the case of district panchayat in case of the claims relating to a period exceeding two years.

3. Payment of arrear claims—The payment of an arrear claim specified in Rule 2 shall not exceed the amount found to be actually due under the claim in respect of a period of one year immediately preceding the date of detection of the under-payment. If, in any particular case, it is considered that for special reason a large concession should be granted, the Executive Authority or the Commissioner or the Secretary, as the case may be, shall obtain the sanction of the Inspector for payment of arrears for a period exceeding two year:

Provided that the sanction of the Inspector shall not be necessary in respect of arrear claim of one thousand rupees which is over one year old, but not more than three years old.

Explanation. For the purpose of this rule, the date of detection of an under-payment shall be the date on which the under-payment is detected by or brought to the notice of the Executive Authority or the Commissioner or the Secretary, as the case may be, or, if it is first detected in audit, the date of detection by the auditor. An arrear claim resulting from an order issued with retrospective effect does not arise until the order is issued and shall not, therefore, be treated as a claim allowed to remain in abeyance during the prior to date of the order. An order passed with retrospective effect shall, for the purposes of this explanation, be deemed to be done which in the circumstances of the case, could not have been passed earlier or which was deliberately held over pending consideration.

4. Restriction for delegation—The power conferred on the panchayat in Rule 2 shall not be delegated by the panchayats to the president of village panchayat or chairman of the panchayat union council or chairman of district panchayat, as the case may be.

5. Submission of audit—(1) Every claim of arrear under Rule 2 shall be submitted by the panchayat concerned to the next audit. In case any amount is found by the audit to have been claimed and disbursed in excess of the eligibility, the same shall be recovered from the claimant by the panchayat concerned.

(2) In case where a claim of arrear under Rule 2, exceeds one lakh, the same shall be submitted for pre-audit to the competent auditor concerned.

(G.O. Ms. No.224 Rural Development (C-4) Department, dated 20th October 1999)

3.6.3 Panchayat Servants Safeguarding of National Security

1. **Short title**—These rules may be called the Tamil Nadu Panchayats (Services Safeguarding of National Security) Rules, 1999.

2. **Definition**—In these rules, unless the context otherwise requires, "employee" means an officer or a servant of a panchayat.

3. **Compulsory retirement**—Where the Government are of the opinion that an employee is engaged in, or is reasonably suspected to be engaged in, subversive activities or is associated with others engaged in subversive activities and that his retention in service is on that account prejudicial to national security, they may make an order compulsorily retiring such employee from service.

4. **Procedure**—Before an order under Rule 3 is made:

(1) the Inspector shall, by notice in writing, inform the employee concerned of the action proposed to be taken against him and give him an opportunity to make any representation in writing against such action to the Government within such period as may be specified in the notice; and

(2) the Government shall take into consideration the representation, if any, so made by such employee.

5. **Suspension**—Where action under these rules is proposed to be taken in regard to an employee, the Inspector shall, before placing him under suspension, permit him to proceed on such leave as may, at that time, be admissible to him, if he opts so.

6. **General rules not to apply**—Nothing contained in these rules relating to the general establishment, appointment and punishment of employees shall apply to, or in respect of, any action taken or proposed to be taken under these rules.

7. **Pension, gratuity, etc.**—Any employee compulsorily retired from service under Rule 3 shall be entitled to such compensation, pension, gratuity or provident fund benefits as would have been admissible to him under the relevant rules on the date of such retirement, if he had been discharged from service due to the abolition of his post without any alternative suitable employment being provided.

(G.O. Ms. No.266, Rural Development (C-4) Department, dated 22nd December 1999)

3.7 SUITS AND PROSECUTION

3.7.1 Limit of Law Charges by Panchayats without Outside Sanction

1. **Short title**—These rules may be called the Tamil Nadu Panchayats (Limit of Law Charges to be incurred by Panchayats without Outside Sanction) Rules, 1999.

2. **Payment of fees to counsel without outside sanction**—Panchayats may pay fees to counsel without outside sanction in accordance with the following scale:

(i) In civil cases, the regulation fee or a fee exceeding the regulation fee but not exceeding one thousand rupees.

(ii) In criminal cases a fee not exceeding two hundred and fifty rupees for each day during which the counsel is engaged in court in connection with the case for not less than three hours, or for less than three hours a different station from that where he usually practices and one hundred rupees for each day in all other cases:

Provided that where the counsel is engaged in the court for more than one case on the same day the total fee payable to him for that day for all cases shall not exceed three hundred and fifty rupees.

(iii) (a) In each case for the work done in examining records and for services rendered out of court, provided no suit or case is instituted or defence entered in continuation of such examination or of such services and where such suit or case is instituted or defence entered, the total fees payable to the counsel for the work done in examining the records, the services rendered out of court and the work in the court, the fees shall not exceed one thousand rupees or the fee payable under Rule 2, whichever is higher; and

(b) in each case in which the subject matter of the claim does not admit of valuation.

3. Payment of fees in special cases—Nothing contained in Rule 2 shall be deemed to restrict the amount payable in special cases, but when the limits fixed in the said rule are proposed to be exceeded, the sanction of the Assistant Director (Panchayats) in case such excess amount does not exceed one thousand rupees and the sanction of the Inspector if the such excess amount exceeds one thousand rupees shall be obtained.

4. Appeal or Revision—In cases where a panchayat desires to prefer an appeal or revision against any judgement order or decree of a court the previous sanction of the Inspector shall be obtained.

(G.O. Ms. No.189, Rural Development (C-4) Department, dated 14th September 1999)

3.7.2 Appointment of Counsel and Payment of Fees in Certain Cases

1. Short title—These rules may be called the Tamil Nadu Panchayats (Appointment of Counsel and Incurring of Law Charges) Rules, 1999.

2. Applicability of the rules—The rules shall apply to village panchayats, panchayat unions and district panchayats

3. Fee payable to the counsel—(1) When both the Government and a panchayat are parties in a civil case in which the correctness of the survey of lands vested in the panchayats is in question and the interest of both are identical, the panchayat shall engage on its behalf only the counsel appointed by Government or the District Collector on behalf of the Government. In such cases the fee payable to the counsel shall be borne by the Government and the panchayat in the proportion of two-thirds and one-third, respectively.

(2) In civil cases other than those mentioned in Rule 3 where both the Government and panchayat are parties and their pleadings are similar, the panchayats shall engage on its behalf only the counsel appointed on behalf of the Government. In such cases the fee payable to the counsel and other incidental charges and any expenses incurred after the proceedings on behalf of the Government and the panchayats become joint and in furtherance of such joint proceedings, shall be borne by the Government and the panchayat in equal shares.

(3) These rules shall not apply to appeals filed by panchayat against the decision of civil courts. In case of appeals by panchayat against the decision of any court, the panchayat concerned shall discuss the legal opinion obtained on the issue from a competent counsel and take a decision. The fee and all allowances to be paid to the counsel shall also be decided by the panchayat.

(4) In cases where Inspector considers of important nature to safeguard the interest of panchayat to be defended or argued by Advocate-General of Tamil Nadu, or the Senior Counsel at a significant cost, the same shall be brought to the notice of the Government. The decision of the Government shall be final. In all such cases, fees shall be fully paid by the panchayat concerned.

(G.O.Ms. No. 166, Rural Development (C-4) Department, dated 9th August 1999)

3.8 AUDIT AND ACCOUNTS

3.8.1 Appointment of Auditors of Panchayats

Notification—In exercise of the powers conferred by sub-section (1) of Section 193 and Section 242 of the Tamil Nadu Panchayats Act, 1994 (Tamil Nadu Act 21 of 1994) and in super session of Rural Development and Local Administration Departments Notification II-2 No.424 of 1960 published at page 222 of Part II-Section 2 of the Fort. St. George Gazette dated the 9th November 1960, the Governor of Tamil Nadu hereby appoints the officers specified in column (2) of the Table below as auditors of the accounts of the receipts and expenditure of the panchayats specified in the corresponding entries in column (1) thereof:-

The Table

Sl. No.	*Nature of Panchayat*	*Name of the Post of Auditing Officer*
1.	Village Panchayat	(a) Deputy Block Development Officer Except Scheme Fund Account (b) Assistant Director of Rural Development (Audit) (Except Scheme Fund Account) Director of Local Fund Audit and his Assistants (Scheme Fund Account only)
2.	Panchayat Union	Director of Local Fund Audit and his Assistants.
3.	District Panchayat	Director of Local Fund Audit and his Assistants.

(G.O. Ms. No. 265 Rural Development (C-3) Department, dated 21st December 1999)

3.8.2 Powers of Auditors, Inspecting and Superintending Officers

1. **Short title**—These rules may be called the Tamil Nadu Panchayats (Powers of Auditors, Inspecting and Superintending Officers) Rules, 1999.

2. **Definition**—In these rules unless the context otherwise requires, "Act" means the Tamil Nadu Panchayats Act, 1994 (Tamil Nadu Act 21 of 1994).

3. **Power of holding inquiries**—All persons authorised by the Act or the rules made thereunder to conduct inquiries and all auditors, inspecting and superintending officers, appointed under the said Act, holding any inquiries into matters falling within the scope of their duties shall have, for the purpose of holding such inquiries, powers:

(1) to summon any person resident within the district whose evidence may appear to them to be necessary for the investigation of any matter under inquiry and also to require the production of any document relevant to the matter under inquiry which may be in the possession or under the control of such person; and

(2) to grant to any such person such allowances as is admissible to a witness summoned by a civil court and to pass orders as to the person by whom or the fund out of which allowance shall be paid.

4. **Issue of summons**—The summons shall be in writing and authenticated by the signature and the seal, if any, of the officer by whom it is issued. It shall require the person summoned to appear before the said officer at a stated time and place and shall specify whether his attendance is required for the purpose of giving evidence or to produce a document, or for both purposes; and any particular document, the production of which is required shall be described in the summons with reasonable certainty.

5. **Serving of summons**—The summons shall be served personally on the person summoned or sent to him by registered post with acknowledgement due or if such person is not found by leaving it at his last known place of residence or by giving or by tendering it to an adult member of his family or if none of the means aforesaid is available by affixing it in some conspicuous part of his last known place of residence.

6. **Production of documents as evidence**—Any person may be summoned to produce a document without being summoned to give evidence, and any person summoned merely to produce a document shall be deemed to have complied with the summons if he causes such document to be produced, instead of attending personally to produce the same.

7. **Circumstances in which summons can be dispensed with**—When the person whose evidence may be required is unable, due to sickness or infirmity, to attend before the officer issuing the summons, or is a person whom by reason of rank or sex it may not be proper to summon, the officer issuing the summons, may of his own motion, or on the application of the person whose evidence is desired, dispense with the appearance of such person, and order him to be examined by a subordinate deputed by such officers for the purpose.

8. **Failure to oblige for summons**—Any person who fails to obey a summon issued under these rules shall be punishable with fine which may extend to one hundred rupees or in case of a continuing breach, with fine not exceeding fifteen rupees for everyday during which, the breach continues after punishment for the first breach.

9. **Savings**—Nothing contained in these rules shall apply to cases for which provision has otherwise been made by or under the Act.

(G.O. Ms. No. 142, Rural Development (C-4) Department, 21st July 1999)

(G.O. Ms. No. 236, Rural Development (C-4) Department, dated 19th September 2001).

3.8.3 Implementation of Concurrent Audit in Panchayats

The high level committee constituted for devolution of power to Local Bodies have suggested to implement of concurrent audit system in panchayats. Accordingly, the Government orders for implementation the concurrent of audit system in all three tiers of Panchayats.

The Deputy Block Development Officer shall audit the village panchayat accounts once in a three months with assistance of his subordinate Officers. The Deputy Block Development Officer shall also audit the Village Panchayat Scheme Fund Accounts. The Officers of Local Fund Audit Department will review the audit conducted by the Deputy Block Development Officers, in circumstances the audit department shall conduct the test check of the audit conducted by the Deputy Block Development Officers.

(1) The Local Fund Audit Department shall audit the accounts of panchayat unions accounts once in a

three months with present staff of Local Fund Audit Department, the plan will be prepared to conduct audit within 90 days, if audit is not conducted within 90 days, that accounts must be audited within next 90 days.

(2) The Local Fund Audit Department shall audit the district panchayat account once in a year based on the volume of transaction and receipt and expenditure of district panchayat.

(3) The quarterly concurrent audit system shall come into force from January 2000 onwards.

(4) The Local Fund Audit Department shall prepare a manual on audit of panchayats.

(G.O. Ms. No. 95, Rural Development (C-3) Department, dated 10th April 2000)

3.8.4 Issue and Disposal of Audit Reports of Panchayat Union Council and District Panchayat

1. Short title—These rules may be called the Tamil Nadu Panchayats (Issue and Disposal of Audit Reports of Panchayat Union Council and District Panchayat) Rules, 2000.

2. Definition—In these rules, unless the context otherwise requires, "Act" means the Tamil Nadu Panchayats Act, 1994.

3. Accounts and records to be produced to the Auditor—The Commissioner of a panchayat union council or Secretary of district panchayat, as the case may be, shall send all accounts and records of the panchayat union council or district panchayat to the Auditor, appointed under sub-section (1) of Section 193 of the Act, as required by him and also to the Accountant General and his subordinate officers, whenever he or his subordinate officers demand the production of records of a panchayat union council or district panchayat.

4. Annual accounts—The Commissioner or Secretary, as the case may be, shall finalise the accounts of a year in respect of all funds, close all the relevant registers and send the annual accounts to the auditor before the end of May of the year following the year to which the accounts relate.

5. Audit of panchayat union council and district panchayat accounts—(1) The auditor shall conduct the audit of accounts of the panchayat union council and district panchayat every year, soon after the Commissioner or Secretary, as the case may be, submits the annual accounts for the previous year in respect of all funds maintained by him or concurrently as and when the bills are passed for payment by the Commissioner or Secretary, as the case may be.

(2) The auditor shall take up the audit of the accounts of the panchayat union council or district panchayat in his jurisdiction from the month of June onwards and complete the audit of all such institutions in his jurisdiction within twelve months of the date of receipt of annual accounts by him. If so, directed by the government, the auditor shall take up concurrent audit of the voucher of the panchayat union or district panchayat soon after payment is made and send audit slips after every voucher is audited by him concurrently.

6. Powers of the auditors—(1) The auditor may, by summons in writing;

(i) require the production of any book, deed, contract, account, voucher receipt or other document, the perusal or examination of which he considers necessary;

(ii) require any person having the custody or control of any such document or person accountable for it to appear in person before him duly specifying the purpose of production; and

(iii) require any person so appearing to make and sign a declaration in respect of such document or to answer any question or to prepare and furnish any statement relating thereto.

(2) Whoever fails to comply with any requisition lawfully made upon him under this rule, shall be punishable with fine which may extend to one hundred rupees or in case of a continuing breach, with fine not exceeding fifteen rupees for every day during which the breach continues after conviction for the first breach.

7. Scrutiny of the records—The auditor shall scrutinize every item of receipts and expenditure subject to checks, prescribed in the audit manual and instructions issued by Rural Development Department from time-to-time and find out whether the Commissioner or Secretary, as the case may be; has conducted the financial transactions of the institution in accordance with the Issue and Disposal of Audit Reports of panchayat union council and district panchayat rules and orders laid down by Government from time-to-time.

8. Preparation and finalization of audit reports—The auditor, during the course of audit shall either in annual audit or concurrent audit issue a copy of the draft of objection on any transaction, which he considers, is not in accordance with the Issue and Disposal of Audit reports of panchayat union council and district panchayat rules and orders laid down by Rural Development Department in Government from time-to-time, to the Commissioner or Secretary, as the case may be, on getting his acknowledgement. On receipt of such draft audit objection, the Commissioner or Secretary, as the case may be, shall take effective action to set right the defects pointed out therein and furnish replies to the auditor, as soon as possible or before the audit is over, as to the nature of action taken for setting right the objection and get his acknowledgement. The auditor shall be bound to consider such replies received from the Commissioner or Secretary, as the case may be, during the course of the audit and may either drop the draft objection or modify the same based on the nature of replies received. At the closure of the audit, the auditor shall compile all the draft audit objections which remain unanswered properly from an audit report present it to the Commissioner or Secretary, as the case may be, and obtain the dated signature of the Commissioner or Secretary, as the case may be, at the end of each page of the audit report. The Commissioner or Secretary, as the case may be, while signing in the audit report, shall write against each objection either "accepted the objection mentioned in this Para", or write "not accepted as the objection lacks authority for the basis of the objection in this Para". The Assistant Director of Local Fund Audit while scrutinising and reviewing the draft audit report in the presence of the Commissioner or Secretary, as the case may be, during local passing shall examine the objections one by one, discuss the contents of the objections with the Commissioner or Secretary, as the case may be, endeavour to convince him as to the correctness of the basis of the objections and finalise the audit report. In case, Commissioner or Secretary as the case may be, is not convinced about the authority for the basis of certain objections, the Assistant Director of Local Fund Audit shall ask the Commissioner or Secretary, as the case may be, to record his views briefly on the objection and then add the same to the audit report. Such views as recorded by the Commissioner or Secretary, as the case may be, shall be part of the audit report.

9. Review of audit report—The reviewing authority namely, the Assistant Director of Local Fund Audit Department, shall not include any objection in the report for which draft audit objection was not furnished to the Commissioner or Secretary, as the case may be, previously in the draft stage and in such cases he shall look into the transaction afresh and decide its proprietary for inclusion in the audit report. In order to avoid such contingency, the Commissioner or Secretary, as the case may be, shall ensure that the records and registers requested in audit are produced systematically during the course of audit.

10. Contents of audit report—The audit report shall contain, besides the names of the Commissioners or Secretaries, as the case may be, who were in office during the period of audit, the names of the engineers, the union overseers and other officers who were also in office during the period of audit. In addition to these, the names of officials who (other than Assistant) recommended payment for an item of expenditure, which is objected to, at the stage prior to the approval by the Commissioner or Secretary, as the case may be, and in the case of loss of revenue and in respect of the defects in the stores accounting the name of the officials including Assistants who are responsible for the loss of revenue or for the maintenance of materials, accounts and custody of such stocks, shall also, be specified at the end of each objection, for facilitating the fixing of proportionate and joint responsibility on the principle of contributory negligence on the officials who are jointly or severally responsible for an irregular or inadmissible expenditure incurred.

11. Sending of audit reports and special report on serious irregularities—(1) The Assistant Director of Local Fund Audit shall send the audit report on the accounts of a panchayat union council, or district panchayat to the Commissioner or Secretary, as the case may be, within thirty days of the completion of audit by the subordinate auditors, send a copy of audit report to the Assistant Director of Rural Development (Audit) of the district and to the Inspector concerned. In addition to this, he shall also submit to the Director of Local Fund Audit, copies of objections involving serious financial and other persistent irregularities for further action, who may communicate such of those audit objections which in his opinion, are serious in nature, to the Government for such action as may be found necessary.

(2) The auditor shall communicate copies of objections to the Commissioner or Secretary, as the case may be, in whose period the expenditure in question, was incurred in cases where it is considered that he is personally responsible for the expenditure and obtain his acknowledgement. The personal responsibility shall arise in a case where

the Commissioner or Secretary, as the case may be, has taken an exceptional or different decision, departing from the office advice, for incurring an expenditure which has given room for the objection or cannot be recovered from the recipient legally. When the present Commissioner or Secretary, as the case may be, can and has to take effective action to fix responsibility and recover the amount either from the recipient of money legally or from the officials who administratively tendered wrong advice, such cases should not be considered as matters for which the past Commissioner or Secretary, as the case may be, is personally responsible. In cases where the limitation of time stands in the way of lawful recovery of an objected expenditure, only the officials who were in office from the date of receipt of audit report to the crucial date of time bar, shall be considered as responsible for not initiating action for recovery before the date of time bar and action shall be taken to fix responsibility for the reported loss, on the principle of contributory negligence and joint responsibility.

12. Actions to be taken on audit objections—(1) The Commissioner or Secretary, as the case may be, soon after the receipt of audit report, shall initiate action and arrange to open one file for each objection in the concerned branch or seat, pursue effective speedy and systematic action to settle the objections and furnish final replies to all the objections raised. No audit file shall be closed before the receipt of orders settling the objections contained therein. Wherever recovery orders are required to be passed by the Commissioner or Secretary, as the case may be, for recovering the amount for settlement of objections, such orders shall be passed immediately, by him after following the prescribed procedure. Incases, where recovery orders have to be passed by an outside authority, the Commissioner or Secretary, as the case may be, shall send proposals with all relevant details to such authority who shall initiate action for issuing recovery orders and pass final orders within two months of the receipt of the proposal from the Commissioner or Secretary, as the case may be, by having recourse to the rules relating to the disciplinary action.

(2) It shall be the bounden duty of the Commissioner or Secretary, as the case may be and his staff who are in office at the time of receipt of audit report issued in concurrent audit to take effective action to settle the audit objections. If the Commissioner or Secretary, as the case may be, in office considers that any orders passed by the previous Commissioner or Secretary, as the case may be, contrary to the office advice, is responsible for the objection in question, he may address the Assistant Director of Rural Development (Audit) concerned, for fixing up of responsibility on the person or persons concerned adhering to the principles of joint responsibility and contributory negligence and passing necessary recovery orders with in a month from the date of receipt of proposals by him. Suitable replies may thereafter be furnished on all those objections.

13. Audit report to be placed before the panchayat union council or district panchayat—The Commissioner or Secretary, as the case may be, after preparing proper and final replies to the objections, place the audit report and the replies to the objections before the panchayat union council or district panchayat, as the case may be, for discussion and suitable decision. He shall send the replies, addressed to the Auditor, in triplicate with a copy of the resolution of the panchayat union council or district panchayat to the Inspector through the Assistant Director of Rural Development (Audit) concerned, within two months from the date of receipt of audit report. The Assistant Director of Rural Development (Audit) concerned shall scrutinize the replies, offer his remarks as to the acceptability of replies or otherwise and communicate the review to the Assistant Director of Local Fund Audit along with a copy of replies received from the Commissioner or Secretary, as the case may be, within fifteen days of the receipt of report. The Assistant Director of Local Fund Audit concerned shall scrutinize the replies of the Commissioner or Secretary, as the case may be, along with the remarks of the Assistant Director (Audit) concerned, pass orders as to the dropping of the objections or their continuance, pending further replies and communicate them to the Commissioner or Secretary, as the case may be, within a month from the date of receipt or report from the Assistant Director of Rural Development (Audit) concerned.

14. Action for settlement of the audit objections—No audit report shall be kept pending for more than two years from the date of receipt of the report by the Commissioner of Secretary as the case may. It shall be the responsibility of the Commissioner or Secretary, as the case may be, to take action to settle audit objection by adopting such speedy and effective measures as are necessary including resource to recovery orders wherever necessary. It is the responsibility of the Inspector concerned to watch effective action at all levels, for the early settlement of the objections and ensure closure of audit report within the period specified above after the settlement of all objections.

15. Restriction for re-audit—After the issue of an audit report on the accounts of the panchayat union council or district panchayat, as the case may be, for a year, the audit of the accounts for the year shall not be re-opened, save with the special orders of the Government.

(G.O.Ms.No.199, Rural Development (C-4) Department, dated 31st July 2000)

3.8.5 Surcharge and Disallowance

1. Short title—These rules may be called the Tamil Nadu Panchayats (Surcharge, Disallowance and Charge) Rules, 2000.

2. Surcharge and disallowance—(1) Any auditor, empowered by the Government, shall carefully and personally examine every case of loss or waste or misapplication of money or property of the village panchayat or panchayat union or district panchayat and may disallow every item contrary to law and surcharge the same on the person making or authorising the making of illegal payments and may charge against any person responsible therefor the amount of any deficiency, loss or unprofitable outlay incurred by the negligence or misconduct of that person or of any sum, which ought to have been, but is not, brought to account by that person and shall, in every such case, certify the amount due from such person.

(2) It shall not be open to an Executive Authority of village panchayat or Commissioner of panchayat union or Secretary of district panchayat whose negligence or misconduct has caused or contributed to any such deficiency or loss, to contend that notwithstanding his negligence or misconduct the deficiency or loss would not have occurred but for the negligence or misconduct of some other person.

3. Power of the Government—(1) The Government prescribe the following officers to exercise the powers referred to in these rules in respect of the funds of every village panchayat or panchayat union or district panchayat within his jurisdiction.

(a) Assistant Director of Rural Development (Audit) in case of village panchayats (General Funds).

(b) Director of Local Fund Audit in case of district panchayats, panchayat union councils and village panchayats (scheme funds).

(2) The auditor shall state in writing the reasons for his decision in respect of every disallowance which shall be based on a stated authority in respect of every disallowance, surcharge or charge, and furnish by registered post, a copy thereof to the person against whom it is made.

(3) Even if the person, to whom a copy of the decision of the auditor is furnished, refuses to receive it, he shall be deemed to have been duly furnished with a copy of such decision within the meaning of sub-rule (2). The period of thirty days fixed in Rules 5 and 6 shall be calculated from the date of such refusal.

4. Issue of surcharge certificate—(1) The auditor who is empowered to issue a surcharge certificate, before issuing a surcharge certificate, shall give a show cause notice to the person concerned calling upon him to state his defence about the proposed notice in writing within a specified time which shall not be less than fifteen days. If such person desires to be heard in person, the opportunity of personal hearing shall be given by the auditor. In such personal hearing the auditor shall record the proceedings of such hearing. The auditor shall issue surcharge certificate after taking into consideration the representation, if any, given by the person concerned and the proceedings by the personal hearing. The show cause notice and the surcharge certificate shall be in Tamil version.

(2) Wherever the Collector, the Inspector or other competent authority takes execution proceedings on behalf of a village panchayat, panchayat union council or district panchayat in respect of which a surcharge certificate has been issued by an auditor, the expenditure for such purpose shall be met from the Government initially and recovered from the funds of the respective village panchayat, panchayat union or district panchayat.

5. Appeal against the surcharge, disallowance or charge—(1) Any person aggrieved by the disallowance, surcharge or charge made, may, within thirty days from the date of the receipt of service of the decision of the auditor, appeal to the Inspector, or any officer authorised by the Government in this behalf to set aside such disallowance, surcharge or charge and the Inspector or such officer, after taking such evidence as is necessary, may confirm, modify or remit such disallowance, surcharge or charge:

Provided that the Inspector or any officer authorised by the Government, may admit an appeal after the expiry of the time specified in this sub-rule, but within sixty days if the appellant satisfies the Inspector or such officer that he has sufficient cause for not preferring the appeal within the specified time:

Provided further that during the pendancy of the appeal made under this rule, the certificate of disallowance, surcharge or charge, as the case may be, shall not be enforced.

(2) Against the order of the Inspector or Officer authorised by Government in this behalf under sub-rule (1), a second appeal shall lie to the Government within thirty days from the date of receipt of such order, the Government may take into account all the fact presented by the appellant and facts of the case and pass such order as they deem fit and proper. Against the order of the Government, an appeal shall lie to the High Court within thirty days from the date of receipt of such order.

(3) Where an appeal is made to the High Court under sub-rule (2) the auditor shall be the sole respondent thereto and the applicant shall not be entitled to make either the Inspector or any officer authorised by the Government or any other person or Government a party to the proceedings.

6. Payment of due—Every sum certified to be due from any person by the auditor under these rules shall be paid by such person into the bank or post office in which the funds of the village panchayat, panchayat union council or district panchayat, as the case may be, are lodged within thirty days from the date of intimation to him of the decision of the auditor unless within that time, such person has appealed against the decision to the Inspector or any officer authorised by the Government, and such sum, if not paid or such sum as the Inspector or such officer shall declare to be due, shall be recoverable in the same way as an amount decreed by a court by filing execution petition.

7. Charge of interest on surcharge, disallowance or charge amount—Interest at the rate specified by the Government, from time-to-time, by general or special order or if no such order is in current at the time of issuing a surcharge certificate at a rate not less than fifteen per cent per annum shall be charged on the amount of disallowance, surcharge or charge due with effect from the day following the last date fixed for payment of the said amount of disallowance, surcharge or charge in the certificate. The interest so charged on the amount of disallowance, surcharge or charge, over due shall be specified in the certificate itself in precise terms as laid down in Section 34 of the Civil Procedure Code, 1908 (Central Act V of 1908).

8. Waiving of amount of disallowance, surcharge or charge—Notwithstanding anything contained in the rules, the Government may at any time direct that the recovery of the whole or any part of the amount of disallowance, surcharge or charge certified to be due from any person by the auditor under these rules shall be waived if, in their opinion that such a course is necessary, considering all the circumstances of the case. The reasons for such waiver shall be conveyed in writing to the village panchayat or panchayat union or district panchayat, as the case may be.

(G.O. Ms. No.32, Rural Development (C-4) Department, dated 11th February 2000)

3.8.6 Recovery of Sums Due to the Panchayat Union Council and the District Panchayats

1. Short title—These rules may be called the Tamil Nadu Panchayats (Recovery of Sums Due to the Panchayat Union Council and the District Panchayats) Rules, 2000.

2. Definition—In these rules, unless the context otherwise requires, "Act" means the Tamil Nadu Panchayats Acts, 1994 (Tamil Nadu Act 21 of 1994).

3. Recovery of sums due to panchayat union councils and the district panchayats—All costs damages, compensations, penalties, charges, fees (other than school fees) expenses, rents, arrears of lease amounts (not being rents for lands and buildings demitted by the panchayat union council or the district panchayat, as the case may be) amounts due or payable on account of contract for execution of any works or supplies made to a panchayat union council or the district panchayat, as the case may be or for any other purposes, made in accordance with the Act, or the rules or bye-laws made thereunder, contributions and other sums which under the Act, or any other law or bye-laws made thereunder are due by any person to the panchayat union council or the district panchayat, as the case may be, if there is no provision in the said Act or the rules made thereunder for their recovery, be demanded by bills which shall be served on the persons concerned and recovered as if it were arrears of land revenue.

(G.O.Ms.No.277, Rural Development (C-4) Department, 24th October 2000)

3.8.7 Constitution of Second State Finance Commission—Terms of Reference

Commission – Second State Finance Commission – Constituted – To study the financial position of

Municipal Corporations, Municipalities, Town Panchayats – Terms of reference – Notified.

1. In the Government Order read above, orders have been issued constituting the Second State Finance Commission with a Chairman and four other Members to study the financial position of Municipal Corporations, Municipalities, Town Panchayats and Panchayats. The Government now issue the notification covering the terms of reference of the Commission.

2. The appended Notification containing terms of reference will be published in an Extraordinary issue of Tamil Nadu Government Gazette, dated the 3rd March 2000.

(G.O.Ms. No. 518, Finance (Resources) Department, dated 1st December 1999)

APPENDIX
NOTIFICATION

In exercise of the powers conferred by sub-clause (a) of clause (1) of Article 243-I and sub-clause (a) of clause (1) of Article 243-Y of the Constitution and in pursuance of sub-section (1) of Section 198 of the Tamil Nadu Panchayats Act, 1994 (Tamil Nadu Act 21 of 1994), read with Rule 6 of the Tamil Nadu State Finance Commission (Chairman and other Members etc.) Rules, 1994, sub-section (1) of Section 162-A of the Madras City Municipal Corporation Act, 1919 (Tamil Nadu Act IV of 1919), sub-section (1) of Section 124-B of the Tamil Nadu District Municipalities Act, 1920 (Tamil Nadu Act V of 1920), sub-section (1) of Section 193-A of the Madurai City Municipal Corporation Act, 1971 (Tamil Nadu Act 15 of 1971), sub-section (1) of Section 193-A of the Coimbatore City Municipal Corporation Act, 1981 (Tamil Nadu Act 25 of 1981), read with Section 8 of the Thiruchirappalli City Municipal Corporation Act, 1994 (Tamil Nadu Act 28 of 1994) and Section 8 of the Salem City Municipal Corporation Act, 1994 (Tamil Nadu Act 29 of 1994), the Governor of Tamil Nadu hereby direct that—

the period of office of the Chairman and other Members of the Second State Finance Commission, constituted with Finance Department Notification No. II (1)/FIN/112(a)/99, dated the 1st December 1999 published at page 1 of Part II –Section 1 of the Tamil Nadu Government Gazette Extraordinary, dated the 2nd December 1999, shall be upto the 31st day of October 2001, from the date on which they respectively assumed charges.

2. The Commission shall review the financial position of the rural and urban local bodies, namely, village panchayats, panchayat union councils, district panchayats, municipal corporations, municipalities and town panchayats and make recommendations as to:

(a) the principles which should govern:
   (i) the distribution between the State and the said local bodies of the net proceeds of the taxes, duties, tolls and fees leviable by the Government which may be divided between them and allocation between the said local bodies of their respective shares of such proceeds;
   (ii) the determination of the taxes, duties, tolls and fees which may be assigned to or appropriated by the said local bodies;
   (iii) the grants-in-aid to the local bodies, from the Consolidated Fund of the State.

(b) the measures needed to improve the financial position of the local bodies taking into account *inter alia*, their level of debt and their ability to service the debt.

2. In reviewing the financial position of the local bodies, the Commission shall assess the financial position of each of the local bodies as on 31st March 2000.

3. In making its recommendations, the Commission shall have regard, to the resources of the State Government, the demand thereon, in particular the expenditure of the State on debt servicing including the debt servicing on behalf of local bodies/other committed expenditure or liabilities of the State Government and the need to generate adequate surplus on revenue account for State's commitments on capital account.

4. The Commission shall also have regard to:

(a) the existing level of devolution and other resource transfer from the State and Central Government and other agencies, including the award and recommendations of the Eleventh Finance Commission to the local bodies and their adequacy;
   (i) the requirement of the local bodies for meeting revenue expenditure including maintenance of capital assets, keeping in

view and need for generating surplus for capital investment.

(ii) revenue resources of the local bodies for the five years commencing from 1st April 2002 on the basis of level of taxation reached in 1999-2000 and the potential for increase in revenue;

(iii) the status of implementation of the recommendations of the First State Finance Commission and then utilization of the local bodies of the resources transferred;

(iv) the scope for better fiscal management consistent with efficiency and economy in major components of recurring and non-recurring items of expenditure.

5. The Commission shall review the present system for assessing the accountability of the local bodies in utilizing the resources raised or received from the State and Central Governments and other agencies.

6. The Commission may suggest changes, if any, on the basis of classification of local bodies as rural and urban.

7. The Commission shall also make suitable recommendations on the changes, if any, needed in the system for payment of pension to the retired employees of local bodies.

8. The Commission can also make suitable recommendations regarding any other issues having bearing on the terms of reference above in parts 2 to 8.

9. The Commission shall make its report available by 31st October 2001, covering the period of five years commencing on 1st April 2002.

(G.O. Ms.No. 518, Finance (Resources) Department, dated 1st December 1999).

3.8.8 Appointment of Chairman and Other Members – Service Conditions

Finance Commission Constitution and Appointment of Chairman and other Members – Framing of rules for the post under the Tamil Nadu Panchayats Act, 1994 – Issued

1. G.O. Ms.No.350 Finance dated 23rd April 1994
2. G.O. Ms.No.101 Rural Development, dated 1st September 1994

Order

The appended notification will be published in an extraordinary issue of the Tamil Nadu Government Gazette dated the 7th September, 1994.

Notification II

In exercise of the powers conferred by sub-section (3) of Section 198 of the Tamil Nadu Panchayats Act, 1994 (Tamil Nadu 21 of 1994) the Governor of Tamil Nadu hereby makes the following rules:

Rules

1. Short title and commencement—(1) These rules may be called the Tamil Nadu State Finance Commission, Chairman and other members (Conditions of Service) Rules, 1994.

(2) They shall come into force on the 7th September, 1994.

2. Definition—In these rules, unless the context otherwise requires,

(a) "Act" means the Tamil Nadu Panchayats Act, 1994 (Tamil Nadu Act 21 of 1994);

(b) "Commission" means the Finance Commission constituted under Section 198 of the Act.

3. Composition of the commission—The commission shall consist of;

(1) Chairman;

(2) Member-Secretary;

(3) Director of Rural Development – *Ex-officio* member;

(4) Director of Municipal Administration – *Ex-officio* member; and

(5) One non-official member.

4. Appointment—The Chairman and other members shall be appointed by the Government.

5. Qualification of the chairman and other members—(1) A person shall not be qualified for appointment as Chairman of the Commission unless;

(i) he is a serving or a retired judge of a High Court, or

(ii) he is a serving or retired government servant; who has served in senior capacities for a period of not less than ten years; or

(iii) he is, a person of eminence with substantial experience in public life as a member of Parliament, State Legislature or in Local Self Government bodies; or

(iv) he is, an eminent academician in economics or public finance or political science or a related area of studies.

(2) A persons shall not be qualified for appointment as a non-official member of the commission unless;

(i) he is a person of eminence with substantial experience in public as a member of Parliament, State Legislature or in Local Self Government bodies; or

(ii) he is an eminent academician in Economics or public finance or political science or a related area of studies.

(3) A person shall not be qualified for appointment as a Member Secretary of the Commission unless he has put in ten years of Government service and who has served as the Collector of a district or a Project Officer in the District Rural Development Agency.

Tenure of Office

The Chairman and other members of the commission other than *ex-officio* members shall hold office from the date on which they respectively assume office till such period as may be fixed by the Government.

6. **Pay**—(1) The Chairman shall receive a pay of rupees six thousand and five hundred per mensem:

Provided that a person who was holding a post under the Government at the time of appointment as Chairman shall, on such appointment as Chairman, receive the pay which he would have drawn from time-to-time under the relevant rules in the scale of pay of the post which he was holding at the time of such appointment or shall receive the pay mentioned in this sub-rule, whichever is higher:

Provided further that in the case of appointment as Chairman, of a person who has retired from service under the Government and who is in receipt of or has received or has become eligible to receive any retirement benefits by way of pension, gratuity, general provident fund, or otherwise, the pay specified in this sub-rule shall be reduced by the gross amount of pension (including any portion of pension which may have been commuted) and the pension equivalent another terms of retirement benefits, if any;

Provided further that a person who was holding a post under the Government at the time of his appointment as Chairman happens from government service on attaining the age of superannuating in the middle of his term as Chairman, shall on and from the date of his retirement, have his pay refixed and regulated in accordance with the second provision to this sub-rule.

(2) The Chairman shall be entitled to draw dearness allowance, house rent allowance, and city compensatory allowance and other allowances, if any at the rates applicable to the highest class of the State Civil Services from time-to-time:

Provided that the dearness allowance, house rent allowance, city compensatory allowance and other allowances, if any, received by a person who was holding a post under the Government at the time of his appointment as Chairman shall be not less than the dearness allowance, house rent allowance, city compensatory allowance or any other allowance admissible, which he would have drawn from time-to-time at the place of headquarters of the Commission, which shall be at Madras under the relevant rules in the scale of pay of the post which he was holding at the time of such appointment.

(3) The Chairman may, if he does not own a house at the headquarters of the Commission, and if he so desires, be provided with an unfurnished residence subject to the payment of rent and other conditions in accordance with the rules applicable to government buildings used as residence.

(4) The pay and allowance shall be paid from government funds and later on reimbursed from such authorities as the government may direct.

(5) A person who on the date of his appointment as Chairman, was in the service of the Government shall be deemed to be on deputation on foreign service terms from such service from the date of his appointment as Chairman.

(6) The non-official member shall be paid on Rs. 500/- per sitting.

(7) The member secretary shall continue to draw his pay and allowances as applicable to his grade in the service to which he belongs;

(8) The *ex-officio* members shall draw their pay and allowances in their respective posts.

7. **Leave**—(1) A person who at the time of his appointment to the Commission was in the service of the Government may be granted leave in accordance with the rules applicable to persons on deputation on foreign service terms and conditions.

(2) The person who at the time of his appointment as Chairman was not in service of the Government may be granted leave admissible to the officers of the highest class of the State Civil Services.

(3) The person who at the time of his appointment as Chairman happens to retire from such service held by him prior to the date of appointment as

Chairman shall be eligible to have leave granted in accordance with sub-rule (2) above.

8. Travelling allowance—(1) The Chairman shall be entitled to draw travelling and daily or other allowances admissible to the officers of the highest class of the State Civil Services while touring on duty in connection with his office.

(2) Travelling allowance bill of the Chairman shall not require the counter signature of any other authority.

(3) The Chairman may avail of leave travel concession admissible to the officers of the highest class of the State Civil Services:

Provided that a person who on the date immediately prior to the date of his appointment as Chairman was holding a post under the Central or State Government and has availed of the benefits of leave travel concession shall not be eligible for further concession until the expiry of the period specified in the relevant leave travel concession rules, which was applicable to him.

9. Advance of travelling allowance and daily allowance—The Chairman shall be entitled to an advance of travelling and daily allowance in respect of journeys undertaken by him in the performance of his functions, whether by road, rail or air.

(2) An advance drawn shall be adjusted in the appropriate travelling allowance bill as per the rule under Article 54 of the Tamil Nadu Financial Code, Volume I.

(3) In respect of the official members, the daily allowance, travelling allowance and other expenditure shall be debited to their respective head of account wherein the travelling allowance, daily allowance are debited.

10. Medical attendance—The Chairman and the non-official member shall be entitled to draw medical attendance benefit as is prescribed from time-to-time for the officers of the highest class of the State Civil Services.

11. Allowance to non-official members—In respect of the non-official member, the Commission shall be treated as first class Commission for the purpose of travelling allowance, daily allowance and other charges. The claim of daily allowance and travelling allowance and other charges of the non-official member will be countersigned by the member secretary of the Commission.

(G.O.Ms.No.162 Rural Development (C.II) Department, dated 6th September 1994)

3.9 CONTROLLING AUTHORITIES

3.9.1 Appointment of District Collector as Inspector of Panchayats

In exercise of the powers conferred by sub-section (1) of Section 199, read with clause (16) of Section 2 of the Tamil Nadu Panchayats Act, 1994 (Tamil Nadu Act 21 of 1994), the Governor of Tamil Nadu hereby appoints the District Collectors to exercise and perform the powers and duties of the Inspectors under said Act in respect of all panchayats in their respective jurisdiction.

(Notification issued *vide* G.O. Ms. No. 149 Rural Development (C1) Department, dated 19th August 1994)

3.9.2 Emergency Power of Collector

The Tamil Nadu Panchayat (Emergency Powers of Collector and Inspector) Rules, 2001.

1. Short title—These rules may be called the Tamil Nadu Panchayats (Control of the Emergency of Powers of Collector or Inspector of Panchayat), Rules, 2001.

2. In these rules unless the context otherwise requires, "Act" means the Tamil Nadu Panchayats Act, 1994 (Tamil Nadu Act 21 of 1994).

3. Intimation after exercise of emergency powers—Collector or the Inspector, shall after exercise of the powers conferred by Section 203 of the Act report forthwith to the Director of Rural Development with the reasons in full, for the exercise of such powers and a copy of the report shall at the same time, be sent to the panchayat for information.

G.O. Ms. No.148, Rural Development (C-4) 31st May 2001.

3.9.3 Appointment of Inspecting and Superintending Officers of Panchayats

Notification—In exercise of the powers conferred by sub-section (1) of Section 199 and Section 242 of the Tamil Nadu Panchayats Act, 1994 (Tamil Nadu Act 21 of 1994) the Governor of Tamil Nadu hereby appoints the officers specified in column (2) of the table below to be the officers for the purpose of inspecting and superintending the operations of the panchayats specified in the corresponding entries in column (1) thereof within their respective jurisdiction).

The Table

Sl. No.	*Nature of Panchayat* (1)	*Name of the Post of Inspecting Officer* (2)
1.	Village Panchayat	(a) Extension Officer (Panchayats) (b) Deputy Block Development Officer (c) Block Development Officer (Village Panchayat) (d) Assistant Director of Rural Development (Panchayats) (e) District Collector (f) Any other officer not below the rank of an Extension Officer nominated by the Inspector (g) Inspector of Panchayats
2.	Panchayat Union Council	Assistant Director of Rural Development (Panchayats) Assistant Director of Rural Development (Audit) Personal Assistant to the District Collector (Development) Personal Assistant to the District Collector (NMP) District Collector Any other officer not below the rank of Assistant Director of Rural Development nominated by the Inspector Inspector of Panchayats
3	District Panchayats	Joint Director of Rural Development Additional Director of Rural Development District Collector Any other officer not below the rank of a Joint Director of Rural Development nominated by the Governments Inspector of Panchayats

(G.O. Ms. No. 264, Rural Development (C3) Department, dated 21st December 1999)

3.9.4 Monthly Report on Exercise of Powers by Inspectors and Controlling Officers

According to Section 202 of the Tamil Nadu Panchayats Act, 1994, the Inspector (i.e.,) District Collector has got powers to cancel a resolution, orders passed, licence issued or permissions granted by the panchayats. Moreover the Inspectors also got powers to stay proceedings of a Panchayat, if they were issued in excess of powers entrusted to them. According to Section 204 of the Act, if a village panchayat president, panchayat union chairman or district panchayat chairman fails to do their duties, the District Collector has got powers to direct them to execute the functions and fix specific period for such execution. Moreover under Sections 205 and 206, of the Tamil Nadu Panchayat Act, 1994, the District Collector has got powers to remove the president or vice-president for the irregularities or failure to do their duties as per the Act and rules made thereunder. Similarly Sections 207, 208, 209 and 210 of Tamil Nadu Panchayats Act, 1994 empower the Inspector to remove the chairman, vice-chairman of panchayat union council and the district panchayat who fails to do the duty.

2. After the introduction of three tier system of panchayat administration, considerable financial resources and administrative powers have been delegated to these local bodies. In order to ensure sustained development of the local bodies, the Government considers that the exercise of powers used by the District collector as per Para 1 shall prepare a Monthly Periodical Report as mentioned in this order.

3. Accordingly, the District Collector shall send a monthly statement on the action taken against the village panchayat president, vice-president, and panchayat union chairman, vice-chairman, district panchayat chairman and vice-chairman in the prescribed form prescribed in this order. The District Collectors shall send the monthly statement to the Director of Rural Development before 10th of every month. The Director of Rural Development shall consolidate all the reports received from the District Collectors and send a consolidated report with is remark before 10th of next month to the Government.

(G.O. Ms. No.286, Rural Development (C1) Department, dated 16th September 1997)

Name of the District

Sl. No.	Name of Village Pt./Pt. Union/District Pt.	Name of Office of the elected representative against whom action has been taken	The stage of the action taken and the relevant sections under which action is taken	The stage of the action at the end of the previous month	Present stage	The authority competent to pass final order	
						District Collector	Government
(1)	(2)	(3)	(4)	(5)	(6)	(7a)	(7b)

Abstract

Number of cases pending at the end of previous month	*No. of cases added during the month*	*Total*	*No. of cases completed during the month*	*Pending*	*Cases pending with Collector*	*Cases pending with Government*
(1)	(2)	(3)	(4)	(5)	(6)	(7)

3.9.5 Limitation of Time for Appeals

1. Shore title—These rules may be called the Tamil Nadu Panchayats (Limitation of Time for Appeals) Rules, 1999.

2. Appellate authority and time limit for appeal—Save as otherwise provided in the Tamil Nadu Panchayats Act 1994 (Tamil Nadu Act 21 of 1994) or in the rules made thereunder, every appeal under that Act, or any such rule shall, subject to the provisions of Section 5 of the Indian Limitation Act, 1908 (Central Act IX of 1908), be presented to the Inspector.

(a) Where the appeal is against an order granting a licence or permission, within thirty days from the date of publication of the order on the notice board of the panchayat; and

(b) In other cases, within thirty days from the date of receipt of the order or proceedings against which the appeal is made.

(G.O.Ms.No.141, Rural Development (C4) Department, dated 21st July 1999)

3.10 MISCELLANEOUS

3.10.1 Display of Portraits

The Government have already issued instructions regarding display of portraits in Government offices and buildings, panchayat union offices and buildings. It is informed that the following portraits of leaders can be displayed in panchayat union offices and buildings after approval of panchayat union council.

(1) Present President of India
(2) Present Prime Minister of India
(3) Mahatma Gandhi
(4) Jawaharlal Nehru
(5) Thiruvalluvar
(6) Peraringer Anna
(7) Perundalaiver Kamarajar
(8) Mootharinger Rajaji
(9) Thanthai Periyar
(10) Dr. B.R. Ambedkar
(11) Muthuramalinger Thevar
(12) V.O. Chidambaram
(13) Quide-e-Millet
(14) Smt. Indira Gandhi

Other than the above said leaders, if the Panchayat desires to display the portraits of other leaders, the concerned panchayat should get prior permission of the Government. The panchayat union Commissioners are directed to communicate this orders to all the village panchayat in their area.

The Government have ordered that the portrait of Dr. B.R. Ambedkar can also be displayed in Public Offices and Buildings in addition to the portraits mentioned earlier. As this is the birth centenary year of Dr. B.R. Ambedkar, it is reminded to all the Government Offices to display the Portrait of Dr. B.R. Ambedkar.

(Govt. Letter No. 235335/91-1, dated 23rd June 1991)

(DRD. Lr. No. 29581/86/H-3, dated 26th March 1986)

3.10.2 Installation and Maintenance of Statues in Panchayat Areas

The Government pass the following orders on the installation of statues and their maintenance in panchayats

(1) Statue, Memorial Pillar, Memorial Mandapam, and Memorial Arches shall be installed only after getting the prior permission of the Government.

(2) The Statues already installed have to be safeguarded and maintained properly. In respect of those Statue, the individuals or institutions or Sangams which installed the Statues shall take up responsibility for maintaining and safeguarding the Statues. To ensure safety to the Statues already installed, they can be taken to safe places and are installed if necessary after getting specific sanction orders of the Government by individuals or organisations.

(3) The above sections will also be applied for Memorial Pillar, Memorial Mandapam or for Memorial Arches.

(G.O.Ms.No.248, Rural Development (C-II) Department, dated 23rd November 1998)

3.10.3 Naming of Panchayat Roads, Buildings, Bus Stand

In the G.O. Ms. No. 113, Municipal Administration and Water Supply Department, dated 13.6.1998 instructions were already issued for postponement of naming of roads, buildings, bus stand etc., situated in Municipality and the Corporation area. The Local Bodies were instructed not to pass any resolutions for naming of roads, buildings, bus stand etc. and to send to Government for necessary approval.

The above instruction is also applicable to village panchayat, panchayat union and district panchayat. The president of village panchayat, the chairman of panchayat union council and district panchayat shall follow the above said instructions. The District Collector is advised to intimate this instruction to the village panchayats, panchayat unions and district panchayats in their district.

(G.O. Ms. No. 137, Rural Development, dated 6th July 1998)

3.10.4 Statues Indiscriminate Installation and Desecration

Sub: Statutes Indiscriminate Installation and Desecration of – reg.

Ref: Government Lr. No. 3174/Home pol. XIII/2001-9 dated 20.7.2001.

G.O. Rt.No.221 M.A.W.S. Department, dated 20.11.1998, instructions were issued, in supersession of all previous instructions, that in Municipalities and Town panchayats.

(i) Prior permission of Government should be obtained for installation of statutes, memorial, pillars, arches, etc.
(ii) The above structures should be protected and that the organisation or individuals who had organised the installation should undertake the responsibility of maintenance of the structures.
(iii) Interested organizers or individuals concerned who want to shift the statues, etc., for repairs of renovation and re-install at the same place may do so with prior permission of the Government.

(2) In the context of installation of a large number of statutes resulting in unscrupulous elements trying to desecrate and the statutes becoming a source of caste conflicts and tensions, instructions were issued in the reference cited for exploring the possibility of removal of shifting of the statutes from their existing locations (public places) in to some other buildings where the chance of desecration may not be there, after forging a consensus among the people concerned. Further, the Collectors and the Unit of Police Department were requested to discourage the setting up of statutes, etc., in future.

(3) The Commissioner of Police, Tirunelveli City (Thiru S.R. Jangidd, IPS) has suggested that the statutes of leaders should be protected by grills and in his jurisdiction, this was completed by the SDOs and the SHOs meeting the villagers and their leaders and explaining to them the advantages of proposed move. When their reaction was not positive, the officers approached philanthropists and other willing and service minded people to supply men and materials for finishing the work. They also obliged. Some statutes were covered with grills by villagers themselves by collecting contribution and at some places the work was carried out by the sponsors who had created the statutes.

(4) In the meantime, precautions were taken against the possible sabotage by unscrupulous elements. At last, all the statues of communal leaders were provided with fool proof grills, steel doors and strong locks. While one key is entrusted with the local leaders of that community another is with the Station House Officer who will set right things in the event of any mischief attempted or rumors spread by anti-social elements. The goal was achieved adroitly despite objections by some undesirable elements. The work of covering statutes with grills on all the 142 statutes of 3 communal leaders located in the three districts of Tirunelveli range and Tirunelveli city was completed in just 10 days from the day it was planned. The task was quite massive as some statutes were erected on very high pedestals. The height ranged from 4-5 feet to 25 feet and accordingly the cost of fixing the grills also ranged from Rs. 5,000 to Rs. 35,000.

(5) It is further reported by the Commissioner of Police, Tirunelveli City that the policemen who were engaged for guarding the statues were withdrawn and diverted to other important police duties as a consequence of this initiative and that the media as well as people from all walks of life have paid encomium.

(6) The above effort is worth emulating by all the Collectors, the Commissioner of Police and the District SPs in their jurisdiction. It may be kept in mind that while covering the statutes with grills it should not look as if the leader has been imprisoned. If the grill structure is designed well, it may lend elegance to the area. The interested organizers or individuals concerned may be advised to provide grills around the statutes.

3.10.5 Awarding of Prizes to the Best Performing Village Panchayats

The State Finance Commission recommended that the Awards may be given to the Presidents and Officers of local bodies to encourage their functioning and also for strengthening their institution from out of the incentive fund of the Government. The Government passed the following orders in this regard.

(a) 3 Village Panchayats in a District, 3 Panchayat Unions in a District level, 3 District Panchayats, and 3 Village Panchayats at State level shall be selected every year and they can be awarded prizes as per Annexure-I of this order.

(b) For awarding of prizes as per Annexure-I, and for conduct of functions at District and State Level and amount of Rs. 10 lakhs is provided. (District level functions at the rate of Rs. 25,000 for 25 Districts Rs. 7 lakhs and for the State level functions Rs. 3 lakhs). Moreover for giving Medals to the selected local bodies sanction is accorded for a sum of Rs. 3.54 lakhs.

(c) For selection of Village Panchayats and Panchayat Unions of District Level, a Committee shall be constituted with the following members.

President – District Collector

Members—1. Additional Collector (Development)/ Project Officer, District Rural Development Agency.

2. One MLA nominated by the District Collector.

3. One Social Worker nominated by the District Collector.

4. One NGO working for the Welfare of Women and Children selected by the President and Members of the District Level Committee.

5. The respective Assistant Director (Panchayats) of the districts.

(d) For selection of the best village panchayats, panchayat unions and district panchayat at State Level Committee shall be constituted with following members.

Chairman – Secretary, Rural Development Department

Members—1. Director of Rural Development

2. One Social Worker nominated by Government.

3. One NGO working for the Welfare of local bodies nominated by Government.

4. One MLA nominated by Government.

(e) The following Time table shall be observed in the election and awarding of best Panchayats as per Annexure-II.

The District Collectors and the Director of Rural Development are requested to take action to form the District level and State Level Committees.

The total expenditure involved in this programme, Rs. 1,95,54,000 (Rupees One Crore Ninety Five Lakhs and Fifty Four Thousand only) shall be sanctioned from equalization and incentive grant sanctioned by the State Government.

ANNEXURE – I
Details of Prizes

Awarding of Prizes to 3 Best Village Panchayats at District Level

1st Prize	Rs. 1.00 lakh
2nd Prize	Rs. 0.50 lakh
3rd Prize	Rs. 0.25 lakh
Rs. 1.75 lakh × 28	Rs. 49.00 lakhs

Awarding of Prizes to 3 Best Panchayat Unions at District Level

1st Prize	Rs. 2.00 lakh
2nd Prize	Rs. 1.00 lakh
3rd Prize	Rs. 0.50 lakh
Rs. 3.50 lakh × 28	Rs. 98.00 lakhs

Awarding of Prizes to 3 Best District Panchayats at State Level

1st Prize	Rs. 10.00 lakhs
2nd Prize	Rs. 5.00 lakhs
3rd Prize	Rs. 3.00 lakhs
	Rs. 18.00 lakhs

Awarding of Prizes to 3 Best Panchayat Unions at State Level

1st Prize	Rs. 6.00 lakhs
2nd Prize	Rs. 3.00 lakhs
3rd Prize	Rs. 2.00 lakhs
	Rs. 11.00 lakhs

Awarding of Prizes to 3 best Town Panchayats at District Level

1st Prize	Rs. 3.00 lakhs
2nd Prize	Rs. 2.00 lakhs
3rd Prize	Rs. 1.00 lakhs
	Rs. 6.00 lakhs
Total	Rs. 182.00 lakhs

ANNEXURE – II
Time Schedule for Giving Awards to Local Bodies

District Level	*Last Date*
Receipt of Application	May
Scrutiny of Application and selection of local bodies	July
Awarding of Prizes	August
State Level	
Receipt of application at state level	August
Scrutiny of application and selection of local bodies	September
Awarding of Prize	October

(G.O.Ms.No.79, Rural Development Department, dated 1st June 1999)

3.10.6 Tamil Nadu Panchayats Act, 1994, receiving of Petitions by the Officers

In exercise of Powers conferred under clause (b), sub-section (1), Section 207 of Tamil Nadu Panchayats Act, 1994 (Tamil Nadu Act 21 of 1994), the Governor of Tamil Nadu hereby appoints the following officers to receive petitions, and petition can be given to any one of the officer.

(1) Secretary, Rural Development Department, Chennai – 9

(2) Director of Rural Development, Chennai – 15

(3) Concerned Inspector mentioned in sub-section (2) of Section 16 of the above Act.

(G.O. Ms. No. 172, Rural Development, dated 13th August 1998)

3.10.7 Panchayats—Complaints on Irregularities Received—Maintenance of Register

It has been brought to notice that the complaints are received against the elected representatives of 3 tier panchayats which are not being monitored properly. Since such cases need to be followed at different level, it is necessary to maintain a register for village panchayats, panchayat union and district panchayats separately under the personal custody of Assistant Director (Panchayat) at the District Level, to ensure timely follow up. The particulars of irregularity reported, action taken and final orders issued should be entered in this register.

A copy of proforma is stated below for opening the register.

PROFORMA

Particulars			
1. Sl. No.			
2. Source and Date of Complaint			
3. Name & Designation against whom complaint received			
4. Nature of Local Body	*Name of the Village Panchayat*	*Panchayat Union*	*District Panchayat*
5. Nature of complaint			
6. Date and No. of reference sent for enquiry			
7. Designation of enquiry officer			
8. Date of receipt of enquiry report			
9. Brief result of enquiry report			
10. Follow up action	*Date*	*Follow up Action Taken*	

(DRD's Circular No.Rc.89507/98/PCA-3, dated 21st October 1998)

3.10.8 Instructions and Guidelines for the Conduct of Functions in Local Bodies

(1) It is brought to the notice of the Government that in the functions conducted in the local bodies, the village panchayat presidents and chairman, panchayat unions have not followed the prescribed protocol and it is resulted in embarrassment to the Government. Functions are conducted without inviting local MLAs and MPs are conducted without informing the District Collector, but invited only the party functionaries as special invitees. It is brought to the notice of the Government that in many panchayat inaugural functions are conducted for small scheme, stone laying for small work or inauguration function conducted for those works which have been completed before long time or some of buildings and institutions not functioning anticipating inauguration by special invitees which are resulted in lot of confusion in the conduct of functions by local bodies. Before the Panchayat Elections were held, there were two tier system of Panchayat Administration, the Panchayat Union Chairman were looking after the conduct of functions in Panchayat Union area. In Urban Municipalities, Municipal Chairman and in Town Panchayats Presidents were conducting the functions. After the conduct of elections in the year

1996, each Panchayats Chair Person of the local bodies area are arranging the functions separately. They are not following the prescribed protocol for conduct of these functions. Moreover each Panchayat Institution invites various VIP for the same function and between the Panchayats, this resulted in lot of field level problems between the local bodies. And the Government officials have to spend a lot of their time in settling the disputes.

(2) In this back-drop, the Government consider that proper Guidelines have to be issued in conduct of functions by the local bodies and to strictly adhere to the prescribed protocol.

(a) *Inaugural functions and foundation stone laying functions selection of schemes*

(i) In local bodies, the works completed during the financial year and the works completed during the previous financial year, (if not put to use so far) inaugural functions can be conducted. Those scheme works completed before the financial year 1996-97, inaugural functions should not be conducted. All these scheme works should be put to use immediately.

(ii) In respect of Government schemes, the Government only shall conduct the function. Instead of the local bodies again conducting functions for these schemes, they can work for bringing the benefits of the newly announced scheme to the people of the area.

(iii) Laying of foundation stone, opening ceremony for Government Scheme works shall not be encouraged. If panchayat considers that the function of laying of foundation is essential for new works for commencement of new schemes before inviting the VIP, the permission of the District Collector should be obtained.

(iv) After completion of Scheme works, they should not be kept pending for use for more than 30 days stating reason that it has not been inaugurated.

(b) *Conduct of functions*

(i) The president of the local bodies before conduct of any functions shall inform the Collector about time, date and the VIPs who have been invited to participate in the function. The Guidelines and protocol for conduct of Government functions and the security arrangements to be maintained, law and order shall be strictly followed in the functions arranged by the local bodies. These formalities shall be strictly observed in the conduct of all functions by village panchayats, town panchayats, panchayat unions, municipalities and district panchayats.

(ii) In respect of schemes implemented under Member of Legislative Assembly Constituency Development Scheme (MLACD), Member of Parliament Local Area Development Programme (MPLAD), the functions shall be conducted by the District Collector after consulting the concerned MLA and MP. In respect of Decentralised District Plan Schemes, the Collectors shall consult the Presidents of local bodies for conducting functions.

(iii) When the local bodies conduct the function, the MLA or the MP of the area shall be invited to participate in the function. After getting their contribution, the names shall be printed in the invitation. In the stone or in the board to be fixed in the building, their names shall be inscribed according to the protocol for the position held by them.

(iv) The names of village panchayat, panchayat union, district panchayat, town panchayat, municipality and corporations, the names of the Chairman, President and Mayor shall be inscribed the stone or board to be opened according to the protocol for the posts held by them.

(v) All the functions shall be conducted without fanfare in a function. Putting up of big Cut-outs, Banners, Arches and decorations can be avoided.

(vi) Presenting Bouquets, garlanding, presenting Shawl can be done in function. But purchase of costly Shawls and Flower Bouquets and purchase of costly gifts shall be avoided.

(vii) In the functions conducted pandal or stage, should not obstruct flow of traffic. The functions shall be conducted only in a public place and not in any private place.

(viii) Advertisement about the functions in Newspapers and in Electronic Medias in a costly manner shall be avoided.

(ix) The expenditure towards conduct of functions can be met from the local bodies or from the allotment fund from the particular scheme.

(x) No collections shall be made for conduct of functions by the local bodies.

(3) The protocol should be observed in the conduct of Government functions as laid down in G.O.Ms.No.1316/Public (Protocol) Department, 12.11.96. The following protocol shall be observed by the local bodies in the conduct of functions by them. This will not be relevant to the day-to-day administration of all the local bodies. According to Section 7 in the conduct of State Level functions, the name of the Chief Minister has to come first before the names of Central Ministers. The following protocol shall be adhered while conduct of function by the panchayats. Incase a new person is added to the statement, they will know their seniority from the date of the inclusion of their name. The names of the members of local bodies shall be arranged according to the Serial No. of the Ward which they represent. In a function whether various representatives of local bodies are taking place priority shall be given to those persons who belongs to the place where functions are conducted. The name of the District Collector shall precede the name of the representatives of the local bodies. Among the Governor, Chief Minister, State Ministers and District Collectors and Mayors, the following Protocol seniority shall be followed.

Protocol Seniority No.	*Name of the Office*
4	Governor of Tamil Nadu
7	Central Minister/Chief Minister of Tamil Nadu
10	Minister of State of Government of India
14	Speaker of Tamil Nadu Legislative Assembly
15	Minister of Tamil Nadu Government and Deputy Ministers of Government of India
16	Mayor of Corporation of Chennai
18	Deputy Speaker, Tamil Nadu Legislative Assembly, Government VIP Tamil Nadu Assembly, Opposition Leader of Tamil Nadu Assembly
21	The Mayors of other Corporations, MPs (Rajya Sabha), MPs (Lok Sabha), MLAs.
28	District Collectors, Deputy Mayor of Corporation, Opposition Leader in the Corporation, Members of Corporation
28(a)	Chairman, District Panchayat, Chairman, Panchayat Union, Chairman, Municipality.
29	Vice-Chairman and Members of District Panchayat and Chairman of Town Panchayats.
29(a)	Village Panchayat President, Vice-Chairman and Members of Panchayat Union, Vice-President and Members of Panchayat Union

(G.O. Ms. No. 355, Rural Development (C-V) Department, dated 16th December 1997)

3.10.9 Preparation of Plans and Estimates for Works and Mode and Conditions of Contracts

1. Short title—These rules may be called the Tamil Nadu Panchayats (Preparation of Plans and Estimates for Works and Mode and Conditions of Contracts) Rules, 1998.

2. Application of rule—In respect of works of village panchayats, panchayat unions and district panchayats for which grant is given by the Government and in respect of works taken up by the village panchayats, panchayat unions and district panchayats for execution from out of their own funds, the procedure laid down in these rules shall apply.

3. Preparation and sanction of estimates—(1) Estimates in respect of village panchayats or panchayat unions or district panchayats works whether original or maintenance works costing upto rupees fifty thousand shall be prepared by the panchayat union overseer of the respective panchayat union and got technically sanctioned by the Block Engineer or Assistant Engineer (Rural Development) of the respective panchayat union.

(2) All estimates costing more than rupees fifty thousand shall be prepared by the Block Engineer or Assistant Engineer (Rural Development) with the assistance of the Union Overseer and sent to the Assistant Executive Engineer (Rural Development) concerned, who shall ensure that administrative and technical sanctions are accorded to the estimates in accordance with Rule 5 below.

Explanation. For purposes of sub-rule (2) of Rule 3, the cost given shall mean the "estimated cost" of the work.

4. Power of the president—During exigencies, the president may prepare estimates with the help of panchayat Assistant, get the approval of the village panchayat and execute works, upto a limit of rupees two thousand at a time and not exceeding rupees five thousand in a year in respect of works executed out of village panchayat fund only. After completion of the work, the details and vouchers shall be placed before the village panchayat in its next meeting.

5. According of administrative sanction and technical sanction to estimates—In respect of estimates including revised estimates for original works, maintenance works and electrical works the authorities competent to accord administrative sanction and technical sanction shall unless the Government has stipulated that the sanction of some other authority is required for a particular scheme or particular fund or above a particular limit, be as specified in Tables I, II, III, IV and V below:

TABLE – I
I. ORIGINAL WORKS

Village Panchayat

Estimate Value	*Authority to Accord Administrative Sanction*	*Authority to Accord Technical Sanction*
(1)	(2)	(3)
1. Estimate costing upto rupees one lakh.	Village Panchayat	(i) Upto rupees fifty thousand—Block Engineer or Assistant Engineer (Rural Development). (ii) More than rupees fifty thousand but not more than rupees one lakh—Assistant Executive Engineer (Rural Development).
2. Estimate costing more than rupees one lakh.	District Collector/ Inspector	(i) Upto rupees three lakhs—Assistant Executive Engineer (Rural Development). (ii) More than rupees three lakhs but not more than rupees six lakhs—Executive Engineer (Rural Development). (iii) More than rupees six lakhs—Superintending Engineer (Rural Development).

TABLE – II
Panchayat Union

Estimate Value	*Authority to Accord Administrative Sanction*	*Authority to Accord Technical Sanction*
(1)	(2)	(3)
1. Estimate costing upto rupees five lakhs	Panchayat Union Council	(i) Upto rupees fifty thousand—Block Engineer or Assistant Engineer (Rural Development). (ii) More than rupees fifty thousand but not more than rupees three lakhs—Assistant Executive Engineer (Rural Development). (iii) More than rupees three lakhs but not more than rupees five lakhs—Executive Engineer (Rural Development).
2. Estimate costing more than rupees five lakhs but not more than rupees ten lakhs.	District Collector/ Inspector	More than rupees five lakhs but not more than rupees ten lakhs—Executive Engineer (Rural Development).
3. Estimate costing more than rupees ten lakhs but not more than rupees one crore.	Director of Rural Development	More than rupees ten lakhs but not more than rupees one crore—Superintending Engineer (Rural Development).
4. More than rupees one crore.	Government	Superintending Engineer (Rural Development).

TABLE – III
District Panchayat

Estimate Value	*Authority to Accord Administrative Sanction*	*Authority to Accord Technical Sanction*
(1)	(2)	(3)
1. Estimate costing upto rupees ten lakhs	District Panchayat	(i) Upto rupees fifty thousand—Block Engineer or Assistant Engineer (Rural Development). (ii) More than rupees fifty thousand but not more than rupees three lakhs—Assistant Executive Engineer (Rural Development). (iii) More than rupees three lakhs but not more than rupees ten lakhs—Executive Engineer (Rural Development).
2. Estimate costing more than rupees ten lakhs but not more than rupees twenty five lakhs.	District Collector/ Inspector	More than rupees ten lakhs—Superintending Engineer (Rural Development).
3. Estimate costing more than rupees twenty five lakhs but not more than rupees one crore.	Director of Rural Development	Superintending Engineer (Rural Development).
4. Estimate costing more than rupees one crore.	Government	Superintending Engineer (Rural Development).

TABLE – IV
II. MAINTENANCE WORKS

Nature of Estimate	*Authority to Accord Administrative Sanction*	*Authority to Accord Technical Sanction*
(1)	(2)	(3)
1. Estimate costing not more than rupees ten thousand.	(i) Village Panchayat, (ii) Panchayat Union Council, (iii) District panchayat, as the case may be, in respect of works vested in it.	Block Engineer or Assistant Engineer (Rural Development).
2. Estimate costing more than rupees ten thousand but not more than rupees fifty thousand.	(iv) Village Panchayat, (v) Panchayat Union Council, (vi) District Panchayat, as the case may be, in respect of works vested in it.	Assistant Executive Engineer (Rural Development).
3. Estimate costing more than rupees fifty thousand but not more than rupees two lakhs.	(vii) Village Panchayat, (viii) Panchayat Union Council, (ix) District panchayat, as the case may be, in respect of works vested in it.	Executive Engineer (Rural Development).
4. Estimate costing more than rupees two lakhs.	(x) Village Panchayat, (xi) Panchayat Union Council, (xii) District Panchayat, as the case may be, in respect of works vested in it.	Superintending Engineer (Rural Development).

TABLE – V
III. ELECTRICAL WORKS

Estimate Value	Authority to Accord Administrative Sanction	Authority to Accord Technical Sanction
(1)	(2)	(3)
1. Estimate costing not more than rupees ten thousand	(i) Village Panchayat, (ii) Panchayat Union Council, (iii) District Panchayat, as the case may be in respect of works vested in it.	Block Engineer or Assistant Engineer (Rural Development).
2. Estimate costing more than rupees ten thousand but not more than rupees twenty-five thousand.	(iv) Village Panchayat, (v) Panchayat Union Council, (vi) District panchayat, as the case may be, in respect of works vested in it.	Assistant Executive Engineer (Rural Development).
3. Estimate costing more than rupees twenty five thousand but not more than rupees fifty thousand.	(vii) Village Panchayat, (viii) Panchayat Union Council, (ix) District Panchayat, as the case may be, in respect of works vested in it.	Executive Engineer (Rural Development).
4. Estimate costing more than rupees fifty thousand.	(x) Village Panchayat, (xi) Panchayat Union Council, (xii) District Panchayat, as the case may be, in respect of works vested in it.	Superintending Engineer (Rural Development).

6. Measurement and check-measurement of works executed by village panchayat, panchayat union and district panchayat—(1) The authorities competent to measure and check-measure all works done or materials supplied whether by contract or by departmental agency shall be as specified in the Table below:

The Table

Name of Work	Measuring Officer	Check-measuring Officer
(1)	(2)	(3)
1. All public works (original, maintenance and electrical works) costing not more than rupees fifty thousand.	Panchayat Union Overseer	Block Engineer or Assistant Engineer (Rural Development).
2. All public works (original, maintenance and electrical works) costing more than rupees fifty thousand.	Block Engineer or Assistant Engineer (Rural Development)	Assistant Executive Engineer (Rural Development).

(2) The Assistant Executive Engineer (Rural Development) shall also super-check not less than twenty five per cent of works costing below rupees fifty thousand check-measured by Block Engineer or Assistant Engineer (Rural Development).

(3) The Assistant Executive Engineer (Rural Development) shall check measure the measurement of works in respect of the first and the final bills for works costing more than rupees fifty thousand and countersign all other intermediate bills after table check, that is after the scrutiny of the calculation and the correctness of the rates adopted. They shall, at the time of the table check of the intermediate bills, invariably examine whether any of the measurements in respect of any work should personally be check-measured by them in view either (i) of the nature and

importance of the portion of the work to which the bill relates or (ii) of the large amount involved. If they consider that such personal check measurements are necessary, they shall carry out such check-measurements.

(4) The Executive Engineer (Rural Development) shall also check at least one of the important works check-measured by the Assistant Executive Engineer (Rural Development) in each panchayat union every year. The Executive Engineer (Rural Development) shall also check some of the works check measured by the Assistant Executive Engineer (Rural Development) in respect of the works executed by the village panchayats and district panchayats.

7. Authorities competent to pass excesses over original estimates

The authorities competent to pass excesses over original estimates are as specified in the Table below:

The Table

Estimate Value	*Authority*	*Powers*
(1)	(2)	(3)
1. Upto rupees fifty thousand.	Assistant Executive Engineer (Rural Development).	Without any excess over technical sanction estimate.
	Executive Engineer (Rural Development).	With five per cent excess over technical sanction estimate.
	Superintending Engineer (Rural Development).	With ten per cent excess over technical sanction estimate.
	Government.	More than ten per cent excess over technical sanction estimate.
2. More than rupees fifty thousand but not more than rupees three lakhs.	Executive Engineer (Rural Development).	With five per cent excess over technical sanction estimate.
	Superintending Engineer (Rural Development).	With ten per cent excess over technical sanction estimate.
	Government.	More than ten per cent excess over technical sanction estimate.
3. More than rupees three lakhs but not more than rupees five lakhs.	Superintending Engineer (Rural Development).	With ten per cent excess over technical sanction estimate.
	Government.	More than ten per cent excess over technical sanction estimate.
4. Exceeding rupees five lakhs.	Government.	—

8. Mode and conditions of contracts—(1) Tenders shall be called for in respect of every work which is to be executed by or on behalf of village panchayat, panchayat union council, district panchayat, as the case may be, on contract and the value of the amount of which is rupees five thousand and above. Any work, the estimated cost of which does not exceed rupees five thousand may be entrusted to a village panchayat within a panchayat union and district panchayat without calling for tenders at rates not exceeding estimate rates.

(2) In respect of works, the value or amount of which is rupees five thousand and above, village panchayat, panchayat union council and district panchayat, as the case may be, may dispense with the calling of tenders in the following cases and entrust the work at rates not exceeding estimate rates:

(a) In the case of any work entrusted for execution for the rates not exceeding annual maintenance, contract fixed by the Government specifically for this purpose;

(b) In the case of a supplemental maintenance work relating to road which is found necessary after the annual maintenance contract for that road has been settled, if the contract amount of the supplemental maintenance work does not exceed fifty per cent of the amount of the original maintenance amount or rupees two thousand five hundred, whichever is less;

(c) In the case of any work to which a village panchayat contributes not less than twenty-five per cent of the estimate cost either from its own resources or by collecting contribution in cash from the public, the work may be entrusted to the village panchayat in which the work lies, if the panchayat passes a resolution to that effect, subject to the condition that where it is not possible to collect a twenty-five per cent cash contribution in advance, the contribution amount may be deducted from the bills at a rate not exceeding twenty five per cent of cash bill;

(d) In the case of any work to which a sponsor contributes not less than twenty five per cent of the estimate cost in cash if he expresses a desire to execute the work and if the panchayat gives prior approval for entrusting it to such sponsor by passing a resolution, the work may be entrusted to such sponsor:

Provided that no part of the contribution which the village panchayat or panchayat union council or district panchayat, as the case may be, may make, shall be taken credit for, to make the twenty five per cent of the contribution of the sponsor:

Provided further that the sponsor shall not entrust the execution of the works to any contractor.

(e) In the case of any work other than those referred to in clauses (a), (b), (c) and (d), the work may be entrusted to a Labour Contract Co-operative Society functioning in the panchayat development block at rates not exceeding estimate rates;

(f) Nothing contained in these rules shall affect the mode of entrustment and execution of works under State Scheme or Centrally Sponsored Scheme, for which specific orders in the entrustment of works are issued.

9. Dispensing with tender—In cases not falling under clauses (a) to (e) of Rule 8, tenders may be dispensed with on the ground of urgency or for any other special reason to be recorded in writing by the Executive Authority or Commissioner or Secretary, as the case may be:

(a) if the value or the amount of the work does not exceed rupees fifty thousand with the previous approval of the Executive Engineer (Rural Development) on the direction from the respective Inspector and Collector of the district concerned; and

(b) if the value or the amount of the work exceeds rupees fifty thousand but does not exceed rupees two lakhs with the previous approval of the Superintending Engineer (Rural Development) on the direction from the Director of Rural Development.

10. Power to entrust the works without tender—Where tenders are not called for or are dispensed with, the Executive Authority or Commissioner or Secretary, as the case may be, shall except in cases falling under clause (a) to (e) of Rule 8, get the work done through a contractor selected from the register of contractors at rates which shall not ordinarily exceed the sanctioned estimate rates. Where on the ground of urgency or for other special reason it is proposed to allow rates exceeding the sanctioned estimate rates, the previous written approval of the authority competent under these rules to approve the acceptance of tenders at such rates shall be obtained.

Provided that any such work may be entrusted to a person in the locality who is not a registered contractor, but who is interested, it its execution, if in the opinion of the Executive Authority or Commissioner or Secretary, as the case may be, its execution through such agency is desirable and if the value or the amount does not exceed rupees two thousand:

Provided further that the selection of contractors for works, the value or the amount of which is rupees two thousand or less shall be made by the Block Engineer or Assistant Engineer (Rural Development):

Provided also that in cases falling under clause (c) of Rule 8, the supplemental maintenance work shall be entrusted to the contractor for the original maintenance work at the same rates as for the original maintenance work.

11. Dispense with further call of tender—(1) Notwithstanding anything contained in these rules, the Executive Authority or Commissioner or Secretary, as the case may be, may upto such date as the State Government may by general or special order specify from time-to-time dispense with further call of tenders either when no tender is received in the first instance or only high premium tenders which are not considered reasonable are received and are rejected:

(a) if the value or the amount of the work does not exceed rupees five lakhs with the approval of the village panchayat or panchayat union council or district panchayat, as the case may be;

(b) if the value or the amount of the work exceeds rupees five lakhs but does not exceed rupees ten lakhs with the approval of the Collector of the district concerned;

(c) if the value or the amount of the work exceeds rupees ten lakhs but does not exceed rupees one crore with the approval of the Director of Rural Development; and

(d) if the value or the amount of the work exceeds rupees one crore with the approval of the State Government.

(2) In case tenders are not dispensed with under sub-rule (1), the Executive Authority or Commissioner or Secretary, as the case may be, may negotiate with the tenderers in order to entrust the work to the most suitable tenderer having regard to all the local conditions and accept an offer at rate other than specified in the tender with approval of the Collector of the district concerned—

(i) if the value or the amount of the work does not exceed rupees five lakhs with the concurrence of village panchayat or panchayat union council or district panchayat, as the case may be;

(ii) if the value or the amount of the work exceeds rupees five lakhs but does not exceed rupees ten lakhs with the concurrence of the collector of the district concerned;

(iii) if the value or the amount of the work exceeds rupees ten lakhs and does not exceed rupees one crore with the approval of Director of Rural Development; and

(iv) if the value of the work exceeds rupees one crore with the concurrence of the State Government.

12. Register of contractors—A register of contractors shall be maintained in the village panchayat, panchayat union and district panchayat offices respectively in Form I as appended to these rules and such register shall be treated as confidential. A copy of the register shall be submitted annually to the Block Engineer/Assistant Engineer (Rural Development) in case of village panchayat, and to the Executive Engineer (Rural Development) in case of panchayat union and district panchayat, by the Executive Authority or Commissioner or Secretary, as the case may be.

13. Scrutiny of registers—(1) The register of contractors shall be kept up-to-date, and when submitted to the authority under Rule 12, such authority shall scrutinise the register at least once in a year and sign it in token of his scrutiny. Any changes in the register considered necessary by such authority shall be referred by him in writing to the Executive Authority or Commissioner or Secretary, as the case may be, for orders. The Executive Authority or Commissioner or Secretary, as the case may be, shall pass orders on the changes, if any, proposed by the said authority and shall record his reasons for the changes, if any, ordered by him. A copy of the corrections made in the register shall be submitted to the Executive Engineer (Rural Development) concerned and shall be filed with the register in his office.

(2) In the remarks column of the register, the qualifications of the contractor, the quality and magnitude of work previously executed by him and all other relevant particulars shall be entered.

(3) Any person desirous of being registered as a contractor shall apply to the concerned village panchayat or panchayat union council or district panchayat, as the case may be, enclosing a receipt from the village panchayat or panchayat union or district panchayat office, as the case may be, for the fee fixed by the village panchayat or panchayat union or district panchayat, as the case may be, under sub-rule (4) and stating his qualifications and previous experience.

(4) The village panchayat or panchayat union council or district panchayat, as the case may be, may fix a fee not exceeding rupees five hundred to be paid by an applicant for registration as a contractor.

(5) On receipt of an application under sub-rule (3), the Executive Authority or Commissioner or Secretary, as the case may be, shall refer such application to Block Engineer or Assistant Engineer (Rural Development), who shall make a full enquiry and submit the application to the Executive Authority or Commissioner or Secretary, as the case may be, with the record of the enquiry made by him and his views on rejections or recommendation in regard to the particulars mentioned in columns (4) and (5) of the register. The Executive Authority or Commissioner or Secretary, as the case may be, shall place the details of enquiry along with the application for consideration of village panchayat or panchayat union council or district panchayat, as the case may be, who shall pass orders on the application after which the same shall be entered in the register by the Executive Authority or Commissioner or Secretary, as the case may be.

(6) The said register and connected records shall be made available for the perusal of the audit or supervising officer, who shall bring to the notice of the Inspector and Superintending Engineer (Rural Development) of any material irregularities. The Superintending Engineer (Rural Development) shall cause the material irregularities to be enquired into and to place the details before the Inspector, who after giving an opportunity to the concerned Executive Authority or Commissioner or Secretary,

as the case may be, shall pass order which will be binding on the respective panchayat.

(7) The names of the contractors may be removed from the register of contractors by the Executive Authority or Commissioner or Secretary, as the case may be, for any proved misconduct or for any financial incapacity or for any other reasons:

Provided that before ordering the removal of the name of any contractor from the register, a notice in writing shall be given to him to show cause against such removal and his explanation be obtained in writing for consideration, and place the details for consideration of the village panchayat or panchayat union council or district panchayat, as the case may be.

14. Tender procedure—(1) Subject to the provisions of Rule 18, tenders in sealed covers shall be invited by the Executive Authority or Commissioner or Secretary, as the case may be in the most open public and transparent manner possible:

(a) by displaying the tender notice in Tamil on the notice board of the village panchayat or panchayat union or district panchayat, as the case may be, and in such other places as the Executive Authority or Commissioner or Secretary, as the case may be, may direct;

(b) by sending copies of the tender notice to the Assistant Executive Engineer (Rural Development) and Executive Engineer (Rural Development) for displaying on the notice board of their offices concerned; and

(c) by publication of the tender notice in the District Gazette:

Provided that tender notice in respect of a work, if the value of which exceeds rupees ten lakhs and does not exceed rupees twenty five lakhs shall be published in two Tamil newspapers at the district level.

(2) Every notice published under sub-rule (1) shall state

(i) When and where the contract documents may be inspected;

(ii) The precise form of tendering, that is, whether it shall be at specified percentage below or above estimate rates, or whether definite rate issued be quoted for each item of work included in the schedule;

(iii) When and where tenders are to be submitted;

(iv) When and where they are to be opened;

(v) The amount of earnest money which shall accompany the tender and the amount and nature of security required in case the tender is accepted; and

(vi) The authority competent to accept the tender, reserve the right to reject any or all of the tenders received without assigning any reasons.

15. Precise form of tender—(1) The precise form of tendering, namely whether it shall be at specified percentage below or above the estimate rates, or whether definite rates shall be quoted for each item of work included in the schedule independently of the rates provided for in the sanctioned estimate, shall be decided by the Executive Authority or Commissioner or Secretary, as the case may be.

(2) Contractors who are required to tender on percentage basis, may be permitted to examine the estimates for a work, but the data statement showing the actual cost of materials and the distance of the leads on which the estimate is really based shall not be shown to them nor shall it form part of the contract documents.

16. Preparation of contract documents—(1) Before tenders are invited for the execution of a work on contract the Executive Authority or Commissioner or Secretary, as the case may be, shall prepare contract documents which shall include

(i) a complete set of drawings showing the general dimensions of the proposed work and so far as necessary details of the various parts;

(ii) a complete specification of the work to be done and of the materials to be used as approved by the Director of Rural Development unless reference can be made to some standard specifications;

(iii) a schedule of the quantities of the various descriptions of the work; and

(iv) a set of conditions of contract to be complied with by the tenderer in case his tender is accepted.

(2) The draft tender schedule and tender conditions shall be got approved from the technical authority concerned competent to accord sanction of estimate before calling for tenders.

17. Valid tenders—No tender shall ordinarily be treated as valid unless it is accompanied either by the earnest money specified in the tender notice or by a receipt in token of the party having remitted the amount of the earnest money into the panchayat office concerned. A separate list of all sums deposited as earnest money shall be maintained under the signature of the officer opening the tender.

18. Tender from the registered contractors—Only tenders from the registered contractors shall be considered. This condition shall not be enforced in the case of capital works the value or amount of which exceeds rupees fifty thousand in the case of steel work, or incases in which the Assistant Engineer (Rural Development) or Block Engineer certifies that the work, requires the use of special plant or materials and specially trained labourer and that tenders from unregistered contractors may be considered. In the case of capital works the value or amount of which exceeds rupees fifty thousand, tenders from engineering firms of standing and from contractors registered in or outside the village panchayat or panchayat union or district panchayat area for such capital works may be considered. A tender register shall be maintained in the village panchayat, panchayat union and district panchayat offices respectively in Form II as appended to these rules and such register shall be treated as confidential.

19. Earnest money deposit—The amount of earnest money to be deposited shall be as specified in tender notice. In case of the contractors failing to furnish the required security within the appointed time after the acceptance of his tender or until the sums due to him form a sufficient guarantee, or fails to execute the work as per the agreement, the earnest money deposit shall be forfeited.

20. Opening of sealed tender cover—The Executive Authority or Commissioner or Secretary, as the case may be, or any responsible official authorised by him in this behalf shall at the time and place specified for the purpose, open the sealed covers containing the tender in the presence of two officials in that office in addition to the presence of such of the tenderers or their authorised agents as may be present. Until the sealed covers containing tenders are so opened, they shall be kept in the personal custody of the Executive Authority or Commissioner or Secretary or of a such official as may be authorised by him in that behalf. On opening the tenders, the Executive Authority or Commissioner or Secretary, as the case may be, or the official authorised by him to open the tenders shall initial all corrections in each tender which may have been made by the tenderer and attested by him. If there are corrections in the tender unattested by the tenderer a note of such corrections shall be made on the tender itself when it is opened. The Executive Authority or Commissioner or Secretary, as the case may be, or the official authorised by him to open the tenders shall enter the total number of tenders received in the tender register against each work.

21. Tender register—(1) After the tenders are opened, they shall be tabulated and posted in a tender register maintained in the village panchayat or panchayat union or district panchayat office, as the case may be, in Form II appended to these rules. The Executive Authority or Commissioner or Secretary, as the case may be, shall scrutinise the entries in the register and certify that the tabulation is correct with reference to the original tenders which shall be preserved and made available for the purpose of audit.

(2) A contractor who withdraws his tender after the acceptance of tender by competent authority without valid reasons to be decided by the Executive Authority or Commissioner or Secretary, as the case may be, shall be liable to have his name removed from the register of contractors for a period ranging from one to five years. The orders of Executive Authority or Commissioner or Secretary, as the case may be, removing the name of the contractor from such register shall be communicated to the contractor concerned by the Executive Authority or Commissioner or Secretary, as the case may be. An appeal shall lie to the Superintending Engineer (Rural Development) against the order of the Executive Authority or Commissioner or Secretary, as the case may be. Such appeal shall be preferred through the Block Engineer or Assistant Engineer (Rural Development) and the Executive Authority or Commissioner or Secretary, as the case may be, and the Executive Engineer (Rural Development), within seven days from the date of receipt by the contractor of the orders of the Executive Authority or Commissioner or Secretary, as the case may be. The orders of the Superintending Engineer (Rural Development) on such appeal shall be final.

22. Acceptance of tender—(1) The lowest tender shall be accepted. Where it is considered undesirable to accept the lowest tender the reasons shall be clearly recorded in writing by the authority competent to accept the tender and the case shall be disposed of in the manner specified in Rules 23 and 24.

(2) Where the capacity for the work and the integrity of a tenderer are not known, his tender need not necessarily be rejected. Such additional security not exceeding ten per cent of the contract amount as the authority competent to accept the tender considers necessary shall, however, be taken from the tenderer if the circumstances warrant such a course.

(3) Where the lowest tender is rejected, the next lowest tender shall be considered. If it is considered

undesirable to accept that tender also, the next higher tender shall be considered. In every case of rejection of a tender under this sub-rule, the reasons therefor shall be recorded in writing by the authority competent to accept tenders.

(4) In no case shall a tender be accepted at rates other than those specified in the tenders. In cases, where the authority competent to accept the tender considers the rate for certain items are pitched too high in the lowest tender, he may negotiate with the above tenderer with the approval of the next superior authority and secure reasonable rates for those items without higher sanction.

(5) There shall be no avoidable delay in the disposal of tenders after they are opened. In cases where the Executive Authority or Commissioner or Secretary, as the case may be, is competent to dispose of tenders without obtaining concurrence of others, the Executive Authority or Commissioner or Secretary, as the case may be, shall do so ordinarily within a week of the date on which they are opened and in any case within a period not exceeding one month. In other cases no tenders shall remain indisposed of for a period exceeding two months from the date on which they are opened.

23. Passing of orders—The Executive Authority or Commissioner or Secretary, as the case may be, with the approval of the village panchayat or panchayat union council or district panchayat, as the case may be, shall pass orders in accordance with the provisions of Rule 22 in the case of works the value or the amount of which does not exceed estimate rate. If the lowest tender is not accepted and the person making such a tender is a person competent according to the register of contractors to execute the works, the matter shall be referred to the Executive Engineer (Rural Development) concerned and the decision of the Executive Engineer (Rural Development) shall be final. The reference and the order thereon shall contain clear and convincing reasons for not accepting the lowest tender.

24. Exceeding the estimate amount—In the case of works the value or the amount of work which exceeds the estimate amount the tender shall be settled after obtaining concurrence from the authority competent to sanction or as specified in Rule 25.

25. Acceptance of tender for special reasons—Tenders which exceed the estimated rate or amount shall not ordinarily be accepted. Where on the ground of urgency or for other special reasons, if it is proposed to accept such tenders, the previous approval of the authority specified in column (2) of the Table below shall be obtained:

Table

	Value or the Amount of the Work		*Authority*
	(1)		(2)
1.	Not exceeding rupees fifty thousand.	(a)	The Assistant Executive Engineer (Rural Development), if the tender rate exceeds the estimate rate by not more than three per cent.
		(b)	The Executive Engineer (Rural Development), if the tender rate exceeds the estimate rate by three per cent but not more than five per cent.
		(c)	The Superintending Engineer (Rural Development), if the tender rate exceeds the estimate rate by five per cent but not more than fifteen per cent.
		(d)	State Government, if the tender rate exceeds the estimate rate by more than fifteen per cent.
2.	Exceeding rupees fifty thousand but not exceeding rupees three lakhs.	(e)	Executive Engineer (Rural Development), if the tender rate exceeds the estimate rate by not more than five per cent.
		(f)	Superintending Engineer (Rural Development), if the tender rate exceeds the estimate rate by more than five per cent but not more than fifteen per cent.
		(g)	State Government, if the tender rate exceeds the estimate rate by more than fifteen per cent.
3.	Exceeding rupees three lakhs but not exceeding rupees five lakhs.	(h)	Superintending Engineer (Rural Development), if the tender rate exceeds the estimate rate by not more than fifteen per cent.
		(i)	State Government, if the tender rate exceeds the estimate rate by more than fifteen per cent.
4.	Exceeding rupees five lakhs.		State Government.

26. Transparent execution of works—(1) all works executed by the respective panchayats shall be placed before the village panchayat, panchayat union council and district panchayat, as the case may be, and necessary follow up action taken.

(2) A display board on each work exceeding rupees fifty thousand executed by the contractor or otherwise in village panchayat, panchayat union, or district panchayat, as the case may be, shall be placed at the work site by the contractor or the executor executing the works at his cost as part of the work contracted with the following details: (a) name of the scheme; (b) name of the work (including year of sanction); (c) estimate value; (d) name of the contractor; (e) date of commencement of work; and (f) date of completion of work.

APPENDIX

Form-I

Register of Contractors

(See Rule 12)

Sl. No.	*Name of the contractor*	*Address*	*Money limit of subsisting contracts which can be safely entrusted to him for execution at any one time in the course of one year*	*Whether fit for supply of materials only or for road works, or for masonry works, or all works in general*	*Number and date of the chalans in which the fee for registration was paid*	*Remarks*
(1)	(2)	(3)	(4)	(5)	(6)	(7)

Form-II

Tender Register

(See Rules 18 and 21)

Name of the Work:
Estimated Amount of the Contract:
Total Number of Tenders Received:

Sl. No.	*Name of the tenderer*	*Whether registered contractor or not and if registered the serial number in the register of contractors*	*Tender percentage*	*Amount of deposit*	*Engineer's recommendations*	*Orders of the authority competent to accept the tender*
(1)	(2)	(3)	(4)	(5)	(6)	(7)

PART IV

GRAMA SABHA

4.1 GRAMA SABHA

4.1.1 Quorum and Procedure for Convening and Conducting of Grama Sabha Meeting

1. Short title—These rules may be called the Tamil Nadu Grama Sabha (Quorum and Procedure for Convening and Conducting of Meetings) Rules, 1998.

2. Venue and day of the meeting—The Grama Sabha in every village panchayat shall meet at a public place within the limits of the village panchayat. Meeting shall be held on official working day. No meeting shall be held on public holidays, unless specially notified by the Inspector, or by the Government.

3. Notice—For holding meeting of the Grama Sabha not less than seven clear days notice prior to the date and time of the meeting and of the subjects to be deliberated shall be given in the manner specified below:

(a) by beat of drum in all the habitations of the village panchayat announcing the place, date, hour and agenda of the meetings;

(b) by a written intimation of the meeting to be displayed by affixture in the office of the village panchayat and in a few other conspicuous public places such as school building, noon meal centre, television room, village temple, over-head tank and so on; and

(c) a copy of the notice and the agenda shall be sent to the Inspector not less than seven clear days before the date of the meeting.

4. Quorum for a meeting—No subject shall be taken up for deliberation at a meeting of the Grama Sabha unless there be present one-tenth of the total number of the members of the Grama Sabha.

5. Adjournment of the meeting—If within half an hour after the time appointed for the meeting, the requisite quorum is not available, the meeting shall stand adjourned to a date and time to be notified to the members by the presiding officer.

6. Agenda—The agenda for the meeting shall be prepared by the president in consultation with the village panchayat. It shall include a report on the action taken on the decisions of the previous meeting of the Grama Sabha.

7. Presiding officer to preserve the orders in the meeting—The presiding officer of the meeting of the Grama Sabha shall preserve order at the meeting and decide all points of order arising at or in connection with the meeting. There shall be no discussion on any point of order if decided by the presiding officer and his decision shall be final.

8. Observer of the meeting—Where the meeting of the Grama Sabha has been convened by the Inspector, the Inspector shall have right to send an officer not below the rank of Block Development Officer as observer who shall submit a report to Inspector within seventy two hours of the completion of the Grama Sabha meeting.

9. Attendance register—The attendance of the members of the Grama Sabha shall cause to be recorded in a register maintained for this purpose by the presiding officer of the meeting.

10. Minutes—The minutes of the meeting shall be recorded in the same register by the presiding officer and it shall be read out before the conclusion of the meeting and the presiding officer shall then sign it. The minutes of the Grama Sabha meeting shall be placed before the village panchayat at its next meeting for consideration and further action.

11. Submission of the minutes—A copy of the minutes of the meeting shall be submitted to the Inspector within three days of the date of the meeting.

(G.O. Ms. No. 150, Rural Development Department, dated 17th July 1998)

4.1.2 Entrustment of Functions to the Grama Sabha

Notification—In exercise of the powers conferred by clause (b) of sub-section (3) of Section 3 of the Tamil Nadu Panchayats Act, 1994 (Tamil Nadu Act

21 of 1994), the Governor of Tamil Nadu hereby entrusts the following other functions to the Grama Sabha:

(1) Approval of the beneficiaries selected and location of institutions and community facilities identified by the village panchayat.

(2) Review of the completed works executed in the previous year by village panchayat and scrutiny of the list of works undertaken in the year by the village panchayat or by any Government Department and agency.

(3) Promotion of communal and social harmony among the various groups of people in the village panchayat.

(4) Mobilisation of voluntary labour, contribution in cash and kind for community welfare and development programmes.

(5) Examining annual statement of accounts and audit report of the village panchayat.

(G.O. Ms. No. 152, Rural Development (C2) Department, dated 20th July 1998)

4.1.3 Guidelines on Quarterly Meeting of Grama Sabha

The Honorable Minister of State Ministry of Rural Employment, Government of India requested Government of Tamil Nadu that meetings of Grama Sabha shall be conducted in every village panchayat once in a quarter, in the day notified by Government. It is also opined that these meetings may be conducted on National holidays of 26th January, (Republic Day), 1st May (Labour Day), 15th August (Independence Day), 2nd October (Mahatma Gandhi Birth Day).

After examining the proposals the Government have decided and issued orders on the dates on which Grama Sabha meeting to be conducted, the subjects to be discussed and the Nodal Officer to be deputed for each Grama Sabha meeting. The Grama Sabha meetings and subjects to be discussed in each meeting shall be as follows:

Period	*Date of Grama Sabha Meeting*	*Subject to be Discussed*
First Quarter (April, May, June)	1st May – Labour Day	Placing the list of beneficiaries for Government welfare programmes and the schemes approved by the village panchayat shall be placed in this meeting.
Second Quarter (July, August, September)	15th August – Independence Day	Explain the nature of benefits for the individuals and the community under each scheme of Poverty Alleviation Programmes as well as other development programmes.
Third Quarter (October, November, December)	2nd October – Mahatma Gandhi Birthday	(i) Interim review of progress in the implementation of development programmes of the Panchayats and other Government Departments. (ii) Placing of Annual Report of village panchayat for the previous year and audit report on receipts and expenditure of village Panchayat.
Fourth Quarter (January, February, March)	26th January – Republic Day	Placing of proposed development plan of village panchayat for next financial year and getting approval of the Grama Sabha.

The District Collectors are requested to depute one Nodal Officer for each Grama Sabha Meeting from among the various department officers working in the District. The Collectors shall send the progress report on the conduct of Grama Sabha meeting within a week to the Director of Rural Development. The Director of Rural Development is requested to consolidate the report on the Grama Sabha meetings and send a report once a quarter to the Government.

(G.O. Ms. No. 245, Rural Development (C1) Department, dated 19th November 1998)

4.1.4 Further Guidelines Issued on Grama Sabha Meeting

Grama Sabha – Instructions on the observation made by the observers sent by the government— The Government sent senior level officers as observers for the Grama Sabha meeting conducted in the district to get their opinions, views and suggestion for successful conduct of the Grama Sabha meeting. They were deputed to the Grama Sabha meeting held on 1.5.1999 and they have submitted the reports with the following suggestions:

(a) The Grama Sabha meeting will be conducted in evening time to enable all the daily labourers to participate in the meeting.

(b) The details of Grama Sabha meeting shall be explained by exhibiting short length film by the Tamil Nadu Film Division in all the Cinema Theatres in the district.

(c) The Nodal Officers of other department may be trained and it shall be made compulsory for them to attend the meeting.

(d) The husband of women president of village panchayat shall not interfere in the meeting.

(e) Information about the Grama Sabha meeting shall be placed in important places in the village.

(f) Formulate rules for rising of questions and getting answer in the Grama Sabha meetings.

(g) The expenditure for conduct of Grama Sabha meeting shall be fixed by the Government.

(h) Creating awareness among the Adidravidar and womenfolk to participate in the Grama Sabha meeting.

The Government issued the following orders on the suggestions of the observers who attended the Grama Sabha meetings:

(a) The women labourers returning to their homes in late hours would always evince interest in handling household activities rather than attending the Grama Sabha meeting. Hence women in the villages may not be able to participate in Grama Sabha meetings in large number. More ever if the Grama Sabha meeting is conducted in evening hours there will be law and order problems. Hence the Government feel that Grama Sabha meeting need not be conducted in the evening hours.

(b) The Director of Rural Development is requested to take action to screen one minute film recorded by the Tamil Nadu Film Division in all the Cinema Theatres during interval time without any additional expenditure.

(c) The Collectors are requested to impart Block level training to all the Nodal Officers deputed to attend Grama Sabha meeting and ensure that the Nodal Officer attend the Grama Sabha meeting without fail.

(d) After enactment of 73rd Constitutional Amendment Act and reservations provided in Tamil Nadu Panchayats Act, 1994, more number of women presidents, vice-presidents and ward members have been elected in the Local body election held in October 1996. As they have been elected for the first time, they may find it difficult to run the administration of village panchayat without any outside help and it may take some more time to get familiarized in the administration of village panchayats. Hence, the Government felt that the present instructions of the husband of women elected representatives restrained to interfere in the matter of village panchayat administration need not be pressed strictly now.

(e) In G.O. Ms. No. 245, Rural Development, dated 29.11.1998, the District Collectors have instructed the village panchayat, to publish the details about the date and subjects to be discussed in Grama Sabha meeting in village panchayat office, T.V. Room, Community Hall and other important public places in the village panchayat area.

(f) The Director of Rural Development and the Collectors have been asked to provide necessary skills for raising the questions and getting proper reply from the Grama Sabha meetings. The president of village panchayat shall be advised to be patient and give responsible answer to all the questions raised by the public.

(g) The presidents of village panchayats are empowered to spend Rs. 500/- (Rupees Five hundred) after approval of the village panchayat for each Grama Sabha meeting.

(h) Organising by village panchayat cultural activities and villuppattu to create awareness among the womenfolk and Adidiravidar will require more expenditure; the Director of Rural Development and the District Collectors are requested to involve Non-Governmental Organisations to create awareness about the importance of Grama Sabha meeting.

(G.O. Ms. No. 76, Rural Development (C4) Department, dated 24th March 2000)

PART V

RULES AND INSTRUCTIONS RELATING TO VILLAGE PANCHAYAT

5.1 FORMATION AND CONSTITUTION

5.1.1 Determination of Population

If any question arises as to the population of any panchayat village or of any part of such village, for the purpose of the Tamil Nadu Panchayats Act, 1994, the question shall be decided with reference to the population of such village, as ascertained at the last preceding census.

(G.O.Ms.No.149, Rural Development (C4) Department, dated 21st July 1999)

5.1.2 Exclusion of Any Local Area from or Inclusion of Any Local Area in a Village Panchayat

The Principles laid down in the following rules shall be followed for exclusion from, or the inclusion of any local area in the village panchayat under sub-section (2) of Section 4 of the Tamil Nadu Panchayats Act, 1994.

(1) No area shall be included in any village except where such area has been excluded from another village and the inclusion of such area in the former village has become necessary or expedient.

(2) No area shall be excluded from any village except for constituting a separate village panchayat or village panchayats for such area or for including such area in another village for which already there is a village panchayat or a village panchayat is proposed to be constituted.

(3) No area shall be excluded from or included in a village unless, in the opinion of the Inspector, the income of a village panchayat concerned after such exclusion or inclusion will be adequate for running the administration of the village in an efficient manner.

(4) No area shall be excluded from a village if, in the opinion of the Inspector, the income of the village panchayat will be substantially reduced by reason of such exclusion.

(5) No area shall be excluded from a village and included in another village unless both the village panchayats concerned have been consulted in regard to such exclusion and inclusion.

(6) Except for special reasons, if a village panchayat has jurisdiction over only a single revenue village; no area shall be excluded from such revenue village.

(7) Where a village panchayat exercises jurisdiction over two or more revenue villages, the exclusion of any area from the jurisdiction of such village panchayat shall be effected in such a way that a separate village panchayat may be constituted for each revenue village or for two or more revenue villages.

(8) Where a village panchayat exercises jurisdiction over one revenue village and a portion or portions of any other revenue village or villages and if the said portions are not contiguous to the revenue village aforesaid, such portion or portions may be excluded from the jurisdiction of the village panchayat and included within the jurisdiction of a village panchayat having jurisdiction over the contiguous area.

(G.O. Ms. No. 147, Rural Development (C4) Department, dated 21st July 1999)

5.1.3 Period within which Appeal to Government Against the Notifications Relating to Formation of Village Panchayats

1. Short title—These rules may be called the Tamil Nadu Panchayats (Limitation for Appeal to Government Against Notifications Relating to Formation of Village Panchayats) Rules, 1999.

2. Period within which an appeal shall be made—Any rate payer or inhabitant of a local area of any village panchayat objecting to a notification under sub-section (1) or sub-section (2) of Section 4 of the Tamil Nadu Panchayats Act, 1994 (Tamil Nadu Act 21 of 1994) in respect of such area or village panchayat may appeal to the Government within thirty days from the date of publication of such notification relating to the formation of village panchayats.

(G.O. Ms. No. 203, Rural Development (C4) Department, dated 28th September 1999)

5.1.4 Alteration in Jurisdiction of Village Panchayat

Changes in the jurisdiction of village panchayat are made at times for administrative purposes and that such changes in administrative boundaries affect the description of the extent of the Parliamentary and Assembly Constituencies, since the proposals for such changes are made without any reference to the boundaries of the Parliamentary and Assembly Constituencies involved.

It is also imperative that the jurisdiction of a village panchayat should be within a single development block forming a panchayat union. In order to avoid administrative difficulties in this regard, it is considered that while constituting, or re-constituting, or bifurcating or otherwise re-defining the jurisdiction of village panchayats, the village panchayat so notified shall lie within the boundary of a single Parliamentary Constituency and Assembly Constituency existing at that time.

Further while constituting village panchayats or for changing the jurisdiction of village panchayats or grouping of villages for purpose of constituting village panchayats, the Inspector of panchayat shall invariably consider the information *inter alia* whether the proposal affects the boundaries of the Parliamentary or Assembly Constituencies existing in the area at that time and if so the extent to which they are affected. Such information should also include the details of area, and income etc., besides the latest published census code units and the population according to latest published census.

(G.O. Ms. No. 146 Rural Development (C1) Department, dated 31st May 2001)

5.1.5 Formation of District Level Committee—Alteration in the Jurisdiction of Village Panchayat

Representations are periodically received indicating that the areas of certain village panchayats and panchayat unions are bigger and unwieldy and it is very difficult to improve the administration and execute plan programmes. It is also necessary to amalgamate or bifurcate these panchayats. The proposals for bifurcation of village panchayats or panchayat union, inclusion or exclusion of areas may be considered by a committee constituted in each district under the Chairmanship of the District Collector and the decisions on the proposals will be taken on the recommendation of the committee and after getting views of the concerned local body. The Government constituted a committee for each district consisting of following members for the purpose.

District Collector	:	Chairman
Project Officer, DRDA	:	Member-Secretary
All the MPs in the District	:	Member
All the MLAs in the District	:	Member
District Panchayat Chairman	:	Member
Five Panchayat Union Ward Members nominated by the District Collector	:	Member
One Village Panchayat President from each Panchayat Union nominated by the District Collector	:	Member
Asst. Director (Panchayats)	:	Member

From among the members to be selected from local bodies, due representation for women, scheduled castes and schedules tribes shall be given. If the Collector desires other Government Officers, President or Chairman of the concerned village panchayat or panchayat union, they may be included as special members in the committee. The District Level Committee shall be considered as class I Committee. The Travelling Allowance of the MPs and MLAs included in the committee shall be met from the Head of Account of Development Section of the Collectorate. The Travelling Allowance of other members may be met from their respective local body.

The Collectors were requested to constitute the District Level Committee for the first time before 15th July, 1999. The Committee shall subject to the following conditions, examine the following subjects and furnish report to the Government within a period of 3 months.

(i) Bifurcation or amalgamation of village panchayats.

(ii) Inclusion of a portion of the village panchayat in another village panchayat or exclusion thereof.

(iii) Bifurcation of panchayat unions or inclusion or exclusion of certain areas.

(iv) While recommending for constitution of new village panchayats or panchayat unions, the committee shall satisfy, that adequate financial resources are available for functioning of village panchayat or panchayat unions. Opinion of the public as well as the resolution of the concerned local body shall be obtained.

(v) The additional expenditure involved due to bifurcation shall be examined and remarks given. The boundaries and population of the recommended new village panchayat or panchayat union shall confirm to those fixed as per Tamil Nadu Panchayats Act, 1994.

(G.O. Ms. No. 113, Rural Development (C1) Department, dated 29th June 1999)

5.1.6 Norms for Classification of Village Panchayat

Section 6(4) of the Tamil Nadu Panchayats Act, 1994 empowers the Government to classify village panchayats into various grades for the purpose of effective administration of the said village panchayats for which Government may prescribe norms.

In the rule notified on 31st March 1999, Government have fixed the norms for Grade I village panchayats.

(1) Village panchayat shall be classified as Grade I village panchayat if,

(a) such a village panchayat is converted as such from town panchayat; or

(b) the annual income of such village panchayat exceeds four lakhs rupees; or

(c) the population of such village panchayat exceeds fifteen thousand.

(2) A village panchayat which does not fulfil the norms specified in sub-rule (1) shall be classified as Grade II village panchayat.

(3) Where the position of a village panchayat classified under sub-rule (1) or (2) is changed subsequently, such village panchayat shall be re-classified, from time-to-time according to its position specified in the said sub-rules.

Explanation. For the purpose of these rules, annual income of village panchayat means the average income of three years preceding the financial year in which the notification is to be issued. The annual income shall not include the receipt of loan, time-barred deposit and non-statutory and development grant allotted to the village panchayat concerned.

(G.O. Ms. No. 62, Rural Development (C4) Department, dated 31st March 1999)

5.2 PRESIDENT, VICE-PRESIDENT, MEMBERS AND EXECUTIVE AUTHORITY

5.2.1 Reporting of Vacancy in the Posts of Elected Representatives of Panchayats

Every vacancy in the office of the president, vice-president or member shall be reported to the District Election Officer by the president/Executive Authority, vice-president or member as the case may be, within two days from the date of occurrence of the vacancy.

(G.O. Ms. No. 66, Rural Development (C4) Department, dated 14th March 2000)

5.2.2 Disclosure of Assets and Liabilities by President, Vice-President and Members of Village Panchayat

1. Short title—These rules may be called the Tamil Nadu Panchayats (Disclosure of Assets and Liabilities by President, Vice-President and Members of Village Panchayat) Rules, 1999.

2. Definition—In these rules, unless the context otherwise requires, Member of the Family means person related whether by blood or marriage to the president, vice-president and members of village panchayat or his wife or her husband and wholly dependant on such president, vice-president and member.

3. Periodical disclosure of assets of president, vice-president and members of village panchayat—The president, vice-president and every member of a village panchayat shall

(a) if he is elected after the date of coming into force of these rules, within a period of thirty days, after such election; and

(b) thereafter, at intervals of every twelve months ending with the 31st day of March, furnish in duplicate to the village panchayat in the Form appended to these rules a return of

(i) all properties owned, acquired or inherited by him or his family members including their liabilities; and

(ii) all properties held on lease or mortgage either in his own name or in the name of his family members, including their liabilities together with details of the means by which, or the sources from which such property was acquired or inherited.

4. Returns to be placed at the meeting and to be public document—(1) After the receipt of the return specified in Rule 3, the Executive Authority shall, cause it be placed at the meeting of the village panchayat and send a copy to the Inspector.

(2) Such return shall be deemed to be a public document and the Executive Authority, with the permission of the village panchayat, may, subject to such condition including payment of fees specified in Rule 5 give to any person on demand a copy of such return.

5. Fee for furnishing return—The fee for furnishing a copy of any return or part thereof shall be ten rupees or the amount to be fixed by the Government from time-to-time.

APPENDIX
Form
(See Rule 3)

Returns of assets and liabilities of the President, Vice-President or Member of the .... Village Panchayat as on the ....

Name of the ....

Date of election:

Part I – Assets and Liabilities of the ....

1. Immovable Property:

(a)	*Land*	*Owned*		*Wet*	*Dry*	*Irrigated dry*
	Extent: Date of acquisition: Value of acquisition: Leased in: Extent: Date of acquisition: Value of acquisition:					
(b)	*Building* Plinth Area: Date of acquisition: Value of acquisition	*Owned*	*Terraced*	*Tiled*	*Thatched*	*Purpose for which the building is used: commercial or residential*
	Plinth Area: Date of acquisition: Value of acquisition:	*Leased in*	*Terraced*	*Tiled*	*Thatched*	*Purpose for which the buildings is used commercial (or) residential*

2. Business interests:
   (a) Shares
   (b) Stock
   (c) Scrip
   (d) Partnership
   (e) Debentures and securities
3. Other interest:
   Bank Account
4. Jewellery:
   (a) Gold
   (b) Precious stones
   (c) Silver Ware
5. Movables (including motor vehicles)
6. Details of Trusts with which he has any connection
7. Remarks any of the .... (Explain the nature of acquisition of properties)
8. Liabilities

Part II – Assets and Liabilities of his family members

Name of the Family member ....

1. Immovable Property:

(a)	*Land*	*Owned*		*Wet*	*Dry*	*Irrigated dry*
	Extent: Date of acquisition: Value of acquisition: Leased in: Extent: Date of acquisition: Value of acquisition:					
(b)	*Building* Plinth Area: Date of acquisition: Value of acquisition	*Owned*	*Terraced*	*Tiled*	*Thatched*	*Purpose for which the building is used: commercial or residential*
	Plinth Area: Date of acquisition: Value of acquisition:	*Leased in*	*Terraced*	*Tiled*	*Thatched*	*Purpose for which the buildings is used commercial (or) residential*

2. Business interests:
   (a) Shares
   (b) Stock
   (c) Scrip
   (d) Partnership
   (e) Debentures and securities

3. Other interest:
   Bank Account
4. Jewellery:
   (a) Gold
   (b) Precious stones
   (c) Silver Ware
5. Movables (including motor vehicles)
6. Details of Trusts with which he has any connection
7. Remarks if any, of the .... (Explain the nature of acquisition of properties)
8. Liabilities

DECLARATION

I .... declare that to the best of any my knowledge and belief, the information furnished in the above return is true and complete.

Place:

Date: **Signature**

(G.O. Ms. No. 181, Rural Development (C4) Department, 30th August 1999)

5.2.3 Removal of Disqualification of Members of Panchayats and Presidents of Village Panchayats Having Certain Subsisting Contracts

1. Short title—These rules may be called the Tamil Nadu Village Panchayats (Removal of Disqualification of Members and President of Village Panchayat Having Certain Subsisting Contracts) Rules, 1999.

2. Exemptions to disqualification on subsisting contract—No member or president of a village panchayat shall cease to hold office as such on the ground that he acquires any interest in a subsisting contract made with or any work being done for the village panchayat by reason of such member or president having a share or interest in

(a) any lease, sale or purchase of immovable property or any agreement for the same; or
(b) any agreement for the loan of money or any security for the payment of money only; or
(c) any newspaper in which any advertisement relating to the affairs of the panchayat is inserted; or
(d) the sale to the panchayat of any article in which he regularly trades or the purchase from the panchayat of any articles to a value in either case not exceeding ten thousand rupees in the aggregate in any year during the period of the contract or work.

(G.O. Ms. No. 144, Rural Development (C4) Department, dated 21st July 1999)

5.2.4 Devolution and Delegation of President's Function

1. Short title—These rules may be called The Tamil Nadu Village Panchayats (Devolution and Delegation of President's Function) Rules, 1999.

2. Definition—In these rules, unless the context otherwise requires, "Act" means the Tamil Nadu Panchayats Act, 1994 (Tamil Nadu Act 21 of 1994).

3. Absence of the president from his jurisdiction—Where the absence of the president from his jurisdiction is within the State of Tamil Nadu and is on business connected with the village panchayat his functions except to the extent, if any, to which the functions have been delegated to the vice-president, shall not devolve on the said vice-president under sub-section (2) of Section 47 of the Act.

4. Delegation of functions—(1) The president shall not delegate under Section 48 of the Act any of his functions including his function as Executive Authority to the vice-president or a member, which the village panchayat expressly forbids him to delegate.

(2) The president may delegate his any function to a member only when there is a vacancy in the office of vice-president or when the vice-president is away from the jurisdiction of the village panchayat for more than thirty days or incapacitated.

5. Nomenclature during delegation period—The member to whom the functions of the president including his function as Executive Authority have been delegated shall be styled, as the president delegate during the period of delegation.

6. Restriction for delegation to another member—When an order of delegation made to a member is in force, no further order of delegation of any function shall be made in favour of any member than the member in whose favour the order of delegation in force was made.

7. Maximum period for delegation—No delegation shall be made by the president to a member for any period exceeding in the aggregate 90 days in any year without special sanction of the village panchayat.

8. Intimation about delegation—(1) Every order of delegation made by the president to the vice-president or a member shall be communicated to the village panchayat at its next meeting and to the Inspector.

(2) This provision of Rules 5 to 7 shall not apply to the delegation by the president of his functions to the vice-president.

9. Restrictions and control imposed on temporary presidents—The temporary president appointed under sub-section (3) of the Section 47 of the Act shall perform the functions of the president subject to the restrictions and conditions that he shall not

(a) appoint, promote or punish any officer or servant of the village panchayat;

(b) conduct public auction of annual sales of leases of markets slaughter houses, fishery rights and other like lease;

(c) enter into contract on behalf of the village panchayat and withdraw any money belonging to the village panchayat by means of cheque except salary bills and electricity consumption charges;

(d) pass final orders of disposal on applications, petitions, and other complaints received from public involving administrative problem;

(e) grant leave other than casual leave to the officers and servants of the village panchayat;

(f) pass orders on petitions for revision of house tax.

(G.O. Ms. No. 178, Rural Development (C4) Department, 30th August 1999)

5.2.5 Appointment of Executive Authority of Village Panchayats

The Government have appointed the president of the village panchayat as the Executive Authority to exercise the powers and perform the functions of the Executive Authority of that village panchayat.

(G.O. Ms. No. 225, Rural Development (C1) Department, dated 15th October 1996)

5.3 PROCEDURE

5.3.1 Procedure for Convening and Conduct of Village Panchayat Meetings

1. Short title—These rules may be called the Tamil Nadu Panchayats (Quorum and Procedure for the Convening and Conduct of Meetings of Village Panchayat) Rules, 1999.

2. Definition—(a) "Act" means the Tamil Nadu Panchayats Act, 1994 (Tamil Nadu Act 21 of 1994);

(b) All other words and expressions used in these rules but not defined therein shall have the meanings respectively assigned to them in the Act.

3. Duration between the meetings—(1) The village panchayat shall meet in its office at least once in every month for the transaction of business on such days and at such times as it may arrange and also at such other times as often as a meeting shall be called by the president.

(2) No meeting shall be held on any day declared by the Government as holiday and other local holidays declared by the Collector.

4. Notice of the meeting—(1) Notice of not less than three clear days shall be given before the day of the meeting specifically indicating the date, and time, the place of meeting and the business to be transacted thereat.

(2) In case of urgency, the president may convene a meeting on giving notice of not less than twenty-four hours clearly indicating the reasons of such urgency, and the place, date and time of the meeting including the business to be transacted thereat.

5. Special meeting—A subject which is to be decided only in a meeting specially convened for a particular purpose as per the provisions of the Act shall be decided only in a special meeting and no other subject shall be placed and decided at such a meeting.

6. Agenda—(1) The agenda for the meeting shall be prepared by the president. The members may also bring agenda for discussion in the meeting and shall furnish details to the president not less than seven days prior to the date of meeting. The president, with his views thereon, shall place the agenda for discussion in the meeting.

(2) The president, while preparing the agenda for the ordinary meeting shall invariably include among others, the following subjects:

(a) A statement showing the monthly receipts and charges of the village panchayat under all accounts upto the month;

(b) Progress of all schemes, programmes and works upto the month;

(c) Administration report of the village panchayat for every financial year within three months in the next year;

(d) Audit report of the village panchayat with explanatory notes thereon at the first meeting of the village panchayat after the receipt of the same;

(e) Tour reports and inspection reports of every higher officer who inspected the schemes, programmes and works of the village panchayat at the first meeting of the village panchayat after their receipt, preparation of development plan for village panchayat.

(3) In order to ensure the successful participation of the members in the administration of village panchayat, the president shall place various instructions, guidelines issued from time-to-time by the Government of India, Government of Tamil Nadu, Director of Rural Development and the Collector of the District concerned before the village panchayat in the agenda.

7. Service of notice of meeting and agenda—The notice of meeting with the agenda shall be served on a member following the procedure specified below, in the order in which it is specified:

(a) by giving or tendering the notice of meeting to the member concerned in person; or

(b) in case personal service could not be effected, by tendering it to an adult member of his family; or

(c) if no adult member of his family is also available for service, the notice of meeting shall be sent by registered post with acknowledgement due, or by affixing it on the conspicuous place of his last known address in the presence of the Village Administrative Officer of that village.

8. Validity of meeting—The entire proceedings shall be invalid if the notice of meeting with the agenda is not served to any member of the village panchayat

9. Requisition meeting—(1) The president shall, on the requisition in writing, of not less than one-third of the members, convene a meeting of the village panchayat provided that the requisition specifies the date on which and the purpose for which the meeting is to be held. The requisition shall be delivered at the village panchayat office during office hours to the president, or any other person who may then be in-charge of the office not less than seven clear days before the day of the meeting.

(2) If the president fails within forty eighty hours from the delivery of such requisition to call a meeting on the day specified therein, or within three days hereafter, the meeting may be called by all the members who signed the requisition on giving the notice as provided in Rule 4 to the other members.

10. Meeting open to public—All meetings shall be open to the public provided that the presiding member may at his discretion or at the request of the village panchayat shall, in any particular case for the reasons to be recorded in the minutes, direct that public generally or any particular person shall withdraw.

11. Attendance of the meeting—The members and the presiding member attending the meeting shall sign in the attendance register. At the closure of the meeting, the presiding member shall close the attendance register by specifying the number of members attended, in the register and sign at the end.

12. Quorum—(1) No business shall be transacted at a meeting unless there be present at least three members or one-third of the number of members then on the village panchayat whichever is higher through out the duration of the meeting.

(2) If within half an hour after the time appointed for a meeting a quorum is not present, the meeting shall stand adjourned unless all the members present agree to wait longer.

(3) If the meeting stands adjourned for want of quorum, the president shall give a fresh notice for such adjourned meeting, as provided in Rule 4.

13. Adjournment of the meeting for other reasons—(1) The presiding member while transacting business at the meeting may adjourn any meeting of village panchayat with the consent of the majority of the members for valid reasons to be recorded in writing in the minutes. When once a meeting is adjourned sine die for valid reasons, it shall not continue its meeting.

(2) While transacting the business, if a meeting is validly adjourned by the presiding member with the consent of the majority of the members present at the meeting, the meeting held on adjourned date shall, for all purposes, be a continuation of the

original meeting and no fresh notice shall be necessary for such an adjourned meeting.

(3) If the president adjourns the meeting contrary to the wishes of the members present and thereby interrupts or leaves un-finished, the business for which the meeting was convened, the remaining members may lawfully continue the business. In the absence of president, the vice-president, in the absence of vice-president, a member elected from among themselves may preside over the meeting and continue the business. Any business which was duly notified in the notice for the meeting shall alone be transacted to completion and if it is so transacted, it shall be valid.

14. Passing of resolution—Every question which may come before the village panchayat at any meeting shall be decided by a majority of the members present and voting at the meeting and, in every case of equality of votes, the presiding member shall have and exercise a second or casting vote. In the case of any resolution not carried unanimously, the names of the members who voted for and against it shall be recorded in the minutes.

15. Modification or cancellation of resolution—No resolution shall be modified or cancelled within three months after the passing thereof except at a meeting specially convened in that behalf and by a resolution supported by not less than one-half of the sanctioned number of members.

16. Minutes—Minutes of the proceedings at each meeting shall be drawn up and entered in a book to be kept for that purpose and as soon as the discussion on a subject is over, the presiding member shall record the decision of the village panchayat then and there, read the text of the decision to the members present and affix his signature immediately below the last line of the resolution. At the end of the meeting he shall record in the minutes that all the resolutions passed have been readout in the open meeting and then only he shall sign at the end of the minutes and shall also obtain the signatures of all the member present at the meeting.

17. Custody of records—The president shall have the custody of the proceedings and records of the meetings of the village panchayat and may grant copies of any such proceedings and records on payment of such fees as the village panchayat may by general or special order, determine. Copies shall be certified by the president as provided in Section 76 of the Indian Evidence Act, 1872 (Central Act I of 1872) and copies so certified may be used to prove the records of the village panchayat in the manner as they may under clause (5) of Section 78 of the said Act, be used to prove the proceedings of that body.

(G.O. Ms. No. 167, Rural Development (C4) Department, dated 9th August 1999)

5.3.2 Sending of Minutes Proceedings and Minutes of Dissent

In the reference first cited rules have been already issued on the procedure for convening and conduct of meeting of village Panchayat. Under Section 92 of Tamil Nadu Panchayats Act, 1994, a copy of the minutes of the proceedings of every meeting of panchayats as well as minutes of dissent in respect of such proceedings received from any member present at the meeting within forty eight hours to the close of the meeting shall be submitted by the President or Chairman as the case may be to the Inspector of panchayats within three days of the date to the meeting. Further in order to effectively monitor this, there is a provision under the same section for further delegation of the power to receive such minutes and scrutiny by any officer empowered by the Inspector in his behalf.

Therefore, all the Collectors (except Chennai) are requested to issue necessary direction under the proviso to Section 92 of the Tamil Nadu Panchayats Act, 1994, that the minutes of the proceedings at every meeting of a village panchayat as well as all minutes of dissent received from any member present at the meeting within 48 hours of the close thereof, shall be submitted to the Block Development Officer (village panchayats), and to the auditor (Deputy Block Development Officer) separately. The president of the village panchayat shall give a copy of the minutes of dissent recorded in the minutes of the meeting as soon as the meeting is over to the member who gave the dissent. The Block Development Officer (village panchayats) may also be directed to file all the minutes of monthly meeting continuously in a separate file for village panchayat-wise. He shall scrutinize all the minutes of the meeting thoroughly to find whether the resolutions confirm to the statutory provisions, instruction, regulations and guidelines issued by the Government from time-to-time and if he notices any resolution contrary to the above, he shall bring it to the notice of the Inspector for cancellation of such resolution as per Section 202 of the Tamil Nadu Panchayats Act, 1994.

The village panchayat member may send the minutes of dissent along with the copy given by the President to the Block Development Officer (village panchayats) citing reasons for the dissent for further action. Moreover immediate follow up action shall be taken on the minutes of dissent if any received by the Block Development Officer (panchayats) thoroughly scrutinising the reasons quoted in the minutes of dissent and decide on the admissibility, or non-admissibility of the resolution. He shall also intimate the panchayat member who gave minutes of dissent on the action taken by him.

(G.O. Ms. No. 167, Rural Development, dated 9th August 1997)

5.3.3 Moving of Resolutions in Village Panchayat Meeting

1. **Short title**—These rules may be called the Tamil Nadu Panchayats (Moving of Resolution at Meetings of Village Panchayats) Rules, 1999.

2. **Procedure of notice**—A member who wishes to move a resolution shall intimate his intention in writing to the president by giving at least ten clear days notice and such notice shall contain a copy of the resolution which he wishes to move:

Provided that the president may allow a resolution with shorter notice than ten days to be entered on the list of business.

3. **Admission of resolution**—No resolution shall be admissible which does not comply with the following conditions, namely

(a) it shall be related to the administration of the village panchayat concerned;
(b) it shall be clearly and precisely expressed and shall raise a definite issue; and
(c) it shall not contain arguments, inferences, ironical expressions or defamatory statements, nor shall it refer to the conduct or character of any person except in his official or public capacity.

4. **Admissibility of resolution**—The president shall decide on the admissibility of a resolution. He may disallow any resolution which, in his opinion, contravenes the provisions of The Tamil Nadu Panchayats Act, 1994 or the rules made thereunder and the decision of the president shall be final:

Provided that if, in the opinion of the president a resolution relates to a matter which is unconnected with the administration of the village panchayat concerned, the president shall refer the resolution to the Inspector and obtain his orders as to its admissibility.

5. **Entry of resolution in the list of business**—A resolution which has been admitted by the president shall be entered in the list of business in the notice for the meeting.

6. **The procedure to move or otherwise of a resolution**—(1) A member in whose name a resolution appears on the list of business shall, when called on either

(i) move the resolution; or
(ii) withdraw the resolution in which case he shall confine himself to a mere statement to that effect.

(2) If the member, when called on is absent or proposes to withdraw or unwilling to move the resolution or if he has ceased to be member before the meeting, any member present at the meeting may move the resolution; and if no member moves it, it shall be considered to have been withdrawn.

(3) Every resolution which has been moved shall be seconded; otherwise it shall not be discussed.

7. **Mode of discussion**—(1) No speech, except with the permission of the president shall exceed five minutes in duration:

Provided that the mover of a resolution when moving the same may speak for not more than ten minutes.

(2) The discussion of a resolution shall be strictly limited to the subject of the resolution moved.

8. **Amendment to a resolution**—(1) When a resolution is under discussion any member may, subject to Rules 3, 4 and 7 move an amendment to such resolution.

(2) Every amendment, which has been moved, shall be seconded; otherwise it shall not be discussed.

(3) A member who has moved a resolution or an amendment to a resolution shall not withdraw the same except by leave of the village panchayat.

(4) No discussion shall be permitted on a motion for leave to withdraw except with the permission of the president.

(5) When an amendment to any resolution is moved or when two or more such amendments are moved, the president shall, before taking the consent of the village panchayat thereon, state or read to the village panchayat the terms of the original motion and of the amendment or amendments proposed.

(6) Ordinarily the president shall put the amendment to vote in the order in which they have been moved and lastly the original motion, if all the amendments are lost. But it shall be in his discretion

in any case to put to vote the original motion and the amendments in such order as he thinks fit.

9. Division of resolution into points for voting—When any resolution involving several points has been discussed, it shall be the discretion of the president to divide the resolution into points and put each of such points separately to vote.

(G.O. Ms. No. 180, Rural Development (C4) Department, dated 30th August 1999)

5.3.4 Interpellation of President of Village Panchayat by the Members

1. Short title—These rules may be called the Tamil Nadu Panchayats (Interpellation of President of Village Panchayat by the Members) Rules, 1999.

2. Restriction on question—No question shall be asked or answered at a meeting of a panchayat as to any matter not concerned with the village panchayat administration and no question shall be asked except as to matters of fact and the answer shall be confined to statement of fact. Except as those provided, any question may be asked by any member of a village panchayat subject to the conditions and restrictions specified in these rules.

3. Notice as to questions—A member of a village panchayat who wishes to ask a question shall intimate his intention in writing to the president by giving ten clear days' notice and such notice shall contain a copy of the question he wishes to ask.

4. Admissible questions—In order that a question may be admissible, it shall satisfy the following conditions, namely:

(1) it shall be related to administration of the village panchayat and that also be based on facts;

(2) it shall not relate to any name or statement not strictly necessary to make the question intelligible;

(3) If a question contains a statement, the member asking it shall make himself responsible for the accuracy of the statement;

(4) It shall not contain arguments, inferences, ironical expressions or defamatory statement;

(5) It shall not ask for an expression of opinion or the solution of an abstract legal question or a hypothetical proposition;

(6) It shall not be asked as to the character or conduct of any person except in his official or public capacity;

(7) It shall not be of excessive in length; and

(8) A question once fully answered shall not be asked again.

5. Decision as to admissibility of questions—The president, shall decide on the admissibility of a question and either allow or disallow it before the date fixed for the next meeting for which it may be in time under Rule 3. He may disallow any question, if in his opinion, it is an abuse of the right of questioning or where in his opinion it cannot be answered consistently in the public interest, and shall disallow any question which in his opinion, contravenes any of these rules; and in such case the question shall not be entered in the proceedings of the village panchayat.

6. Agenda—Questions allowed by the president, shall be entered in the agenda and the president shall answer every question so entered, if not previously withdrawn by the member putting it, in the order in which it stands in the paper, before any business is entered upon at the meeting. The answer shall be confined to a statement of facts only:

Provided that the president may, at his discretion, on the ground of public interest, answer a question on the agenda, even though the question may have been withdrawn.

7. Supplementary questions—Any member may put a supplementary question for the purpose of further elucidating any matter of fact regarding which an answer has been given:

Provided that the president shall disallow any supplementary question, if, in his opinion, it infringes the rules as to the subject matter of questions and does not confirm to the conditions specified under rule:

Provided further that he may decline to answer a supplementary question without notice, in which case it may be put only in the form of a fresh question at a subsequent meeting of the village panchayat.

8. Bar on discussion of answered questions—No discussion shall be permitted in respect of any question or of any answer given to a question, asked under these rules.

9. Minutes—The question asked and the answer given to it shall be entered in the minutes of the village panchayat.

(G.O. Ms. No. 33, Rural Development (C4) Department, dated 15th February 1999)

5.3.5. Constitution of Committees of Village Panchayats and Delegation of Functions

1. Short title—(1) These rules may be called the Tamil Nadu Panchayats (Constitution of Committees of Village Panchayats and Delegation of Functions to such Committees) Rules, 2005.

2. **Definition**—In these rules, unless the context otherwise requires, "Act" means the Tamil Nadu Panchayats Act, 1994 (Tamil Nadu Act 21 of 1994).

3. **Constitution of Committees**—(1) Every village Panchayat shall constitute the following committees, namely—

(i) Appointment Committee
(ii) Development Committee
(iii) Agricultural and Watershed Committee
(iv) Works Committee
(v) Education Committee

(2) The village Panchayat shall select members for each Committee as indicated in the respective provisions of these rules. The president and members of the village panchayat may serve in one or more Committees. No member of a Committee shall act as Chairman for more than three Committees. The President shall be ex-officio member of all the Committees constituted under sub-rule (1).

4. **Appointment Committee**—(1) The Appointment Committee shall consist of the president of the village panchayat and two of its members selected from among its members annually.

(2) The Appointment Committee may select candidates for appointment to any of the posts sanctioned in the village panchayats as prescribed in section 101 of the Act (except the posts which are specifically excluded from the purview of the provisions of the Act or the rules made thereunder) and the pay of which is debitable to the funds of the village panchayat.

5. **Development Committee**—(1) (a) The Chairman of the Development Committee shall be selected from among the women members of the village panchayat.

(b) The Development Committee shall consist of the following members, namely—

(i) Two members of the village panchayat.
(ii) One Noon Meal Organiser.
(iii) One Head Master or Headmistress of Local Primary or Middle School.
(iv) One Non-Governmental Organiser or Social Worker.
(v) Representative from one Self Help Group.
(vi) One Village Health Nurse.
(vii) One Rural Welfare Officer.
(viii) Secretary of the Primary Agriculture Co-operative Society.

(2) The Development Committee shall—

(a) promote community maintenance of assets in the field of health, drinking water and sanitation.

(b) supervise the protected drinking water supply to all the areas of the panchayat village to ensure prevention of communicable diseases;

(c) organise immunisation and vaccination camps and promote better health care;

(d) create awareness to promote, organise campaign relating to public health, water and rural sanitation;

(e) inspect health sub-centres and health centres located in the panchayat village and submit its observations and suggestions for discussion in the village panchayat;

(f) promote participation of the users of drinking water in maintenance of water supply system;

(g) promote individual household toilets, group toilets, school and community sanitation and women sanitary complex;

(h) process and recommend the resolution passed by the habitation or ward Committees;

(i) promote the Welfare of Women, children, physically handicapped, destitute, widows, aged people, bonded labourers, scheduled castes and scheduled tribes;

(j) form self help groups;

(k) take action for eradication of child labour, prohibition of liquor, prevent female infanticide, promotion of anti dowry, promotion of communal harmony, eradication of untouchability and implementation of Poverty Reduction Project;

(l) assist the village panchayat in the maintenance of hand pumps, power pumps, over head tanks, drinking water ooranies and any other means of drinking water supply in the panchayat village;

(m) assist the village panchayat to watch the functioning of ration shop under Public Distribution System in the panchayat village and monitor timely supply of goods in prescribed quantity and quality, display of daily stock position in retail shop, price of each commodity sold, supply among the card holders and suggest steps to redress the public grievances;

(n) assist the village panchayat for the preparation of comprehensive village development plan.

(3) The Committee may visit and inspect such centre, establishment or institution within the area of the panchayat village. The Chairman of the Committee shall intimate in writing to the Head of the Centre, establishment or institution three days in advance indicating the date, time and purpose of visit or inspection.

(6) Agricultural and Watershed Committee—(1) (a) The Chairman of the Agricultural and Watershed Committee shall be selected by the members of the Committee among themselves.

(b) The Committee shall consist of the following members, namely—

(i) one member (from General category) of the village panchayat;

(ii) one member (from Scheduled Castes or Scheduled Tribes Members) of the village panchayat;

(iii) Village Administrative Officer;

(iv) a representative from Non-Governmental Organisation;

(v) a representative from Self Help Group (Women);

(vi) Assistant Agricultural Officer or his representative;

(vii) a representative from Watershed Association.

(2) The Agricultural and Watershed Committee shall—

(a) Plan and assist for the implementation of programmes relating to agriculture, horticulture, sericulture, floriculture, pisciculture, dairy development, poultry development, drought prone area development, watershed, wasteland development, social forestry, soil conservation and water management.

(b) Organize farmers forum in panchayat village to promote application of latest technologies, improved irrigation system in minor irrigation tanks, Public Works Department Tanks, etc.;

(c) Process and recommend the resolution passed by the habitation/Ward Committees.

7. Works Committee—(1) (a) The Chairman of the Works Committee shall be selected by the members of the Committee from among themselves.

(b) The committee shall consist of the following members, namely—

(i) One member of the village panchayat (from General category);

(ii) One member of the village panchayat (from Scheduled Castes and Scheduled Tribes women members);

(iii) One representative from Non-Governmental Organisation;

(iv) One representative from Self Help Group;

(v) One Noon Meal Organiser;

(vi) One Head Mistress or Headmaster of the local Primary or Middle School;

(vii) One Rural Welfare Officer;

(viii) Village Administrative Officer;

(ix) One Village Health Nurse.

(2) The Works Committee shall:

(a) Assist the village panchayat to execute centrally and state sponsored schemes where the guidelines prescribed for the execution of works through public and monitor other works executed in the panchayat village including works related to Government Departments and organisations to ensure quality and timely execution;

(b) Assist the village panchayat in the preparation of village development plan based on the requirements and available local resources;

(c) Process and recommend the resolution passed by the habitation/Ward Committees.

8. Education Committee—(1) (a) The Chairman of the Education Committee shall be selected by the village panchayat from among its members.

(b) the Committee shall consist of the following members, namely—

(i) One Representative from Parent-Teacher Association;

(ii) One representative from Self Help Groups;

(iii) One representative from Non-Governmental Organisations;

(iv) One Headmaster or Headmistress of local primary or middle school;

(v) One Noon Meal Organiser;

(2) The Education Committee shall—

(a) Monitor the functioning of all schools in its area;

(b) Plan and organise public participation to develop school infrastructure including building;

(c) Organise campaign for universal education, non-formal education, maintenance of libraries and promote the literacy and reading habit among public.

9. Constitution of Temporary Committee—A Village Panchayat may constitute any Committee other than the Committee specified in sub-rule (1) of Rule 3 for any specific purpose of exercising such powers, discharging such duties and performing such functions as it may delegate (except irrigation) to such Committee and may also constitute any Committee as and when required to inquire into and report or advise on any matter which may be referred to it. The tenure of such Committee shall not exceed six months from the date of its constitution. If a Committee needs to function for a period longer than six months, prior sanction of the Inspector of Panchayats shall be obtained.

10. Constitution of Sub-Committees—(1) A Village Panchayat may constitute any sub-committee other than the Committees specified in sub-rule (1) of Rule 3 for any specific or general purpose of exercising such powers, discharging such duties and performing such functions as it may delegate (except irrigation) to such Committee and may also constitute any Committee as and when required at habitation or ward level. The ward member of the Village Panchayat concerned will be the Chairman of the Sub-Committee.

(2) The sub-committee shall;

(a) Suggest any improvement to promote the purpose for which it has been constituted;

(b) Monitor the programme implementation, etc.;

(c) Forward the recommendation to panchayat level committees for consideration and recommendation to village panchayat.

11. Inspection—Every Committee may visit and inspect such centre, establishment or institution within the area of the panchayat village. The Chairman of the Committee shall intimate in writing to the head of the centre, establishment or institution, as the case may be, three days in advance.

12. Notice and Agenda for Committee—The Chairman of the Committee shall fix the date, time and venue of the meeting of the Committee and circulate the agenda for discussion atleast three days in advance.

13. Periodicity of meeting—Every Committee except the Appointment Committee shall meet once in two months. The Appointment Committee shall meet whenever selection for any post in the village panchayat is to be made.

14. Plan Preparation—Every Committee shall prepare respective sectoral annual and perspective development plan for panchayat village. The Chairman of each Committee shall submit such plan to the village panchayat for discussion and decision.

15. Approval of Panchayat—Every observation, suggestion or recommendation of each committee shall be placed in the meeting of the Village Panchayat for consideration and decision.

16. Appraisal to Grama Sabha—Grama Sabha to be appraised about the recommendations of the Committees. The Village Panchayat shall compile the recommendations of the Committees every year and appraise the Grama Sabha during its meeting to be held in the quarter of January to March.

[G.O. (Ms.) No.102, Rural Development (C4), 12th July 2005]

5.4 ESTABLISHMENT

5.4.1 Appointment of Common Officer or Servant for Two or More Village Panchayats

1. Short title—These rules may be called the Tamil Nadu Village Panchayats (Appointment of Common Officer or Servant for Two or More Village Panchayats) Rules, 1999.

2. Definition—In these rules unless the context otherwise requires, "Act" means the Tamil Nadu Panchayats Act, 1994 (Tamil Nadu Act 21 of 1994).

3. Power of the inspector to appoint common officer or servant for two or more village panchayats—The Inspector may, when necessary require two or more village panchayats to appoint the same officer or servant to exercise or discharge any powers or duties of a similar nature for both or all of them:

Provided that the Inspector shall consult the officer not below the rank of a Deputy Director of Public Health in respect of appointment, in the public health establishment.

4. Salary and allowances payable to the officer or servant—The village panchayat concerned shall meet the salary and allowances payable to such officer or servant together with contributions payable towards his leave salary or provident fund in such proportion and in such manner as may be laid down by the Inspector with reference to the income of the village panchayats, the out turn of work of such officer or servant or any other data which the Inspector may consider suitable for the purpose.

5. Power to punish the officer or servant—The Inspector shall specify the Executive Authority of one of the village panchayats concerned for the purpose of exercising the powers referred to in Section 106 of the Act.

6. Power of the inspector—If any of the village panchayats concerned is not satisfied with the exercise of the powers referred to in Rule 5 by the Executive Authority specified under the rule, the panchayat first mentioned may refer the matter to the Inspector whose decision on such reference shall be final.

(G.O. Ms. No. 139, Rural Development (C-4) Department, dated 21st July 1999)

5.4.2 Procedure of Appointment of Part-time Clerk in Village Panchayats

Government permits the village panchayat president to make appointment of part-time clerk of village panchayat if there is no panchayat Assistant. Moreover whenever there is vacancy in the post of panchayat assistant, the president may appoint part-time clerk in that place. The panchayat assistant and the part-time clerk shall work under the control of village panchayat president. Similarly all the duties and responsibilities of the panchayat assistant will also be looked after by the part-time panchayat clerk. The pay of part-time clerk shall be paid from village panchayat fund account according to the norms fixed by the Government on population basis as fixed by the Government from time-to-time.

(G.O. Ms. No. 230, Rural Development (E5) Department, dated 15th October 1996)

5.4.3 Qualification for Appointment of Part-time Clerk

The qualification prescribed for appointment of part-time clerk of village panchayat is

1. Pass in 10th standard (S.S.L.C.)
2. Should not exceed 28 years of age
3. Shall be a resident of concerned village panchayat

For SC, ST, Backward class and MBC candidates age limit is raised by five years and the maximum age limit is prescribed as 33 years. For all others age limit is prescribed as 28 years.

(G.O. Ms. No. 245, Rural Development (E-5) Department, dated 4th March 1997)

5.4.4 Honorarium for Panchayat Assistant/Part-time Clerk

The honorarium for village panchayat assistant is raised to Rs. 750/- (Seven hundred and fifty only) per month.

The honorarium for part-time clerk of village panchayat shall be paid at the following rates:

Population of Village Panchayat	*Honorarium*
2000 and less than 2000	Rs. 450/-
2001 to 3000	Rs. 500/-
3001 to 4000	Rs. 550/-
4001 to 5000	Rs. 600/-
5001 and above	Rs. 650/-

The expenditure on payment of honorarium shall be met from the village panchayat fund account.

(G.O. Ms. No. 86, Rural Development (E-5) Department, dated 8th May, 1998)

5.4.5 Increase of Pay for Panchayat Assistant/Part-time Clerk

In the Government orders referred above, the honorarium was fixed for village panchayat/part-time clerk/sweepers/power pump/OHT Operators. The Government now enhances the honorarium as follows:

(a) The honorarium of village panchayat assistant working in Grade 2 village panchayat is increased from Rs. 750/- to Rs. 800/- per month.

(b) The honorarium for the village panchayat part-time clerk working in Grade 2 village panchayat is enhanced as follows:

Population of Village Panchayat	*The Present Honorarium Amount*	*Increased Honorarium*
Less than 2000	Rs. 450/-	Rs. 500/-
2001-3000	Rs. 500/-	Rs. 550/-
3001-4000	Rs. 550/-	Rs. 600/-
4001-5000	Rs. 600/-	Rs. 650/-
5000 and above	Rs. 650/-	Rs. 700/-

The expenditure on payment of honorarium shall be met from the village panchayat fund account.

The Government have given permission to village panchayat to enhance the honorarium upto Rs. 800/- per month for the village panchayat part-time clerk/assistant depending upon the revenue and work load of the village panchayat.

The village panchayat assistant and bill collectors working in Kanyakumari District and the panchayat assistant/bill collectors who have been appointed on time scale by the Collector as per sub-section (3) of Section 57 of Tamil Nadu Panchayat Act, 1958 (whether the village is Grade I or Grade II), they are permitted to draw their salary continuously. In arising vacancy of these posts in Grade I village panchayats shall appoint village panchayat assistant and an amount of Rs. 1,800/- p.m. or 10 per cent revenue of village panchayat whichever is less may be paid. In vacancy arising in Grade II village panchayats, the village panchayat part-time clerk shall be appointed and a maximum honorarium amount of Rs. 800/- shall be given to them. The expenditure shall be incurred from the village panchayat fund only.

(G.O. Ms. No.117, Rural Development (E-5) Department, dated 10th May 2000)

Note—As per G.O. Ms. No. 60 RD dated 3.5.2005, an uniform increase of Rs. 200/- has been sanctioned to all the employees mentioned in the statement furnished above.

5.4.6 Appointment of Full Time Clerk in Certain Village Panchayats

The Government considered the additional responsibilities and duties entrusted to the village panchayats after the enactment of Tamil Nadu Panchayats Act, 1994 and have decided that full time clerk may be appointed for those Grade-I village panchayats with an annual income of more than Rs. 3 lakhs, subject to the condition, the expenditure towards salary shall not exceed 10 per cent of its income.

They can be paid consolidated pay as fixed by the Government from time-to-time. The Grade-I village panchayats with an income of Rs. 3 lakhs shall appoint the present panchayat assistant or part-time clerk as full time village panchayat clerk on consolidated pay.

(G.O. Ms. No. 122, Rural Development (E-5) Department, dated 6th July 1999)

5.4.7 Honorarium for Full Time Clerk

The honorarium for the full time panchayat assistant shall be given based on the financial position and work load of the village panchayat. However, the honorarium amount shall not exceed 10 per cent of total revenue of the village panchayat or shall not exceed Rs. 1,800/- per month, and this expenditure shall be incurred only from the concerned village panchayat fund account only.

(G.O. Ms. No. 116, Rural Development (E-5) Department, dated 10th May 2000)

Note—As per G.O. Ms. No. 60 RD dated 3.5.2005 an uniform increase of Rs. 200/- has been sanctioned.

5.4.8 Procedure for Filling up Vacancies of the Post Junior Assistant/Junior Assistant-*cum*-Typist/Cashier/Typist from Among Panchayat Clerks

1. In the G.O. fourth read above, Government have issued order, *inter alia*, framing guidelines in drawing the panel of candidates for appointment to the vacancies reserved for the part-time/full time clerks of the village panchayats in the posts of Junior Assistants, Rural Welfare Officer, Grade-II and Cashiers. Among the guidelines, it has been specified that person to be eligible for appointment as Junior Assistant/Rural Welfare Officer/Grade-II/Cashier should have rendered not less than 5 years of service in the lower categories and that he should have been in the first instance recruited through Employment Exchange.

2. Based on the observation of the Tamil Nadu Administrative Tribunal for prescribing a longer period of qualifying experience in the lower category, it was ordered, *inter alia*, in the G.O. Ms. No. 43, Personnel & Administrative Reforms Department, dated 16.2.94, that the existing qualifying experience of 5 years be enhanced to 7 years and that persons appointed as Junior Assistant/Junior Assistant-*cum*-Typist by recruitment by transfer from the post of Record Clerk, Office Assistant etc., shall undergo training in the Civil Service Training Institute, Bhavanisagar for the period that may be prescribed by the Government from time-to-time. The Government have decided that the orders issued in G.O. Ms. No. 43, Personnel & Administrative Reforms Department, dated 15.2.94 be made applicable to the categories of Part-time/Full time Clerks of village panchayats also.

3. There shall be no temporary appointment from the above categories to the post of Junior Assistant, Junior Assistant-*cum*-Typist, Cashier and typist under any circumstances and appointments shall be made only from the panel approved by the Tamil Nadu Public Service Commission as aforesaid.

4. The Part-time/Full time Clerks who were appointed as Junior Assistant, Junior Assistant-*cum*-Typist/Cashier/Typist by transfer shall undergo training in the Civil Service Training Institute, Bhavanisagar for the period that may be prescribed by the Government from time-to-time.

5. The seniority of the persons, who were appointed as Junior Assistant/Junior Assistant-*cum*-Typist/Cashier/Typist by transfer from the posts of Part-time/Full time Clerks for village panchayats, shall be fixed on the basis of date of appointment to the Ministerial Service.

6. These revised guidelines shall come into effect from the date of issue of this order.

(G.O. Ms. No. 52, Rural Development (E-5) Department, dated 20th March 1998)

5.4.9 Fixation of Pay for Part-time Operator of Power Pumps/Over-head Tank Operators

(1) In G.O. Ms. No. 148, Rural Development (E-3) Department, dated 9.7.1999, the Government have fixed the honorarium of Rs. 330/- per month for village panchayat part-time power pump, OHT operators and sanitary workers.

The Government passed the following Orders on the pay for Part-time Operator of Power Pumps and Over-head Tanks in village panchayats.

(a) In future instead of appointing one Operator for each Power Pump, village panchayats may appoint one Operator for all the power pumps in village panchayats.

(b) The pay of Part-time power pump operators is raised as Rs. 400.

(c) He will be paid Rs. 150/- per extra power pump operated by him.

(2) The expenditure involved for the payment mentioned above shall be met from the village panchayat funds account.

(3) In G.O. Ms. No. 191, Finance Department, dated 29.4.1998, the following associations have filed writ petition in the court, claiming that the Government order is applicable to village panchayat sanitary workers and power pump operators, the court has dismissed the writ as withdrawn.

Sl. No.	*Name of the Association*	*Writ petition*
1.	**Vellore District** Panchayat Union Power Pump/OHT operators association	High Court writ petition No. 15917/98
2.	**Dharmapuri District** Panchayat Union Power Pump/OHT operators association	High Court writ petition No. 16965/98
3.	**Dharmapuri District Panchayat** Assistant Association	High Court writ petition No. 17118/98

The High court have not stayed the Government order. The following writ petitions are still pending with High court.

Sl. No.	*Name of the Association*	*Writ petition*
1.	Thiru. T.R. Ramnath, General Secretary, Tamil Nadu Panchayat Union Power Pump Operators and Sanitary Workers Association, Chennai, Thiruvannamalai District.	Writ petition No. 16307/98. The High Court gave stay order on 30.10.1998
2.	Thiru. R. Rengraj Tamil Nadu Rural Development Employees Association	High Court writ petition No. 9025/99. The High Court have stayed the Government order for six weeks from 10.6.1999
3.	Tamil Nadu Panchayat OHT Operators and Sanitary Workers Association (Reg. No. 441/ Director of Rural Development) The Secretary, Vellore District Panchayat	On the writ petition No. 14976/99, the High Court have given interim judgment on 8.9.1999, directed to pay the honorarium already given continuously until the final judgment is delivered.

Hence, except in the above said cases, the remaining employees are eligible to receive the increased honorarium amount of Rs. 400/- per month.

(G.O. Ms. No. 119, Rural Development (E-5) Department, dated 10th May 2000)

Note—As per G.O. Ms. No. 60 RD dated 3.5.2005 an increase of Rs. 200/- has been sanctioned to power pump operators and Rs. 100/- has been sanctioned to every addl. power pump looked after by him.

5.4.10 Fixation of Pay for Sanitary Workers in Village Panchayats and Regulation of the Sanitary Workers

(a) The Part-time Sanitary Workers already working in village panchayat shall be continued.
(b) The total expenditure on sanitary workers pay and other items of sanitary worker shall not exceed 20 per cent of House tax collection in the village panchayat.
(c) The consolidated pay so paid to the part-time sanitary workers, subject to the condition laid in (b) above shall be fixed not exceeding Rs. 400/–.

The additional expenditure involved in this regard shall be met from the village panchayat fund account.

(G.O. Ms. No. 4, Rural Development (E-5) Department, dated 1st March 1999)

Note: As per G.O. Ms. No. 60 RD dated 3.5.2005 an increase of Rs. 200 has been sanctioned.

5.4.11 Maintenance of Radio and Televisions in Village Panchayats

(a) The Government have decided that there need not be any separate persons employed in village panchayat, for operating the Television and Radio in village panchayat.
(b) The operation of Television and Radio can be entrusted by the village panchayat to Volunteers, Members of Women Group and Over-head Tank Operators.
(c) No expenditure shall be incurred towards this purpose from the funds of the village panchayats.
(d) It will be responsibility of the village panchayat president to supervise and monitor the operation of Radio and Television by the above mentioned volunteers etc.

(G.O. Ms. No. 125, Rural Development (Planning-3) Department, dated 16th May 2000)

5.4.12 Group Insurance Scheme for Employees of Village Panchayat

The Group Insurance Scheme is being implemented for the employees of local bodies, aided schools, aided colleges, and aided technical educational institutions and employees working under the nutritious meal programme. The Scheme does not; however apply to the employees of village panchayats.

The Government extend Group Insurance Scheme to the Panchayat Assistant/Part-time clerk and other part-time panchayat employees like sanitary workers, over head tank/power pump operators drawing consolidated pay/honorarium from village panchayat. The Group Insurance Scheme for the employees of village panchayat shall come into force from 1.7.1997.

The rules and other instructions so far issued in respect of the Group Insurance Scheme for local body employees shall apply *mutatis mutandis* to these employees also.

The expenditure towards payment of premium shall be debited to the head of account "2235. Social Security and Welfare – 60. Other Security Welfare Programmes – 110. Other Insurance Scheme – I. Non-Plan – BU. Payment of premium to the Life Insurance Corporation of India under Group Insurance Scheme – 10. Contribution. (DP Code 2235 60 110 BU 1006)"

The employees contribution and local body contribution shall be credited to the head of account "0075.00. Miscellaneous General Services – 800. Other Receipts – AW. Contribution under Group Insurance Scheme for employees of Local Bodies. Aided Schools, Aided Colleges and Aided Technical Institutions – 10. Employees of Local Bodies – Panchayat Assistant/Part-time Clerks and Panchayat Employees like Sanitary Worker, Over Head/Power Pump Operators.

Employees Contribution
(DP Code 0075 00 800 AW 1011)

Management Contribution (Village Panchayat)
(DP Code 0075 00 800 AW 1022)"

(G.O. Ms. No.326, Rural Development Department, dated 23rd June 1997)

5.4.13 Village Panchayat Employees not Covered Under Labour Act

Non-implication of provisions of Minimum Wages Act to employees employed in any local authority.

No.II (2) LAB 426vs4 – In exercise of the powers conferred by sub-section (2) of Section 26 of the Minimum Wages Act, 1948 (Central Act XI of 1948), the Governor of Tamil Nadu hereby directs that the provisions of the said Act shall not apply to employees employed in any local authority.

(G.O. Ms. No. 1403, Labour, 26th June 1984)

5.5 POWERS AND FUNCTIONS

5.5.1 Building Rules

1. Short title, extent and commencement— (1) These rules may be called the Tamil Nadu Panchayats Building Rules, 1997.

(2) They shall apply to the whole of the areas which come under the purview of the Tamil Nadu Panchayats, 1994 (Tamil Nadu Act 21 of 1994), excluding the areas to which the provisions of chapters IX and X of the Tamil Nadu District Municipalities Act, 1920 (Tamil Nadu Act V of 1920) are extended and are applicable.

(3) They shall come into force at once.

2. Definitions—In these rules, unless there is anything repugnant in the subject or context

(a) "Appendix" means an appendix to these rules,

(b) "continuous type" means a series of buildings in a continuous row where there will be:

(i) open space left in the front and rear sides and interior portion; and

(ii) no open space on either side by such buildings except in the side of the first and the last building,

(c) "detached type" means a single house with open space on all sides,

(d) "dwelling house" means a house designed or intended to be used wholly or principally for human habitation together with such outbuildings, latrines and other erections as are ordinarily used or intended to be used there with or building used for cottage industries,

(e) "executive authority" means the president of the village panchayat,

(f) "Government means the State Government,

(g) "Public building" means any building to which the public or any class of section of the public are granted access or any building which is open to the public or any class or section of the public and includes any building

(a) used as a:

(i) Educational institution including school or college;

(ii) Hostel;

(iii) Library;

(iv) Hospital, nursing home, dispensary clinic maternity centre or any other like institution;

(v) Club;

(vi) Lodging house;

(vii) Coffee house, boarding house or hotel or an eating house,

(b) used by any association,

(c) Ordinarily used by the,

(i) Central or any State Government or any local authority or any body corporate, owned or controlled by the Central or any State Government;

(ii) Public or any class or section of the public for religious worship or for religious congregation;

(iii) "Plot" means a continuous portion of land held in single or joint ownership other than land used allotted or set apart for any street, lane, passage, pathway or other common public purposes; and

(iv) "site for building" includes all the land within the cartilage of the building and forming its appurtenances such as out-buildings, yard, court open space and garden attached thereto or intended to be occupied therewith.

3. Application for approval of layout of sites— (1) No owner or other persons shall layout a street, lane passage or pathway or sub-divide or utilise the land or any portion or portions of the same on the site or sites for building purposes until a layout plan has been approved by the Executive Authority who shall get prior concurrence of the Director of Town and Country Planning or his authorised Joint Director or Deputy Director of Town & Country Planning for such approval. In cases of lay out abutting National Highways, State Highways and Bye Pass Roads thereof, the concurrence of the Divisional Engineer (Highways and Rural Works) under whom the control of the road is vested shall also be obtained by the Executive Authority. The application for approval or such layout plan or sub-division shall be submitted to the Executive Authority in the form specified in Appendix A with such variation as circumstances may require.

(2) The application shall be accompanied by a layout plan or plans (in triplicate) of the land to be laid out into house-sites, as far as may be necessary.

(3) The application for layout approval shall be accompanied by a late encumbrance certificate of the land specifying ownership and also the authenticated survey sketch. It shall be entertained only from the owner of the land or from any other person who possesses the power of attorney duly registered.

(4) The owner of the land to be laid out shall while submitting the application and plans required under sub-rule (1) submit a letter of consent relinquishing the land required for such streets, lanes, passage common construction and pathways in favour of the Executive Authority.

(5) Every street, lane, passage and pathway shall be demarcated formed and constructed including paving, metalling, flagging, channelling, sewering draining conserving and lighting by the owner of the land in accordance with the provision of the layout for the proper development of the area ensuring safety and convenience of the public and all expenses incurred thereof shall be paid by the owner of the land at his expense, while submitting the application required under sub-rule (1).

(6) The owner of the land to be laid out shall not proceed to sub-divide or utilise the site or sites intended for building purposes unless he has complied with the requirements of sub-rules (1), (2), (3), (4), and (5).

(7) The Executive Authority may require the applicant to furnish any information which has not already been furnished or to satisfy him that there are no objections which may lawfully be taken to the grant of approval.

(8) If, any information required under sub-rule (7) is in the opinion of the Executive Authority, incomplete or defective, he may require further information to be furnished.

(9) If, any requisition made under sub-rule (7) or (8) is not complied with within one month, the application shall be rejected.

(10) The Executive Authority may as soon as may be after sixty days from the date of receipt of the application.

(a) grant the approval applied for either absolutely or subject to such conditions as he thinks fit to impose; or

(b) refuse approval if he is of opinion that such work is contrary to the conditions specified under the approved plan.

(11) No site or any new layout of site lying within a distance of thirty metres from the Railway boundary shall be used as site for the construction of a building or to a hut masonry constructions.

4. Application for approval of sites for buildings and huts—(1) Every person who intends, to construct or reconstruct or alter or add to a building or to a hut shall submit an application to the Executive Authority for the approval of the site and for permission to execute the work, in the form specified in Appendix B. with such variations as circumstances may require which shall be accompanied by,

(a) a site plan (in triplicate) of the land on which the building or hut is to be constructed, re-constructed or altered or added to as far as may be necessary, complying with the requirements specified in Appendix C;

(b) a plan or plans (in triplicate) of the building, or hut to be constructed, reconstructed or altered or added to as far as may be necessary, complying with the requirements specified in Appendix D;

(c) a specification (in triplicate) as far as may be necessary complying with the requirements specified in Appendix E; and

(d) the information as to the purpose for which the building or hut is proposed to be constructed, reconstructed or altered or added to.

(Provided that the construction or reconstruction or addition or alteration to residential houses, all such as other public buildings like commercial buildings, hotels, resort and factory buildings excluding a plinth area of 250 sq. metres in the panchayats of Nilgiris district shall be approved by the Executive Authority after obtaining the permission of the committee for architectural and aesthetic aspects headed by the Collector of Nilgiris district).

(G.O. Ms. No. 360, Rural Development Department, dated 18th December, 1997)

(2) The application as well as plan specifications and the information as required under items (a), (b), (c) and (d) of sub-rule (1) shall be signed by the owner of the site or accompanied by a letter of authority or consent from the owner of the site, if the applicant himself is not the owner.

(3) No site shall be used for the construction of a building intended for public worship or religious purposes without the prior approval of the Collector of the district who may refuse such approval if in his opinion, the use purpose of the site and building is likely to endanger public peace and order.

(4) No site which is situated within a distance of ninety metres from a place used as a burning or burial place or ground shall be used for construction of any building, without the previous approval of the Executive Authority and no building intended for human habitation shall be built within ninety metres of such burning or burial place or ground, unless such burning or burial place or ground was

closed for burning or burial of corpses and remained so closed for a period of not less than five years as ascertained from the record maintained by the village panchayat. Provided that no existing building situated within ninety metres from any burning or burial place or ground shall be reconstructed or added to without the previous approval of the Executive Authority.

(5) No approval to the construction or reconstruction or addition or alteration to a building shall be given in case where the clearance between the building and the Aerial line has less than:

(a) 1.5 metres for low tension lines, 1.75 metres from high tension lines from accessible portions or buildings measured horizontally and 1.25 metres for both low tension and high tension from inaccessible portions measured horizontally;

(b) 2.5 metres from portions of buildings not accessible to portions measured vertically; and

(c) 4.5 metres from accessible portions of buildings measured vertically.

(6) For effective conservation of rain water, no approval to the construction or reconstruction or addition or alteration to a building (other than a hut) including houses constructed by Government for below poverty line families under the poverty alleviation programmes or building constructed by any agency under the control of the Government, shall be given, if the application for construction, re-construction, alteration or addition to such a building does not contain provision for water conservation and rain water harvesting as specified below.

5. Street, lanes, passages and pathways—(1) The streets and access to be provided in the development layout shall connect with an existing access way, street or road. The main access to the development shall be well defined and as far as possible proceeding to a suitable central location of the immediate adjacent village or human habitation.

(2) No street or access shall normally be less than 7 metres in width, if the length of the access is not more than 120 metres.

(3) The main street or access to the development shall have a width of not less than 9 metres if the length of the said access or main development street is not more than 200 metres.

(4) The main accesses and other street, whose length will be in excess of 200 metres, shall be provided with a width of not less than 12 metres.

(5) All the streets shall be provided with open side drains and shall be formed with metal, gravel or other hard surfacing.

(6) The streets and access ways shall be properly lighted.

(7) Culverts shall be provided wherever required. The width of such culverts shall as far as possible be less than 3.6 metres and they shall be provided with parapet walls at both ends a height of not less than 0.5 metres from the road level.

(8) The corners of two streets shall be shamphered with a 1.5 metres scamper.

(9) Streets ending blindly shall be avoided unless the length of such street is less than 45 metres.

(10) All streets which have width of 9 metres and over shall be provided with marginal trees planted alternately on the opposite sides and at a distance of not less than 9 metres and at a distance of 1 metre from the street edge.

(11) The trees for the avenues should be selected in accordance with the local conditions and should be the fast growing and good shade giving trees yielding flowers of varying colours and hues as recommended in the layout and to the satisfaction of the Executive Authority.

6. Space about building—(1) The building shall be erected in a site whose minimum size shall be 9 metres width and 15 metres depth.

(2) Continuous type building shall be allowed with a minimum rear open space of 3 metres.

(3) Semi-detached type building shall be allowed with a minimum rear open space of 3 metres and side open space of 1.5 metres.

(4) Detached buildings may be allowed as per the table for all category of buildings.

The open space around the building shall be as follows:

Plot abutting road margin	*Front open space*	*Rear open space*	*Side open space*
(1)	(2)	(3)	(4)
For plots abutting roads of width 9 metres	1.5 metres	2.00 metres	1.00 metre
For plots abutting roads of width 12 metres	3.0 metres	2.00 metres	1.00 metre
For plots abutting roads of width above 12 metres	4.5 metres	2.00 metres	1.00 metre

7. Foundation and basement—The building shall be built on proper foundations and shall be provided with a basement of not less than 0.5 metres height, from the adjacent ground level.

8. Flooring—Flooring shall be made of such impervious material or be of well rammed earth with cow dung wash or of tiles, cement and such other flooring material.

9. Minimum size of rooms—Every room intended for human habitation shall have an area of not less than 7.2 square metres provided that the kitchen room may have an area of not less than 3.6 square metres.

10. Walls—Walls shall be built of such materials as may be approved by the concerned authority with suitable damp proofing at the basement level.

11. Height of rooms—The average height between the floor and the under side of the roof of a living room shall be not less than 2.4 metres.

12. Ventilation—Every living room shall be provided with adequate windows and ventilators for securing effective ventilation. In no case shall the total area of windows and ventilators of a room be less than 1/5th of its floor area. Only ventilators or windows that connect directly with external air and about on an open space shall be deemed to ventilate the room provided that ventilator or window opening into an open verandah or other overhead covering, the width of which is not over 2.4 metres shall also be deemed to connect with external air.

13. Flues and chimneys—Every kitchen or every room where a fire is lit shall be provided with sufficient means for the escape of smoke or the products of combustion, directly above every fire place.

14. Sanitation—(1) The site shall be well drained and all sullage water shall be collected and drained off into the street drain unless separate provision is made for utilisation of domestic sullage for cultivation or gardening purposes. In no case shall water be allowed to stagnate in the site or to form pools.

(2) Every site appurtenant to a house shall be laid out with such garden or cultivation or shall otherwise be kept clean and tidy at all times and also be kept free from water logging. Removal of earth from the site and creation of hollows shall be forbidden.

15. Latrine—(1) Every house shall be provided with a latrine of such specifications and size as may be determined by the Executive Authority and every latrine shall be located only at the rear corner of the site.

(2) Where a latrine provided is of a hand removal type such latrine shall not be provided with trap doors opening into a conservancy lane or a street. As far as possible independent means of access should be provided to the conservancy cleaning staff for entering the latrine and for under taking the cleaning operations.

16. Cattle-shed—Every cow shed or cattle-shed shall be provided with an impervious flooring and adequate facilities for drainage of urine and removal of refuses which should be collected and disposed of as may be determined by the concerned authority.

17. Fencing and compound wall—Each site shall be fenced suitably either with live fencing or other fencing or a compound wall. No such fencing and compound wall shall have heights at more than 1.5 metres from the ground level. A gateway shall be provided in the front where the site abuts on a street and in addition suitable door way shall be provided at the rear where the site abuts on a conservancy or rear access lane.

18. Common amenities—In every layout which has a provision for more than 10 houses, the following minimum standard of amenities shall be provided.

(1) An open space for common public use as park, playground or recreation ground to an extent not less than 10 per cent of the total area of the layout.

(2) Such open spaces and common amenities shall be so distributed in order that one such open space shall be available for every group of 25 houses.

(3) There shall be provided one or more public wells, public baths and latrines in every layout to the satisfaction of the Executive Authority.

(4) Facilities such as shopping, recreation centre, community hall and library shall be provided in accordance with the size of the development and based on the following standards:

(a) For every 100 persons, there shall be at least one shop; and

(b) For every 1,000 persons, there shall be a common children playground, a primary school, a community hall, a library and a recreation centre.

(5) Separate provision shall be made in every development site specifically reserved for temple, church, mosque and other religious institutions as may be necessary:

Provision shall be made for burial of the dead or their cremation at suitable locations away from the residential and other developments and no burial or burning shall be permissible within 90 metres of the development.

19. Space about huts—No portion of a hut shall be placed with 1.75 metres of a masonry or wooden building provided that there shall be a minimum open space of 1.25 metres between the lanes or between the eaves of the hut and a masonry wall, as the case may be.

20. Heights of huts—(1) No hut shall be of more than one storey not exceeding 3.75 metres in height measured from the top of the plinth to the junction of the eaves and wall.

(2) The wall of the hut, at a junction of the eaves and wall shall in no place be less than 1.75 metres in height measured from the top level of the plinth.

21. Alignment of huts—On the land exclusively set apart for the construction of huts, the huts shall be built in continuous lines in accordance with the alignment to be determined by the panchayat.

22. Passage between rows of huts—Where an alignment determined under Rule 21 does not correspond with the alignment of the street, a passage of at least 6 metres measured from eave to eave, shall be left between the rows of huts abutting on such alignment.

23. Open courtyard among huts—Not withstanding anything contained in Rule 21, huts may with the special sanction of the panchayat, be built so as to form an open court yard comprising at least one-fourth of the whole area occupied by the huts and courtyard.

24. Space between huts—Between any two huts, there shall be a space of at least 1.25 metres measured eave to eave.

25. Multi-storeyed and public buildings—Every person intending to construct, reconstruct, add to or alter any public building other than Government building shall follow the provisions of the Multi-storeyed and Public Building Rules, 1973 issued under the Tamil Nadu District Municipalities Act, 1920 (Tamil Nadu Act V of 1920):

Provided that the Executive Authority shall not grant approval for construction, reconstruction, addition or alteration of any such building without consulting the concerned Joint Director or Deputy Director of Town and Country Planning.

26. Aisles and spacing row of seats—(a) Clear aisles not less than 1.2 metres in width shall be provided at right angles to the line of seating in such number and such manner that no seat shall be more than 3.8 metres away from an aisle measured in the line of seating.

(b) Where all the aisles do not directly meet the exit doors cross aisles of minimum 1 metre width and at the rate of one cross aisle for every 10 rows of seats shall be provided parallel to the line of seating so as to provide direct access to the exit.

(c) Rows of seats between aisles shall not have more than 14 seats and in the case of such rows opening to an aisle at one end, shall not have more than 7 seats.

(d) There shall be a minimum space of 85 cm between the backs of any two rows of seats and a minimum of 35 cm between the back of any seat and the front of the seat immediately behind it as measured between plumb lines.

27. Fire detecting and extinguishing systems—Every public building having a capacity of one thousand persons or more, shall be provided with either a manually operated fire alarm system coded to alert employers or attendants or with an automatic fire detection system to conform to the standards and recommendations laid down in the National Building Code of India, 2005 and to the satisfaction of the Directorate of Fire Services.

28. Extension of Tamil Nadu Special Building Rules to panchayat area—The provision pertaining to the Tamil Nadu Cyclone Prone Areas Special Buildings Rules, 1982 and the Tamil Nadu Industrial Township Area Development Authority Act, 1997 and the rules made thereunder shall apply to such of those panchayat falling in these special areas.

29. Grant of approval by Executive Authority—(1) All approvals granted under these rules in the panchayat shall be placed in the next panchayat meeting for information.

(2) Any appeal against the orders of the Executive Authority under sub-rule (1) shall be made to the Collector of Revenue District concerned within thirty days from the date of receipt of such orders. The orders of the Collector on such appeal shall be final.

30. Lapse of permission—If the construction or reconstruction of any building is not completed within the period specified, the permission shall lapse and a fresh application shall be made before the work is continued.

31. Penalty for breach of rules—Any breach of these rules shall be punishable with fine which may extend to Rs. 100 or in case of continuing breach with fine not exceeding Rs. 15 for everyday during which breach continues after conviction for the first breach.

32. Power of Executive Authority to require alteration of work—(1) If the Executive Authority finds that the work:

(a) is otherwise than in accordance with the plans or specifications which have been approved or

(b) contravene any of the provisions of this rule or any of the rule or declaration made thereunder he may by notice, require the owner of the building with in a period stated either
  (i) to make such alterations as may be specified in the said notice with the object of bringing the work into conformity with the said plans or provision; or
  (ii) to show cause why such an alteration should not be made.

(2) If the owner does not show cause as aforesaid he shall be bound to make the alterations specified in such notice referred to in clause (i) of sub-rule (1).

33. Stoppage of work endangering human life—Notwithstanding anything contained in any of the preceding provisions the Executive Authority may at any time stop the construction or reconstruction of any building if in his opinion the work in progress endangers human life.

34. Demolition or alteration of building works unlawfully commenced, carried on or completed—(1) If the Executive Authority is satisfied:

(i) that the construction or re-construction of any building:
  (a) has been commenced without obtaining the permission of the Executive Authority; or
  (b) is being carried or has been completed otherwise than in accordance with the plans and particulars on which such approval or order was passed; or
  (c) is being carried on, or has been completed in breach of any of the provisions of this rule;

(ii) that any alterations required by any notice issued under these rules have not been duly made; or

(iii) that any alteration of or addition to any building or any other work made or done for any purpose, into or upon any building has been commenced or is being carried on or being completed in breach of rules, he may make a provisional order requiring that owner or the builder to demolish that work done or so much of it as in the opinion of the Executive Authority, has been unlawfully executed or to make such alteration as may in the opinion of the Executive Authority be necessary to bring the work into conformity with the rules, direction or requisitions as aforesaid or with the plans and particulars on which such permission or order was passed, and may also direct that until the said order is complied with the owner or builder shall refrain from proceeding with the building.

(2) The Executive Authority shall serve a copy of the provisional order made under sub-rule (1) on the owner of the building together with a notice requiring him to show cause within a reasonable time to be named in such notice why the order should not be confirmed.

(3) If the owner fails to show cause to the satisfaction of the Executive Authority, the Executive Authority may confirm the order with any modification as he may think fit to make and such order shall then be binding on the owner.

35. Levy of fees by village panchayats—The Inspector of the village panchayats shall notify the maximum and minimum rates specified in Appendix F for adoption by the village panchayats taking into consideration the proximity of the village panchayats to the nearest municipality and ensure that the rates so determined by the village panchayats do not exceed the prevailing rates of the neighbouring Municipality.

(G.O. Ms. No. 255, Rural Development (C-2) Department, dated 18th August 1997)

APPENDIX A

[See Rule 3 (1)]

Application under Rule 3 (1) of the Tamil Nadu Panchayats Building Rules, 1997

From

(Name of the Applicant) and Address.

To

The Executive Authority,

____________________ Village Panchayats

Sir,

I intend to layout the plot of land or lands in Survey No.__________Street or road named__________measuring________under Rule 3(1) of the Tamil Nadu Panchayat Building Rules, 1997.

I forward herewith in triplicate a layout plan/plans of the plot of land to be laid out.

I intend to use the layout sites for the purpose.

I request that the layout plan may be approved and permission may be accorded to execute the said work.

Place:

Date:

Signature of the applicant

CONDITIONS

(i) I agree not to proceed with layout of the house-sites or plots until the approval signed by the Executive Authority required under the Tamil Nadu Panchayat Building Rules, 1997.

(ii) I agree not to dispose of any house-site or plot unless the layout has been approved by the Executive Authority.

(iii) I agree not to do any work otherwise than in accordance with the layout plan which has been approved or in contravention of any of the provision of the Act or any rule, bye-law order or other declaration made thereunder or any direction or requisition lawfully given or made under the said Act, rules or bye-laws.

(iv) I agree to make any alterations which may be required by any notice issued or by any order confirmed by the Executive Authority.

(v) I agree to keep my site open at all times for the inspection of the Executive Authority or any officer authorised by him in that behalf.

(vi) I agree to relinquish the lands required for streets, lanes, passages and pathways in favour of the Executive Authority authorising him, making of such streets lanes, passages and pathways.

(vii) I agree to carry out demarcation, formation and construction of street, lanes passages and pathways including levelling paving metalling flagging channelling severing conserving and lighting in accordance with the provisions of the layout approved.

(viii) I agree to furnish any information which may be required by the Executive Authority for the grant of permission to execute the work and also while executing the work.

(ix) I also agree to provide for all the common amenities as required under the Tamil Nadu Panchayat Building Rules, 1997.

I certify that the land in question belongs/does not belong to a Wakf, Hindu or Christian religious or charitable institution or to any other religious or charitable institution or Government, Quasi-Government or local bodies. I also certify that the plan of the building is in accordance with the terms of the lease agreement or is with the prior concurrence of the Tamil Nadu State Wakf Board, Chennai or the Commissioner of the Hindu Religious and Charitable Endowment Department, Chennai or Christian Religious Institution or other competent authority, as the case may be I furnish copies of the agreement/letter of concurrence/ plan of the building as approved by the aforesaid authority.

[The certificate is necessary only when the land belongs to any of the religious or charitable institution or to Government, Quasi-Government or local bodies).

APPENDIX B

[See Rule 4 (1)]

Application under Rule 4(1) of the Tamil Nadu Panchayat Building Rules, 1997

From

Name of the Applicant,

Address,

To
The Executive Authority,
_______________ Village Panchayat.

Sir,

I intend to construct/reconstruct/make alteration or additions to a building/hut in the site measuring in revenue Survey No._______street or road named_______________________________________ under Rule 4(1) of the Tamil Nadu Panchayat Building Rules, 1997.

I forward herewith in triplicate:

(a) a site plan of the land on which the building or hut is to be constructed or reconstructed or altered or added to complying with the requirement of Appendix 'C' to the rules;

(b) a plan or plans, of the building showing the ground plan of each floor elevation and section: (complying with the requirements of Appendix 'E' to the rules); and

(c) a specification of the work (complying with the requirement of Appendix 'E' to the rules).

I intend to use the building only for__________as________a dwelling house/not as a dwelling house but for the purpose of_______________________________________

I request that the site plan may be approved and permission may be accorded to execute the said work.

Place:

Date: **Signature of the applicant**

Items (b) and (c) are not applicable in case of huts.

CONDITIONS

(i) I agree not to proceed with the execution of the work until approval is signed by the Executive Authority required under the Tamil Nadu Panchayat Building Rules, 1997 or permission is granted by the said authority.

(ii) I agree not to do any work otherwise than in accordance with the site and building plan and specifications which have been approved, or in contravention of any of the provisions of the Tamil Nadu Panchayat Act, 1994 (Tamil Nadu Act 21 of 1994) or any rule bye-law, order or other declaration made thereunder, or of any direction or requisition lawfully given or made under the said Act, rules or bye-laws.

(iii) I agree to make any alterations which may be required by any notice issued or by any order confirmed by the Executive Authority.

(iv) I agree to keep one copy of the approved site plan and one set of copies of the sanctioned plans of the building at the site at all times when the work is in progress and also agree to see that plans are available and the building is open at all time for the inspection of the Executive Authority or any officer authorised by him in that behalf.

(v) I agree to give notice to the Executive Authority and furnish a set of completion plans within fifteen days from the date of completion or occupation of the building, whichever is earlier.

(vi) I also agree not to occupy the building that will be constructed or reconstructed by me or cause or permit it to be occupied until I have obtained a certificate from an officer of the Public Health Department of the area as required by Sections 26 and 33 of the Tamil Nadu Public Health Act, 1939 [Tamil Nadu Act III of 1939].

I certify that the land in question belongs/does not belong to a Wakf, Hindu or Christian religious or charitable institution or to any other religious or charitable institution or Government, Quasi-Government or local bodies. I also certify that the plan of the building is in accordance with the terms of the lease agreement or is with the prior concurrence of the Tamil Nadu State Wakf Board, Chennai or the Commissioner of the Hindu Religious and Charitable Endowment Department, Chennai or Christian Religious Institution or other competent authority, as the case may be I furnish copies of the lease agreement/letter of concurrence plan of the building as approved by the aforesaid authority.

(The certificate is necessary only when the land belongs to any of the religious or charitable institution or by Government, Quasi-Government or local bodies.)

APPENDIX C

[See Rule 4 (1)(a)]

The Site Plan

The site plan shall comply with the following requirements:

1. It shall be drawn to scale of not less than one centimetre to 4 metres, provided that where circumstances are such as to make a smaller scale necessary or sufficient the plan may with the counsel of the Executive Authority be a scale of one centimetre to 8 metres.
2. It shall show the boundaries of the site or plot for the building.
3. It shall give the survey number or numbers of the site or plot.
4. It shall show the street or streets with name or names, on which the site or plot abuts or those from which access to the site or plot is proposed to be obtained.
5. It shall give accurately the dimension of the site or plot.
6. It shall give the width of the street or streets on which the site or plot abuts or those from which access is proposed to be obtained.
7. It shall show whether the street or streets on which the site of plot abuts, or those from access is proposed to be obtained are public or private and if the latter what the names of the owners of the land occupied by them are and whether they have been formed and metalled, the existing proposed or approved minimum building lines on each side of the street or streets, shall also be shown.
8. It shall show the location of the proposed building on the site or plot and also the location of latrines, urinals stables cow-sheds and other appurtenances of the building as well as the position dimensions of the open spaces including the courtyards is left in the site or plot forming the cartilage or appurtenance of the building.

   It shall show the position of wells, tanks water course if any in the site or plot and
9. Within a distance of twenty metre from it in any direction.
10. It shall show the position and approximate height of all buildings within twelve metres of the site or plot.
11. It shall incorporate the position and sections of trial pits taken within the site or plot describing so far as may be necessary and possible, the extent nature of soil and sub soils met with.
12. It shall, so far as may be necessary and possible, record the water-level in the well if any on the site or plot or in the adjoining well, if any with the date on which the observation was taken.
13. It shall give the relating levels of the site or plot with reference to the crown of the street or streets on which the building abuts or those from which access to the building is proposed to be obtained.
14. It shall also show other particulars required under any bye-laws made by the panchayat.
15. The Executive Authority may require the owner to furnish him with any further information which has not already been given.
16. It shall not be necessary to comply with requirements of conditions 10 to 12 in the case of an application for the construction or reconstruction of a hut.
17. In the case of an application for a hut, only a ground plan and section, of the proposed hut showing the position, from and dimensions of the walls, rooms and roofs and the position and dimensions of windows or door ways need be furnished unless otherwise required by the Executive Authority.

APPENDIX D

[See Rule (4) (1)(b)]

Building Plans

1. The ground plan, plans of each floor elevations and sections of the proposed building shall be neatly and accurately drawn to a scale or not less than one centimetre to one metre.
2. The plans and sections shall show:
   (i) the depth and width of the foundation and the nature of the soil on which the foundation is to rest.
   (ii) the level of the lowest floor of the building and the level of all courtyards and open spaces with reference to the level of the surface of the site or ground adjoining the building and, where possible, to the level of the crown of the abutting street or streets or those form which access to the building is proposed to be obtained.

(iii) the position, form and dimensions of the walls, rooms floor roofs, chimney's and the several parts of the building and also the form and dimensions of any water closet, earth closet, privy ash-pit or cesspool to be constructed in connection with the building.

(iv) the lines of drainage of the building and the position and level of the out fall of the drains and the position of any sewer with which the drainage is intended to be connected.

3. If the construction or re-construction of a building or any temporary or permanent additions thereto will render any aerial electricity supply line accessible to such building or structure, such line shall be shown both in the plan and section of the building or structures.
4. If it is intended to use the building or part thereof for any purpose other than a dwelling house, the information shall be shown in the plans.
5. The plan shall also show the position and dimensions of window, doorways and ventilators.
6. The Executive Authority may require the owner to furnish him any further information so far as may be necessary to show whether the building complies with any of the provisions of the Act and the rules and bye-laws made thereunder.

APPENDIX E

[See Rule 4(1) (c)]

Specification

The following particulars shall be incorporated in the specification:

1. The materials and the methods of construction to be used for the various parts of the building.
2. The manner in which the roof and house drainage and the surface drainage of the site are proposed to be disposed of.
3. The means to access that will be available for conservancy.
4 The use or uses for which the building is intended.
5. Whether there is within the building or site, or with in a reasonable distance therefrom a supply of wholesome water sufficient for the domestic purposes of the inmates of the building if it is intended to be used as a dwelling house.
6. If the building is intended to be used as dwelling for two or more families or as a place for carrying on any trade, business or industry in which not less than twenty people may be employed or as a place of public resort entertainment or other similar purposes the means of ingress and egress in case of emergency proposed to be provided.
7. The correct extent of the site as a whole, the area occupied by the existing building or buildings if any and the total area that will be occupied by all building in the site excluding the buildings if any exempted under these rules.
8. The above specification shall be required only in the case of a building other than a hut.
9. The Executive Authority may require the owner to furnish him with any further information so far as may be necessary to know whether the building satisfied all the requirements of safety and stability.

APPENDIX F

(See Rule 35)

Sl. No	*Category*	*Nature of construction/activity*	*Maximum rates*	*Minimum rates*
(1)	(2)	(3)	(4)	(5)
1.	Building Plan approved	1. Building area 2. Construction of wall 3. Compound wall 4. Inspection Fees 5. Plan copy for more than 3 copies	Rs. 100 per sq. metre or part thereof Rs. 100 Rs. 100 [Lump sum] Rs. 50 Rs. 10 per additional copy	Rs. 5 per sq. metre or part thereof Rs. 25 Rs. 25 [Lump sum] Rs. 25 Rs. 5 additional copy
2.	Layout approval		Rs. 1000 per acre	Rs. 500 per acre

5.5.2 Building Rules, 1997 – Amendment

(A) Tiled and Sloped Terrace Building—(1) In the tiled or sloped building, semicircular gutters of width 15 to 25 centimetres of plastic or any other material shall be provided on the down side roof slopes of the building for harvesting rain water. The gutter shall be connected at the down stream end with a down pipe of 75 to 100 millimetres diameter, depending upon roof area and size of tank to convey the harvested rainwater from gutters to a plastic or other material storage tank or sump (through a filter unit). An inlet screen (wire mesh) to prevent entry of dry leaves and other debris into the down-pipe shall be fitted. The collected rainwater from the roof shall be allowed to pass through a filter unit. The filter unit shall be filled with suitable filter material such as well-burnt broken bricks (or pebbles) upto 15 centimetres from top. The top 15 centimetres shall be filled up with coarse sand. The filter unit shall be placed either over a storage tank or at bottom of the down pipe.

(2) The filtered rain water shall be collected in a collection tank or storage tank placed over the ground or underground. The shape of the tank shall be cylindrical, rectangular or square of suitable size/capacity ranging from 1,000 to 10,000 litres or even higher depending on the roof area. The material of construction shall be brick work, stone work, cement bricks, ferro-cement, High Density Polyethylene (HDPE), plain cement concrete or reinforced cement concrete. The storage tanks/ collection tank shall be provided with pipe fixtures at appropriate places to draw the water to clean the tank and to dispose of the excess water depending upon use/re-use either to open well/ bore well or to a percolation pit.

(B) Ordinary Building (Ground + First Floor)—(1) Percolation pits of 30 to 45 centimetres diameter and of depth adequate not less than one metre to recharge the ground, shall be made. This pit shall be filled with suitable filter material such as well burnt broken bricks (or pebbles) upto 15 centimetres from top. The top 15 centimetres shall be filled up with coarse sand. The top of this pit shall be covered with perforated reinforced concrete (RCC) slab or of any other material, wherever considered necessary. The number of such percolation pits shall be provided on the basis of one pit per 30 square metres of available open terrace area/plinth area. The cross distance between the pits shall be minimum 3 metres.

(2) Wherever an open well or bore well as the case may be is available within the building premises the rain water collected from the open terrace shall be collected through pipes 150 millimetres diameter or other suitable sizes and led to a filter pit of size 60 centimetres × 60 centimetres × 60 centimetres (with appropriate filter material) and then led into the open well/bore well through 150 millimetres diameter or other suitable pipes.

(3) Wherever existing water storage sumps are available, the rain water so collected, after it passes through the filter, shall be allowed to flow to the sump through closed pipes. An overflow pipe shall be provided to the storage sump so that the surplus water is led into the nearby open well/bore well/ percolation pit.

(C) Ordinary Building (Ground + 2 Floors and above) and Multi-storeyed Building—(1) The specification detailed in item 'B' above for Ordinary building (Ground + First Floor) shall also be applicable to building specified in this category.

(2) In addition to the percolation pits of 30 centimetres diameter shall be provided at 3 metre interval, a pit of 1 to 1.5 metres width and appropriate depth, so as to recharge the ground, shall be provided all along the plinth boundary depending upon the soil classification below ground. This pit shall be filled with appropriate filter material, namely broken bricks, pebbles, broken stones etc., at the bottom and the top 15 to 25 centimetres shall be filled with coarse sand. The ground/pavement surface around the building shall be sloped towards the percolation pit so that rain water from terrace and sides, open spaces etc., flow over this sloped surfaces and spread into the filter bed all around. Masonry dwarf walls of 5 to 7.5 centimetres or of suitable height depending upon the site conditions shall be constructed, if necessary, at the entrance and exit gates to allow the rain water collected within the compound to recharge the ground within the premises itself, and from draining out to the road.

(3) If the sub-soil is not a permeable one (namely clay or black cotton) appropriate recharge structures, namely recharge shaft or bore pit shall be provided below the filtration pits so as to recharge the ground.

(D) Group Development, Industries and Institutional Building—(1) For buildings for ground + first floor or ground + 2 and above located within group development institutional and industrial premises, the specification detailed in items A, B and C above shall apply.

(2) The surface run off rain water, in the open spaces within the group development/industrial/ institutional premises shall be allowed to run towards collection drains of suitable size and these drains shall be constructed as rain water friendly storm water drains. All the approach and access roads to the buildings within the group development/industrial/institutional premises shall also be provided with rain water friendly storm water drains. These rain water-friendly storm water drains shall not have paved bottom. If adequate spaces are available in low lying areas, percolation ponds of suitable size shall be formed and these rain water-friendly storm water drains shall be led into the percolation ponds for recharging the ground.

(3) For other localized low lying areas, recharge pits of size of minimum 1 metre × 1 metre × 1 metre or 1 metre diameter shall be provided wherever needed, so as to prevent rainwater stagnation around the building. For other places catch water pit structures of size 30 centimetres diameter and 30 centimetres depth or higher depth as necessary shall be provided wherever necessary. For existing paved storm water drains, catch water pits of 30 centimetres diameter and 30 centimetres depth or higher depth, as necessary, shall be provided at the bottom of these drains at 10 to 15 metre intervals. These catch water pits shall be filled with appropriate filter material as described in item 'B' above for Ordinary building (Ground + First Floor).

Explanation. Any other modifications, additional structures or alternative designs, furnished by the applicant shall be considered for approval, if it conforms to rain water harvesting concept to the satisfaction of the competent authority for building plan approval. Provision of water harvesting structures for re-use of used water like water emanating from kitchens and bathrooms for flushing toilets gardening etc., shall be considered for approval on its merits:

Provided that the Government may grant one year time to comply with rain water harvesting in all existing buildings which may be extendable upto two years in case of below poverty line families.

(G.O. Ms. No. 121, Rural Development Department, dated 13th November, 2002)

5.5.3 Licensing of Pandal and Temporary Structure on Road Margins

1. Short title—These rules may be called the Tamil Nadu Panchayats (Licensing of Pandals and Temporary Structures on Road Margins Vested in the Highways and Rural Works Department, in Village Panchayat Areas) Rules, 1999.

2. Grant of Licence for erection of pandals or temporary structure on public road—(1) No pandal or other temporary structure on public road vested in any village panchayat or panchayat union, or Highways and Rural Works Department or Public Works Department within the limits of such village panchayat shall be erected without the licence granted by the Executive Authority of the village panchayat concerned. He shall grant such licence subject to such condition as may be imposed by the village panchayat, which shall be in addition to the general directions, which may be issued by the officers of the Highways and Rural Development or Public Works Department from time-to-time.

(2) A copy of the application for the grant of such licence shall be simultaneously made to the local police also. The Executive Authority of the village panchayat shall consult the local police authority before granting such licence. The recommendation of the police authorities shall be sent to the village panchayat within five days of the reference. If no reply is received from the local police authority within five days of the reference, it shall be presumed that the police have no objection to the grant of licence applied.

3. Period of licence—The occupation of such sites shall be allowed only temporarily during a fair or festival. The period for which such occupation is permitted shall, in no case, exceed three days before the commencement and three days after the termination of the fair or festival exclusive of the actual period of its duration.

4. Licence fees—The village panchayat shall fix the rate of licence fee for the occupation of the site for erection of pandal or temporary structure at a rate not below of one rupee per square metre area of pandal or temporary structure, as the case may be for a period of three days or part thereof. The village panchayat may increase the above rate from time-to-time.

5. Collection of licence fee—The licence fee shall be paid to the village panchayat in advance; otherwise the licence applied for shall be refused. The acceptance of the pre-payment of the fee for licence shall not by itself entitle the person making such pre-payment, to the licence in case of refusal of the licence. The income derived from the levy of licence fee and the expenditure incurred there from shall be shown under separate account.

6. Payment of the deposit—Any person applying for a licence shall, in addition to the payment of the licence fee, deposit a sum equivalent to twenty-five per cent of that fee, which shall be refunded to him at the time of his vacating the site, subject to the provision of sub-rule (2) of Rule 10.

7. Provision of sanitary arrangements and lighting—The income derived by the levy of licence fee shall be used primarily for special sanitary arrangements and lighting connected with fairs or festivals, and the balance remaining, if any, shall be utilised for the improvement of the general sanitary condition of the village in which such fairs or festivals are conducted.

8. Loss or Damage to trees or usufructs—The village panchayat shall have no right to trees, if any, standing on the public road or to the usufructs therefor. It shall be solely responsible for any loss or damage to trees or produce, if any, caused by a licensee, during the period of occupation of the site and shall be liable to pay such compensation as may be fixed by the Highways and Rural Works Department or Public Works Department in respect of the loss or damage. The village panchayat shall recover such loss or damage from the licensee.

9. Prohibition of permanent structure on public road—No masonry or other permanent structure shall be erected on a public road except by the village panchayat or the Highways and Rural Works Department or Public Works Department.

10. Removal of the temporary structure—(1) The village panchayat shall cause the temporary pandal or structures if any, erected on any public road in connection with the fairs or festivals to be removed by the licensee and restore the site to its original condition on the completion of the fair or festival.

(2) In case the licensee fails to remove pandal or structure on the expiry of the period of licence, the Executive Authority shall have power to dismantle it at the cost of the licensee. The cost of dismantle shall be adjusted from the deposit amount. If, in the event of deposit amount not being adequate for such cost, the balance shall be recovered from the licensee by means of a bill as an arrears of taxes due to the village panchayat.

(G.O.Ms.No.150, Rural Development (C-4) Department, dated 21st July 1999)

5.5.4 Licensing of Dogs

1. Short title—These rules may be called the Tamil Nadu Panchayats (Licensing of Dogs) Rules, 1999.

2. Grant or Renewal of licence—Within thirty days from the commencement of every succeeding half-year the owner or custodian of every dog shall apply to the Executive Authority for the grant or renewal of the licence on payment of a licence fee of ten rupees. The Executive Authority of the village panchayat may grant a licence and a badge showing the number of the licence. The badge shall be tied to the neck of the dog.

3. Issue of public notice—Every village panchayat may, or if so directed by the Inspector shall, give public notice in the manner provided for in Rule 5 relating to the manner of publication of notice, that unlicensed dogs straying within the village panchayat limits shall be destroyed. When a notice has been given, the owner or custodian of every dog within such limits shall apply to the Executive Authority within thirty days from the date of such notice for grant or renewal of licence for the dog under his custody. After receipt of the application the Executive Authority shall grant or renew licence as specified in Rule 2.

4. Seizure of unlicensed dogs—Any dog found straying in any public place without the badge duly obtained under Rule 2 shall be liable to be seized by any person authorized by the Executive Authority in that behalf.

5. Detention of dogs seized—When a dog is seized, the Executive Authority shall display a notice in the notice board of the village panchayat and in other public places like chavadi, informing the seizure of the unlicensed dogs and detention thereof and also informing the time within which such dogs may be resumed on payment of licence fee with a penalty of five rupees per dog together with a detention charge of two rupees for every twenty-four hours of detention or part thereof.

6. Recovery, sale and destruction of seized dogs—On payment of the licence fee penalty and detention charge specified in Rule 5, the Executive Authority shall return the dog to its owner or custodian. In default of such payment within the period specified under Rule 5, the Executive Authority shall sell the dog in public auction, adjust the proceeds thereof to the payment of the licence fee, penalty and detention charge due to the village panchayat and shall return to the owner or custodian of the dog, the balance if any. If the sale proceeds are not sufficient to meet the licence fees, penalty and detention charge dues to the village panchayat, the entire sum shall be credited to the village panchayat funds. If any dog is not sold in auction, the Executive Authority shall cause its destruction and burial and in such cases the amount due on licence fee, penalty and detention charge may be caused to be written off by the village panchayat.

7. Seizure and destruction of dogs in certain circumstances—If in any village panchayat notified under sub-section (1) of Section 76 of the Tamil Nadu Public Health Act, 1939 (Tamil Nadu Act III of 1939), regarding the out-break of rabies, the Executive authority may, or if so required by the Deputy Director of Health Services and Preventive Medicine shall, make such arrangements as may be necessary for the seizure, detention, destruction or disposal of dogs in accordance with the Rabies (Prevention and Control) Rules, 1941.

8. Powers of the Executive Authority to seize the dogs suffering from rabies—(1) The Executive Authority of the village panchayat or any person authorized by him may seize or destroy any stray dog which, in his opinion, is suffering from rabies or detain any such dog if he suspects it to be showing symptoms of rabies. In all such cases, the Executive Authority shall consult the Block Health Supervisor or the officer of the Animal Husbandry Department, having jurisdiction over the area and carry out any suggestions made by him.

(2) The Executive Authority may direct that any dog which he knows or suspects to be suffering from rabies or which has been bitten or snapped at by any rabies or suspicious dog, jackal or other animal shall either be destroyed or at the option of its owner detained under observation at the expense of its owner in the place appointed for the purpose for such period as the Executive Authority may fix. Any dog kept under observation may be destroyed immediately if it is found to be suffering from rabies or developing rabies. When any such direction made by the Executive Authority is not compiled with, he shall make arrangements for such destruction or detention and the owner or other person in possession of the dog shall be bound to comply with such directions as may be given by the Executive Authority.

(3) Any person who has in his possession any dog which he knows or has reason to believe to be suffering from rabies or to have been bitten or snapped at any rabies or suspicious dog, jackal or other animal shall immediately intimate the fact in writing to the Executive Authority.

9. Penalty—Whoever commits a breach of sub-rules (2) and (3) of Rule 8 shall be punishable with fine which may extend to one hundred rupees and in case of a continuing breach with fine which may extend to fifteen rupees for every day during which the breach continues after conviction for the first offence.

10. Maintenance of register—(1) Every licence granted under Rule 2 shall be entered in a register to be maintained for this purpose and it shall contain the name and address of the owner or custodian of the dog, the name if any, and other particulars of the dog, the number and the date of issue of licence and the fee collected therefor.

(2) The Executive Authority shall also maintain a separate register showing the description of the dog seized, the time of its seizure, the name and address of its owner or custodian, the fee or charge collected, if any, the date of such collection, the time and date of its release, particulars of auction, or destruction and the amount, if any, realized in the auction.

(G.O.Ms.No.202, Rural Development (C-4) Department, dated 28th September 1999)

5.5.5 Licensing of Pigs and Destruction of Unlicensed Pigs

1. Short title extent and commencement—(1) These rules may be called the Tamil Nadu Panchayats (Licensing of Pigs and Destruction of Unlicensed or Infected Pigs) Rules, 1996.

(2) They extend to all areas declared as panchayat villages under the provisions of the Tamil Nadu Panchayats Act, 1994 (Tamil Nadu Act 21 of 1994).

(3) They shall come into force at once.

2. Definitions—In these rules, unless the context otherwise requires

- (a) "Act" means the Tamil Nadu Panchayats Act, 1994 (Tamil Nadu Act 21of 1994).
- (b) Collector means the Collector of Revenue Districts.
- (c) "Detention charges" means the charges calculated at the rates specified in these rules and includes the feeding and other charges spent by the Executive Authority towards the detention of pigs.
- (d) "Half Year" means the period of six months commencing from the month of April and ending with September or from the month of October and ending with March of a year.
- (e) "Infected pig" means a pig whether licensed or not under these rules, which in the opinion of the Executive Authority will be cause for

spreading of diseases like Encephalitis or any other communicable diseases for the spreading of which pigs are considered as carriers.

3. Issue of public notice—Every panchayat may and if so directed by the Collector shall publish notice in the official gazette of the District in English and Tamil that unlicensed or infected pigs straying within the Panchayat Limits specified in the notice will be destroyed after the date specified in such notice.

4. Taking of licence—When a Notice under Rule 3 has been published the owner or custodian of every pig with in the limits of the panchayat, shall within fifteen days from the date of such publication of notice take out from the Executive Authority of the panchayat, a licence badge showing the following particulars and such other particulars if any, as the Collector may prescribe, on payment of a licence fee not exceeding five rupees per pig for the half year in which such notice was given.

(1) Name of the Panchayat in an abbreviated form if the name is too long;

(2) Number of licence issued; and

(3) Particulars of the year and half year for which the licence is issued.

The badge shall be fixed to any one of the ear of the pig for purposes of inspection and verification by the Executive Authority of the panchayat or any person authorised by him:

Provided that the Collector may for special reasons, reduce the period within which a licence shall be taken from the Executive Authority after the publication of the notice.

5. Application for licence—With in fifteen days from the commencement of every succeeding half year or with in such reduced period as the collector may fix for special reasons the owner or custodian of every pig shall apply to the Executive Authority for the grant or renewal of the licence on payment of the fee specified in Rule 4.

6. Seizure of unlicensed pigs—Any pig found straying in any public place with in the limits of the panchayat with out the licence badge obtained under Rule 4 shall be liable to be sized by any person or persons authorised by the Executive Authority in that behalf.

7. Intimation as to seizure of pigs—When a pig is seized, the Executive Authority shall intimate, its owner or custodian (if his name address are known) of its detention and on payment of the licence fee with a penalty of rupees five require the owner or custodian to remove it within seven days from the date of detention together with a detention charge of rupees three for every twenty-four hours of detention or part thereof.

8. Restoration of possession of the pigs seized—On payment of the licence fee, penalty and detention charges specified in Rule 7, the Executive Authority shall release the pig to its owner or its custodian. In default of such payments within a period of seven days specified in Rule of 7 of these rules or if the name and address of the owner or custodian are not known, the Executive Authority may sell the pig in public auction, apply the proceeds thereof to the payment of the licence fees, penalty and detention charges due to the panchayat and shall return to the owner or custodian of the pig, the balance, if any. If the sale proceeds are not sufficient to meet the licence fees, penalty and detention charges due to the panchayat or if the name and address of the owner or custodian are not known, the entire sum shall be credited to the panchayat funds.

9. Seizure and destruction of pigs during the out break of encephalitis—Not withstanding anything contained in these rules, if in any panchayat or in the panchayat adjoining it, there is an outbreak of encephalitis disease or any other disease for the spreading of which pigs are considered as carriers of the disease the Executive Authority may, and if so required by the District Health Officer or the Collector, shall make such arrangements as may be necessary for the seizure, detention, destruction and disposal of pigs irrespective of the fact whether they are licensed or not and the owners of the pigs whether licensed or not have no claim, what so ever against the Executive Authority, ordering the destruction of such pigs.

10. Destruction of pigs by the Executive Authorities—The Executive Authority of the panchayat or any other person or persons authorised by him, may seize or destroy a pig, irrespective of the fact whether the pig is licensed or not under these rules which in his opinion will be a cause, for the spreading of the disease specified in Rule 9 or detain for observation any pig if he suspects it to be a cause for the spread of the said disease. In all such cases, the Executive Authority shall consult the Health Officer or the Officer of the Animal Husbandry Department having jurisdiction over the panchayat and carry out any suggestion made by him.

11. Destruction of pigs by the owner or custodian—The Executive Authority may direct the owner or custodian of any pig he knows or suspect to be a cause for the spread of the diseases referred to in Rule 9 to destroy the pig immediately irrespective of the fact whether the pig is licensed or not under these rules, when such a direction has not been complied with by the owner or custodian with in a reasonable period or when the owner or custodian of any pig which is suspected to be a cause for the spread of the disease referred to the Executive Authority shall make arrangements for the seizure and destruction of these pigs.

12. Duty of the owners to intimate about the pigs which cause spreading diseases—Every person who has in his possession any pig which he knows or has reasons to believe to be a cause for the spread of the disease specified in Rule 9 shall intimate the fact to the Executive Authority in writing.

13. Punishments—Whosoever commits a breach of Rules 11 and 12 shall be punishable with a fine which may extend to seventy five rupees and in case a continuing offence, with a fine which may extend to rupees fifteen for every day during which the offence continues after the date of issue of notice for the first offence.

14. Maintenance of register—The Executive Authority shall maintain a register to enter every licence granted under Rule 4 and it shall contain the names and addresses of the owners or custodians of the pigs, description of the pig by which it can be identified, the number and date of issue of licence and the badge and the amount collected.

15. Maintenance of register showing the particulars of pigs seized—The Executive Authority shall also maintain a separate register showing description of pigs seized and the time of its seizure, the name and addresses of their owners or custodians, the fees and charges collected, if any, the date of such collection the time and date of their release, auction or destruction and the amount, if any realized, in the auction.

(G.O. Ms. No. 174, Rural Development (C-1) Department, dated 23rd August 1996)

5.5.6 Public Landing Places, Halting Places and Cart Stands

1. Short title—These rules may be called the Tamil Nadu Panchayats (Public Landing Places, Halting Places, Cart Stands) Rules, 1999.

2. Definition—For the purposes of the rules, cart means any conveyance suitable for use on road and includes any kinds of carriage, cart wagon, vehicle, bicycle, tricycle rickshaw both pedalled or motorized, motor cycle, scooter and moped.

3. Application to provide public landing places, halting places and cart stands—(1) When a village panchayat proposes to provide a public landing place, halting place or cart stand shall submit an application to the Inspector. The application shall contain

(a) the survey number extent and classification of the land in which the village panchayat proposes to provide the landing place or halting place, cart stand, and shall be accompanied by a sketch indicating the position or location of the land with reference to the important roads and other lands in the neighborhood; and

(b) any other particulars which the Inspector may specifically require.

(2) Before according sanction, the Inspector shall consult the Regional Transport Authority concerned in the case of stands intended solely or partly for motor vehicles and shall have due regard to its opinion.

(3) No village panchayat shall close public landing place, public halting place or cart stand: whether temporarily or permanently without the previous permission of the Inspector.

4. Places not to be declared as public landing place and halting places and cart stand—(1) A road or road margin shall not ordinarily be declared as a public landing place, public halting place or cart stand

Provided that in a special case, the Inspector, in consultation with the authority in whom the road is vested, permit a village panchayat to provide a public landing place, halting place or cart stand if in his opinion, that there is sufficient space available for road purpose, after making provision for such purposes.

(2) No village panchayat shall declare the entire village to be a public landing place, a public halting place or cart stand.

5. Prohibition for use of public landing place, halting place or cart stand—Where a village panchayat has provided a public landing place, halting place or cart stand, it may prohibit the use for the same purpose by any person, within one kilometre thereof, of any public place or the sides of any public road:

Provided that nothing contained in this rule shall apply to any motor vehicle which is not a stage carriage within the meaning of the Motor Vehicles Act, 1988 (Central Act 59 of 1988).

Explanation. A public place or the sides of a public road shall not be deemed to be used as a public landing place, halting place or cart stand if a vehicle used for the carriage of passenger stops therein for a period not exceeding two minutes for the purpose of getting down or picking up passengers or their luggage, or if a vehicle used for the carriage of goods stops there in only for the period required for the loading or unloading of goods.

6. Notification for opening of public landing place, halting place or cart stand—When a village panchayat provides a public landing place, halting place or cart stand, it shall give due publicity by publishing a notice in the office of the village panchayat and in the District Gazette, with informations as to the place where such landing place, halting place or cart stand is to be opened and the rates of fees payable for its use. A notice specifying the rates fixed by the village panchayat, the name of the person authorized to collect fees therein and the prohibited distance shall be put up on notice board in a conspicuous place in such public landing place, halting place or cart stand.

7. Rate and fees to be fixed for public landing place, halting place and cart stand—Fees for the use of a public landing place, halting place and cart stand shall be levied at the rate not lower on the rate prescribed in this rule specified in the Table, below:

Table

	Description of cart/vehicle	*Minimum rate per diem*
	(1)	(2)
1.	For every hand drawn cart	4.00
2	For every cart or vehicle drawn by one or more animals	8.00
3.	For every motor vehicle (Heavy)	
	Class A Bus stand	15.00
	Class B Bus stand	12.00
	Class C Bus stand	8.00
	Class D Bus stand	5.00
	For every motor vehicle (Light)	
	Class A Bus stand	10.00
	Class B Bus stand	8.00
	Class C Bus stand	5.00
	Class D Bus stand	5.00
	For every Auto-rickshaw and two wheeler	4.00
4.	For every tricycle or cycle rickshaw	2.00
5.	For every horse, mule, bullock, bull, cow or buffalo	2.00

8. Amenities—There shall be provided amenities in every public landing place, halting place and cart stand such as shelter facility for passengers, vehicles and animals, lighting facility, drinking water facility and toilet facility.

9. Seizure and detention of property—(1) If the fee leviable under these rules read with clause (a) of Section 154 of the Tamil Nadu Panchayats Act, 1994, (Tamil Nadu Act 21 of 1994) in respect of vehicle or animal is not paid on demand, the person authorized to collect such fee may seize and detain such portion of the appurtenance or load of such vehicle or animal as will, in his opinion suffice to defray the amount due and in the absence of any such appurtenance or load or in the event of this value being insufficient to defray the amount due may seize and detain the vehicle or animal.

(2) Any property seized under sub-rule (1) shall be sent, within twenty four hours of it seizure to the Executive Authority or to such person as may be authorized to receive and sell such property and the Executive Authority shall forth with give notice to the owner of the property seized or if the owner, is not known, or is not present within the village, to the person who was in charge of the said property at the time of its seizure or if such person cannot be found, publish by beat of drum, that after the expiry of two days, exclusive, of Sunday from the date of service or publication of such notice the property shall be sold by public auction at a place to be

specified in the notice and the proceeds of the sale shall be appropriated towards,

(i) the amount due on account of the fee;

(ii) such penalty not exceeding the amount of the fee as the Executive Authority may direct; and

(iii) a sum of rupees five on account of charge incurred in connection with the seizure, detention and sale.

The surplus, if any, shall be paid to the owner of the property or to the person who was in charge of the property at the time of its seizure.

(3) If, at any time before the sale has begun, the amount due on accounts of the fee together with a sum of rupees five on an account of charges incurred in connection with the seizure and detention is tendered to the Executive Authority or other person authorized as aforesaid, the property, seized shall be forthwith released.

(4) If no such tender is made, the property may be sold.

(G.O. Ms. No. 184, Rural Development (C-4) Department, dated 30th August 1999)

5.5.7 Prohibition or Regulation of the Use of Places for Slaughtering Animals and Licensing of Slaughterers

1. Short title—These rules may be called the Tamil Nadu Village Panchayats (Prohibition or Regulation of the Use of Places for Slaughtering Animals and Licensing of Slaughterers), Rules 1999.

2. Definition—In these rules unless the context otherwise requires 'form' means a form appended to these rules.

3. Regulation of slaughtering by issue of licence—No person shall without a licence issued by the Executive Authority slaughter cut up or skin or permit to be slaughtered cut up or skinned any cattle, horse sheep, go at or pig or poultry or fish in any place in the village other than in a public slaughter house if any provided by the village panchayat:

Provided that the Executive Authority may allow any animal to be slaughtered in such places other than temples or their precincts within the village as he thinks fit on occasions of festivals and ceremonies or as a special measure:

Provided further that nothing contained in this rule shall be deemed to prohibit the slaughter of animals for private use but not for sale:

Provided also that nothing contained in this rule shall apply to places used by the Central or the State Government for the purposes specified in these rules.

4. Licence from the Executive Authority—(1) Every person who intends to obtain a licence under these rules shall apply to the Executive Authority in Form 1 along with such fee as may be fixed by the village panchayat with the prior approval of the Inspector.

(2) On receipt of the application specified in sub-rule (1) the Executive Authority shall if he is satisfied with the particulars specified therein issue a licence to the applicant in Form 2 subject to such condition as may be specified in the licence.

5. Certificate to be issued by veterinary assistant surgeon—It shall be the duty of the village panchayat that an animal to be slaughtered at the slaughter house provided by it is brought to the authorized Veterinary Assistant Surgeon atleast twenty-four hours before slaughtering and is certified in Form 3 as to whether such animal is free from any contagious disease by a qualified Veterinary Assistant Surgeon who is either employed by itself or employed in a Government Veterinary Institution or panchayat union near its jurisdiction and whose services are requisitioned by it for the purpose. The veterinary assistant surgeon so employed shall examine the carcass of an animal slaughtered and certify in Form 4 as to its fitness for human consumption. If the village panchayat which employed qualified veterinary assistant surgeon for the purpose aforesaid shall without any outside sanction pay to him a remuneration at the rate not exceeding that which is fixed by the village panchayat from time to time in this behalf.

6. Responsibility of the licensee to dispose of the unusable of the slaughtered animal—It is the responsibility of the person who slaughters any animal aforesaid to remove any unusable remains of the slaughtered animal from the premises of the slaughter house and dispose them in the manner specified by the village panchayat failing which licence shall be liable to be cancelled or suspended for such period as the Executive Authority may decide

(G.O. Ms. No.212, Rural Development (C-4) Department, dated 5th October 1999)

APPENDIX

FORM 1

Application for Licence

[See Rule 4(1)]

To
The Executive Authority,
________________Village Panchayat.
________________District.

1. Name of person/firm
2. Father's Name
3. Address

House No.	Street
Village	Post
District	Pin

4. Purpose for which licence is applied.
5. Number, type and description of animals intended for slaughtering.
6. This is to certify that ____________number of ____________will be presented by me on (date)____________and I am to inform that all these animals are free from contagious diseases and request to issue of licence for slaughtering at ____________slaughter house on ____________(date), I shall abide by all the terms and conditions of the licence.

Date:
Place: **Signature of the applicant**

FORM 2

[See Rule 4 (2)]

Licence for Slaughter of Animal, etc.

____________Village Panchayat ____________District. Licence is issued in favour of Thiru/Tmt____________Address ____________for slaughtering ____________number of cattle/horse/sheep/goat/pig/poultry/fish in ____________slaughter house located at____________(place) coming under the jurisdiction of this village panchayat on ____________between ____________to ____________Time for which a fee of Rs.____________(Rupees ____________) has been paid vide this village panchayat receipt No.____________dated ____________

Date

Signature of the Executive Authority and Designation
Original to the licence
Counterfoil Office copy

TERMS AND CONDITIONS OF LICENCE

1. Slaughtering of animal shall be done as per the laws and rules in force
2. No slaughtering of animals is allowed between ____________p.m. to____________a.m.
3. Slaughtering time as permitted herein shall be followed.
4. This licence is liable for cancellation in case the license violates any of the conditions of the licence.
5. This licensee shall get the carcasses of animals slaughtered for examination by the Veterinary Assistant Surgeon who will issue a certificate to their fitness for human consumption.

FORM 3

(See Rule 5)

Certificate of Animals Free of Contagious Diseases

This is to certify that____________cattle/horse/sheep/goat/pig/poultry/fish belonging to Thiru____________permitted by their village panchayat through its licence No.____________dated____________were examined by me today and found to be free from contagious disease and fit for slaughtering before____________(date).

Name ____________________ **Signature of Veterinary Assistant Surgeon**
Date ____________________

(Counterfoil shall be retained to the village panchayat)

FORM 4

(See Rule 5)

Certificate the Carcasses of Animals Slaughtered as to their Fitness for Human Consumption

This is to certify that the slaughtered carcasses of____________________cattle/horse/sheep/goat/pig/poultry/fish belonging to______________permitted by the village panchayat, slaughtered to ________________________slaughter house were examined by me today at____________________________(time) and were found fit for human consumption before____________________________(time) of____________________(date)

Name ____________________ **Signature of Veterinary Assistant Surgeon**

Date____________________

5.5.8 Form and Contents of Licence and Permission

1. Short title—These rules may be called the Tamil Nadu Village Panchayats (Form and Contents of Licence and Permission, etc.) Rules, 1999.

2. Definition—In these rules, unless the context otherwise requires, 'Act' means the Tamil Nadu Panchayats Act, 1994 (Tamil Nadu Act 21 of 1994).

3. Licence to be in writing—Every licence, permission or notice granted or issued under the Act, any rule or bye-law made thereunder shall be in writing.

4. Specification of period for licence and permission—Every licence or permission granted under the Act or any rule or bye-law made there under shall specify the period, if any, for which, and the restrictions, limitations and conditions subject to which the same is granted and shall be signed by the Executive Authority and every order granting such licence or permission shall be displayed on the notice board of the village panchayat.

5. Suspension or cancellation of licence and permission—(1) Any licence or permission granted under the Act or any rule or bye-law made thereunder may, at any time, be modified, suspended or cancelled by the Executive Authority, if any of its restrictions, limitations or conditions are violated or infringed or if the grantee is convicted of a breach of any of the provision of the Act, or of any rule, bye-law or regulation made thereunder in any manner to which such licence or permission relates, or if the grantee has obtained the same by misrepresentation or fraud.

(2) An appeal shall lie to the village panchayat against any order of the Executive Authority under this rule modifying, suspending or cancelling a licence and no such appeal shall be heard unless it is received in the office of the village panchayat with in ten days from the date of receipt by the grantee of the order appealed against. The village panchayat shall pass a final order within thirty days, after the receipt of such appeals, failing which the appeal shall be deemed to have been allowed.

(3) A second appeal shall lie to the Assistant Director (Panchayats) against the orders of the village panchayat under sub-rule (2) within fifteen day from the date of receipt by the grantee of the order appealed against. The Assistant Director (Panchayat) shall pass final orders within thirty days after the receipt of such second appeal, failing which the appeal shall be deemed to have been allowed.

(4) Every order of the authority competent under the Act or any rule or bye-law made thereunder to pass an order refusing, modifying, suspending or cancelling a licence or permission shall be in writing and shall state the grounds on which such order is passed.

(5) When any licence or permission is suspended or cancelled or when the period for which it was granted or with which application for renewal should be made, has expired, the grantee, shall, for all purposes of the Act, or any rule or bye-law made thereunder be deemed to be without a licence or permission until the order suspending or altering the licence or permission is cancelled or until the licence or permission is renewed, as the case may be.

(6) The grantee of every licence or permission shall at all reasonable times, while such licence or permission remains in force, produce the same at the request of the Executive Authority or any person authorized by it in this behalf.

6. Procedure for sending of notice—(1) When any notice is required by the Act or by any rule, bye-law, regulation or order made thereunder to be served on, or sent to any person, the service or sending thereof may be effected,

(i) by giving or tendering the said notice to such person; or

(ii) if such person is not found, by leaving such notice at his last known place of abode or business, or by giving or tendering the same to some adult member or servant of his family or place of business; or

(iii) if such person does not reside in the village and his address elsewhere is known to the Executive Authority by sending the same to him in such address by registered post; or

(iv) if none of the modes of service is available, by affixing the notice in any conspicuous part of such place of abode or business of the person concerned in the address last known.

(2) When the person is an owner or occupier of any building or land, it shall not be necessary to name the owner or occupier in the notice and in the case of joint owners or occupiers, it shall be sufficient to serve it on, or sent it to, one of such owners or occupiers.

(3) Whenever any bill, notice, form or other document is served or sent, and a period is fixed within which any tax or other sum is to be paid or any work to be executed, or anything to be provided such period shall, in the absence of any provision to the contrary in the Act or the rules framed thereunder, be calculated from the date of receipt of such bill, notice, form or other document, as the case may be.

(4) Whoever fails to produce a licence or permission on demand under sub-rule (6) of Rule 5, shall be punishable with fine which may extend to hundred rupees, or in case of a continuing breach, with fine not exceeding fifteen rupees for everyday during which the breach continues after conviction for the first breech.

[G.O.Ms.No.221, Rural Development (C-4) Department, dated 20th October 1999]

5.5.9 Provision of Burial and Burning Grounds

1. Short title—These rules may be called the Tamil Nadu Village Panchayats (Provision of Burial and Burning Grounds) Rules, 1999.

2. Definition—In these rules, unless the context otherwise requires "Act" means the Tamil Nadu Panchayats Act, 1994 (Tamil Nadu Act 21 of 1994).

3. Provision and collection of rent and fees for burial and burning grounds—A village panchayat shall, if no sufficient provision exists, provide at its cost, places to be used as burial or burning grounds and may charge rents and fees for the use thereof.

4. Registration of burial and burning grounds—(1) Every owner or other person having the control over any place used as a place for burying or burning of the dead shall, if such place is not already registered under the Act or any other Act apply to the village Panchayat to have such place registered.

(2) If it appears to the village panchayat that there is no owner or person having the control of such place, the village panchayat shall assume such control and register such place or may, with the sanction of the Assistant Director (Panchayats) close it.

5. Conditions for opening of burial and burning ground—(1) No new place for burying or burning the dead, whether private or public, shall be opened, formed, constructed or used, unless a licence has been obtained from the village panchayat on application.

(2) Such application for a licence shall be accompanied by the plan of the place for which licence is required showing the locality, boundary and extent thereof, the name of the owner or person or community interested therein, the system of management and such further particulars as the village panchayat may require.

(3) The village panchayat to which an application is made may:

(a) grant or, if there is valid reason to be recorded in writing, refuse to grant a licence, or

(b) postpone the grant of a licence until the objection if any to the site has been cleared or any particulars called for by it have been furnished.

(4) The Assistant Director (Panchayats) may cancel or modify any order passed by a panchayat under sub-rule (3):

Provided that no order either on application or *suo moto* prejudicial to the appellant shall be passed without giving reasonable opportunity to the appellant under this sub-rule or sub-rule (3).

6. Registers to be maintained—(1) A register shall be maintained at the office of every village panchayat showing places provided, registered or licensed under Rules 3 to 5 and all such places provided, registered or licensed before the commencement of the Act which are used as burial or burning grounds.

(2) A notice in Tamil and in English that such place has been provided, registered or licensed as aforesaid shall be displayed on some conspicuous place at or near the entrance to the burial or burning ground.

7. Place for burial and burning grounds—(1) No person shall bury or burn or cause to be buried burnt any corpse in any place within ninety metres of a dwelling place or source of drinking water supply other than a place licensed as a burial and burning ground.

(2) The person having control of a place for burying or burning the dead shall give information of every burial or burning of a corpse at such a place to any officer appointed by the village panchayat for this purpose.

(3) If a village panchayat is satisfied:

(a) that any registered or licensed place burying or burning of the dead is in such a state or situation as to be or likely to become, dangerous to the health of persons living in the neighbourhood thereof, or

(b) that any burial ground is overcrowded with graves and if in the case of a public burial or burning grounds, another convenient place duly authorised for burying or burning of the dead exists or has been provided for the persons who would ordinarily make use of such place, it may with the previous sanction of the Assistant Director (Panchayats) give notice that it shall be not lawful after the expiry of a period of not less than two months to be specified in such notice to bury or burn any corpse at such place.

(4) Every notice given under sub-rule (3) shall be published by affixture to the notice board of the village panchayat and by beat of drum in the village.

(5) No person shall in contravention of any notice under sub-rule (3) and after expiration of the period specified in such notice bury or burn or cause or permit to be buried or burnt any corpse at such place.

(6) The Inspector may cancel or modify any notice issued by a village panchayat under sub-rule (3).

(7) Whoever contravenes any of the provisions of those rules shall be punishable with fine which may extend to one hundred rupees or in case of a continuing breach with fine not exceeding fifteen rupees for everyday during which the breach, continues after conviction of the first breach:

Provided that no prosecution shall be instituted for contravening the provision of sub-rule (1) of Rule 7 without the written sanction of the Executive Authority of the village panchayat concerned.

(G.O. Ms. No. 213, Rural Development (C-4) Department, dated 5th October 1999)

5.5.10 Cleaning of Private Soak Pit and Cesspools

1. Short title—These rules may be called the Tamil Nadu Village Panchayats (Cleaning of Private Soak Pit and Cesspools) Rules, 1999.

2. Arrangements by village panchayats—Every village panchayat shall make adequate arrangement for the regular cleaning of soak pit and cesspools in private premises.

3. Levy of fee—(1) The village panchayat may levy a fee from the owner or occupier of the said premises or place at the rate calculated to cover the cost of the service.

(2) In calculating the rate of the fees to be levied under sub-rule (1), the village panchayat shall take into account the area and or depth of the soak pit and cesspools and the quantum of waste material or dirty material to be cleaned.

(G.O. Ms. No. 36, Rural Development (C-4) Department, dated 22nd February 1999)

5.5.11 Restrictions and Control Over Execution of Kudimaramat and Levy of Fees by Village Panchayats

1. Short title—These rules may be called the Tamil Nadu Village Panchayats (Restrictions and Control Over Execution of Kudimaramat by Village Panchayat-Levy of Fees by Village Panchayats) Rules, 1999.

2. Definition—In these rules, unless the context otherwise requires–

(1) "Act" mean the Tamil Nadu Panchayats Act, 1994 (Tamil Nadu Act 21 of 1994).

(2) "Government" means the Government of Tamil Nadu.

3. Levy of annual fee—(1) The village panchayat may levy an annual fee from all the registered holders of lands served by any irrigation work at such rate per acre as the Collector of the revenue district may from time-to-time determine having regard to the nature of Kudimaramat work executed or proposed to be executed by the panchayat.

(2) The fee shall be levied at one flat rate per acre in the case of wet and dry lands irrigated from the irrigation work concerned by direct flow, and at one-half of such rate in the case of wet and dry lands irrigated from such work by baling.

Explanation. The fee shall be in addition to the wet or dry assessment and the water rate, if any, chargeable on the land.

4. Collection of fees—The fee shall be collected by the village panchayat through the Village Administrative Officer or any other person of the Land Revenue Department having jurisdiction over the village panchayat or any part thereof and shall be administered and expended by the village panchayat under the general or special order of the Collector. The Village Administrative Officer shall furnish the demand account relating to the fee to the village panchayat and he shall also collect it. The Village Administrative Officer or any other person belonging to the staff of the Land Revenue Department shall be paid such remuneration, as may be determined by the Collector either by general or special order in this behalf under Section 177 of the Act.

5. Non-payment of fees—The fee shall, on demand shall be payable by the registered holder or of the joint registered holders, as the case may be and if not paid, may be recovered from such holder or any holders, as it were arrear of land revenue.

6. Rights of the village panchayat to spend the proceeds of the fee—The proceeds of the fee shall be constituted into a separate fund and shall be spent at the discretion of the village panchayat on the maintenance or repair of the irrigation work concerned and shall not be utilised for any other purpose.

7. Accounts to be maintained by the village panchayat—Proper accounts shall be maintained by the village panchayat for the transactions relating to the fund and the accounts audited by the auditor appointed by Government under sub-section (1) of Section 193 of the Act.

8. Inspection by the Government officials—The village panchayat shall at all times allow the Officers of the Public Works and Revenue Department of the Government to inspect the irrigation work and all or any other works concerned therewith.

9. Facilities to be provided for any repairs—The village panchayat shall at all times allow facilities to any contractor who may be employed by the Public Works or Revenue Department of the Government to effect any repairs to the irrigation work or other works connected therewith.

(G.O. Ms. No. 214, Rural Development (C-4) Department, dated 5th October 1999).

5.5.12 Execution of Kudimaramat Works

The Government issued the rules on execution of Kudimaramat norms by village panchayats as per the reference first cited.

The Government consider it necessary, as part of the policy underlying the entrustment of agricultural development work to panchayat unions, that the provisions, contained in Section 133 (1) of the Tamil Nadu Panchayats Act, 1994, regarding the transfer of irrigation works should be utilised adequately.

In the context of implementation of the Tamil Nadu Panchayats Act, Government also consider it very important that village panchayats should be advised to take over Kudimaramat in their villages in every case. The need for panchayat unions taking up Kudimaramat obligation fall on the ryots of more than one panchayat villages collectively and the village panchayats concerned are unable to divide up the responsibility among themselves.

The Government accordingly pass the following orders:

(1) Section 133 (1) of the Tamil Nadu Panchayats Act, 1994, empowers the Government to transfer to the village panchayat or the panchayat union the functions relating to (a) the protection and maintenance of irrigation works, (b) the management of turns of irrigation, and (c) the regulation of distribution of water from the irrigation work to the fields depending on it. The Government have decided that these functions should be transferred to the panchayat unions and not to the village panchayats. The Government have, however, no objection to the panchayat union entrusting to the local panchayat under Section 119 (2) of the Act, the execution of maintenance works, the management of turns of irrigation and the regulation of distribution of water from the irrigation work, if the ayacutdars of the irrigation source request in writing that such entrustment should be effected and if the village panchayat concerned agrees (by a resolution passed by it at a meeting specially convened for the purpose) to take over the said functions and to abide by the conditions upon which the irrigation source has been transferred by the panchayat union.

(2) The Collectors have already transferred minor irrigation sources with an ayacut of 100 acres to the panchayat unions and they are maintaining the tanks under the cycle system.

(i) In order to enable the panchayat union to discharge the responsibility thus entrusted, a special annual grant which may be referred to as the "Local Irrigation Grant" is be made available to the panchayat union besides scheme funds.

(ii) The panchayat union shall not effect any alteration in the sluice of the irrigation work interfere with standard and specifications laid down in the Tank Restoration Scheme Memories in respect of such work or raise lower or extend the weirs or claingulas or make any material alterations in or interfere with the headwork, if any, of the channels.

(iii) The panchayat union shall be responsible for keeping watch over the bund of irrigation work during the rainy season.

(iv) The panchayat union shall make good any damage to the sluices weirs calingulas, channels, head-works, bund or other works forming part of or connected with the irrigation work resulting from its misfeasance or non-feasance, the decision of the District Collector as to whether any particular item of damage was the result of any misfeasance or non-feasance on the part of the panchayat union being final.

(v) The panchayat union shall not excavate earth at any time for any purpose within thirty feet of either toe of the bund of the irrigation work.

(vi) The panchayat union shall have power to regulate the manner and order in which the land under the irrigation work shall be irrigated, the time at which the supply of water shall continue and the total quantity of water to be supplied but this power shall not be exercised so as adversely to affect any established or customary right to preferential or proportional supply.

(vii) Any function in respect of a village irrigation work transferred to a panchayat union may at any time be resumed without assigning any reason by the Government or their delegate the Collector.

(viii) A resolution of the panchayat union council agreeing to abide by the conditions referred to above shall be obtained before the minor irrigation sources are transferred to the panchayats.

Kudimaramat—

(i) The Tamil Nadu Compulsory Labour Act, 1858, refers to the existence of a customary obligation to provide free labour for certain types of work on irrigation sources. The law provides that, where the customary obligation was not discharged, the necessary works should be carried out by the Tehsildar and the costs apportioned among the land holder responsible and recovered from them as arrears of land revenue. Section 133 (2) of the Tamil Nadu Panchayats Act, 1994, makes it possible for the village panchayats or panchayat union councils to take over this customary obligation, discharge it and meet the cost by levying a statutory fee for the purpose. Tamil Nadu Panchayats Act, 1994, specially provides that this assumption of responsibility by the village panchayat or the panchayat union council as the case may be does not exempt the land holders from liability to enforcement of the rules by the Tehsildar in the event of the village panchayat or the panchayat union councils failing to discharge the obligation assumed by them.

(ii) Collectors of districts are requested to take action to bring to the notice of every village panchayat the provisions of Section 133 (2) of the Act and induce the village panchayats to assume responsibility for executing Kudimaramat and for discharging their obligation periodically in order to keep irrigation works in good condition. The village panchayats may be informed of the provisions of the Act enabling them to levy suitable fees for executing Kudimaramat. The question of panchayat union councils taking up this obligation need not be considered until the result of the approach to panchayats has become clear.

(iii) In order to prevent the customary obligation lapsing by disuse, a record should be maintained by the panchayat union Commissioner specifying the existence of customary obligation and its precise nature in respect of each source in which it existed. The nature of the customary obligation will be available in the settlement registers of the village and records in the Taluk Office. The particulars in respect of each source should be obtained from the Tehsildar and entered in the said registers.

(iv) Sub-paragraph (5) under Board's Standing Order No. 86 and Appendix I and Appendix II to that Standing Order prescribed the maintenance of two registers in Taluk Office, namely:

(a) The Kudimaramat Register for the Taluk with a page for each village; and

(b) Register showing penalties recovered under the Act and its disposal. The Board of Revenue has reported that these two registers will be useful for the village panchayats when they take over the responsibility for executing Kudimaramat and the maintenance of such registers will be necessary to show what works should be regarded as coming under the preview of the Kudimaramat liability. The Government direct that these two registers now maintained in the Taluk office should also be maintained with such modifications as the Board of Revenue may consider to be necessary for every panchayat development block, by the panchayat union Commissioner concerned. If any panchayat in the block after assuming power and responsibility under Section 133 (2) of the Act fails to execute Kudimaramat in respect of any irrigation source the panchayat union Commissioner should bring the matter to the notice of the panchayat union council and suggest that the latter may assume the power and responsibility and to execute Kudimaramat in that case. It is only in the very unlikely event of even this attempt failing that it would be necessary for the panchayat union Commissioner to bring the fact to the notice of the Tehsildar for enforcing the provisions of the Madras Compulsory Labour Act, 1858.

(G.O. No. 711, Local Administration, dated 16th April 1960)

5.5.13 Village Panchayats to Run Fair Price Shops under Public Distribution System

In exercise of the powers conferred under clause (h) of Section 110 and Section 257 of the Tamil Nadu Panchayats Act, 1994 (Tamil Nadu Act 21 of 1994), the Governor of Tamil Nadu hereby imposes the duty and entrust on the village panchayats to run fair price shops under Public Distribution System subject to the following conditions, namely:

(1) (i) The village panchayats which are willing to run the fair price shops under Public Distribution System (hereinafter referred to as "shop") located in the panchayat village may be identified by the Collector and he shall grant permission to run the said shop:

Provided that the Collector before grant of such permission shall ensure that the authorisation, if any, issued to the Co-operative Society is terminated following the procedures laid down in the Tamil Nadu Scheduled Commodities (Regulation of Distribution by Card System) Order, 1982.

(ii) The village panchayats shall be adequately solvent to meet the working capital and running expenditure of the said shop as evidenced by the statement of the village panchayat fund account and a projected one year receipt and expenditure of the village panchayat to arrive at the surplus fund to run the said shops proposed to take over. The village panchayat may use the village panchayat fund account for running the shops under Public Distribution System including purchase and other incidental expenses like transport etc.

(iii) The village panchayat should not have come to an adverse notice in the past in respect of its financial transactions;

(iv) The village panchayat President's Credentials and past records are good;

(v) The village panchayat shall pass a resolution to run the shop on self-lifting basis without claiming any subsidy from the Government. The resolution shall indicate the following, namely:

(a) The village panchayat shall take over the stocks from the concerned Co-operative Society on the date ordered by the District Collector and in the presence of officers nominated by the District Collector. While taking over the commodities the value of the commodities shall be paid to the concerned Co-operative Society.

(b) The village panchayats shall adhere to all the requirements of the Tamil Nadu Scheduled Commodities (Distribution by Card System) Order, 1982.

(c) The village panchayats planning to operate the shop in the same building shall take steps to transfer the agreements with the landlords in their favour, if the landlord is willing for such transfer and if any advance has been paid by the concerned Co-operative Society, such advances shall be refunded to the co-operatives.

(d) Furnitures and fixtures for the shop shall be provided by the village panchayats at their cost. As the co-operative department shall withdraw the existing furniture in the shops after a period of one year of handing over, the village panchayats shall make suitable arrangements in the interim period. Assets taken over by the village panchayat shall be paid for at book value and liabilities after detailing shall remain with the respective Co-operative Societies.

(e) The village panchayat shall make its own arrangement for running the shop including payment of the workers with no nexus to the emoluments in other organisations or agencies.

(2) The village panchayat shall maintain all the Records that are normally maintained in the shop run by the Co-operative Societies. The shop shall be subject to control and supervision by the Civil Supplies Department or any other Department authorised by the Government, from time-to-time. The village panchayat shall submit the details of the distribution and accounts of such shop in every Grama Sabha meeting for social auditing. The Collector shall closely monitor the shop run by the village panchayat and ensure effective control over the system.

(3) The village panchayat shall not sell scheduled commodities obtained from source other than the Government or any agency appointed by the Collector. Provided that the District Collector or any authorised officer by him from time-to-time may grant special permission with conditions, if any, to sell commodities obtained from other source.

(4) The village panchayat shall take adequate measure to ensure that the scheduled commodities are stored and maintained in good condition and damage to them due to ground moisture, rain, insects, rodents, birds, fire etc, shall be avoided.

Explanation. "Scheduled Commodities" means the commodity specified in the schedule to this order and supplied by the Government by an agency authorised by the Government on this behalf to any authorised dealer for issue to consumers.

(5) The village panchayats, without reasonable cause, shall not abruptly stop the working of the shop or allow the shop to remain closed during working hours on any working day without prior approval of the Collector.

(6) The village panchayats shall also strictly adhere to such other conditions as may be imposed by the Government or the Collector in the running of the shops.

(7) The Collector may revoke the permission granted to village panchayats to run the shop any time under the following circumstances:

(i) In the case of serious irregularities committed by village panchayats in running the shop;

(ii) Wherever the village panchayat is unable to run the shop effectively due to financial constraints or any other reasons.

The Collector may grant permissions to run such shop to the Self-Help Group or to the near by Co-operatives, who are willing to run the shop.

(8) The Collector may grant permission to the village panchayat to run an existing shop or to run a newly created full time shop. The part-time shop attached to such shop also shall be transferred to the respective village panchayat. The Collector shall not grant permission to a village panchayat to run a part-time shop, if the main shop to which such part-time shop is attached is run by either self-help groups or society. The shops run by the village panchayat shall be treated as a stand alone self- lifting shop.

Explanation. "Stand alone self-lifting shop" means an independent shop not attached to any other lead societies for lifting essential commodities on its own for public distribution.

(9) The Collector, in consultation with the Joint Registrar of Co-operatives, shall identify the shop to be run by the village panchayat if the following conditions are satisfied, namely:

(i) the shop identified for transfer from a Co-operative Society would be those, where irregularities have been continuously noticed; or

(ii) where they are attached to Co-operative Societies which have shortage of personnel or are financially weak; or

(iii) where the Commissioner of Civil Supplies finds such a transfer would be in the interest of the consumer; or

(iv) if it is full time shop, the shop shall have a minimum number of five hundred cards; or

(v) where a Co-operative Society satisfies either

or both conditions (i) and (ii) the Collector may give priority to the Co-operative Society holding shops in excess of six to be run by a village panchayat.

(10) The village panchayat shall make its own arrangement for lifting the materials directly from the Tamil Nadu Civil Supplies godown either in single movement or two and more movements according to its convenience. Liftment shall be made after making necessary payment directly to the Tamil Nadu Civil Supplies Corporation by the village panchayats. Kerosene also shall be lifted following the procedure of stand alone self lifting shops.

(11) The village panchayat is entitled for the commission on par with similarly run shops by the Co-operative Society as fixed by the Registrar of Cooperative Societies from time-to-time.

(12) The village panchayat may engage a person to run the shop on daily wages basis after getting the due approval from the Collector who shall ensure that he is engaged on temporary basis and paid wages at the rates normally fixed by the Collector for non-farm works from time-to-time. The village panchayat can use the Public Distribution System buildings already constructed under Rural Development Programmes, wherever such buildings are available to run the shop.

(G.O. Ms. No. 57, Rural Development (C-4) Department, dated 22nd February 2001)

(G.O. Ms. No. 209, Rural Development (C-4) Department, dated 14th August, 2001).

THE SCHEDULE

[See explanation under conditions (3) and (4)]

1. Rice (including paddy) Whole or Broken or the Flour Products Thereof
2. Wheat
3. Jawar including milo
4. Bajra
5. Maize
6. Ragi
7. Sugar
8. Gram
9. Gramdhall
10. Toor
11. Toordhall
12. Green gram
13. Urid
14. Uriddhall
15. Baby Food
16. Groundnut Oil, Gingelly, coconut oil and imported edible oils including palmolein and R.P.D. Palm Oil
17. Toilet and washing soaps
18. Kerosene
19. Iodised salt

5.5.14 Village Panchayats to Run Fair Price Shops under Public Distribution System—Amendment to Notification

In exercise of the powers conferred under clause (h) of Section 110 and Section 257 of the Tamil Nadu Panchayats Act, 1994 (Tamil Nadu Act 21 of 1994), the Governor of Tamil Nadu hereby makes the following Amendment to the Rural Development Department Notification No.II (2)/RUL/254(e)/2001, published at pages 1-4 of Part II-Section-2 of the Tamil Nadu Government Extraordinary, dated the 26th February 2001.

AMENDMENT

In the said Notification in clause (i) of Condition (1) for the words "he shall grant" the words "he may grant" shall be substituted.

(G.O. Ms. No. 209, Rural Development (C4), 14th August 2001)

5.5.15 Furnishing Details of Monthly Receipt and Issue of Commodities in the Fair Price Shops to Elected Representatives of the Local Bodies

The Government permit all the Civil Supplies authorities including Tamil Nadu Civil Supplies Corporation:

(i) to furnish, free of cost, details of monthly receipt and issue of commodities in the Fair Price Shops of the Corporation in various regions to elected representatives of the Local Bodies and legislature in respect of shops within the jurisdiction;

(ii) to supply these details to any interested cardholder in respect of the shops to which his card is attached, for a moderate fee;

(iii) to make available, for a moderate fee, to any cardholder to extract of drawal register in respect of his card; and

(iv) to make available copies of the 'A' register to any interested cardholder, Consumer Association, Voluntary Organisation, Welfare Associates of the locality where the shop is situated.

2. The Government direct that "Copies of 'A' register or any other document listed in para 4 (ii), (iii) and (iv) above be issued on payment of Re. 1 per page and if entire 'A' register is required on payment of Rs. 50/- if it contains 100 pages or less, Rs. 100/- if it contains more than 100 pages.

(G.O. Ms. No. 225 dated 26th August, 1997)

5.5.16 Certain Clarifications on Public Distribution System

Sub: Public Distribution Systems—Targeted Public Distribution System – Measures of Transparency – Supply of 'A' Register and Drawal Register to the consumers and Voluntary Organisations – Clarification Issued.

Orders issued in the Government Order (G.O. Ms. No. 225 dated 26.8.1997) will also apply to the Fair Price Shops run by the Cooperatives with equal force.

(Government letter No.35677/F/97-1 dated 4.12.97 addressed to the Registrar of Cooperative Societies, Chennai)

5.5.17 Authority for Numbering of Buildings

1. Short title—These rules may be called the Tamil Nadu Panchayats (Authority for Numbering of Buildings) Rules, 1999.

2. Authority for numbering of buildings—

(i) The authority for the purpose of sub-section (1) of Section 158 of the Tamil Nadu Panchayats Act, 1994 (Tamil Nadu Act 21 of 1994) shall be the Executive Authority of the village panchayat concerned.

(ii) The expenditure in connection with the numbering of buildings shall be borne from the fund of the village panchayat concerned.

(G.O. Ms. No. 143, Rural Development (C-4) Department, dated 21st July 1999)

5.5.18 Procedure for Numbering of Buildings

As per the sub-section (1) of Section 158 of Tamil Nadu Panchayats Act, 1994, each village panchayat has to assign the door number for each building in their area. As the door number for each building has been assigned 10 years before, now new door numbers are assigned as sub-numbers (i.e.) A, B, C, D, the new buildings constructed later have not been assigned any door numbers. Hence the Government like that the door numbers have to be assigned before the commencement of the Census enumeration and order as follows:

(1) In each street or road, the building situated in one side door number have to be assigned as Odd numbers (1, 3, 5, 7, 9, 11, 13, 15, 17, 19), the another side of streets or road the door number have to be assigned as even numbers (2, 4, 6, 8, 10, 12, 14, 16, 18, 20).

(2) While assigning the door number, to avoid confusion, both old door number and new number have to be marked as follows:

Old Number	9
New Number	21

After familarisation of the new number, the old number may be deleted.

(3) While assigning the door number, the numbers have to be started from left side of street or road. As the village panchayat assign the new door number providing number as A, B, C, D, shall be avoided. After assigning the new number, if any new building

is constructed near by, the new door number has to be assigned with suffix of the near by buildings with A, B, C, D, like that.

(4) If any site is vacant in the street or road, the door number need not be assigned.

(5) If any building has more than one door, only one door number shall be given, in each house of that multi-stored building, the numbers can be assigned like 18/1, 18/2, 18/3, 18/4, and it shall be marked in out side of each building. The owner of the building can do this mark themselves. The Owner of building shall not assign the sub-door number as A, B, C, and D, in their buildings.

(6) While providing the door number for each building, initially white background may be painted, afterwards both old and new numbers may be written in the black letters. After completion of all this work, the District Collector may intimate this matter to the Director of Census Operations (Tamil Nadu), E Wing, Third Floor, ABC Blocks, Rajaji Bhavan, Besent Nagar, Chennai–600 090. As the new door number have to be noted in the Legislative Assembly Voter list, this matter may be intimated to Legislative Assembly Voter Registration Office and Tamil Nadu State Election Commission.

(7) The expenditure for this exercise shall be met from the Village Panchayat Funds only.

(G.O. Ms. No. 238, Rural Development (C-2) Department, dated 10th November 1999)

5.6 PROPERTIES OF VILLAGE PANCHAYAT

5.6.1 Restriction and Control to Regulate the Use of Porambokes in Ryotwari Tracts

1. Short title—These rules may be called the Tamil Nadu Panchayats (Restriction and Control to Regulate the Use of Porambokes in Ryotwari Tracts) Rules, 2000.

2. Definition—In these rules, unless the context otherwise requires

(a) "Act" means the Tamil Nadu Panchayat Act, 1994 (Tamil Nadu Act, 21 of 1994).

(b) "Memo" means the statement showing the details of unauthorised encroachments on Government lands, the use of which is regulated by village panchayats.

3. Regulation of poramboke land—No poramboke at the disposal of the Government, the use of which is regulated by the village panchayat, shall be used for any purpose other than that for which it was originally intended except with the prior approval of the Collector and such use shall be subject to such conditions and restrictions as may be imposed by the Collector.

4. Procedure for alternate use of poramboke land—(1) If a village panchayat considers that a poramboke mentioned in sub-section (2) of Section 134 of the Act, is no longer required for the purpose for which it was originally intended and that it may be used for any other specified public purpose, it shall cause a notice to be published in the village panchayat in which the land is situated, specifying its survey number and the purpose for which it is required and inviting objections to the proposal with in a specified date which shall not be less than thirty days from the date of publication of the notice. The notice shall be published by beat of tom tom and by displaying it in some conspicuous part of the building in which the office of the village panchayat is located.

(2) On expiry of the date fixed for the receipt of objections, the village panchayat shall forward the proposal together with the objections received thereon to the Collector for issue of such orders as may be deemed fit.

(3) When a village panchayat desires to regulate the use of a poramboke mentioned in sub-section (4) of Section 134 of the Act, it may apply to the Collector with a copy of its resolution on the subject specifying

(a) the survey number or numbers the boundaries and the extent of the porambokes;

(b) the purpose for which the poramboke is used; and

(c) a list and description of the trees, if any, standing on it.

(4) The Collector shall after satisfying himself that the poramboke is at the disposal of the Government and that the particulars specified in the resolution are correct, issue such orders as he may deem fit.

5. Maintenance of list of poramboke—The village panchayat shall maintain list of the porambokes with details of survey number, boundaries, extent, the purpose for which each poramboke is used and the trees there on the use of which is regulated by it under sub-sections (2) and (4) of Section 134 of the Act.

6. Inspecting of poramboke lands—The village Administrative Officer or any inspecting officer of the Revenue Department shall have the right to inspect at any time, any poramboke, the use of which is regulated by the village panchayat.

7. Levy of fees on the use of poramboke land—The village panchayat may levy a fee for the use of any poramboke in accordance with the schedule of rate approved by the Collector, which shall not be less than seven per cent of the market value of the land for non-commercial purpose and fourteen per cent for commercial purpose.

8. Maintenance of certain poramboke lands—(1) The village panchayat shall maintain thrashing floors, cart stands, cattle-stands and burning and burial grounds in a sanitary condition and shall carry out any direction issued by the Deputy Director of Public Health and Preventive Medicine in this behalf.

(2) The village panchayat shall take all measures to maintain the topes in good condition and plant new trees in the place of wind fallen or withered or dead trees.

(3) The village panchayat may lease the topes subject to suitable conditions and enjoy the income from the usufruct of the trees in the topes.

(4) The rules framed under clause [xxxv] of sub-section [2] of Section 242 of the Act shall *mutatis mutandis* apply in relation to the leasing, cutting and planting of trees by the village panchayat on any poramboke, the use of which is regulated by it.

9. Removal of encroachment on poramboke—The village panchayat shall take steps to remove encroachments on any poramboke, the use of which is vested and regulated by the Act. If the village panchayat commits and defaults in doing so, the Village Administrative Officer shall issue B. Memo to the encroachment and after three months from the date of receipt of B. Memo by the village panchayat, the Tehsildar concerned shall order the removal of such of those encroachments as are considered objectionable by him. An appeal shall lie to the Revenue Divisional Officer against the orders passed by the Tehsildar. A second appeal shall lie against the order of the Revenue Divisional Officer with the District Collector.

10. Revision—A revision shall lie to the Commissioner of Land Administration against the orders of the Collector under Rule 9 and a second revision to the Government against the orders of the Commissioner of Land Administration.

11. Power of the Government—The Government in respect of an order passed by the Commissioner of Land Administration may either *suo moto* or an application by the aggrieved party, call for and examine the records and for reasons to be recorded in writing annul or modify or remit for reconsideration of such order on grounds of material irregularity or mistake of fact or misrepresentation or on the ground of public interest:

Provided that no order prejudicial to any person shall be passed unless the person concerned is given a reasonable opportunity of showing cause.

(G.O.Ms. No. 317, Rural Development (C-4) Department, dated 6th December 2000)

5.6.2 Regulation of the Use of Communal Lands by Panchayats in Estates

1. Short title—These rules may be called the Tamil Nadu Panchayats (Regulation of the Use of Communal Lands by Panchayats in Estates) Rules, 1999.

2. Definition—In these rules, unless the context otherwise requires (1) "Act" means the Tamil Nadu Panchayats Act, 1994 (Tamil Nadu Act 21 of 1994).

(2) "Estate Villages" means the villages notified as Estate village under the Tamil Nadu Estate Land Act, 1908 (Tamil Nadu Act 1 of 1908) and as specified in the appendix appended to this rule.

3. Applicability of other rules—The rules framed under sub-section (2) of Section 134 of the Act, shall apply *mutatis mutandis* to the regulation of the use of lands referred to in clause (a) of sub-section (1) of Section 135 of the Act and the rules framed under clause (xxxv) of sub-section (2) of Section 242 of the Act shall apply *mutatis mutandis* for the regulation of the planting of trees on lands referred to in clause (a) of sub-section (1) of Section 135 of the Act.

4. Restriction of village panchayat to use of communal lands—In exercise of the powers under clause (a) of sub-section (1) of Section 135 of the Act, in respect of any land, the village panchayat shall not do any act which would affect the revisionary right, if any, of the land holder of such land and if the land is in a town or village site, his right to assign as house-site any vacant portion of it which is not in the common use of the inhabitants for any lawful purpose.

5. Disputes in the description of land—If any question arises whether or not any land is of the description mentioned in sub-clause (b) of clause (16) of Section 3 of the Tamil Nadu Estates Land Act, 1908, the village panchayats shall not exercise its powers under Section 135 (1) (a) of the Act, in respect of that land until that question is decided under Section 20 of the Tamil Nadu Estates Land Act, 1908.

6. Action taken on the disputed land—Any action taken under clause (a) of sub-section (1) of Section 135 of the Act shall be subject to the control of the district collector and he may, if so, desires, in consultation with the Executive Authority of the panchayat, alter or modify or any of the action taken by the panchayat.

7. Rights of the village panchayat to use of communal land—(1) A village panchayat either *suo moto* or on a representation made by any of the persons residing within its limits, considers that any land set apart for any purpose referred to in sub-clause (b) of clause (16) of Section 3 of the Tamil Nadu Estates Land Act, 1908, namely thrashing fields, cattle stand, village sites and other lands in the village which are set apart is no longer required for that purpose and that it should obtain the sanction of the Collector to issue an order under clause (b) of sub-section (1) of Section 135 of the Act directing that it shall be used for any other specified communal purpose, it shall, by a notice to be published in the village in which the land is situated by beat of drum and by affixture in the building in which the office of the village panchayat is located, invite objection if any, to the proposed order within a specified date which shall not be less than thirty days from the date of such publication of the notice. The notice shall also specify the time and date on which the objection will be heard. A copy of the notice shall be served on the land holder or any person having possession or control over the land either in person or by registered post with acknowledgement giving thirty days time from the date of service to file his objection, if any.

(2) The date of hearing under sub-rule (1) shall be after the expiry of fifteen days from the date on which the time allowed for filing objection.

(3) The village panchayat shall hear every objection that may be received on or before the date fixed in sub-rule (1) and in doing so; give all reasonable opportunity to the parties concerned to produce both oral and documentary evidences in proof of their claim.

8. Application to the Collector by the village panchayat—After the completion, of the enquiry if the village panchayat decides that the objections are to be over-ruled and that a direction under clause (b) of sub-section (1) of Section 135 of the Act is necessary, it shall record a finding to that giving full reasons therefor and submit an application to the Collector for his sanction to issue such a direction, along with a copy of its findings, the records of enquiry including documents to prove the service and issue of notices referred to in sub-rule (1) of Rule 7, and a certificate to the effect that it has taken into consideration all the other customary rights of the landholder, the ryots in the use of such land or portion and that it has satisfied itself that the exercise of such rights would otherwise be provided for, adequately if such a direction is given.

9. Declaration by the Collector—On receipt of such an application, the Collector may after such enquiry as he deems fit, issue a declaration under clause (1) of sub-section (a) of Section 20-A of the Tamil Nadu Estates Land Act, 1908, that the land is no longer required for its original purpose, and permit the village panchayat to issue an order under clause (b) of sub-section (1) of Section 135 of the Act directing that it shall be used for the purpose specified in the application. The village panchayat shall thereupon issue an order accordingly. If the collector is not satisfied with the proposal of the village panchayat, he shall record his reason for doing so and reject the application and communicate a copy of his order to the village panchayat.

(G.O. Ms. No. 273, Rural Development (C-4) Department, dated 28th December 1999)

APPENDIX

(See Rule 2)

List of Estate Villages Under the Tamil Nadu Estates Land Act, 1908

Sl. No.	*Name of the district villages*	*Name of the estate*
(1)	(2)	(3)
1.	Madurai	(1) Karanapatti (2) Kalanivoipatti
2.	Tirunelveli	Easanamadam
3.	Ramanathapuram	Tharikombam
4.	Dharmapuri	(1) Marasandiram (2) Elayansandiram

Sl. No.	Name of the district villages	Name of the estate
(1)	(2)	(3)
		(3) Bairasandiram (4) Chinnasandiram (5) Uliyalam (6) Thimmasandiram
5.	Thanjavur	(1) Arayapuram – Thattimalpadugai (2) Suryanarayanapuram
6.	Nagapattinam	Ramachandrankoilpathu
7.	Pudukkottai	(1) Perunjunai (2) Kothandaramapuram (3) Nilayapatti (4) Karanapatti (5) Varpattu

5.6.3 Administration and Regulation of Village Panchayat Vested Properties

The Government have already issued rules relating to restriction and control to regulate the porambokes in ryotwari tracts and communal lands in estate by the village panchayat. Detailed instruction regarding the village panchayat vested properties and its use regulations were already issued and is in force now. Further the procedure to regulate the use of such village panchayat vested porambokes in ryotwari areas and communal land in estate areas were already issued.

Therefore to regulate such of those public properties following guidelines can be issued and earlier instructions may be reiterated.

A. Village Panchayat Vested Properties

1. Details of panchayat vested properties—The properties mentioned below are statutorily vested in panchayats:

(i) Unreserved forests;
(ii) Porambokes classified as grazing grounds, thrashing floors, burning and burial grounds, cattle-stands, cart-stands and topes; and
(iii) Public roads other than National Highways, State Highways, Major District Roads and Panchayat Union Roads.

2. Village Panchayat-vested unreserved forests—Under Section 120 (1) (a) of the Tamil Nadu Panchayat Act, 1994, all "unreserved forests" in the village at the commencement of the Act shall vest in the village panchayat and shall be administered by it for the benefit of such village. It is necessary to be clear about the categories of land referred to as "unreserved forests". Under Section 2 (35) of the term "unreserved forests" means a forest not notified under Section 4 of the Tamil Nadu Forest Act, 1882 and also includes "unreserved land" at the disposal of the Government. Land at the disposal of Government includes all unoccupied land whether assessed or unassessed, but does not include patta lands and other lands owned by private persons – *vide* Section 2 of the Tamil Nadu Forest Act, 1882. Lands which are classified in the Revenue Accounts as "porambokes" should be deemed (subject to one exception which is referred to presently) to be lands reserved for the particular purposes for which they are so classified. As such all porambokes (other than forest porambokes) should be deemed to fall outside the scope of the term "unreserved land" at the disposal of the Government. There remain assessed wastes or unassessed wastes, assessed wastes are distinguished from unassessed wastes as being lands which are reserved for assignment on a permanent basis. Assessed wastes also cannot, therefore be deemed to be "unreserved forests" automatically vesting as such in the panchayat. It is necessary that all lands of the nature thus referred to which are situated within the limits of every panchayat village should be identified, listed and formally placed under the administration of the village panchayat concerned.

The unassessed waste lands should be deemed to be unreserved land vesting in the village panchayat concerned under the Act. All unassessed wastelands will, therefore, normally vest in the village panchayat. The village panchayat will be fully free to utilise these unassessed wastelands for any public purpose.

3. Village panchayat-vested porambokes—Section 134 (2) of the Act empowered the village panchayat to regulate the use of the following porambokes subject to such restrictions and control as may be prescribed:

(i) grazing grounds;
(ii) threshing floors;
(iii) burning and burial grounds;
(iv) cattle-stands;
(v) cart-stands; and
(vi) topes.

These porambokes are now vested in the village panchayats. They may accordingly be referred to as panchayat-vested porambokes. Action has therefore to be taken to get lists of village panchayat-vested porambokes for every panchayat villages prepared with particulars of survey numbers, etc., and to hand over lists to the village panchayats concerned. Thereafter, the village panchayats will regulate the use of such village panchayat-vested porambokes subject to such restrictions and control as may be prescribed by rules.

4. Village panchayat-vested public roads—Under Section 125(1) of the Tamil Nadu Panchayat Act, 1994, all public roads in a panchayat village other than panchayat union roads and roads classified by the Government as National Highways and State Highways are vested in village panchayats. With reference to these orders, lists should be prepared, with particulars of survey numbers, etc., of village panchayat roads vesting in every village panchayat separately.

5. Other village panchayat-vested lands—There may be other lands already vested in village panchayats or which may hereafter be vested in village panchayats, as a result of alienation proceedings under the Board's standing orders. Though as stated already, assessed waste land do not automatically vest in village panchayats, it will be open to village panchayats to get such lands vested in them and they may apply to the Collector for this purpose. Such applications should be freely granted, unless there are special objections in particular cases.

6. Power of village panchayats regarding utilisation of assessed waste, etc.—The intention of Government that all available public lands at the disposal of Government (which it is not necessary in the public interest to continue to be directly administered by the Government through any of its Departments), should be made available to the village panchayats for the utilisation by the village panchayat for the common benefit of the village. Keeping this main purpose in view, the Government has examined the question of utilisation of the assessed wastes; and directs that the following orders should be put into effect:

(i) *Assessed wastes* — Assessed wastelands are public lands in the village not held on patta by any private individual but classified as assessed waste in view of the fact that such lands are considered fit for cultivation at such time as some person so interested may apply. The Board's standing orders and various orders of Government in the matter regulate the question of assignment of such assessed wastelands to deserving applicants. Government have examined the question whether such lands should be made over to the village panchayats and if so in what form. It would be in the public interest if the village panchayats are enabled to utilise these lands for a suitable public purpose. Such public purposes would include the raising of fuel, fodder or green manurial plantations in the promotion of agriculture or animal husbandry. At the same time, it has to be kept in mind that there is continuous demand for the assignment of these lands to private persons for cultivation. Taking these factors into consideration Government direct that all lands classified, as assessed waste in the village should be available to the village panchayat for any public purpose. In so utilising such assessed wastes for public purposes, the village panchayats will not be expected to obtain the permission of any authorities in the matter. It should, however, be distinctly understood that it is not the intention of Government that the village panchayat should be given the power to permit the creation of rights by private parties in such assessed wastes. The assessed wastes will, therefore, be made available to the village panchayats subject to the specific understanding that it will not be open to the village panchayat to permit the creation of any private right in such lands by assignment lease or any other form of private ownership. The creation of any such rights will not be binding on the State Government. It should also be clearly understood that Government through the

Revenue Divisional Officer will, at all times, be entitled to revoke the permission on due notice and resume for such purposes as they deem fit, any or all portions of such assessed wastes for use by Government Departments, for assignment to private individuals or for any other purposes. In such case the village panchayat will not be entitled to any form of compensation.

7. Power of village panchayat regarding utilisation of natham poramboke—The present rules relating to natham porambokes are governed by the rules relating to the assignment of house sites under the Board's standing orders. In dealing with the question of utilisation of natham porambokes, it is to be remembered that except for the general survey sketches relating to the survey numbers included in the natham porambokes, detailed survey sketches relating to the areas actually occupied in the natham are not available in respect of many villages. Government, however, direct that in respect of all portions of natham porambokes which were unoccupied as on the 1st January 1961 it will be open to the village panchayat to utilise any such portion of the natham poramboke for any public purpose relating to village panchayat administration without prior permission from any authority. If in any case in which a dispute exists or likely to arise as to whether any particular portion of the natham porambokes is unoccupied or forms part of a private house site the village panchayat should take care not to get involved in the dispute, it should refer the matter for a decision by the Revenue Divisional Officer before taking any action on the utilisation of that portion of the natham poramboke by the village panchayat. The restriction regarding the creation of private rights mentioned above in respect of assessed wastes will apply fully in this case also. Government will also be entitled to resume any portion of the natham poramboke unoccupied. If it forms part of a private house-site, the village panchayat should take care not to get involved in the dispute; it should refer the matter for a decision by the Revenue Divisional Officer before taking any action on the utilisation of that portion of the natham porambokes by the village panchayat. The restrictions regarding the creation of private rights mentioned above in respect of assessed wastes will apply fully in this case also. Government will also be entitled to resume any portion of the natham poramboke for any purpose as they deem fit without the village panchayat being entitled to payment of any compensation for the land.

8. Rights of village panchayats-vested properties—The properties vested in the village panchayats either under the Act—*vide* paragraphs 2 to 6 above or those vested as a result of alienation proceedings under the Board's standing orders are intended to be used by the village panchayats for the purposes or purposes for which they are vested or alienated. The village panchayats will have no right to assign or alienate the properties to other persons.

9. Preparation of lists of village panchayat-vested properties—A list of all properties vested with the village panchayat shall be prepared by the Village Administrative Officer. "The list shall mention in the remarks column opened for the purpose the name of encroachers, if any, at the time it is prepared. The Revenue Inspectors in the ryotwari tract and the Estate Manager or the Assistant Manager not below the rank of a Deputy Tehsildar in the areas not yet settled under the Tamil Nadu Estates (Abolition and Conversion into Ryotwari) Act, 1948, shall authenticate the correctness of the list.

Where there are trees on these porambokes, they may either be held on tree patta or the right to their usufruct may be sold in each fasli. The Village Administrative Officer should prepare separate lists in duplicate for each class of trees. These lists should be got approved by the Revenue Inspectors in the ryotwari tract, or by the Estate Manager or the Assistant Manager in the estate areas not yet settled under the Tamil Nadu Estates (Abolition and Conversion into Ryotwari) Act, 1948. The Revenue Inspector, the Estate Manager or the Assistant Manager, as the case may be, should examine them with reference to special orders, if any, issued in the matter.

The list in respect of trees other than those held on tree-tax system will enable the village panchayat to take appropriate action in regard to them. Trees held on tree-tax system will of course be borne on the revenue accounts and the list of these trees sent to village panchayats are only intended for their information.

The Collectors are requested to take action urgently for the preparation by the Village Administrative Officers of the list of village panchayat-vested properties on the line referred to above and see that the list of the properties are checked during the next jamabandi, and that they are handed over to Village Panchayat President, and their acknowledgements obtained and filed in the Taluk office for records soon after the jamabandi is over.

If, for any reason, any list prepared and checked at the next jamabandi happens to be incomplete, a supplemental list may be prepared as soon as possible thereafter and issued to the panchayats concerned. Under Section 225 of the Tamil Nadu Panchayats Act, 1994, the Executive Authority or the Commissioner may, by an order in writing, require the Village Administrative Officer Revenue Inspector or both of any revenue village comprised within the jurisdiction of the village panchayat or panchayat union council to furnish him with information on any matter falling within such categories as may be prescribed in respect of such or any part thereof or any person or property therein.

B. Village Panchayat – Regulated Properties

10. Village panchayat-regulated porambokes— Section 134 (4) of the Tamil Nadu Panchayats Act, 1994, empowers the village panchayats to regulate the use of any poramboke other than those referred above, if the village panchayat is authorised in that behalf by an order of the Government. Orders have been issued separately in G.O. No. 76, L.A., dated the 12th January 1960, delegating to the District Collectors the power of the Government to issue orders under Section 86 (4) of the Tamil Nadu Panchayats Act, 1958 which even at present holds good as per the saving clause provision under Section 215 of the Tamil Nadu Panchayats Act, 1994.

Collectors are requested to make known to all the panchayats in the district the provision of this section. If and when any panchayat applies for authorisation to regulate the use of any poramboke for the benefit of the village, Collectors are requested ordinarily to issue such authorisation unless there are special reasons to the contrary in any particular case. The issue of such authorisation may be subject to such conditions and restrictions as Collectors may find it necessary, from time-to-time, to stipulate.

11. Manner of dealing with encroachments— In respect of these classes of public lands, it is likely that encroachments exist as on the date of the implementation of this order. Wherever such encroachments exist, the power of the village panchayat in the utilisation of such public lands on the basis of this order will not become operative until such time as the encroachment is dealt with by the Revenue Department and a decision taken either regularising the encroachment by the grant of necessary pattas or by carrying out an eviction. In respect of encroachments made by private persons in these lands after this order becomes operative, it will be open the village panchayat to complain against such encroachments to the Officers of the Revenue Department and to seek eviction under the Tamil Nadu Land Encroachments Act, 1905. This procedure would apply in respect of all lands entrusted to the village panchayat under executive instructions. In respect of lands statutorily vested in the village panchayat it will be open to the village panchayat to follow the procedure laid down in the Act, and the rules framed thereunder for getting the encroachments evicted. Whenever a dispute exists regarding the occupation of any portion of the public lands dealt with in this order, the village panchayat will refer the matter to the Revenue Divisional Officer concerned for a decision and the decision of the Revenue Divisional Officer shall be final.

12. Planting and preservation of trees on village panchayat vested properties and village panchayat-regulated properties

(i) Planting of trees on road — One of the discretionary functions vested in panchayats under Section 111 of the Tamil Nadu Panchayats Act, 1994, is the "planting and preservation of trees" on the sides of public roads in a village. The village panchayat may undertake planting and preservation of trees on the sides of all public roads in the village subject to mutually agreed terms and conditions between the village panchayat and the authority which maintains the road in case the road is not maintained by the panchayat itself.

(ii) Planting of trees, on village panchayat-vested properties and village panchayat-regulated properties — Sub-section (5) of Section 134 of the Tamil Nadu Panchayats Act, 1994, provides that the village panchayat subject to such restrictions and control as may be prescribed plant trees on any poramboke whether vested in it or not, provided the use of such poramboke is regulated by it under sub-section (2) or sub-section (4) of the Section 134 of the Act.

(iii) Government attach great importance to these provisions. They consider it essential that every village panchayat should do its best to plant and preserve trees on porambokes or wastelands, whether or not they are vested in them. This is necessary in order to increase the fuel, fodder and manurial resources in the village to the maximum practicable extent and thus contribute to the sustainable development environment and increasing the agricultural production in the village. The tree plantations thus developed will constitute valuable community assets, yielding income for the panchayats in future.

(iv) Collectors of districts are requested to bring to the notice of all village panchayats the provisions of the Act referred to above and issue instructions to them to undertake a systematic programme of plantation and preservation of trees in the villages.

(G.O. Ms. No. 317, Rural Development, dated 6th December 2000)

(G.O. Ms. No. 273, Rural Development, dated 28th December 1999)

(G.O. Ms. No. 608, Rural Development and Local Administration, dated 4th April 1960)

(G.O. Ms. No. 972, Rural Development and Local Administration, dated 4th April 1961)

5.6.4 Entrustment or Vesting of State Owned Trees to Village Panchayat

The Government have issued instructions regarding entrustment or vesting of state owned trees to village panchayat. In these instructions the Government directed that regarding trees the village panchayats be given the various responsibilities and rights mentioned against each category. Therefore, these instructions may be reiterated again.

1. The following classification of lands will be adopted for this purpose

(a) Patta land.

(b) Privately occupied land as on 1st January 1961.

(c) Road porambokes under the custody of the Highways and Rural Works Department relating to categories of roads under the direct. maintenance of the State Government.

(d) Public Works Department porambokes.

(e) Poramboke lands vested in the panchayats, in pursuance of the Tamil Nadu Panchayats Act, 1994.

(f) Land, the use regulation of which has been entrusted to the village panchayat under Section 134 (4) of the Tamil Nadu Panchayats Act, 1994.

(g) Non-vested and unentrusted public land other than those mentioned above.

(A) Patta Land

The village panchayats will have no rights over trees on patta lands. These orders will not in any way alter the rights of pattadars or Government in respect of such trees. Other privately occupied land — If trees have been planted on Government lands by private persons before 1st January 1961 or if there are trees within portions of Government land privately occupied prior to 1st January 1961, then the village panchayats or panchayat unions will have no night over such trees until the private occupation is regularised or evicted. In case the private occupation is legalised by assignment of the land to the encroacher or to any other, the village panchayat or the panchayat union is *suo motu* vacated, then the village panchayat will have the rights over the trees in accordance with the provisions of the rest of these orders depending on the category in which the land falls.

(B) Road Porambokes of the Highways and Rural Works Department

The responsibility for planting as well as protection and maintenance of trees on road margins of all highways now rests with the Department of Highways and Rural Works. According to the present procedure, the usufruct of trees as well as withered and wind-fallen trees are sold in public auction. The control over the ownership, maintenance, etc., of all standing trees on such roads should continue with the Highways and Rural Works Department. The department will also continue to be responsible for the planting of new trees and for their protection and growth. Government now direct that the Highways and Rural Works Department should lease out all trees standing on road porambokes of the Highways and Rural Works Department to the village panchayat for the exploitation of the usufructs of such trees on payment of rent by the village panchayat equal to the average annual rent realised by sale of usufructs of these trees for the last four years. Withered and wind-fallen trees will also be handed over to the panchayats for sale on payment of a price by the panchayats to the Highways and Rural Works Department. Such price will be calculated on the basis of a Seigniorage rates to be fixed. The Junior

Engineer in-Charge of the Highways should certify that the tree in question is withered or wind-fallen and will notify the concerned panchayat union to take over the tree and effect the sale. Under Section 111 (a) of the Tamil Nadu Panchayats Act, 1994, any village panchayat which desires to plant trees on such road margins may do so subject to such terms and conditions as may be laid down by the Highways and Rural Works Department. Government direct that the Assistant Engineers of the Highways and Rural Works Department be authorised to determine suitable terms and conditions for the planting of such trees by the panchayats wherever the panchayat so desire. These arrangements will relate only to road porambokes and not to other classes of porambokes in the custody and control of the Highways and Rural Works Department.

(C) Lease of Avenue Trees to Panchayats

Procedure towards the payment as well as collection of lease amount prescribed.

The usufructs of trees standing on Highways road margin can be leased out to village panchayats and in following procedure is prescribed for the lease.

(i) 60 days prior to the date of expiry of current lease, the Divisional Engineer will issue a notice (to be sent by registered post acknowledgement) to the panchayats concerned within 30 days from the date of receipt of such notice, whether the Panchayats are willing to take trees on lease for the exploitation of the usufructs and if so, remit the prescribed sum. On receipt of the letter and remittance, the Divisional Engineer will issue necessary Orders permitting the lease in favour of the panchayats.

(ii) If no reply to the said notice is received within 30 days from the panchayats concerned the Divisional Engineer will pass orders to lease out the usufructs of trees by public auction in accordance with the normal rules fixing the date of auction or some suitable date immediately after the expiry of the current lease, sending a copy of the notice to the panchayats concerned so as to enable them to write to the Divisional Engineer in this regard, if they so desire before the date of auction to reconsider his orders and to lease the usufructs to the panchayats concerned or to sell the usufructs by public auctions; and

(iii) The Divisional Engineer will pass orders for the sale of usufructs of the tree by public auction in the usual manner in accordance with the rules immediately on the expiry of 30 days in the absence of a communication from the village panchayats concerned.

(D) Public Works Department Porambokes

In respect of porambokes under the control of the Public Works Department the arrangements detailed below will apply to land appurtenant to water spreads and water-sources and will not apply to other types of lands like those appurtenant to buildings, etc. Even in respect of water spreads and water courses, the Public Works Department will lay down certain classes of lands which will be exempt for the application of this order. The areas required for the formation of Korambus or for other departmental work will be excluded from the preview of these arrangements. The Public Works Department will communicate to the Collector of the district concerned a list of exempted categories of Public Works poramboke lands for the purposes of these arrangements. In respect of all lands not so exempted, the entire rights relating to the planting, protection, maintenance, enjoyment of usufructs, sale and appropriation of the proceeds of withered and wind-fallen trees, will, in future vest with the village panchayat, concerned. Subject to such instructions as may be given by the Public Works Department it will be open to village panchayats concerned to plant trees on these lands, enjoy the usufructs, dispose of withered and wind-fallen trees and do all other things that may be necessary, for the promotion of planned tree growth. Auction sales in respect of usufructs of trees standing on these lands as well as of withered and wind-fallen trees will be conducted by the panchayat itself.

(E) Vested Public Lands

Some categories of poramboke lands including cattle-stands, cart-stands, burning and burial ground, tope and unreserved forests vest in the village panchayats under the provisions of the Tamil Nadu Panchayats Act, 1994. In respect of trees standing on all such lands vested, the entire rights of Government will stand transferred to the concerned village panchayat. The village panchayat will be entitled to the exploitation of the usufructs of trees standing on such porambokes. The village panchayat will also be entitled to the withered and wind-fallen trees on these lands. The village panchayat will conduct auctions for the sale of the usufructs as well as for the sale of withered trees and will be entitled to credit the proceeds of such sale to its own funds.

(F) Poramboke Lands Entrusted to the Village Panchayat for Use – Regulation

The provisions set out above in respect of vested land will also apply in this case.

(G) Non-vested and Unentrusted Public Lands Other Than Those Mentioned Above

The village panchayats will have no right over trees on these lands and the planting, protection, maintenance and utilisation of these trees will continue to remain with the department concerned.

(H) Private Rights by 2-C Patta, etc.

1. All existing private right by way of 2-C patta in respect of trees standing on public land (whether vested, entrusted or otherwise) will continue to remain wholly unaffected by these orders. The entire amount of 2-C tax revenue collected from private parties will hereafter be credited to the panchayats. No new 2-C patta will be granted subsequent to 30th May 1961 except on the recommendation of the village panchayat concerned. 2-C patta, if any, will be granted subject to the payment of tax at rates to be specified by the village panchayats which shall not be less than those leviable under the existing rules relating to this subject.

2. The Revenue Divisional Officer may by an order and after giving the village panchayats due notice withdraw the right of the panchayat over trees in all classes of non-vested public land including the trees planted by the village panchayats or by others, if in his opinion the trees entrusted to the village panchayat in pursuance of this order are not being properly safeguarded or maintained. In respect of the porambokes belonging to the Highways and Rural Works Department and the Public Works Department similar powers of withdrawal will also be exercised by the Divisional Engineer or the Executive Engineer concerned in consultation with the Revenue Divisional Officer. Where the Revenue Divisional Officer differs from the Divisional Engineer or the Executive Engineer the matter will be referred to the Collector whose decision in the matter shall be final. When trees are so withdrawn from the village panchayat the village panchayat shall not be entitled to claim any compensation whatsoever, even in respect of trees planted by the village panchayat itself.

3. If the immediate removal of a tree or trees on any non-vested public land including those of the Public Works Department or the Highways Department becomes necessary in the interest of public safety or public convenience, then the Revenue Divisional Officer or the Divisional Engineer or the Executive Engineer as the case may be will have the power to have the tree or trees cut and removed. Such felled trees will be handed over to the village panchayat to be sold in public auction and for crediting the proceeds of such sale to the village panchayat funds. The village panchayat will not be entitled to any compensation whatsoever even in respect of trees planted by the village panchayats.

4. When a non-vested public land is assigned by Government to a private party the order of assignment shall be deemed to cover the transfer of rights relating to the trees standing on such lands to the assignee. The village panchayat will not be entitled to the payment of any compensation in respect of such trees. The same provision will also apply in case where such public land is taken over for the use of a department of Government.

5. The ownership of all sandal wood trees on any public land existing at present or which may grow subsequent to the date of this order in the special tracts noted below will continue to be reserved to Government and village panchayats shall have no right for such trees:

Vellore
Thiruvannamalai
Cuddalore
Villupuram
Thirunelveli
Salem
Coimbatore
The Nilgiris

The Government may also by specific orders declare that specified species of trees are exempted from the application of this order and reserve such trees for exploitation by specified departments of Government.

6. In respect of trees transferred to the village panchayats in accordance with this order the village panchayats shall have the power to lease out the

usufruct and effect sale by auction of withered and wind-fallen trees. Such lease or auction will have to be done with the approval of the village panchayat and shall not be done by the village panchayat president acting solely in his capacity as Executive Authority of the panchayat. All leases auctions, sales, etc., will have to be confirmed by legal resolution of the panchayats.

Entrustment of trees standing on beds/bunds of minor irrigation sources transferred to panchayat union

The Government have considered that the entrustment of trees standing on the beds and bunds of the minor irrigation sources be transferred to the panchayat union – the concerned local bodies — will awaken among the rural public a sense of public ownership and will thereby constitute effective safeguard against their destruction. The Government, therefore, direct that all trees excepting trees held by private persons on 2-C pattas standing on the beds and bunds of minor irrigation sources transferred to the panchayat unions be entrusted to the custody and management of the panchayat union concerned.

The Government have also considered the question whether the panchayat unions in turn should be permitted to effect sub-entrustment of these trees to the village panchayats concerned in their respective areas. The Government observe that there are two issues involved in this question, *viz.*

(i) the planting of trees on the beds and bunds of the minor irrigation sources transferred to the panchayat unions and the exploitation of their usufructs, and
(ii) the exploitation of the usufructs of the trees already standing on the beds and bunds of the minor irrigation sources.

In both these cases the Government wish to make it clear that the rights and responsibilities involved vest only in the panchayat unions concerned. If, however, the village panchayats are willing to plant trees on beds and bunds of the minor irrigation sources and to protect and maintain the trees already standing on the beds and bunds of the minor irrigation sources as well as to enjoy the usufructs therefrom the Government permit the panchayat unions to effect the sub-entrustment to the village panchayats concerned for the purpose of planting trees on beds and bunds and for exploiting the usufructs of the trees already standing thereon provided the village panchayats pass necessary resolutions to that effect and apply for such entrustment. In these resolutions the village panchayats should agree to abide by any condition that may be imposed by the panchayat unions in this regard in order to ensure the safety of the beds and bunds of the minor irrigation sources. In case where the village panchayat unions make a sub-entrustment, the village panchayats shall have the responsibility to maintain the trees in proper condition and auction their usufructs from time-to-time. The proceeds of the auction shall be shared between the village panchayats and the panchayat unions on a 50: 50 basis. Where, however, the trees standing on the beds and bunds of these minor irrigation sources are maintained solely by the panchayat unions, they shall be responsible for the maintenance of the trees in good condition and they shall auction the usufructs of the trees from time-to-time. The proceeds of such auction shall be appropriated by the panchayat unions only.

As regards withered and wind-fallen trees, etc., standing on the beds and bunds of the minor irrigation sources the panchayat unions shall have the right to dispose of them and appropriate the income if their maintenance is looked after by the panchayat unions themselves. If, however, the maintenance has been entrusted to the village panchayats, the right of disposal of the withered and wind fallen trees shall be that of the village panchayats. The income out of these shall be shared as indicated above, viz., on a 50: 50 basis.

(I) Planting of trees on the beds of major irrigation sources by panchayats

Government direct that the village panchayats be permitted to undertake plantations on the beds of the Major Irrigation Sources, maintain them and enjoy the usufructs thereof subject to the following conditions:

1. The village panchayats should be permitted to occupy beds only after Public Works Department certified that the undertaking of the plantations in these portions of bed does not affect the waterway and also does not interfere with the region of the bed of the safety of the banks.
2. The Public Works Department will have the right to remove any tree if the same is found to endanger the safety of the bund or irrigation structures.
3. The trees may be planted between F.W.L. and M.W.L of the tank in the foreshore.
4. The rights of village panchayats to grow plantation will automatically cease in the

foreshore lands once such tanks are taken up under Desilting-*cum*-Reclamation Scheme. But, if plantation has been done, the Public Works Department will have the right to clear away to enable reclamation work to be done.

The Panchayats are not only entitled to plant new trees and enjoy the usufructs thereof but also entitled to the usufructs of trees already standing on the beds of the Major Irrigation sources and sale and appropriation of withered and wind-fallen trees on these tank beds.

(J) Lease of trees standing on the panchayat union road margins

The Government permit the panchayat union councils to lease out the usufructs of the trees standing on the panchayat union road margins to the village panchayats on payment of lease amount equal to the average rent realised by sale of usufructs of trees for the preceding four years.

(K) Lease of trees standing on non-vested or unentrusted poramboke land

Government direct that the trees standing on non-vested or unentrusted poramboke land under the control of the Revenue Department be leased to the village panchayats based on the average lease of the previous three years and also subject to the following conditions:

1. A proper list of the trees standing on such poramboke be made and the acknowledgment of the village panchayats be obtained.
2. The Collector should hand over only those trees which are yielding or have begun to yield.
3. Periodical inspection as specified by the Collector be made by the Staff of the Revenue Department.
4. Periodical inspection of the rental may be also be made, as there will be considerable increase in value of the usufructs after a certain period.

(L) Sale proceeds of usufructs of trees standing in non-vested porambokes

Government direct that the auction sale of usufructs of trees standing in non-vested or unentrusted porambokes in the panchayats jurisdiction shall be conducted by the Revenue Department and the panchayat concerned in the manner indicated below:

If the amount fetched in the auction by the Revenue Department is less than the amount now derived it shall be paid over to the panchayat and if the amount fetched is higher than this amount, a sum equal to this amount and 1/3 of the excess amount shall be paid to the panchayats, the balance being retained by Government in the Revenue Department, subject to the condition that the highest amount to lease got by the panchayat in any of the last three years shall be specified as the amount now derived.

(G.O. Ms. No.1150, Rural Development and Local Administration, dated 30th May 1961)

(Govt. Memo. No. 243179-P-2/61-10, Rural Development and Local Administration, dated 17th November 1962)

(G.O. Ms. No. 2526, Rural Development and Local Administration, dated 19th November 1962)

(G.O. Ms. No. 6, Rural Development and Local Administration, dated 2nd January 1964)

(Govt. Memo. No. 245170/70/P2/63-10, Rural Development and Local Administration, dated 4th April 1994)

(G.O. Ms. No. 1146, Rural Development and Local Administration, dated 26th June 1969)

(G.O. Ms. No. 2339, Rural Development and Local Administration, dated 6th November 1972)

(G.O. Ms. No. 789, Rural Development and Local Administration, dated 13th April 1967)

(G.O. Ms. No. 2172, Revenue Department, dated 4th November 1977)

5.6.5 Determination of Claim to Trees Growing on Public Roads Rules

1. Short title—These rules may be called the Tamil Nadu Panchayats (Determination of Claim to Trees Growing on Public Roads or other Property Vesting in or Belonging to Village Panchayats) Rules, 2001.

2. Definition—In these rules, unless the context, otherwise requires:

(a) "Act" means the Tamil Nadu Panchayats Act, 1994 (Tamil Nadu Act 21 of 1994);

(b) "Trees-tax system" means the trees-tax system as defined in clause (e) (ii) of paragraph 2 of Revenue Standing Order No.18, Appendix-XI of the Revenue Standing Orders, Volume I.

3. Presumption of ownership on trees standing on public roads—It shall be presumed that the Government own the trees (except those granted on tree-tax system) standing on any public road vested in a village panchayat under sub-section (1) of Section 125 of the Act and such trees shall vest in the village panchayat:

Provided the Government may, if they consider that the village panchayat has abused its rights under this rule, withdraw any such trees from the control of the village panchayat, after giving a notice to the village panchayat and considering the representation given by the village panchayat.

4. Rights of the Government to remove any tree—The Government may cut and remove any tree planted by the village panchayat on any poramboke which is vested in it under sub-section (2) of Section 134 of the Act or the use of which is regulated by the panchayat under sub-section (4) of Section 134 of the Act, on the grounds of public interest. The Government shall not be liable to pay any compensation for any tree so cut and removed. The trees so cut and removed may either be handed over to the village panchayat or be sold in public auction and where they are sold in public auction, the proceeds of such sale shall be credited to the village panchayat fund.

5. Grant of licence—The village panchayat shall have power to grant licence to any owner of land adjoining public road vested in it under sub-section (1) of Section 125 of the Act or any poramboke which is vested in the village panchayat under sub-section (2) of Section 134 of the Act or the use of which is regulated by the panchayat under sub-section 4 of Section 134 or any estate under Section 135 of the Act, for planting fruit bearing trees, for a period within which the trees may reach the fruit bearing stage on such public road or poramboke or estate subject to the proper maintenance and upkeep of the trees and other suitable terms and conditions as may be imposed.

6. Usufruct and lease of trees by village panchayat—The village panchayat shall be entitled to the usufruct of the trees on the margin of any public road vested in it under sub-section (1) of Section 125 of the Act and on the porambokes which are vested in it under sub-section (2) of Section 134 of this Act or the use of which is regulated by it under sub-section 4 of Section 134 or an estate under clause (a) of sub-section (1) of Section 135 of the Act except those held on tree-tax system and the village panchayat may lease such trees as per the procedure prescribed in the Tamil Nadu Panchayats Rules for conducting public auction of lease and sales to any person. The village panchayats shall be entitled to the income from such lease.

7. Auction of trees—(1) The village panchayat shall have the powers to cut down or sell by auction:

(a) Wind-fallen and withered trees irrespective of the fact whether they are fruit bearing trees or non-fruit bearing trees;

(b) live trees on road margins which are considered as dangerous to traffic or a danger to life or health or for executing any work by or on behalf of village panchayat, and

(c) live trees on the bunds of small tank which serve as sources of supply of drinking water, if the leaves of such trees fall into the tanks and render them unfit for drinking purposes;

(2) The income derived from the sale of the trees under sub-rule (1) shall be appropriated by the village panchayats;

(3) When the village panchayat proposes to cut or sell live trees under clause (b) or (c) of sub-rule (1), it shall obtain the sanction of the Revenue Divisional Officer:

Provided that no such sanction shall be accorded except on a report from the Tehsildar of the taluk concerned, after his personal inspection of the trees.

(4) In respect of trees fallen as a result of a cyclone, the village panchayat shall report to the Revenue Divisional Officer and obtain sanction as in sub-rule (3) to sell the trees. The income derived from the sale of such trees under this rule shall be credited to the village panchayat fund.

(G.O. Ms. No.108, Rural Development (C-4) Department, dated 28th March 2001)

5.6.6 Action against Illicit Cutting of Trees

Rules

1. Short title—These rules may be called the Tamil Nadu Panchayats (Action against Illicit Cutting of Trees) Rules, 2001.

2. Reporting of illicit cutting of tree—The Panchayat Assistant/Rural Welfare Officer Grade-I shall report every case of illicit cutting of trees standing on road margins and lands belonging to or vesting with the village panchayat or in panchayat union council or in district panchayat, as the case may be to the Executive Authority or the Commissioner or the Secretary, as the case may be. The Executive Authority or the Commissioner or the Secretary as the case may be shall there upon send a report based on such reports received from the Panchayat Assistant/Rural Welfare Officer Grade-II to the Tehsildar. The Executive Authority or the Commissioner or the Secretary, as the case may be, shall within seven days from the date on which the said report has been sent, inform the Tehsildhar of the action taken or proposed to be taken against the person or persons responsible for the illicit cutting. If no communication is received from the Executive Authority or the Commissioner or the Secretary, as the case may be within seven days from the date of the report received by him, the Tehsildar shall after ascertaining the factual position, he himself lay the complaint of the said offence before the appropriate Judicial Magistrate. Whenever the Panchayat Assistant/Rural Welfare Officer, Grade-II apprehends an offender in the act of illicit cutting of trees, seize the cut tree trunk and branches and handover them to the Executive Authority or the Commissioner or the Secretary, as the case may be, or to any person authorized by him for that purpose.

3. Failure of panchayat Assistant/Rural Welfare Officer Grade-II to report about illicit cutting of tree— In a case of illicit cutting of tree, in the panchayat area, wherein the Panchayat Assistant/Rural Welfare Officer Grade-II, fails to report the same and where the Executive Authority or the Commissioner or the Secretary, as the case may be, notices the incident, the Executive Authority or the Commissioner or the Secretary, as the case may be shall be competent to take action as specified in these rules.

4. Assessment of value of the tree and compounding of offences—The Executive Authority or the Commissioner or the Secretary, as the case may be, within two days from the receipt of the report of illicit cutting of tree from the Panchayat Assistant/Rural Welfare Officer Grade-II, shall inspect the site of the offence, satisfy himself about the truth of the report, take measurements of the trunk of the tree in question, conduct enquiries in the vicinity, record statements of any possible witnesses, if available, who might disclose the identity and the name of the offender, if mentioned in the report of the Panchayat Assistant/Rural Welfare Officer Grade-II or revealed from the evidence of the witnesses, the Executive Authority or the Commissioner or the Secretary, as the case may be, shall decide whether to prosecute the offender or to compound the offence as per Rule 2 of the Tamil Nadu Panchayats (Composition of Offence) Rules, 2000. In case the cut tree parts are seized by the Panchayat Assistant/Rural Welfare Officer Grade-II, and handed over to the Executive Authority or the Commissioner or the Secretary as the case may be and where he decides to compound the offence the Panchayat Assistant/Rural Welfare Officer Grade-II as the case may be shall assess the value of the tree parts by following the procedure prevailing in the Revenue Department and communicate the same to the Executive Authority or the Commissioner or the Secretary, as the case may be. The Executive Authority or the Commissioner or the Secretary, as the case may be shall measure the cut tree parts, assess all the value of the tree parts and decide quantum of penalty by way of compounding fee to be imposed which shall represent the compensation for the offence committed and shall be in terms of number of times the value of tree, which shall not be less than twice the value of the tree assessed and then pass orders for compounding of the offence. The orders so passed shall be communicated to the offender by means of a written notice, to be served on him in the manner specified in the Annexure, informing him of the offence committed, enquiries made thereon, the decision made requiring the offender to pay the value of cut tree parts assessed and the amount of the compounding fee imposed. These amounts shall be mentioned separately in the said notice for remittance by the offender within a time to be specified in the notice of the period being not less than fifteen days, or in default, face imminent prosecution. If it is decided to confiscate the seized tree parts, the offender shall not be asked to pay the value of the tree parts seized. So such a notice shall also indicate whether the seizure of the tree parts involved in the offence will be returned to the offender or will be confiscated. In case, the offender remits the amount mentioned in the above notice, into the funds of the village panchayat or the panchayat union council or the district panchayat as the case may be, within the period prescribed, it shall be at the discretion of the administration, either to accept the compounding of the offence or proceed with the prosecution. The fact of compounding the offence and the payment of amount by the offender shall be reported to the Tehsildar. Where an offender after receiving the notice referred to above, fails to respond to the notice within the period specified thereon or where the Executive Authority or the Commissioner or the Secretary, as the case may be, desires to prosecute the offender instead of adopting the method of compounding the offence, the Executive Authority or the Commissioner or the Secretary, as the case may be, shall lay a complaint with the concerned Judicial Magistrate.

5. Filing of complaint with the police—Where the name of the offender is not mentioned in the report of the Panchayat Assistant/Rural Welfare Officer Grade-II or could not even be identified during the enquiries conducted by the Executive Authority or the Commissioner or the Secretary, as the case may be, he shall file a complaint with the police having jurisdiction over the place of crime within five days of the date of receipt of report of the Panchayat Assistant/Rural Welfare Officer Grade-II, obtain a copy of first information report from the police station and intimate the fact to the Tehsildar.

ANNEXURE

(See Rule 4)

Notice for compounding of offence for illicit cutting of tree standing on the road margins and lands belonging to or vesting with the Village Panchayat or Panchayat Union Councillor, District Panchayat.

__________ Village Panchayat/Panchayat Union/District Panchayat __________

District.
Post
Pin Code
To
Thiru/Tmt./Messrs.
Village
Post
District
Sir,

Whereas this Village Panchayat/Panchayat Union/District Panchayat has decided illicit cutting of trees standing on the road margins and lands belonging to or vesting with the Village Panchayat/Panchayat Union/Panchayat Union Council.

And whereas, the Executive Authority/the Commissioner or the Secretary has inspected the site where illicit cutting of trees to place and satisfied about the truth of the report of illicit cutting trees.

And whereas, the Executive Authority/the Commissioner or the Secretary has come to conclusion that you have committed the said offence of the illicit cutting of trees.

And whereas, it is decided to compound the offence of the illicit cutting of trees in rule of the Tamil Nadu Panchayat (Composition of the Offence) Rules, 2000.

This notice is issued to you that the value of the tree illicit cut is assessed at Rs.__________ (Rupees__________only) and the set offence is compounded __________times (Not less than two times) of the value of the illicitly cut tree and you are informed that the illicitly cut tree will be confiscated/returned you are informed to pay totaly Rs. __________(Rupees__________only) in the office of the undersigned within __________days (Not less than fifteen days), failing which action will be taken against you as per the Tamil Nadu Panchayat (Action against Illicit Cutting of Tree), Rules 2001.

Yours faithfully
Executive Authority for Commissioner
__________Village Panchayat/Panchayat Union Council

(G.O. Ms. No.179, Rural Development (C4), dated 13th August 2001)

5.7 TAXATION, ACCOUNTS AND AUDIT

5.7.1 Assessment and Collection of Taxes

1. Short title—These rules may be called the Tamil Nadu Village Panchayats (Assessment and Collection of Taxes) Rules, 1999.

2. Definition—In these rules, unless the context otherwise requires:

(a) "Act" means, the Tamil Nadu Panchayats Act, 1994 (Tamil Nadu Act, 21 of 1994).

(b) "Schedule" means, the schedule appended to these rules; and

(c) "Form" means, the form appended to these rules.

3. Determination of tax—The Executive Authority shall, save as otherwise provided in these rules, determine the tax to which each person or property is liable:

Provided that in the case of taxes payable by the person exercising the functions of the Executive

Authority, the assessment shall be made by the village panchayat.

4. Power to amend assessment—(1) If at any time it appears to the village panchayat that any person or property has been inadequately assessed or inadvertently or improperly omitted from the assessment book relating to any tax, or that there is any clerical or arithmetical error in the said book, it may direct the Executive Authority to amend the said book in such manner as it deems just or necessary:

Provided that no such direction shall be given, where it involves an increase in the assessment, unless the person concerned shall have been afforded a reasonable opportunity to show cause to the village panchayat as to why the assessment book should not be amended as proposed.

(2) Such amendment shall be deemed to have taken effect on the earliest date

(i) In the current year or in the two years immediately preceding it, if the house tax is levied annually, and

(ii) In the half year or in the two half years immediately preceding in the house tax is levied half yearly. In the case of other taxes which the circumstances justifying the amendment existed.

5. Receipt for payment of tax—(1) The Executive Authority shall give to every person making payment of a tax a receipt therefor signed by him or by some person duly authorized by him in that behalf.

(2) Such receipt shall specify

(i) the date of payment of the tax;

(ii) the name of the person to whom it is issued;

(iii) the tax in respect of which the payment has been made;

(iv) the period for which payment had been made; and

(v) the amount paid as tax and the amount of interest, if any, collected under sub-rule (3) of Rule 17.

A. Assessment of Tax

6. Basis of levy of house-tax—(1) Every village panchayat shall have power to assess the levy and collect the house-tax on the basis referred to under Section 172 of the Act and in accordance with the other provisions of the Act. The village panchayat concerned shall decide on the basis of plinth area of house at the rate specified in schedule 1 of the Act subject to provision of sub-section (3) Section 172 of the Act.

(2) House-tax shall be levied by the village panchayat either on half yearly or on annual basis as notified by the Government as per sub-section (3) of Section 172 of the Act.

(3) Any house-tax so levied shall not be altered or modified during the period of assessment year except with the prior approval of the Inspector:

Provided that no such prior approval of the Inspector is required if the enhancement of the tax is ordered by the village panchayat under sub-rule (1) of Rule 3.

7. Classification of houses—(1) When a proportionate rate has been adopted by the village panchayat, it may group the houses in the village into classes to simplify the calculation and the collection of the tax.

(2) When a progressive rate has been adopted by the village panchayat, it shall

(i) specify principles of classification (as that a certain sum, which shall be tax-free, shall be deducted from the assessment of each house, or that progression shall be from a certain percentage in the lowest to a certain percentage in the highest class); and

(ii) settle the precise number and limits of each class.

(3) The village panchayat shall not in either case so arrange the classes as to affect substantially the principle of taxation, whether proportionate or progressive, and the number of classes shall in no case be less than six.

(4) Before passing a resolution imposing a tax for the first time or increasing the rate of an existing tax, the village panchayat shall publish a notice in at least one Tamil Newspaper and also on the notice board of the office of the village panchayat and in such other places within the village panchayat limits as may be specified by the village panchayat and by beat of drum, of its intention proposed to levy any tax or increase the existing rate of tax, fixing a reasonable period, not being less than one month for submission of objections and consider such objection, if any received within the stipulated period before passing the said resolution.

8. Preparation of house-tax assessment list—The panchayat assistant or part-time clerk or any other person specified by the Government having jurisdiction over the village panchayat shall prepare and furnish to the Executive Authority, the house-tax assessment list in such Form as may be specified by the Government from time-to-time, duly signed. The Executive Authority shall approve the house-tax assessment list so prepared by him.

9. Preparation of assessment book—The Executive Authority shall on the receipt of the list specified in Rule 8, cause the assessment book (House-tax Demand Register) to be prepared. Such assessment book will show in distinct columns, the name of the owner and of the occupier of such house, the class, if any under which such house is taxed, the amount of the tax due and the yearly or half year for which the tax is payable.

10. Notice for inspection of the assessment book—As soon as the assessment book is prepared, the Executive Authority shall, by beat of drum in the village panchayat, give public notice thereof, the place and the time where the book may be inspected.

11. Manner of amendment of assessment book—(1) The Executive Authority may amend the assessment book at any time between one general revision and another by inserting any house therein or removing any house therefrom or by altering the valuation or classification of any house, or the amount of tax payable in respect thereof, subject to any other rules which the Government may make in this behalf, by substituting therein for the name of the owner of any house, the name of any other person who has succeeded by transfer or otherwise to the ownership of the house.

(2) Such amendment shall be deemed to have taken effect on the first day of the half year or year in which it is made:

Provided that, where the amendment is rendered necessary by reason of the fixation of the fair rent of a house under the Tamil Nadu Buildings (Lease and Rent Control) Act, 1960 (Tamil Nadu Act 18 of 1960), the amendment shall have effect as from the date on which the fair rent was so fixed:

Provided further that the decision of the Executive Authority, in any disputed case of transfer of ownership of a house shall not give the transferee a legal title to the house.

(3) In every case in which, between one general revision and another, the Executive Authority assesses any house-tax for the first time or increases the tax levied on any house other than in consequence of a general enhancement of the rates at which the house-tax is leviable, the Executive Authority shall issue a special notice to the owner or occupier of such house. Any objection or representation against such levy or increase in tax received shall be considered by the Executive Authority if it reaches the office of the village panchayat within sixty days from the date of service of such notice in the case of the Government, a Railway Administration or a Company and within thirty days in other cases.

(4) When the assessment book has been prepared for the first time and whenever a general revision of such book has been completed, the Executive Authority shall give public notice stating that any revision petition shall be considered if they reach the office of the village panchayat within a period of sixty days from the date of such notice in the case of the Government, Railway Administration or a Company and thirty days in other cases. The notice shall also be displayed on the notice board of the village panchayat and on the same day be announced in the village by beat of drum:

Provided that in every case where there is an enhancement in the assessment already levied, the Executive Authority shall also send in writing to the owner and occupier of house concerned:

Provided further that in every case where a special notice is required to be served on the owner or occupier under the first proviso, the period of sixty days and thirty days as the case may be referred to in this rule shall be calculated from the date of service of such special notice.

12. Revision petition against assessment—Any person may, at any time not being less than thirty days or more than sixty days before the end of a half year or year, move the Executive Authority by a revision petition to reduce the tax to which he is liable for the forthcoming half year or year on the ground that the annual rental value or capital value or on the plinth areas, as the case may be, of the house in respect of which the tax is imposed has decreased since the assessment of the house was last made or revised.

13. Intimation of the result of the revision petition—Immediately after the receipt of a revision petition preferred under sub-rule (3) of Rule 11 or Rule 12 the Executive Authority shall pass final orders on such revision petition within two months of its receipt and shall inform the petitioner or his authorised agent in writing, of the orders passed thereon, and shall direct him to pay the amount fixed on revision within fifteen days after the date of receipt of such intimation, or, if the amount is not yet due within fifteen days from the date on which it becomes due, and shall, if necessary cause the assessment book to be corrected:

Provided that, in exceptional circumstances, if any, to be specified in writing, no revision petition may be kept pending the half year or year to which such revision petition relates to.

14. General revision of assessment book—(1) The Executive Authority shall not be bound to cause new list or assessment book to be prepared every half year or year but may adopt those of the preceding half year or year with such amendment as has been or may be made for the preceding half year or year.

(2) A general revision of assessment book shall be made by the Executive Authority once in every five years:

Provided that this provision shall not apply to a fresh revision ordered by the Inspector under sub-rule (6).

(3) (a) Notwithstanding anything contained in sub-rule (2), the Inspector may for sufficient cause, from time-to-time by order,

(i) Postpone the general revision of assessment book, or

(ii) Stay the proceedings relating to the general revision of assessment book, for a period of one or more half years at a time but not exceeding in any case four half-years:

Provided that such postponement or stay shall not affect any subsequent general revision of assessment book.

(b) Where the stay is vacated or the period of stay expires, the Inspector may direct that proceedings for the general revision of assessment book shall be either commenced *de novo* or continued from the stage at which such proceedings were stayed.

(4) The Executive Authority shall give public notice of the amendment referred to in sub-rule (1) and of the general assessment referred to in sub-rule (2) in the manner provided in Rule 11.

(5) The general assessment shall be deemed to have taken effect on the first day of the half-year or year in which the notice under sub-rule (4) is given.

(6) The Inspector may, by order in writing, cancel the general revision made under sub-rule (2). If in his opinion, the revision made discloses that the assessment has been enhanced or reduced without reasonable basis and shall direct the conduct of fresh revision by any person authorized by him in this behalf (other than the person whose revision is cancelled under this rule) in respect of such period as he considers necessary. The procedure for the revision so ordered by the Inspector shall be in the manner provided for in these rules for the assessment of house-tax:

Provided that the revision ordered by the Inspector under this rule shall not have the effect of postponing the next general revision.

15. Exemption of specified classes of houses from house-tax—The following buildings shall, if they fall within the meaning of house as defined in the Act, be exempt from the house-tax

(a) Buildings set apart for public worship and either actually so used or used for no other purpose.

(b) Choultries for the occupation of which no rent is charged and choultries where the rent charged for the occupation is used exclusively for charitable purposes.

(c) Buildings used for educational purposes including hostels and libraries which are open to the public, and public buildings used for charitable purpose of sheltering the destitute or animals.

(d) Such ancient monuments protected under the Ancient Monuments Preservation Act, 1904, or parts thereof, as are not used as residential quarters or as public offices.

(e) Charitable hospitals and dispensaries and other buildings exclusively used for charitable purposes.

(f) Such hospitals and dispensaries maintained by Railway Administrations as may, from time-to-time be notified by the Government.

(g) Buildings, belonging to village panchayats.

(h) Building of the Forest Department situated within the forest area which are within the jurisdiction of a village panchayat.

(i) Light houses,

(ii) All cattle pounds maintained by the Revenue Department, and

(iii) Cyclone shelters:

Provided that nothing contained in clauses (a) and (c) shall be deemed to exempt from house-tax if any building for which rent is payable by the person or persons using the same for the purposes referred to in the said clauses:

Provided further that educational institution (not commercial in nature) exempted from levy of house-tax, immediately before the commencement of the Act shall continue to be exempted under the said Act.

Explanation. The exemption granted under this rule shall not extend to residential quarters attached to schools or colleges not being the hostels or residential quarters attached to hospitals, dispensaries and libraries.

16. Manner of ascertaining the annual or capital value of houses—(1) For purposes of assessment of house-tax, the capital value of a house shall be deemed to be the total of the estimated value of the land determined in accordance with the procedure laid down in the rules prescribed for such purpose and the present estimated cost of erecting the house after deducting for depreciation a reasonable amount which shall in no case be less than ten per cent of such cost.

(2) Machinery and furniture shall be excluded for purpose of determining the value under this rule.

(a) The annual rental value of house shall be deemed to be the gross annual rent at which the house may reasonably be expected to let from month to month, or from year to year less a deduction of ten per cent of such annual rent and the said deduction shall be in lieu of all allowances for repairs or on any other account whatsoever.

(b) In the case of:

(i) Any Government or railway building falling within the definition of house under the Act.

(ii) Any building falling within the definition aforesaid of a class not ordinarily let and the gross annual rent which cannot in the opinion of the Executive Authority be estimated, the annual value shall be deemed to be six per cent of its capital value:

Provided that in the case of buildings in industrial estates and developed plot estates, where the amenities are provided by the Industries Department or any other authority, the annual value shall be deemed to be four per cent of its capital value.

17. Persons liable to pay house-tax—(1) The house-tax shall be paid by the owner of the house within thirty days after the commencement of the half year of sixty days after the commencement of the year according to the period of levy.

(2) If the owner of a house fails to pay the whole or any part of the house-tax due thereon within the stipulated time, the Executive Authority may, if the said tax has remained unpaid for more than twelve months, require by a notice in writing the occupier for the time being of such house, to pay the amount within a specified period, not being less than fifteen days in the case of half yearly levy and thirty days in the case of annual levy.

(3) Every village panchayat may collect an interest for the belated payment of tax due to it at rupees one and fifty paise or two rupees as may be decided by the village panchayat concerned for every hundred rupees of the tax for every month of belated payment. The interest shall be levied after thirty days of the commencement of the year if the tax is levied on half yearly basis or sixty days of the commencement of the year if the tax is levied on yearly basis.

18. Obligation of transferor and transferee to give notice of transfer—(1) Whenever the title of any person, primarily liable to the payment of house-tax for any house to or over such house is transferred, the person whose title is transferred and the person to whom the title is transferred shall, within three months after the execution of the instrument of transfer or after it registration if it is registered or after the transfer is effected if no instrument is executed, give notice of such transfer to the Executive Authority.

(2) In the event of the death of any person primarily liable as aforesaid, the person to whom the title of the deceased is transferred or inherited as heir or otherwise, shall give written notice of such transfer to the Executive Authority within one year from the date of death of the deceased.

(3) The notice to be given under this rule shall be in such Forms as the Executive Authority may specify and the transferee or the person to whom the title passes as the case may be, shall, if so required, be bound to produce before the Executive Authority any document evidencing the transfer or succession.

(4) Every person who makes a transfer as aforesaid fails to give such notice to the Executive Authority shall, in addition to any other liability which he incurs through such failure, continue to be liable for the payment of house-tax assessed on the house transferred until he gives notice or until the transfer shall have been recorded in the village panchayat registers, but nothing in this rule shall be held to affect the liability of the transferee for the payment of the said tax.

19. Vacancy remission—(1) When any house or portion of a house has been vacant for ninety or more consecutive days in a half year or one hundred and eighty or more consecutive days in a year, the Executive Authority shall, on demand by the assessed, remit to so much, not exceeding two-thirds of the amount of the tax, as is proportionate to the number of days during which the house was vacant in the half year or year.

(2) Every demand for remission under sub-rule (1) shall be made during the half year or year in respect of which the remission is sought or in the following half year or year and not afterwards.

(3) (a) No demand for such remission shall be entertained unless the owner of the house or his agent has previously given notice to the Executive Authority, the house is vacant and the period in respect of which the remission is made shall be calculated from the date of delivery of such notice.

(b) Every such notice shall expire in a half year or year during which it is so delivered and shall take no effect thereafter.

20. Owners obligation to give notice of construction, re-construction or demolition of buildings—

(1) (a) If any house in the village panchayat is constructed or re-constructed the owner shall give notice thereof to the Executive Authority within fifteen days from the date of completion or occupation of the house, whichever is earlier.

(b) If such date falls within the last two months of a half year or four months of a year the owner shall subject to notice being given under clause (a) be entitled to a remission of the whole of the tax or enhanced tax, as the case may be payable in respect of the house for that half year or year.

(c) If such date falls within the first four months of a half year or eight months of a year the owner shall, subject to notice being given under clause (b) be entitled to a remission of so much not exceeding a half of the tax or enhanced tax as the case may be payable in respect of the house for that half year or year as is proportionate to the number of days in that half year or year preceding such date.

(d) Any owner who commits a breach of the provisions of this rule shall be punishable with fine which may extend to one hundred rupees. Or in case of a continuing breach, with fine not exceeding fifteen rupees for everyday during which the breach continues after conviction for the first breach.

(2) (a) If any house in a village is demolished or destroyed, the owner shall, until notice thereof is given to the Executive Authority be liable at his discretion for the payment of the tax which would have been payable had the house not been demolished or destroyed.

(b) If such notice is given within the first two months of a half year or four months of a year, the owner shall be entitled for a remission of the whole of the tax payable in respect of the house for that half year or year.

(c) If such notice is given within the last four months of a half year or eight months of a year, the owner shall be entitled to a remission of so much not exceeding a half of the tax payable in respect of the house for that half year or year as is proportionate to the number of days in that half year or year succeeding the demolition of destruction as the case may be.

21. Remission of tax in areas included or excluded in the middle of a half year—(1) If any area is included within a panchayat village in the middle of a half year the owner of every house in such area shall

(a) If the date of such inclusion falls within the last two months of a half year or four months of a year, not be liable to pay any house-tax in respect thereof for that half year or year; and

(b) If such date falls within the first four months of a half year or eight months of a year, be entitled to a remission of so much not exceeding a half of the house-tax payable in respect thereof for that half year or year, as is proportionate to the number of days in that half year or year preceding such date.

(2) If any area is excluded from a panchayat village the owner of every house in such area shall be entitled

(a) If the date falls of such exclusion within first two months of a half year or four months of a year, to a remission of the whole of the house tax payable for that half year or year; and

(b) If such date falls within the last four months of a half year, or eight months of a year, to remission of so much amount not exceeding a half of the house-tax payable in respect of thereof for that half year or year to the number of days in that half year or year succeeding such days.

(3) No remission shall be granted under sub-rule (2) in respect of any house unless an application for such remission is made to the Executive Authority within three months from the date of the exclusion of the area in which the house is situated.

22. Transfer of registry of ownership of houses—In effecting changes in the ownership of properties in the assessment book on the application of any party, whether at a general revision or between one general revision and another, the Executive Authority shall observe the following provisions, namely

(a) In every case of absolute transfer of title, the registry of properties may be altered to correspond with the transfer of its ownership on the application of both the parties to the transfer or either of them, provided that the application for change of registry is in every case made in writing and is signed by the party or parties making it. It may be sent by post or presented in person or by duly authorized agent, or through an officer of the Registration department. Where such an application is presented by both the parties and one of them is the registered owner, change of registry as requested may be ordered at once. But where only one of the parties to the transfer makes the application, notice shall be served on the other party. Where the registered owner is not a party to the transaction notice shall also be issued to him whether the application for transfer of registry is presented by both the parties or one of them. If the registered owner objects to the proposed transfer, no change shall be made unless the person who claims to be the owner produces satisfactory legal evidence. Where only one party of the transaction applies and the other either objects or is silent, the parties should be connected by a complete chain of documents. When the chain is not complete, it should be filled in by other evidence, such as statements of respectable persons and tax receipts. A month's time shall be allowed for filing objections and if any objection is found to be valid transfer or registry shall not be made.

(b) In the case of transfer of title of properties in the name of a decree holder with reference to a decree of a civil court or of purchaser in auction sales held in execution of a civil court decree, change of registry may be made at once on the application of any of the parties to the suite or of the auction purchaser and on the production of an authenticated copy of the decree or a certificate of sale, as the case may be, and a certificate of delivery of possession in pursuance thereof provided the transfer is from the registered owner. When the transfer is from a person who is not the registered owner, notice shall be given to the registered owner in the manner provided in sub-rule (2) before a change of registry is made. Where, however a certificate of delivery of possession cannot be produced, as for instance, where on decree passed possession is conceded without execution proceedings and the decree is apparently final, the case shall be dealt with as provided in sub-rule (2) in regard to application for change of registry presented only by one of the parties of the transfer.

(c) In cases where transfer of registry is sought under a declaratory decree on which no execution can be taken out namely, where the decree merely declares the title to be vested in a particular person, so as to entitle him to registration the Executive Authority may, on the production of any authenticated copy of such decree, at once make the transfer of registry.

(d) (1) The Executive Authority may on production of satisfactory proof, order transfer or registry in the case of transfers which accrue by succession.

(2) There shall be an appeal to the village panchayat against the order of the Executive Authority under the rule making or refusing to make a transfer of registry. Such appeal shall be presented within thirty days after the date of receipt of the order appealed against.

23. A tax on agricultural land—(1) The tax on agricultural land as referred to in sub-section (3) of Section 171 of the Act shall be leviable by the village panchayat for a specific purpose and shall decide the rate of tax, period of tax and total period to levy of such tax based on the purpose and paying capacity of the assessee

(a) repairs to irrigation channels and tanks in respect of which no Kudimaramat fee is levied under sub-section (2) of Section 133 of the Act.

(b) construction, maintenance repair, extension or improvement of water works or drainage works.

(c) lighting by electricity or any other means.

(d) construction of a road, or a bridge or culvert.

(e) protection of trees, plants and crops.

(f) raising matching contribution for any programme of development specified in panchayat development Schematic Budget or that may be included in it from time-to-time and the levy of such tax shall take effect from the first day of the half year or the year following that in which it is sanctioned.

(g) construction or maintenance of soil conservation works:

Provided that the tax for the purpose specified in clause (g) shall be leviable on such agricultural land as is benefited by the construction or maintenance of works referred to in that clause.

(h) for any other purpose which will subserve the causes of agricultural development and improve the productivity of agricultural land.

Explanation. (1) For the purpose of this rule, the tax on agricultural land levied by the village panchayat is in no way related to land revenue, local cess or local cess surcharge collected by the Revenue Department.

(2) The rate of the tax shall be on the basis of the extent and classification of land and the source of irrigation of land as provided in the revenue record:

Provided that for the purpose of adopting different rates for different classes of lands under this sub-rule, such lands may be classified according to the number and nature of crops raised there on or the nature of the sources of irrigation.

(3) (a) Every proposal for the levy of the tax shall be submitted to the Assistant Director (Panchayats) through the Block Development Officer (village panchayats). The Assistant Director (panchayats) shall forward it to the District Collector who is the sanctioning authority for the levy of tax on agricultural lands.

(b) Every such proposal shall be accompanied by

(i) resolution of the village panchayat passed at a meeting specially convened for the purpose and supported by not less than one-half of the sanctioned strength of the village panchayat specifying the levy of tax either half yearly or yearly the purpose for which the rate at which and the total levy period for which the tax is to be levied.

(ii) a Statement showing the receipts and charges under the various heads of accounts for the three years preceding the year in which the proposal is made.

(iii) the budget estimate for the year in which the proposal is made.

(iv) particulars of the approximate or estimated cost of the work in respect of which the tax is proposed to be levied and the amount of tax likely to be realised in a half year or a year.

(4) The rate at which and the period for which the tax to be levied shall be specified in the order sanctioning the levy of the tax. The period specified in the order may be extended from time-to-time, if necessary, in order that the purpose for which the tax is levied may be fulfilled:

Provided that the village panchayat may for sufficient reason, and with the approval of the sanctioning authority, alter the rate, suspend or cancel the levy of the tax within the period so specified in the order.

(5) The proceeds of the tax shall form a separate fund, earmarked for the purpose for which it is levied and a separate account shall be maintained for the transactions relating to the fund.

(6) The rules relating to levy and collection of taxes on house shall apply *mutatis mutandis* to the assessment and collection of the tax on agricultural land.

24. Appeal against imposition of taxes—An appeal shall lie to the village panchayat against the levy or an enhancement of the tax in respect of the following taxes:

(a) The assessment and imposition of house-tax and an order of the Executive Authority under Rule 13 upon a revision petition.

(b) The assessment and levy of tax on agricultural land.

(c) Any person who is aggrieved by the decision of the village panchayat under clause (a) or (b) may prefer a petition of revision within thirty days after receipt of orders of the village panchayat to the Inspector. The Inspector shall pass orders on such revision petition on the merits of the claims within a reasonable time and such orders of the Inspector shall be final.

25. Limitation for appeal

(1) (i) No appeal to village panchayat shall be entertained (1) unless it reaches the office of the village panchayat within fifteen days after the receipt of demand notice or an order under Rule 13 as the case may be, and

(ii) Unless, except when the Executive Authority otherwise directs on the ground of poverty, the tax in respect of which the appeal is presented has been paid or deposited at the office of the village panchayat within the period specified in clause (1).

(2) The village panchayat may admit an appeal presented after the expiry of the period specified sub-rule (1) but not exceeding fifteen days thereafter if it is satisfied that the party concerned had sufficient cause for not presenting it within the said period.

(3) On receipt of an appeal made under sub-rule (1) or (2) the village panchayat may, after giving the appellant an opportunity of being heard, shall pass appropriate orders on merits by allowing the appeal or modify the orders appealed against or rejecting the appeal.

26. Powers of a panchayat to cancel or modify the orders of the Executive Authority—The village panchayat may, of its own motion or otherwise, cancel or modify any order passed by the Executive Authority reducing or remitting a tax.

27. Correction of assessment book and refund of house-tax on appeal— (1) The assessment book in respect of house-tax shall be corrected in accordance with any orders passed by the village panchayat on appeal, in the event of the amount of any tax being reduced or remitted by the village panchayat, the Executive Authority shall grant a refund of the tax already paid.

(2) The village panchayat may, on appeal pass orders reducing such tax to such an extent upto which such, enhanced amount assessed by the Executive Authority could be justified.

28. Assessment of tax when final—Subject to the provisions of the Act when no appeal or revision is made as herein before provided the tax determined by the Executive Authority shall be final. When an appeal or revision is made, the order passed in appeal or in revision against assessment of tax made by the village panchayat thereon shall be final:

Provided that where any assessment or demand is not in accordance with the assessment book, nothing in this rule shall be deemed to prohibit a fresh assessment or demand of the tax being made in accordance therewith.

B. Collection of Tax

29. Collection of tax or fee due to a village panchayat— Any tax or fee due to village panchayat shall be collected by the panchayat Assistant or part-time clerk of the village panchayat appointed for this purpose.

30. Mode of collection—(1) When house-tax or tax on agricultural land is due from any person and where coercive action becomes absolutely necessary the panchayat Assistant or part-time clerk as the case may be shall serve upon such person a demand notice for house-tax or tax on agricultural land for the sum due before he proceeds to enforce the provisions of Rule 31.

(2) A demand notice for house-tax or tax on agricultural land under sub-rule (1) shall be signed by the Executive Authority or bear his facsimile, and also by the panchayat Assistant or part-time clerk as the case may be and shall contain

(a) a description of the house or agricultural land and a statement of the period for which the tax is due; and

(b) a notice of the liability incurred in default of payment.

(3) No tax for any year or half years whichever is applicable shall be recovered from any person in the manner laid down in Rule 31 unless the bill is served upon such person either within that year or half years or in the succeeding year or half years whichever is applicable:

Provided that where the assessment book has been amended under Rule 3, the bill may be served either in the year or half years whichever is applicable in which the amendment was made or in the succeeding year or half year whichever is applicable.

(4) Nothing contained in this rule or in Rule 31 shall preclude the village panchayat from taking appropriate legal proceedings in a Court for the tax due to it.

31. Distraint and sale of movable property— (1) If the amount of the tax demanded is not paid within fifteen days from the service of the demand notice referred in Rule 13 and if the person from whom the tax is due has not shown sufficient cause to the satisfaction of the Executive Authority of the village panchayat concerned for non-payment of tax the Executive Authority may recover by taking distraint proceedings under his warrant and sale of the movable property of the defaulter. The amount due on account of the tax together with the warrant fee and the distraint fee and with such further sum as will satisfy the probable charges that will be incurred in connection with the detention and sale of the property so distrained:

Provided that the movable property described in the proviso to sub-section (1) of Section 60 of the

Code of Civil Procedure, 1908 (Central Act V of 1908) shall not be liable to distraint.

(2) If for any reason the distraint or a sufficient distraint of the defaulter's properties is impracticable, the Executive Authority may prosecute the defaulter before the Criminal Court having jurisdiction.

(3) The warrant under sub-rule (1) shall be in Form I and for each such warrant a fee of one rupee shall be levied.

(4) Under a special order in writing of the Executive Authority who signed the distraint warrant, the panchayat Assistant or part-time clerk as the case may be, between sunrise and sunset, break open any outer or inner door or window of any building in order to make the distraint, if he has reasonable grounds for believing that such building contains property which is liable to seizure and if, after notifying, his authority and purpose and duly demanding admittance, he cannot otherwise obtain admittance:

Provided that he shall not enter or break open the door of any apartment appropriated to women until he has given three hours notice of his intention and has given such women an opportunity to withdraw.

32. Seizure of property—(1) The panchayat Assistant or part-time clerk as the case may be shall, before making the distraint demand payment of the tax due and warrant fee. If the tax and fee are paid, no distraint shall be made, but if the tax or fee is not paid the panchayat Assistant or part-time clerk as the case may be shall

(a) seize such movable property of the defaulter as he may think necessary having regard to the tax arrears,

(b) make an inventory of the property seized, and

(c) give to the person in possession of the property seized at the time of seizer, a copy of the inventory and the notice of sale in the Form II:

Provided that a period of seven days shall be allowed for paying the amount due and redeeming the property seized.

(2) The distraint shall not be excessive, that is to say the property distrained shall be as nearly as possible equal in value to the tax due by the defaulter together with all expenses incidental to the warrant distraint detention and sale.

33. Sale of property seized—(1) If the amount due by the defaulter on account of the tax, the warrant fee and distraint fee and expenses incidental to the detention of the property are not paid within the period of seven days specified in the notice given under Rule 32 and if the distraint warrant is not suspended by the Executive Authority, the property seized or a sufficient portion thereof shall be sold by public auction under the orders of the Executive Authority who shall apply the proceeds of the sale to the payment of the amount due on account of the tax, the warrant fee, the distraint fee and the expenses incidental to the detention and the sale of the property and shall return to the person in whose possession the property was at the time of seizure, any property or sum which may remain after the sale and the application of the proceeds thereof as aforesaid. If the proceeds for the sale are insufficient for the payment of the amount due on account of the tax, the warrant fee and distraint fee and the expenses incidental to the detention and sale of the property, then, the Executive Authority may again proceed under Rule 31 in respect of the sum remaining unpaid.

(2) When the property is subject to speedy and natural decay, the Executive Authority may sell it at any time before the expiry of the said period seven days, unless the amount due is sooner paid.

(3) The Executive Authority shall consider any objection to the distraint of any property which is made within the said period of seven days and may postpone the sale pending investigation thereof. If the Executive Authority decides that the property attached was not liable to distraint, he shall return it, or if it has already been sold, the proceeds of the sale, to the person appearing to be entitled thereto and may again proceed under Rule 31 and all fees and expenses connected with the first distraint and sale shall be recoverable from the defaulter if it shall appear, to the Executive Authority that he willfully permitted the distraint of the property when to his knowledge it was not liable to distraint.

34. Distraint fees—(1) The distraint fees shall be payable at such rates as are specified in Form III.

(2) Such fees shall not be held to include the expenses incidental to the detention of any property distrained.

35. Property to be distrained within the area of the village panchayat—The property of a person in default under sub-rule (1) of Rule 31 may be distrained wherever it may be found within the area of the village panchayat.

36. Liability of occupier to pay house-tax—If the tax due on account of any house remains unpaid in whole or in part at the end of the period specified in sub-rule (1) of Rule 31, the official who is authorized to sign the warrant may if the said tax has remained unpaid for more than twelve months, require the occupier, for the time being, of such building to pay the amount within a specified period, not being less than fifteen days, and if the occupier fails to comply with such requisition, the Executive Authority may distriant and sell any movable property found on the building, and the provisions of the foregoing rules shall, *mutatis mutandis* apply to all distraints and sales effected under this rule:

Provided that no occupier shall be liable to prosecution or any proceedings in a civil suit in respect of any sum recoverable from him under this rule, unless he has willfully prevented distraint or a sufficient distraint.

37. Recovery of arrears of tax—If any tax due from any person remains unpaid in whole or in part at the end of the period specified in sub-rule (1) of Rule 31 and if such person has left India or cannot be found, the said tax or such part thereof as remains unpaid together with all sum payable in connection therewith shall be recoverable as if it were an arrear of land revenue.

38. Imposition of fine—(1) Every person who is prosecuted under sub-rule (2) of Rule 31 shall be liable, on proof to the satisfaction of the Court that he willfully omitted to pay the amount due by him, to pay a fine not less than five times of the amount which may be due by him on account of:

(a) the tax and the warrant fee, if any; and

(b) if distraint has taken place, the distraint fee and the expenses incidental to the detention and sale, if any, of the property distrained.

(2) Whenever any person is convicted of an offence under sub-rule (1) the Court shall in addition to any fine which may be imposed, recover summarily and pay over to the village panchayat the amount, if any, due under the heads specified in clauses (a) and (b) of sub-rule (1) and also recover summarily and pay the village panchayat such amount, as it may fix as the cost of the prosecution in its discretion.

39. Prohibition to purchase distrained property in certain cases—Neither the Executive Authority nor any officer who signed the warrant or servant of the village panchayat shall directly or indirectly purchase any property at any sale distrained held under the foregoing rules.

(G.O. Ms. No. 255, Rural Development Department, dated 13th December 1999)

FORM I

[See Rule 31 (3)]

Distraint Warrant

Warrant No.

To

(Name of Officer charged with execution of warrant)

(State tax or taxes due and premises, if any, in respect of which the tax is or taxes are due)

Whereas of ________________________has not paid or shown sufficient cause for the non-payment of the sum of Rs.________________Paise________________________due for the tax or taxes noted above for the

1. Although the said sum has been duly demanded from the said and fifteen days have elapsed since such demand was made. This is to command you to demand the said sum of Rs.________________________and Paise________________together with One Rupee for warrant fee, failing which you are to distraint the goods and chattels of the said (or as the case may be, any goods and chattels found on the premises referred to) to the amount of the said sum of Rs.________________________Paise________________________together with Rs.____________Paise______for warrant fee and distraint fee making sufficient to defray the charges of keeping and selling such distraint and if within seven days next after such distraint, the amount due on account of the said tax or taxes and fees shall not be paid together with such further sum as may be sufficient to defray the charges of keeping such distraint, to sell the said goods and chattels under orders to be hereafter issued by me, and to remit to the village panchayat the sale proceeds of the distrained property, out of which the amount due on account of the said tax or taxes and fees, namely Rupees __________________Paise____________and the charges of keeping and selling such distraint, will be deducted and credited to the fund and the surplus if any, returned to the owner of the goods and chattels distrained. If distraint or sufficient distraint cannot be found of the goods and the chattels of the said you are to certify the same together with this warrant.

Signature of the Executive Authority

Station:

Date:

Form II
[See Rule 32(1)]
Form of Inventory and Notice of Sale
(State Particulars of Goods and Chattels Seized)

Take notice that I have this day seized the goods and chattels specified in the above inventory for the sum of Rupees....................and Paise............... due towards the tax or taxes specified for the period ending. And that unless you pay into the Office of the Village Panchayat the amount due together with the warrant fee, the distraint fee and the cost of keeping the goods and chattels within seven days from the date of this notice, the goods and chattels will be sold on the day of .... at the office of the village panchayat as the Executive Authority may direct and that the goods and chattels may be sold at any previous date if they are liable to speedy and natural decay.

Signature of the Executive Authority

Station:
Date:

Form III
[See Rule 34]
Table of Maximum Fee Payable on Distraint

Sums Distrained For (1)	*Distraint Fees* (2) Rs. P.
Under Rs. 30	6.00
Above Rs. 30 and Rs. 70	10.00
Above Rs. 70 and Rs. 100	20.00
Above Rs. 100 and Rs. 150	30.00
Above Rs. 150 and Rs. 200	40.00
Above Rs. 200 and Rs. 250	50.00
Above Rs. 250 and Rs. 300	60.00
Above Rs. 300	At the rate of twenty per cent of tax rounded off to the next whole rupee.

The above charge includes all expenses, except when menials are kept in charge of property distrained, in which case Rs. 5 shall be paid daily for each menial.

5.7.2 Assessment of Railway, Central and State Government Properties

Assessment of Railway Properties to House-tax Guide Lines—Issued

The following principles should be observed while assessing railway properties in panchayats to house-tax:

(i) Railway property acquired by the Central Government after the 25th January 1950 are exempt from local taxes.

(ii) Railway property vested in the Central Government which was not liable to taxes on 25th January 1950 is exempt from the taxes.

(iii) Railway buildings constructed after the 25th January 1950 are exempt from local taxes.

(iv) In the case of complete or substantially complete demolition of buildings, new railway buildings constructed in their stead after 25th January 1950 are exempt from taxes.

(v) Extension made to railway buildings after 25th January 1950 are exempt from taxes.

(vi) Railway buildings partially demolished after 25th January 1950 where such demolition is necessary to effect adequate repairs will continue to be liable to tax although the effect of such demolition may be to enhance the amount of tax on account of the taxable value of the building increasing thereby.

(vii) With regard to improvements and partial demolitions which come in the category of improvements, made after the 25th January 1950 the liability to tax would depend in each case on whether the property in its final stage is not substantially the same property as originally vested.

(viii) The Government of India have agreed to pay enhanced rates of tax with effect from 1st April 1948 in respect of buildings which were in existance.

As regards payment of service charges in respect of railway properties of the Central Government, the following principles should be observed.

Water and Drainage Tax

(a) Where a Railway administration derives no direct benefit—One-third of the tax.
(b) Where a Railway administration derives only partial benefit—Half of the tax.
(c) Where a Railway administration derives full benefit—Full tax.

Scavenging Tax

(a) Where a Railway administration has made efficient arrangements of its own for the daily removal and disposal of rubbish, filth, etc., from its premises – No tax.
(b) Where the Railway administration does not take power from the local authority for lighting its premises and where the roads leading to the Railway station are lit by the local authority – Half of the tax.
(c) Where the Railway administration takes power from the local authority for lighting its premises – Full tax in addition to the charges for energy consumed.

(G.O. No.1280, L.A., dated 26th 1951)
(G.O. No. 1386, L.A., dated 8th October 1954)
(G.O. No. 1628, L.A., dated 22nd November 1954)

5.7.3 Assessment of Central Government Properties other than Railway Properties

The Government of India have accepted liability only of such taxes as were being paid before 1st April 1937 in respect of only such buildings which existed as government buildings before that date. They have stated that they are not liable to pay taxes in respect of improvements and additions to the buildings which existed on 1st April 1937 and on which taxes were beings levied. The Government of India have now agreed to pay enhanced taxes with effect from 1st April 1948 in respect of their buildings which existed on 1st April 1937 and on which taxes were being levied. The Government of India have now agreed to pay enhanced taxes with effect from 1st April 1948 in respect of their buildings which were liable to tax before 1st April 1937, where such increase is due either to a general increase in the valuation of such properties or a general increase in the rate of levy of the tax applicable to all properties within the jurisdiction of the panchayat concerned.

(G.O. No. 2200 L.A., dated 25th October 1949)
(G.O. No. 1386 L.A., dated 8th October 1964)

5.7.4 Assessment of Government Buildings

For purposes of assessment to house tax, the Executive Engineer in the case of Government buildings borne on the books of the Public Works Department and the officers of the department concerned in the case of other Government buildings should ascertain from the Tahsildar of the taluk concerned, the estimated capital value of the sites of such buildings and communicate such valuation of the Executive Authority of the concerned along with the figures as to the estimated present cost of erecting the buildings.

The Executive Authority of the panchayat should intimate to the officer or officers who are to make the valuation at least three months before the date on which the revision of the assessment books is to come in force, the particulars of the buildings and other properties to be valued for the purposes of the revision. The officer or officers should see that the valuation is communicated to the Executive Authority sufficiently early to enable the latter to show the revised assessment books on the date on which the revision comes into force.

(G.O. No.3651, L and M., dated 12th September 1932)
(G.O. No.3098, L.A. dated 31st August 1940)

5.7.5 Assessment of Railways, other Central Government and State Government Properties for House-Tax

In the reference one to nine cited the Government have already issued various instructions for assessment of Railway properties, Central Government properties other than State Government Railway properties and panchayat properties for levy of house-tax by the village panchayat under Tamil Nadu Panchayats Act, 1958. In the reference tenth cited the Government have issued rules for assessment and collection of house tax by the village panchayat under Tamil Nadu Panchayats Act, 1994.

1. Assessment of Railway properties by village panchayat. The following principles should be observed while assessing railway properties in panchayats to house-tax.

(i) Railway property acquired by the Central Government after 25th January 1950 are exempted from local taxes.
(ii) Railway property vested in the Central Government which was not liable to taxes on 25th January 1950 are exempt from taxes.
(iii) Railway buildings constructed after the 25th January 1950 are exempt from local taxes.
(iv) In the case of complete or substantially complete demolition of buildings, new railway buildings constructed in their stead after 25th January 1950 are exempt from taxes.
(v) Extensions made to Railway buildings after 25th January 1950 are exempt from taxes.
(vi) Railway buildings partially demolished after 25th January 1950, where such demolition is necessary to effect adequate repairs will continue to be liable to tax although the effect such demolition may be to enhance the amount of tax on account of the taxable value of the building increasing thereby.
(vii) With regard to improvement and partial demolitions which come in the category of improvements made after the 25th January 1950 the liability to tax would depend in each case on whether the property in its initial state is not substantially the same property as originally vested.
(viii) The Government of India have agreed to pay enhanced rates of tax with effect from 1st April 1948 in respect of buildings which were liable to tax on 25th January 1950.

As regard payments of service charges in respect of railway properties of the Central Government, the following principles should be observed:

(a) where a Railway administration derives no direct benefit—One-third of the tax.
(b) where a Railway administration derives only partial benefits—Half of the tax.
(c) where a Railway administration derives full benefits—Full tax.

I. Scavenging Tax

(a) Where a Railway administration has made efficient arrangements of its run for the daily removal and disposal of rubbish, filth etc., from its premises—No tax.
(b) Where the Railway administration has made arrangements for removal of filth etc., but where the local authority is responsible for its final disposal—Half of the tax.
(c) Where the Railway administration does not take power from the local authority for lighting its premises and where the roads leading to the Railway station are also not hit by the local authority—No tax.

II. Lighting-Tax

(a) Where the Railway administration does not take power from the local authority for lighting its premises and where the roads, leading to the Railway station are also not hit by the local authority—No tax.
(b) Where the Railway administration does not take power from the local authority for lighting its premises, but the roads leading the Railway station are lit by the local authority—Half of the tax.
(c) Where the Railway administration taken power from the local authority for lighting its premises—Full tax in addition to the charges for the energy consumed.

III. Procedure for Collection of Service Charges in Respect of Central Government Properties

The service charges in regard to various government building located in village panchayat area should be claimed properly. The Executive Authority should ensure that there are no omissions in the claims. In order to ensure thus the procedure mentioned below should be adopted.

1. The Executive Authority should verify the buildings of the Union Government located in the village panchayat.
2. A list of the Union Government building located in village panchayat should be drawn up for each district by the Assistant Director (Panchayats) concerned.
3. The panchayats concerned should be asked to make formal claims of service charges. There should be separate claims for the properties of Railway are properties other than those belonging to the Railways.
4. The Assistant Director (Panchayats) shall verify whether the claims are proper and in

order. After verification he shall transmit them to the District Collectors concerned.

5. The Collectors should consolidate the claims of the village panchayats under the jurisdiction and forward them to the concerned local department office of the Union Ministries for payment.

IV. Assessment of State Government Buildings for House-Tax

For purpose of assessment to house-tax, the Executive Engineer in the case of Government buildings borne on the books of the Public Works Development and the officers of the department concerned in the case of other government buildings should ascertain from the Tehsildar of the Taluk concerned the estimated capital value of the sites of such buildings and communicate such valuation to the Executive Authority of the concerned panchayat along with the figures as to the estimated present cost of evicting the building.

The Executive Authority of the panchayat should intimate to the officer or officers who are to make the valuation at least three months before the date on which the revisions of the assessment books into come into force, the particulars of the buildings and other properties to be valued for the purpose of the revision. The officer or officers should see that the valuations is communicated to the Executive Authority sufficiently easily to enable the latter to show the revised assessment books on the date on which the revision comes into force.

V. Assessment of Panchayat Union Buildings for House-Tax

In the case of panchayat union buildings, which are liable to house-tax on the basis of the annual value and which is re-lit out for rent, the actual gross annual rent less a deduction of 10 per centum of such annual rent should be taken as the annual value of the building for purposes of assessment to house-tax. In the case of panchayat union buildings which are liable to house-tax and which are not let out for rent, the annual value or the capital value, as the case may be, estimated by the Divisional Engineer (Highways and Rural Works) of the division concerned should be adopted for purposes of assessment to the tax, in order to avoid disputes in valuation. For this purpose the Divisional Engineer himself need not inspect the buildings, in all cases. He may depute an Assistant Engineer for making the valuation and forward the valuation statement with his counter signature, to the commission of the panchayat union and the Executive Authority of the panchayat concerned. The valuation furnished by the Divisional Engineer (Highways and Rural Works) should be adopted till the next quin quennnial general revision of assessments. At each quin quennnial general revision the Executive Authority of the panchayat should obtain from the Divisional Engineer (Highways and Rural Works) a fresh statement of valuation.

In the case of weekly markets only such panchayat union buildings as fall with in the definition of house in Section 2 (14) of the Tamil Nadu Panchayats Act, 1994 are liable to house-tax.

(G.O. No. 280 Local Administration dated 26th March 1951)

(G.O. No. 1386, Local Administration, dated 8th October 1954)

(G.O. No. 1628, Local Administration, dated 22nd November 1954)

(G.O. No. 2200, Local Administration, dated 25th October 1949)

(G.O. No. 1386, Local Administration, dated 8th October 1964)

(G.O. No. 3651, Local Administration, dated 12th September 1932)

(G.O. No. 398 Local Administration, dated 31st August 1940)

(G.O. No. 843 Local Administration, dated 28th April 1962)

(Govt. Lr.No. 63750/C2/67-2 Rural Development & Local Administration, dated 19th January 1968)

(G.O. Ms. No.255, Rural Development, dated 13th December 1999)

(Commissioner of Rural Development-tax-letter No. 88788/2000/PCA-4, dated 31 March 2001)

5.7.6 Levy and Collection of Library Cess

Under Section 12 of the Madras Public Libraries Act, 1948 levy of the library cess by village panchayat is obligatory and the library cess has to be collected by the village panchayats in the form of a surcharge on the entire house-tax in the panchayat area at the rate of 10 paise for every whole rupee in the house-tax. No cess is leviable on a single assessment of less than a rupee. A notification regarding levy of library cess is not necessary. The monthly library cess collections less refunds should be remitted in to the treasury to the credit of the Local Library Authority every month soon after the accounts for that month are closed.

(G.O. Ms. No.1191 Education, 1st May 1951)

(G.O. Ms. No.3020 Education, 20th November 1951)

(G.O. Ms. No. 2591 Education, 11th November 1952)

(G.O. Ms. No. 5158 E/52-24, Education 25th February 1953)

5.7.7 Test Check of Original Receipts of Collection

In village panchayats, the collection of taxes and other revenues are made by the panchayat assistants or part-time clerks based on the receipt with the facsimile of the Executive Authority of the village panchayat/president. The Executive Authority of village panchayat has to test check at least five per cent of the original receipts granted to tax payers in each month and in addition receipts in respect of all assessment of Rs. 100 and above should be compared in that month to verify and find out that the tax collected and credited to the village panchayat General Fund Account and tax collected as per the original receipt granted to the party is one and the same. If any difference is noticed between the two, it will amount to misappropriation of tax collection by the panchayat assistant and the Executive Authority shall take immediate action to verify cent per cent of all the original receipts and take further action to arrive at the amount misappropriated and to recover it from the person responsible besides taking criminal action against him.

The Executive Authority of the village panchayat shall maintain a record of original receipts verified. The Extension Officer (panchayats) during the inspection of the village panchayat and the Deputy Block Development Officer (panchayats) during the audit of the village panchayat shall verify whether the works has been carried out and the record of verification is maintained. He shall also comment on this in the inspection as well as audit report.

(G.O. Ms. No.945 L.A., dated 14th May 1948)

5.7.8 House-tax—Educational Institutions run on Commercial Basis—Not Exempted from Levy of House-tax

(1) Petitioner is an educational trust, which is running various educational institutions in Perumalpattu village, within the respondent panchayat union in Tiruvallur District. It has constructed several buildings for the purpose of running the classes for the educational institutions, hostels, laboratories and for other purposes in connection with running of the educational institutions. The respondent panchayat issued a notice dated 19.2.2001 claiming that the panchayat union is assessing property tax for the buildings. At that stage, the petitioner had filed O.S.No.85 of 2001 for injunction and an interim order of injunction was passed. Subsequently, a further notice had been issued by the respondent giving rise to filing of O.S.No. 270 of 2001 against the present respondent as well as other officials such as the Deputy Director of Rural Development and the District Collector for injunction. However, subsequently the Advocate who had conducting the suit had expired; both the suits were dismissed for default. While the matter stood thus, the respondent has served impugned proceedings dated 9.12.2002 claiming that the petitioner should pay a sum of Rs. 72,16,920/- as tax for the period from 1985 to 2003. The aforesaid proceedings is being challenged in the present writ petition.

(2) It is the contention of the petitioner that as per Rule 15(c) of the Tamil Nadu Panchayat (Assessment and Collection of Taxes) Rules, 1999 framed in exercise of the power conferred under Sections 171, 172, 174, 176 and 242(1) of the Tamil Nadu Panchayat Act, 1994, buildings used for educational purpose, including hostels, libraries, which are open to the public are exempted from house-tax. It is submitted in alternative that even if tax is payable the impugned proceedings to collect taxes from 1983 to 2003 is barred by limitation.

(3) On behalf of the respondent a petition for vacating the stay has been filed and in the said petitions, the contentions raised in the writ petition have been refused.

(4) The entire writ petition was heard on merit while considering the question of vacating the order to stay.

(5) Section 172 of the Tamil Nadu Panchayats Act empowers the panchayat to levy the house-tax. Section 172(4) empowers the Government to make rules which being relevant is extracted hereunder.

"172(4) The Government may make rules providing for:

(a) the persons who should be able to pay the tax and the giving of notices of transfer of houses;
(b) the grant of vacancy and other remissions;

(c) the circumstances in which and condition subject to which, houses, constructed or demolished or situated in areas included in or excluded from the panchayat village during any half-year or year, shall be liable to the whole or any portion of the tax".

(6) It is not disputed that the Tamil Nadu Panchayat (Assessment and Collection Taxes Rules) Rules, 1999 have been framed pursuant to aforesaid provision. Learned counsel for the petitioner has relied upon Rule 15, particularly Rule 15(c) and claimed exemption on the ground that the buildings used for educational purpose or for library purpose are not liable to be assessed to the house-tax. The provisions contained in Rule 15(c) are quoted hereunder:

"15. Exemption of specified classes of houses from house-tax:

(a) ....

(b) ...

(c) buildings used for educational purposes including hostels and libraries which are open to the public, and public buildings used for charitable purpose of sheltering the destitutes or animals.

(d) to (k)....

Provided that nothing contained in clauses (a) and (c) shall be demand to except from house-tax if any building for which rent is payable by the person or persons using the same for the purposes referred to in the said clauses:

Provided further that education institution (not commercial in nature) exempted form levy of house tax, immediately before the commencement of the Act shall continue to be exempted under the said Act.

Explanation. The exemption granted under this rule shall not extend to resident quarters attached to schools or colleges not being the hostels or residential quarters attached in hospitals, dispensaries and libraries.

(7) It is the contention of the petitioner that since the hostels and libraries are open to public, as per clause (c) of Rule 15, no house-tax is payable. A reading of the entire provisions make it clear that the intention is to exempt charitable organizations which are running such hostels or libraries or shelters for animals. Where, however the persons using the hostels and libraries are paying rent. It cannot be said that tax is not leviable. The intention seems to be for the benefit of the charitable organizations and not for the organisations which are collecting money for particular use.

(8) Learned counsel for the petitioner has relied upon the decision of this court reported on 1992. MLU 381 (NEPCO SCHLENK ENGINEERING COLLEGE, SIVAKASI. THE PRESIDENT, KERISERI PANCHAYAT AND OTHERS). The question related to notices issued regarding two hostels and one canteen for the purpose of determining the property tax for the year 1989-90 under the Tamil Nadu Panchayats Act, 1958. Under the relevant rules then applicable, it was provided:

"Provided that nothing contained in clauses (a), (c) and (e) shall be deemed to exempt house-tax any building for which rent is payable by the person of persons using the same for the purposes referred to in the clause":

"Provided further that the buildings used for educational purposes including hostels owned and run for such purpose irrespective of the fact whether any rent is payable by the person or persons using the same for educational purposes or not shall be exempt from tax".

(9) While considering the aforesaid provisions, it was observed

"The second provision is mandatory in its terms and even if the educational agency of the management of the institution charges rent for the occupation of the hostels from the occupants thereof, the buildings are exempt from property tax. Hence the demand made by the first respondent on the petitioner for payment of tax as well as for production of certificate of valuation with respect to the two hostel buildings is unsustainable as they have to be quashed".

(10) It has to be seen that under the new provisions, the second provision upon which reliance had been placed in the decision has now been deleted. Therefore, the aforesaid decisions would no longer be, applicable in view of the relevant provisions contained in the present Rules.

(11) Even though the main contention regarding total exemption is not justified in view of the changed Rules, the contention to the effect that demand for payment of house-tax for the entire period, *i.e.* 1985 to 2003, appears to be unjustified. The decision of justice M. Srinivasan, as His Lordship then was, cited supra was obviously applicable to the present institution under the old Act. Even though the old Act was replaced in the year 1994, the savings clause and the Rules made under the old Act continue to remain in force and the Rules under the new Act, were only framed in 1999. Therefore, all the new Rules were framed in

1999 in view of the earlier decision reported above, there was no liability to pay tax, even through the educational agency was charging rent from the occupants of the hostel. The second proviso new incorporating itself indicates that only if any organisation was being run on charitable basis, such exemption would continue in the present case, it is not the case of the petitioner that the trust is running the educational institution on charitable basis.

(12) Now that the position has been clarified, there shall be assessment in respect of the liability subsequent to the enforcement of Tamil Nadu Panchayat (Assessment and Correction of Taxes Rules), 1999 and thereafter if would be open to the respondent to collect tax in accordance with the Rules, demand notice dated 9.12.2002 is accordingly quashed.

(13) For the aforesaid reasons, the writ petition is allowed in part. It is made clear that the petitioner is liable to pay tax with effect from the enforcement of Tamil Nadu Panchayat (Assessment and Collection of Taxes Rules) Rules, 1999 and there is no liability to pay tax for the earlier period. No costs.

(Judgment of the Madras High Court)

5.7.9 Collection of Tax on Profession, Trade, Calling and Employment

1. Short title and application—(1) These rules may be called the Tamil Nadu Village Panchayat (Collection of Tax on Profession, Trade, Calling and Employment) Rules, 2000.

(2) They shall apply to all village panchayats.

2. Definition—(1) In these rules, unless the context otherwise requires

(i) 'Act' means the Tamil Nadu Panchayats Act, 1994 (Tamil Nadu Act 21 of 1994);

(ii) 'Average half-yearly income' means the average of the total gross income for the year earned by a person;

(iii) 'Director' means the Director of Rural Development;

(iv) 'drawing and disbursing officer' means an officer in Central or State Government Department quasi Government or private company or organization who is in charge of passing of the pay bills and disbursement of pay to the employees;

(v) 'form' means form appended to these rules;

(vi) 'general revision' means the revision of tax once in five years by the panchayat concerned;

(vii) 'Panchayat' means village panchayat constituted under the Act;

(viii) 'place of work' means the place where a person liable to pay tax ordinarily carries on his profession, trade calling or employment; and

(ix) 'tax' means the tax fixed on profession, trade, calling or employment by the panchayat concerned, under sub-section (2) of Section 198-B of the Act.

(2) Words and expression used but not defined in these rules shall have the meanings respectively assigned to them in the Act.

3. Fixation of tax—The Executive Authority of the panchayat shall fix the rate of tax in accordance with the provision of the Act, before a general revision of tax is started. The first general revision of tax under these rules shall be taken up for the half-year commencing from the First October 1998.

4. Publication of tax—The Inspector shall make arrangements for publication of the tax fixed by the panchayat under Rule 3 in the panchayat office and in one or more conspicuous place of the wards concerned. He shall also give wide publicity through tom tom, loud speakers as approved by the panchayat for information of the public.

5. Mode of payment of tax—(1) The drawing and disbursing officer of the office concerned shall recover the tax for the half-year from the pay of the employees concerned in the months of August and January of every year. He shall remit the tax amount for the half-year in full to the Executive Authority concerned by means of cheque or demand draft on or before the 15th September and 15th February respectively every year along with the return as in Form-1.

(2) Every self-drawing officer of the Central or State Government or quasi Government undertaking shall pay the tax for the half-year from the pay for the months of August and January every year by means of cheque or demand draft drawn in favour of the Executive Authority concerned before the 15th September and 15th of February, respectively. While presenting his pay bill for the months of September and February respectively, he shall be given a certificate for having paid the tax to the Executive Authority concerned indicating the number and date of the cheque or demand draft in his pay bill. The Treasury officer shall honour the pay bill of such self-drawing officer for the months of September and February only if such certificate is enclosed along with the pay bill.

(3) If the pay of an employee for the month of January or August of a year was not drawn, the tax shall be recovered as and when his pay for such month is drawn subsequently and the cheque or demand draft for the tax amount shall be sent to the Executive Authority concerned together with Form-1 within fifteen days of the recovery of such tax.

(4) Every trader or professional or an employer having an average half-yearly income of Rs. 21,001 (Rupees Twenty one thousand and one only) and above shall file a return in Form 2 within thirty days from 1st December 1999 or the date to be notified by the panchayat concerned or whichever is earlier. The return shall be acknowledged by the panchayat:

Provided that the Executive Authority may extend the time for filing of returns for another thirty days.

(5) (a) The person filing a return under sub-rule (4) shall remit the tax on the basis of his average half-yearly income in the office of the panchayat concerned by means of chalan or by cheque or demand draft. The return shall be accompanied by the chalan or cheque or demand draft for the tax amount due for the half-year for which the return is filed in the office of the panchayat. The return not accompanied by the chalan or cheque or demand draft shall be deemed to have been not duly filed.

(b) The return filed by a person under sub-rule (4) shall be valid for a period of five years.

(c) The tax for the subsequent half-year shall be paid within the period of half-year concerned as provided in clause (a) but without filing the return.

(6) If there is a change in the average half-yearly income or if there is a change in the place of trade or profession or employment, the person concerned shall file a fresh return as provided in clause (a) of sub-rule (5). Such change shall take effect from the next half-year period and it shall be valid the next general revision of tax.

(7) The Executive Authority may, on its own motion or on an application, rectify any error on the fact of the record of any return or cancel the assessment and re-assess the tax in accordance with these rules. The excess amount if any, paid by the person concerned shall be adjusted towards tax that may be payable by him in future within such period as may be specified by the Executive Authority:

Provided that no such re-assessment of tax which has the effect of enhancing the tax as assessed by the person concerned in the return filed by him shall be made unless he has been given an opportunity of being heard and within thirty days from the date of receipt of the notice by him.

6. Assignment of permanent account number and issue of pass book—(1) The Executive Authority after receiving the returns filed under sub-rules (1) and (4) of Rule 5 shall issue a pass book or card valid for five years as in Form-3 with thirty days from the date of receipt of such return.

(2) The Executive Authority shall assign a permanent account number for a person who files a return under sub-rules (1) and (4) of Rule 5 and in accordance with the guidelines issued by the Director or the Government, from time-to-time. The permanent account number so assigned shall be indicated in the pass book or card. The Executive Authority shall maintain a permanent account register to record the details of each permanent account number holder.

(3) The pass book or card issued to a person in the middle of the period of a general revision of tax shall be valid for the period the next general revision of tax is taken up.

(4) If any pass book or card is lost or mutilated, the person concerned may apply to the Executive Authority for a duplicate pass book or card along with a chalan for rupees ten paid in the office of the panchayat concerned. In the case of mutilated pass book or card shall also be enclosed along with the application. The Executive Authority shall furnish the duplicate pass book or card within fifteen days from the date of receipt of such application and such duplicate pass book or card shall be valid the issue of a new pass book or card after a general revision of tax.

7. Checking of return—The Executive Authority shall verify the return filed by the persons concerned under sub-rules (1) and (4) of Rule 5 in the following manner:

(a) If a person has filed a return for the maximum amount of tax filed or where the return is accompanied by proper evidence as proof for his gross income, such returns need not be verified.

(b) Among the returns which are not of the kind specified in clause (a), he shall select at random ten per cent of the total number of such returns under each slab rate fixed in the Act, and verify the correctness of the contents of such returns. Such ten per cent verification shall be completed within the next half-year period and in the case of general revision of tax within the next half-year period after the general revision is over. For this purpose he may require the person concerned to produce copies of income tax or sales tax returns or any other relevant documents.

(c) If the Executive Authority, while checking, the returns, finds any error relating to the quantum of tax payable in the assessment made by the person or employer concerned, he shall rectify such error after giving an opportunity to the person or employer concerned of being heard.

(d) In addition to the rectification of error in the return under clause (c) the Executive Authority shall levy penalty on such person or drawing and disbursing officer under sub-rule (2) of Rule 9 treating such return as incorrect or incomplete under these rules.

8. Time limit for payment of half-yearly tax—The half-yearly tax shall be paid on or before the 30th September for the first half-year and on or before the 31st March for the second half-year, respectively.

9. Levy of penalty for belated payment—(1) When a person or drawing and disbursing officer fails to pay the tax within the period, Executive Authority shall levy a penalty at the rate of one rupee per mensum or part of a month for the tax amount of every hundred rupees or part thereof due to be paid.

(2) If a person or drawing and disbursing officer files an incomplete or incorrect return under Rule 5 and if the same is detected during checking done under Rule 7 the Executive Authority shall revise the tax amount and shall collect from the person or drawing and disbursing officers concerned a penalty of one hundred per cent of the difference of the tax revised and the tax paid as per the return filed by him.

10. Failure to file return by any person or drawing and disbursing officer—If any person or drawing and disbursing officer fails to file a return in Form-1, the Executive Authority shall direct the Panchayat Assistant to visit the place of work of the person or disbursing officer concerned and after making such enquiries as may be considered necessary he shall prepare a return. A copy of such return so prepared shall be furnished to the person of drawing and disbursing officer concerned along with a notice for payment of the tax as assessed.

11. Maintenance of registers for collection of tax—The assessment book for collection of tax shall be kept in the office of the panchayat concerned which shall be used from one general revision to the next general revision. This register shall be maintained in accordance with the general instruction issued by the Government or the Director, from time-to-time.

12. Appeal—If any person or drawing and disbursing officer is aggrieved by any order or decision of the Executive Authority relating to the payment of tax including penalty he may, with in thirty days from the receipt of such order or decision of the Executive Authority, appeal in writing to village panchayat.

13. Time limit for disposal of appeal—Every appeal preferred under Rule 11 shall be disposed of by the appellate authority before the end of the succeeding half-year period prescribed in Rule 8.

14. Revision of rate of tax by the panchayat—(1) The panchayat shall revise the rate of tax once in five years for the period commencing from the 1st October 1998* by increasing the rate not less than twenty-five per cent and not more than thirty-five per cent of the rate of tax fixed in the Act. The panchayat shall not change or revise the slabs of average half-yearly income fixed in the Act.

(2) The percentage of increase in the tax once fixed by the panchayat under sub-rule (1) shall not be reduced without prior permission of the Government.

15. Interpretation of these rules by Government—If any question arises as to the interpretation of these rules, the question shall be referred to the Government whose decision thereon shall be final.

(G.O.Ms.No.8, Rural Development (C4) Department, dated 19th January 2000)

*(Amended by the G.O.Ms.No.315, Rural Development (C2) Department, and dated 4th December 2003).

(G.O.Ms.No.6, Rural Development (C2) Department, dated 12th January 2004).

APPENDIX

FORM-1

[See Rule 5(1) and (3)]

Return for recovery of tax from the employees and officers working in ______________________for the half-year period______________________(Name of the Company/Organization/Central/State Government Offices with address)

Sl. No.	*Name and designation of the employee or officer*	*Gross half-yearly income Rs.*	*Amount of tax and deducted and paid Rs.*	*Details of chalan if paid in cash in the Panchayat Office or Cheque/Demand draft number in which amount is remitted*
(1)	(2)	(3)	(4)	(5)

Total __________

Number of employees for whom half-yearly tax was deducted and paid in the immediate previous half-year and amount thereof.

Copy of receipts for such payment.

FORM-2

[See Rule 5 (4)]

Return for Payment of Tax on Profession, Trade, Calling and Employment

1. Name (Trade/Firm/Company/Organsiation/Professional)
2. Address: Ward No. Ward Office
3. Nature of profession, trade, calling and employment (in brief)
4. Half-yearly gross income (indicate the average six months gross income of the previous financial year) (Photocopy of the proof for the gross income to be enclosed)
5. Amount of half-year tax to be paid
6. Whether all the tax amount due for the previous half-years have been paid, if not, whether return has been filed for arrears of tax due
7. Details of chalan or demand draft/cheque for payment of the half-yearly tax relating to the period in which this return is being filed.

CERTIFICATE

I ______________________certify that the particulars given above are true to the best of my knowledge.

Signature

ACKNOWLEDGEMENT

Received Return for payment of tax on profession, trade calling and employment along with/chalan No. ____________a sum of Rs. ____________being the tax for the half-year ____________from Thiru/Thirumathi ______________in the profession of ______________on ____________This acknowledgement is deemed to be the assessment subject to verification.

Signature and designation

Details of slab rates of tax on profession, trade, calling and employment and mode of payment of tax, penalty of returns by the panchayats, etc. (will be retained by the person filling the return).

FORM-3
(See Rule 6)

.... Panchayat
Pass Book or Card for payment of tax on Profession, Trade, Calling and Employment.
Ward no. Permanent Account No............................. Ward No..............................
And name (if any)

Name:
Address:
Profession/trade/calling and employment:
Half-year average:
Gross Income:
Amount of tax

Half	*Tax Amount Rs.*	*Fine Rs.*	*Receipt Number of Chalan number or Demand Draft Number with date and other details*	*Signature of the official who makes the entry along with his designation*

Columns for 10 half-years.
(G.O. Ms. No. 8, Rural Development Department, dated 19th January 2000)

5.7.10 Collection of Arrears of Tax on Professions, Trades, Callings and Employment

1. Short title, application and commencement—(1) These rules may be called the Tamil Nadu Village Panchayats (Collection of Arrears of Tax on Professions, Trades, Callings and Employment) Rules, 1999.

(2) These rules shall apply to all village panchayats in this State.

2. Filing of return for payment of arrears of tax on professions, trades, callings and employments Every trader or professional, who is in arrears of profession tax, shall file a return furnishing the details of amount due by him at the rate already determined under the provisions of the Tamil Nadu Tax on Professions, Trades, Callings, and Employment Act, 1992 (Tamil Nadu Act 24 of 1992) which was in force for the period from the 1st April 1992 to the 30th September, 1998, to the Executive Authority of the village panchayat in Form-1 appended to these rules on or before the 31st January 1999. The Executive Authority may if necessary extend the period for filing the return beyond the 31st January 1999 and the period so extended shall not be beyond 28th February 1999.

3. Mode of payment of tax—(1) The return under Rule 2 shall be accompanied by a challan, in support of payment of arrears of profession tax due by a trader or a professional for the first two half years commencing from the 1st April 1992. The payment shall be made in the office of the respective village panchayats during the office hours on all working day.

(2) A trader or professional shall pay the remaining arrears of profession tax due by the 30th September 1998 during every current half-year along with the arrears for the periods not less than of two half years:

Provided that the entire arrears of tax due under the repealed Tamil Nadu Tax on Professions, Trades, Callings and Employment Act, 1992 (Tamil Nadu Act 24 of 1992) shall be paid not later than three years period commencing from the 1st October 1998.

(3) The Executive Authority shall accept and acknowledge the return and the arrears of tax amount paid by the trader of professional in Form-2, appended to these rules.

4.Interpretation of these rules by the Government—If any question arises as to the interpretation of these rules, the question shall be referred to the Government, whose decision shall be final.

(G.O. Ms. No. 9, Rural Development Department, dated 18th January 1999)

FORM-1

(See Rule 2)

Profession Tax Arrears Return Form

1. Name:
   [Individual/Firm]
2. Address:
3. Profession/Trade/Calling/Employment:
4. Half-year which profession Tax paid under Tamil Nadu Act 24 of 1992:
5. Details of Half-Years for which profession: tax not paid — I/92-93: II/92-93; I/93-94: II/93-94; I/94-95: II/94-95; I/95-96: II/95-96; I/96-97: II/96-97; I/97-98: II/97-98
   [Tick the half-years concerned]
6. The number of half-yearly profession Tax due as per Tamil Nadu Act 24 of 1992;
   (a) Total arrears due (Number of half-years × amount):
   (b) Number of half-yearly instalments which arrears to be cleared (Please Tick one):
   (c) Details of number and date of chalan Receiving 1st instalment:

CERTIFICATE

I certify that the particulars given above are true to the best of my knowledge and belief.

Signature

FORM-2

[See Rule 3 (3)]

Acknowledgement

Received statement of arrears of profession tax along with Chalan No.________________dated being the 1st instalment from Thiru/Tmt________________________doing business at________________________engaged in the profession of ________________________on ________________

Signature

5.7.11 Licensing of Hoarding and Levy and Collection of Advertisement Tax

1. Short title and application—(1) These Rules may be called the Tamil Nadu Panchayats (Licensing of Hoardings and Levy and Collection of Advertisement Tax) Rules, 1999.

(2) These rules shall apply to all the village panchayats constituted under the Tamil Nadu Panchayats Act, 1994.

2. Definitions—In these rules, unless the context otherwise requires—

(a) "Act" means the Tamil Nadu Panchayats Act, 1994 (Tamil Nadu Act 21 of 1994);

(b) "Advertisement" means any information exhibited on any screen or boards, wall or building either private or pubic or on any hoarding erected on any private or public land or building or on any frame work or other support wholly or in part over any private or public land or building visible to public wholly or partly and will exclude advertisements made in newspapers, broadcast made over radio or telecast in television;

(c) "Form" means the Form appended to these rules;

(d) "hoarding" means any screen or boards at any private or public place used or intended to be used for exhibiting advertisement including the frame works or other support erected wholly or in part upon or over any land, building, wall or structure visible to public wholly or partly;

(e) "Licence" means the licence granted under Rule 3;

(f) Words and expressions used but not defined in these rules shall have the meanings respectively assigned to them in the Act. In the absence of such meaning the Tamil Nadu General Clauses Act, 1891 (Tamil Nadu Act 1 of 1891) shall apply for the interpretation of these rules.

3. Issue of provisional permission and licence—(1) Any person including a State or Central Government Department intends to exhibit any advertisement shall apply to the executive authority in Form-I for obtaining a provisional permission.

(2) Every application for a licence under sub-rule (1) shall be accompanied by:

(a) The Licence fee as may be fixed by the village panchayat in the manner specified in Rule 12;

(b) A plan of the hoardings to be erected indicating the height and other dimensions and the material proposed to be used as approved by a qualified engineer;

(c) A no objection certificate from the owner of the land where the hoarding is to be erected in a private land or building or a no objection certificate from an officer of the State or Central Government Department not below the rank of an Assistant Executive Engineer or Commissioner of the panchayat union as the case may be, if the hoarding is to be erected on a State or Central Government or panchayat union land or a no objection certificate from the Executive Authority if the hoarding is to be erected on a village panchayat land;

(d) No objection certificate from the traffic police issued by an officer not below the rank of an Inspector of Police where the hoarding is to be erected on the important roads in village panchayats areas and where the size of the hoarding to be erected is above 3 square metres; and

(e) a topo sketch indicating the proposed location of the hoarding.

(3) The Executive Authority shall on receipt of such application scrutinise the application and inspect or cause to be inspected the place where the hoarding is proposed to be erected.

(4) After such scrutiny and inspection if the Executive Authority is satisfied that the hoarding proposed to be erected confirms with the particulars specified in the application form and other documents furnished by the applicant fulfil the requirements of sub-rule (2) the Executive Authority shall grant a provisional permission in Form-II with such condition as may be necessary for erection of a hoarding in that place which shall be valid for thirty days from the date of grant thereof:

Provided that on representation from the applicant the period of thirty days may be extended by another thirty days by the Executive Authority.

(5) Within thirty days form the date of receipt of such provisional permission or within such extended period under the proviso to sub-rule (4) the applicant shall erect the hoarding in accordance with the conditions, if any, specified in the provisional permission and shall apply in Form-III for a licence along with a certificate of structural stability issued by a qualified Engineer.

(6) On satisfying that the hoarding has been erected in accordance with the condition specified in the provisional permission issued under sub-rule (4) the executive authority shall issue a licence in Form-IV with such condition as may be necessary.

4. Period of validity of licence—The licence shall be valid for one year from the date of issue.

5. Renewal of licence—Every application for renewal of the licence shall be made to the Executive Authority before two months prior to the expiry of the validity of the licence in Form V along with the fee fixed by the village panchayat. The Executive Authority shall dispose of all such renewal applications received by him before the expiry of the validity of the licence.

6. Maximum height and size of the hoardings to be erected—The height of a hoarding to be erected shall not exceed thirty metres from the ground level and the message to be exhibited shall be at a height of not less than three metres from the ground level.

7. Cancellation of licence or refusal for renewal of licence—(1) Where the Executive Authority, either *suo motu* or on public representation has reason to believe that the licensee has violated or failed to comply with the conditions of the licence or any provision of the Act or these rules, he shall call upon the licensee by notice in writing, addressed by registered post to the address given in his licence and stating grounds, to show cause within such period not less than fifteen days from the date or receipt of such notice as to why the licence shall not be cancelled or the renewal of the licence shall not be refused and also shall give the licensee an opportunity of being heard.

(2) If the Executive Authority does not satisfy with the reply received form the licensee within the time limit specified in sub-rule (1) it may cancel the licence or refuse to renew the licence.

8. Removal of unauthorised obscene or objectionable hoardings—(1) On cancellation of licence or refusal to renew the licence under sub-rule (2) of Rule 7, the owner of such hoarding shall remove it within seven days from the receipt of the order or cancellation or refusal, failing which the Executive Authority shall cause to remove such hoarding and recover the cost of such removal from the owner or user of such hoarding.

(2) The Executive Authority may, either *suo motu* or on any representation, shall direct the licensee to remove an advertisement in a hoarding within seven days from the date of receipt of such direction, if the contents of such advertisement is considered to be obscene or objectionable. If the licensee does not remove such advertisement within seven days, the Executive Authority shall remove the hoarding and recover the costs from the owner or user of such hoarding.

9. Notification of area prohibited for erection of hoardings—(1) The inspector may notify any area within the village panchayat as a prohibited area for erection of any hoarding. The Executive Authority shall not grant licence for erection of a hoarding in such area.

(2) If there is a hoarding, which is already existing in such notified prohibited area the licensee shall be liable to remove such hoarding within fifteen days of the date of such notification. If the licensee does not remove such hoarding within such time limit, the Executive Authority shall cause to remove it and recover costs for such removal from the licensee concerned. No individual notice is required before such removal. The excess amount of advertisement tax, if any shall be refunded to the owner of such hoarding removed.

10. Appeal against the order refusing to issue or to renew licence cancellation of the licence—An appeal to the village panchayat in Form-VI shall be made within thirty days from the date on which the order of refusal of licence or renewal of the licence or cancellation of the licence. Such an appeal shall be accompanied by fee of two hundred rupees, and the statement of the grounds of appeal. Such appeal shall be disposed of in the next meeting of the village panchayat or not later than sixty days from the date of receipt of such appeal.

11. Mode of payment—All fees and advertisement taxes to be paid under these rules shall be paid either by cash or in the form of bank draft payable to the village panchayat.

12. Rate of advertisement tax to be fixed by the village panchayat—(1) The village panchayat shall fix the yearly advertisement tax on an advertisement within the minimum and maximum limits as stated in the following Table:

Table

Sl. No.	*Area*	*Minimum* (Per square metre) Rs.	*Maximum* (Per square metre) Rs.
1.	If the village panchayat lies within 30 km radius from any Municipal Corporation	20	250
2.	If the village panchayat lies within 10 km radius from a Municipality	15	200
3.	Other village panchayats	10	150

(2) While fixing the rate of tax, the village panchayat shall take into consideration the location and type of the hoarding and fix different rates of tax for different places and different types of hoarding.

(3) The rate as fixed by the village panchayat shall be published in the notice board of the village panchayat concerned and in conspicuous place in the village panchayat area and also by beat of tom and maintain such record of publication in the village panchayat office.

(4) If a hoarding is kept erected for a period of less than six months, fifty per cent of the annual tax shall be collected.

13. Issue of advertisement tax assessment order—The Executive Authority shall issue the assessment order for payment of yearly advertisement tax in Form-VII and issue along with the licence for erection of a hoarding.

14. Period within which the advertisement tax has to be paid—The advertisement tax shall be paid within thirty days from the date of issue of licence.

15. Liability of the user of the hoarding for payment of advertisement tax—The owner user or advertiser shall be liable to pay the tax within the period specified in Rule 14, failing which the Executive Authority shall make arrangements to remove such advertisement after giving a notice in writing to the owner or user or advertiser

16. Refund of tax—Where the annual tax has been paid in respect of the hoarding specified in sub-rule (4) of Rule 12, the balance amount shall be refunded while removing the hoarding.

17. Maintenance of register for issue of licence for collection of advertisement tax—A register in Form-VIII shall be maintained by the Executive Authority in the village panchayat which shall be used for a period of five years for issue of licences for erection of hoarding and for collection of advertisement tax for all hoardings.

18. Periodical inspection of hoarding—The Executive Authority shall make periodical inspection of the hoardings erected. During such inspection if it is noticed that any hoarding is not in accordance with the provisions of the Act or these rules or the conditions of licence the Executive Authority shall take immediate action for removal of such hoarding after giving notice in writing to the owner or user or advertiser of such hoarding.

(G.O.Ms.No. 218, Rural Development (C-4) Department, dated 14th October 1999)

APPENDIX

FORM-I

[See Rule 3(1)]

Application for Provisional Permission to Erect a Hoarding

1. Name and address of the Applicant/Company/Government Department________________
2. Exact location with land mark identification and direction of facing frontage of the hoarding________________Place of erection of hoarding (if private property, address of the building) ________________
3. Name of the land/building owner on which the hoarding is to be erected________________
4. Size of the hoarding proposed to be erected (length, breadth and width to be mentioned) ________________
5. Nature of the materials to be used________________
6. Indicate whether the following documents have been enclosed with the application:
   (i) Licence Fees________________
   (ii) Plan of the hoarding indicating width, height, etc., duly approved by the qualified Engineer________________
   (iii) No Objection Certificate from the land owner________________
   (iv) No Objection Certificate from the Traffic Police not below the rank of an Inspector of the area concerned for erection of hoarding in the important roads in village panchayat area in respect of hoarding above 3 square metre ________________
   (v) A topo sketch indicating the proposed location of the hoarding ________________

ACKNOWLEDGEMENT

Received the application for provisional permission for erection of hoarding at ________________ from Thiru/ Thirumathi________________

Executive Authority

FORM-II
[See Rule 3(4)]

No.____________________
Dated__________________

Provisional Permission for Erection of a Hoarding

Reference: Application No. ________________ dated______________________
Provisional permission is granted to ___________ for the erection of hoarding of size____________________ at ______________________ on the land belonging to ________________________ This provisional permission is valid for thirty days from the date of issue. The applicant after erection of the hoarding as per this permission shall apply in Form-III for licence.

Executive Authority

FORM-III
[See Rule 3(5)]
Application for Licence to the Hoarding Erected

1. Name of the applicant______________________
   Number and date of provisional permission (along with the copy thereof) ____________
2. Location of hoarding, number and other details____________________
3. Name of the Land Owner/Competent Authority_______________________
4. Size of the hoarding erected________________________________
5. Whether Licence fees has been paid (Draft number or Receipt Number and date to be specified)_____________
6. Whether annual rent paid for land belonging to Government or panchayat union or village panchayat, if so, the date of payment and other details_________________________
   Whether the following documents have been enclosed with the application_____________
   (i) Structural stability certificate from the qualified Engineer_________________
   (ii) Copy of the provisional order issued in Form-II___________

Signature of the Applicant

FORM-IV
[See Rule 3(6)]
Licence for Erection of the Hoarding

No.______________________
Dated____________________

Reference: Application number and date of Form-III.
Licence is granted to ________________ for erection of hoarding of size______________ at ______________on the land belonging to subject to the following conditions:

CONDITIONS

This licence is not transferable.
The licence should on no account change the ownership of the hoarding without prior permission of the Executive Authority.
This Licence is valid for the period from __________________ to __________________

Executive Authority

FORM-V
(See Rule 5)

No.________________ Dated__________________

Application for Renewal of the Licence

1. Name and address of the licensee of the existing hoarding
2. Place of erection of hoarding
3. Exact location with landmarks identification of the hoarding

4. Permitted size of the existing hoarding
5. Details of existing licence issued under Form-IV
6. Number and date of the tax assessment order issue under Form-VI
7. Details of rent and tax paid

Signature of the Applicant

FORM-VI

(See Rule 10)

Appeal Against the Orders of the Executive Authority Refusing to Issue or to Renew Licence or Cancelling the Licence for Errection of Haording

From

Date:

____

____

____

To

____________ Village Panchayat

Reference: Orders of the Executive Authority No.__________ dated____________

Sir,

I hereby appeal against the order of the Executive Authority, dated _______ refusing to grant or renew a licence or cancellation of the licence applied by me (copy enclosed).

I enclose herewith a copy of Demand Draft No.__________ dated________ for Rs. 200 towards the fee for filing appeal.

Under the following grounds only I am filing an appeal to the village panchayat for suitable orders (Details of the Grounds)

1.
2.
3.
4.
5.

Signature of the Licensee

FORM-VII

(See Rule 13)

No.

Date:

Assessment Order for the Payment of Yearly Advertisemnt Tax

This order is for payment of advertisement tax for the advertisement exhibited on Hoarding/Signboard/Television/Neon Board/Balloon/Arches/Half-arches at______________of size____________ for Rs. ______________ payable yearly. The mode of payment of the tax shall be by cash or demand draft in favour of the village panchayat. Non-payment of advertisement tax shall attract removal of the advertisement by the Executive Authority.

Executive Authority

FORM VIII

(See Rule 17)

Register for Collection of Licence Fee and Advertisement Tax

1. Name of the Licensee __________
2. Location of the hoarding __________
3. Name of the land owner or competent authority if on Government land __________
   Name and address of the building owner (if it is on private building) __________
4. Licence number and date and licence fees paid __________
5. Assessment number and date __________
6. Size __________

Year (1)	*Advertisement Tax (Yearly) (Rupees)* (2)
1999-2000	
2000-2001	
2001-2002	
2002-2003	
2003-2004	

(G.O. Ms. No. 218, Rural Development (C-4) Department, dated 14th October 1999).

5.7.12 Duty on Transfer of Property

1. Short title—These rules may be called the Tamil Nadu Panchayats (Duty on Transfer of Property) Rules, 2001.

2. Definition—In these rules, unless there is anything repugnant in the subject or context

(a) 'Act' means the Tamil Nadu Panchayats Act, 1994 (Tamil Nadu Act 21 of 1994);

(b) 'Instruments' means an instrument of sale, exchange, gift, mortgage with possession or lease in perpetuity of immovable property on which transfer duty is leviable under Section 175;

(c) 'Section' means a section of the Act;

(d) 'Stamp Act' means the Indian Stamp Act, 1899 (Central Act II of 1899), as in force in the State of Tamil Nadu;

(e) 'Transfer duty' means the duty on transfer of property leviable under Section 175; and all words and expressions used herein but not defined in these rules shall have the meanings respectively assigned to them in the Stamp Act and the rules made thereunder.

3. Provisions of Stamp Act to apply to transfer duty—(1) All the provisions of the Stamp Act and the rules made thereunder shall, so far as may be, apply in relation to the transfer duty as they apply in relation to the duty chargeable under that Act.

(2) Where the transfer duty or any portion thereof is less than a rupee, such duty or such portion shall not be collected.

4. Duties of registering officers in regard to the particulars to be set forth in instruments—(1) Whenever any instrument is presented for registration to any registering officer, he shall ensure whether the particulars referred to in Section 27 of the Stamp Act are set forth in the instrument separately as required by the said Section 27 read with clause (a) of sub-section (2) of Section 175 of the Act and shall also ensure that the village panchayat within whose jurisdiction the property concerned is situated, is set forth clearly in the instrument.

(2) If the said particulars are not so separately set forth in the instrument, the registering officer shall impound it and forward it in original to the Collector, of the district concerned calling his attention to Section 64 of the Stamp Act, read with clause (b) of sub-section (2) of Section 175 of the Act.

(3) The duty leviable on an instrument of exchange shall be regulated as follows:

(a) if the value of the property exchanged is unequal, the duty shall be levied on the value of the property of the greater value;

(b) if the value of the property exchanged is equal, the higher amount of duty leviable shall be levied.

5. Maintenance and consolidation of accounts in respect of transfer duty—(1) (a) Every registering officer shall maintain an account of the duty paid in respect of each instrument registered by him showing separately the duty imposed by the Stamp Act and the transfer duty levied under Section 175 of the Act. He shall also maintain a separate account for each village panchayat within whose jurisdiction the property concerned is situated, ascertaining from the party concerned wherever necessary and the amount on which the transfer duty is to be levied.

(b) The Inspector General of Registration may issue instructions regarding the maintenance of accounts by a registering officer in this behalf land the form in which the consolidated accounts for each quarter are to be forwarded to the Collector of the district concerned.

(2) In the case of an instrument which does not come into the hands of a registering officer owing to the fact that is not compulsorily registerable under Section 17 of the Registration Act, 1908 (Central Act XVI of 1908), the Collector before whom any such instrument is produced under Section 31 or 41 of

the Stamp Act or who impounds any such instrument under Section 33 of the said Act or receives a certificate of the duty and penalty paid in respect of any such instrument or the original of any such instrument under Section 38 of that Act, shall keep an account of the duty paid in respect of each such instrument showing separately the duty imposed by the Stamp Act and the transfer duty and forward to the District Registrar of Assurances concerned within one month after the close of each quarter, a quarterly consolidated account with particulars in the case of each such instrument regarding the names of the executant and claimant, the date of execution, the nature of the transaction, the amount on which the transfer duty is leviable and the description of the property situated within the limits of the village panchayat or outside such limits.

(3) If in any case it becomes impossible to recover the full duty payable on any instrument, then, only such portion of the duty realised on such instrument as is in excess of the duty imposed by the Stamp Act shall be treated in the accounts referred to in these rules as transfer duty.

6. Collector to forward to the District Registrar concerned quarterly statement of refunds of transfer duty—Every Collector who sanctions a refund of the transfer duty of the transfer duty paid on any instrument shall forward to the District Registrar of Assurances concerned within one month after the close of each quarter, a statement of instruments in respect of which such refunds were sanctioned during the quarter noting therein the amount of the transfer duty refunded and the particulars referred to in sub-rule (2) of Rule 5 in respect of each such instrument.

7. District Registrars to send intimation to the Collectors of the districts concerned in respect of the amounts payable to the village panchayat—(1) The District Registrar at the headquarters of the Revenue district shall, in respect of the instruments referred to in sub-rules (1) and (2) of Rule 5, within one month after the close of each quarter, send,

(a) an intimation regarding the amount payable quarterly to the village panchayats, to the Collectors of the district concerned and the Inspector General of Registration; and

(b) an intimation regarding the amount of deduction on account of the collection of the transfer duty to be credited to the Government by the Inspector General of Registration.

(2) The amount payable to the village panchayat shall represent the transfer duty paid less a deduction of three per cent thereon on account of the charges for collection of transfer duty and the amount of refunds referred to in Rule 6, if any.

(3) The intimation set by the District Registrar to the Collector and the Inspector General of Registration shall contain the particulars of the amount payable to the village panchayat and that to be adjusted to the Registration department, distinctly and separately.

8. Payment to village panchayats by the Collector—(1) The Collector of the district shall check the arithmetical accuracy of the figures in the intimation sent by the District Registrar with reference to Rule 7 and prepare a consolidated bill in triplicate with full details of the amount due to each village panchayat as transfer duty as furnished in the intimation of the District Registrar and send to the Treasury Officer for payment to the village panchayat by Bank Demand Draft. The Treasury Officer concerned shall send an intimation to the Inspector General of Registration of such payment of the amount to the village panchayats.

(2) The Registrar at the headquarters of the Revenue district concerned shall prepare a consolidated bill for the amount of collection charges forming three per cent of the gross collections as arrived at by him and intimate to the Inspector General of Registration to be credited to the Government and send it to the Treasury Officer who shall credit the amount to the head to be specified from time-to-time and send an intimation to the Inspector General of Registration of full details of the credit so made.

(3) The statement of accounts sent by the Inspector General of Registration shall contain particulars of the amount payable to the village panchayat and that adjustable to the Registration department distinctly and separately. A copy of the statement shall also be sent to the Collector of the district concerned.

(G.O. Ms. No. 77, Rural Development (C4) Department, dated 20th March 2001)

5.7.13 Reduction of Surcharge on Stamp Duty by Village Panchayats

Under sub-section (1) of Section 175 of the Tamil Nadu Panchayats Act, 1994 (Tamil Nadu Act 21 of 1994), the Governor of Tamil Nadu hereby fixes the rate of duty on transfer of property to be levied in the form of a surcharge on the duty imposed by the Indian Stamp Act, 1899 (Central Act II of 1899), on every instrument of the description specified in the said sub-section at two per centum on the amount specified in that sub-section against such instrument.

Sl. No.	*Art. No.*	*Description*	*Rate of Stamp Duty*	*Transfer Duty*	*Old Rate of Total Duty*
1.	23	Conveyance on sale	6%	2%	13% or 12%
2.	31	Exchange	6%	2%	13% or 12%
3.	32(a), (b)1	Further charge	6%	2%	13% or 12%
4.	33	Gift	6%	2%	13% or 12%
5.	40(a)	Mortgage with possession	6%	2%	13% or 12%
6.	35(ix)	Perpetual lease	6%	2%	13% or 12%
7.	18	Certificate of sale	6%		8% or 7%
8.	48(e)	Power for consideration	6%		8% or 7%
9.	63	Transfer of lease	6%		8% or 7%
10.	35(a)(iii) (iv), (v), (vi), (vii), (viii) 35(b), (c)	Lease	6%		8% or 7%
11.	46(B)(i)	Dissolution of partnership—Non-family member	8%		13% or 12%
12.	5(i)	Agreement relating to construction of a flat/multi-unit house	8%		13% or 12%
13.	55(B)–(a) &(b)	Release of benami right	8%		13% or 12%
14.	55(c)–(i) & (ii)	Release of right in favour of co-owner	8%		13% or 12%
15.	55(D)(ii)	Release of right in favour of partners who are not family members	8%		13% or 12%
16.	58(a) (ii) (A) & (B)	Settlement other than family members	8%		13% or 12%

(G.O. Ms. No. 309, Rural Development Department, dated 21st November 2003)

5.7.14 Receipts and Expenditure and Maintenance of the Accounts of Village Panchayats

1. Short title—These rules may be called the Tamil Nadu Village Panchayat (Receipts and Expenditure and Maintenance of the Accounts of Village Panchayats) Rules, 2000.

Part I—Receipts

2. Definitions—In these rules, unless the context otherwise requires—

(a) "Act" means the Tamil Nadu Panchayat Act, 1994 (Tamil Nadu Act 21 of 1994).

(b) "Form" means the Form appended to these rules.

3. Maintenance of accounts and registers—Every village panchayat shall have as many accounts and maintain separate cash books and other registers for each one of the accounts as the Government may direct from time-to-time in the specified forms.

4. Collection and remittance of taxes—(1) The house-tax levied under Sections 171 and 172 of the Act, the profession tax levied under Section 198-A of the Act the tax on agricultural land levied under sub-section (3) of Section 171 of the Act or any other tax which may be levied in future shall be collected from the assessee by granting a printed receipt, using double side carbon, in the form prescribed by the Government. As and when receipts are granted the details of collection shall be entered in a collection register maintained for this purpose. The receipt for the collection of taxes shall bear the signature of the Executive Authority in the form of facsimile and shall be signed in ink by the Panchayat Assistant/Part-time clerk of the village panchayat.

(2) The amounts collected shall be entered in the tax and miscellaneous items collection register and in the cash book. The amount collected shall be remitted to the credit of the village panchayat fund account. Whenever the remittances are made and credited to the fund accounts of village panchayat,

the details of the remittance shall be entered on the debit side of the cash book on the date of remittance.

(3) No part of receipt received in cash shall be directly appropriated for any expenditure.

5. Fees for licence and permission—(1) The fee payable in respect of every licence or permission granted under the act or any rule or regulations, made thereunder shall be collected in advance when the application for the licence or permission is presented.

(2) The particulars relating to the collection of fee and to the grant of such licence or permission shall be entered consecutively in the register of licences and permissions which shall be maintained in such form as may be laid down by the government from time-to-time.

6. Income from endowments and trusts—(1) The Executive Authority of the village panchayat shall maintain or cause to be maintained in the office of the village panchayat, an up-to-date record of every endowment or trust managed by it. Such record shall show:

(a) the authority and sources of income of the endowment or trust; and the expenditure chargeable to the endowment or trust;

(b) the assets and sources of income of the endowment or trust; and

(c) the expenditure chargeable to the endowment or trust.

(2) The Executive Authority of the village panchayat shall, in addition to the record in sub-rule (1), maintain or cause to be maintained in the office of the village panchayat a register of endowments and trusts showing in separate pages, the yearly transactions relating to each endowment or trust.

7. Contributions—The receipt of contributions payable to a village panchayat from the Government, other panchayat, municipal councils, other local authorities and private persons shall be watched through the miscellaneous demand collection and balance register.

8. Sale-proceeds of tools and plant, sweeping, old store materials—The orders of the village panchayat shall be taken for the disposal of old and unserviceable tools and plants, stores and materials, sweepings, wind fallen and withered trees and usufruct of avenue trees over which the village panchayat has control or ownership and they shall be sold in public auction unless otherwise ordered by the village panchayat, for specific reasons to be recorded. The sales shall be subject to confirmation by the village panchayat. The receipt from all such sales shall be shown in the register of taxes and miscellaneous items collection register.

9. Fees from markets, cart-stands, landing or halting places, slaughter houses, fisheries and ferries—(1) the village panchayat shall collect fees in respect of the use of any market, cart-stand, landing or halting place, slaughter house, fishery or ferry through lease by public auctions as per the rules prescribed by the Government. Collection of amounts due shall be watched through the miscellaneous demand register.

10. Collection of fees by village panchayat—(1) Where any market cart-stand, landing or halting place, slaughter house, fishery or ferry is managed directly by village panchayat, all fees levied in respect of the use thereof shall be collected by means of tickets printed and supplied by the Executive Authority.

(2) The tickets shall be printed in foil and counterfoil in different colours for different rates of fees, the rates being printed in each case. Each kind of ticket shall be bound in books of 10 each and shall bear consecutive machine numbers. Before issue to the collecting officers they shall be stamped, with the common seal of the village panchayat in the presence of the Executive Authority or any person authorized by him in this behalf.

(3) A register in two parts shall be maintained in the office of the village panchayat in respect of these tickets.

(a) The first part shall be a stock register, the entries for receipts being attested by the Executive Authority or an officer authorized by him and the entries for issue being attested by the collecting officer concerned.

(b) The second part shall be a personal ledger account for each officer entrusted with the collection of revenue by means of these tickets. It shall be debited with the number and value of each kind of ticket issued to each collecting officer and shall be credited with the amount of the collections paid by him into the office of the village panchayat. Remittances shall be made by the collecting officer every day and shall be accompanied by the details of the number and value of each kind of ticket issued by him.

(4) Where any ticket book has been completely used, the counter foil shall be sent to the office of the village panchayat for check with actual credits.

(5) The collecting officer shall also keep an account of the tickets, entrusted to him and the

collection made by him. The daily collections by each kind of ticket shall be entered in such account and the balances struck at the end of everyday. The account and the stock of tickets shall be verified at regular intervals by the Executive Authority or any officer authorized by him who shall certify to such verification.

11. Income from buildings, lands and other immovable property—(1) If any building belonging to a village panchayat is rented out the prompt recovery of the rent of such building shall be watched through the miscellaneous demand collection and balance register.

(2) A register in such form as may be laid down by the Government, from time-to-time shall be maintained in every traveller's bungalow, rest-house or chatram under the control of the village panchayat and person occupying such traveller's bungalow, rest house or chatram shall be required to enter the particulars specified in the register, fees shall be charged for such occupation at the rates determined by the village panchayat.

12. Advance collection for services to be rendered—Save as the otherwise provided in the Act, no work for any private individual or body shall be undertaken by a village panchayat unless the estimated cost and service charges thereof has been paid in advance.

13. Tax and miscellaneous item collection register—All transactions relating to miscellaneous dues for which miscellaneous receipts are issued shall be recorded in the tax and miscellaneous item collection register.

14. Utilization of moneys—No moneys received on behalf of the village panchayat shall be utilized for its expenditure without first being brought into the concerned account. No part of any receipt in cash shall directly be appropriated for expenditure.

15. Refunds of revenue—(1) No item of revenue received by a village panchayat shall be refunded without the sanction of the village panchayat. The sanction accorded by the village panchayat shall lapse after one year from the date of grant thereof and hereafter a fresh sanction shall be necessary.

(2) Bills for refunds of revenue shall be drawn in village panchayat Form 34 (Appendix-XIII) As soon as refund is made, a note of the grant thereof shall be made against the original credit entry in the relevant accounts.

16. Sale of usufruct of trees, wind fallen trees, etc.—(1) All sales of:

(a) the produce or usufruct of trees;

(b) wind fallen and withered trees;

(c) sweepings;

(d) tools and plant;

(e) old stores and materials

belonging to village panchayat shall be effected by public auction by the Executive Authority of the village panchayat as per the procedure laid down by the Government.

(2) The sale proceeds realized by the Executive Authority of the village panchayat shall be remitted immediately in the village panchayat fund.

17. Security for collection of fees—Security adequate in the opinion of the Executive Authority shall in all cases be taken for the due fulfilment of the terms of a lease of the produce or usufruct of trees or of the right to collect fees in respect of markets cart-stands, landing places, halting places-slaughter house, fisheries or of any other similar right. The security so taken shall not be repaid to the lessee unless and until he has satisfactorily complied with all the terms of the lease. But the amount of security may be adjusted towards the last instalment due under the lease.

18. Duty on transfers of poverty—(1) Each village panchayat shall be entitled to receive a duty on transfer of property in the form of surcharge on the duty imposed by the Indian Stamps Act, 1899 (Central Act II of 1899) on all transfers of immovable property situated in the area under the jurisdiction of village panchayat.

(2) The duty shall be adjusted once a quarter by the District Collector based on the collection details from the District Registrar. The amount shall be credited to village panchayat fund.

19. Local cess—(1) Each village panchayat shall receive the entire collection of local cess levied under Section 167 of the Act which shall be credited to the Village Panchayat Fund.

(2) Local cess shall be adjusted once a quarter in advance by the District Collector based on the average collection of local cess for the past three fasli years. The final adjustment of local cess shall be made after finalisation of collection under local cess in the Jamabandi, held for every fasli year.

20. Entertainment tax—(1) Each village panchayat shall receive the proportionate share of the proceeds of entertainment tax as may be fixed by the Government from time-to-time of the said tax collected in the panchayat village.

21. Seigniorage fees—(1) The village panchayat shall receive a sum equivalent to the seigniorage fees collected by the Government every year from persons permitted to quarry minor minerals in the panchayat village.

(2) The District Collector shall adjust the seigniorage fees to the Village Panchayat Fund once a year.

22. Devolution grant by the State Government—(1) Each village panchayat shall receive a devolution grant based on the recommendation of the State Finance Commission based on the norms fixed by the Government from time-to-time. This grant shall be credited to Village Panchayat Fund.

(2) The Government may also sanction equalization and incentive grant to the village panchayat based on the norms as may be fixed by the Government, from time-to-time.

23. Devolution grant by the Government of India—(1) Each village panchayat shall receive a devolution grant based on the recommendation of the 11th Finance Commission as per the norms fixed by the Government of India from time-to-time. The grant and other such amounts shall be credited to Village Panchayat Earmarked Funds.

24. Receipt of money—All money received by the Executive Authority or under his authority by an officer or servant of the village panchayat including a Government servant, whose services have been placed at the disposal of the village panchayat in his capacity as such, shall be brought into account as soon as they are received. All money so received shall be credited into the village panchayat office daily.

25. Payment into Co-operative Bank, Regional Rural Bank, Post Office Savings Bank or Nationalized Bank—Every payment into a Co-operative Bank, Regional Rural Bank, Post Office Savings Bank or Nationalized Bank shall be accompanied by a Chalan, which shall show the amount of the payment made the nature thereof and the person or office on whose account it is made.

26. Application of capital receipts to ordinary expenditure—No village panchayat shall apply its capital receipts, such as sale proceeds of land, building or machinery, to ordinary expenditure without the previous sanction of the Inspector.

27. Supply of collection book—Every village panchayat servant or the Village Administrative Officer entrusted with the collection of revenue due to village panchayat shall be supplied with a collection book.

28. Collection of taxes and other revenues—Collection of taxes and other village panchayat revenues made by Bill-Collectors or Village Administrative Officer or his subordinates or any other persons shall be remitted into the village panchayat office through the taxes and miscellaneous items collection register maintained in the village panchayat office.

29. Issue of receipts—Receipts in the form laid down by the Government shall be given for all moneys received in the village panchayat office from the public except in the case of the receipts acknowledged in the taxes and miscellaneous item collection register. Such receipts shall be signed by the executive authority or by official of village panchayat authorized by him.

30. Cash book and subsidiary registers—The Executive Authority shall maintain or cause to be maintained such accounts and registers in the village panchayat office in such form be laid down by the Government.

Part II – Expenditure

31. Payments from village panchayat—All payments out of the Village Panchayat Fund against bills presented to the village panchayat shall be made only after the bills are passed by the Executive Authority or by any person authorized by Government in respect of any particular scheme or fund.

32. Payments by cheque—(1) Payments shall be made only by crossed accounts payee cheque drawn in favour of the parties as per the procedure laid down by Government from time-to-time. The Executive Authority may draw amounts in self cheque only in respect of the following payments:

1. Salaries to the village panchayat staff.
2. Travelling allowance payable to Executive Authority, members and staff of the village panchayat.
3. Petty office contingent expenditure.
4. Advances to the staff for festival.

33. Drawal of cheque—Where the Executive authority or other persons of a village panchayat who is authorized to draw cheques against the funds of the village panchayat hands over charges of the office either temporarily or permanently, he shall send a specimen of the signature of the relieving person together with a certificate in the Form-1 to the local official of the bank, or the postmaster or secretary of the co-operative bank, as the case may be.

34. Maintenance of cheque books—Cheque books shall be kept in the personal custody of the drawing authority and when a transfer of charge takes places, a note shall be recorded in the book over the signature of both the relieved and the relieving persons showing the number of unused cheques and cheque books made over and received by them respectively.

35. Procedure for claims against the Village Panchayat Fund—(1) Every person having any claim against the Village Panchayat Fund shall present a bill in village panchayat office.

(2) Wherever possible printed forms shall be used in preparing bills.

(3) Where a claimant presents a bill in a form different from the form provided for the purpose, a separate bill in the proper form shall be prepared by the officer incurring the expenditure and the claimant's bill attached thereto as sub-voucher.

(4) Every bill shall be presented to the Executive Authority of the village panchayat who shall enter it in the register of bills and then check and examine the bill as regards its admissibility with reference to sanction or other documents, the propriety of the claim and the arithmetical accuracy. If on such check and examination the bill is found to be correct the Executive Authority shall pass the bill.

(5) In respect of scheme fund, where the bill is to be scrutinized and passed by a person authorized by Government, the Executive Authority shall send such bill to the authorized person, who shall thoroughly scrutinize the bills as a foresaid and if the bill is found to be correct and in order, pass and send it back to the Executive Authority within three days for drawing the cheque for the amount passed by the notified person.

36. Acknowledgement for receiving of money—(1) Separate acknowledgements (stamped where necessary) shall be taken in the acquitance register from each officer or servant of the village panchayat to whom any salary or allowance is paid except where the drawer of the bill is the sole payee and has already furnished a receipt (stamped where necessary) on the bill itself.

(2) Where any officer or servant of a village panchayat makes any payment from any sum drawn by him, he shall unless a receipt (stamped where necessary) has been furnished on the bill itself obtain and attach to the bill a separate receipt (stamped where necessary).

37. Sanction of expenditure—Where any item of expenditure requires the sanction of any authority higher than the officer or servant drawing the bill, such sanction shall be obtained and the terms thereof shall be quoted on the bill.

38. Certificate for sanctioning of expenditure—(1) No item of expenditure shall be sanctioned by a village panchayat unless a certificate furnished by the executive authority in Form-2.

If there is no budget provision under the head concerned and the Executive Authority of the village panchayat decides to find the amount by re-appropriation from another head, the words "by re-appropriation" shall be added after the word "met".

The certificate shall be entered in the agenda, circulated before the meeting and if accepted by the village panchayat need not be written again as part of the resolution in the minutes book. If, however, the village panchayat makes any alteration either in the amount of expenditure or in the head from which the expenditure is to be met, the certificate shall form part of the resolution of the village panchayat and be entered as such in the minutes book.

(2) A sanction for any fresh charge which has not been acted on for a year shall be held to have lapse unless it is specifically renewed:

Provided that this sub-rules shall not apply to the expenditure on works which shall be governed by the provisions laid down in sub-rule (3).

(3)(a) The sanction to an ordinary annual maintenance estimate shall lapse on the last day of the financial year to which is relates. If however inconvenience would a rise in any exceptional case from stoppage of the work on that date, the repairs; may be carried on to completion, the expenditure incurred after the date being treated as expenditure against a fresh repair estimate.

(b) Estimate for special repairs shall remain current till the completion of the repairs in the same manner as estimates for original works.

(c) The approval of sanction to an estimate for any public work other than annual maintenance shall, unless such work has been commenced, cease to operate after a period of three years from the date from which it was accorded.

39. Limitation of claims—No claim made against a village panchayat other than one relating to any officer or servant of the village panchayat which will be governed by rules separately framed in that behalf, shall be laid:

(1) Where the bill in respect of them is presented more than six months; but not more than one year

from the date on which the claim became due without the order of the executive authority.

(2) Where such bill is presented more than one year from the date on which the claim became due without the order of the village panchayat.

40. Over payment—The responsibility for the over payment shall rest primarily with the drawer of a bill who shall be required to make good the over payment and increase where the bill is passed by a person notified by Government in respect of any scheme of fund, the over payment shall be recovered from such notified person.

41. Defalcation or loss of moneys or stamp—(1) Any defalcation or loss of moneys or stamps belonging to a village panchayat shall be reported immediately after discovery by the president or any one of the inspecting officer to the Inspector and Auditor appointed under Section 193 of the Act. A further and complete report shall also be submitted to such auditor as soon as may be after the matter has been fully enquired into by such inspecting officer settingforth nature and the extent of the defalcation or loss, the errors, neglect of rules by which such defalcation or loss was rendered possible, and the prospects or effecting a recovery.

(2) Loss by theft or otherwise of any property belonging to a village panchayat shall also be reported by the president or inspecting officer to the auditor, if the loss of the property exceeds rupees one thousand.

(3) The submission of the reports prescribed by the sub-rules (1) and (2) shall not be deemed to debar the village panchayat or the Executive Authority from taking such further action as may be considered necessary.

42. Loss of property due to other causes—(1) Any loss to any immovable property belonging to village panchayats due to calamity, such as fire or flood or cyclone other than wear and tear shall be reported to the Inspector and Auditor appointed under Section 193 of the Act in Form III.

(2) In case of loss by way of damage to any portion of any immovable property belonging to village panchayats, it shall not be necessary to write off the value of the damage of portion if the damaged portion is replaced or reconstructed within a period of two years from the date of such damage.

(3) For the purpose of write off, the value of the temporary structures damaged or destroyed which have served the period intended for and which are therefore not proposed to be replaced or reconstructed the value of such structures shall be assessed by the Block Engineer/Assistant Engineer (Rural Development) as on the date of damage or destruction.

43. Establishment bills—(1) Pay bills shall be prepared in such form as may be laid down by the Government from time-to-time. The monthly pay bill of the establishments shall be supported either by an absentee statement in such form as may be laid down by the Government from time-to-time or by a certificate in the bill that no leave has been granted to any member of the establishment.

44. Increment certificate form—To the first pay bill in which a periodical increment is drawn, an increment certificate in such form as may be laid down by the Government from time-to-time shall be attached.

45. Drawal of pay of officers—The pay of an officer or servant lent by the Government to a village panchayat or transferred to it from any other local body shall be drawn only after the receipt of the last pay certificate which shall be in such form as may be laid drown by the Government, from time-to-time, granted by the head of his former office. Such certificate shall be attached to the first pay bill drawn after such loan or transfers.

46. Payment due to a deceased officer or servant—(1) Pay, leave salary and allowances may be drawn for the day of death of an officer or servant of the village panchayat. The hour at which death takes places does not affect the claims.

(2) Payment due to a deceased officer or a servant of a village panchayat shall not be made except on the production of an authority of the nature specified in clause (i), (ii), (iii), (iv), (v), or (vi) of sub-section (1) of Section 214 of the Indian Succession Act, 1925 (Central Act XXXIX of 1925):

(i) Provided that payment may be made without the production of such authority (i) to the extent of Rs. 250 under the orders of the village panchayat if it is satisfied after such enquiry as it may consider sufficient, about the right and title of the claimant; and

(ii) above Rs. 250 under the orders of the Inspector on the execution of an indemnity bond with such security or securities as he may require if he is satisfied, after such enquiry as he may consider sufficient, about the right and title of the claimant and considers that undue delay and hardship would be caused by insisting on the production of such authority.

47. Drawal of arrears of pay—Arrears pay shall be drawn not in the monthly bill but in a separate bill which shall quote the bill from which the charge was omitted or with held or on which it was refunded by deduction.

48. Authority to sign and pass pay bills—Pay bills shall be signed and passed by the Executive Authority.

49. Date of payment of salaries and allowances—Payment of salaries and fixed allowances shall be made on the last working day of the month to which the payment relates:

Provided that in the event of an officer or servant finally quitting the service of the village panchayat or being transferred to the service of another local body payment shall be made on the date of such event.

50. Responsibility of the drawer of a bill—The drawer of a bill for salary and allowances shall be personally responsible for the amount so drawn until it has been disbursal to the proper person or person concerned and the acquittances have been obtained. If the payee does not present himself within thirty days of drawl of money the amount drawn for him shall be refunded by short drawal in the next bill. The amount of salary and allowances drawn shall not in any circumstances be placed under deposit.

51. Audit register—In order to facilitate the check of monthly bills for recurring charges, such as establishment, house-rent and conveyance, an audit register shall be maintained in the office of every village panchayat.

52. Drawal of travelling allowance—Travelling allowances other than fixed travelling allowances shall be drawn in a separate bill in such form as may be laid down by the Government from time-to-time.

53. Drawal of conveyance allowance—Conveyance allowance shall be drawn in the pay bill of the Officer or servant concerned and not on travelling allowance bills. To every bill of conveyance allowance a certificate shall be attached that the conveyance was actually maintained in good condition and used by him during the month.

54. Placing of all bills before the village panchayat—All bills for expenditure incurred in a month whether with or without the sanction of the village panchayat shall be placed before it as early as possible for being passed after such scrutiny as it may consider necessary.

Part III—General

55. Limited number of accounts—Every village panchayat shall have accounts preferably Saving Bank Account in the Post Office, Co-operative Bank, the Nationalized Bank available in the panchayat village. Total number of Accounts to be opened and operated by village panchayat shall on no occasion be more than five.

56. Reconciliation of receipt and expenditure—The Executive Authority of village panchayat shall be responsible to reconcile village panchayat funds with receipt and bank accounts he shall be responsible to reconcile all expenditure accounts.

57. Placing receipts and expenditure details before the Grama Sabha—The president of each village panchayat shall present in every Grama Sabha meeting the receipts and expenditure of village panchayat upto previous month of the financial year. Once in a year president of the village panchayat shall present the report of the village panchayat for the previous financial year which will include the Annual Accounts clearly indicating the receipts and expenditure.

(G.O.Ms.No.43 Rural Development (C4) Department, dated 21st February 2000)

FORM – 1

(See Rule 33)

Form of Certificate (Signed) A.B.

Signature and designation of the relieving person

I certify that above is the signature of the individual to whom I have made over charge of my office with effect from the forenoon/afternoon of __________(date) of __________(month) __________ of __________(year).

Signed CD

Signature of the authority handing over charge with date

FORM – 2

(See Rule 38)

Certificate for Sanctioning Expenditure

The amount may be met from the budget allotment of under the head	Rs. ....
The amount spent under this head up-to-date is	Rs...............
The amount sanctioned up-to-date but not spent is	Rs. ....
The amount to be sanctioned now is	Rs. ....
	Total ....

The balance remaining amount will be Rs. ....

FORM – 3

(See Rule 33)

Report of Damage to Immovable Property Belonging to Village Panchayat

1. Name of the village panchayat.
2. Name any location of the property damaged or destroyed.
3. Description of property damaged or destroyed.
4. Cause of the damage or destruction.
5. Value of the damaged or destroyed portion of the property at the time of damage or destruction.
6. (a) Is it proposed to replace or reconstruct the damaged or destroyed portion?
   (b) If so, what is the estimated cost of the replacement or reconstruction?
7. If it is not proposed to replace or reconstruct the damaged or destroyed portion of the property, what is the amount to be written of in the capital value of the property in the accounts?
8. What action is being taken to effect such write-off, if any?

5.7.15 Opening of Village Panchayat Fund Accounts

According to sub-section (2) of Section 188 of Tamil Nadu Panchayats Act, 1994, the Government notify that the following separate Accounts shall be opened and operated in all the village panchayats.

(1) Village Panchayat Fund Account
(2) Village Panchayat Earmarked Fund Account
(3) Village Panchayat Scheme Fund Account.

(G.O.Ms.No.233, Rural Development (C-3) Department, dated 17th July 1997)

5.7.16 Use of Grants Recommended by the State Finance Commission and Abolition of Certain Grants to Village Panchayats and Panchayat Unions

1. The Government examined the recommendations of the State Finance Commission and decided to allot 8 per cent of the Pool 'B' Tax Collection excepting Entertainment Tax to the panchayats.

2. As a result of the above decision, the grants hitherto received by village panchayats and panchayat unions will not be sanctioned by Government from 1.4.97 onwards. The following grants shall not be sanctioned to the panchayats.

Village Panchayats

(i) Hand Pump Maintenance Grant
(ii) Power Pump Maintenance Grant
(iii) Grant for Salary for Panchayat Assistant
(iv) Street Light Grant for Weaker Panchayats
(v) Compensation for Surcharge on Sales Tax sanctioned to Village Panchayats
(vi) House Tax Matching Grant.

Panchayat Unions

(i) Local Cess Surcharge Matching Grant
(ii) Local Roads Grant.

3. The panchayats already met the expenditure from the particular hereafter shall grant incur the expenditure on grants allotted as per recommendations of the State Finance Commission.

4. Other Grants shall continuously be sanctioned by Government.

5. The Grant sanctioned as per the recommendations of the State Finance Commission shall be utilised only for the following purposes:

Village Panchayats

(i) Salary and Wages of sanctioned staff.
(ii) Maintenance of Drinking Water Sources including Hand pump and Power pump.
(iii) Maintenance of Street Lights and remittance of current consumption charges.
(iv) To fulfil various obligatory functions as per Tamil Nadu Panchayat Act, 1994 like Public Health, Sanitation, Drainage etc.
(v) Office Maintenance including stationery.

Panchayat Unions

(i) Salary and Wages for sanctioned employees of Panchayat Union
(ii) Provident Fund and Pension Contribution, Travelling Allowance, Daily Allowance and other expenditure of Panchayat Union employees.
(iii) Expenditure on Office maintenance, Stationery, Current Consumption charges, Telephone Charges etc.
(iv) Maintenance of Panchayat Union Buildings and other buildings entrusted to Panchayat Unions.
(v) Maintenance of Panchayat Union Roads.
(vi) Maintenance of Minor Irrigation Tanks transferred to Panchayat Unions.

6. The following instructions have to be strictly followed by all the panchayats:

(i) Salary of staff, Pension and Provident Fund Contribution, Office expenditure shall be the first charge in this grant.
(ii) In respect of village panchayats, the following items shall be given priority:
  (a) Maintenance of Drinking Water Sources like Bore Wells, Hand pumps and Power pumps.
  (b) Street Lights
  (c) Public Health Sanitation
  (d) Other obligatory functions
(iii) In respect of panchayat unions, the maintenance of buildings shall be given the next preference
(iv) After providing for all the items only the maintenance of Roads and Minor Irrigation Tanks can be taken up.

7. Unless provided in the Government Orders, no Part-time/Full time/NMR/Temporary employees shall be appointed newly.

8. The District Collectors as Inspector of panchayats and panchayat unions shall strictly follow the above instructions.

9. If there is surplus fund after providing or after incurring expenditure on all the above items. The panchayat shall take up the works as suggested by the Director of Rural Development.

10. Besides the State Finance Commission Grant, village panchayats will be having their own finance resource like House Tax, Professional tax, License Fee etc.,

11. Local Cess, Surcharge on Stamp duty share of entertainment tax seigniorage fee on mining of minor minerals etc., will also be received by village panchayats. Local Cess Surcharge and share of entertainment tax will be continuously be sanctioned to the panchayat unions.

12. There shall be no transaction after 31.3.97 between village panchayats and panchayat unions. No adjustment shall be made between the accounts of village panchayats and panchayat unions after 31.3.97. The balance amount as on 1.4.97 in the Village Panchayat Consolidated Fund shall be transferred to the new Savings Bank Account opened as per G.O.Ms.No.92, Rural Development Department, dated 26.3.97 by the village panchayats in Co-operative Bank/Regional Rural Bank/Post Office Savings Bank/Nationalised Bank and credited to that account.

13. Separate Committee shall be formed to look after the amount to be transferred from panchayat unions to village panchayats and from village panchayats to panchayat unions.

(G.O. Ms. No. 93, Rural Development (C-3) Department, dated 26th March 1997)

5.7.17 Procedure for Expenditure of Surplus Funds

The Government issued orders specifying authorities competent to sanction expenditure from the surplus funds of village panchayats and also prescribing conditions for such sanctions as follows:

Sl. No.	*Work and Amount*	*Authority competent to sanction*
1.	Individual work costing upto Rs. 1 lakh	Village Panchayat
2.	Individual work costing more than Rs. 1 lakh	Inspector of Panchayat (District Collector)

Conditions for Sanction

(1) Village panchayat shall sanction the individual capital work

(2) Village panchayat Administration shall first ensure that adequate funds are available for running day today administration before sending proposal for sanction of works under Surplus fund.

(G.O. Ms. No. 189, Rural Development Department, dated 3rd September 1998)

5.7.18 Opening of Bank Account and Lodging of the Panchayat Funds – Regarding

In G.O. Ms. No. 92, Rural Development (C3) Department, dated 26.3.97 orders have been issued prescribing the accounting procedure to the village panchayat. In Para 2 of Annexure–I to that Government Order it has been ordered among others that "these accounts may be permitted to be opened in a branch of

— Any Co-operative Bank
— Any Branch of Regional Rural Banks
— Post Office Savings Bank
— Nationalised Bank

in the above order of priority, depending upon the convenience of the village panchayat, either in the same village or in the nearby village.

The Government hereby clarify that the above of priority should be strictly followed. In respect of the first priority (Co-operative Banks) the accounts may be opened in a branch of Primary Agricultural Co-operative Society, Co-operative Land Development or Land Mortgage Bank or any Co-operative Bank, either in the same panchayat or in the adjacent village. If there is no co-operative bank as mentioned above either in the same village or in the nearby village, the accounts may be permitted to be opened in a branch of

— Any Regional Rural Banks
— Post Office Savings Banks
— Nationalised Banks

in the panchayat in the above order of priority, depending upon the convenience of the village panchayat.

This clarification is being issued to safeguard against village panchayats attempting to open the account in distant places.

(Government Lr. No. 19857/C3/97-1, Rural Development Department, dated 22nd May 1997)

5.7.19 Form and Content of Budget of Village Panchayats

1. ____________________
2. ____________________
3. Form and content

(1) The Executive Authority of every village panchayat shall, before the 31st December of each year frame a budget showing the probable receipts and expenditure during the following financial year in such form as the Government may specify, from time-to-time, and place the same before the village panchayat and Grama Sabha.

(2) A working balance of not less than five per cent of the estimated receipts excluding those from endowments, Government grants and debt heads of the year for which the budget has been prepared shall be provided for in the budget. While preparing the budget the village panchayat shall make adequate provision for the obligatory functions of the village panchayat stipulated under Section 110 of the Act.

3. Placing the Budget before Grama Sabha—The Executive Authority shall place the draft budget of the village panchayat before the Grama Sabha on or before the 26th January and carry out any modification, if any, in the budget and place it before the village panchayat for approval before the 31st January of the year preceding the year for which the budget is prepared.

5. Prescribed officer for scrutiny of budget—Three copies of the draft budget so prepared by the village panchayat, and approved by the Grama Sabha under Rule 4 shall be sent by the executive authority of the village panchayat to the Deputy Block Development Officer (Panchayats) on or before the 31st January preceding the budget year.

6. Time limit for approval of the budget—If the Deputy Block Development Officer (Panchayats) fails either to scrutinize and send it to the village panchayat the draft budget or return, the same for modification, with in thirty days of its receipt, it may be construed that the draft budget is approved and the village panchayat may proceed further. In the case of return, the Executive Authority shall immediately modify the draft budget and send it back as mentioned previously for getting approval. In any case remarks of the scrutinising officer on the draft budget in respect of every village panchayat under his jurisdiction shall be sent by the Deputy Block Development Officer (Panchayats) not later than 8th February of each year. The Executive

Authority of the village panchayat shall obtain the sanction of the village panchayat for the budget approved by the Deputy Block Development Officer (Panchayats) before the 15th March of the year. Copies of the sanctioned budget shall be sent to the Inspector, Auditor, Assistant Director (Panchayats) Deputy Block Development Officer (Panchayats) within seven days of the passing of the budget is prepared.

7. **No Expenditure in Village Panchayat, without the Budget Provisions**—(1) No village panchayat shall authorise any item of expenditure not included in the budget or which is in excess of the budget allotment and without indicating source from which money required for proposed expenditure is to be found.

(2) No village panchayat shall without the previous sanction of the Inspector, divert even temporarily any part of the following earmarked funds for purposes other than those for which they are collected:

(a) Proceeds of the tax levied on agricultural land under sub-section (3) of Section 171 of the Act for the purposes specific.
(b) Loan amounts.
(c) Deposits (including provident fund).
(d) Surplus under the special tax accounts for specific purpose.
(e) Receipts derived from the sale of capital assets.
(f) Income from endowments and trusts.
(g) Proceeds of the water tax specially levied as surcharge on house-tax for the purpose of providing for expenses connected with water supply scheme and works.
(h) Government grants and subsidies sanctioned for specific purposes.

8. **Outside sanction to be obtained wherever prescribed**—(1) The sanctioning of the budget shall not by itself be deemed to authorise the village panchayat to incur all the expenditure provided for therein and where the sanction of the Government or of any other authority is required for incurring any expenditure, for which the provision has been included in the budget, and such sanction has not been specifically accorded, it shall be duty of the village panchayat to obtain such sanction before the expenditure is incurred.

(2) The Executive Authority shall pay prompt attention to the remarks, if any, made by the auditor in regard to expenditure as compared with the budget allotment.

9. **Lapse of budget provision**—(1) All allotments made in the budget shall lapse at the end of the financial year. Parts of allotments remaining unexpended at the end of the financial year shall not be reserved for disbursement after the end of the financial year, nor shall they be appropriated by transfer to deposits or any other head or drawn in advance in order to avoid lapse.

(2) All expenditure during the course of the year shall be regulated in accordance with the allotments made in the budget for the year sanctioned by the village panchayat with modifications suggested, if any, by the Deputy Block Development Officer (Panchayats) or as modified by the Inspector under sub-section (3) of the Section 192 of the Act.

10. **Excess over budget provision**—Each case of excess expenditure which does not exceed five per cent of the provision in the budget estimate shall be got ratified by the Deputy Block Development Officer (Panchayats) concerned after obtaining the sanction of the village panchayat concerned. Each case of excess expenditure which exceeds five per cent of the provision in the budget estimate shall be got approved by the Inspector.

11. **Revised Budget**—If, in the course of the year, any village panchayat find it necessary to alter or modify provisions shown in the budget, a revised budget may be prepared and placed before the village panchayat and Grama Sabha for approval and then submit three copies to the Deputy Block Development Officer (Panchayats) before the 31st December of the budget year.

(G.O.Ms.No.223, Rural Development (C4) Department, 20th October 1999)

5.7.20 Issue and Disposal of Audit Report of Village Panchayats

1. **Short title**—These rules may be called the Tamil Nadu Panchayats (Issue and Disposal of Audit Report of Village Panchayats) Rules, 2000.

2. **Definition**—In these rules unless the context otherwise requires

(i) "Act" means The Tamil Nadu Panchayats Act, 1994 (Tamil Nadu Act 21 of 1994);
(ii) "Auditor" means the Deputy Block Development Officer of the panchayat union in whose jurisdiction the village panchayat lies appointed by the Government under sub-section (1) of Section 193 of the Act.

3. **Submission of accounts and records of the village panchayat**—The Executive Authority of a

village panchayat shall produce all accounts and records of the village panchayat to the auditor, as required by him and also to the Accountant General and his subordinate officers whenever he or his subordinate officers demand the production of the records of a village panchayat.

4. Conduct of audit of village panchayat— (1) The Executive Authority shall report in writing to the auditor before the end of May of every year regarding the closure of the accounts for the previous year along with the copy of the annual accounts. The auditor shall conduct the audit of the village panchayats every year, within two months from the receipt of the report but not later than 30th September of that year.

(2) If so directed by the Government, the auditor shall take up concurrent audit of vouchers of a village panchayat soon after the payment is made and send audit slips after such audit is done by him, to the Inspector for sending the same to Government with his remarks thereon.

5. Powers of the auditor—(1) The auditor may, by summons in writing

(i) require the production of any book, deed, contract, account, voucher, receipt or other documents, the perusal or examination thereof which he considers necessary;

(ii) require any person having the custody or control of any such document or person accountable for it to appear in person before him and require him to make and sign a declaration in respect of such document or to answer any question or to prepare and furnish any statement relating thereto.

(2) Whoever fails to comply with any requisition lawfully made upon him under this rule, shall be punishable with fine which may extend to one hundred rupees, or in case of continuing breach, with fine not exceeding fifteen rupees for everyday during which the breach continues after conviction of the first breach.

6. Procedure for conduct of audit—(1) The auditor shall scrutinise every item of expenditure and decide whether the Executive Authority has conducted the financial transactions of the village panchayat in accordance with rules and orders, issued by the Government and other competent authorities, from time-to-time, and also with the approval of the village panchayat. As far as the receipts are concerned, the auditor shall verify whether the Executive Authority has properly assessed all the eligible persons or properties under various taxes leviable by the village panchayat. He shall decide items of expenditure which are not admissible and items of loss of revenue, or leakage of revenue which are attributable to the negligence of the Executive Authority and clearly establish the persons responsible for the loss of income or irregular and inadmissible expenditure.

(2) The auditor shall specify the grounds or the basis of authority or the non-observance or violation of rules, instructions, norms or orders which has led to a material impropriety or irregularity in a transaction involving financial implications which he find in any financial transaction, item of expenditure of or revenue receipt to the village panchayat.

(3) The auditor shall report to the village panchayat any loss, waste or misapplication of money or other property owned by or vested in the village panchayat if such loss, waste or misapplication is a direct consequence of the neglect or misconduct of the Executive Authority or any other subordinates with names of persons directly or indirectly responsible for such loss, waste or misapplication.

(4) The audit report on the accounts of the village panchayat for a financial year shall be sent to the Executive Authority and a copy of the same sent to Assistant Director of Rural Development (Audit) within fifteen days of the completion of audit.

(5) The Assistant Director of Rural Development (Audit) shall check the audit report of not less than ten per cent of the total number of village panchayats in the district and verify the correctness of audit done by the auditor.

(6) During the course of audit, when the auditor of the village panchayat notices, any defalcation or misappropriation of the fund of the village panchayat, he shall immediately bring the fact to the notice of the Inspector for taking necessary action under the Act including prosecution of the Executive Authority. Copy of such report shall also be sent to the Assistant Director of Rural Development (Panchayats) and Assistant Director of Rural Development (Audit).

(7) The Executive Authority shall forthwith rectify the defects or irregularities, if any, which may be pointed out by the auditors and report the same to the village panchayat.

7. Placing of audit report before Grama Sabha— (1) The Executive Authority shall place the audit report of the village panchayat along with the replies furnished to auditor, in the meeting of the Grama Sabha.

(2) The Grama Sabha shall scrutinise, review and approve the audit report with replies.

(3) The Grama Sabha shall also take stock of the completed works and benefits intended to the beneficiaries and issue necessary completion report.

8. Action on audit objections—(1) The Executive Authority shall take prompt and effective action to set right the objections raised in the audit report. He shall prepare suitable replies to the objections and place the report along with his replies before the village panchayat and Grama Sabha for their approval. He shall submit three copies of the replies with a copy of resolution, to the Assistant Director of Rural Development (Audit), through the auditor within two months of the date of receipt of the audit report. The auditor shall submit two copies of the replies of the Executive Authority after verifying the correctness of the replies, with his remarks to the Assistant Director of Rural Development (Audit) within thirty days from the date of receipt of the replies.

(2) The Assistant Director of Rural Development (Audit) shall scrutinise the replies to the audit objections, keeping in view the remarks of the auditor, and pass suitable orders accepting or rejecting the replies to objections raised. He shall also send a copy of such orders to the auditor.

(3) Thereupon, it is the responsibility of the Assistant Director of Rural Development (Audit), to pursue further action on the pending audit objections, if any, and initiate surcharge proceedings against the Executive Authority and any other person responsible in respect of audit objections for which the Executive Authority has not submitted acceptable replies. Initiating such proceeding shall not be delayed beyond three months from the issue of final order on the replies.

(4) After the issue of an audit report on the accounts of a village panchayat, the audit of the accounts of that village panchayat shall not be reopened, save with special orders of the Inspector.

(G.O. Ms. No. 59, Rural Development (C4) Department, dated 7th March 2000)

5.7.21 Implementation of Concurrent Audit System

The hig level committe constituted for devolution of power to Local Bodies have suggested to implement concurrent audit system in panchayats. Accordingly, the Government orders for implementation the concurrent of audit system in all three tiers of panchayats.

(1) The Deputy Block Development Officer shall audit the village panchayat accounts once in three months with assistance of his subordinate Officers. The Deputy Block Development Officer shall also audit the Village Panchayat Scheme Fund Accounts. The Officers of Local Fund Audit Department will review the audit conducted by the Deputy Block Development Officers, in circumstances the audit department shall conduct the test check of the audit conducted by the Deputy Block Development Officers.

(2) The Local Fund Audit Department shall audit the accounts of panchayat unions accounts once in a three months with present staff of Local Fund Audit Department, the plan will be prepared to conduct audit within 90 days, if audit is not conducted within 90 days, that accounts must be audited within next 90 days.

(3) The Local Fund Audit Department shall audit the district panchayat account once in a year based on the volume of transaction and receipt and expenditure of district panchayat.

(4) The quarterly concurrent audit system shall come into force from January 2000 onwards.

(5) The Local Fund Audit Department shall prepare a manual on audit of panchayats.

(G.O. Ms. No. 95, Rural Development (C3) Department, dated 10th April 2000)

5.7.22 Surcharge and Disallowance Rules

1. Short title—These rules may be called the Tamil Nadu Panchayats (Surcharge, Disallowance and Charge) Rules, 2000.

2. Surcharge and disallowance—(1) Any auditor, empowered by the Government, shall carefully and personally examine every case of loss or waste or misapplication of money or property of the village panchayat or panchayat union or district panchayat and may disallow every item contrary to law and surcharge the same on the person making or authorising the making of illegal payments and may charge against any person responsible therefor the amount of any deficiency, loss or unprofitable outlay incurred by the negligence or misconduct of that person or of any sum, which ought to have been, but is not, brought to account by that person and shall, in every such case, certify the amount due from such person.

(2) It shall not be open to an Executive Authority of village panchayat or Commissioner of panchayat union or Secretary of district panchayat whose

negligence or misconduct has caused or contributed to any such deficiency or loss, to contend that notwithstanding his negligence or misconduct the deficiency or loss would not have occurred but for the negligence or misconduct of some other person.

3. Power of the Government—(1) The Government prescribe the following officers to exercise the powers referred to in these rules in respect of the funds of every village panchayat or panchayat union or district panchayat within his jurisdiction.

(a) Assistant Director of Rural Development (Audit) in case of Village Panchayats (General Funds).

(b) Director of Local Fund Audit in case of District Panchayats, Panchayat Union Councils and Village Panchayats (Scheme Funds).

(2) The auditor shall state in writing the reasons for his decision in respect of every disallowance which shall be based on a stated authority in respect of every disallowance, surcharge or charge, and furnish by registered post, a copy thereof to the person against whom it is made.

(3) Even if the person to whom a copy of the decision of the auditor is furnished, refuses to receive it, he shall be deemed to have been duly furnished with a copy of such decision within the meaning of sub-rule (2). The period of thirty days fixed in Rules 5 and 6 shall be calculated from the date of such refusal.

4. Issue of surcharge certificate—(1) The auditor who is empowered to issue a surcharge certificate, before issuing a surcharge certificate, shall give a show cause notice to the person concerned calling upon him to state his defence about the proposed notice in writing within a specified time which shall not be less than fifteen days. If such person desires to be heard in person, the opportunity of personal hearing shall be given by the auditor. In such personal hearing the auditor shall record the proceedings of such hearing. The auditor shall issue surcharge certificate after taking into consideration the representation, if any, given by the person concerned and the proceedings by the personal hearing. The show cause notice and the surcharge certificate shall be in Tamil version.

(2) Wherever the Collector, the Inspector or other competent authority takes execution proceedings on behalf of a village panchayat, panchayat union council or district panchayat in respect of which a surcharge certificate has been issued by an auditor, the expenditure for such purpose shall be met from the Government initially and recovered from the funds of the respective village panchayat, panchayat union or district panchayat.

5. Appeal against the surcharge, disallowance or charge—(1) Any person aggrieved by the disallowance, surcharge or charge made, may, within thirty days from the date of the receipt of service of the decision of the auditor, appeal to the Inspector, or any officer authorised by the Government in this behalf to set aside such disallowance, surcharge or charge and the Inspector or such officer, after taking such evidence as is necessary, may confirm, modify or remit such disallowance, surcharge or charge:

Provided that the Inspector or any officer authorised by the Government, may admit an appeal after the expiry of the time specified in this sub-rule, but within sixty days if the appellant satisfies the Inspector or such officer that he has sufficient cause for not preferring the appeal within the specified time:

Provided further that during the pendency of the appeal made under this rule, the certificate of disallowance, surcharge or charge, as the case may be, shall not be enforced.

(2) Against the order of the Inspector or Officer authorised by Government in this behalf under sub-rule (1), a second appeal shall lie to the Government within thirty days from the date of receipt of such order, the Government may take into account all the fact presented by the appellant and facts of the case and pass such order as they deem fit and proper. Against the order of the Government, an appeal shall lie to the High Court within thirty days from the date of receipt of such order.

(3) Where an appeal is made to the High Court under sub-rule (2) the auditor shall be the sole respondent thereto and the applicant shall not be entitled to make either the Inspector or any officer authorised by the Government or any other person or Government as a party to the proceedings.

6. Payment of due—Every sum certified to be due from any person by the auditor under these rules shall be paid by such person into the bank or post office in which the funds of the village panchayat, panchayat union council or district panchayat, as the case may be, are lodged within thirty days from the date of intimation to him of the decision of the auditor unless within that time, such person has appealed against the decision to the Inspector or any officer authorised by the Government, and such sum, if not paid or such sum as the Inspector or such officer shall declare to be due, shall be recoverable in the same way as an amount decreed by a court by filing execution petition.

7. **Charge of interest on surcharge, disallowance or charge amount**—Interest at the rate specified by the Government, from time-to-time, by general or special order or if no such order is in current at the time of issuing a surcharge certificate at a rate not less than fifteen per cent per annum shall be charged on the amount of disallowance, surcharge or charge due with effect from the day following the last date fixed for payment of the said amount of disallowance, surcharge or charge in the certificate. The interest so charged on the amount of disallowance, surcharge or charge, over due shall be specified in the certificate itself in precise terms as laid down in Section 34 of the Civil Procedure Code, 1908 (Central Act V of 1908).

8. **Waiving of amount of disallowance, surcharge or charge**—Notwithstanding anything contained in the rules, the Government may at any time direct that the recovery of the whole or any part of the amount of disallowance, surcharge or charge certified to be due from any person by the auditor under these rules shall be waived if, in their opinion that such a course is necessary, considering all the circumstances of the case. The reasons for such waiver shall be conveyed in writing to the village panchayat or panchayat union or district panchayat, as the case may be.

(G.O. Ms. No. 32, Rural Development (C4) Department, dated 11th February 2000)

5.7.23 Surcharge and Disallowance Rules—Amendment to Notification

No.SRO A-70(a-3)/2000

In exercise of the powers conferred by clause (xvii) of sub-section (2) of Section 242 of the Tamil Nadu Panchayat Act, 1994 (Tamil Nadu Act 21 of 1994), the Government of Tamil Nadu hereby makes the following amendment to the Tamil Nadu Panchayats (Surcharge, Disallowance and Charges), 2000:

Amendment

In the said rules, in clause (a) in sub-rules (1) in Rule 3, for the expression "Assistant Director of Rural Development (Panchayats), the expression "Assistant Director of Rural Development (Audit)" shall be substituted.

(G.O. Ms. No.207, Rural Development (C-4) dated 17th August 2000)

5.7.24 Power to Write-Off Properties Lost Due to Theft, Fire etc.

1. G.O. Ms. No.1512, Local Administration Department, dated 31.7.1951.

2. G.O. Ms. No.2691, Rural Development and Local Administration Department, dated 1.2.1973.

3. From the Director of Rural Development, Chennai, Letter Roc No.88788 2002/PCA-4, dated 29th March 2001.

Order

In the G.O. first read above, instructions were issued prescribing monetary limit and delegation of powers to write-off in the case of loss of property belonging to the panchayat due to theft, fire or other accidents. In the GO 2nd read above, revised orders were issued delegating powers to officers to write-off losses due to theft, fire or other accident.

2. In his letter 3rd read above, the Director of Rural Development has proposed that a ceiling as detailed below may be fixed requiring the sanction of authorities, viz. Assistant Director of Rural Development (Panchayat) and Collector.

Assistant Collector of Rural Development (Panchayats) upto Rs. 1000/-

Collector above Rs. 1000/-

3. The Government have carefully examined the proposal of the Director of Rural Development and sanction the following delegation of powers to the officers noted against each in regard to writing-off losses due to theft, fire, or other accidents in the panchayats.

Assistant Director of Rural Development (Panchayats) upto Rs. 1000/-

Collector from Rs. 1001 to Rs. 5000/-

Director of Rural Development from Rs. 5001/- to Rs. 10,000/-

Government above Rs. 10,000/-

Sanction of Government should be in all cases exceeding Rs. 10,000/-

4. This order issues with the concurrence of Finance Department — *vide* their U.O.No.78/JS (SF)/01 dated the 30th April 2001.

(By order of the Governor)

5.7.25 Contribution to Charitable Institution

Village panchayat may with the sanction of the Inspector contribute from their general funds to the extent to which their finances permit to charitable institutions provided:

(i) that the institutions are rendering services, which are the functions of the village panchayat under the Tamil Nadu Panchayat Act, 1994;
(ii) that the institutions are situated within the jurisdiction of the village panchayat; or
(iii) that the institutions are serving the people in the jurisdiction of the village panchayat;
(iv) that the object of the contribution is of proved meritoriousness; and
(v) that the village panchayat has no deficits in its general funds and can meet the expenditure on the contribution without any grant from Government towards the administrative expenditure of village panchayat.

(G.O. Ms. No. 1939, Local Administration, dated 3rd October 1952)

5.8 CONTROLLING AUTHORITIES

5.8.1 Procedure for Conduct of Cursory and Annual Inspection

The Government issued notification under Section 199 of Tamil Nadu Panchayat Act, 1994 appointing the inspecting officers for all three tiers of panchayats. The Commissioner of Rural Development has sent the detailed proposals for inspection of village panchayat with formats for cursory and annual inspection, fixing responsibility on officers for inspection and periodicity and number of village panchayats to be inspected. The Government examined the proposals sent by the Commissioner of Rural Development and issues the following orders.

After the enactment of Tamil Nadu Panchayat Act 1994, several financial responsibilities have been delegated to village panchayats. Village panchayats have been allowed to function independently without any interference from other 2 tiers of panchayats. The Executive Authority of the village panchayats, *i.e.* panchayat presidents have been clothed with enormous powers. The village panchayats have been authorized to give administrative sanction to take up works costing upto Rs. One Lakh from its general fund without any other sanction from other authorities.

All the above devolution and delegation of powers to the village panchayats presidents require close monitoring and, effective guidance. The Government in the GO first cited have issued orders under Section 199 of the Tamil Nadu Panchayats Act, 1994 nominating inspecting officers for the village panchayats with detailed guidance on the periodicity of the inspections to be made. As per the orders the main responsibilities of inspection of village panchayats is given to the Extension Officer (Panchayats) and the Deputy Block Development Officer (Panchayats) have to inspect all the village panchayats in the panchayat union twice a month. The Block Development Officer (VPts) has to inspect all the village panchayats in his area once in a month. Besides these, directions have been given for pooling up the various account books, Panchayat Registers and Cash Books of village panchayats in one area and reconciling the transaction by the Extension Officer (Panchayats) and the Block Development Officer (Village Panchayats) once in a month.

In order to streamline the above inspections the following guidelines may be issued for the proper conduct of all the inspections and verifications of records.

1. Cursory inspection—Every Extension Officer (Panchayat) and the Block Development Officer (Village Panchayats) or any other officer while visiting the Panchayats in their area to take up notes of the inspection should record his notes of inspections in the format prescribed for such cursory inspection as enclosed. The Extension Officer (Panchayats) and the Block Development Officer (Village Panchayats) or any other officer shall fill up the inspection format carefully after studying and perusing in detail, the accounts and the various registers maintained by the village panchayats. They should not leave any column unfilled. While taking up cursory inspection of village panchayat the inspecting officers, i.e. Extension Officer (Panchayats) and Block Development Officers (Panchayats) or another officer shall first look at the notes of the previous cursory inspection or annual inspection and verify whether all the defects pointed out in those notes are rectified. They must add on a special note in the cursory inspection about the action taken by the village panchayats presidents on the defects pointed out in the earlier inspections. More over if any serious irregularities committed by the village panchayats presidents are noticed and omitted to be pointed out by the inspecting officers in inspection notes to the Assistant Director (Panchayats) or the Collector severe disciplinary action will be taken against the inspecting Officer, besides taking action against the village panchayats presidents who committed this irregularity.

It must be noted that the Extension Officer (Panchayats) has to take up cursory inspection of all the village panchayats in his area once in a month and the Block Development Officers (Village Panchayats) should cover all the village panchayats atleast once in two months.

2. Annual inspection—It is the statutory responsibility of the inspecting Officers to take up annual inspection of village panchayats every year as indicated below. The Format for Annual inspection enclosed herewith shall be used for this purpose.

The annual inspection of the village panchayats shall be taken up by all the Officers of the Rural Development Department working in the district including the District Collector. Under the direction of the Inspector of Panchayat, the Assistant Director (Panchayats) shall in the beginning of the year draft a programme of inspection of all the village panchayats in the district fixing the number of village panchayats to be inspected every year as detailed below and obtain the orders of the Collector and communicate to all the Officers and the village panchayats:

	Name of the Officer	*Annual Inspection to be done in a year*
1.	District Collector	10 Village Panchayats
2.	Project Officer, DRDA	10 Village Panchayats
3.	Assistant Directors (Panchayats)	36 Village Panchayats
4.	Assistant Director (Audit)	36 Village Panchayats
5.	Personal Assistant (NMP)	25 Village Panchayats
6.	Block Development Officer (Regular) Block Development Officer [PTs/EO(P)]	Balance Panchayat in the Union

The notes of annual inspection and the conduct of inspection by all the officers have to be done in a detailed manner by verifying all the Registers in the village panchayat office besides making a short visit of the Streets in the village panchayat area to write observations on the condition of the roads, sanitation and water supply.

If any incident comes to the notice of the government here the inspecting officer while inspecting the village panchayats has failed to notice the misappropriation done by the village panchayat assistant and the president because of lack of proper inspection severe action will be taken against the officials who have conducted Inspection. Therefore, all the officers shall be careful in conducting inspection either cursory or annual inspection of village panchayats.

The responsibility of conducting cursory inspection of village panchayats has been given only to the Extension Officer (Panchayats) and the Block Development Officers (Village Panchayats). The Assistant Director (Panchayats) has therefore to test check the cursory inspection taken by the Extension Officer (Panchayats) and the Block Development Officer (Village Panchayats).

An important thing to be noted in the conduct of inspection of village panchayats, whenever the inspecting Officers notice any serious lapses or misappropriation of funds shall immediately send a special repot to the District Collector and the Assistant Director (Panchayats) besides writing up cursory inspection notes or annual inspection notes.

(G.O. Ms. No. 238/Rural Development (E5) Department, dated 25th July 1997)

(Commissioner of Rural Development)

Lr. No.88788/2000/PCA-4, dated 30th March 2001

Name of the Village Panchayat:	*Date of Inspection*
Inspecting Officer:	*Previous Inspecting Officer/date:*

1. Meetings

1.	Are the meetings conducted not allowing 60 days gap as per rules?	
2.	Was the meeting conducted every month?	
3.	If not, reasons therefor	
4.	Action taken	
5.	Date of meeting conducted lastly	
6.	Are the members informed of the agenda of the meeting before three days of the meeting?	
7.	If not, action taken to avoid this defect	
8.	Is the Grama Sabha meetings conducted 4 times in a year as per Government instructions? Date of last meeting Is a register maintained to monitor the conduct of the meeting?	
9.	If not, action taken	
10.	Whether the agenda for the Grama Sabha discussed after approval by Village Panchayat?	
11.	Whether the meeting adjourned for want of quorum?	
12.	If so, meeting conducted again	
13.	In the Grama Sabha meeting, whether the subjects of other departments discussed?	
14.	Whether further action taken on the resolution passed in the Grama Sabha? If not, action taken to avoid this lapse	
15.	Whether the accounts and vouchers are placed before the Grama Sabha for Social Audit?	
16.	Whether the details of completion of previous year's works placed in Grama Sabha and the completion certificate approved by Grama Sabha?	

2. Registers

1.	Whether the 31 register/forms maintained properly as per Government instructions? (Indicate the lapse in the maintenance of register if any by random check)	

3. Accounts

1	Indicate the closing balance in the following accounts on the date of inspection						
		Opening Balance on ¼	Receipt	Expen-diture	Closing Balance as per Cash Book	As per Bank/ Post Office Account	Bank/ Post Office Account
	Whether there is difference between the total of cash book, balance with bank/post office, cash on hand and details furnished in Form 30?						

	Village Panchayat Fund Account Village Panchayat Earmarked Fund Account Village Panchayat Scheme Fund Account Village Panchayat Drinking Water Supply Fund Account						
2.	How much of amount is released as State Finance Commission grant? Verify the allocation orders and credit in Bank Account and Cash Book						
3.	Whether credited in full						
4.	Verify the allocation order, Bank Account and Cash Book						
5.	Whether 20 per cent on the House Tax collected credited to Drinking Water Supply Fund Account?						
6.	Whether the amount of incentive fund on House Tax collection credited to Village Panchayat Fund Account?						
7.	Whether the funds allotted are credited to concerned account verify						
8.	Whether the funds for schemes credited as allocated. (Verify the Funds release order, Cash Book and Bank Account)						
9	Whether any advance is drawn from scheme fund? Details and based on which order						
10.	Whether the approval of the Block Development Officer obtained for all expenditure under scheme fund? If not, furnish the details						
11.	Details of advances to be refunded to Panchayat Union						
	Amount received from the funds of Panchayat Union as advance	Rs. P.					
	Adjustment upto the date of inspection	Rs. P.					
	Closing Balance	Rs. P.					
	Furnish the details of action taken to wipe-off the dues						
12.	Whether all the expenditure exceeding Rs. 500/- is incurred from Village Panchayat Fund after approval by Village Panchayat? If not, furnish details						
13.	Whether Bill passed register is maintained separately for each Fund Account?						
14.	Whether the Earmarked Fund is credited in the respective account in full?						
15.	Furnish details of Earmarked Fund utilized for the purposes other than the purposes for which it was sanctioned if any. Also indicate the action taken						
	Deposit	Total Deposits collected on Household water connection in one lumpsum	Other Deposits lapsed after (6 years)	Refunded	Balance		

4. Tax Collection

		Arrears			Current		
1.	Indicate the details of Tax Collection and other receipts on the date of inspection	Demand	Collection	Arrears	Demand	Collection	Arrears
(i)	House Tax						
(ii)	Profession Tax						
(iii)	Advertisement Tax						
(iv)	Tax on Cable TV connection						
(v)	Other taxes						
(vi)	Water charges						
(vii)	Licence on Trade						
(viii)	Building Licence						
(ix)	Shandies						
(x)	Topes						
(xi)	Other Miscellaneous Receipts						
2.	Whether house tax demand fixed without delay and notice issued?						
3.	If not, which month the notice was issued?						
4.	Action taken to avoid delay						
5.	Whether demand for profession tax fixed without delay?						
6.	Whether the report of remittance of profession tax received in February and August from the salary-disbursing officers?						
7.	Furnish details of action taken by Village Panchayats to augment the advertisement tax						
8.	Whether the tax collected remitted into account in full periodically? (Verify receipt book, collection chitta challan and cash book) (Furnish details of delay and omission if any in remittance)						

5. Maintenance of Basic Amenities

1.	Indicate the maintenance in the following items in the current year upto the date of inspection	

		Numbers	Total number under use	Maintenance upto inspection date in the current year	Average expenditure monthly	Average expenditure per unit
1.	Drinking Water					
	Hand Pump					
	Power Pump					
	Other category					

		Numbers	Total number under use	Maintenance upto inspection date in the current year	Average expenditure monthly	Average expenditure per unit
2.	Street Light					
	Incandescent light					
	Tube Light					
	Sodium vapour lamp					
	Mercury lamp					
3.	Roads					
	A. Village Roads					
(i)	Mud Road					
(ii)	Gravel Road					
(iii)	Metalled Road					
(iv)	Black Topped Road					
	B. Streets					
(i)	Cement street					
4.	Television					
5.	Radio					
6.	Drainage					
7.	Public latrine					
8.	How many house connections are recommended by TWAD Board					
9.	How many connections are given?					
10.	Whether all the deposits credited to account @ Rs. 1,000/- for all permitted connections					
11.	Indicate whether the average expenditure on hand pump Rs. 25/- per month has been exceeded. Furnish reasons					
12.	Power pump – Rs. 7, 000/- per annum per pump. Amount of maintenance expenditure?					
13.	Whether the spares are purchased following the procedures with the approval of Village Panchayats? If, not, furnish details.					
14.	Street light – whether purchased with fixed rates, with ISI mark and with the approval of Village Panchayats?					
15.	Stock Register – Whether the quality and quantity of goods purchased are verified chalan wise and entered in the stock register. Indicate whether the stock of materials on date of inspection tallies with the Stock Register.					
16.	Verify Cash Book and Stock Register and find out whether materials purchased are brought to Stock Register?					
17.	Details of payment of current consumption charges	Demand		Remitted		Balance
	Street lights					
	Power Pumps					
	Buildings					
18.	Details of hamlets having drinking water scarcity	Below 10 LPCD		10-55 LPCD		Specify hamlets where ground water source is not available
19.	Indicate the village not having link roads	Name of village	Length in km required		Population	
20.	Furnish the details of villagers not having street lights	Name of village	No of lights required		Adi Dravidas	Number
21.	Number of families not having houses	SC/ST	Others		Total	
22.	Number of huts improved					
23.	Number of houses where toilets are to be provided					

6. Scheme Works

1.	Details of works completed on the date of inspection						
		Spill Over			Current Year		
		Total	Completed	Balance	Taken Up	Completed	Balance
		Fund	Work	Fund	Work	Fund	Work
(a)	Central Finance Commission Grant						
(b)	Jawahar Gram Samridhi Yojana						
(c)	Indira Awas Yojana						
(d)	Central Rural Sanitation Programme						
(e)	Equalization Fund						
(f)	Other Schemes						
2.	Whether estimate and allotment Register maintained properly? (Verify with bills passed register)						
3.	Make spot inspection on certain completed work and works in progress and furnish details on lapses, if any						
4.	Furnish details of efforts taken by Village Panchayats for the participation of people in Namakku Naame Thittam						
5.	Furnish note on the lapses if any after inspection of works executed in Village Panchayats through Panchayat Unions or Line Departments under Anna Marmumalarchi Thittam, Member of Legislative Assembly constituency Development Scheme, Member of Parliament Local Area Development Programme, Employment Assurance Scheme etc.						

7. Audit

1.	Upto which year audit is completed?	
2.	Whether serious irregularities and financial loss, if any, pointed out?	
3.	Details of surcharge amount certificate pending against the president	

8. General

1.	Is the information board put up? Whether information's and general details are written in the board	
2.	Whether of works under execution with estimates are written in the wall of the Panchayat office?	
3.	Whether Ayyan Thiruvalluvar Noolagam maintained and utilized properly?	

9. General Remarks of Inspecting Officer

Inspecting Officer/Signature
Date:

INDEX

I.	GENERAL INFORMATION	
II.	CONSTITUTION	
III.	FUNCTIONS	
IV.	BASIC AMENITIES	
V.	POWERS	
VI.	FINANCIAL ADMINISTRATION	
VII.	LEVY OF TAX AND COLLECTION	
VIII.	REMUNERATIVE ENTERPRISES	
IX.	SCHEMES	
X.	ACCOUNTS – REGISTERS	
XI.	AUDIT	
XII.	MAINTENANCE OF ASSETS	
XIII	ADMINISTRATION REPORT	

Notes on Annual Inspection of Village Panchayats

I. General Information

1. Name of the Panchayat Union
2. Name of the Village Panchayat and Grade
3. Name of President
4. Name of Vice-President
5. Date of last inspection
6. Name, Designation of officer and date of inspection whether the defects pointed out in previous annual inspection and cursory inspection rectified? If not, furnish details
7. Date of inspection
8. Period of inspection
9. Name and Designation of the Inspecting Officer

II. Constitution

(a) 1. Area (in Hectare)

2. Total Population of Village Panchayat as per last census — Total:
Male:
Female:

3. Number of hamlets with name and also population of each hamlet — 1.
2.
3.

4. Number of wards and members

5. Details of Village Panchayat President and members wardwise

	Sanctioned Strength						Number of Members						Date from which vacancy occurred and to whom reserved					
	SC/ST		W		General		SC/ST		W		General		SC/ST		W		General	
	M	F	M	F	M	F	M	F	M	F	M	F	M	F	M	F	M	F
President																		
Ward 1																		
Ward 2																		
Ward 3																		
Ward 4																		
Ward 5																		

6. Action taken to fill up the vacancy
7. Whether removal of President and no confidence motion against Vice-President occurred during the period under inspection?
8. Details of general and casual election held

III. **Functions**

1. **Village Panchayat Meetings** — Ordinary Urgent Special
   - (a) Dates on which meetings conducted during the inspection period
   - (b) Whether meetings adjourned for want of quorum as per attendance Register. If so, furnish details
   - (c) Whether meetings conducted in every month and within 60 days as per Panchayat Act. Verify and furnish remarks
   - (d) Whether follow up action taken on the resolutions passed
   - (e) Whether meeting intimation served properly?
2. **Committees**
   - (a) Constitution of committees, details president, number of members, indicate committeewise
   - (b) Details of meetings convened committeewise (with date and number of resolutions)
   - (c) Whether the resolutions of committees placed in the next meeting of village panchayats?
   - (d) Which are the Committees that have helped in the administration of panchayat/If so, in what manner
3. **Grama Sabha**
   - (a) Date of Conduct of Grama Sabha meeting
   - (b) Whether any Grama Sabha adjourned for want of quorum as per attendance
   - (c) Whether the resolutions of Grama Sabha placed in the Village Panchayat meeting for further action? Give details
   - (d) Whether follow up action taken in the resolutions
4. **Administration**
   - (a) Whether panchayat office is in its own building or rented building. If rented, the amount of rent? Is toilet facility available
5. **Employees**

	Designation	Name of the Employee	Period of service from to
(a) Details of sanctioned posts, salary, service etc.			

   - (b) Furnish details of excess salary paid over and above the sanctioned amount, if any
   - (c) Whether the allowances paid to president, members and employees are in proper order?

IV. **Basic Amenities**

1. **Drinking water facility**
   1. What are the drinking water sources in Village Panchayat? Status of them on the date of inspection (enclose list)
   2. Number of hamlets benefited under comprehensive water supply scheme? Population benefited. Whether supply of water sufficient?
   3. Number of open wells
   4. Number of protected water schemes
   5. Number of hand pumps

   5a. Annual maintenance expenditure

6. Number of power pumps
6a. Annual maintenance expenditure
7. Number of public fountains
8. Number of household water supply connections. Date of last connection given
9. Annual income from the connections
10. Whether account maintained separately and expenditure incurred for drinking water supply?

11. **Deposit**
    (a) Total deposit to be collected
    (b) Balance to be collected numbers—Amount
    (c) Whether 20 per cent of house tax collected credited into water supply account? If not, reasons thereof

12. Present stage of the drinking water facility
13. Average monthly total quantity supplied
14. How much amount paid to TNEB for Power pumps? Monthly Average
15. Furnish details of amount paid previously. Are there arrears?
16. Whether any drinking water works are pending? If so, give details and stage.

2. **Street Lights**

1. Status of street light on the date of inspection

		Burning	Not Burning	Expenditure upto the date of inspection	Expenditure per unit
(a)	Incandescent lights				
(b)	Tube lights				
(c)	Mercury lights				
(d)	Sodium vapour lamps				

2. Whether street light facilities provided for all hamlets
3. Number of hamlets provided with facility in full
4. Facility provided partly
5. Street lights not provided name of hamlet/population
6. Total per annum/monthly average of .... remittance of full amount of current consumption charges. Are there arrears to be settled?
7. Details of stock of spares
   (a) 40 watts incandescent light
   (b) 40 watts chokes
   (c) Starters
   (d) Others (Specify name) verify the stock and record it in the stock register

3. **Village Roads**

1. Whether Registers of roads maintained properly?

Name of Road	Nos.	Length
(a) Concrete street		
(b) Black topped road		
(c) Mud road		
(d) Gravel road		
(e) Earthen road		
(f) Streets		
Total		

2. Name of hamlet and population not provided with link road, length of road required
3. What are the schemes in the current year for improvement of roads? Indicate estimated cost

Spill over of last year				In current year			
		Taken up		Completed		Balance	
Nos.	Amount.	Nos.	Amount.	Nos.	Amount.	Nos.	Amount.

4. Whether there are encroachments in roads and streets? And whether encroachment register is maintained
5. Whether action taken to remove the objectionable encroachments?
6. Whether details of encroachment fees collected maintained as per register?

4. Public Sanitation Facilities

1. Number of public toilets
   Whether water, electricity, provided for these toilets? Are they maintained properly?
2. How many number of sanitary latrines available in individual houses
3. Indicate the efforts taken to provide toilets in all households
4. Whether toilet facility provided in all primary/ middle schools? If not, what is the action taken?
5. Number of Public Health/sanitation employees
6. Salary and annual expenditure Rs.......
7. Whether drainage facilities provided in all hamlets

...............Drainage	
Nos.	Length

8. Number of hamlets provided with these facilities
9. Whether facilities provided for cleaning of private cess pool? How many houses covered under this?

5. Burial Ground, Burning Ground

1. Whether roads, formed to burning and burial ground, specifically for SC/ST
2. Whether water and electricity facility are available near the burning and burial grounds
3. Details of burial grounds utilized commonly by all communities

6. Reading Rooms/Libraries

1. Number of reading rooms/libraries available in village
2. Number of persons daily utilizing Ayyan Thiruvallur Padippagam and dailies, magazines supplied daily

7. **Television and Radios**

   1. Total number of colour and black television installed
   2. Total number of radio sets actions taken to repairs/ condemn the radio set not functioning

Colour or Black and White

Functioning	Not Functioning	Maintenance	Average Expenditure per set	Salary of Operator

V. Powers

House Tax—Whether quinquinniel revision being done? Date of previous revision of tax. Action taken to levy on the plinth area basis.

Profession Tax—Whether tax revised once in five years. When was the revision done lastly?

Advertisement Tax—Rate of levy of advertisement tax revision date.

Date of resolution of village panchayat fixing fees for the following items.

Licence fees on Trades Building, Fees on layout approval, Fees on advertisement boards.

VI. Financial Management

1. **Monthly Accounts**—(a) Whether the receipts and payments classified in village panchayat Form 30. Are three accounts consolidated monthly and placed in monthly meeting of village Panchayat and Grama Sabha meeting
   Furnish Details:
   Date of Monthly Meeting:
   Date of Grama Sabha Meeting
   Accounts relate to which month:
   Whether the copy of the monthly report sent to the Collector and Deputy BDO (Audit) within seven days from the date of meeting.

2. **Annual Accounts**

   (a) Whether accounts closed annually and sent to audit
   (b) Action taken if particulars are placed late in Gram Sabha

VII. Levy of Tax and Demand Collection

Items	Collection	Balance
1. House-Tax		
2. Profession Tax		
3. Advertisement Tax		
4. Tax on Cable TV Connection		
5. Fees		
6. Water Charges		
7. Licence fees on D & O Trade		
8. Fees on building licence		
9. Other fees		

10. Fines
11. Shandy auction/share amount
12. Topes, Social Forestry
13. Other miscellaneous tax receipts
14. What is the action taken to collect the arrears
15. Whether special action taken on the time barred arrears?

VIII. Remunerative Enterprises

Action taken to increates the revenue of Village Panchayat and to increase the facilities needed by the public.

1. **Shandies**—Whether shandies are opened where facilities available?
   Whether revenue increases annually in existing shandies. If so, amount realized in the past three years. Amount due from panchayat union and amount received.
2. **Fisheries**—Whether sufficient water sources available for fishery?
   If so, whether action taken to rear fish in the sources to augment the income.
3. Whether there is possibility of income by opening cart-stand, ferries, bus stand etc.
   If so, the action taken thereof.
4. Whether poramboke lands are utilized for the purpose specified in the registers
   Whether poramboke lands fully utilized.
   Whether Social Forestry, tree growing, orchards, etc. raised? If so, the income received in the past three years.
   Whether there are encroachments in porambokes? If so, action taken to remove them.
5. Other remunerative enterprises taken if any may be specified.

IX. Schemes

Schemes Implemented in Village Panchayat

1. **Scheme Works**	Funds allotted	No. of works taken up	Completed	Balance
(a) Village Panchayat fund works				
(b) Earmarked Fund Accounts works Capital works under Tenth Finance Commission Grant				
(c) Jawahar Grama Samridhi Yojana				
(d) Indira Awaas Yojana				
(e) Central Rural Sanitation Programme				
(f) Namakku Naame Thittam				
(g) Other Schemes				

2. **Beneficiary Oriented Schemes**	No. of Beneficiaries	Loan Amount	Grant
(a) Swarna Jayanthi Gram Swarozgar Yojana			
(b) Grant for funeral rites			
(c) One hut one light			

3. **Other Social Services**

   (a) Whether this village selected for Anna Marumalarchi Thittam? If so, furnish list of works taken up under this scheme.

(b) Furnish details of works taken up under Namakku Naame Thittam/Estimated cost. What is the amount of public contribution?

(c) Whether details of scheme works with estimates executed in panchayat area or exhibited in panchayat office building compound wall?

4. **Planning**

1. Whether the annual plan is prepared as per instructions, date of sending to panchayat unions
2. Whether the resolution of Grama Sabha and the village panchayat obtained for the plan prepared? Furnish resolution number and date.

X. **Accounts Registers**

(a) Indicate the name of the bank branch and account number in which four fund accounts are maintained. Whether Bank is within 5 kms. distance. If so, whether the daily collections remitted by next day itself. If the bank is exceeding 5 kms. whether the collection of Rs. 1000/- or more than Rs. 1000/- whether any lapses found in this procedure and pointed out in the cursory inspection and whether action taken or objection raised in Audit?

1. Whether both the president and vice-president are signing the cheque?
2. Whether the approval of the village panchayat and the Collector, obtained for the person nominated as co-signatory in the absence of vice-president?

(b) Furnish the closing balance in the following fund accounts on the date of inspection. Furnish remarks after verifying the closing balance.

1. Village Panchayat Fund Account Rs.
2. Village Panchayat Earmarked Fund Account Rs.
3. Village Panchayat Scheme Fund Account Rs.
4. Water Supply Maintenance Account Rs.

(c) Furnish the receipt for the following items for the current year
As per the recommendations of State Finance Commission, the grant devolved under Pool B, the quarterly grant received, which quarter?
Equalization and Incentive Fund.

1. **Incentive Grant on House Tax Collected**

Provision of Infrastructure Facilities

1.
2.
3.
4.

2. **Grant Released to the Panchayat as per the recommendation of Central Finance Commission**

3. **Grant released under the following Centrally Sponsored Schemes**

(a) Jawahar Gram Samridhi Yojana
(b) Indira Awaas Yojana

4. **Indicate the amount of assigned revenues**

(a) Entertainment tax
(b) Local Cess
(c) Surcharge on Stamp Duty on transfer of property
(d) Seigniorage fees on minor minerals
(e) Other items

(f) Whether the registers/forms (V.Pt.No.1 to 31) ordered by DRD maintained properly? Whether entries made upto the date of inspection? Examine each item and furnish remarks

Date of last inspection and remarks lastly	Action taken on the remarks in the inspection Details of rectification	Other remarks

1. Demand Notice for House tax
2. House tax receipts
3. House tax (arrears and current) demand register
4. For Profession Report
5. Profession Tax (arrears of amount, current Demand Registers)

(a) Advertisement Tax

6. Miscellaneous Receipts
7. Register of taxes and miscellaneous receipts
8. Register of grants, assigned revenues, upto which quarter, grant received.
9. Village Panchayat Fund chitta
10. Miscellaneous demand, collection, balance register
11. Cash books (Village Panchayat Fund Account)
12. Advances Recoverable Register
13. Register of classified payments
14. Acquittance Register
15. Register of estimates and allotments
16. Register of assets of village panchayat
17. Register of maintenance
18. Stock Register of street light materials
19. Vouchers
20. Stock register of money value forms
21. Registers of non-saleable materials
22. Stock register of materials for construction
23. Cash book
24. Register of classified receipts
25. Register of estimates and allotment
26. Classified receipts and payments (Scheme Fund Account)
27. Register of scheme works
28. Beneficiary list
29. Statement of monthly receipt and expenditure after approval by village panchayat
30. Budget of village panchayat date sent to Deputy BDO
31. Date of approval by village panchayat with resolution number

XI. Audit

1. Whether village panchayat accounts are audited before 31st July?
2. Whether the audit paras and replies to audit paras placed in Grama Sabha before 30th September
3. Pending objection raised during current years

Total

Dropped in the current year

Balance

4. Whether financial loss if any pointed out?
   Whether surcharge notice received from Assistant Director (Audit)?
   Action taken on the certificate

XII. Maintenance of Assets

	Lands	Buildings	Water sources
1. What are the community assets			
2. What is the annual maintenance cost for this? Percentage to total expenditure			
3. Details of utilization of lands			

XIII. Administrative Report

1. Date of sending annual administrative report to panchayat union prepared as per instructions
   Verify the closing balance of the following fund accounts and note them in the cash book

		Village Panchayat Fund Account	*Earmarked Fund Account*	*Scheme Fund Account*
1.	Bank			
2.	Post Office			
3.	Cash on hand			

General Remarks of Inspecting Officer

Signature of the Inspecting Officer
Name and Designation

Place:

5.8.2 Duties and Responsibilities of Inspecting Officers

1. The Government appoint Block Development Officer (VP) and Extension Officer (Panchayat) as Inspecting Officers of Village Panchayats.

2. According to Section 202 of The Tamil Nadu Panchayats Act, 1994, the Officers specified above shall visit village panchayat, inspect works, verify registers and assets and shall be empowered to collect required information from the village panchayats. (It is the duty of the village panchayat to furnish required information, registers and records to the Officers authorised under the above Section.)

3. The Deputy Block Development Officer has been notified as the Auditor of the village panchayat. The Block Development Officer (Village Panchayat) and the Extension Officer (Panchayat) shall attend to the works fixed by the Collector and the Director of Rural Development and shall also attend to the following works giving due importance:

(a) Inspection of village panchayats

(i) The Extension Officers (Panchayat) shall visit all the village panchayats in the block atleast twice a month. [In those panchayat unions, where there are two Extension Officers, 50 per cent village panchayats shall be allotted to one and the other 50 per cent shall be allotted to the other Extension Officer (Panchayat) by the Block Development Officer (Village Panchayat)].

(ii) The Block Development Officer (Village Panchayat) shall visit every village panchayat in his area atleast once in a month.

(b) Ensuring payment of salaries to panchayat employees—The S.F.C Grant sanctioned as per G.O. Ms. No. 93, Rural Development

Department, dated 26.3.97 by subsequence Government orders shall be utilised for payment of salaries to the employees of village panchayats. The Inspecting Officers shall ensure that the salary is disbursed every month without omission.

(c) **Inspection of works**—The inspecting officers shall inspect drinking water hand pumps, power pumps, street lights, roads, libraries, and reading rooms and shall verify all the assets maintained by the village panchayat to find out whether they are maintained properly. He shall also inspect the capital works taken up by the village panchayat and review that the work is done without any stagnation or delay.

(d) **Inspection of registers**—The registers to be maintained by the village panchayat have been prescribed in G.O.Ms.No.92, Rural Development Department, dated 26.4.97. The Inspecting Officers shall verify whether all the registers are maintained.

(e) **Village panchayats—Meetings and resolutions**—He shall verify that the village panchayat meetings are conducted regularly and the resolutions are recorded properly. All the resolutions shall be examined and if necessary further report may be sent to the District Collector.

(f) **Revenue collection and expenditure – Verification**—The Extension Officer (Panchayat) and the Block Development Officer (Village Panchayat) shall verify all the village panchayat accounts of the 25 per cent of the total number of panchayats in the area by getting all the records in a central place in one day in every week. They shall verify all the pass books, cash books, cheque books, tax collection receipts, registers, challan etc., during such inspections.

(i) The record and registers of all the 3 accounts shall be verified. Irregular or expenditure incurred without sanction shall be reported to the District Collector immediately.

(ii) They shall examine whether all the taxes and fees are collected regularly and whether all the collected amounts are remitted into panchayat accounts immediately. If they notice any collection amount not remitted and not brought to account, a special report shall be sent to the District Collector.

These Officers shall verify the panchayat accounts in all the panchayats in 4 centres once in a month without fail.

(g) The Extension Officer (Panchayats) and the Block Development Officer (Village Panchayats) while inspecting the village panchayat shall record all the defects noticed in the concerned registers and sign them with date. They shall also issue instructions to rectify the defects pointed and during next inspection shall verify whether the defects have been rectified.

The Extension Officer (Panchayat) shall maintain a diary on the inspections done by them and shall submit to Block Development Officer (Village Panchayat) every week for his review.

(h) **Training of village panchayat presidents and vice-presidents**—The Block Development Officer (Village Panchayats) and the Extension Officer (Panchayats) shall conduct training to all the presidents and vice-presidents in the panchayat union for one or two days at the Block Headquarters, once a year on the rules issued, registers prescribed for maintenance of accounts, maintenance of assets, implementation of schemes etc. The first training shall be completed within a period of two months.

4. **Fixing responsibility**—The serious irregularities or misappropriation, if noticed subsequently besides taking action against the responsible Panchayat Assistants, the Extension Officer (Panchayat) and the Block Development Officer (Village Panchayat) will also be held responsible for the irregularities.

(G.O.Ms.No.238, Rural Development (E5) Department, Dated 25th August 1997)

5.9 MISCELLANEOUS

5.9.1 Preparation and Submission of Administration Report of Village Panchayats

1. **Short title**—These rules may be called the Tamil Nadu Panchayats (Preparation and Submission of Administration Report of Village Panchayats) Rules, 1999.

2. **Definition**—In these rules, unless the context otherwise requires, "Act" means the Tamil Nadu Panchayats Act, 1994 (Tamil Nadu Act 21 of 1994).

3. **Submission of Administration report of village panchayats**—The Executive Authority of

every village panchayat shall, after the close of each financial year, prepare the administration report of the village panchayat concerned in two parts, namely (a) the report embodying the particulars specified in Appendix A, and (b) the annual account indicating income and expenditure for the year as per audited accounts as specified in Appendix B.

4. Procedure of submission and processing—The administration report shall be placed before the village panchayat which shall consider the report and pass a resolution thereon. The president shall sign the report with seal and send three copies of the administration report to the panchayat union concerned through the Deputy Block Development Officer (Panchayats) concerned not later than the 30th June of the year following the year to which the report relates.

(G.O. Ms. No.248, Rural Development (C-4), Department, dated 3rd December 1999)

APPENDIX A

(See Rule 3)

Administration report of_______________village panchayat within_______________Panchayat union__________________district panchayat, for the year__________

I. Constitution and Management

(1) (a) What is the number and date of order constituting the village panchayat; (b) What is the area of the village panchayat? Was there any change in jurisdiction during the year? Quote the number and the date of order; (c) What is its population according to the latest census figures available.

(2) (a) What is the total sanctioned strength of the village panchayat? (b) Was there any change in its strength during the year? (c) Was any revision of wards ordered during the year? (d) The number of seats, if any, reserved for Scheduled Caste/Scheduled Tribe/Women. Was this number changed during the year? State the ward members to which these seats are allotted. (e) The number of elected women members of Scheduled Caste/Scheduled Tribe/General. (f) Is there any vacancy and if so how long? (g) Was any election of members, ordinary or casual held during the year and was there any election dispute?

(3) President, Vice-president and members (a) Is the office of the President reserved? If so, to whom Scheduled Caste/Scheduled Tribe/Women? (b) Was there any election of President or Vice-president during the year and was there any election dispute? If so what was the result? (c) Was the President or Vice-President removed from Office during the year? If so, reasons for the same and details may be furnished. (d) Was any motion expressing want of confidence in the Vice-President passed? (e) Vice-President in charge of the office of president or whether any temporary president appointed and if so, for what period? (f) Was any member disqualified during the year? (g) Was any member restored to office during the year?

(4) Meetings of Grama Sabha and Village Panchayat (a) Did Grama Sabha meet on 4 occasions as stipulated by Government? If yes, provide briefs about the resolution passed and action taken thereon. If no, what are the reasons? Did Women, Scheduled Caste, and Scheduled Tribe members participate – give number of participants. (b) Number of village panchayat meetings held during the year with dates and how many meetings were ordinary, urgent and special? How many were adjourned for want of a quorum and date of such meeting?

(5) How many committees are functioned? Was any Committee formed during the year; and if so, for what purpose? How many times the committees met and nature of discussion. Are there any joint committees with other village panchayats? If yes, furnish details.

(6) Management (a) Where is the village panchayat office located? Is the building owned or rented? If rented what is the amount paid? Is it accessible to all communities? (b) Are the prescribed registers and forms maintained? (c) Establishment (i) State the number of ministerial and contingent staff employed (both full time and part-time) and what is the salary paid to them and annual expenditure for the same? (ii) Are the number of ministerial staff and contingent staff and salary of pay/honorarium is paid in accordance with the orders of the Inspector or Government? (iii) Has the village panchayat, along with any other village panchayat employed any common staff? If so, furnish details of such staff with information regarding the proportion of cost thereof met by the other village panchayat(s).

II. Communications

(1) (a) Any road newly formed or bridges and culverts constructed during the year and at what cost? How were they financed? (b) What is the total length of roads and streets maintained by the village panchayat? Give break-up details in respect of cement concrete/black topped/metalled/gravelled/earthen. (c) Number of encroachments pending at the beginning of the year, detected during the year, evicted during the year, and pending at the close of the year. (d) What is the general condition of roads? (e) What are the budget provision and the percentage to the total budget of the village panchayat for road maintenance?

(2) Are there any canals and ferries in the village and is the management of such ferries entrusted to the village panchayats? What is the income derived from the source?

(3) Is the right to collect the usufruct of avenue trees leased out? What is the income and expenditure?

III. Lighting

State the number of electric lights, details of lights maintained ordinary, tube lights, sodium vapour lamp, mercury lights, what is the total expenditure on street lighting?

IV. Education

(1) (a) What are the number of primary, elementary, secondary and higher secondary schools in the panchayat village? (b) By whom are they maintained? (c) Are the schools adequate? Are the buildings adequate? (d) What is the total number of boys and girls attending the schools? (2) How many Scheduled Caste/ Scheduled Tribe girls are studying in the schools? (3) Is there any reading room in the village panchayat? Give details of Journals supplied. (4) (a) Is there any adult literacy center in the village panchayat? If so, how many and by whom they are conducted? What is the literacy per cent in the village? (b) What was the strength of these Adult literacy centre during the year? (c) Whether any illiterate adult turned literate in the village panchayat during the year; and if so, how many?

V. Public Health

(1) Streets—(a) Are streets swept regularly? (b) What is the number of sweepers employed and at what cost? (c) What is the budget provision and percentage to the total budget?

(2) Sanitary Latrines—(a) How many houses are there in the village panchayat? How many of there have household flush out toilets? How many families constructed toilets during the year? (b) Are there any public latrines? If so, how many? For how many latrines water supply connection has been given? How many are put under use? Are they maintained properly? As a result of abolition of private scavenging the living condition and working conditions of the sweepers in the employment of the village panchayat satisfactory? Whether as a result of these improvements any scavenger was thrown out of employment. If so how many of them have been absorbed in any other suitable work of employment under the control of village panchayat?

(3) Water supply—(a) What are the drinking water sources and are they adequate? Give details of sources – Public open wells, power pumps, hand pumps, tube wells, bore wells, moraines ground level reservoirs, overhead tanks with number of public water taps provided. (b) How many house service connections have been given and amount collected as water charges? Are there any irregular connection? If so, what action has been taken? (c) Have measures been taken to prevent water sources from pollution? Whether any prosecutions launched, and if so, the number and the result? (d) What is the total expenditure on drinking water supply and total receipt on water charges? What is the budget provision and the percentage to the total budget?

(4) Drainage—Is there any drain in the village panchayat and are they cleaned regularly and maintained properly? If there are no drains, what arrangements are made for the disposal of sludge?

(5) Burial and burning grounds—(a) Is there any common burial ground? Is the space adequate? (b) Is there a common burning ground? (c) What is the expenditure incurred in improving and maintaining them? What is the budget provision and state the percentage to total budget?

(6) Fairs and festivals—What are the principal fairs and festivals in the village panchayat? Were sanitary arrangements made during such fairs and festivals? If so, by whom and at what cost?

(7) Medical Relief Epidemics—(a) Is there any hospital or dispensary in the village panchayat? How are these maintained? How many medical and para medical personnel working and the annual expenditure on these? (b) Were there any epidemics during the year and what preventive measures were taken by the village panchayat?

(8) Dangerous and offensive trades—Has the village panchayat notified any industrial area? What are the trades controlled by the village panchayat? How many licences were issued during the year and what is the income derived from them? Has the village panchayat framed any bye-laws?

(9) What is the income derived from Public Resort Act Licence Fees—What is the income derived from entertainment tax?

(10) How many new building licences were issued during the year and of which how many houses were completed? What is the total income derived from building licence fees? Was there any layout approved and if so the extent and number of plots? Is there any housing scheme? If so, the number of houses constructed for Schedule Caste, Schedule Tribe, Backward, Most Backward and others.

(11) Irrigation Source Maintenance—How many village panchayat tanks and other irrigation sources are there and how are they maintained?

VI. Remunerative Enterprises

(1) Did the village panchayat open any new markets, bus stands, cart-stands, or slaughter houses during the year?

(2) Markets—(a) How many public markets are there in the village panchayat? Is the village panchayat maintaining any market and has it constructed any stall? What is the income therefrom? (b) Is the village panchayat receiving contribution from the panchayat union council on account of markets classified as panchayat union markets? (c) Furnish details on private markets, their number, and income derived by way of licence fees levied on them?

(3) Cart-stand or Bus stand—Is the village panchayat maintaining any bus stand or cart-stand? What is the method of collecting fees? What is the income therefrom and the cost of establishment?

(4) Slaughter houses—State the number of slaughter houses maintained by the village panchayat and private and the revenue derived therefrom.

(5) Cottage industries—What are all cottage industries in the village panchayat? Describe the steps taken, if any, by the village panchayat to improve them.

(6) Is any rent paid for the unreserved forest and social forest under the control of the village panchayat, and if so, state the income realised and other expenditure incurred.

(7) Is compost manufactured in the panchayat village? If so, state the income derived therefrom and expenditure incurred.

(8) How many trees were planted during the year? Give details of programme under which such trees were planted? What is the experience on maintenance and revenue realized?

(9) Number and name of public parks and gardens maintained, (i) Expenditure incurred on their maintenance; (ii) Income, if any, derived from them; and (iii) Proposal, if any, to open new parks or gardens.

(10) How many private parks and gardens are there in village panchayat ? Furnish information briefly.

VII. General Revenues

Taxes—(a) Give particulars of rates at which house-tax, profession-tax and advertisement tax are levied, and the amount collected during the year under each head. (b) State the number of coercive process taken for the recovery of tax. (c) Is any tax levied on agricultural land for specific purpose under sub-section (3) of Section 17 of the Tamil Nadu Panchayats Act, 1994, and if so, what is the income derived from it?

Other Income—State the following (a) The amount of local cess credited to the Village Panchayat Account, (b) Income from duty on transfers of property, (c) Income from fisheries, (d) Income from communal porambokes, (e) Income from endowments and trusts, (f) Any *ex-gratia* grants paid by Government,

(g) Government grants under Section 183 of the Tamil Nadu Panchayats Act, 1994 (Tamil Nadu Act 21 of 1994), and (h) any other income.

(3) (a) The amount of contribution, if any paid by the panchayat union council and on what account, (b) The amount of contribution, if any, paid by private individuals and for what purpose.

VIII. Accounts and Audit

(1) (a) State the name of the co-operative bank, regional rural bank, post office savings bank, Nationalised bank in which the funds of the village panchayat are maintained. (b) Is the village panchayat maintaining separate bank accounts and the separate cash books? Give details of the accounts opened and maintained as specified by the Government. (c) Give details of investment, if any, of village panchayat fund, quoting the authority in support of such investment. (d) When were the accounts of the village panchayat last audited and what is the result of the audit? Give a brief abstract of receipts and charges separately under all accounts during the year together with the opening and closing cash balance. (The heads and the amount furnished in the audit report for the year under report to be entered here – if audit has been completed already). This information should be inconsonance with the facts furnished in Appendix B.

IX. Miscellaneous Functions

(1) Was any unreserved forest withdrawn from the control of the village panchayat during the year?

(2) Are there any institutions or works transferred to the management of the village panchayat?

(3) Are there any charitable endowments or inams under the management and superintendence of the village panchayat?

(4) Was any donation accepted during the years if so, state details.

(5) Are there any trusts under the management of the village panchayat?

(6) Is protection and maintenance of any village irrigation work, managerial turns of irrigation or rotation of distribution if irrigation water transferred to the village panchayat?

(7) Was any poramboke grazing ground, threshing floor, burning and burial ground, cattle-stand, bus stand, cart-stand and tope excluded by the Collector from the operation of the Act during the year?

(8) Was any Kudimaramat work executed?

(9) What are the steps taken for improving the economic status and control of population in the village panchayat? What are the steps taken for effecting family welfare in the village panchayat?

(10) What are the steps taken for eradicating of untouchability and communal harmony?

(11) Was village plan prepared and sent to the panchayat union council?

X. Implementation of Schemes and Programmes

(a) How many works were under State Government and Government of India sponsored programmes and schemes. How many are completed? Provide details of physical and financial aspects of each scheme and programme. (b) How many houses are constructed under State and Government of India Schemes (IAY)? What is the total amount spent on this scheme? How many houses are completed? (c) How many toilets are taken up under CRSP and how many completed? What is the total expenditure under this scheme? (d) How many villagers got the benefit under SGSY Scheme and what is the total subsidy involved? Are there self help groups? If yes, give details. (e) Give details of State plan schemes implemented in the panchayat village, Namakku Naame Thittam, Anna Marumalarchi Thittam, Member of Legislative Assembly Constituency Development Scheme and Scheme of other departments implemented in the village. (f) How many households have got bio-gas plants and are they working well?

XI. General Administration

(1) Was the village panchayat dissolved during the year? If so, state the period. (2) Was there any occasion for the Executive Authority or the inspector to exercise emergency powers under Section 86 or Section 203 of the Tamil Nadu Panchayats Act, 1994 (Tamil Nadu Act 21 of 1994)? If so furnish details. (3) Was any

resolution, licence or permission cancelled during the year? If yes give details. (4) Was there any occasion for the Inspector or other competent authority to direct the performance of any duty in default of the village panchayat president or Executive Authority performing the same? (5) Are weights and measures tested in the panchayat village and if so give details? (6) Were any bye-laws framed? If so, state their nature. (7) General remarks, if any.

APPENDIX B

(See Rule 3)

Income and Expenditure of Village Panchayat (Year ....)

Sl. No.	*Source of Income*	*Amount Rs.*	*Serial No.*	*Head of Account for expenditure*	*Amount Rs.*
1	2	3	4	5	6

5.9.2 Household Drinking Water Supply Connections

As per the policy of the Government, a detailed survey has been conducted in all the hamlets to provide Household water supply connections. Out of 66,631 hamlets, 32,274 hamlets are provided with the water supply at the rate of 40 LPCD. The Managing Director, Tamil Nadu Water Supply and Drainage Board (TWAD) has sent a proposal to provide household connections for the remaining 34,357 hamlets. The recommendation of Managing Director, TWAD Board was considered and the Government issue following orders:

(a) The TWAD Board may conduct detailed survey in all the hamlets to identify the feasibility of the drinking water supply to the required number of household connection. After conduct of the survey, the detailed report can be sent to the concerned village panchayats through the District Collector.

(b) The village panchayat can regulate the water supply charges and provide house connections after the concerned households make deposits to the village panchayat.

(c) For each household connection, Rs. 1,000/- may be collected as a non-refundable deposit amount. The Owner or Occupier of the house shall pay the cost required for giving connection to that house. Also the Owner or Occupier may be permitted to undertake connection work. However, the village panchayat may verify whether the work is done as per the norms and procedures laid by the village panchayats.

(d) For each household connections, Rs. 30/- per month may be collected as a water charge.

(e) If any village panchayat desires to give connection for more number of houses, the concerned village panchayat should analyse the matter intensively and may get prior permission from the Executive Engineer, TWAD Board for providing household connection additionally.

(f) The village panchayats should undertake the work from their own fund only. If village panchayat desires to implement the same through TWAD Board, they are permitted to do so.

(g) After completion of the waters supply extension work, the village panchayat may give household connections.

(h) The village panchayat may avoid providing household connection from the Public Water Supply outlets particularly those situated in economically backward area. If any village panchayat gives more number of household connections than it is admissible, the District Collector may consider this as an unlawful connection and order to disconnect such of those household connections.

(i) As far as the new schemes are concerned, the TWAD Board should be consulted for fixing of the number of household connections.

(j) The expenditure for providing household connection can be met from the income derived as deposit and monthly water supply charges. The village panchayat should maintain separate accounts for this purpose.

(G.O. Ms. No. 260, Rural Development (W.S.1) Department, dated 9th December 1998)

5.9.3 Implementation of Group Insurance Scheme through Village Panchayats

The Government have accorded administrative sanction for implementation of Rural Group Life Insurance Scheme – RGLIS in Tamil Nadu from 1998-99 though village panchayats in all the villages in Tamil Nadu with the help of LIC of India. This scheme is implemented in two categories as follows:

(A) Common Scheme (Persons above poverty line)

The persons between the age group of 20 to 50 years are eligible to join in this scheme. Those who join the scheme shall pay the premium annually as noted below:

Scheme	*Group*	*Age*	*Annual amount of premium to be remitted by subscription*
General Scheme	A	20 to 40 years	Rs. 60/-
	B	40 to 50 years	Rs. 70/-

(B) Scheme with Assistance (for Persons below poverty line)

1. The following persons are eligible to join this scheme. The persons should be below poverty line as per the norms prescribed by Government of India and should be identified by the village panchayats who will be the implementing agency and they shall be the implementing agency and they shall be allowed to join in the scheme.
2. The eligible age shall be 20 to 50 years.
3. The scheme—The participant shall pay annual premium as noted below:

Scheme	*Group*	*Age*	*Premium*	*Amount to be paid*	*Government Subsidy*	
					State Share	*Central Share*
Grant Scheme	A	20 to 40 years	Rs. 60/-	Rs. 30/-	Rs. 15/-	Rs. 15/-
	B	40 to 50 years	Rs. 70/-	Rs. 35/-	Rs. 17.50/-	Rs. 17.50/-

(C) The above scheme will be implemented from 15th August 1998 to 14th August 1999. The subscription of members shall be collected within the scheme period noted above.

(D) The persons those who are covered in any of the two schemes expire before attaining the age of 60, an insured amount of Rs. 5,000/- will be paid to the family.

(E) More than one person from the same family can join in the common scheme, whereas only one person from BPL family can join under grant scheme.

These schemes will be implemented through the Block Level Officers of LIC through village panchayats.

The village level officer shall receive the premium and receipt shall be given to the members. Separate register shall be maintained in every village panchayat. Money shall be kept under the custody of village level officer till the remittance to LIC branch. The village level officer shall responsible to remit the premium amounts to the LIC through panchayat union periodically. Honorarium will be paid the village level officer at the rate of Rs. 6/- in the first year for the enrolment of new member and at the rate of Rs. 3/- per member for the second and subsequent years. Moreover village level officers shall maintain proper register for the implementation of the scheme.

Subscription amount collected from the members shall be remitted in the Block Level LIC Office situated in that area. A proposal will be sent to Government through Directorate of Rural

Development based on the subscription remitted, fixing the grant to be sanctioned by the State Government description of the Scheme to the Group Insurance Department, Southern Region, LIC of India, Chennai–2.

The LIC of India has prescribed certain administrative rules in this regard. (31.12.96)

(i) No Commission shall be paid to the panchayat for the implementation of the scheme.

(ii) The printing charges for the registers will not be paid by the LIC of India.

(iii) Honorarium will be paid to the village level workers as per the rules.

The scheme will be named as a "new scheme". A token allotment of Rs. 1000/- will be provided in the supplementary demand for 1998-99 and approval State legislature may be obtained later.

The expenditure for the scheme under demand No. 27 will be debited under the following Head of Account.

2501 – RD Special Scheme 0/-
IRDP – 800 – Other expenditure
IXth Five year plan works
State Scheme – J1 – Contribution to Rural Group Life Insurance Scheme
Contributions – (DPC – 2501 – 60-800 – J1 – 1105)

The above Head of Account will be operated and controlled by the Director of Rural Development.

(G.O.MS.No.153, Rural Development (IRDP-I) Department, dated 20th July 1998)

5.9.4 Electricity—Shifting of Poles—Electricity Board not to Collect Shifting Charges from Panchayats

Electricity—Shifting of electric poles, lines, cables, transformers etc. Bearing the cost of shifting by the Tamil Nadu Electricity Board—regarding highways and rural works and other local bodies – revised orders – issued.

The government have examined the request of the Chairman, Tamil Nadu Electricity Board to meet the expenses in shifting of poles, lines and transformers etc., by the intending department like highways and rural works and other local bodies concerned under Deposit Contributory work basis.

In supersession of the orders issued in the Government Orders 1 & 2 read above, the Government order that the entire cost of shifting of Electric Poles, Cables etc., on account of widening the roads etc., should be borne by the Tamil Nadu Electricity Board only since the Tamil Nadu Electricity Board is collecting the electric current consumption charges from the public, industries, commercial institutions etc.

(G.O. Ms. No.101, Energy (C3) Department, dated 18th December 2001)

5.9.5 Guidelines for Selection of Best Village Panchayats for Awarding of Prize

(1) G.O. Ms. No. 97, Rural Development Department, dated 1.6.99

(2) G.O. Ms. No.151, Rural Development Department, dated 22.7.99

To encourage the performances of panchayats, the Government have decided to select three best performing village panchayats and three panchayat unions at District Level and three best performing village panchayats, three panchayat union councils and three district panchayats at State Level, and time schedule for selection of panchayats is narrated in the Government order first cited. The selection committee at District Level and State Level is also constituted in that order. In the Government order second cited, the Government has allotted Rs. 1.69 crores from out of Equalisation and Incentive grant.

For selection of best performing village panchayats, the following criteria shall be adopted.

I. CONDUCT OF GRAMA SABHA MEETING

Total Marks – 20
(Each shall carry 2 Marks)

Sl. No.	*Item*	*Two Marks*	*One Mark*	*No Mark*
1.	Number of Grama Sabha meetings held in last year	4 and above Grama Sabha meetings	3 meetings	Less than 3 meetings
2.	Out of total voters participated percentage of women voters in Grama Sabha meeting	More than 51%	30 to 50%	Less than 30%
3.	Out of total voters participated percentage of Scheduled Caste/ Scheduled Tribes voters in Grama Sabha meetings	More than 51%	30 to 50%	Less than 30%
4.	Preparation of plan for implementation of Scheme according to requirement of the public	Selection of all the works by Grama Sabha	75% to 99% of the works have been selected by the Grama Sabha	Less than 75% of the works have been selected by the Grama Sabha
5.	Permitted the Grama Sabha for selection beneficiaries under Rural Development Programmes	All the beneficiaries have been selected by the Grama Sabha	75% to 99% of Beneficiaries have been selected by the Grama Sabha	Less than 75% of beneficiaries have been selected by the Grama Sabha
6.	Whether minutes of the Grama Sabha meeting is recorded properly and whether it has been read and approved by the Grama Sabha	In Grama Sabha meeting itself, the minutes has been recorded properly and approved by the Grama Sabha	—	Minutes of Grama Sabha meeting has not been recorded
7.	Whether Administrative Report, Annual Accounts and Audit of previous financial year approved by Grama Sabha	The Grama Sabha approved the Administrative Report, Annual Accounts and Audit Report related to home previous financial year	—	Not approved by the Grama Sabha
8.	Whether the annual plan of Village panchayat for the next year is approved by the Gram Sabha	Grama Sabha has approved the annual plan of village panchayat	—	Not approved by the Grama Sabha
9.	Social Audit – Whether the public have been permitted to see all the records, registers, vouchers and measurement book have maintained by the village panchayat	All registers, vouchers, Measurement Book and other records have been placed before Grama Sabha meeting and the public have been permitted to see the records	—	Not placed before Grama Sabha meeting
10.	Whether Reports, opposition views, criticism are handled properly and responsible answer is provided for each views	The Presidents has handled properly	—	The President has not responded properly

II. VILLAGE PANCHAYAT FUNCTIONS

Total Marks – 20
(Each shall carry two marks)

Sl. No.	Function	Two Marks	One Mark	No Mark
1.	In last one year, how many village panchayat meeting have been conducted with participants all the member of village panchayats?	All the member of the village panchayats have participated in 12 or more than 12 village panchayat meetings	12 village panchayat meetings have been conducted but all the member shall not participated in the meetings	Conducted less than 12 village panchayat meetings
2.	Whether the village panchayat president functions independently	Village panchayats president functions independently	—	Village panchayat president depending on others
3.	Participation of women members in village panchayat meeting	All the women member have participated in all the meetings conducting in the year	More than 50% of women member have participated in the meeting	Less than 50% women member have participated in the meeting
4.	Whether the village panchayat constituted sub-committees and they function regularly	Committees have been constituted and functions regularly (All the committee meeting held once in a month properly)	Committees have been constituted but the meeting have not been held regularly	Conducted no sub-committees meeting
5.	Whether the Audit of village panchayat is completed	Audit has been completed and no audit objections are pending	Audit has been completed and some audit objections are pending	Audit has not been completed
6.	If contribution of village panchayat Fund for creation of community works	50% of village panchayat fund is spent for creation of community assets	42% to 50% of village panchayat fund is spent for creation of community assets	Less than 40% of village panchayat fund is spent for creation of community assets
7.	Whether the works have taken up by the village panchayat is completed with participation of public or works committee	Works are completed with participation of the public and works committee	—	Works are not completed with the participation of public or works committee
8.	Whether the remunerative enterprises have been started by the village panchayat and any income is derived from such enterprises	Out of total revenue 10% of the income is derived from remunerative enterprises	Out of total revenue 5% of the income is derived from remunerative enterprises	Less than 5% of the income is derived from remunerative enterprises
9.	Assessment of demand from dangerous and the offensive traders	100% assessment is made (1 mark)	—	Less than 100% assessment is made
10.	Whether the house-tax is revised and revised the house tax is collected	Yes (1 mark)	—	No
11.	Whether the village panchayat has collected full demand of professional tax	Yes (1 mark)	Collected more than 75% (1/2 mark)	Collected less than 75%
12.	Advertisement tax is collected for properly	Yes (1 mark)	Collected more than 75% of tax demand (1/2 mark)	Collected less than 75% of tax demand

(Serial No. 9, 10, 11 and 12 shall carry maximum of 1 mark only)

III. OTHER ACTIVITIES OF VILLAGE PANCHAYAT

Total Marks – 23
(Each shall carry 1.5 marks)

Sl. No.	*Item*	*1.5 Marks*	*1 Mark*	*No Mark*
1.	Number of Hand Pumps, Power Pumps in use	100%	75%–99%	Less than 75%
2.	School going children out of total children inclusive of girls children	100%	75%–99%	Less than 75%
3.	Number of street lights burning	100%	75%–99%	Less than 75%
4.	Identification of malnourished children and out of them number of children were brought to non-malnourished category	Above 50%	30%–49%	Less than 30%
5.	Steps taken for good maintenance and upgradation of causeway, public roads, tanks, ooranies, social forestry	More than 15% of Village Panchayat Fund is earmarked for this purpose	10–14% of Village Panchayat Fund is earmarked	Less than 10% is earmarked
6.	Sending of village panchayat reports properly	Yes – Village panchayat sent all the reports properly	Yes Few reports were sent by the village panchayat	No
7.	Whether SHGs formed? Percentage or number of women below poverty line have been included in Self-Help Groups	100%	75%-99%	Less than 75%
8.	Whether the village panchayat has taken steps to increase the income of unorganised labourers and scheduled castes	Yes	—	No
9.	Abolition of Child Labour in village panchayat area	Yes	—	No
10.	Abolition of illicit preparation of arrack and usage by the local people	Conducted awareness camp and people were explained about effect of alcoholism	Assisted with police for eradication of illicit aracking	No steps taken
11.	The expenditure incurred on maintenance of power pumps is within admissible expenditure	Yes	—	No
12.	The expenditure incurred on maintenance of Hand pumps is within admissible expenditure	Yes	—	No
13.	The expenditure incurred on maintenance of street light is within admissible limit	Yes	—	No
14.	The village panchayat maintain the primary school building properly	Yes	—	No
15.	Noon meal centres are maintained properly	Yes	—	No

IV. TRANSPARENT ADMINISTATION OF VILLAGE PANCHAYATS

Total Marks – 12
(Each shall carry 2 marks)

Sl. No.	*Item*	*2 Marks*	*1 Mark*	*No Mark*
1.	In Grama Sabha meeting Accounts, Statements, Attendance, Vouchers and other items are read and discussed elaborately	Yes. In all the Grama Sabha meetings, all the accounts, attendance, vouchers and other related matters are read and discussed elaborately	Only in three Grama Sabha meeting, the account, attendance and vouchers were read and discussed	In less than 3 meetings, the accounts, attendance and vouchers were read and discussed
2.	All the records are available at village panchayat office for inspection	All the records are scrutinized and available for inspection	All the records are available but only one part of the records were scrutinized	Records are not kept for inspection
3.	Whether all the certified forms are available for the residents of village panchayats	Yes	—	No
4.	Notifications and Notices issued by all three tier panchayats, Tender publication and other public information are displayed in notice board of village panchayat	Yes	Only notice issued by village panchayat is published in the notice board	Notice Board is not in use
5.	Whether the list of beneficiaries selected by the village panchayats published in important places and notice board of village panchayat	Yes	—	No
6.	Whether the works completed in each year is published properly in village panchayat buildings	The village panchayat published the list of works completed and basic information about the village panchayat	Only the works completed is published	Not published

V. SPECIAL PARAMETERS

Total Marks – 25
(Each shall carry 5 marks)

Sl. No.	*Item*	*5 Marks*	*2 Marks*	*No Mark*
1.	Bringing of individual contribution for the development of village panchayat	Above Rs. 250/-	Rs. 50/– Rs. 250/-	Less than Rs. 50/-
2.	Tax, Non-Tax Revenue (Arrears + Collection)	100%	80%	Less than 80%
3.	In Namakku Namme Thittam Public contribution in terms of cash/labour and kind	Above Rs. 250/-	Rs. 50 to Rs. 250/-	Less than Rs. 50/-
4.	Contract works completed adjustment of expenditure in last year expenditure statement	100%	—	Less than 100%
5.	Under Rural sanitation programme Household and school toilets	All the households and schools are provided with toilet facilities	50% of households are covered	Less than 50% of household are covered

(G.O. Ms. No. 27, Rural Development (C1) Department, dated 8th February 2000)

5.9.6 Conduct of Sports by Village Panchayats—Certain Instructions

The Government permit the village panchayats and the panchayat unions to conduct Sports Competition at village panchayat and at panchayat union level for Valley Ball, Badminton, Kabady, Foot Ball, Basket Ball and other Athletic events. Those who win the Competitions at the village panchayat level, Prize value of Rs. 50/- may be sanctioned from village panchayats. In respect of the panchayat union level prize value of Rs. 100/- may be given from panchayat union funds.

All the expenditure for the conduct of Sports at village panchayats and panchayat union level shall be met from village panchayat Fund or panchayat union General Fund Account. Those village panchayats or panchayat unions which do not have sufficient financial resources for conduct of Sports may seek the help of reputed industrial institutions located in the District.

(G.O.Ms.No.76, Rural Development Department, dated 24th April 1998)

5.9.7 Ceiling of Expenditure for Conduct of Sports

(1) The Government fixed the following ceiling of expenditure for conduct of Sports by various local bodies.

(a) Village Panchayat —Rs. 1,000/- per year
(b) Panchayat Unions —Rs. 10,000/- per year
(c) District Panchayat —Rs. 25,000/- per year

(2) The expenditure shall be met from the general funds of the concerned Panchayat.

(3) Before incurring expenditure, the sanction of the Village Panchayat/Panchayat Union Council/District Panchayat shall be obtained.

(G.O.Ms.No.1, Rural Development (C-2) Department, dated 7th January 1999)

PART VI

RULES RELATING TO PANCHAYAT UNION COUNCIL

6.1 CONSTITUTION OF PANCHAYAT UNION COUNCIL

6.1.1 Constitution of Panchayat Union Council

Sl. No.	*1. Kancheepuram District*
1.	Kancheepuram
2.	Wallajabad
3.	Uthiramerur
4.	Sriperumbudur
5.	Kunrathur
6.	Kattankolathur
7.	Thiruporur
8.	Thirukalukundram
9.	Maduranthagam
10.	Acharapakkam
11.	Chithamur
12.	Lathur
13.	St. Thomas Mount

Sl. No.	*2. Tiruvallur District*
1.	Villivakkam
2.	Pozhal
3.	Minjur
4.	Sholavaram
5.	Gummidipoondi
6.	Tiruvallur
7.	Poonamallee
8.	Kadambattur
9.	Poondi
10.	Ellapuram
11.	Tiruthani
12.	Thiruvalankadu
13.	R.K. Pet
14.	Pallipet

Sl. No.	*3. Vellore District*
1.	Vellore
2.	Kaniambadi
3.	Anaicut
4.	Madhanur
5.	Gudiyattam
6.	Pernampet
7.	K.V. Kuppam
8.	Katpadi
9.	Wallajapet
10.	Sholingur
11.	Arakkonam
12.	Nemili
13.	Kaveripakkam
14.	Arcot
15.	Timiri
16.	Tiruppathur
17.	Kandhili
18.	Natrampalli
19.	Alangayam
20.	Jolarpet

Sl. No.	*4. Tiruvannamalai District*
1.	Tiruvannamalai
2.	Keelpennathur
3.	Thurijapuram
4.	Chengam
5.	Pudupalayam
6.	Thandarampet
7.	Polur
8.	Kalasapakkam
9.	Chetpet
10.	Jawadhu Hills
11.	Cheyyar
12.	Anakkavur
13.	Vembakkam
14.	Wandavasi
15.	Pernamallur
16.	Thellar
17.	Arani
18.	Arani (West)

Sl. No.	*5. Cuddalore District*
1.	Cuddalore
2.	Kurinjipadi
3.	Panruti
4.	Annagramam
5.	Vridachalam

6.	Kammapuram
7.	Nallur
8.	Mangalur
9.	Keerapalayam
10.	Portnovo
11.	Melbhuvanagiri
12.	Kattumannarkoil
13.	Komartchi
14.	Arcot
15.	Timiri
16.	Tiruppathur
17.	Kandhili
18.	Natrampalli
19.	Alangayam
20.	Jolarpet

Sl. No.	*6. Villupuram District*
1.	Thirukoilur
2.	Mugaiyur
3.	Thiruvennainallur
4.	Kolianur
5.	Kanai
6.	Vikaravandi
7.	Kandamangalam
8.	Ulundurpet
9.	Thirunavalur
10.	Olakkur
11.	Mailam
12.	Vanur
13.	Marakanam
14.	Gingee
15.	Melmalayanur
16.	Vallam
17.	Kallakurichi
18.	Chinnasalem
19.	Thiyuagadurgam
20.	Sankarapuram
21.	Rishivandiyam
22.	Kalrayan Hills

Sl. No.	*7. Dharmapuri District*
1.	Dharmapuri
2.	Pennagaram
3.	Nallampalli
4.	Harur
5.	Morapppur
6.	Pappireddipatti
7.	Hosur
8.	Thally
9.	Kelamangalam
10.	Shoolagiri
11.	Krishnagiri
12.	Veppanapalli
13.	Bargur
14.	Kaveripattinam
15.	Palacode
16.	Karimangalam
17.	Uthangarai
18.	Mathur

Sl. No.	*8. Salem District*
1.	Salem
2.	Veerapandi
3.	Panamarathukpatti
4.	Ayothipattinam
5.	Vaalapady
6.	Athur
7.	Peddanaickenpalayam
8.	Talaivasal
9.	Gangavalli
10.	Mecheri
11.	Nangavalli
12.	Kolathur
13.	Omalur
14.	Tharamangalam
15.	Kadaiyampatti
16.	Sankari
17.	Edapadi
18.	Konganapuram
19.	Mac. Donald Choultry
20.	Yercaud

Sl. No.	*9. Namakkal District*
1.	Tiruchengodu
2.	Mallasamuddram
3.	Elachipalayam
4.	Pallipalayam
5.	Namakkal
6.	Sendamangalam
7.	Kolli Hills
8.	Puduchatram
9.	Erumaipatty
10.	Paramathyk
11.	Mohanur
12.	Kabilamalai
13.	Rasipuram
14.	Vennandur
15.	Namagiripet

Sl. No.	*10. Erode District*
1.	Erode
2.	Modakurichi
3.	Kodumudi
4.	Perundurai

5.	Ukthukuli
6.	Chennimalai
7.	Dharapuram
8.	Mulanur
9.	Kundadam
10.	Kangeyam
11.	Vellakoil
12.	Gobichettipalayam
13.	Nambiyur
14.	Thookkanaickenpalayam
15.	Sathyamangalam
16.	Bhavanisagar
17.	Thalavadi
18.	Bhavani
19.	Anthiyur
20.	Ammapet

Sl. No.	*11. Coimbatore District*
1.	Palladam
2.	Pongalur
3.	Sulur
4.	Sultanpet
5.	Tiruppur
6.	Annur
7.	Avinashi
8.	Pollachi North
9.	Pollachi South
10.	Kinthukadavu
11.	Anamalai
12.	Gudimangalam
13.	Udumalpet
14.	Mathankulam
15.	Madukkarai
16.	Karamadai
17.	S.S. Kulam
18.	Thondamuthur
19.	P.N. Palayam

Sl. No.	*12. Niligris District*
1.	Gudalur
2.	Coonoor
3.	Uthagamandalam
4.	Kothagiri

Sl. No.	*13. Thanjavur District*
1.	Thanjavur
2.	Budalur
3.	Thiruvaiyaru
4.	Orathanadu
5.	Thiruvonam
6.	Kumbakonam
7.	Thiruvidaimaruthur
8.	Thirupanandal
9.	Papanasam
10.	Ammapettai
11.	Pattukottai
12.	Madukkur
13.	Peravurni
14.	Sethubavachatram

Sl. No.	*14. Nagapattinam District*
1.	Nagapattinam
2.	Keelaiyur
3.	Kivelur
4.	Thirumarugal
5.	Mayiladuthurai
6.	Kuttalam
7.	Sembanarkoil
8.	Sirkali
9.	Kollidam
10.	Vedaranyam
11.	Talanayar

Sl. No.	*15. Thiruvarur District*
1.	Thiruvarur
2.	Thiruthuraipoondi
3.	Muthupettai
4.	Kottur
5.	Manargudi
6.	Needamangalam
7.	Valangaiman
8.	Koradachery
9.	Kodavasal
10.	Nannilam

Sl. No.	*16. Tiruchirapall District*
1.	Anthanallur
2.	Manikandam
3.	Manapparai
4.	Marungapuri
5.	Vaiyampatti
6.	Lalgudi
7.	Pullambadi
8.	Manachanallur
9.	Thiruverumbur
10.	Musiri
11.	Thottaim
12.	Thathiengar Pettai
13.	Thuraiyur
14.	Uppliliapuram

Sl. No.	*17. Karur District*
1.	Karur
2.	Thanthoni

3.	Aravakurichi
4.	K. Paramathi
5.	Kulithalai
6.	Krishnayapuram
7.	Kadavur
8.	Thogaimalai

Sl. No.	*18. Perambalur District*
1.	Ariyalur
2.	Thirumanur
3.	Alathur
4.	Veppur
5.	Perambalur
6.	Veppanathattai
7.	Jayamkondam
8.	T. Palur
9.	Sendurai
10.	Andimadam

Sl. No.	*19. Pudukottai District*
1.	Pudukottai
2.	Viralimalai
3.	Kunnandarkoil
4.	Annavasal
5.	Thirumayam
6.	Ponnamaraavathy
7.	Arimalam
8.	Thiruvarankulam
9.	Karambakudi
10.	Aranthangi
11.	Gandaravakottai
12.	Avudayarkoil
13.	Manalmelkudi
14.	Kaveripattinam
15.	Palacode
16.	Karimangalam
17.	Uthangarai
18.	Mathur

Sl. No.	*20. Madurai District*
1.	Thirukpparankundram
2.	Madurai East
3.	Madurai West
4.	Melur
5.	Kottampatti
6.	Vadipatti
7.	Allanganallur
8.	Usilampatti
9.	Sedapatti
10.	Chellampatti
11.	Thirumangalam
12.	T. Kallupatti
13.	Kallikudi

Sl. No.	*21. Theni District*
1.	Periyakulam
2.	Andipatti
3.	Theni
4.	Bodinayakkanur
5.	Chinnamanur
6.	Uthamapalayam
7.	Cumbum
8.	Kadamalaikundu Mayilaadum-parai

Sl. No.	*22. Dindigul District*
1.	Reddiarchattram
2.	Authur
3.	Dindigul
4.	Shanarpatti
5.	Natham
6.	Nilakottai
7.	Batlagundu
8.	Ottanchatram
9.	Palani
10.	Thoppampatti
11.	Vedasandur
12.	Vadamadurai
13.	Guziliamparai
14.	Kodaikanal

Sl. No.	*23. Ramanathapuram District*
1.	Ramanathapuram
2.	Tirupullani
3.	Mandapam
4.	Tiruvadanai
5.	R.S. Mangalam
6.	Paramakudi
7.	Bogalur
8.	Nainarkoil
9.	Mudukulathur
10.	Kadaladi
11.	Kamuthi

Sl. No.	*24. Sivagangai District*
1.	Sivagangai
2.	Kalayarkoil
3.	Manamadurai
4.	Thirupuvanam
5.	Ilayangudi
6.	Devakottai
7.	Kannangudi

8. Sakkottai
9. Kallal
10. Thirupathur
11. Singampuneri
12. S. Pudur

Sl. No.	*25. Virudhunagar District*
1.	Arukppukkottai
2.	Kariapatti
3.	Tiruchulai
4.	Narikudi
5.	Virudhunagar
6.	Sattur
7.	Sivakasi
8.	Vembakkottai
9.	Srivilliputhur
10.	Watrap
11.	Rajapalayam
12.	Kabilamalai
13.	Rasipuram
14.	Vennandur
15.	Namagiripet

Sl. No.	*26. Tirunelveli District*
1.	Palayamkottai
2.	Mannur
3.	Sankarankoil
4.	Kuruvikulam
5.	Melaneelithanallur
6.	Cheranmahadevi
7.	Ambasamudram
8.	Kadayam
9.	Pappakudi
10.	Nanguneri
11.	Kalakadu
12.	Valliyur
13.	Radapuram
14.	Tenkasi
15.	Kadayanallur
16.	Alangulam
17.	Keelapavoor
18.	Shencottai
19.	Vasudevanallur

Sl. No.	*27. Tuticorin District*
1.	Tuticorin
2.	Srivaikuntam
3.	Karunkulam
4.	Tiruchendur
5.	Alwarthirunagari
6.	Udangudi
7.	Sathankulam
8.	Kovilpatti
9.	Kayathar
10.	Vilathikulam
11.	Pudur
12.	Ottapidaram

Sl. No.	*28. Kanniyakumari District*
1.	Agastheeswaram
2.	Rajakkamangalam
3.	Thovalai
4.	Thuckalay
5.	Thiruvattar
6.	Kurunthencode
7.	Melpuram
8.	Munchirai
9.	Killiyur

6.1.2 Delegation of Powers for Constitution of Panchayat Union Council

The Government authorise the District Collectors to exercise powers vested in Government in respect of all panchayat unions in their jurisdiction under certain sections of Tamil Nadu Panchayats Act, 1994, and issue the following notification;

Notification—In exercise of the powers conferred by sub-section (1) of Section 218 of the Tamil Nadu Panchayats Act, 1994 (Tamil Nadu Act 21 of 1994), the Governor of Tamil Nadu hereby authorises the District Collectors to exercise the powers vested in the Government under Sections 16 and 19 of the said Act in respect of all Panchayat Unions in their respective jurisdiction.

(G.O. Ms. No. 166, Rural Development (C1) Department, dated 28th August 1995)

6.1.3 Alteration in the Jurisdiction of Panchayat—Formation of District Level Committee

Representations are periodically received indicating that the areas of certain village panchayats and panchayat unions are bigger and unwieldy and it is very difficult to improve the administration and execute plan programmes. It is also necessary to amalgamate or bifurcate these panchayats. The proposals for bifurcation of village panchayats or panchayat union, inclusion or exclusion of areas may be considered by a committee constituted in each district under the Chairmanship of the District Collector and the decisions on the proposals will be taken on the recommendation of the committee and after getting views of the concerned local body. The Government constituted a committee for each district consisting of following members for the purpose.

District Collector	:	Chairman
Project Officer, DRDA	:	Member-Secretary
All the MPs in the District	:	Member
All the MLAs in the District	:	Member
District Panchayat Chairman	:	Member
Five Panchayat Union Chairmen nominated by the District Collector	:	Members
One Village Panchayat President from each Panchayat Union nominated by the District Collector	:	Members
Asstt. Director (Panchayats)	:	Member

From among the members to be selected from local bodies, due representation for women, scheduled castes and schedules tribes shall be given. If the Collector desires other Government Officers, President or Chairman of the concerned village panchayat or panchayat union, they may be included as special members in the committee. The District Level committee shall be considered as class I Committee. The Travelling Allowance of the MPs and MLAs included in the committee shall be met from the Head of Account of Development Section of the Collectorate. The Travelling Allowance of other members may be met from their respective local body.

The Collectors were requested to constitute the District Level Committee for the first time before 15th July, 1999. The Committee shall subject to the following conditions, examine the following subjects and furnish report to the Government within a period of 3 months.

(i) Bifurcation or amalgamation of village panchayats.

(ii) Inclusion of a portion of the village panchayat in another village panchayat or exclusion thereof.

(iii) Bifurcation of panchayat unions or inclusion or exclusion of certain areas.

(iv) While recommending for constitution of new village panchayats or panchayat unions, the committee shall satisfy, that adequate financial resources are available for functioning of village panchayat or panchayat unions. Opinion of the public as well as the resolution of the concerned local body shall be obtained.

(v) The additional expenditure involved due to bifurcation shall be examined and remarks given. The boundaries and population of the recommended new village panchayat or panchayat union shall confirm to those fixed as per Tamil Nadu Panchayats Act, 1994.

(G.O.Ms.No.113, Rural Development (C1) Department, Dated 29th June 1999)

6.2 ELECTED REPRESENTATIVES OF PANCHAYAT UNION COUNCIL

6.2.1 Disclosure of Assets and Liabilities by Chairman and Members of Panchayat Union council

1. Short title—These rules may be called the Tamil Nadu Panchayats (Disclosure of Assets and Liabilities, by Chairman and Members of Panchayat Union Council) Rules, 1999.

2. Definition—In these rules, unless the context otherwise requires, Member of the Family means person related whether by blood or marriage to the chairman, vice-chairman and members of panchayat union council or his wife or her husband and wholly dependant on such chairman, vice-chairman and member.

3. Periodical disclosure of assets of chairman, vice-chairman and members of panchayat union Council—The chairman, vice-chairman and every member of a panchayat union council shall

(i) if he is elected after the date of coming into force of these rules, within a period of thirty days, after such election;

(ii) thereafter, at intervals of every twelve months ending with the 31st day of march, furnish in duplicate to the panchayat union council in the Form appended to these rules a return of;

(iii) all properties owned, acquired or inherited by him or his family members including their liabilities; and

(iv) all properties held on lease or mortgage either

in his own name or in the name of his family members, including their liabilities together with details of the means by which, or the sources from which such property was acquired or inherited.

4. Returns to be placed at the meeting and to be public document—(1) After the receipt of the return specified in Rule 3 the Commissioner shall, cause it be placed at the meeting of the panchayat union council and send a copy to the Inspector.

(2) Such return shall be deemed to be a public document and the Commissioner, with the permission of the panchayat union council, may, subject to such condition including payment of fees specified in Rule 5 give to any person on demand a copy of such return.

5. Fee for furnishing return—The fee for furnishing a copy of any return or part thereof shall be ten rupees or the amount to be fixed by the Government from time-to-time.

(G.O.Ms. No. 183, Rural Development (C-4) Department, dated 30th August 1999)

APPENDIX

Form

(See Rule 3)

Returns of Assets and Liabilities of the Chairman, Vice-Chairman or Member of the .... District Panchayat as on the ....

Name of the ....

Date of election:

Part I – Assets and Liabilities of the ....

1. Immovable Property

(a)	*Land*	*Owned*		*Wet*	*Dry*	*Irrigated dry*
	Extent:					
	Date of acquisition:					
	Value of acquisition:					
	Leased in:					
	Extent:					
	Date of acquisition:					
	Value of acquisition:					
(b)	*Building*	*Owned*	*Terraced*	*Tiled*	*Thatched*	*Purpose for which the building is used: commercial or residential*
	Plinth Area:					
	Date of acquisition:					
	Value of acquisition					
	Plinth Area:	*Leased in*	*Terraced*	*Tiled*	*Thatched*	*Purpose for which the buildings is used commercial (or) residential*
	Date of acquisition:					
	Value of acquisition:					

2. Business interests:
   (a) Shares
   (b) Stock
   (c) Scrip
   (d) Partnership
   (e) Debentures and securities
3. Other interest:
   Bank Account
4. Jewellery:
   (i) Gold
   (ii) Precious stones
   (iii) Silver Ware
5. Movables (including motor vehicles)
6. Details of Trusts with which he has any connection
7. Remarks, if any, of the ____________________(Explain the nature of acquisition of properties)
8. Liabilities

Part II – Assets and Liabilities of his family members

Name of the Family member ....

1. Immovable Property

(a)	*Land*	*Owned*		*Wet*	*Dry*	*Irrigated dry*
	Extent:					
	Date of acquisition:					
	Value of acquisition:					
	Leased in:					
	Extent:					
	Date of acquisition:					
	Value of acquisition:					
(b)	*Building*	*Owned*	*Terraced*	*Tiled*	*Thatched*	*Purpose for which the building is used: commercial or residential*
	Plinth Area:					
	Date of acquisition:					
	Value of acquisition					
	Plinth Area:	*Leased in*	*Terraced*	*Tiled*	*Thatched*	*Purpose for which the buildings is used commercial (or) residential*
	Date of acquisition:					
	Value of acquisition:					

2. Business interests:
   (a) Shares
   (b) Stock
   (c) Scrip
   (d) Partnership
   (e) Debentures and securities

3. Other interest:
   Bank Account
4. Jewellery:
   (i) Gold
   (ii) Precious stones
   (iii) Silver Ware
5. Movables (including motor vehicles)
6. Details of Trusts with which he has any connection
7. Remarks, if any, of the ______________________(Explain the nature of acquisition of properties)
8. Liabilities

DECLARATION

I __________________declare that to the best of any my knowledge and belief and the information furnished in the above return is true and complete.

Place

Date: **Signature**

6.3 PROCEDURE

6.3.1 Procedure for Convening and Conduct of Meeting of Panchayat Union Council and its Committees

1. Short title—These rules may be called the Tamil Nadu Panchayats (Procedure for the Convening and Conduct of Meetings of Panchayat Union Council and its Committees) Rules, 1999.

2. Definition—In these rules, unless the context otherwise requires,

(a) "Act" means the Tamil Nadu Panchayats Act, 1994 (Tamil Nadu Act 2 of 1994);

(b) All other words and expressions used in these rules but not defined therein shall have the meaning respectively assigned to them in the Act.

3. Location of the office and the meetings—(1) Unless the Government by order otherwise direct, the office of the panchayat union council shall be located in the Block Development Office concerned.

(2) No meeting shall be held on any day declared by the Government as holiday and other local holidays declared by the Collector.

(3) The panchayat union council shall meet in the office so located at least once in every month for the transaction of the business on such days and at such times as it may arrange and also at such other times as often as a meeting shall be called by the chairman.

4. Notice of the meeting—(1) No meeting shall be held unless notice of the day and time when the meeting is to be held and of the business to be transacted thereat has been given atleast five clear days before the day of the meeting.

(2) Provided that in cases of urgency, the chairman may convene a meeting on giving a notice of not less than twenty-four hours clearly indicating in writing the reason of urgency and the date, and time including the business to be transacted thereat.

5. Special meeting—The subject which is to be decided only in a meeting specially convened for a particular purpose as per the provisions of the Act shall be decided only in a special meeting and no other subject shall be placed and decided at such a meeting.

6. Agenda—(1) The agenda for the meeting shall be prepared by the Commissioner and approved by the chairman. The Commissioner may include in the agenda any subject which, as per the provision of the Act and in his opinion should be considered by the panchayat union council and shall include therein any subject specified by the chairman. On any subject included in the agenda, the chairman as well as the Commissioner shall have the right of recording his views in a note and such note shall be circulated to the members or placed before the council before or at the time of the consideration of such subject by the panchayat union council.

(2) If a member of the panchayat union council is desirous of bringing in a subject for discussion, shall send detailed note to the Commissioner fifteen days in advance; and the Commissioner on receipt of the same, shall examine the relevance and furnish his views and get the views of the chairman in writing before placing the agenda for the meeting.

(3) The Commissioner, while preparing the agenda for the ordinary meeting shall invariably include among others, the following subjects:

(a) A statement showing the monthly receipts and charges of the panchayat union under all accounts during the month and upto the month for every financial year;

(b) preparation of development plan for panchayat union;

(c) progress of all schemes, programmes and works during the month and upto the month;

(d) audit report of the panchayat union with explanatory notes on the audit objection at the first meeting of the panchayat union council after the receipt of the same;

(e) administration report of panchayat union for each financial year;

(f) diaries of the Commissioner and other subordinate officers of the previous months;

(g) tour reports and inspection reports of all higher officers who inspected the schemes, programmes and works of the panchayat union at the first meeting of the panchayat union council after their receipt;

(h) review of schemes, programmes and other activities executed in the panchayat union area for which Government have by order entrusted the review powers to the panchayat union council.

(4) In order to ensure the successful participation of the chairman and members of the panchayat union council in the administration of panchayat union, the Commissioner shall place the various instructions, guidelines issued, from time-to-time by the Government of India, Government of Tamil Nadu, Director of Rural Development and the Collector, before the panchayat union council.

7. Service of notice of the meeting and agenda—(1) The notice of the meeting with the agenda shall be served on all the members of the panchayat union council following the procedure specified below, in the order in which it is specified:

(a) by giving or tendering the notice of the meeting to the member concerned in person; or

(b) in case personal service could not be effected, by tendering it to an adult member of his family, or

(c) if no adult member of his family is available for service, it shall be sent by registered post with acknowledgement due; and if the notice with the agenda returns back from the post, the same may be affixed on the conspicuous place of his last known address in the presence of village administrative officer of the village concerned.

(2) The copies of the notice of the meeting and agenda of the meeting of the panchayat union council may be supplied to the local press representatives.

(3) The entire proceedings of the meeting of the panchayat union council shall be invalid if the notice with the agenda of the meeting is not served to any member of the panchayat union council.

8. Requisition meeting—(1) The chairman shall, on the requisition in writing, of not less than one-third of the members of the council, convene a meeting of the council, provided the requisition specifies the day when and the purpose for which the meeting is to be held. The requisition shall be delivered at the panchayat union office during office hours to the chairman, or any other person who may then be in charge of the office, not less than fifteen clear days before the date of the meeting.

(2) If the chairman fails within forty-eight hours from the delivery of such requisition to call a meeting on the date specified therein, or within three days, thereafter, the meeting may be called by all the members who signed the requisition on giving the notice as provided in Rule 4 to the other members of the panchayat union council.

9. Meetings open to public—Every meeting of the panchayat union council shall be open to the public, provided the presiding member may, and at the request of the panchayat union council shall in any particular case, for reasons to be recorded in the minutes book, restrict the number of public to witness the meeting or direct that the public generally or any particular person, shall withdraw.

10. Attendance of the meeting—The members and the presiding member attending the meeting shall sign in the attendance register. At the closure of the meeting the presiding member shall close the attendance register by specifying the number of members attended in the register and sign at the end.

11. Commissioner to be present and responsible for other subordinate officers and other Government officers to be present—(1) The Commissioner shall attend the meeting. It is the responsibility of the Commissioner to make available at the meeting of the panchayat union council and the committees thereof all information which may be required at such meetings. The block engineer shall also attend the meeting. If the Commissioner considers that the presence of any other subordinate officers working under him at any of the meeting may be necessary, it is his responsibility to make arrangement for their presence provided the council or the committee, as the case may be, has no objection to their presence.

(2) The Commissioner shall request the Government Officer concerned in the panchayat union area to attend the meeting for review of the programmes. In all such cases, the Commissioner shall get the order of the chairman and communicate the same to the officer concerned in advance.

12. Quorum—(1) No business shall be transacted at a meeting unless there be present not less than one-third of the number of members of the panchayat union council throughout the duration of the meeting.

(2) If, within half an hour after the time appointed for a meeting, a quorum is not present, the meeting shall stand adjourned unless all the members present agree to wait longer.

(3) If the meeting stands adjourned for want of quorum, the chairman shall give a fresh notice for the adjourned meeting.

13. Adjournment of the meeting for other reasons—(1) The presiding member of a panchayat union council, while transacting business at the meeting, may adjourn any meeting of a panchayat union council with the consent of the majority of the members for valid reasons to be recorded in writing in the minutes book. Once a meeting is adjourned *sine die* for valid reasons, it shall not continue its meeting.

(2) While transacting the business, if a meeting is validly adjourned by the presiding member with the consent of the majority of the members present at the meeting, the meeting held on, the adjourned date shall, for all purposes, be a continuation of the original meeting and no fresh notice shall be necessary for such an adjourned meeting.

(3) If the chairman adjourns the meeting contrary to the wishes of the members present and thereby interrupts or leaves the meeting unfinished, the remaining members may lawfully continue the business for which the meeting was convened. In the absence of chairman or vice-chairman, a member elected from among them may preside over the meeting and continue the business. Any business which was duly notified in the notice of the meeting shall be transacted to the completion and if it is so transacted, it shall be valid.

14. Passing of resolution—Every question which may come before the panchayat union council at any meeting shall be decided by a majority of the members present and voting at the meeting and, in every case of equality of votes, the presiding member shall have and exercise a second or casting vote. In the case of any resolution not carried unanimously, the names of the members who voted for and against it shall be recorded in the minutes.

15. Modification or cancellation of resolution—No resolution of the panchayat union council shall be modified or cancelled within three months after the passing thereof except at a meeting specially convened in that behalf and by a resolution of the panchayat union council supported by not less than one-half of the number of members.

16. Minutes—Minutes of the proceedings at each meeting of the panchayat union council shall be drawn up and entered in a book to be kept for that purpose and as soon as the discussions on a subject are over, the presiding member shall record the decision of the panchayat union council then and there, read the text of the decision to the members present and affix his signature immediately below the last line of the resolution. At the end of the meeting he shall record in the minutes that all the resolutions passed have been read out in the open meeting and then only he shall sign at the end of the minutes and shall also obtain the signatures of all the members present at the meeting.

17. Custody of records—The Commissioner shall have the custody of the proceedings and records of the panchayat union council and may grant copies of any such proceedings and records on payment of such fees as the panchayat union council may by general or special order, determine. Copies shall be certified by the Commissioner as provided in Section 76 of the Indian Evidence Act, 1872, and copies so certified may be used to prove the records of the panchayat union council in the same manner as they may under sub-section (5) of Section 78 of the said Act, be used to prove the proceedings of that body.

18. Procedure for committee meetings—Every committee constituted by the panchayat union council under Section 96 of the Act shall meet in the panchayat union office and shall follow all the procedure laid down for the meetings of panchayat union council in these rules, for the transaction of its business.

19. Placing of minutes of the meeting of the committee—A copy of the minutes of proceedings of every meeting of any committee of the panchayat union council shall be placed before the panchayat union council at its first meeting to be held, after the receipt thereof, for its approval. The panchayat union council shall have the power to modify, alter or rescind any resolution of the committee.

(G.O. Ms. No. 260, Rural Development Department, dated 17th December 1999)

6.3.2 Attendance in Panchayat Union Council Meeting

In order to promote the effective transaction of business at the meetings of the panchayat union council and of the committees of the council, Government consider it desirable that the Commissioner should attend as far as possible, every such meetings of the council and of the committees of the council even if he is not specifically required by the chairman to attend.

It is the responsibility of the panchayat union Commissioner, as the administrative head of the union, to make available at the meetings of the panchayat union council and of the committees thereof all information that will be required at such meetings. The Commissioner has to discharge this function irrespective of the fact whether he attends a particular meeting or not. If the Commissioner considers that the presence of any Officer of the panchayat union or any of the other departmental officers are necessary at any of the meetings, it is his responsibility to make arrangements for inviting such officers to ensure their presence in the meeting.

(Govt. Memo No.249429, Rural Development (E-4) Department, dated 29th January 1962)

6.3.3 Supply of Agenda Copies to Local Press

The Government direct that copies of the meeting notices and agenda of the meeting of the panchayat union councils be supplied to the Local Press representatives.

(G.O. Ms. No. 587, Rural Development and Local Administration Department, dated 14th March 1962)

6.3.4 Furnishing Important Orders to Panchayat Union Council

In order to ensure the effective participation of the Chairman and members of the panchayat union councils in the administration of the panchayat union, it is necessary that they are kept regularly and sufficiently informed of the various instructions and Government orders issued from time-to-time by Government Department.

Important Government orders, Government Memoranda and instructions which should be made known to every member of the panchayat union council will in future be specifically addressed to the panchayat union councils. The panchayat union Commissioner shall ensure that all such references thus addressed to, and other references which are considered as important, shall be collected from the date of the previous meeting and are read out and explained to the members at the next meeting of the Panchayat Union Council and formally recorded after thus being read.

(Govt. Memo No. 14528/L.Sp./61-1, Rural Development and Local Administration Department, dated 20th December 1961)

6.3.5 Moving of Resolutions at Meetings of Panchayat Union Council

1. Short title—These rules may be called the Tamil

Nadu Panchayats (Moving of Resolutions at Meetings of Panchayat Union Council) Rules, 1999.

2. Procedure of note—A member who wishes to move a resolution shall intimate his intention in writing to the chairman by giving at least ten clear days notice and such notice shall contain a copy of the resolution which he wishes to move:

Provided that the chairman may allow a resolution with shorter notice than ten days to be entered on the list of business.

3. Admission of resolution—No resolution shall be admissible which does no comply with the following conditions, namely:

(a) It shall be related to the administration of the panchayat union council concerned;

(b) It shall be clearly and precisely be expressed and shall raise a definite issue; and

(c) It shall not contain arguments, inferences ironical expressions for defamatory statements nor shall it refer to the conduct or character of any person except in his official or public capacity.

4. Admissibility of resolution—The chairman shall decide on the admissibility of a resolution. He may disallow any resolution which in his opinion contravenes the provisions of the Tamil Nadu Panchayats Act, 1994, or the rules made thereunder and the decision of the chairman shall be final:

Provided that if in the opinion of the chairman a resolution relates to a matter which is unconnected with the administration of the panchayat union concerned the chairman shall refer the resolution to the Inspector and obtain his orders as to its admissibility.

5. Entry of resolution in the list of business—A resolution which has been admitted by the chairman shall be entered in the list of business in the notice for the meeting.

6. Procedure to move or otherwise of a resolution—(1) A member in whose name a resolution appears on the list of business shall, when called on, either

(a) move the resolution; or

(b) withdraw the resolution in which cast he shall confine himself to a mere statement to that effect.

(2) If the member, when called on is absent or proposes to withdraw or is unwilling to move the resolution, or of he has ceased to be a member before the meeting any, member present at the meeting may move the resolution and if no member moves it, it shall be considered to have been withdrawn.

(3) Every resolution, which has been moved, shall be seconded otherwise it shall not be discussed.

7. Mode of discussion—(1) No speech, except which the permission of the chairman shall exceed five minutes in duration:

Provided that the mover of a resolution when moving the same may speak for not more than ten minutes.

(2) The discussion of a resolution shall be strictly limited to the subject of the resolution.

8. Amendment to a resolution—(1) When a resolution is under discussion any member may, subject to Rules 3, 4 and 7 move an amendment to such resolution.

(2) Every amendment which, has been moved, shall be seconded, otherwise it shall not be discussed.

(3) A member who has moved a resolution or an amendment to a resolution shall not withdraw the same except leave of the panchayat union council.

(4) No discussion shall be permitted on a motion for leave to withdraw except with the permission of the chairman.

(5) When an amendment to any resolution is moved or when two or more such amendments are moved, the chairman shall, before taking the consent of the panchayat union council thereon, state or read to the panchayat union council the terms of ordinal motion and of the amendment or amendments proposed.

(6) Ordinarily, the chairman shall put the amendment to vote in the order in which they have been moved and lastly the original motion if all the amendments are lost. But it shall be in his discretion in any case to put to vote the original motion and the amendments in such order as he thinks fit.

9. Division of resolution into points for voting—When any resolution involving several points has been discussed it shall be in the discretion of the chairman to divide the resolutions into points and put each of such points separately to vote.

(G.O. Ms. No. 201, Rural Development (C-4) Department, dated 28th September 1999)

6.3.6 Interpellation of Chairman of Panchayat Union Council by the Members

1. Short title—These rules may be called the Tamil Nadu Panchayats (Interpellation of Chairman of Panchayat Union Council by the Members) Rules, 1999.

2. Restriction on questions—No question shall

be asked or answered at a meeting of a panchayat union council as to any matter not connected with the administration of. the panchayat union council and no question shall be asked except as to matters of fact and the answer shall be confined to a statement of facts. Except as thus provided, any question may be asked by any member, subject to the conditions and restrictions specified in these rules.

3. **Intimation about to questions**—A member of panchayat union council who wishes to ask a question shall intimate his intention in writing to the chairman by giving prior notice of not less than ten clear days and such notice shall contain a copy of the question he wishes to ask.

4. **Admissible questions**—In order that a question may be admissible, it shall satisfy the following conditions, namely:

(i) it shall be related to the administration of the panchayat union and it shall be based on facts;
(ii) it shall not relate to any name or statement not strictly necessary to make the question intelligible;
(iii) if a question contains a statement, the member asking it shall make himself responsible for the accuracy of the statement;
(iv) it shall not contain arguments, inferences, ironical, satirical expressions or defamatory statements;
(v) it shall not ask for an expression of opinion or the solution of an abstract legal question or of a hypothetical proposition;
(vi) it shall not be asked as to the character or conduct of any person except in his official or public capacity;
(vii) it shall be short and brief and shall not be of excessive in length; and
(viii) a question once fully answered may not be asked again.

5. **Decision as to admissibility of questions**—The chairman shall decide on admissibility of a question and either allow or disallow it before date fixed for the next meeting for which it may be within the time specified under Rule 3. He may disallow any question, if in his opinion, it is an abuse of the right of questioning or where in his opinion it cannot be answered consistently in the public interest, and shall disallow any question which in his opinion, contravenes any of these rules; and in such case the question shall not be entered in the proceedings of the panchayat union council.

6. **Entry of questions into the agenda**—Questions allowed by the chairman, shall be entered in the agenda and the chairman shall answer every question so entered, if not previously withdrawn by the member putting it, in the order in which it stands in the paper, before any business is entered upon at the meeting. The answer shall be confined to a statement of facts only:

Provided that the chairman may, at his discretion, on the ground of public interest, answer a question on the agenda, even though the question may have been withdrawn.

7. **Supplementary questions**—Any member may put a supplementary question for the purpose of further elucidating any matter of fact regarding which an answer has been given:

Provided that the chairman, shall disallow any supplementary question if, in his opinion, it infringes the rules as to the subject matter of question and does not confirm to the conditions specified under Rule 4:

Provided further that the chairman may decline to answer a supplementary question without notice, in which case it may be put only in the form of a fresh question at a subsequent meeting of the panchayat union council.

7. **Bar of discussion on answered questions**—No discussion shall be permitted in respect of any question or of any answer given to a question, asked under these rules.

8. **Minutes**—The question asked and the answer given to it shall be entered in the minutes of the panchayat union council.

(G.O.Ms.No.145, Rural Development (C-1) Department, dated 14th July 1998)

6.4 COMMITTEES

6.4.1 Election of Members to the Committees of Panchayat Union (Other than Appointment Committee) Rules, 1998

1. **Short title**—These rules may be called the Election of Members to the Committees of Panchayat Union (Other than Appointment Committee) Rules, 1998.

2. **Definition**—In these rules unless the context otherwise requires:

(a) "Act" means the Tamil Nadu Panchayats Act, 1994 (Tami Nadu Act 21 of 1994);
(b) "Committee" means the committee constituted under clause (c) of sub-section (1) of Section 96 of the Act;
(c) "President" means the president of the meeting;

(d) "Meeting" means the meeting specially convened for the purpose of the election.

3. Holding of election of members—The election of members to each of the committees shall be held in the offices of the panchayat union and shall be from among the elected members of the panchayat union council at a meeting.

4. Convening of meeting

(a) The meeting shall be convened by the chairman of the panchayat union council within thirty days of the occurrence of a vacancy:

Provided that where the chairman of a panchayat union council fails to convene the meeting, the inspector shall convene the same.

(b) Notice of the day and hour of the meeting shall be given to all the elected members and to the inspector under acknowledgement at least seven clear days previous to the date of the meeting.

(c) The Inspector shall depute an observer not below the rank of an Assistant Director of Rural Development or Revenue Divisional Officer to be present at the meeting to ensure that the election is conducted in a free and fair manner.

5. Nominations

(a) Every candidate for election shall file a nomination in Form I appended to these and rules shall be proposed by a member. No proposer shall sign nomination for more than the number of candidates to be elected.

(b) The president shall record the names of members so proposed in the minutes of the meeting after ascertaining in writing their willingness to serve in the committee. He shall readout the names of candidates proposed to the members present at the meeting.

6. Procedure in contested and uncontested election

(a) If the number of contesting candidates is equal to the number of seats to be elected, the president shall forthwith declare all such candidates to be duly elected to the committee.

(b) If the number of contesting candidates is more than the number of seats to be elected, a poll shall be taken.

(c) If the number of contesting candidates is less than the number of seats to be elected, the president shall forthwith declare all the contesting candidates to be duly elected and arrange for the conduct of election in respect of the remaining seats.

7. Provision of voting compartment—The president shall provide in the place where the meeting is held, a voting compartment in which the members can record their votes screened from observation. The president shall also place a ballot box for the receipt of ballot papers in the view of the president and the members. The ballot box shall be so constructed that the ballot papers can be introduced therein but cannot be withdrawn there from without the box being unlocked or opened.

8. Ballot box to be shown empty—The president shall immediately before the votes are taken, show the ballot box empty to such members as may be present so that they may see that it is empty and shall then lock it up, and place a seal upon it in such a manner as to prevent its being opened without breaking such seal.

9. Ballot paper—Every member wishing to vote shall be supplied with a ballot paper of uniform size and colour in the Form II in the Appendix to these rules on which the names of all the candidates shall be legibly written or type written or cyclostyled in Tamil and signed by the president before being handed over to the member.

10. Procedure for voting—The member shall, on receiving the ballot paper proceed to the voting compartment for the purpose of recording his vote by putting a cross mark on the ballot paper against the name of the candidate or candidates for whom he wishes to vote by using the seal supplied by the president. He shall, before leaving the voting compartment, fold up the ballot paper so as to conceal the cross mark and put the ballot paper so folded up into the ballot box in the presence of the president.

11. Voting by illiterate, blind, etc., persons—

(a) If owing to illiteracy or blindness or other physical infirmity, a member is unable to read the ballot paper and make a cross mark thereon, and seeks assistance for doing so, the president shall record the vote in the ballot paper in accordance with the wishes of the member and fold it up so as to conceal the vote.

(b) The member shall then himself or with the assistance of the president insert the ballot paper into the ballot box.

(c) While acting under this rule, the president shall observe as much secrecy as is feasible and shall keep a brief record of each such instance but shall not indicate therein the manner in which any vote has been given.

12. Recording of votes—After voting by members is over, the president shall open the ballot box in the presence of members present, take out the ballot papers therefrom and, record the number of votes obtained by each candidate in a statement.

13. Invalidation of ballot papers—A ballot paper shall be treated as invalid on which

(a) there is no cross mark; or

(b) if votes are given on it in favour of more candidates than the number of candidates to be elected; or

(c) a cross mark and some other mark are put opposite the name of the same candidate; or

(d) any mark is made by which the member may afterwards be identified; or

(e) if it is uncertain to which candidate the mark is intended to apply; or

(f) the mark has been made by any seal other than the one provided for this purpose.

14. Declaration of result of election—When the counting of votes has been completed, the president shall forthwith declare the candidate or candidates to whom the largest number of valid votes has been given, to be elected.

15. Procedure in case of equality of votes—If after the counting of the votes is completed, any candidates are found to have secured equal number of votes and the addition of one vote will entitle one of these candidate to be declared elected, the president shall forthwith decide between these candidates by lot, and proceed as if the candidates on whom the lot falls had received an additional vote.

16. Reporting of the result of the election—Immediately after the meeting, the president shall

(a) prepare a record of the proceeding of the meeting in the minutes book read out the minutes aloud, sign it, attesting with his initial every correction made therein; and also permit any member present at the meeting to affix his signature on such record if he expresses his desire to do so;

(b) send a report of the result of the election to the Inspector and to such other officer or authority as may be specified by the Government by general or special order; and

(c) publish on the notice board of the office of the panchayat union, a notification signed by him stating the name(s) of the person(s) elected as member(s) of the committee;

(d) The observer of the election shall separately send a detailed report to the inspector within twenty four hours as to whether the election was conducted in a free and fair manner:

Provided that where the Government is satisfied based on the report of the Inspector that the election has not been conducted in a free and fair manner, the Government may cancel the result of the election and order a fresh election.

17. Disposal of ballot papers

(a) The president shall then, make up the ballot papers into a separate packet, seal up the packet and note thereon a description of its contents, the election to which it relates and the date thereof.

(b) These packets shall not be opened and their contents inspected or produced except under the order of a competent court.

(c) The packets shall be retained in safe custody in the office of the panchayat union for a year and shall then, unless otherwise directed by the orders of a competent court, be destroyed.

APPENDIX

Form I

[See Rule 5(a)]

Nomination Paper for Election of Members of the ____________Committee

I, ______________________________an elected member from ___________________________ward of the ____Panchayat Union hereby nominate Thiru/Tmt/ Selvi______________________________a member elected from _________________________ward of the ______________________________________Panchayat Union as a candidate for election as a member of the ______________________________committee.

Signature of the Proposer

Declaration of the Candidate

I,____ a member elected from ______________________ward of the ___________________________Panchayat Union hereby give my consent to this nomination.

Signature of the Candidate

Form II
(See Rule 9)

Ballot Paper

___________________PANCHAYAT UNION COUNCIL.

DATE OF ELECTION_______________________

Name of the candidates duly nominated for election as members of the ________________committee.

1.
2.
3.
4.

President

6.4.2 Election of Members of Appointment Committee

1. Short title—These rules may be called the Appointments Committee of the Panchayat Union Council (Election of Member) Rules, 1997.

2. Definition—In these rules, unless the context otherwise requires:

(a) "Committee" means the appointment committee of the panchayat union council.

(b) "President" means the president of the meeting.

3. Holding of election of member—The election of a member to the committee shall be held in the office of the panchayat union and shall be from among the elected members of the panchayat union council at a meeting especially convened for the purpose.

4. Convening of meeting—The meeting for the election of a member to the committee shall be convened by the chairman of the panchayat union council within thirty days of the occurrence of a casual vacancy. Provided that where the chairman of the panchayat union council fails to convene the meeting, the Inspector shall convene the same.

(a) Notice of the day and hour of the meeting shall be given to all the elected members and to the Inspector under acknowledgement at least seven clear days previous to the date of the meeting.

(b) The Inspector shall depute an "Observer" in the rank of Assistant Director of Rural Development or Revenue Divisional Officer to be present at this meeting in order to ensure that the election is conducted in a free and fair manner.

5. Presiding over the meeting—The meeting shall be presided over by the chairman or in the absence of the chairman, the vice-chairman, or in the absence of both the chairman and vice-chairman by a member not intending to contest as a candidate at the election an chosen by the members present at the meeting to preside for the occasion. Such a person may be styled as the President.

6. Nominations

(a) Every candidate for election shall be nominated in the form given in Appendix I below by a member as proposer. There is no need for a seconder. No proposer shall sign more than one nomination.

(b) The president of the meeting shall record the names of members so proposed in the minutes of the meeting after ascertaining in writing their willingness to serve in the committee for a period of one year from the date of election. He shall read out the name of the candidates proposed to the hearing of the members present at the meeting.

7. Procedure in contested and uncontested election

(a) If the number of contesting candidates is more than one, a poll shall be taken.

(b) If there is only one contesting candidate, the president shall forthwith declare the candidate to be duly elected to the committee.

(c) If no candidates are forthcoming, then the president shall arrange for the conduct of election at the next meeting, which should be convened within fifteen days.

8. Provision of voting compartment—For conducting the poll, the president shall provide in the place where the meeting is held a voting compartment in which the members can record their votes screened from observation. The president shall also place a ballot box for the receipt of the ballot papers in the view of the president and the members. The ballot box shall be so constructed that the ballot papers can be inserted therein but cannot be withdrawn there from without the box being unlocked or opened.

9. Ballot box to be shown empty—The president shall immediately before the votes are taken, show the ballot box empty to such members as may be present so that they may see that it is empty and shall then lock it up, and place a seal upon it in such a manner as to prevent it being opened without breaking such seal.

10. Ballot paper—Every member wishing to vote shall be supplied with a ballot paper of uniform size in the form given in Appendix II and colour on which the names of all the candidates shall be legibly written or typewritten or cyclostyled in Tamil, and signed by the president before being handed over to the members.

11. Procedure for voting—Every member shall, on receiving the ballot paper proceed to the voting compartment and record his vote by putting a cross mark on the ballot paper against the name of the candidate for whom he wishes to vote by using the seal supplied by the president. He shall, before leaving the voting compartment, fold up the ballot paper so as to conceal the cross mark and put the ballot paper so folded up into the ballot box in the presence of the president.

12. Voting by illiterate, blind, etc., persons—If owing to illiteracy or blindness or other physical infirmity, a member is unable to read the ballot paper and make a cross mark thereon, and seeks for assistance for doing so, the president shall record the vote in the ballot paper in accordance with the wishes of the member and fold it up so as to conceal the vote.

(a) The member shall then himself or with the assistance of the president insert the ballot paper into the ballot box.

(b) While acting under this rule, the president shall observe as much secrecy as if feasible and shall keep a brief record of each such instance but shall not indicate therein the manner in which any vote has been given.

13. Recording of votes—After the voting by members is over, the president shall open the ballot box in the presence of the members present, take out the ballot papers there from, record the number of votes obtained by each candidate in a statement.

14. Invalidation of ballot papers—A ballot paper shall be treated as invalid on which

(a) there is no cross mark; or

(b) if votes are given on it in favour of more candidates than one; or

(c) a cross mark and some other mark are put opposite the name of the same candidate; or

(d) any mark is made by which the member may afterwards be identified; or

(e) if it is uncertain to which candidate the mark is intended to apply; or

(f) the mark has been made by and seal other than the one provided for this purpose.

15. Declaration of result of election—After the completion of the counting of votes, the president shall forthwith declare the candidate to whom the largest number of valid votes has been given to be duly elected.

16. Procedure in case of equality of votes—After the counting of the votes is completed, and in the event of there being an equality of votes between any two or more candidates and the addition of one vote will entitle one of these candidates to be declared elected, the president shall forthwith decide between these candidates by lot and proceed as if the candidates on whom the lot falls had received an additional vote and declare him elected.

17. Reporting of the result of the election—After completion of the voting, immediately after the counting, the president shall

(a) prepare a record of the proceedings of the meeting in the minutes book, read out the minutes aloud, sign it, attesting with his initials every correction made therein; and also permit any member present at the meeting to affix his signature to such record if he express his desire to do so;

(b) send a report of the result of the election to the Inspector and to such other officer or authority as may be specified by the Government by general or special order;

(c) publish on the notice board of the office of the panchayat union, a notification signed by him stating the name of the person elected as member of the committee; and

(d) the observer of the election shall separately send a detailed report to the Inspector within twenty four hours as to whether the election was conducted in a free and fair manner:

Provided that where the Government is satisfied based on the report of the Inspector that the election has not been conducted in a free and fair manner, the Government may cancel the result of the election and order a fresh election.

18. Disposal of ballot paper

(a) The president shall then make up the ballot papers into a separate packet, seal up the packet and note thereon a description of its contents, the election to which it relates and the date thereof.

(b) These packets shall not be opened and their contents inspected or produced except under the order of a competent court.

(c) These packets shall be retained in safe custody in the office of the panchayat union for a year and shall then unless otherwise directed by the orders of a competent court, be destroyed.

APPENDIX I

Form

[See Rule 6 (a)]

Nomination Paper for Election of Member to the Committee

I__________an_________Elected_________member from________ward of the said council hereby nominate Thiru/Tmt./Selvi____________a member elected from______________ward of the above said council as a candidate for election as a member of the Committee of the above said council.

Signature of the Proposer

Declaration of the Candidate

I,______________a member elected from_____________ward of the said council hereby give my consent to this nomination.

Signature of the Candidate

APPENDIX II

Form

(See Rule 10)

Ballot Paper

Panchayat Union Council

Date of election__________

Names of candidates duly nominated for election as member of the Appointments Committee.

1.

2.

3.

4.

President of the meeting

(G.O. Ms. No. 336, Rural Development (C-1) Department, dated 26th November 1997)

6.5 ADMINISTRATION

6.5.1 Preparation and Submission of Administration Report of Panchayat Union Councils

1. **Short title**—These rules may be called the Tamil Nadu Panchayats (Preparation and Submission of Administration Report of Panchayat Union Councils) Rules, 1999.

2. **Definition**—In these rules, unless the context otherwise requires, "Act" means the Tamil Nadu Panchayat Act, 1994 (Tamil Nadu Act 21 of 1994)

3. **Preparation of consolidated administration report**—The Commissioner of every panchayat union council shall, as soon as may be not later than 30th June every year, prepare a consolidated report on the administration of the panchayat union council and on the administration of all village panchayats in the panchayat union during the preceding year in two parts, namely (a) embodying the particulars specified in Appendix A; and (b) the annual account indicating income and expenditure of the panchayat union during the year in Appendix B.

4. **Prescribed date for submission of report**—Once the Administration Report along with audit report is ready, their copies shall be supplied to the members of the panchayat union council in advance before they meet to consider the report. Ten copies of the report together with a copy of the resolution of the panchayat union council shall be submitted to the district panchayat not later than the 30th September of the year following that to which the report relates. The report and the resolution of the council thereon shall be kept in places accessible to the public, one such copy being affixed to the notice board of the office of the panchayat union council.

5. **Prescribed date for submission of general report on the administration by district panchayat**—The date before which the district panchayat shall submit the general report on the administration of panchayat union councils and village panchayats to the panchayat district to the Government, with a copy of the Inspector referred to in sub-section (3) of Section 99 of the Tamil Nadu Panchayats Act, 1994 (Tamil Nadu Act 21 of 1994) shall be the 30th October of the year following that to which the report relates.

6. **Publishing the general report on the administration**—The general report and the resolution of the district panchayat shall be published in the district gazette and be kept in places accessible to the public in the district, copies being affixed in the notice board of the office of the district panchayat and Inspector.

(G.O. Ms. No. 247, Rural Development (C-4) Department, dated 3rd December 1999)

APPENDIX A
(See Rule 3)

Consolidated Report on the Administration of the ______________ Panchayat Union Council and Village Panchayats in the said Panchayat Union in the __________________________ District Panchayat for the year ________________________

I. Constitution and Management

1. **Juriсidiction**
   - (i) The area of the panchayat union as on 31st March of the year to which the report relates in square kilometres.
   - (ii) Changes in the jurisdiction of the panchayat union during the year under report, if any.
   - (iii) Total number of wards.
   - (iv) Number and names of village panchayat coming with in the panchayat union.
   - (v) Details of population (as per latest available census figures), (a) Male, (b) Female, (c) Total, (d) Density of population per square metre, (e) Schedule Caste/Schedule Tribe population, (f) Percentage of women population in total population, (g) Percentage of Schedule Caste/Schedule Tribe population in total population.
2. **Personnel**—
   - (i) The council, break up details of members and (a) Number of Scheduled Caste and Scheduled Tribe members including women, (b) Number of other women members, (c) Others, (d) Vacancy, if any, (e) Total number of members items (a)+(b)+(c)+(d).

(ii) Changes, if any, in the total strength.

(iii) Number of seats fell vacant (with ward members and category of reservation) and date from which they are/were vacant.

(iv) Was election of members ordinary or casual, held during the year and if so date of election?

(v) Whether elections have been held and seats filled up with in six months from the date of vacancy?

(vi) Date of first meeting of the ordinary election.

3. Holders of different office—

(i) *Chairman and vice-chairman*: Briefly state on each of them mainly on the following.

- (a) Name and party affiliation,
- (b) Date of election and ward he represents,
- (c) Date of taking oath and date of first meeting after ordinary election,
- (d) Removal of chairman, if any, and
- (e) No-confidence motion, if any, moved.

(ii) Panchayat Union Commissioner, Block Development Officer (Panchayats), Deputy Block Development Officer Extension Officers: Indicate names, date of joining etc. on each of them.

4. Election—(i) Ordinary election, (ii) Casual Elections, and (iii) Election disputes. Provide brief on the elected members and election disputes, if any.

5. Panchayat union council meeting—Provide details of meeting conducted, ordinary, urgent special with dates and subjects decided, attendance of members at meetings—average percentage of attendance; and number of meetings adjourned if any for want of quorum with dates, total number of subjects (a) Taken up in agenda, (b) Number disposed of, (c) Number of items adjourned once or more with reasons therefor, and (d) Number of items on which action needs to be initiated, number disposed of and number pending.

6. Committees—Details of statutory committees and other committees formed, meeting held, with summary of working of the committees. Furnish details on Joint Committees, if any, and the work done by them.

7. Establishment—What is the sanctioned strength? What is the cost of establishment? Expenditure incurred on plaints and suits and on law charges. Location of the panchayat union office was the building repaired during the year and if so the expenditure incurred. Are the prescribed forms and registers maintained?

8. Roads, Bridges, Ferries and Buildings—

(a) *Roads*

(*i*) Provide details on road density and facilities of (a) National Highway, (b) State Highways, (c) Major district roads, (d) Other district roads, (e) Panchayat union roads, and (f) Village panchayat roads.

Furnish the following information on Panchayat Union Roads:

(a)	Cement concrete	No....length
(b)	B.T.	No....length
(c)	Metalled	No....length
(d)	Gravelled	No....length
(e)	Earthen	No....length
	Total	No....length

(ii) Bus route roads—No.... length, Number of hamlets covered by route buses and town buses,

(iii) The expenditure on the maintenance of Panchayat Union roads, with comparative figures for the last three years,

(iv) Whether a programme has been drawn up for block-topping of metalled roads and unmetalled roads,

(v) Was any road transferred to the control of State Government and if so the length? Was any road taken over from village panchayats and if so, the number and length,

(vi) Any encroachments of roads and the condition of roads,

(vii) Details of gangmazdoors and road inspectors employed and expenditure incurred on them.

(b) *Bridges*

(i) Details of capital works such as bridges, causeway and culverts incurred in the year. Percentage of such expenditure to the total amount spent on roads,

(ii) Number of bridges, culverts, causeways etc; improved repaired and the expenditure incurred during the year,

(iii) Amount spent on:

- (1) new works,
- (2) repairs.

(c) *Ferries*

What is the total receipt and charges, the rate of charges, the method of collection and the convenience offered?

(d) *Panchayat Union Buildings and Other Assets*

(i) The building and other assets that are maintained by the panchayat union;

(ii) Any work of improvement and maintenance like white washing, colour washing, painting carried out and the expenditure thereon;

(iii) Whether any maintenance grant received under any scheme, and give details;

(iv) Was any new asset created or new building completed and if so under which scheme?

9. Choultries, Rest Sheds, Bus Shelters and Watersheds—(i) Number of choultries, rest sheds, bus shelters and watersheds maintained; the receipt and charges there from; (ii) Endowments if any for choultries and water shed and their condition; (iii) Cost of free feeding, if any and number of person fed.

10. Tools—*Plant machinery and stores:* (i) Total ordinary expenditure on tools, plants, and stores; (ii) Percentage of such expenditure on communication; capital expenditure on tools plants and machinery or vehicle; and expenditure on repair charges, Petrol, Oil and Lubricant charges and their maintenance.

11. Lighting—(i) Number of street lights installed, under different category. Expenditure incurred on new installation and cost of maintenance of existing street lights.

12. Medical—(i) Number of PHCs, rural dispensaries and other public medical institutions in union area, the average population served by each institution; (ii) Number medical officers and other para medical and contingent staff of panchayat union; (iii) Number of private medical institutions, hospitals, dispensaries and practitioners in the panchayat union area.

13. Health service— (i) Number of patients treated for minor ailments by the rural dispensary and the expenditure per patient, expenditure on doctors, non-medical staff and medicines. (ii) Is there any maternity ward, or inpatient facility available and if so the number treated as inpatients and deliveries in the maternity ward? (iii) Accommodation equipment etc. details may be given.

14. Maternity relief and family welfare—(i) Number of maternity and child welfare centres functioning. Do they workout to one centre for every 10,000 population. Do they have own building and facilities? Number of panchayat union staff employed for these centres and the expenditure incurred by the panchayat union.(ii) Family welfare: (a) What is the birth rate, death rate, net population growth rate, infant mortality rate, maternity mortality rate in the panchayat union area, (b) Number of vasectomy and sterilisation done in the union area.

15. Endemic and epidemic diseases—(i) The steps taken on the preventive measures to control diseases affecting pregnant women, mother and children, and on communicable diseases.

(ii) Value of medicines, vaccines and other materials supplied to the public health staff for prevention of diseases.

16. Sanitation— (a) Number of houses and percentage of houses having house flush out toilets and school toilets. What is the general sanitary condition in the panchayat union? Name the villages where all houses have toilets.

(b) *Food adulteration:* (i) Steps taken to control food adulteration by means of licensing of hotels, sweet meat shop etc. (ii) Whether the Food Adulteration Act has been extended to the union area? (iii) Whether the conditions of licence enforced?

(c) *Dangerous and offensive trades:* (i) What are all the trades identified and number of licences issued tradewise, amount collected by way of fees village panchayatwise, and furnish other details? (ii) Indicate details an industrial pollution affection the environments and if so what steps taken by the union to prevent such pollution.

17. Water supply—(i) Total number of habitation having 300 population and above and of which how many have piped water supply and 40 litres per capita water supply. (ii) Total number of habitation having bore well pumps, hand pumps. (iii) Number of water supply installations available in the union (hand pumps, power pumps, ground level reservoir, over head tank etc.). (iv) Number of houses having water supply connections and water charges collected by village panchayats during the year.

18. Fairs and festivals—Notified fairs and festivals controlled by the panchayat union, dates of such festivals, estimated number of persons visiting the festivals, special arrangements made for the health and comfort of such persons, the expenditure incurred for such arrangements and the receipt by way of auctioning and issuing licences to shops in the fair and other receipts.

19. Veterinary service and dairy development—(i) Number of veterinary dispensaries functioning with location, number of animals treated? (ii) Artificial insemination centres and sub-centres functioning. (iii) Is the veterinary relief adequate? (iv) Number of milch animals in the panchayat union dairy co-operative and furnish information on the same.

20. Eradication of untouchability—(i) Protection of Civil Rights Act, 1955, state the steps taken to eradicate untouchability in the union, with special reference to service of tea in tea stalls and meals in hotels, and (ii) number of prosecution filed under the Protection of Civil Rights Act and the result of prosecution?

21. Markets—(i) Panchayat union and village panchayat markets, location, periodicity, receipt and charges from the markets, improvements carried in the year and the development needed for better services and income; (ii) Private markets, number, licence fee realised, enforcement of licence conditions; (iii) Factories and industries located in the panchayat union; (iv) Industrial units run by this panchayat union production, sales, expenditure, and profit loss may be furnished.

22. Social forestry—(i) Number and variety of trees available in panchayat union roads and tanks, (ii) What is the auction amount fetched by way of leasing the enjoyment of the usufructs of such trees for the last three years? (iii) Steps taken to plant more trees on vacant road sides and tank beds, (iv) Whether forest department has been permitted to raise social forestry in tanks and if so the name of tank extent covered? (v) Number of prosecution launched for illicit tree cuttings.

23. Land encroachment—(i) *Road side stalls:* Are those obstructing traffic flow? What is the receipt by way of collection of fees from such stalls? (ii) *Encroachments:* (a) Number of encroachments existing, licensed and pending; (b) Number of encroachment found to be objectionable on inspection by Commissioner; and (c) Number of encroachments reported by Village Administrative Officer and action taken to remove such encroachments.

24. Land Utilisation and irrigation—Extent of land cultivated (i) Extent of land: (a) Wet (b) Dry, (ii) Net cultivated area: (a) Wet, (b) Dry, (iii) Gross cultivated area: (a) Wet, (b) Dry, (iv) Source of irrigation: (a) Wells (b) Tanks (c) Channels (Length in km) (d) others, (v) Number of tanks vested with panchayat union and village panchayats, (vi) Number improved or desisted during the year, and expenditure incurred. Execution of Kudimaramath. Amount of excess Kudimaramath grant sanctioned by Government. Number of sources taken up for Kudimaramath, number completed and area covered, amount of Kudimaramath fees levied by panchayats.

25. Financial position—(1) Income: (i) Land revenue, (ii) Rate of local cess surcharge, (iii) Rate of local irrigation fees, (2) The opening and closing balances and the extent of the total receipts and expenditure during the year, (3) Balance pertaining to remunerative enterprises government grants and loans due by the union, (4) Ways and means position during the year, (5) (i) Receipt and expenditure on all accounts, and (ii) Receipts and expenditure under general account ordinary.

26. Capital expenditure—(a) Total expenditure on capital works (i) on development works entrusted, (ii) other items, (iii) government grant received on the development works and contribution if any paid from panchayat union funds, and (iv) expenditure incurred from loans.

27. Debt—Debt at the beginning of the year, incurred during the year, repaid during the year and balance at the close of the year. Total interest paid on debt on account of the arrears of previous year and for the year under reports.

28. Investment—Details of amount invested, year of investment, nature of securities, interest, date of maturity etc.

29. Audit—Inspection remarks of Assistant Director of Local Fund Account.

30. Furnish details of assets and liabilities.

31. Visit of distinguished persons notable activities of the panchayat union council during the year.

APPENDIX B

(See Rule 3)

Income and Expenditure of Panchayat Union

Sl. No.	*Source of Income*	*Amount Rs.*	*Sl. No.*	*Head of Account for Expenditure*	*Year*	*Amount Rs.*
(1)	(2)	(3)	(4)	(5)	(6)	(7)

6.5.2 Use of Perforating Machine by the Panchayat Union Council

The Government direct that the letters "L.F.D." be perforated on ordinary postage stamps used on all official correspondence of panchayat unions. The Commissioners of panchayat unions are requested to adopt the procedure laid down in the rules issued for Receipt and Expenditure Accounting procedure of panchayat unions for the purchase of postage stamps and keeping accounts.

Panchayat unions should obtain the perforating machines from Public Works Workshops only.

(Govt.Memo.No.70579/E III/66-5 Rural Development Department & Local Administration, dated 16th December 1966)

6.5.3 Priority in Installation of Telephone in the Office and Residence of Panchayat Union Chairman

In G.O.Ms.No.696, Rural Development and Local Administration Department, dated 16.3.66, the District Collectors have been authorised to permit the panchayat union councils to install direct line telephones at the residences of the chairman of panchayat union councils provided the panchayat union councils concerned passes a resolution to that effect and also express their willingness to meet the entire expenditure from the concerned panchayat union councils funds. The Government now considered that this position is equally applicable in respect of the installation of the separate direct line telephone for the office room of the chairman also. The General Manager, Telecommunications, Tamil Nadu Circle, Chennai 600002 has been requested to issue suitable instructions to all those concerned in the telephone department in the State to give a priority to install direct line telephone to the residences and office rooms of the newly elected panchayat union councils chairmen.

(Govt.Lr.No.44237/C1/96-2 Rural Development Department, dated 8th January 1997)

6.6 ESTABLISHMENT

6.6.1 Staffing Pattern of Panchayat Union Council

After the introduction of the three-tier system of Panchayat Administration, the Government issued the following orders on the staffing pattern in panchayat union.

The Post of RWO Gr.I which is equivalent to Assistant post and the RWO Gr.II which is equivalent to Junior Assistant is ordered to convert as Assistant and Junior Assistant and they are directed to work in the panchayat union office. The existing establishment in panchayat unions is broadly divided into 2 categories, *i.e.* Category 1 panchayat union (block panchayat) work to be attended to by BDO, Category 2, village panchayat works and audit of village panchayats to be attended to by ABDO. The staffing pattern in the Panchayat union will be as follows:

(a) Panchayat Union Section (Block Panchayat)

Sl.No.	*Name of the Post*	*Number*
1.	BDO	1
2.	EO (Admn)	1
3.	EO (SS & PR)	1
4.	EO (ADW)	1
5.	Assistants	4
6.	Junior Assistant	3
7.	Cashier	1
8.	Typist	1
9.	Accountant	1
10.	Junior Assistant-cum-Typist	1

(b) Village Panchayats Section

Sl.No.	*Name of the Post*	*Number*
1.	ABDO	1
2.	EO (Pts.)	1
3.	E.O. (JVVT)	1
4.	Cashier	1
5.	Assistants	2
6.	Junior Assistant-cum-Typist	1
7.	Audit	1
8.	Dy. BDO (Pts.)	1
9.	Assistant	1
10.	Junior Asst.	1
11.	Office Asst.	2

In those panchayat unions while there is Addl. EO (P), the post will be under the control of ABDO, the existing orders of panchayat union set up is hereby abolished. In future, the establishment pattern shall be uniform for all the panchayat unions in the State.

The existing post of EO (AH), EO(C), EO (NMP), EO(SW), RWO(W) and other staff sanctioned to assist the above categories of staff and the staff relating to Rural Water Supply Maintenance like Electrician, Fitter, Tailoring Instructors, School

Conductress shall be continued to be under the control of BDO.

From the available 2 Union Engineers and 2 Overseers, 1 Engineer and 1 Overseer will work under the control of BDO and the other Engineer and Overseer will work under the control of ABDO. The Road Inspectors will work under the control of BDO (BP).

The Panchayat Union Rural Dispensaries and Carpentry and Blacksmithy Unit shall be under the control of BDO (BP). Apart from the staff mentioned above, if there is any other post of Junior Assistant or Junior Assistant-cum-Typist in the Panchayat union office they will work under the control of ABDO.

If there is any shortfall in the number of posts as per the above staffing pattern action will be taken separately to transfer the surplus posts available in the panchayat union to fill up the shortfall.

This changed establishment pattern shall come into effect from 1.7.97. The natures of work to be allotted to various staff as per the new staffing pattern are indicated in the Annexure. The District Collectors may make changes in the model work allocation between BDO (BP) and ABDO without changing the staffing pattern between the 2 categories of each panchayat union.

The Government permitted the ABDO to draw salary for the staff working under his control.

(G.O.Ms.No.180, Rural Development (E-5) Department)

6.6.2 Appointment of Rural Welfare Officers for Implementation of Schemes

The Government ordered for conversion of 1448 posts of Assistants and 1020 posts of Junior Assistants as RWO Gr.I and RWO Gr.II to work in all the panchayat union in the State.

Each RWO on an average has to work with a jurisdiction of 6 village panchayats to look after the scheme works of panchayat union. But the required number of RWOs as per the above norm is not sufficient and therefore the tentative allocation of RWOs and the number of panchayats to be looked after by them are worked out and is enclosed.

The District Collectors are authorised to make arrangements according to occurrence of vacancies so that one RWO look after the work in 6 village panchayats. Similarly, the DRD is empowered to transfer staff from one district to another district in the course of time to ensure that each RWO looks after 6 village panchayats in a panchayat union.

The Government accepted the proposals of DRD and sanctions 1816 posts as indicated in Annexure II and the Director Rural Development is requested to take action to distribute the posts to each district according to requirement.

(G.O.Ms.No.249 Rural Development (E-5) Department, dated 24th November 1998)

6.6.3 Filling Up of the Post of Additional Jeep Drivers

While filling up the post of additional jeep drivers through Appointment Committee, priority may be given to the Panchayat Union Office Assistants, Tractor Drivers, Roller Drivers, and Cleaners who are fully qualified and employed through Employment Exchange to hold the post of Jeep Drivers. The receipt of this letter may please be acknowledged.

(Govt. Lr. No. 42003/P-4/97-2, dated 17th December 1997)

6.6.4 Appointment of Road Roller Drivers in Panchayat Unions

The Government permit the panchayat unions having sufficient funds to convert the temporary posts of Road Roller Drivers created and appointed with proper sanction to Road Roller post with time scale of pay of Rs. 975-25-1150-30-1660. All the expenditure relating to this post shall be met from the General Funds of the panchayat union.

(G.O.Ms.No.126, Rural Development (E-5) Department, dated 16th April 1997)

6.6.5 Regular Scale of Pay for the Post of Gangmazdoors

1. G.O.Ms.No. 1661, R.D. & L.A. dated 17.10.79.
2. Representation dated 4.2.80 from Tamil Nadu Highways Workers Progressive Union Ramnad.
3. From the Director of Rural Development, Letter Roc.No. 39716/80/H4 dated 7.4.81.
4. From the Examiner of Local Fund Accounts Letter Roc.No. 16545/14/81 dated 20.5.81.
5. From the Director of Rural Development Letter Roc.No. 37974/80/H4 dated 13.2.81.

6. From the Chief Engineer (H & RW) S2/81-2 dated 20.7.81 and letter dated 23.11.81.
7. From the Director of Rural Development Letter No. 37943/80/H4 dated 18.12.82.

1. In G.O.Ms.No. 1661 RD & LA, dated 17.10.79, the Government have issued orders brining the Gangmazdoors in panchayat unions who had put in service of ten years as on 1.4.79 into regular scale of pay of Rs. 200-5-300 subject to certain conditions stipulated therein.

2. The President, Tamil Nadu Highways Workers Union has requested to regularise the services of the Gangmazdoor, in panchayat unions who have put in five years service, as in the case of Gangmazdoors of Highways Department besides extending the concessions and privileges provided in G.O.Ms.No. 51 Finance dated 14.1.77.

3. The Government have examined the requests in consultation with Director of Rural Development and the Chief Engineer (Highways and Rural Works) and the Examiner of Local Fund Accounts, Madras.

4. The Director of Rural Development has brought to the notice of Government that there are 1443 Gangmazdoors who have completed 10 years of service to be absorbed into regular establishment. He has also furnished detail of 959 persons who have completed five years of service as on 1.4.79. He has also pointed out that it is not known whether there is break in service of the above Gangmazdoors. But there may be a few cases where they might have been ousted for want of allotment funds under Local Roads Grant at the end of financial year and subsequently employed at the commencement of the next financial year. In such cases, the break in service has to be condoned. He has further requested, that the Director of Rural Development as Inspector of Panchayat Unions may be permitted to condone such break in service of deserving Gangmazdoors. He has therefore requested the Government to issue orders:

(a) Sanctioning the creation of 1443 posts of Gangmazdoors in orders to bring the persons who have completed 10 years of service as on 1.4.79 into regular establishment.

5. The Government have examined the suggestion of the Examiner of Local Fund Accounts and the Commissioner of Rural Development and issue the following orders:

(*i*) The orders issued in para 4 of G.O.Ms.No. 2131 RD & LA dated 19.10.76 laying down the collection of the lump sum contribution of Rs. 2000/- (Rupees two thousand only) in respect of Gangmazdoors working in panchayat union be dispensed with and that the Gangmazdoors working in panchayat union who have completed 10 years of service and 5 years of service as on 1.4.79 will be eligible to count their qualifying service for pension from 1.4.79 the date on which the time scale of pay was granted to them and those retiring on or after 1.4.89 alone will get monthly pension. Those retiring in between 1.4.79 and 31.3.89 will be eligible to get only service gratuity.

(*ii*) The monthly pension contribution of 10% of the maximum of the time scale in respect of the said Gangmazdoors working in panchayat unions for the subsequent period, *i.e.* 1.4.79 should be paid to the panchayat union employees pension fund from the funds of the local bodies.

6. The Commissioner of Rural Development, Madras is requested to send necessary draft amendment to Tamil Nadu Panchayat Union and Panchayat Services Pension Rules, 1976 of Local Fund Accounts, Madras.

(G.O. Ms. No. 868, Rural Development Department, dated 17th June 1983)

6.6.6 Regularisation of Services of Panchayat Union Gangmazdoors

Government have decided that the Gangmazdoors working in panchayat unions who have put in ten years of service be brought under regular establishment with the time scale of pay. They accordingly direct that the services of the Gang-mazdoors working in panchayat unions who have put in ten years of service be brought under regular establishment with the time scale of pay. They accordingly direct that the services of the Gang-mazdoors working in panchayat unions who have put in Ten years of service as on 1.4.79 be brought in the time scale of pay of Rs. 200-5-300 subject to the following conditions:

(i) that the ban of fresh recruitment of Gang-mazdoors shall continue, and
(ii) that the total number of Gangmazdoors is brought to the level justified by the work load norms.

They will also be allowed to draw Dearness Allowance, House Rent Allowance etc., at the rates admissible under the orders in force from time-to-time and additional benefits as detailed below:

(a) Joining time
(b) House Rent Allowance
(c) Earned Leave at the rate of 1-22 of duty and accumulation of leave upto 60 days

(d) Unearned Leave on medical certificate for six months
(e) Maternity leave

Separate orders will be issued sanctioning specific number of Gangmazdoors on time scale of pay under various Panchayat Unions.

(G.O. Ms. No. 1661, RD & LA Department, dated 17th October, 1999)

6.6.7 Creation of Posts of Electrician and Helpers in Panchayat Unions

The Government sanctioned the creation of 384 posts of Electricians in the scale of pay of Rs. 950-20-1180-25-1500 and 768 posts of helpers in the scale of pay of Rs. 750-12-870-14-945 for a period upto 31.3.96. The Government also direct that expenditure in connection with the pay and allowances of Electricians and Helpers shall be borne by the respective panchayat unions.

The staff required for these posts, i.e. 384 posts of electricians and 768 posts of helpers have to be identified by re-deployment of staff already working at the Mobile Team of the Divisional Development Office and obtain additional staff from the Tamil Nadu Electricity Board on deputation basis. Therefore the Government pass the following consequential orders to give effect to the above decision:

(i) All the Mobile Teams functioning under the control of Divisional Development Officer shall hereby stand cancelled. The Director of Rural Development shall make use of 123 posts of Electricians and 114 posts of fitters and helpers for re-deployment as electricians and helpers respectively in the blocks against the posts sanctioned above.

(ii) The Government authorise the Director of Rural Development to obtain electricians from Tamil Nadu Electricity Board on deputation to fill up the balance of 261 posts after deployment of 123 posts of electricians functioning in the Mobile Teams. The Director of Rural Development is also authorised to obtain the services of helpers from the Tamil Nadu Electricity Board on deputation to fill up 654 posts after re-deployment of 1143 posts now functioning in the Mobile Teams. The deputation of staff from the Tamil Nadu Electricity Board shall be for a period upto 31.3.96.

(iii) The Assistant Engineers looking after the Divisional Level Mobile Teams shall be reverted to Tamil Nadu Water Supply and Drainage Board consequent on the abolition of these Mobile Team.

(iv) The Drivers now working in the Mobile Teams shall be re-deployed in the existing or future vacancies in the Rural Development Department.

2. The Director of Rural Development is requested to indicate the number of posts of Electricians and Helpers required after re-deployment of staff from the Mobile Teams and indicate to the Tamil Nadu Electricity Board the additional posts required on deputation basis. The District-wise break up of these posts may be furnished to the Tamil Nadu Electricity Board for identifying the available staff from the respective district itself.

3. The Electricians and Helpers who are either re-deployed from the Mobile Teams or on deputation from Tamil Nadu Electricity Board shall be under the administrative control of the Block Development Officers. The Collectors shall issue posting orders allotting the Electricians and Helpers to the respective blocks.

4. The Director of Rural Development is requested to organise the positioning of the Electricians and Helpers in the blocks as expeditiously as possible.

(G.O. Ms. No. 141, Rural Development (P-3) Department, dated 3rd August 1995)

6.6.8 Guidelines for Recruitment of Persons by the Appointment Committee

The Government issue the following guidelines for recruitment of persons by the Appointment Committee of panchayat union to have a transparent transaction in the selection of eligible persons.

(1) 'Communal Rotation' shall be strictly followed in the selection of persons for appointment.

(2) The list of eligible persons having prescribed educational and age, qualification shall be obtained from the Employment Exchange and selection may be made only from the list of obtained.

(3) The persons from the list received from Employment Exchange shall be selected only on the basis of seniority of registration. If a candidate will be crossing the maximum age limit prescribed for the post with in next six months from the date of holding of meeting of appointment committee, he shall be given preference in selection.

(4) Appointment committee may be convened by the Chairman of the Committee whenever necessary. But appointment orders for the selected candidates as per the guidelines in para 1 to 3 above shall be issued by the Commissioner within 3 days from the date of selection by the appointment Committee.

(5) The Government orders and guideline issued on appointment committee shall be followed strictly.

(G.O. Ms. No. 191, Rural Development (E-5) Department, dated 7th September 1998)

6.6.9 Norms for Filling Up of Posts of Office Assistants in Panchayat Unions

1. G.O. Ms. No. 745, Finance (Ze-bag) Department, dated 22.9.1995
2. G.O. Ms. No. 180, Rural Development Department, dated 9.6.1997
3. This office Lr.No.70774/94/- B-1, dated 21.5.1998.

Government have issued orders fixing the norms for the appointment of Office Assistants at the ratio of 15:1. Against this order, the Tamil Nadu Panchayat Union Office Assistant State Association has filed Writ Petition in the High Court and obtained stay orders.

In the reference second cited, 4 Office Assistants were allotted to each panchayat union and in the office letter No. 70774/94/B.I, dated 21.5.98, proposal have been sent to Government for reallotment of left out post of office assistant. Proposals have also been sent to Government that instructions issued in the G.O. first cited need not be insisted in respect of panchayat unions.

Pending receipt of orders from Government, I request you to take necessary steps to fill up the post of Office Assistants in panchayat union not exceeding three posts. While filling up these posts the instructions already issued by the Government should be followed scrupulously.

(RC. No. 90215/96/F-1, dated 9th April 1999)

6.6.10 Instructions for Filling Up of Certain Posts in Panchayat Union

The panchayat unions are permitted to fill up the posts paid from the panchayat union funds excepting Junior Assistants/Cashier/Typists coming under the purview of TNPSC, subject to the following conditions with the prior approval of the Inspector of panchayat unions/District Collector.

(1) All the posts have been filled up only through appointment committed after getting list from Employment Exchange and subject to rules and regulations prescribed by Government in this regard.

(2) These posts should have been sanctioned by the Government and continuity for the posts should have been obtained from the Government.

(3) These posts should not be a vanishing post as notified by the Government.

(4) From the posts sanction, by the Government only those posts which have fallen vacant due to promotion, superannuation or death shall only be filled up. No temporary basis have been filled up.

Besides the following conditions stated above, the panchayat unions can fill up the posts only after getting prior approval of the Inspector of panchayat unions/District Collector. At the time of granting approval, the Collector shall ensure that post has already sanctioned post, is not a vanishing post and the request satisfied other conditions imposed by the Government in this regard.

Separate order should be issued for fill up the post of Office Assistant.

(DRD Lr.No.71628/98/E-1, dated 10th September 1998)

6.6.11 Filling Up of the Posts of Rural Medical Officers

The Government ordered that all the posts for which the expenditure on salary is met from the general funds of the panchayat union shall be filled up according to Section 53(1) of the Tamil Nadu Panchayat Act, through the appointment committee of the panchayat union. While appointing Medical Officers, the appointment committee shall consult the concerned District Medical Officers or if the post relates to Siddha or Ayurvedha system of medicine, the District Siddha Medical Officer and only after their approval of the qualification of the selected persons, appointment orders shall be issued.

(G.O.Ms.No. 99, Rural Development (E-5) Department, dated 24th April 1992)

6.6.12 Opening of Rural Dispensaries and Filling Up of the Post of Rural Medical Officers

The Government issued the following orders on the opening of new Rural Dispensaries and filling up the post of Rural Medical Officers.

(a) The norm for starting of Government dispensaries is available in the Health and Family Welfare Department. No evaluation is so far been made on the functioning of existing Rural Dispensaries in panchayat unions. The DRD has been requested to conduct an evaluation and send the report pending detailed examination of the result of evaluation no new rural dispensaries or no new post in rural dispensaries shall be created and it is banned.

(b) In as much as there is sufficient number of primary health centres and additional primary health centres in each panchayat union area the existing panchayat union rural dispensaries shall continue to function only as part time rural dispensary.

(c) Whenever vacancy arises in the post of Rural Medical Officers, the panchayat union council shall appoint only part time Rural Medical Officer, through Appointment Committee. They should get technical guidance for filling up the post of Rural Medical Officers from the district level Medical Officers of Health and Family Welfare Department.

(d) All the existing rural medical officers shall be paid the salary as fixed by the Government in G.O.Ms.No.16, Rural Development Department dated 29.1.98 without any variation on educational qualification of the Medical Officers.

(e) The retirement benefits, selection grade, special grade, compassionate ground appointment, group insurance, General Provident Fund, Encashment of Earned Leave and Half pay leave are eligible only to full time employees of the panchayat union. In as much as the post of Rural Medical Officer is a part-time post they are eligible for any of the above benefits.

(f) The DRD is authorised to fix the working hours of the rural dispensaries after consulting Health & Family Welfare Department in this regard.

(g) The Regular Medical Officers and the part-time Medical Officers working in the panchayat union do not require higher qualification according to the nature of existing work done by them. Therefore those Medical Officers of panchayat union who are deputed for higher studies are eligible only to get stipend for higher studies. During the period of higher studies they are not eligible to get the time scale of pay from the funds of the panchayat union.

(h) The Rural Medical Officers appointed by the panchayat union were selected from the list of persons in the panchayat union area only. The duties and responsibilities of these Medical Officers are less than that of regular Medical Officers working in the primary health centres. Therefore they are not eligible to get the rural allowances or personal pay.

(G.O.Ms.No.250, Rural Development (E-5) Department, dated 14th September 2000)

6.6.13 Regularisation of Contingent Staff of Panchayat Union

The orders in G.O. Ms. No. 52, Finance (F-4), dated 14-1-77 provide for bringing all the contingent employees in Government Departments who have put in five years of service or more to regular establishment with a time scale of pay etc. on a systematic orderly and uniform basis. Director of Rural Development, Madras was requested to examine the question of making applicable to the above orders to the employees of the panchayat institutions (viz.) panchayats unions, town panchayats and panchayat townships. Representation has also been received from the service Associations of the employees of the panchayats and panchayat unions for regularising the services of the contingent staff in the panchayats and panchayat unions.

2. The Director of Rural Development, Madras has recommended that orders may be issued bringing the contingent workers on the rolls of the panchayat union councils, panchayats and panchayat townships to regular establishment as has been done in the case of the contingent employees of municipal councils in G.O. Ms. No.1644 RD & LA dated 12.12.79 according to which the employees in Municipal councils and Municipal Township committee and under contingencies who have completed ten years of service without break as on 1.10.79 were brought under regular establishment of the municipality or the Municipal Township committee concerned on a time scale of pay of Rs. 200-5-300 with other usual allowances from 1.10.79 based on their seniority in the respective categories subject certain conditions stipulated therein.

3. The Government have carefully considered the matter in the light of the remarks of the Director of Rural Development, Madras and the orders issued in respect of the contingent employees of the

Municipal councils referred to in paragraph 2 above and have decided that the full time contingent staff of the panchayat union, town panchayats and panchayat townships should also be similarly brought into regular establishment. Accordingly they direct that the full time contingent staff in the above Panchayat institutions who have put in ten years of service and more without break as on 1.4.81 be brought into regular establishment with a time scale of pay Rs. 200-5-300 with usual allowance subject to the following conditions.

(*i*) The contingent staff will be brought into regular establishment based on the seniority in the respective category of the concerned panchayat institutions and their pay on the above scale of pay shall be fixed based on the total emoluments or wagers last drawn by them.

(*ii*) They shall be eligible for benefits like leave and medical facilities applicable to the employees in local bodies having a scale of pay Rs. 200-5-300.

(*iii*) The present strength should be frozen at the existing level and the surplus should be utilised in filling up vacancies arrived at after fixing the cadre strength as per needs. The Director of Rural Development is requested to send a report in this regard within 3 months without fail.

(*iv*) No new posts in the category of contingent establishment after 1.4.81 should be created and the vacancies after 1.4.81 should not be filled up.

(*v*) Those in the category of contingent establishment who have put in less than 10 years of continuous service as on 1.4.81 and who have not been regularised now should be paid the fixed pay and usual allowances or the play eligible under the Minimum Wages Act whichever is advantageous to them.

(*vi*) The Director of Rural Development is empowered to fix the total strength of the employee under contingent establishment in each panchayat unions and the collector of the district in respect of each town panchayats and panchayat township lying in his jurisdiction based on the work load and the actual need therefore as on 1.4.81 taking into account the financial position of the panchayat institution concerned. The Director of Rural Development should send in report to Government on the fixation of Cadre strength of each panchayat institutions (panchayat union, town panchayat and panchayat township) in due course.

(*vii*) In future as and when the employees borne on the contingent establishment complete 10 years of service, the executing authority of the panchayat institution should send necessary proposal to bring them to time scale of pay through the collector of the district concerned and Director of Rural Development, Madras for approval of the Government after the total strength in each category is fixed by the Collector or the Director of Rural Development as the case may be.

(*viii*) The panchayat institutions should bear the additional cost from their own funds without affecting their other programmes.

4. This order shall take effect from 1.4.1981.

5. The Director of Rural Development is requested to send necessary draft amendments to the relevant panchayat and panchayat union service rules consequent on these orders for the regularisation of the contingent staff.

(G.O. Ms. No. 873, Rural Development & Local Administration Department, dated 15th May 1981)

6.6.14 Contingent Staff Appointed as on 1.4.1981 in Panchayat Union

The Government prohibited the appointment of contingent staff or filling up of vacancies in contingent staff in panchayat union service after 1.4.81 in G.O. Ms. No. 878, Rural Development, dated 15.5.1981.

Based on the proposals sent by the Director of Rural Development, the Government issued orders that the contingent staff appointed in panchayat union service prior to 1.4.81 and who will be completing 10 years of service after 1.4.81 can be brought to the regular service with time scale of pay and the Collectors are authorized to bring such of those employees in to regular service and time scale to pay subject to the following conditions.

(a) While regularizing services, the Collector shall strictly follow the Government instructions prescribed in G.O. Ms. No. 878, Rural Development, dated 15.5.1981.

(b) If any contingent employee is appointed after 1.4.81, his services shall not be regularised and brought to time scale of pay.

(c) The employees on consolidated pay working in Government offices shall not be regularized and brought to time scale of pay.

(d) The Collectors shall obtain ratification of Government for the regularization orders issued by him with in 3 months from the date of orders.

(G.O. Ms. No. 217, Rural Development (E-5) Department, dated 3rd July 1997)

6.6.15 Redeployment of Fitters at Block Level—Protection of Scale of Pay

1. As per the Government order, 57 posts of Fitters and 57 posts of Helpers in the Rural Water Supply Maintenance Mobile Teams at Division level were redeployed at Block level as Helpers to Electricians, among others, in the scale of pay of Rs. 750-12-870-14-945. The fitters of Division level redeployed as Helpers at Block level have represented to Government to review the G.O. and retain them as Fitters at Division level, as the scale of pay of Helper is lesser than that of Fitter.

2. In compliance with the direction of the Tamil Nadu administrative Tribunal in O.A.No.5426/97 the Government have considered the above request of the Fitters. As maintenance of hand pumps and power pumps is the responsibility of the panchayats, the necessity for Fitters of Division level ceased to exist. There is already a Mechanic-*cum*-Fitter at Block level. In the circumstances the Government direct that the Fitters who have drawn pay in the scale of pay of Rs. 950-1500 with effect from 1.6.88 but redeployed at Block level as Helpers to Electricians in the scale of pay of Rs. 750-945 shall be given protection of the scale of pay of Rs. 950-1500 as personal to them.

3. The status of the 57 Fitters as panchayat union employees and that of the Electricians and 57 Helpers as Government employees accorded in the Government Orders first and second read above prior to the redeployment will continue irrespective of the fact that they are paid from devolution grant of panchayats.

(G.O.Ms.No. 42, Rural Development (E-5) Department, dated 1st March 1999)

6.6.16 Scale of Pay for Conductress

(1) Government have issued orders to bring full-time contingent staff to regular establishment on time scale of pay on completion of 10 years of service as on 1.4.1981. In the same Government order, the Government have specifically agreed in principle to bring in future all other contingent staff also into regular establishment on time scale of pay, as and when they complete 10 years of service.

(2) The Conductresses working in panchayat union schools are paid from contingencies treating them as part-time employees. Various service associations represented this issue for converting them into regular contingent staff and thereby getting the benefits of time scale of pay, by bringing them into regular establishment. The Government negatived the above requests.

(3) But certain Executive Authorities before issue of the instruction in Lr.No.4318/E5/90-7 Rural Development Department dated 11.4.1991 had applied the G.O.Ms.No.878, Rural Development and Local Administration Department dated 15.5.1981 and issued orders bringing some of the part-time Conductresses into regular establishment with time scale of pay. In some cases, it was not done, which resulted in an anomaly. A few Conductresses have also gone to the Tribunal in O.A.No.2804, 2805, 2843 and 3434 of 1993 and the Tribunal has directed that in the case of Conductresses whose services had already been regularised in the light of G.O.Ms.No. 878, Rural Development and Local Administration Department dated 15.5.1981, the subsequent order cannot retrospectively cancel the regularisation already ordered. It has further directed that the applicants, if regularised already, should continue to be paid in the time scale of pay as fixed.

(4) Meanwhile, in the light of the Judgment of the High Court, dated 14.6.1991, the Government in the Government order fourth cited have issued orders in favour of certain Conductresses who were party in the Writ Petition No.4746 of 1989 that they may be brought into regular establishment in the time scale of pay from the date on which they have completed 10 years of service as per the orders to G.O.Ms.No.878, Rural Development and Local Administration Department dated 15.5.1981 without monetary benefits. Based on these orders, many of the Conductresses are now seeking remedy in legal forums.

(5) In these circumstances the Government have decided to examine the whole issue in detail. The posts of Conductresses are vanishing category and recruitment to the above posts was already stopped in the year 1975 and thereafter no further recruitments were made. All the Conductresses now working have, therefore completed 10 years of service in 1985 and would have become eligible for time scale of pay, provided the executive authorities of Panchayat Institutions have sent necessary proposals in time with reference to the orders issued (para 7) in G.O.Ms.No.875, Rural Development and Local Administration Department dated 15.5.1981. But the issuance of letter ROC. 43118/E5/91-1 Rural Development Department dated 11.4.1991 has created certain anomalies, viz. some Conductresses

had already got their services regularised and some others, due to administrative reasons, could not get their services regularised before the issue of the letter. The letter lost its standing per the orders of the Tribunal in O.A.Nos. 2804, 2805, 2843 and 3434 of 1993. Further these whose services were not regularised cannot also be denied their right on par with these whose services were already regularised and protected by the Tribunal, since they have already completed 10 years of service and the delay in their regularisation is purely on administrative one. Taking into consideration all these factors, to avoid further litigations and to preserve natural justice, the Government direct that the clarification issued in Lr.No.4318/E5/90-7 Rural Development Department dated 11.4.1991 shall stand cancelled.

It is therefore directed that the orders issued in G.O.Ms.No.878, Rural Development Local Administration Department dated 15.5.1981 (para 7) with regard to bringing contingent staff into regular establishment should be adhered to scrupulously.

(Govt. Lr. No. 33302/E5/93-12, Rural Development Department, dated 23rd November 1994)

6.6.17 Bringing of Conductress to Regular Establishment of Panchayat Union

1. The District Collectors have brought the Panchayat Union School Conductresses to regular establishment as authorised in the Government order second cited. The Government have been informed that some of the panchayat union Commissioners have raised doubts regarding eligibility of the Panchayat Union School Conductresses to draw increment, arrears of pay, Pongal Bonus leave and retirement benefits like Pension, DCRG etc.

2. The Government have examined the matter and clarify as follows:

(i) The Panchayat Union School Conductresses brought to regular establishment with reference to G.O. Ms. No. 878, Rural Development and Local Administration Department dated 15.5.1981 and G.O. Ms. No. 87 Rural Development dated 6.5.1995 are eligible to draw increment and arrears of pay, if any consequent on the retrospective regularization with effect from the date of completion of 10 years of continuous service in the contingent category. They are eligible for other benefits like Earned Leave, Provident Fund, Group Insurance, Pongal Bonus etc., as is admissible to other last grade servants like Office Assistants borne on the regular establishment of panchayat unions.

(ii) The Rule 2 of the Tamil Nadu Panchayat Union and Town Panchayat Services Pension Rules, 1976 which came into force with effect from 1.4.74 stipulates that the said rules shall apply to Officers and servants (both in superior and last grade service) under all panchayat union councils (except Panchayat Union Teacher, Contingent Employees, Contract Officers, Casual employees and officers and servants under work charged establishment). Hence the School Conductresses brought to regular establishment of the panchayat union councils are eligible for pensionary benefit also, subject to satisfying the relevant rules and conditions.

(iii) Proposals for the sanction of pension shall be sent to the Director of Local Fund Audit.

(Govt.Lr.No.190 Rural Development (E-5) Department, dated 10th June 1997)

6.6.18 Procedure for Filling Up of Vacancies for the Post of Junior Assistant/Junior Assistant-*cum*-Typist/Cashier/Typist from Among the Part-time/Full-time Clerks of Village Panchayats

G.O. Ms. No. 349, Personnel & Administrative Reforms Department, dated 12.4.84

G.O. Ms. No. 208, Rural Development Department, dated 20.3.88

G.O. Ms. No. 373, Rural Development Department, dated 13.5.87

G.O. Ms. No. 964, Rural Development Department, dated 28.11.90

G.O. Ms. No. 43, Personnel & Administrative Reforms Department, dated 15.2.94

From Tamil Nadu Administrative Tribunal Judgement in O.A.No.664/95, dated 7.10.96

From Secretary, Tamil Nadu Public Service Commission, Lr.No.4689/CDB 194.

1. In the G.O. fourth read above, Government have issued order, *inter alia*, framing guidelines in drawing the panel of candidates for appointment to the vacancies reserved for the Part-time/Full-time Clerks of the village panchayats in the posts of Junior Assistants, Rural Welfare Officer, Grade-II and Cashiers. Among the guidelines, it has been specified that person to be eligible for appointment as Junior Assistant/Rural Welfare Officer/Grade-II/Cashiėr should have rendered not less than 5 years of service in the lower categories

and that he should have been in the first instance recruited through Employment Exchange.

2. Based on the observation of the Tamil Nadu Administrative Tribunal for prescribing a longer period of qualifying experience in the lower category, it was ordered, *inter alia*, in the G.O. Ms.No.43, Personnel & Administrative Reforms Department, dated 16.2.94, that the existing qualifying experience of 5 years be enhanced to 7 years and that persons appointed as Junior Assistant/Junior Assistant-*cum*-Typist by recruitment by transfer from the post of Record Clerk, Office Assistant etc., shall undergo training in the Civil Service Training Institute, Bhavanisagar for the period that may be prescribed by the Government from time-to-time. The Government have decided that the orders issued in G.O.Ms.No.43, Personnel and Administrative Reforms Department, dated 15.2.94 be made applicable to the categories of Part-time/Full-time Clerks of village panchayats also.

3. There shall be no temporary appointment from the above categories to the post of Junior Assistant, Junior Assistant-*cum*-Typist, Cashier and Typist under any circumstances and appointments shall be made only from the panel approved by the Tamil Nadu Public Service Commission as aforesaid.

4. The Part-time/Full-time Clerks who were appointed as Junior Assistant, Junior Assistant-*cum*-Typist/Cashier/Typist by transfer shall undergo training in the Civil Service Training Institute, Bhavanisagar for the period that may be prescribed by the Government from time-to-time.

5. The seniority of the persons who were appointed as Junior Assistant/Junior Assistant-*cum*-Typist/Cashier/Typist by transfer from the posts of Part-time/Full-time Clerks of Village Panchayats, shall be fixed on the basis of date of appointment to the Ministerial Service.

6. These revised guidelines shall come into effect from the date of issue of this order.

(G.O. Ms. No. 52, Rural Development (E-5) Department, dated 20th March 1998)

6.6.19 Sanction of Additional Post of Typist to Panchayat Union

The District Collector should be authorised to sanction additional Typist in the scale of pay of Rs. 975-25-1160-30-1660. Wherever the norms fixed by the Government for the creation of the posts of Typist is satisfied in panchayat union. The entire expenditure on the post of Additional Typist shall be met from the funds of the panchayat union. The panchayat union council shall pass a resolution requesting the Collector to create the post of Additional Typist and passed on that the Collector shall issue orders. Copy of the sanction orders of the Collector shall be marked to the Director of Rural Development.

Both the Typist and additional Typist shall attend all the works relating to Panchayat Union Administration in both of the Commissioner of Panchayat Union and the Block Development Officer-Village Panchayats.

(G.O.Ms.No.186, Rural Development (E-4) Department, dated 10th June 1977)

6.6.20 Upgradation of Record Clerks as Record Assistants

The Government Orders for upgradation of one Record Clerk for every six Record Clerks as Record Assistants is extended to the Record Clerks working in panchayat unions.

The Director of Rural Development shall follow the instructions issued in Government Order No.2, P & AR Department, dated 2.1.96, while implementing these Orders for upgradation of Record Clerks as Record Assistants.

The additional expenditure to be incurred because of upgradation of the post of Record Clerk as Record Assistant shall be met from the same head of account from which the pay of the Record Clerk is met. Similarly in panchayat unions, the additional expenditure shall be met from the general funds of the panchayat unions.

(G.O.Ms.No.188, Rural Development (E-5) Department, dated 10th June 1997)

6.6.21 Revision of Scale of Pay for Fitter and Fitter-*cum*-Mechanic

The Fitters and Mechanic-*cum*-Fitters employed under the Rural Water Supply Maintenance Wing at Block and Divisional level have represented to the Government, pointing out certain anomalies in the scales of pay allowed to them as per Tamil Nadu Revised scales of pay Rules, 1985 and 1989 and requested to revise the scales of pay with effect from 1.10.84 and to sanction Personal Pay at 5 per cent. Even when their representation was under consideration, they filed O.A.No.5426/97 and the Tamil Nadu Administrative Tribunal in its order dated 17.7.97 as modified in its order dated 31.7.97

directed the Government to consider the representation and pass orders as per rules.

2. In compliance with the orders of the Tamil Nadu Administrative Tribunal, the Government have carefully considered and request of the Fitters/Mechanic-*cum*-Fitters employed in the Rural Water Supply Maintenance Wing at Division and Block level. The Government direct that the scale of pay of the post of Mechanic-*cum*-Fitter/ Fitters employed in Rural Water Supply Maintenance Wing at Block and Division level be revised as follows:

Name of Post	*Existing scale of pay*	*Revised scale of pay*
Mechanic-*cum*-Fitter/Fitter	Rs. 555-970 (with effect from 1.10.84) Rs. 610-1075 (Selection Grade)	Rs. 610-1075 (Notional effect from 1.10.84 and monetary benefit from 1.4.86) Rs. 705-1230 (Selection Grade)
		Rs. 950-1500(with effect from 1.6.88)

The revised scale of pay ordered above shall take notional effect from 1.10.84 and monetary benefit from 1.4.86. The fixation and arrears in the revised scale shall be made as per Tamil Nadu Revised Scales of Pay Rules 1985 and 1989.

3. Selection Grade pay shall be regulated based on the ordinary grade scale of pay as per the G.O. fourth read above as amended in G.O. seventh read above, subject to proviso therein.

4. Granting of Personal pay to the Fitters/ Mechanic-*cum*-Fitters in the Rural Water Supply Maintenance Wing will be governed by the orders issued in the G.O. sixth read above as amended in the G.O. eighth read above.

5. Necessary amendment to the Pay schedule 1985 and 1989 will be issued separately by the Government in Finance Department.

6. This order issues with the concurrence of the Finance Department *vide* its U.O.No.632/JS/99, dated 20.2.99.

(G.O.Ms.No. 41, Rural Development (E-5) Department, dated 1st March 1999)

6.6.22 Counting of Service Rendered by Fitters in TWAD

Consequent to entrusting of maintenance the hand pumps and power pumps under the Rural Water Supply Programme to the panchayat unions the staff appointed by Tamil Nadu Water Supply and Drainage Board already for the past several years were absorbed in panchayat union service in compliance with the direction of the Hon'ble Tamil Nadu Administrative Tribunal at 17.7. 97 and 31.7.97 in O.A.No.5426/97, a the Government considered the requests of the Tamil Nadu Rural Water Supply Hand Pump and Power Pump Maintenance Staff Association which includes regularisation of service from the date of appointment in Tamil Nadu Water Supply and Drainage Board, the Government in the letter second read above clarified, among others, that the period of service in Tamil Nadu Water Supply and Drainage Board will be counted for increment and pension as far as the Hand Pump and Power Pump Maintenance staff of Tamil Nadu Water Supply and Drainage Board absorbed in Panchayat Union/ Government Service, subject to payment of pension contribution by Tamil Nadu Water Supply and Drainage Board to the local bodies concerned as payment of pension will be a burden for the panchayat unions in respect of staff absorbed in panchayat union service, that the existing instructions apply in respect of staff absorbed in Government service from Tamil Nadu Water Supply and Drainage Board and that however regularisation of service from the date of appointment in Tamil Nadu Water Supply and Drainage Board is not possible.

2. The Action Forum of the Tamil Nadu Rural Development Department Associations have demanded to regularise the service of the staff absorbed from Tamil Nadu Water Supply and Drainage Board from the date of appointment in Tamil Nadu Water Supply and Drainage Board. The Government considered the matter in detail. O.A.No.2683/98 filed already in Tamil Nadu Administrative Tribunal by the Tamil Nadu Water Supply Hand Pump and Power Pump Maintenance Staff Association praying for direction to regularise the service of the members of the Association (Fitters) from the date of their initial appointment

in Tamil Nadu Water Supply and Drainage Board till 29.11.82 is pending. There are no interim orders staying operation of the clarification issued in the Government letter second read above.

3. In the circumstances the Government direct that the period of service of the Tamil Nadu Water Supply and Drainage Board staff prior to absorption in Panchayat Union/Government Service shall be counted for purpose of increment and pension only, without prejudice to the decision to be taken by Hon'ble Tamil Nadu Administrative Tribunal in O.A.No.2683/98 and subject to the condition that pension contribution for the period shall be paid by the Tamil Nadu Water Supply and Drainage Board to the local bodies. As regards the Tamil Nadu Water Supply and Drainage Board staff absorbed in Government service the existing instructions will apply.

4. The Director of Rural Development is directed to workout in consultation with the Director of Local Fund Accounts and claim from the Tamil Nadu Water Supply and Drainage Board the pension contribution payable by it and remit to the pension Fund maintained by the Director of Local Fund Accounts.

(G.O.Ms.No.136, Rural Development (E-5) Department, dated 19th July 1999)

6.6.23 Creation of Additional Technical Posts to Panchayat Union

1. The Director of Rural Development in his letters read above has pointed out that technical supervision of works related to Rural Development Department is inadequate as currently there is only one post of Union Engineer in the panchayat union. The works taken up per panchayat union exceed Rs. 1.5 crore and this requires close technical monitoring supervision and control to ensure timely execution of works as well as implementation quality. In the circumstances, he is pressed for the strengthening of the technical wing in Rural Development by providing for a full fledged office of a Divisional Engineer/Executive Engineer in each district, a sub-division headed by Assistant Divisional Engineer/Assistant Executive Engineer in each division and atleast two Union Engineers for each block. He has also proposed the creation of a technical wing at the Directorate of Rural Development, Chennai headed by a Superintending Engineer.

2. The proposals of the Director of Rural Development were considered by the Staff Committee presided over by Chief Secretary and the Staff Committee recommended the creation of the following posts:

(*i*) One post of Union Engineer (Assistant Engineer) for each block;

(*ii*) 15 Technical sub-division in those Development divisions where these sub-divisions should not exist;

(*iii*) A technical division headed by Divisional Engineer/Executive Engineer in each district.

3. The Government after careful consideration order the creation of the following posts for a period of three years of till the need therefor ceases whichever is earlier:

(a) At the panchayat union level, 384 posts of additional Union Engineer in the rank of Assistant Engineer at the rate of one additional Union Engineer per panchayat union.

(b) At the Divisional level, 15 sub-divisions at the rate of one sub-division to each of the development division which do not have technical staff at present (viz., Cuddalore, Krishnagiri, Lalgudi, Palani, Dharmapuri, Perambalur, Madurantakam, Tiruttani, Uthamapalayam, Tiruchengode, Tiruvarur, Kulithalai, Paramakudi, Tenkasi, Udayarpalayam).

For each sub-division the following posts are created:

Sl. No.	*Category*	*No. of post(s) for each sub-division*	*Total No. of posts*
	Technical Posts		
1.	Assistant Divisional Engineer/ Assistant Executive Engineer	1	15
2.	Assistant Engineer	1	15
3.	Junior Draughting Officer	1	15
	Non-Technical Posts		
4.	Assistant	1	15
6.	Junior Assistant	1	15
7.	Office Assistant	2	30
8.	Watchman	1	15

(c) The non-technical staff, sanctioned above will be filled by way of redeployment from the Rural Development Department staff and equal number of equivalent posts should be surrendered by Director of Rural Development.

(d) At the District level, a District Level Technical Unit at the rate of one unit per district with the following posts.

Sl. No.	*Category*	*No. of post(s) per unit*	*Total No. of posts*
1.	Divisional Engineer/Executive Engineer	1	28
2.	Personal Assistant to Divisional Engineer in the cadre of Assistant Divisional Engineer/ Assistant Executive Engineer	1	28
3.	Senior Draughting Officer	1	28
4.	Junior Draughting Officer	2	56
5.	Driver	1	28

Non-technical posts, if any, required for this unit will be provided by the Director of Rural Development by re-deployment from the Rural Development staff and equal number of equivalent posts should be surrendered by Director of Rural Development.

At the Directorate level, there will be a Technical Unit to advise and assist the Director of Rural Development in all technical matters with the following technical staff:

Sl. No.	*Category*	*No. of post(s)*
1.	Superintending Engineer with the powers of the Chief Engineer (Highways)	1
2.	Assistant Divisional Engineer/Assistant Executive Engineer	1
3.	Assistant Engineer	1
4.	Junior Draughting Officer	1
5.	Jeep Driver	1
Non-technical		
6.	Superintendent	1
7.	Assistant	1
8.	Junior Assistant/Typist	2
9.	Office Assistant	2

All the non-technical posts required by this technical unit will be provided by the Director of Rural Development from the existing staff and equal number of equivalent posts should be surrendered by Director of Rural Development.

5. The Government also order that the additional technical posts sanctioned will be filled up on deputation/by transfer of service basis for a period of three years on temporary basis. The staff for these posts will be drawn from various departments viz. Highways and Rural Works, Public Works Department, Agricultural Engineering, Tamil Nadu Water Supply and Drainage Board and other Allied Technical Departments. Staff will be placed at the disposal of the Rural Development Department by concerned cadre controlling authority. For the period under deputation, Rural Development Department will be the controlling authority in respect of transfer, postings etc., Rural Development Department will in turn issue orders placing the staff at the disposal of Director of Rural Development/Collector for suitable posting. The technical unit at Director of Rural Development Office will approve the Type design, model estimates, adopting the schedule of rates followed in Public Works Department.

6. The performance of the newly created Technical Wing of Rural Development Department will be reviewed at the end of one year.

7. The incumbents of the above posts are eligible to draw in addition to their pay and dearness allowance other usual allowances admissible to them under the orders from time-to-time.

8. The expenditure shall be debited to

"2505 Rural Employment-01. National Programmes-

702. Jawahar Rozgar Yojana – Schemes in the eighth five year Plan-II State Plan-JA. Jawahar Velai Vaippu Thittam-01-Salaries (DPC 2505 01 702-JA 0000)"

9. This order issues with the concurrence of Finance Department vide its U.O.No.23/ADS (G)/96, dated 27.12.96.

(G.O.Ms.No.263, Rural Development (CSS-I) Department, dated 27th December 1996)

6.6.24 Absorption and Recruitment of Engineering Staff in Rural Development Department

(1) At present the Engineering Staff working in Rural Development Department are drawn from various other departments on transfer of service on deputation basis. It had been experienced some administrative difficulties in implementing the various pivotal schemes of the State as well as Centre without adequate powers to the implementing authorities to control over the Engineering staff of other departments. It has become imperative need, from a purely administrative point of view, that Rural Development Department should have an Engineering Wing of its own. As a first steps in G.O.Ms.No.263, Rural Development (CSS-I) Department dated 27.12.96, Government created 384 additional posts of Union Engineers, *i.e.* Assistant Engineers at the rate of one for each Block, 156 additional posts of Assistant Executive Engineers for those sub-divisions which did not have the post, 28 posts of Executive Engineers at the District level (one for each district) and one Superintending Engineer with the powers of a Chief Engineer.

(2) The Engineers required for these posts were drawn from Highways and Rural Works, Public Works Department, Agricultural Engineers, Tamil Nadu Water Supply and Drainage Board and other Allied Technical Departments. The required number of Engineers could not be filled from these departments since they do not have adequate technical staff for Rural Development Department posts.

(3) After a detailed deliberations with the senior officials of the Departments concerned, it has been proposed, among other things, that the technical posts in Rural Development Department could be categorised into "New Posts" (*i.e.* those sanctioned by G.O.Ms.No.263, Rural Development (CSS-I) Department dated 27.12.96) and "Original Posts" (i.e. those sanctioned dated prior to the said G.O.) the powers to do postings and transfers of officers manning the "New Posts" is vested in Collectors/Director of Rural Development/Government in Rural Development Department and in respect of "Original Posts" now manned by personnel drawn from Highways Department, whose postings are done by the Divisional Engineers (Highways)/Chief Engineer (Highways and Rural Works)/Government in Highways Department. The present system of "dual control" of the technical posts in Rural Development Department with the "New Posts" being controlled by Rural Development Department and the "Old Posts" by Highways Department was creating administrative confusion and was not conducive to good administration.

(4) The Government examined the issues in details and hereby order as follows:

(i) The Chief Engineer (Highways & Rural Works) Government in Highways Department shall stop posting personnel directly to the "Original" 53 posts of assistant Executive Engineers (RD) 384 posts of Block Engineers; 768 posts of overseers; 53 posts of Junior Draughtsman (one in each technical sub-division) and all the posts of Road Inspectors, which are borne on Panchayat Union General Funds, with immediate effect. The Chief Engineer (H&RW) Government in Highways Department should instead place these personnel at the disposal of the Director of Rural Development/Collectors on transfer of service basis and the Director of Rural Development/Collectors will, in turn, discharge the duty and powers of postings and transfer.

(ii) In orders to avert reversions with in Highways Department, the "Original", 53 posts of Assistant Executive Engineers (RD); 384 posts of Block Engineers; 768 posts of overseers; 53 posts of Junior Engineers/Assistant Engineers and 53 posts of Junior Draughtsman (one in each technical sub-division) will be earmarked for personnel from Highways Department but if that department is not able to sponsor candidates within 2 months from the date of request made by the Director of Rural Development, then Rural Development Department will fill up these posts by drawing personnel from other departments. All future vacancies arising out of promotions retirement or otherwise will be filled up only by Rural Development Department.

(iii) Although the posts of Overseers found only in the panchayat unions, the incumbents cannot be promoted against a part of the Block Engineers, Assistant Engineers (RD) because they are presently staff of Highways Department. They need to be permanently absorbed into Rural Development Department by getting individual options and only thereafter can the question of their promotions be taken up. Similar individual options may be obtained from the draughtsmen of Highways Department for permanent absorption against the 53 posts of Junior draughtsmen in the office of the AEE (RD)/EE (RD) also. The Road Inspectors/ Assistant Draughtsmen (the scales of these 2 posts are the same) in Highways Department will also be given an opportunity for permanent absorption against the posts of Road Inspectors in the panchayat unions. These posts will be the feeder categories for appointment (by promotions) of overseers. The Chief Engineer (H&RW) may be requested to obtain options from all those personnel and place them at the disposal of Rural Development Department.

(iv) 209 posts in the category of Block Engineers/ Assistant Engineer (RD) will be earmarked to be filled up by promotion from the feeder categories of Overseers and Junior Draughtsmen. But this route would be available to them only after they exercise their option and permanently absorbed in Rural Development Department. This number of 209 would be out of the 384 posts of Block Engineers suggested in item (i.e.) above to be earmarked for engineers from Highways Department.

(5) The Director of Rural Development is directed to explore the possibility and report to Government of permanently absorbing Assistant Engineer from other Technical Departments giving them a 1:1 weightage for service already put in by them in their respective departments. This would enable Rural Development Department to have officers of varying seniorities and the promotion channels will not be clogged as happens when bulk retirement is done.

(6) This order will come into force from the date of issue of order.

(G.O. Ms:No. 102, Rural Development (E-4) Department, dated 25th May 1998)

6.6.25 Adhoc Rules for the Post of Engineering Establishment

Notification-I—1. In exercise of the powers conferred by the proviso Article 309 of the Constitution of India, the Governor of Tamil Nadu hereby makes the following rules:

2. The rules hereby made shall be deemed to have come into force in the 25th May 1998.

1. **Rules**—The General and the special rules applicable to the holders of the permanent posts in the Tamil Nadu Panchayat Development Service shall apply to the holder of the temporary post of Superintending Engineer in Rural Development Department sanctioned from time-to-time, for the Engineering Branch of the Rural Development Department subject to the modifications specified in the following rules.

2. **Constitution**—The post shall constitute a separate category in the said service.

3. **Appointment**

(a) Appointment to the post shall be made by promotion from the category of Executive Engineer in the Rural Development Department.

(b) Promotions to the post shall be made on the basis of merit and ability and the seniority shall be considered only where the merit and ability are approximately equal.

4. **Qualification**—No person shall be eligible for the appointment to the post unless he possesses the following qualifications, namely:

(1) A degree in Civil Engineering or a pass in Section A and B Examinations (AMIE) conducted by the Institution of Engineers (India), and

(2) Service as Executive Engineer for period of not less than three years on duty.

5. **Pay**—There shall be paid to the holder of the post a monthly pay calculated in the scale of Rs. 14,300-400-18,300.

Notification-II—1. In exercise of the powers conferred by the proviso to Article 309 of the Constitution of India, the Governor of Tamil Nadu hereby makes the following rules:

2. The rules hereby made shall be deemed to have come into force on the 25th May 1998.

1. **Rules**—The General and the special rules applicable to the holders of permanent posts in the Tamil Nadu Panchayat Development Service shall apply to the holder of the temporary post of Executive Engineer in the Rural Development Department, sanctioned from time-to-time, for the Engineering Branch of the Rural Development Department subject to the modifications specified in the following rules.

2. **Constitution**—The post shall constitute a separate category in the said service.

3. Appointment

(a) Appointment to the post shall be made by promotion from the category of Assistant Executive Engineer in the Rural Development Department.

(b) Promotion to the post shall be made on the basis of merit and ability and seniority shall be considered only where the merit and ability are approximately equal.

4. Qualification—No person shall be eligible for the appointment to the post unless he possesses the following qualifications, namely:

(1) A degree in Civil Engineering or a pass in Section A and B Examinations (AMIE) conducted by the Institution of Engineers (India), and

(2) Service as Assistant Executive Engineer for a period of not less than five years on duty.

5. Pay—There shall be paid to the holder of the post a monthly pay calculated in the scale of Rs. 10,000-325-15,200.

Notification-III—1. In exercise of powers conferred by the proviso to Article 309 of the Constitution of India, the Governor of Tamil Nadu hereby makes the following rules:

2. The rules hereby made shall be deemed to have come into force on the 25th May 1998.

1. Rules—The General and the special rules applicable to the holders of the permanent posts in the Tamil Nadu Panchayat Development Service shall apply to the holder of the temporary post of Assistant Executive Engineer in the Rural Development Department, sanctioned from time-to-time, for the Engineering Branch of the Rural Development Department subject to the modifications specified in the following rules:

2. Constitution—The post shall constitute a separate category in the said service.

3. Appointment—Appointment to the post shall be made by:

(a) recruitment by transfer from the categories of Junior Engineer and Senior Draughting officer of the Tamil Nadu Rural Development Department, and

(b) promotion from the category of Assistant Engineer in the Rural Development Department.

(2) The ratio for appointment to the posts by promotion from the category of Assistant Engineer and by recruitment by transfer from the categories of Junior Engineer and Senior Draughting Officer shall be 6:2:1. The following rotation shall be followed while filling up of the vacancies arising in a year.

(a) Promotion from the category of Assistant Engineer.

(b) Promotion from the category of Assistant Engineer.

(c) Recruitment by transfer from the category of Junior Engineer.

(d) Promotion from the category of Assistant Engineer.

(e) Promotion from the category of Assistant Engineer.

(f) Recruitment by transfer from the category of Senior Draughting Officer.

(g) Promotion from the category of Assistant Engineer.

(h) Promotion from the category of Assistant Engineer.

(i) Recruitment by transfer from the category of Junior Engineer.

(3) Promotion to the post shall be made on the basis of merit and ability and seniority shall be considered only where the merit and ability are approximately equal.

4. Qualification—No person shall be eligible for the appointment to the post by the method specified in column (1) of the Table below, unless he possesses the qualifications specified in the corresponding entries in column (2) thereof.

The Table

Method of appointment (1)	*Qualification* (2)
(a) Promotion from Assistant Engineer in the Rural Development Department	(1) A degree in Civil Engineering or a pass in Sections A and B examinations (AMIE) conducted by the Institution of Engineers (India); and (2) Service as Assistant Engineer for a period of not less than five years on duty.
(b) Recruitment by transfer from Junior Engineer and Senior Draughting Officer in the Rural Development Department	(1) A diploma in Civil Engineering; and (2) Service as Junior Engineer or Senior Draughting Officer, as the case may be, for a period of not less than five years on duty in the Tamil Nadu Rural Development Department.

5. **Pay**—There shall be paid to the holder of the post a monthly pay calculated in the scale of Rs. 8000-275-10500.

Notification-IV—1. In exercise of the powers conferred by the proviso to Article 309 of the Constitution of India, the Governor of Tamil Nadu hereby makes the following rules:

2. The rules hereby made shall be deemed to have come into force on the 26th September 1997.

2. **Constitution**—The post shall constitute a separate category in the said service.

3. **Appointment**—Appointment to the post shall be made by

(a) direct recruitment,
(b) recruitment by transfer from Overseer in the Rural Development Department, and
(c) the ratio for appointment to the post by direct recruitment and recruitment by transfer shall be 1:1.

4. **Appointing authority**—The appointing authority for the post shall be the Director of Rural Development.

5. **Qualifications**

(a) *Age*: No person shall be eligible for the appointment to the post by direct recruitment, if he has completed or will complete the age of thirty five years on the first day of July of the year in which the selection for appointment to the post is made.
(b) *Other Qualification*: No person shall be eligible for the appointment to the post by the method specified in column (1) of the Table below, unless he possesses the qualification specified in the corresponding entries in column (2) thereof.

The Table

Method of appointment (1)	*Qualification* (2)
(a) Direct Recruitment	(1) A degree in Civil Engineering from a recognised University, or a pass in Sections A and B examination (AMIE) conducted by the Institution of Engineers (India); and (2) Practical training in surveying for a period of not less than one year: Provided that other things being equal preference shall be given for appointment to a person who has undergone one year apprenticeship training under the Government of India Scheme or State Government Apprenticeship Scheme.
(b) Recruitment by transfer from Overseer/ Junior Draughting Officer in Tamil Nadu Rural Development Department	(1) A degree in Civil Engineering; or a pass in Sections A and B examination (AMIE) conducted by the Institution of Engineers (India) (or) Service as overseer of Junior Draughting Officer, as the case may be for a period of not less than five years; and (2) Practical training in surveying for period not less than one year.

3. **Reservation of appointment**—The rule of reservation (General Rule 22) shall apply for appointment to the post by direct recruitment.

4. **Probation**

(i) Every person appointed to the post by direct recruitment shall, from the date on which he joins duty, be on probation for a total period of two years on duty, within a continuous period of three years.
(ii) Every person appointed to the post by recruitment by transfer shall from the date on which he joins duty, be on probation for a total period of one year on duty within a continuous period of two years.

5. **Tests**—(1) Every person appointed to the category of Assistant Engineer by direct recruitment shall within the period of probation pass the following tests, namely:

(a) The account test for Public Works Department Officers and Subordinates; and
(b) The Tamil Nadu Panchayats Act, 1994.

(2) The incumbents recruited as Assistant Engineer post pass the above tests within the period of probation of two years.

6. Pay—There shall be paid to the holder of the post a monthly pay calculated in the scale of Rs. 6500-200-10500.

(G.O. Ms. No. 15, Rural Development (E-I) Department, dated 25th January 2000)

6.6.26 Guidelines to Avoid Delay in Regularisation of Appointment Made on Compassionate Ground

The Government issue the following orders to avoid delay in regularisation of services – persons temporarily appointed on compassionate grounds.

(a) Before giving appointment on temporary post, the authority shall verify whether the applicant requesting appointment on compassionate grounds contains required certificates and affidavits before issuing appointment order.

(b) If a person is appointed on compassionate grounds to a post under the purview of Tamil Nadu Public Service Commission, the Officer issuing the appointment order shall send proposals for getting concurrence of Tamil Nadu Public Service Commission within one month of the date of issuing of appointment order.

(c) The Director of Rural Development shall monitor every month as to the number of persons appointed on compassionate grounds, number of proposals received for regularisation of services and whether all the conditions and rules prescribed for such appointment have been followed scrupulously. The periodical report may be prescribed for these purpose and if any delay and irregularity in the appointment is noticed responsibilities have been fixed and further action may be initiated.

(d) Similarly, the Director of Rural Development shall send a report before 31st January every year on the number of compassionate ground appointment made, number of proposals received for regularisation of services within prescribed time limit, delay or irregularities if any noticed on the appointment and the follow up action take on those cases and the result of action.

(e) While sending proposals received with delay, the persons responsible for the delay and the action taken against them for the delay shall also be sent along with the proposals.

(G.O.Ms.No.181, Rural Development (E-V) Department, dated 10th June 1997)

6.6.27 Release of 25 Per cent of Gratuity with held for Audit Objections

The Government ordered that withholding of 25 per cent of the Death-*cum*-Retirement Gratuity at the time of retirement for pending of audit objections need not be followed and that full gratuity may be released to them on the date of retirement.

The personnel of Rural Development Department allowed to retire without any disciplinary action against them may be sanctioned full gratuity at the time of retirement. Severe disciplinary action shall be initiated against the persons involved in serious irregularities as per audit objections or on any irregularity committed with intention or due to lack of supervision or financial loss caused to the Government.

The Government also ordered that those Block Development Officers who retired earlier and against whom no disciplinary action is pending 25 per cent gratuity withheld shall be released to them immediately.

(G.O.Ms.No.187, Rural Development (E-6) Department, dated 7th September 1999)

6.6.28 Record Clerks, Office Assistant and Watchman Permission to Write a Special Examination

Tamil Nadu Ministerial Services – RD Unit – Record Clerk, Office Assistants, Night Watchman of Panchayat Union Service who do not possess minimum general educational qualification-Permission to write the common examination for acquiring general educational qualification conducted by TNPSC orders.

The Record Clerk, Office Assistants, Night Watchman and other Panchayat Union Employees who do not possess minimum general educational qualification prescribed for the post of Junior Assistant-*cum*-Typist/Cashier and those who promoted on the 10 per cent quota reserved for such promotion are allowed to write the special examination, equivalent to X standard conducted by the TNPSC.

(G.O. Ms. No. 108 Rural Development (E-5) Department, dated 19th May 1988)

6.6.29 Rejection of Time Scale of Pay for Cholera Gang Mazdoors

(1) Thiru. V. Manivel engaged as Cholera Mazdoor by the Panchayat Union Commissioner, Andanallur panchayat union for short period from time-to-time on daily wage basis, filed O.A.No.2455/2000 in the

Tamil Nadu Administrative Tribunal, Chennai seeking direction to bring him to time scale of pay and regularise his service from the date of initial appointment. In its order dated 13.4.2000 in the above said O.A. the respondent Government was directed to dispose of the representation dated 4.7.1999 of the applicant within a period of five months.

(2) Thiru. V. Manivel, applicant in the above O.A. submitted a copy of his representation dated 4.7.1999 together with a copy of the direction of Tamil Nadu Administrative Tribunal. In his representation, he has requested to grant him time scale of pay and to regularise his service.

(3) In compliance with the direction of Tamil Nadu Administrative Tribunal, in the order first read above the Government examined the matter carefully. Cholera Mazdoors are casual labourers, engaged on daily wage basis by panchayat unions for short period ranging from 15 days to 3 months when epidemic conditions exist. Such a condition is not a feature existing regularly or permanently. Therefore, necessity for continuous employment of a person for this purpose does not exist. Cholera Mazdoors are NMR Workers and are not contingent employees and hence G.O.Ms.No.52, Finance, dated 14.1.1977 and G.O. Ms. No. 878, R.D.L.A., dated 15.5.1981 are not applicable to them.

(4) In the circumstances the Government decided, that the request of the applicant in the O.A.No. 2455/2000 is not feasible of compliance. Accordingly, the Government hereby reject the request of the applicant in O.A.No.2455/2000, as it is not feasible of acceptance.

(G.O. Ms. No. 23, Rural Development (E-5) Department, dated 23rd January 2001)

6.6.30 Formation of Technical Service Cell at Panchayat Union Office for Maintenance of Hand-pumps and Power-pumps

(a) The Technical Service Cell will be formed at panchayat union level including Hand-pump Fitters and his Assistants, Electricians who were looking after the maintenance of power pump Supervisor for looking after this work.

(b) The maintenance of all the hand-pumps and power-pumps in village panchayats shall be done by the village panchayat presidents utilising the service of the technical service cell looked at panchayat union level office.

(c) The charges for the repairs shall be decided according to the nature of repairs by the technical service cell.

(d) The technical service cell will work under the control of Block Development Officer, village panchayats with the technical Assistance of Union Engineer.

(e) The spare power pumps will be with the technical service cell and it will be maintained by them. In case of the village panchayats can requisition the spare power-pumps and use them for supplying water.

The revolving fund will be created at each panchayat union and during current year 2000-2001, Rs. One lakh initially shall be allotted from the village panchayat drinking water supply maintenance grant and equalisation of incentive fund.

The service charges collected by the village panchayat shall be credited into the revolving fund.

The hand-pump Fitters, his helpers, Electricians and his Assistants shall be paid at the rates already received by them from out of this revolving fund.

(G.O.Ms.No.121, Rural Development (P-III) Department, dated 10th May 2000)

6.7 AUDIT AND ACCOUNTS

6.7.1 Recovery of Advances Sanctioned from Panchayat Union Funds

The Government consider that it is not necessary to open a register of recoveries in the case of advances granted to Government servants in panchayat union councils and that it would be sufficient if a register of recoveries and remittance of advances is opened for servants paid out of panchayat unions in the form annexed to this order, in respect of the advances sanctioned by the order local bodies from which the staff concerned have been transferred, the initial entries in the register should be made with reference to the particulars of advances shown in the last pay certificates. The Executive Authorities should check the register periodically and take necessary steps to eliminate delays in recovering the advance and remitting them to the concerned local body.

ANNEXURE

Register to watch recovery and remittances of advances drawn by incumbents from local bodies from which they have been transferred.

Name of the person and designation (1)	*Name of the Local body from which transferred* (2)	*Nature of advance* (3)	*Total amount to be recovered* (4)	*Number of installments* (5)
Amount and date of recovery (6)	*Total amount recovered* (7)	*Amount remitted to the concerned local body* (8)	*Particulars of remittance* (9)	*Initials of Executive Authorities* (10)

6.7.2 Power to Write-off Irrecoverable Taxes, Fees, etc., by Panchayat Union Councils

1. Short title—These rules may be called the Tamil Nadu Panchayats (Power to Write-off Irrecoverable Taxes, Fees, etc., Restrictions and Control) Rules, 2000.

2. Approval of the panchayat union council for the proposal to write-off the irrecoverable amounts—Any amounts found irrecoverable shall be reported by the person entrusted with the responsibility of collection of such amount with reasons thereof, which shall be verified by the Commissioner. A list of all such amounts shall be prepared once a quarter and submitted to the panchayat union council in its next meeting for approval with the reasons and recommendations of the Commissioner for writing-off the same. The Commissioner shall ensure that the defaulter has no attachable property within the village and that all means of recovery have been tried and found unsuccessful, before recommending the write-off of the amount:

Provided that before recommending the write-off in case where any single item of tax or fee or other amount found to be irrecoverable exceeds Rs. 250 the Commissioner shall obtain the sanction of the Inspector.

3. Maintenance of register—(1) A register for recording the amounts written-off shall be maintained in the form specified in the Appendix.

(2) When a panchayat union council sanctions that any amount be written-off, particulars as to the nature of the tax, fee or other amount (with assessment number in the case of items relating to tax), the amount written-off and the period to which it relates shall be written in detail in the minutes book. The total amount authorized to be written-off each time shall be specified in words, in every case.

(3) The bills and warrants (both foil and counterfoil) for the taxes, fees or other amount written-off, shall, as soon as possible after sanction for the write-off is given by the panchayat union council be stamped with the words "Written-Off" and necessary entries shall, at the same time, be made in the demand register.

4. Powers of the Commissioner of land administration—Notwithstanding anything contained in these rules, where the Collector or any of his subordinates is responsible for the collection of any tax, fees, or other amount as provided in the proviso to Section 177of the Tamil Nadu Panchayats Act, 1994 (Tamil Nadu Act 21 of 1994) the power to write-off such amounts shall be subject to a limit of Rs. 100 for the Revenue Divisional Officer and Rs. 500 for the Collector. The authority sanctioning such write-off shall inform in writing to the panchayat union council, the reasons for such write-off, within two months from the date of sanction of write-off.

5. Writing-off of the amounts payable by the lessees and contractors—(1) Any amount payable by any lessee or contractor may be written off only in cases where such lessee or contractor is prevented from carrying out his part of the lease or contract by reason of the occurrence of some extraordinary, extrinsic cause which could not reasonably have been anticipated.

(2) The amount of write-off shall not exceed the proportionate amount payable under the lease or contract for the period for which the lessee or contractor was prevented from carrying out his part of the lease or contract on account of such extraordinary cause.

(3) When the amount proposed to be written-off exceeds five hundred rupees, in each case the previous sanction of the Inspector shall be obtained.

6. **Penalities**—Penalities provided in the lease or contract shall be strictly enforced in accordance with terms of the lease or contract. Penalities for late payment of the amount due to the panchayat union council under the lease or contract shall not be written-off except in cases where the payments of instalments, of the amount due, are in the opinion of the panchayat union council, fairly regular and the whole amount due to the panchayat union council under the lease or contract is paid before the end of the period to which the lease or contract relates.

(G.O.Ms.No.206, Rural Development (C4) Department, dated 17th August 2000)

6.7.3 Use of Grants Recommended by the State Finance Commission and Abolition of Certain Grants to Panchayat Union

(1) The Government examined the recommendations of the State Finance Commission and decided to allot 8 per cent of the Pool 'B' Tax Collection excepting Entertainment Tax to the panchayats.

(2) As a result of the above decision, the grants hitherto received by village panchayats and panchayat unions will not be sanctioned by Government from 1.4.97 onwards. The following grants shall not be sanctioned to the panchayats.

Village Panchayats

(i) Hand Pump Maintenance Grant
(ii) Power Pump Maintenance Grant
(iii) Grant for Salary for Panchayat Assistant
(iv) Street Light Grant for Weaker Panchayats
(v) Compensation for Surcharge on Sales Tax Sanctioned to Village Panchayats
(vi) House Tax Matching Grant.

Panchayat Unions

(i) Local Cess Surcharge Matching Grant
(ii) Local Roads Grant.

(3) The panchayats which incurred expenditure from the above grants shall incur expenditure from the grants allotted as per recommendations of the State Finance Commission.

(4) Other Grants shall continuously be sanctioned by Government.

(5) The Grant sanctioned as per the recommendations of the State Finance Commission shall be utilised only for the following purposes:

Village Panchayats

(i) Salary and Wages of sanctioned staff.
(ii) Maintenance of Drinking Water Sources including hand pump and power pump
(iii) Maintenance of Street Lights and remittance of current consumption charges
(iv) To fulfil various obligatory functions as per Tamil Nadu Panchayat Act, 1994 like Public Health, Sanitation, Drainage etc.
(v) Office Maintenance including stationery.

Panchayat Unions

(i) Salary and Wages for sanctioned employees of panchayat union.
(ii) Provident Fund and Pension Contribution, Travelling Allowance, Daily Allowance and other expenditure of panchayat union employees.
(iii) Expenditure on Office maintenance, Stationery, Current Consumption charges, Telephone Charges etc.
(iv) Maintenance of Panchayat Union Buildings and other buildings entrusted to panchayat unions.
(v) Maintenance of panchayat union roads.
(vi) Maintenance of Minor Irrigation Tanks transferred to panchayat unions.

(6) The following instructions have to be strictly followed by all the panchayats.

(i) Salary of staff, Pension and Provident Fund Contribution, Office expenditure shall be the first charge in this grant.
(ii) In respect of village panchayats, the following items shall be given priority:
   (a) Maintenance of Drinking Water Sources like Bore Wells, Hand pumps and Power pumps
   (b) Street Lights
   (c) Public Health Sanitation
   (d) Other obligatory functions
(iii) In respect of panchayat unions, the maintenance of buildings shall be given the next preference.
(iv) After providing for all the items only the maintenance of Roads and Minor Irrigation Tanks can be taken up.

(7) Unless provided in the Government Orders, no Part-time/Full-time/NMR/Temporary employees shall be appointed newly.

(8) The District Collectors as Inspector of panchayats shall strictly follow the above instructions.

(9) If there is surplus fund after providing or after incurring expenditure on all the above items, the panchayat shall take up the works as suggested by the Director of Rural Development.

(10) Besides the State Finance Commission Grant, village panchayats will be having their own finance resource like House-tax, Professional tax, Licence Fee etc.

(11) Local Cess, Surcharge on Stamp duty share of entertainment tax seigniorage fee on mining of minor minerals etc., will also be received by village panchayats. Local Cess Surcharge and share of entertainment tax will be continuously be sanctioned to the panchayat unions.

(12) There shall be no transaction after 31.3.97 between village panchayats and panchayat unions. No adjustment shall be made between the accounts of village panchayats and panchayat unions after 31.3.97. The balance amount as on 1.4.97 in the Village Panchayat Consolidated Fund shall be transferred to the new Savings Bank Account opened as per G.O.Ms.No.92, Rural Development Department, dated 26.3.97 by the village panchayats in Co-operative Bank/Regional Rural Bank/Post Office Savings Bank/Nationalised Bank and credited to that account.

Separate Committee shall be formed to look after the amount to be transferred from panchayat unions to village panchayats and from village panchayats to panchayat unions.

(G.O. Ms. No. 93, Rural Development (C-3) Department, dated 26th March 1997)

6.7.4 Procedure for Expenditure of Surplus Funds of Panchayat Union Council

The authority competent to sanction works from the surplus funds of the panchayat union with monetary limit for sanction shall be as follows:

Sl. No.	*Amount*	*Competent Authority*
sanction		
1.	Individual works cost upto Rs. 5 lakhs	Panchayat Unions
2.	Individual works cost above Rs. 5 lakhs and upto Rs. 10.00 lakhs	District Collector
3.	Individual works cost above Rs. 10 lakhs and upto Rs. 1 crore	DRD
4.	Individual works cost above Rs. 1 crore	Government

For incurring expenditure of works from the surplus funds of the panchayats they shall follow the guidelines and the conditions prescribed below:

(a) Prior approval of the panchayat union council shall be obtained.

(b) The works mentioned in G.O.Ms.No.229, Rural Development Department, dated 15.10.96 and G.O. Ms. No. 363 Rural Development Department, dated 22.12.97 shall alone be sanctioned. After reserving Rs. 5 lakhs from the surplus funds of the panchayat unions 50 per cent of the balance amount shall alone be spent on surplus fund works. This will be specific responsibility of the panchayat union Commissioner and the panchayat union council. While sending proposals for sanction, a special certificate shall be included in the resolution sanction in the proposal.

(c) The panchayat union Commissioner shall send a copy of the resolution of the panchayat union council within 7 days after the conduct of the meeting to the Inspector of panchayats.

(G.O.Ms.No.85, Rural Development Department, dated 6th May 1998)

6.8 CONTROLLING AUTHORITIES

6.8.1 Procedure for Conduct of Cursory and Annual Inspection

After the enactment of Tamil Nadu Panchayats Act, 1994 all the three tiers of panchayat unions function independently of each other. The panchayat union council has been empowered with various duties and responsibilities and financial resources and responsibilities for implementation of various Government schemes. There must be a system of frequent inspection of the accounts and the various registers, besides field inspection of all the schemes implemented through panchayat unions. Hence the questionnaire for Cursory Inspection and Annual

Inspection of Panchayat Union is prescribed and given in the Annexure I and II respectively.

Inspecting Officers of Panchayat Union

The Government have notified in G.O.Ms. No. 264 Rural Development (C3) Department dated: 21.12.99, the following Officers as the Inspecting Officers of the panchayat union council. They are viz.

(1) Assistant Director of Rural Development (Panchayat).
(2) Assistant Director of Rural Development (Audit).
(3) Personal Assistant to the District Collector (Development).
(4) Personal Assistant to the District Collector (NMP).
(5) District Collector.
(6) Other Officers not below the rank of Assistant Director of Rural Development nominated by the Inspector of Panchayat.

Cursory Inspection

Cursory Inspection of all panchayat unions in the district shall be done by the Assistant Director of Rural Development (Panchayat) and Assistant Director of Rural Development (Audit), Personal Assistant to Collector (Development) Personal Assistant to Collector (NMP) and any other officers not below the rank of Assistant Director Rural Development nominated by the District Collector. The Personal Assistant to Collector (Development) shall draw programme for Cursory Inspection of all the panchayat unions in the District in such a way that each panchayat union is inspected once in three months and obtain orders of the Collector and communicate to all the Inspecting Officers of the panchayat unions well in advance at the beginning of the financial year itself. The Inspecting Officers shall be strictly instructed to verify all the Records and Registers particularly Cash Books, Pass Books and Reconciliation of various accounts works etc. and Stock Registers of materials and test check the stock held, pendency of the advances etc. If any serious irregularities are noticed at the time of cursory inspection the Inspecting Officers shall immediately bring it to the notice of the District Collector for immediate action. The Assistant Director of Rural Development (Panchayats) shall be responsible for taking follow up action on the cursory inspection notes issued by the Inspecting Officers.

Annual Inspection

Further, the Personal Assistant to Collector (Development) shall draw a programme for annual inspection of all the panchayat unions every year before February in order to complete all inspection before June, and fix responsibilities for inspections by the Project Officers (DRDA) and all the Assistant Director Rural Development working in their district for the approval for the District Collector. After getting approval of the Collector for the programme and after getting Collectors concurrence, any two of the panchayat unions in the District may be allotted for annual Inspection by the District Collector. Similarly, Project Officer, District Rural Development Agency shall take annual inspection of not less than three blocks every year. The notes of annual inspection shall be submitted to the District Collector through the Assistant Director (Panchayats) by the Inspecting Officers and if they notice any irregularities, special report shall be sent to the District Collector for taking follow up action. While taking up annual inspection by the panchayat unions special verification may be made by the Inspecting Officers on the rectification of defects pointed out in the earlier annual inspection as well as cursory inspection by the Inspecting Officers.

The receipt of the circular shall be acknowledged by all the District Collectors and immediate action shall be taken to draw programme for the conduct of cursory as well as annual inspection of all the panchayat unions. A consolidated report may also be sent in this regard to this office for every year before June of the succeeding year.

ANNEXURE - I
Cursory Inspection of Panchayat Union

1. General Particulars
2. Office Administration
3. Meetings
4. Financial Administration
5. Implementation of Schemes

6. Accounts – Deposits – Advances – Audit
7. Registers

Inspecting Officer

Name: ______________________

Designation: ______________________

Date of Inspection

Cursory Inspection Notes of Panchayat Union Office

I. General Information

1 Name of the of Panchayat Union :
2 Name of the Inspecting Officer/ Designation :
3. Date of last Inspection :
4. Persons holding offices during the period of inspection :
5. (a) Block Development Officer (Panchayats) :
   (b) Block Development Officer (Panchayat Union) :
   (c) Union Engineer :
   (d) Additional Union Engineer :

II. Office Administration

1. Is attendance register maintained properly?
2. Are proper entries made in the Casual Leave register?
3. Is log book for vehicles maintained properly?
4. Have Panchayat Union Commissioner, Extension Officers, Union Engineers, Deputy B.D.O's, and Overseers submitted their monthly diaries in time?
5. Action taken against the persons who have failed to submit their dairies in time.
6. Is review of diaries undertaken? If so any special item noticed?
7. Is register of increment and service registers maintained properly?
8. Has increment been sanctioned on the due dates?
9. Has anybody failed to submit their P.R. for check on the due date?
10. Action taken against such persons?
11. Is there vacancy of posts in Panchayat Union Office? Action taken to fill up such vacancies.
12. If any new appointment is made? Has selection been made by the approval of appointment committee? Note resolution number and date.

III. Meetings

1. Have meetings been conducted within 60 days interval? If not conducted what action was taken to avoid such delays?
2. (a) Has meeting notice been served properly and on all the members?
   (b) Has notice been served on those members who have failed to attend three panchayat union council meetings continuously?
   (c) Is there vacancy in members and if so, from which date?
   (d) Action taken to fill up the vacancy.

IV. Accounts

1. Financial position in the various accounts on the date of inspection

(In Rupees)

Panchayat Union	*Opening Balance*	*Receipt*	*Expenditure*	*Closing Balance*	*As per Bank/Post Office A/c*	*Account of Bank/ Post Office*
General Fund						
Educational Fund						
Noon meals Fund						
Closing balance under all schemes						
Fund Accounts on the date of inspection						

Anna Marumalarchi Thittam
Namakku Name Thittam
M.L.A Constituency
Development Scheme
Equalisation grant of SFC
Employment Assurance Scheme
Member of Parliament Local Area Development Scheme
Central Rural Sanitation Programme/Bio Gas Programme
Chulah
Central Finance Commission Grant
Other Schemes

2. Have Bank Accounts of Discontinued schemes viz. Special Self Sufficiency Scheme, IRDP, DWRCA, Million Well Scheme, Social Forestry, Jawahar Rozgar Yojana, closed, and whether the balance have been remitted to the various Accounts as per Govt. Orders?
3. Is cash book of scheme funds/general funds maintained properly? Has reconciliation of balance as per Bank/Treasury Accounts made and B.D.O has certified in reconciliation?
4. Is register of bills passed for payment maintained account-wise/scheme-wise properly? This register shall be verified with the entries in cash book?
5. Is Miscellaneous demand register/Register of miscellaneous collection maintained properly?
6. Has monthly accounts been closed, account-wise and report sent to Assistant Director of Local Fund Audit? Date of dispatch of monthly accounts during last month.
7. Has diversion of funds been made from scheme funds/general funds for the other Accounts? Please verify and furnish remarks.

V. Financial and Tax Administration

1. (a) Local cess surcharge adjusted upto what fasli?
   (b) Amount pending for adjustment with details of fasli.
   (c) Action taken to adjust the amounts due and present stage.
2. (a) Demand collection and balance of licence fee for Factories and installation of machinery.
   (b) Is D and O Trade Licence fees adjusted to Village Panchayats Accounts?
   (c) Is there any expenditure without sanction of the panchayat union council? Furnish details.
3. Has Budget estimate of panchayat union for current year approved by the competent authority?

VI. Implementation of Schemes

List of works pending implementation on the date of Inspection

	Arrear			Current year			Current year allotment		
Name of Scheme	Number pending	Completed	Balance	Taken up	Completed	Balance	Allocation	Expenditure	Balance
General Fund	Number Pending	Completed	Balance	Taken up	Completed	Balance	Allotment	Expenditure	Balance
Equalisation Fund-wise	Number pending	Completed	Balance	Taken up	Completed	Balance	Allotment	Expenditure	Balance

This should be verified with reference to Allotment and Estimate Registers of the respective schemes and years.

VII. Equalisation Fund Works

1. Have all works taken up under schemes entered in Estimate and Allotment register? Yes/No (Give details).
2. Have pending works of previous years carried forward in Estimate and Allotment Register? Yes/No (Give details).
3. Have details of entries made in register of bills passed register and cash book entered in estimate and allotment register?
4. Details of final bills for completed works and date of completion noted in Estimate Allotment Register.
5. Has the register been verified and certified by B.D.O.?
6. Deposit Amount.

Total deposit Amount received	*Deposit amount— Purchase of materials*	*Amount received at the beginning of the year*	*Amount refunded*	*Balance on the date of inspection*
Deposit amount received for works	*Amount received at the beginning of the year*	*Amount adjusted*	*Amount refunded*	*Balance*

7. Advances
   (a) Advances to individuals
   (b) Advance for purchase of materials
   (c) Advance given to village panchayats (List to be given Panchayat-wise)

VIII. Registers

(a) Verify Tender registers. If there is a gap of more than one month from the date of administrative sanction and date of finalisation of tender, find out the reasons.

(b) Verify Estimate, Technical register of the Engineers and if there is more than one month delay from the date of administrative sanction and the technical sanction, indicate such cases and state reasons.

(c) Are all Overseers and Engineers maintaining Technical Sanction Register?

(d) If there is delay of more than one month from the date of issue of work order between, the tender finalisation date and beneficiary selection date; note down such cases.

(e) Is bills received register maintained properly and are all bills entered in the register (Please compare with Bills passed Register)?

(f) If there are cases of bills pending for more than 7 days from the date of receipt as per bills received register, furnish details.

(g) Is Asset Register and Roads register maintained properly? Verify Estimate and Allotment Register of the Last and Current year furnish details. (Scheme-wise verification may be done)

(h) Materials Purchase and Stock Register
   (i) Cement
   (ii) Steel
   (iii) Bitumen
   (iv) Door
   (v) Window
   (vi) Pane
   (vii) Others

(i) Date of last verification of Stock/Designation of Officers/Audit.

(j) No. of Audits completed by Deputy B.D.O/ and numbers pending.

Verify stock of excess motors and furnished details	Total	Issued temporarily	Balance as on date	
			As per stock register	Number During inspection

IX. Inspection of Village Panchayats

Officer	*No. of inspection made*	*No. inspected*	*Balance*	*No. of Cases Action taken under Section 205 of the Act*
B.D.O. (Block Panchayat)				
B.D.O. (Village Panchayat)				
Extension Officer (Panchayat)				
Extension Officer (Small Savings)				
Extension Officer (Animal Husbandry)				

X. Swarna Jayanthi Gram Swa Rozgar Yojana

1. Is regular monthly S.G.S.Y meeting conducted?
   Yes/ No (Give details)
2. Is B.L.B.C meeting conducted monthly?
3. Total number of trades selected as per Annual action plan?
4. No. of self-help groups selected?
5. No. of S.H.G's selected for awarding Revolving Fund
6. No. of S.H.G's selected for financial assistance

7. No. of S.H.G's sanctioned loans?
   (a) No. of S.H.G's
   (b) Total Subsidy
   (c) Total Loan
   (d) Total Assistance
   (e) Details of persons assisted for individual schemes
      (i) Number
      (ii) Subsidy
      (iii) Loan
      (iv) Total
8. Amount spent for formation of S.H.G.
9. Amount spent in Training
10. No. of Infrastructures created
11. Total Cost
12. Details of Infrastructure works pending
13. Is the scheme improving standard of living?

XI. General

Inspection Remarks:

(Give narrative note of strength, weakness, opportunity and threat to the local body perceived during inspection)

ANNEXURE - II

Annual Inspection

Date of Inspection: | | | |

Inspecting Officer

Name ....
Designation...........................

GENERAL
Annual Inspection Notes of Panchayat Union

1. Name of Office
2. Date of Inspection | | | |
3. Period of Inspection From | | | | To | | | |
4. Name
   Designation of
   Officer taking up Inspection
5. Names of Commissioners who worked during the period of Inspection.

   (1) From | | | | To | | | |

   (2) From | | | | To | | | |

   (3) From | | | | To | | | |
6. Date of last Inspection by District Collector/ other Officer—Details of Inspection.
   (i) District Collector's Name
   Period of Inspection From | | | | To | | | |

(ii) Other Officers

	Name	Designation	From	To
(1)				
(2)				
(3)				

7. Action taken on Inspection Notes of previous years
   (a) Have replies been sent and review on them received?
   (b) Have all the defects pointed out fully rectified?
   (c) Whether rectification report was verified by the Inspecting Officer?

PART - I

1. Office Procedure

1.1 Extension Officer (Administration)/Accountant

Sl. No.	*Name*	*Designation*	*Period*	
			From	*To*

1.2 Extension Officer

Sl. No.	*Name*	*Designation*	*Period*	
			From	*To*
1.				
2.				
3.				
4.				
5.				
6.				

1.3 Office Staff

Sl. No.	*Section*	*Name*	*Designation*	*Period*	
				From	*To*
1.					
2.					
3.					
4.					
5.					
6.					
7.					
8.					
9.					
10.					

1.4 *Office Assistants*

Sl. No.	*Name*	*Designation*	*Period*	
			From	*To*
1.				
2.				
3.				

1.5 *Panchayat Union Employees*

Dispensary/Maternity ayahs

Sl. No.	*Name*	*Designation*	*Period*	
			From	*To*
1.				
2.				
3.				

Night Watchman

Sl. No.	*Name*	*Designation*	*Period*	
			From	*To*
1.				
2.				

Pump Mechanic

Sl. No.	*Name*	*Designation*	*Period*	
			From	*To*
1.				
2.				
3.				

1.6 *Other Employees*

(Carpentry/Blacksmithy/Tractor/Shandy)

2. Attendance, Leave and Vacancies

A Is attendance register closed daily and submitted for the approval of the Commissioner/Block Development Officer (Village Panchayats)?

B Is Casual Leave register and Attendance register compared and certificate furnished in the attendance register in the month end?

C Is delayed attendance taken into accounts for deducting Casual Leave?

D Upto what month the above action has been taken?

E Whether list of persons who are continuously absent reported to the District Collector? (Leave without Pay/Absence without any intimation, etc.)

F Has action been taken to fill up the vacancy due to continuous absence?

3. Distribution Register

A Is Distribution Register maintained properly? Yes/No

If No, give reasons

B Are all tapals numbered, distributed, and acknowledgement obtained from all the employees? Yes/No

If No, indicate specifications

C Whether in volume 2 enclosure in registered tapal noted? Yes/No
If No, please indicate instances

D Has the Manager checked the tapal register daily? Yes/No
If No, please indicate instance

E Has the Commissioner verified the tapal and distribution of register in the week end? Yes/No

F Whether brought forward D.R. is maintained? Yes/No

G Is the list of over 3 months current tallied with the actual number of currents?
(1) Section:
(2) Name:
(3) Period:

H Whether entries in the D.R. are rounded once a month? Yes/No

4. Personal Register

Sl. No.	*Name*	*Section*	*Duty period*	*Subjects dealt with*

4.1 Is There Abnormal Delay in Initial Action? If So Point Out

Section	*Current number*	*Date of receipt of tapal*	*First action taken*	*Delay*

4.2 Is There Delay in Taken of Follow Up Action? If So, Point Out Cases

Section	*Current number*	*Date of last action*	*Date of next action*	*Delay*

4.3 Is There Delay in Handing Over Closed Files to Record?

Section	*Current number*	*Date of closing the file*	*Date of handing over to record*	*Delay*

4.4 Is reminder diary maintained? Yes/No

4.5 Is there any premature closure of files? Comment to be given after verifying. Closed files. Yes/No

4.6 Are Block Development Officer (Block Panchayat), BDO (Village Panchayat) and Extension Officers taking up inspection of Noon Meal, Village Panchayat/Scheme works/as per advance tour programme?

4.7 Are these inspections instructive and making true evaluation?

4.8 Whether defects pointed out have been rectified?

4.9 Has Extension Officer/Administration/Noon Meals/Schemes checked the Personal Register of the Clerks with the pending Currents?

4.10 Whether the subject heads noted in the Personal Registers are apt?

4.11 Is there any meaningless or unavoidable correspondence?

4.12 While disposing of complaints and petitions, whether proper reasons are recorded and orders obtained?

5. Periodical Register

5.1 Is consolidated periodical register maintained?

5.2 Whether all the periodicals are entered in the register maintained by the Clerk?

Section	*Year*	*Half yearly*	*Annual*	*Monthly*	*Weekly*

5.3 Is calendar of periodicals due for the month is prepared in advance and their dispatch watched by E.O. (Admn.)

5.4 Has certificate been given by the Clerk that all the periodicals entered in the previous years register are entered in the new register?

5.5 Is calendar for periodicals to be sent prepared and posted in the front page of the register? Is there delay in sending periodicals? If so, such cases shall be pointed out.

5.6 Has action been taken to reduce the number of periodicals and to change the periodicity of them?

5.7 Has the periodical register been checked along with personal register as per already drawn up programme?

6. Stock Files

6.1 Has Office order been issued prescribing subjects for which stock files are to be maintained by the Clerks and are the stock files maintained accordingly?

Section	*Stock File*	*Subject*

6.2 Whether index is prepared for Stock File upto the date of inspection?

6.3 Have obsolete and irrelevant orders removed from Stock File?

6.4 If amendments are issued to the earlier orders, whether such amendments are noted in the original reference?

6.5 Is Head of Office checking the stock file during the check of Personal Register?

6.6 Is Stock File maintained properly and orders arranged neatly?

7. Fair Copy Register

7.1 Is the Fair Copy Register maintained in the prescribed form separately for English and Tamil?

7.2 Is the register checked daily by the E.O. (Admn.) and by the BDO once a week?

7.3 Is there delay in Fair copying?

7.4 Note down the delays.

Fair Copy Register

Sl. No. in Fair Copy Register	*Date of Receipt*	*Date of Fair Copying*	*Delay*

8. Attendance Register

8.1 Is attendance register submitted to the BDO (Block Panchayat) and BDO (Village Panchayat) for check?

8.2 Is delayed attendance register maintained

and while signing the register whether Time is noted? For continued delay in Attendance has deduction been made in the Casual Leave or Earned Leave?

8.3 Is the Casual Leave Register maintained properly in the prescribed format.

8.4 Have entries of leave taken checked with attendance register?

8.5 Has additional Casual Leave taken regularised by sanctioning Earned Leave?

9. Establishment Service Registers

9.1 Is Register of Service Register maintained properly?
Whether Service Registers have been opened for all eligible persons as per Fundamental Rules? Is there any person for whom Service Register not opened? Total number of employees, Number of Service Registers opened, Details of appointment, Joining date, Date of Regularisation, Date of Increment sanction, sanction of surrender of Earned Leave, Promotion Details. Have all been entered in the Service Register?
Has any punishment been awarded and if so entry made in the Service Register?

9.2 Whether according to Establishment Rule and Fundamental Rule verification of service. Particulars made and certificate given in the Service Register?

9.3 No. of Service Registers verified during Inspection?

9.4 Whether once in 5 years signature of the Employee obtained in the Service Register?

9.5 Whether in all the Service Registers nomination for G.P.F., DCRG, Special P.F., Family Benefit Fund obtained from the concerned employee and recorded?

9.6 Note down other defects if any noticed in the Maintenance of Service Register? (Example whether Immovable Property Statement obtained) Failure to make Entries of General Educational Qualification, Passing of Special Tests prescribed for qualifying for the post shall be noted.

10. Increment

10.1 Is Increment Register maintained in the prescribed format? Are entries made quarterly? Has the register been checked once a quarter?

10.2 Is there delay in sanction of increment? If so follow up action taken to get them sanctioned?

11. Probation Register

11.1 Is Probation Register maintained to watch declaration of completion of probation?

11.2 Whether this register is checked at the time of P.R. check?

11.3 Is there delay in issuing orders of completion of probation?

12. Register of Superannuation

12.1 Furnish the names of person due for retirement with the details of post held?

Sl. No.	*Name and Post held*	*Whether no objection certificate is obtained from the officers where the individual has previously worked?*	*Date of retirement*	*Whether any audit objection is pending?*

12.2 Is there delay in sanction of pension/gratuity to any persons who have expired after superannuation?

12.3 Is the register maintained in the proper form?

12.4 Has any Officer retired during the period of inspection?

12.5 Has the following terminal benefits been sanctioned to them?
(1) Pension,
(2) GPF,
(3) Encashment of Leave,
(4) Leave on Private Affairs.

13. Temporary Establishment

13.1 Whether temporary establishment register is maintained
13.2 Whether anybody has been suspended from service? If so date of suspension and the present stage of suspension may be furnished.
13.3 Has suspension been ordered on public interest?
13.4 Has action taken to quickly dispose of the disciplinary action taken against the suspended person?
13.5 Whether subsistence allowance is paid as per F.R.53? Is detailed verification done in the above cases.

14. Disciplinary Action

14.1 How many disciplinary actions initiated during the period of inspection?
14.2 Whether proper action taken to dispose of such cases?

15. Office Order Book

15.1 Is Office Order Book maintained?
15.2 Have obsolete orders been removed?

16. Call Book

16.1 Is the register maintained properly?
16.2 Have currents been reopened on the due dates and entered in the P.R.?
16.3 Has the register been checked once in a week by the E.O. (Admn.) and once in a month by the Commissioner?

17. Stamp Account

17.1 Is Stamp Account maintained properly?
17.2 Is the register checked daily by the E.O. (Admn.)?
17.3 While preparing indent for postage stamp whether stamp available is verified by the BDO?
17.4 Does the actual stamps available tally with the Stock as per stamp account?
17.5 Has postage stamps been perforated?
17.6 Is Local Tapal register maintained properly?

18. Local and Outstation Postal Register

18.1 Is the register maintained properly?
18.2 Has the register been checked by E.O. (Admn.), E.O. (Noon Meal), E.O. (Panchayat) and B.D.O.?

19. Arrear List

19.1 Is arrear list as prescribed in G.O. No. 100 P & AR Department, dated 24.2.78 maintained by each individual clerk and is consolidated arrear list prepared?
19.2 Has the consolidated arrear list checked properly?
19.3 Have instructions been given to dispose of currents pending for more than six months?
19.4 List out over six months clerk wise in the format given below?

Section	*Over six months*	*Over one year*	*Total*

20. Office Library

20.1 Have all the books in the Office library verified once a half year?
20.2 Have the Officers not returned the books taken out for a long period?
20.3 Has action been taken to collect the cost of missing books from persons responsible and to return it from the register?

21. Record Room

21.1 Is separate record room maintained?
21.2 Are D.Dis files maintained properly? Are files, ripe for destruction identified and kept ready for destruction?
21.3 Has the B.D.O. approved the list of files ripe for destruction?
21.4 Whether "D.Dis" files converted as "R.Dis"

files are taken to "R.Dis." bundle for the year?

21.5 Are any "D.Dis" or "R.Dis" identified as not necessary to be retained and before this destruction whether BDOs orders obtained?

21.6 Has the BDO signed the list of files destroyed with certificate?

21.7 Has the list of files to be destroyed entered in a register?

21.8 Are there files which has not been returned for more than 3 months?

21.9 Is the Record Issue Register maintained in the proper Form?

22. Diary

22.1 Have all the Officers undertaken tour in all the months during inspection?

22.2 Have Diaries been submitted monthly to the District Collector in time?

22.3 List of Panchayats visited for more than once in a month and purpose of visit?

Month	*Name of the village visited more than once a month*	*Date of visit*	*Purpose*

22.4 Have the BDO (Block Panchayat) and the BDO (Village Panchayat) conducted cursory inspection of not less than 10 village panchayats.

23. Special Tapal Register

23.1 Is a separate register maintained for tapals received from Government and other special letters?

23.2 Is the Head of Office verifying the register everyday?

23.3 Is there delay in sending replies to the special tapals?

Sl. No. in Register	*Section Clerk*	*File No.*	*Date of receipt*	*Date of taking final action*	*Delay*

24. Record Sheets

24.1 Are the Record Sheets maintained and entries have been made upto date?

24.2 Is Defaulter sheet maintained for Basic Servants?

25. Vehicle

25.1 Registration number of vehicle with date of receipt.

25.2 Has the Log Book been written upto date?

25.3 Has abstract been recorded in the Log Book with the average of kilometre per 1 litre of Petrol or Diesel worked out?

25.4 Is Petrol/Diesel issue register maintained?

25.5 Is Expenditure register maintained properly?

25.6 Has the vehicle met with any accident during the period of inspection? Is Accident Register maintained?

25.7 Whether the register of changed spare parts maintained? Has action been taken to remove them from the Stock register and for auction them?

25.8 Is Log Book Part II maintained properly?

25.9 Is attendance register of vehicle maintained?

25.10 (*i*) Has verification of stock of vehicles been made?

(*ii*) Is the quarterly expenditure on vehicle according to the Government Order?

(*iii*) If there is any excess expenditure, has ratification been obtained?

(*iv*) Has the Petrol/Diesel consumption exceeded the ceiling limit?

(*v*) Is monthly servicing done regularly?

(*vi*) Has the vehicle been taken outside the jurisdiction?

(*vii*) Has the vehicle been used for other purpose? Whether proportionate charges have been recovered?

(*viii*) Is Tools and Plant Register maintained?

(*ix*) Has the vehicle been repaired in Private

Workshop? Has any repair been undertaken without the Director's order?

(*x*) Have tyres or battery purchased from private persons?

(*xi*) If Tyres and Batteries are purchased furnish those details.

(*xii*) Is the advance tour programme for the vehicle sent to the Collector?

(*xiii*) Is "C" Form certificate renewed once in 3 years and kept safely?

(*xiv*) Has the vehicle been condemned? Details of condemnation and replacement vehicle to be furnished?

26. Tools

26.1 If sufficient tools and plant required for Office available?

26.2 Whether all the tools and plants entered in the Stock Register and annual stock verification done and certificate given?

27. Stationery

27.1 Is the Stock of Stationery Register maintained in the prescribed form?

27.2 Has Stock verification made every half year?

28. Office Building

28.1 Is there sufficient space available for construction of office building?

28.2 Action taken to construct staff quarters.

28.3 When were the buildings last maintained?

28.4 Have the buildings been constructed in Government land?

29. Accounts Maintenance (Government Fund)

29.1 Verify and comment whether the following Registers are maintained properly?

(a) TNTC.70

(b) Bill Register

(c) Travelling Allowance Register

(d) Acquittance Register

(e) Advances Register

(f) Festival Advance, Handloom, Khadi Advance, Marriage Advance, Cycle Advance Registers

(g) Last Pay Certificate

(h) Cash Book

(i) Family Benefit Fund/Special Provident Fund

(j) Permanent Advance Register

(i) Is Permanent Advance Register maintained properly?

(ii) Whether cash on hand and paid vouchers verified?

(iii) Is there any irregular or unauthorised expenditure from Permanent Advance?

(iv) Are all vouchers exceeding Rs. 500/- Revenue Stamps for Re. 1.00 affixed and cancelled by the BDO.

(k) Contingent Register

(i) Is Contingent Register maintained properly?

(ii) Are the vouchers spent from Permanent Advance recouped by taking the expenditure to Budget Head of Account.

(iii) Whether all adjustment entries are made in Red Ink.

(l) Security Register

(i) Is Security Register maintained in the prescribed format?

(ii) Whether all the securities as entered in Register are physically verified in the year end and certificate furnished?

(iii) Whether these securities have been verified during credit.

(m) Life Insurance Register

(i) Is the monthly recovery of L.I.C. premium of staff watched, recovered and remitted properly and in time by making entries in the register.

(ii) Has the BDO checked the register once in a month?

(n) Cash chest

(i) Is the cash received in the Office kept in the Chest under double lock system?

(ii) Whether cash chest is permanently embedded in the wall?

(iii) Whether any money exceeding Rs. 1000/- available in excess of the limit remitted to the Treasury?

30. Register of Assets

30.1 For all the building works taken up and completed from scheme funds entered in the Register of Assets?

31. Roads-Bridges Register

31.1 Are all the road and bridge works taken up and completed under Scheme Fund entered in the Roads-Bridges Register?

32. Trusts and Contributions Register

32.1 Are all the trust endeavoured Panchayat Union entered in the register and the income from the trust is utilised only for the purpose for which trust is created?

32.2 Are all contributions received entered in the register and its utilisation watched?

33. Lands

33.1 A Register showing lands received by gift maintained?

33.2 Whether all the gift lands received with government permission (or) whether legal opinion was obtained that the Panchayat Union Council will be able to fulfil the purpose.

33.3 Whether the files are closed only after ensuring that all the gift lands are legally transferred to the Panchayat Union?

33.4 Whether all the roads newly formed transferred to Panchayat Union or Village Panchayat or other department for maintenance?

33.5 Whether all the new Survey numbers of lands where road work is done has been properly acquired and rights of Government are proved?

33.6 Whether the register is maintained in the form prescribed in G.O.172, R.D. dated 24.5.1967.

33.7 Whether the lands obtained by acquisition or gift for various purpose are entered village-wise in the Register prescribed in Annexure 2 in G.O.No.172, R.D. dated 24.5.1967?

33.8 Whether Panchayat Union has constructed School Buildings, New Wells or Roads in lands for which Panchayat Union has no right?

33.9 Whether Panchayat Union has taken steps to obtain land on gift for all the works? Attach a list showing the details.

34. Office Procedure

34.1 Whether any post in Panchayat Union Office is vacant? What is the action taken to fill it up?

34.2 Tractor Driver

34.3 Before making any new appointment, is the Panchayat Union consulting Employment Exchange?

34.4 Have all new appointments been made only through Appointment Commission?

35. Village Visiting Roaster

35.1 Are all the villages visited by the Commissioner and all the Extension Officers?

35.2 Has the Commissioner visited atleast one time the village not visited by the Extension Officer? Jeep (Separate particulars to be furnished for each vehicle)

35.3 Registration Number

35.4 Date of supply

35.5 Place of Registration

36. Whether the Following Registers are Maintained Properly?

(a) Log Book

(b) Expenditure Register

(c) Expenditure Register (Repair)

(d) Stock Register

(e) Battery and Tyre Register

(f) Accident Register

(g) Whether monthly periodical on Jeeps sent to Collector?

(h) Register unusable spare parts

(i) Is 'C' Form Certificate kept safely?

(j) As repairs of Jeeps been undertaken in local workshop? If so, is it approval workshop?

(k) Any repair has been undertaken in a private workshop not approved by the Director of Motor Vehicle Maintenance Organisation?

(l) Whether tyres and pumps have been purchased locally?

(m) Whether the conditions for re-treading and condemning of tyres have been fulfilled in purchase of tyres.

(n) As any accident occurred if so, whether due intimation has been sent to the Higher Officer?

(o) Has Advance Tour Programme been drawn up for the Jeep?

(p) Whether it is followed?

(q) As a fuel Petrol or Diesel used? Is the ceiling fixed by the Government? If not whether ratification orders of higher authorities have been obtained?

37. Motor Cycle (Scheme Section)

37.1 Registration Number of Motor Cycle
37.2 Date of supply of Motor Cycle
37.3 Log Book
37.4 Petrol Expenditure Register
37.5 Repair Expenditure Register
37.6 Maintenance of Service Registers of Employees:
(a) Have Service Registers been opened for all the employees?
(b) If any defects in the maintenance of Service Registers.

38. Establishment

38.1 Family Benefit Fund Nomination Register
38.2 As service verification certificate been written in Service Register
38.3 As any entry in Service Register omitted to be attested
38.4 Is Probation Register maintained?
38.5 Is Increment Register maintained?
38.6 Is Superannuation Register maintained?
38.7 Is Temporary Appointment Register maintained?
38.8 Is Record Sheet maintained for the employees?

39. Family Benefit Fund Scheme

39.1 No. of employees included	*Panchayat Union employees*	*Government Servants*	*Total*
(a) No. of sanctioned staff			
(b) No. of staff available			
(c) Is all the eligible staff including staff on foreign service been included in the scheme			
(d) List of amount recovered and remitted into the Treasury tallied with the number of persons included in the scheme.			

39.2 *Nomination:*
(a) Has nomination been received from the persons included in the Scheme
(b) Are the nomination forms been countersigned by the Officer and pasted in the Service Register along with the necessary entries?

40. Accounts Maintenance

(a) Is register of recovery of contribution maintained in Form IV?
(b) Whether the amount recovered is remitted into the Treasury within 15 days from the date of recovery?
(c) Is Sanction and Distribution Register maintained?

41. Union Engineers

41.1 Name of the Union Engineer
41.2 Period of service in the Union during Inspection.
41.3 Is he mantaining the following Registers?
41.4 Register of Estimates (Estimates prepared by the Union Engineer)
Panchayat Union
Village Panchayat
Total
41.5 How many Estimates were sent to the Assistant Executive Engineer for technical sanction?
Union Engineer
Assistant Executive Engineer
Executive Engineer
Total
41.6 How many Estimates prepared by the Union Overseer and how many were technically sanctioned by the Union Engineer?
Panchayat Union
Village Panchayat
Total

41.7 Is register of Bills prepared maintained?

41.8 How many Bills during the current year were prepared and sent to higher Officers for counter signature?

Part Bill

Final Bill

Panchayat Village

Union Panchayat

Total

41.9 Has Administrative sanction been received before according technical sanction?

41.10 Has bill been prepared more than the estimate amount?

41.11 No. of estimates prepared scheme-wise.

Name of the Scheme	*Estimates prepared*	*Works taken up*	*Completed*	*Balance*	*Last year work pending*	*Total (*)*

(*) 1. The balance shall be compared from the estimate and allotment register

2. Has completion report been attached with the final bill?

41.12 (i) Is register of Measurement Books maintained?

(ii) Is list been prepared Measurement Book-wise and the number of works recorded in the each measurement book?

41.13 Has register of check measurement maintained?

41.14 Has Union Engineer test checked the works which are check measured by the Union Overseer?

41.15 Is Stock Register of materials prepared for construction maintained separately?

(1) Cement
(2) Steel
(3) Bitumen
(4) Other items
(5) Engineering Stock Register

41.16 Has the stock been verified by Assistant Director level Officer once in 3 months? Date of last verification sought for and excess details to be furnished.

41.17 As a separate Register to watch the recovery of cost of materials supplied for execution of work maintained and is it checked once in a month with cash book by Extension Officer (Admn.)/Scheme.

41.18 Are the following registers maintained?

42. Registers

(1) Register of Usufruct Trees
(2) Register of Measurement Book
(3) Register of Sanction of Estimates
(4) Register of Tools and Plants
(5) Stock Register of materials on work spot
(6) Contract Register
(7) Periodical Register
(8) Register of check measurement of works by Assistant Engineer
(9) Buildings Register
(10) Roads/Bridges Register
(11) Minor Irrigation Tanks Register
(12) Wells Register
(13) Irrigation Register
(14) Asset Register
(15) Check Measurement Register
(16) Encashment Register
(17) Agreement Register
(18) Schedule of Rate Data Book
(19) Data Book
(20) Register of Supply of Materials Work-wise with Details of Recovery of Cost
(21) Register of Bills Received for Payment
(22) Register of Bills Passed for Payment
(23) Muster Roll for the works taken up under EAS, JGSY etc.
(24) Man-days Generated Register
(25) Person Seeking Employment Register
(26) Block Listed Contractors Register

43. Deputy Block Development Officer

(1) Name of the Deputy Block Development Officer
(2) Period of Service in the Panchayat Union
(3) Total number of Village Panchayats
(4) Is he maintaining the monthly Diary
(5) Is he visiting all the village panchayats in the union atleast once in a month?
(6) Is village visiting roaster maintained?
(7) Is he sent a report on the defects noticed by him during inspection of village panchayats?
(8) Is he obtained proper replies for the Inspection Notes and taking further action?

(9) If serious irregularities are noticed as he taken the notice of Assistant Director (Panchayat) or Assistant Director (Audit)

(10) How many audits completed during current year?

(11) Furnishing the following particulars
1995-96 1996-97 1997-98 1998-99
1999-2000 Total

(12) (a) No. of panchayats to be audited in previous years

(b) No. of panchayats to be audited during current year

(c) Total

(d) No. of audit completed
No. of pending

(e) Reasons for pending

(f) Is audit objection register maintained in village panchayat-wise?

(g) How many objections are pending?

44. Audit Objections Settled and Pending

Year	*No. of objections pending*	*No settled*	*Balance pending*
1995-96			
1996-97			
1997-98			
1998-99			
Total			

44.1 Are separate files maintained for audit objections involving monetary loss?

45. Budget

45.1 Has Budget of the Panchayat Union prepared? If not, action taken to send the budget?

45.2 Has Administration report been received from all the village panchayat? If not, why it has not been received?

46. Extension Officer (Panchayats)

(1) Name

(2) Period of service in the panchayat union

(3) Is he submitting monthly diary regularly?

(4) Is village-visiting register maintained?

(5) Is he inspecting all the village panchayat once a month?

(6) Is general information register of village panchayats maintained?

(7) Is the register verified and additions and deletions carried out?

(8) Is statement in village panchayat Form No.30 received from all the village panchayats in time? Are all vouchers verified once a month?

(9) Is a separate register maintained to watch whether village panchayat conducts monthly meeting regularly?

(10) Whether defects noticed during inspection entered in a register and further action watched?

(11) Whether serious irregularities noticed during inspection listed out and follow up action taken?

(12) Against how many village panchayat presidents action under Section 204 initiated? Furnish details.

(13) How many presidents were removed from service?

(14) Whether additional charge arrangement is made in case of removal of president?

(15) Against how many vice-presidents of village panchayat action taken?

(16) Is proportionate amount of tax collection made every month and how it is monitored?

(17) How many building licences were issued and whether tax assessment is made on completion of construction?

(18) Is layout approval by village panchayat taken up with the approval of Director of Town Planning?

(19) Is proper monitoring done to watch the receipt of grants to the village panchayats by maintaining a separate register?

47. Panchayat Election

(1) Is Electoral Roll of village panchayat available ward-wise and panchayat-wise?

(2) Is register showing the jurisdiction of village panchayat maintained?
(3) Is register of reservation for president/members/SC/woman maintained?
(4) Is the Register of strength of wards maintained?
(5) How many vacancies during current year?
  (i) By resignation
  (ii) By removal
  (iii) Other reasons
(6) Has proposal been sent to the Collector and Election Commission to full up the vacancy?
(7) Is election expenditure proper and with in all limits?
(8) Has he inspected any panchayat work under execution?
(9) Has he visited the Noon Meal Centre allotted to him two times in a month?
(10) Is the register to watch Grama Sabha meetings maintained? Has action been taken against village panchayat who has/which has not conducted Grama Sabha?
(11) Has action been taken to take up works by panchayats under Namakku Namme Thittam?
(12) Has he checked the works of hand pump fitters? Is the register or repairs under taken maintained?

48. Extension Officer (Public Relation)

(1) Name
(2) Service in the Panchayat Union
(3) Is diary submitted every month?
(4) Is the rotation register for visit of village panchayat maintained?
(5) Details of small savings agent register whether maintained and renewed?
How many new agents were appointed in the current year?
(6) How many appointments of small savings agent renewed in time?
(7) Is monthly meeting of agent conducted for review of small savings collection?
(8) How many villages in the panchayat union became cent per cent covered under Rural Development scheme?
(9) Are all the IRDP beneficiaries having Rural Development Accounts?
(10) Is a register showing the number of persons employed both private and Government maintained?
(11) Have all of them been enrolled in pay roll savings scheme? If not, action taken to enroll them.
(12) Is a register of investors in NSC and other small savings securities maintained?
(13) What action is taken to enroll all the villagers under small savings in AMT village?
(14) Is he visiting all the Noon Meal Centre atleast once a month?
(15) What is the target and achievement under Eye camp and other similar camps?
  (i) Medical Camp :
  (ii) Date :
  (iii) No. of beneficiaries :
  Males/Women/Children

49. Extension Officer (Adi Dravida Welfare)

(1) Name
(2) Period of service in the panchayat union
(3) Is monthly diary submitted in time and reviewed?
(4) Is village visiting roaster maintained?
(5) Is register of AD colonies maintained?
(6) Is register of general particulars of AD colonies maintained and is it made update?
(7) Is the register of huts in AD colonies maintained?
(8) Have applications received for group houses entered in a register?
(9) For how many houses one light scheme extended? What is the balance number of such application pending?
(10) Eye camp, small saving camp achievement details.
(11) Has he taken action to get loan sanctioned to Adi Dravidars under IRDP?
(12) Details of action taken to get 'Thadco' loan sanction to Adi Dravidars.
(13) Whether eradication of untouchability camp conducted?

Other Works

(14) Has he taken action to take up works under "Namakku Namme Thittam"?
(15) Is register of bio-gas plant maintained?
(16) What is the target and achievement in the current year?
(17) Is beneficiary register of Chulah scheme maintained?

(18) What is the target and achievement with current year?
(19) What is the target under house hold sanitary latrine and achievement?

50. Extension Officer (Social Welfare)

(1) Name
(2) Period of service
(3) Is every month diary submitted and reviewed?
(4) Is village visiting roaster maintained?
(5) Is the Mahalir Mandrams, Chairperson, members register maintained?
(6) Has any new president been appointed?
(7) What is the target and achievement under the following schemes? Separate statement should be given.
(8) Whether applications rejected intimated to the applicant with reasons for rejection?
(9) Movalur Ramamirthammal marriage assistance
(10) Anjugam Ammiar Inter Caste marriage assistance
(11) Widow's daughter's marriage scheme
(12) Dr. Dharmambal widow's remarriage scheme
(13) Blind persons assistance
 (i) Tricycle
 (ii) Free schoolbooks
 (iii) Free uniforms
 (iv) Free chappals
 (v) Other schemes
(14) Has the E.O. visited all the Noon Meal Centres allotted? If not give reasons?
(15) Is monthly meeting conducted in all Mahalir Mandrams?
(16) Is a meeting conducted monthly once for all Mahalir Mandrams and review of their functioning made?
(17) Has Honorary Award been given once in 3 months?
(18) Whether baby show/women's tour conducted?
(19) Has the entire allotted grant fully been spent?
(20) How many Self-Help Groups are under S.G.S.Y. Scheme? How many are functioning? What action was taken to review them?
(21) Is repayment of revolving fund monitored? Function details of refund bank-wise/Self-Help Group-wise?
(22) Have all the members of Mahalir Mandrams enrolled in constituency development works?
(23) How many small saving camps conducted and what is the collection?
(24) What is the action taken to appoint Mahalir agents?
(25) What is the target and achievement under special camps like Eye camp, Medical camp etc.?

51. Extension Officer (Co-operation)

(1) Name
(2) Period of service
(3) Has monthly diary been submitted in time and reviewed?
(4) What is the target under S.G.S.Y for co-operation institutions?
(5) How many assets were verified?
(6) What is the action taken to put bio-gas plant?
(7) Is recovery camp conducted? In how many camps did he participate and what is the collection?
(8) Are milk animals purchased and attached to milk supply societies for recovery of loan?
(9) Other co-operation department works attended
 (i) Total number of co-operative societies
 (ii) Cultural service society
 (iii) Milk supply society
 (iv) Sheep farming society
 (v) House building society
 (vi) Students co-operative store
 (vii) Vegetable growers society
 (viii) Other co-operative society

52. Extension Officer (Animal Husbandry)

(1) Name
(2) Period of service
(3) Is monthly diary submitted in time and reviewed?
(4) General information register
(5) Is village visiting roaster maintained?
(6) Name of banks, co-operative societies in the panchayat union to be furnished
(7) How many applications are received under S.G.S.Y and how many are sanctioned and asset created? Furnish details in the statement given below.

Asset Verification Target

Month	*Application received*	*Sent to Bank*	*No. of Form III sent*	*Loans sanctioned*	*Asset created*	*Asset verified*
April						
May						
June						
July						
August						
September						
October						
November						
December						
January						
February						
March						

(8) How many applications are received for bio-gas plants and how many are sanctioned? (Order No.____________________)

53. Schemes/Accounts Branch

(1) Name of the Block Development Officer (Panchayats)
(2) Period of service
(3) Name of the Accountant
Extension Officer (Scheme)
(4) Period of service
(5) Are following registers maintained separately for each scheme?
  (i) Cash Book
  (ii) Register of Bills passed for payment
  (iii) Advance recoverable register
  (iv) Deposit register
  (v) Grants received register
  (vi) Miscellaneous receipts register
  (vii) Posting register
  (viii) Pass book
(6) Are all registers closed every month and approval of Commissioner obtained?
(7) Are monthly accounts sent by 10th of every month to the Audit Department and the Panchayat Office?
(8) What is the action taken to adjust advance?
(9) Has any file been closed before adjustment of advance?
(10) Is permit issued for supply of steel/cement? Verify stock register and the actual stock in godown?
(11) Recovery of cost of cement/steel made and voucher number noted in the stock register.
(12) Is audit objection register maintained and updated entries are made?
(13) Year-wise pendency of audit objections to be furnished
Year
Pending
Settled
Balance
(14) Is proper follow up action taken on audit objections?
(15) Wherever loss is pointed out, is separate file opened and follow up action taken?
(16) Has any expenditure in violation of rules pointed out? What is the action taken to get it ratified?

54. Seat Number

(1) Name of Assistant/Junior Assistant
(2) Period of service
(3) Are following registers maintained?
(4) Personal register
(5) Periodical register
(6) Follow up register
(7) Stock file (subject-wise)
(8) Running note file
(9) Are the registers submitted to the Block Development Officer/Commissioner for check on the fixed date?
(10) Has special attention been given on over six months/over one year files?
(11) Is delay noticed in initial action? (Note down some cases)
(12) Is delay noticed in follow up action (Note down some cases)
(13) Is delay noticed in handing over closed files to record? (Note down a few cases)

(14) Is there time delay in sending periodical reports? (Note down few cases)

(15) What are other registers to be maintained in the section and have they been checked by the Commissioner or BDO?

(16) How many audit objections relating to this seat are pending and what is action taken. Verify pending files and give report?

(17) What is the action taken by the Commissioner where proper action has not been taken?

6.9 MISCELLANEOUS

6.9.1 Guidelines for Execution of Works

There are instances that the records and registers (Registers of Measurement Book, Registers of C.M., etc.) maintained by technical wing at various levels are not maintained uptodate. Field level Engineers, viz, UE/AE, Overseers are not submitting their diary properly. Further, instances are many where unusual delay is noticed in estimate preparation, according technical sanction, issue of tender concurrence etc. which causes disrepute to the organization. In some places bills are transmitted through unauthorised person for passing instead of forwarding through official channel. Similarly while measuring the work, necessary entries are not made in the M-Book in the site itself which raises suspicion on the integrity of the staff attending measurement. Surprisingly, Executive Engineers (RD) who are responsible for the control and supervision of the engineering staff are not at all exercising their control resulting in the steady deterioration of work quality at field level. Therefore following instructions are issued for strict compliance.

Executive Engineer (RD), DRDA, is responsible for the overall control and supervision of the activities of technical wing in the district. He should ensure proper quality in the work as per the technical specification of the estimates. He shall immediately after issue of administrative sanction by Collector, segregate the works according to the technical sanctioning authority and issue instructions to prepare estimates to accord technical sanction at appropriate level. He should ensure that in all such cases technical sanctions are accorded within 30 days from date of issue of administrative sanction. Executive Engineer shall cross check the estimate and technical sanction details coming under purview of ADE, UE/AE, Overseers atleast in 5 per cent of the cases after conducting detailed field inspection apart from supervising the progress of these works. The Executive Engineer (RD) should super check atleast 2 works per month costing more than Rs. 3 lakhs.

In the case of tendered works, Executive Engineer shall ensure that estimates are prepared quickly and tender process is competed within 40 days of according Administrative sanction. He shall ensure, tender concurrence is accorded by appropriate authority within 5 days from the date of receipt of this reference and BDO to send the proposal for tender concurrence to the competent authority within 5 days from the date of opening tender. All AEEs/EEs should maintain tender concurrence register in the prescribed proforma scheme-wise.

Executive Engineer (RD) should conduct periodical review meeting of technical wing to ensure prompt action on estimate preparation, according technical sanction etc., and conduct intensive field visit to cross check the quality of work. Following registers relevant to technical side shall be maintained by the appropriate authorities as indicated below:

- BDO – Register of Measurement Book (M-Book)
- UE/AE – Tender register (Scheme-wise)
  – Estimate register (Scheme-wise)
  – Register of check measurement
  – Measurement books
  – Stock registers
- ADE/AEE – Tender register (Scheme-wise)
  – Estimate register (Scheme-wise)
  – Register of check measurement
- EE – Tender register (Scheme-wise)
  – Estimate register (Scheme-wise)
  – Register of check measurement

Tender register, Estimate register at all level shall be maintained scheme-wise in the serial order of date of receipt of such references for easy follow up. Register of measurement book should be maintained by concerned Block Development Officers to keep track of the persons to whom M-Books were issued.

These registers and forms can be printed locally by unions or through District level Co-operative Printing Press by consolidating the indent at district level.

The EEs/AEEs (RD) shall also check stock of materials with the stock register in the Panchayat Unions and add remarks in their notes.

As and when any work reaches stage for measurement, entries should be made directly in the M-Book after ensuring quality and quantity. It should be check measured by the competent authority in the M-Book at the site itself. Check measuring authority shall maintain the register of check measurement in the prescribed format.

When the bills are prepared it should be sent to higher authority through official channel with covering letter for passing of bills. After passing bills, it should be sent to Block Development Officers with covering letter for making payments. Transmitting bills through unauthorized persons will be treated as serious lapse. Any delay in bill preparation, passing of bills and payments, etc will be viewed seriously.

All Overseers, AE/UE, ADE/AEE should submit Fortnightly Progress Reports (FNPR) in the prescribed proforma to their higher authority for review, FNPRs of Overseers, UE/AE will be reviewed by AEE and that of AEE shall be reviewed by EE. Executive Engineer shall send a detailed report every month to Superintending Engineer, covering various aspects of their performance in the district. Sufficient number of copies of FNPRs can be prepared by blocks and circulated for use. Executive Engineer (RD) should take regular inspection of ADE office once in six months and inspect Technical wing of the block office at least once in six months.

The District Collectors, Project Officers are also requested to undertake office inspection of technical wing and ensure that the procedure prescribed are being followed strictly. They are also requested to inspect the on-going and completed works and take deterrent action against the erring officials.

Any violation of the above guidelines will be viewed seriously and would entail disciplinary action.

(CRD Circular No. 106290/98/TU-RD, dated 9th December 1998)

ANNEXURE - I
Register of Check Measurement

Sl. No.	*Name of Work*	*Estimate Sanction No. & Date*	*Estimate Amount (Rs. in lakhs)*	*Value of work done*	*Value check measured, super check measured with date*	*M-Book Page No.*	*Remarks*

ANNEXURE - II
M-Book Register

Sl. No.	*M-Book No.*	*Date of Receipt*	*Date of Issue*	*Issued to*	*Initials*	*Remarks*

Note: M-Book Serial No. should be given from April to March. For example the first M-Book issued in financial year should have serial No.1/98-99 and so forth and so on.

ANNEXURE - III
Part I

Division
Sub-division
Section

Progress Reports of works ——————— in charge of———————
——————————————— from ——— to ——— 19

No. Dated 19

Submitted to the Sub-division Officer / Executive Engineer

Sub-division Officer / Executive Engineer

No. Dated 19

Forwarded to the Executive Engineer / Superintending Engineer

Sub-division Officer / Executive Engineer

No. Dated 19

Returned to the Sub-division Officer / Executive Engineer with remarks

Executive Engineer / Superintending Engineer

No. Dated 19

Forwarded to the Section Officer / Sub-divisional Officer

For note of

Executive Engineer's Superintending Engineers

Remarks and return

Sub-division Officer / Executive Engineer

No. Dated 19

Noted and returned. Sub-divisional
Section Officer

Sub-divisional Officer

Part - II
Memorandum

A. Tanks, Channels and Building inspected for preparation of estimates:
   (1) Number in charge, Tanks – Channels and Building
   (2) Number inspected up-to-date
   (3) Number inspected during the period

B. Preparation of estimates:
   (1) Number of estimates to be prepared
   (2) Number submitted to Sub-divisional Officer or Executive Engineer and sanctioned during the period.
   (3) Number yet to be prepared
   (4) Number of estimates checked

C. Unanswered references.
   Over 10 days old
   Below 10 days old
   Balance at end of last period
   Number received during the period
   Total
   Number disposed of during the period
   Balance

D. Bills:
   (1) Number of works in execution
   (2) Number inspected during the days

(3) Number $\frac{\text{Billed}}{\text{Paid}}$ for

(4) Number of bills check-measured (To be filled by S.D.Os only)

Part - III

Name of work and date of inspection (Date-wise)	*Report by Section or Sub-Divisional Officer*	*Remarks by Sub-Divisional Officer, Executive Engineer or Superintending Engineer*

6.9.2 Maintenance of Panchayat Union Office Building and Other Panchayat Union Buildings by the Panchayat Union

The Government ordered that all the buildings under the control of panchayats and panchayat unions shall be maintained by the concerned local bodies to avoid delay for getting them maintained through Highways and Rural Works Department or other departments who previously maintained them.

(G.O. Ms. No. 22, Rural Development (P-4) Department, dated 22nd January 1997)

6.9.3 Awarding of Prizes to the Best Performing Panchayat Union

The State Finance Commission recommended that the Awards may be given to the presidents and officers of local bodies to encourage their functioning and also for strengthening their institution from out of the incentive fund of the Government. The Government passed the following orders in this regard.

(a) 3 Village Panchayats in a District, 3 Panchayat Unions in a District Level, 3 District Panchayats, 3 Panchayat Unions and 3 Village Panchayats at State Level shall be selected every year and they can be awarded prizes as per Annexure-I of this order.

(b) For awarding of prizes as per Annexure-I, and for conduct of functions at District and State Level an amount of Rs. 10 lakhs is provided. (District level functions at the rate of Rs. 25,000 for 25 Districts, Rs. 7 lakhs and for the State level function Rs. 3 lakhs). Moreover for giving Medals to the selected local bodies sanction is accorded for a sum of Rs. 3.54 lakhs.

(c) For selection of Village Panchayats and Panchayat Unions of District Level, a Committee shall be constituted with the following Members.

President-District Collector

Members:

(1) Additional Collector (Development)/ Project Officer, District Rural Development Agency.

(2) One MLA nominated by the District Collector.

(3) One Social Worker nominated by the District Collector.

(4) One NGO working for the Welfare of Women and Children selected by the President and Members of the District Level Committee.

(5) The respective Assistant Director (Panchayats) of the Districts.

(d) For selection of the best village panchayats, panchayat unions and district panchayat at State Level Committee shall be constituted with following members.

Chairman-Secretary, Rural Development Department

Members:

(1) Director of Rural Development.

(2) One Social Worker nominated by Government.

(3) One NGO working for the Welfare of local bodies nominated by Government.

(4) One MLA nominated by Government.

(e) The following Time-table shall be observed in the selection and awarding of best panchayats as per Annexure-II.

The District Collectors and the Director of Rural Development are requested to take action to form the District Level and the State Level Committees.

The total expenditure involved in this programme, Rs. 1,95,54,000/- (Rupees One Crore Ninety Five Lakhs and Fifty Four Thousand only) shall be sanctioned from Equalisation and incentive grant sanctioned by the State Government.

ANNEXURE-I
Details of Prizes

Awarding of Prizes to 3 Best Village Panchayats at District Level

1st Prize	Rs. 1.00 lakh
2nd Prize	Rs. 0.50 lakh
3rd Prize	Rs. 0.25 lakh
Rs. 1.75 lakhs × 28	Rs. 49.00 lakhs

Awarding of Prizes to 3 Best Panchayat Unions at District Level

1st Prize	Rs. 2.00 lakhs
2nd Prize	Rs. 1.00 lakh
3rd Prize	Rs. 0.50 lakh
Rs. 3.50 lakhs × 28	Rs. 98.00 lakhs

Awarding of Prizes to 3 Best District Panchayats at State Level

1st Prize	Rs. 10.00 lakhs
2nd Prize	Rs. 5.00 lakhs
3rd Prize	Rs. 3.00 lakhs
	Rs. 18.00 lakhs

Awarding of Prizes to 3 Best Panchayat Unions at State Level

1st Prize	Rs. 6.00 lakhs
2nd Prize	Rs. 3.00 lakhs
3rd Prize	Rs. 2.00 lakhs
	Rs. 11.00 lakhs

Awarding of Prizes to 3 Best Town Panchayats at District Level

1st Prize	Rs. 3.00 lakhs
2nd Prize	Rs. 2.00 lakhs
3rd Prize	Rs. 1.00 lakh
	Rs. 6.00 lakhs
Total	Rs. 182.00 lakhs

ANNEXURE-II
Time Schedule for Giving Awards to Loal Bodies

District Level	Last Date
Receipt of Application	May
Scrutiny of Application and selection of Local Bodies	July
Awarding of Prize	August
State Level	
Receipt of application at State level	August
Scrutiny of Application and Selection of Local Bodies	September
Awarding of prize	October

(G.O. Ms. No. 97, Rural Development Department, dated 1st June 1999)

6.9.4 Guidelines for Selection of Best Performing Panchayat Union

(1) The following two methods can be adopted for selection of best performing panchayat union at district level and state level.

(a) Fixing basic criteria for selection of best panchayat union.

(b) Adoption of five point scale to assess the best performing panchayat union.

The panchayat unions which have crossed the stage of (a) only, shall be eligible to enter into the stage; (b) which consists of 100 marks in five point scale.

(2) If any panchayat union has reached any of one or more of the following stages, it shall not be eligible for assessment for selection of best panchayat union.

(a) If any action is taken for removal of chairman or vice-chairman of panchayat union council or pending action of removal of chairman or vice-chairman of panchayat union council under Sections 207, 208 and 212 of the Tamil Nadu Panchayats Act, 1994.

(b) The panchayat union which is not collected its full due of tax and non-tax revenue entitled to the panchayat union.

(c) If any allegation is found while conduct of audit or inspection of panchayat union council in the last year.

(3) After deletion of in eligible panchayat unions, the following scoring method may be adopted and assess the performance of panchayat union.

After assessment is made, the best performing three-panchayat union (1st, 2nd and 3rd) may be selected, according to the marks scored out of 100 marks. If any two panchayat unions have scored the same mark, the maintenance of registers and records of the panchayat union can be assessed and select the panchayat union. If any two or more number of panchayat unions have scored the same marks and if the selection committee is unable to select the best panchayat union, this matter may be entered in the mark meet.

(4) For selection of best performing panchayat union, the following five-point scale questionnaire may be adopted.

Monitoring Indicator for Assessment of Best Panchayat Union

I. Statutory Functions

100 Marks
Each question 4 Marks

Sl. No.	*Item*	*4 Marks*	*3 Marks*	*2 Marks*	*1 Mark*	*Normal*
(1)	(2)	(3)	(4)	(5)	(6)	(7)
1.	Whether council meetings are conducted regularly	6 and above meetings	5 meetings	4 meetings	3 meetings	Less than 3 meetings
2.	Average percentage attendance of members	100%	75% to 99%	50% to 74%	40% to 49%	Less than 40%
3.	Average percentage of women members	100%	75% to 99%	50% to 74%	40% to 49%	Less than 40%
4.	Average percentage of SC/ST members	100%	75% to 99%	50% to 74%	40% to 49%	Less than 40%
5.	Approval of scheme works floating and approval of tender works within stipulated time	100%	75% to 99%	50% to 74%	40% to 49%	Less than 40%
6.	Whether standing committee formed and functioning smoothly	Standing committees formed and all the committees are functioning	Standing committees formed, only 75% of the committees are functioning	Standing committees formed, only 50% of the committees are functioning	Standing committees formed, less than 50% of committees are functioning	Standing committee not formed
7.	Whether panchayat union prepared Annual Plan in time	Yes	–	–	–	No
8.	Whether panchayat union budget approved in due date	Yes	–	–	–	No
9.	Whether any serious audit irregularities pointed during the period under consideration	No	–	–	–	Yes
10.	Whether any complaints about council meeting or council functioning	No	–	–	–	Yes

II. Functions

Sl. No.	Item	4 Marks	3 Marks	2 Marks	1 Mark	Normal
1.	Whether repairs and maintenance of panchayat union schools are carried out properly	Yes	–	–	–	No
2.	Whether repairs and maintenance of sub-centres are carried out and all centres are functioning	Yes	–	–	–	No
3.	Whether all irrigation tanks are maintained properly?	Maintained MI tanks in cycle system properly	Only 15% tanks were maintained	Only 10% tanks were maintained	Only 5% tanks were maintained	Less than 5% of tanks were maintained
4.	Percentage collection of non-tax revenue	100%	75%-99%	50%-74%	41%-50%	Less than 50%
5.	Number of villages in which NNT implemented against total villages and per capital public contribution mobilized	12 villages	9 villages	6 villages	3 villages	Less than 3 villages

III. Scheme Implementation

Sl. No.	Item	4 Marks	3 Marks	2 Marks	1 Mark	Normal
1.	Whether schemes are entrusted within stipulated time for implementation	All the works	75%-99%	50%-74%	30%-50%	Less than 30%
2.	Per Capita investment from General Fund	Out of total General Fund 25% above invested for capital works	Out of total General Fund 20 – 24% invested for capital works	Out of total General Fund 15 – 19% invested for capital works	Out of total General Fund 10 – 14% invested for capital works	Out of total General Fund less than 10% invested for capital works
3.	Whether scheme completed in time percentage completion of works (both Centrally and State sponsored financial)	100%	75%-99%	50%-74%	30%-49%	Less than 30%
4.	Whether active campaign organized as per calendar chart in ANT village	Yes	–	–	–	No
5.	Achievement under Small Savings	100% and above	75%-99%	50%-75%	30%-40%	Less than 30%
6.	Whether any complaints on quality of works received or detected during inspection	No	–	–	–	Yes
7.	Timely settlement of bills	Yes	–	–	–	No
8.	Prompt maintenance of accounts	Yes	–	–	–	No
9.	Whether information on schemes works accessible to public	Yes	–	–	–	No
10.	Involvement of elected representation in inspection and execution of works to keep up quality and time scheme	Yes	–	–	–	No

(G.O. Ms. No. 27, Rural Development (C-1) Department, dated 8th February 2000)

6.9.5 Allotment of Room to M.L.A. in Panchayat Union Office

The Government examined the proposal for providing a separate room for MLAs in panchayat union office and has decided that they need not be given separate room in the panchayat union office. But they permit MLAs to use the meeting hall of the panchayat union in a specific day in a week to hear the grievances of the people and receive petition from the public. The panchayat union council meeting may be avoided on those days in which MLA proposes to use the meeting hall.

(G.O.Ms.No.35, Rural Development (C-l) Department, dated 31st January 1997).

PART VII

RULES AND INSTRUCTIONS RELATING TO DISTRICT PANCHAYAT

7.1 CONSTITUTION OF DISTRICT PANCHAYATS

7.1.1 Constitution of District Panchayat for Chengalpattu – M.G.R. District*

In exercise of the powers conferred by sub-section (1) of Section 24 of the Tamil Nadu Panchayats Act, 1994 (Tamil Nadu Act 21 of 1994), the Governor of Tamil Nadu hereby constitutes with effect on and from the 14th April 1995, a district panchayat for the Chengalpattu – M.G.R. District comprising the local areas forming the panchayat unions specified below, namely:

Name of the panchayat unions:

1. Kancheepuram
2. Wallajabad
3. Uthiramerur
4. Sriperumpudur
5. Poonamallee
6. Kunrathur
7. Kattankulathur
8. Thiruporur
9. Thirukalikundram
10. Maduranthagam
11. Acharapakkam
12. Chithamur
13. Lathur
14. St. Thomas Mount
15. Villivakkam
16. Puzhal
17. Minjur
18. Sholavaram
19. Gummidipoondi
20. Thiruvallur
21. Kadambathur
22. Poondi
23. Ellapuram
24. Thiruthani
25. Thiruvalangadu
26. R.K. Pet
27. Pallipet

(G.O. Ms. No. 56, Rural Development (C-1) Department, dated 13th April 1995)

(*The name of the district has since been changed as Kancheepuram)

7.1.2 Constitution of District Panchayat for North Arcot – Ambedhkar District*

In exercise of the powers conferred by sub-section (1) of Section 24 of the Tamil Nadu Panchayats Act, 1994 (Tamil Nadu Act 21 of 1994), the Governor of Tamil Nadu hereby constitutes with effect on and from the 14th April 1995, a district panchayat for the North Arcot – Ambedhkar District comprising the local areas forming the panchayat unions specified below, namely:

Name of the panchayat unions:

1. Vellore
2. Kaniambadi
3. Anaicut
4. Madhunur
5. Gudiyatham
6. Pernampet
7. K.V. Kuppam
8. Katpadi
9. Wallajapet
10. Sholingur
11. Arakonam
12. Nemili
13. Kaveripakkam
14. Arcot
15. Timiri
16. Tiruppathur
17. Kandhili
18. Natrampalli
19. Alangayam
20. Jolarpet

(G.O. Ms. No. 58, Rural Development (C-1) Department, dated 13th April 1995)

(*The name of the district has since been changed as Vellore)

7.1.3 Constitution of District Panchayat for Thiruvannamalai – Sumbuvarayar District*

In exercise of the powers conferred by sub-section (1) of Section 24 of the Tamil Nadu Panchayats Act, 1994 (Tamil Nadu Act 21 of 1994), the Governor of Tamil Nadu hereby constitutes with effect on and from the 14th April 1995, a district panchayat for the Thiruvannamalai – Sambuvarayar District comprising the local areas forming the panchayat unions specified below, namely:

Name of the panchayat unions:

1. Thiruvannamalai
2. Keelpennathur
3. Thurinjapuram
4. Chengam
5. Pudupalayam
6. Thandarampet
7. Polur
10. Jawadhu Hills
11. Cheyyar
12. Anakkavur
13. Vembakkam
14. Wandavasi
15. Pernamallur
16. Thellar

8. Kalasapakkam
9. Chetput
17. Arani
18. Arani West

(G.O. Ms. No. 60, Rural Development (C-1) Department, dated 13th April 1995)

(*The name of the district has since been changed as Tiruvannamalai)

7.1.4 Constitution of District Panchayat for South Arcot – Vallalar District*

In exercise of the powers conferred by sub-section (1) of Section 24 of the Tamil Nadu Panchayats Act, 1994 (Tamil Nadu Act 21 of 1994), the Governor of Tamil Nadu hereby constitutes with effect on and from the 14th April 1995, a district panchayat for the South Arcot – Vallalar District comprising the local areas forming the panchayat unions specified below, namely:

Name of the Panchayat Union:

1. Cuddalore
2. Gurinjipadi
3. Panruti
4. Annagramam
5. Virudhachalam
6. Kammapuram
7. Nallur
8. Mangalur
9. Keerapalayam
10. Melbhuvanagiri
11. Portanova
12. Kattumannarkoil
13. Komaratchi

(G.O. Ms. No. 62, Rural Development (C-1) Department, dated 13th April 1995)

(*The name of the district has since been changed as Cuddalore)

7.1.5 Constitution of District Panchayat for Villupuram – Ramasamy Padayachiyar District*

In exercise of the powers conferred by sub-section (1) of Section 24 of the Tamil Nadu Panchayats Act, 1994 (Tamil Nadu Act 21 of 1994), the Governor of Tamil Nadu hereby constitutes with effect on and from the 14th April 1995, a district panchayat for the Villupuram Ramasamy Padayachiyar District comprising the local areas forming the panchayat unions specified below, namely:

Name of the panchayat unions:

1. Thirukoilur
2. Mugaiyur
3. Thiruvennainallur
4. Kolianur
5. Kanai
6. Vikravandi
7. Kandamangalam
8. Ulundurpet
9. Thirunavalur
10. Olakkur
11. Mailam
12. Vanur
13. Marakkanam
14. Gingee
15. Melmalayanur
16. Vallam
17. Kallakurichi
18. Chinnasalem
19. Thiagadurgam
20. Sankarapuram
21. Rishivandiyam
22. Kalrayan Hills

(G.O. Ms. No. 64, Rural Development (C-1) Department, dated 13th April 1995)

(*The name of the district has since been changed as Villupuram)

7.1.6 Constitution of District Panchayat for Dharmapuri District

In exercise of the powers conferred by sub-section (1) of Section 24 of the Tamil Nadu Panchayats Act, 1994 (Tamil Nadu Act 21 of 1994), the Governor of Tamil Nadu hereby makes the following amendment to the Rural Development Department Notification No.II/(2)/RUL/1439/(B-11)/95, published at page 8 in Part II-Section 2 of the Tamil Nadu Government Gazette, Extraordinary, dated the 13th April 1995.

2. The amendment hereby made shall come into force on the 28th January, 2004.

Amendment

In the said Notification, for the heading "Name of the Panchayat Unions" and the entries thereunder, the following heading and entries shall be substituted, namely:

"Name of the panchayat unions:

1. Dharmapuri
2. Nallampalli
3. Pennagaram
4. Harur
5. Morappur
6. Pappireddipatti
7. Karimangalam
8. Palacode"

(G.O. Ms. No. 18, Rural Development (C-1) Department, dated 28th January 2004)

7.1.7 Constitution of District Panchayat for Krishnagiri District

In exercise of the powers conferred by sub-section (1) of Section 24 of the Tamil Nadu Panchayats Act, 1994 (Tamil Nadu Act 21 of 1994), the Governor of Tamil Nadu hereby constitutes with effect on and from the 28th January, 2004, a district panchayat for the Krishnagiri District, comprising the local areas forming the panchayat unions specified below, namely:

Name of the panchayat unions:

1. Krishnagiri
2. Kaveripattinam
3. Veppanapalli
4. Bargur
5. Mathur
6. Uthangarai
7. Hosur
8. Shoolagiri
9. Kelamangalam
10. Thally

(G.O. Ms. No. 18, Rural Development (C-1) Department, dated 28th January 2004)

7.1.8 Constitution of District Panchayat for Salem District

In exercise of the powers conferred by sub-section (1) of Section 24 of the Tamil Nadu Panchayats Act, 1994 (Tamil Nadu Act 21 of 1994), the Governor of Tamil Nadu hereby constitutes with effect on and from the 14th April 1995, a district panchayat for the Salem District comprising the local areas forming the panchayat unions specified below, namely:

Name of the panchayat unions:

1. Salem
2. Veerapandi
3. Panamarathupatti
4. Ayothiapattinam
5. Valapady
6. Athur
7. Peddanaickenpalayam
8. Thalaivasal
9. Gangavalli
10. Mecheri
11. Nangavalli
12. Kolathur
13. Omalur
14. Tharamangalam
15. Kadaiyampatty
16. Sankari
17. Edappadi
18. Konganapuram
19. Mac.Donald Choultry
20. Thiruchengodu
21. Mallasamudram
22. Elachipalayam
23. Pallipalayam
24. Namakkal
25. Sendamangalam
26. Kolli Hills
27. Puduchatram
28. Erumaipatty
29. Paramathy
30. Mohanur
31. Kabilamalai
32. Rasipuram
33. Vennandur
34. Namagiripet

(G.O. Ms. No. 68, Rural Development (C-1) Department, dated 13th April 1995)

7.1.9 Constitution of District Panchayat for Periyar District*

In exercise of the powers conferred by sub-section (1) of Section 24 of the Tamil Nadu Panchayats Act, 1994 (Tamil Nadu Act 21 of 1994), the Governor of Tamil Nadu hereby constitutes with effect on and from the 14th April 1995, a district panchayat for the Periyar District comprising the local areas forming the panchayat unions specified below, namely:

Name of the panchayat unions:

1. Erode
2. Modakkurichi
3. Kodumudi
4. Perundurai
5. Uthukuli
6. Chennimalai
7. Dharapuram
8. Mulanur
9. Kundadam
10. Kangeyam
11. Vellakoil
12. Gobichetti-palayam
13. Nambiyur
14. Thookkanaicken-palayam
15. Sathyamangalam
16. Bhavanisagar
17. Talavadi
18. Bhavani
19. Anthiyur
20. Ammapet

(G.O. Ms. No. 70, Rural Development (C-1) Department, dated 13th April 1995)

(*The name of the district has since been changed as Erode)

7.1.10 Constitution of District Panchayat for Coimbatore District

In exercise of the powers conferred by sub-section (1) of Section 24 of the Tamil Nadu Panchayats Act, 1994 (Tamil Nadu Act 21 of 1994), the Governor of Tamil Nadu hereby constitutes with effect on and from the 14th April 1995, a district panchayat for the Coimbatore District comprising the local areas forming the panchayat unions specified below, namely:

Name of the panchayat unions:

1. Palladam
2. Pongalur
3. Sulur
4. Sultanpet
5. Tiruppur
6. Annur
7. Avinashi
8. Pollachi (North)
9. Pollachi (South)
10. Kinathukadavu
11. Gudimangalam
12. Anamalai
13. Udumalpet
14. Madathukulam
15. Madukkarai
16. Karamadai
17. S.S. Kulam
18. Thondamuthur
19. P.N. Palayam

(G.O. Ms. No. 72, Rural Development (C-1) Department, dated 13th April 1995)

7.1.11 Constitution of District Panchayat for Nilgris District

In exercise of the powers conferred by sub-section

(1) of Section 24 of the Tamil Nadu Panchayats Act, 1994 (Tamil Nadu Act 21 of 1994), the Governor of Tamil Nadu hereby constitutes with effect on and from the 14th April 1995, a district panchayat for the Nilgris District comprising the local areas forming the panchayat unions specified below, namely:

Name of the panchayat unions:

1. Gudalur
2. Coonoor
3. Uthagamandalam
4. Kothagiri

(G.O. Ms. No. 74, Rural Development (C-1) Department, dated 13th April 1995)

7.1.12 Constitution of District Panchayat for Thanjavur District

In exercise of the powers conferred by sub-section (1) of Section 24 of the Tamil Nadu Panchayats Act, 1994 (Tamil Nadu Act 21 of 1994), the Governor of Tamil Nadu hereby constitutes with effect on and from the 14th April 1995, a district panchayat for the Thanjavur District comprising the local areas forming the panchayat unions specified below, namely:

Name of the panchayat unions:

1. Thanjavur
2. Budalur
3. Thiruvaiyaru
4. Orathanadu
5. Thiruvonam
6. Kumbakonam
7. Thiruvidaimarudur
8. Thiruppanandal
9. Papanasam
10. Valangaiman
11. Ammapettai
12. Pattukootai
13. Madukkur
14. Peravurani
15. Sethubha-vachatram

(G.O. Ms. No. 76, Rural Development (C-1) Department, dated 13th April 1995)

7.1.13 Constitution of District Panchayat for Nagapattinam – Quaid-E-Milleth District*

In exercise of the powers conferred by sub-section (1) of Section 24 of the Tamil Nadu Panchayats Act, 1994 (Tamil Nadu Act 21 of 1994), the Governor of Tamil Nadu hereby constitutes with effect on and from the 14th April 1995, a district panchayat for the Nagapattinam – Quaid-E-Milleth District comprising the local areas forming the panchayat unions specified below, namely:

Name of the panchayat unions:

1. Nagapattinam
2. Keelaiyur
3. Tiruvarur
4. Kilvelur
5. Nannilam
6. Thirumarugal
7. Kodavasal
8. Koradachery
9. Mayiladuthurai
10. Kuttalam
11. Sembanarkoil
12. Sirkali
13. Kollidam
14. Mannargudi
15. Kottur
16. Needamangalam
17. Thiruthuraipoondi
18. Muthupet
19. Vedaranyam
20. Talanayar

(G.O. Ms. No. 78, Rural Development (C-1) Department, dated 13th April 1995)

(*The name of the district has since been changed as Nagapattinam)

7.1.14 Constitution of District Panchayat for Thiruchirappalli District

In exercise of the powers conferred by sub-section (1) of Section 24 of the Tamil Nadu Panchayats Act, 1994 (Tamil Nadu Act 21 of 1994), the Governor of Tamil Nadu hereby constitutes with effect on and from the 14th April 1995, a district panchayat for the Thiruchirappalli District comprising the local areas forming the panchayat unions specified below, namely:

Name of the panchayat unions:

1. Thiruverumbur
2. Andanallur
3. Manikandam
4. Manaparai
5. Vaiyampatti
6. Marungapuri
7. Musiri
8. Thathaiyangarpet
9. Thottiam
10. Thuraiyur
11. Uppiliapuram
12. Lalgudi
13. Manachanallur
14. Pullampadi
15. Karur
16. K. Paramathy
17. Thanthoni
18. Aravakurichi
19. Kulithalai
20. Krishnaraya-puram
21. Kadavur
22. Thogaimalai
23. Ariyalur
24. Sendurai
25. Thirumanur
26. Jayamkondam
27. Andimadam
28. T. palur
29. Perambalur
30. Veppur
31. Veppanthattai
32. Alathur

(G.O. Ms. No. 80, Rural Development (C-1) Department, dated 13th April 1995)

7.1.15 Constitution of District Panchayat for Perambalur District

In exercise of the powers conferred by sub-section (1) of Section 24 of the Tamil Nadu Panchayats Act, 1994 (Tamil Nadu Act 21 of 1994), the Governor of Tamil Nadu hereby makes the following amendment to the

Rural Development Department Notification No.II(2)/RUL/3318/(G-5), dated the 9th October 1995, published at page of 4 of Part II-Section 2 of the Tamil Nadu Government Gazette, Extraordinary, dated the 9th October 1995, as subsequently amended.

Name of the panchayat unions:

1. Veppanthattai
2. Veppur
3. Perambalur
4. Alathur

(G.O. Ms. No. 1, Rural Development (C-1) Department, dated 1st January 2001)

7.1.16 Constitution of District Panchayat for Ariyalur District

In exercise of the powers conferred by sub-section (1) of Section 24 of the Tamil Nadu Panchayats Act, 1994 (Tamil Nadu Act 21 of 1994), the Governor of Tamil Nadu hereby constitutes with effect on and from the 1st January 2001, a district panchayat for the Ariyalur district, comprising the local areas forming the panchayat unions specified below, namely:

Name of the panchayat unions:

1. Andimadam
2. Sendurai
3. Jayamkondam
4. Ariyalur
5. T. Palur
6. Thirumanur

(G.O. Ms. No.1, Rural Development (C-1) Department, dated 1st January 2001)

7.1.17 Constitution of District Panchayat for Pudukkottai District

In exercise of the powers conferred by sub-section (1) of Section 24 of the Tamil Nadu Panchayats Act, 1994 (Tamil Nadu Act 21 of 1994), the Governor of Tamil Nadu hereby constitutes with effect on and from the 14th April 1995, a district panchayat for the Pudukkottai District comprising the local areas forming the panchayat unions specified below, namely:

Name of the panchayat unions:

1. Pudukkottai
2. Viralimalai
3. Kunnandarkoil
4. Annavasal
5. Thirumayam
6. Ponnamaravathy
7. Arimalam
8. Thiruvarankulam
9. Karambakudi
10. Aranthangi
11. Gandarvakottai
12. Avudayarkoil
13. Manelmelkudi

(G.O. Ms. No. 82, Rural Development (C-1) Department, dated 13th April 1995)

7.1.18 Constitution of District Panchayat for Madurai District

In exercise of the powers conferred by sub-section (1) of Section 24 of the Tamil Nadu Panchayats Act, 1994 (Tamil Nadu Act 21 of 1994), the Governor of Tamil Nadu hereby constitutes with effect on and from the 14th April 1995, a district panchayat for the Madurai District comprising the local areas forming the panchayat unions specified below, namely:

Name of the panchayat unions:

1. Thirupparan-kundram
2. Madurai East
3. Madurai West
4. Melur
5. Kottampatti
6. Vadipatti
7. Alanganallur
8. Usilampatti
9. Sedapatti
10. Chellampatti
11. Thirumangalam
12. T. Kallupatti
13. Kallikudi
14. Periyakulam
15. Andipatti
16. Theni
17. Bodinayakanur
18. Chinnamanur
19. Uthamapalayam
20. Cumbum
21. Kadamalaikundu Myladumparai

(G.O. Ms. No. 84, Rural Development (C-1) Department, dated 13th April 1995)

7.1.19 Constitution of District Panchayat for Dindigul-Anna District*

In exercise of the powers conferred by sub-section (1) of Section 24 of the Tamil Nadu Panchayats Act, 1994 (Tamil Nadu Act 21 of 1994), the Governor of Tamil Nadu hereby constitutes with effect on and from the 14th April 1995, a district panchayat for the Dindigul-Anna District comprising the local areas forming the panchayat unions specified below, namely:

Name of the panchayat unions:

1. Reddiarchatram
2. Athur
3. Dindigul
4. Shanarpatti
5. Natham
6. Nilakottai
7. Batlagundu
8. Oddanchatram
9. Palani
10. Thoppampatti
11. Vedasandur
12. Vadamadurai
13. Guzillamparai
14. Kodaikanal

(G.O. Ms. No. 86, Rural Development (C-1) Department, dated 13th April 1995)

(*The name of the district has since been changed as Dindigul)

7.1.20 Constitution of District Panchayat for Ramanathapuram District

In exercise of the powers conferred by sub-section (1) of Section 24 of the Tamil Nadu Panchayats Act, 1994 (Tamil Nadu Act 21 of 1994), the Governor of Tamil Nadu hereby constitutes with effect on and from the 14th April 1995, a district panchayat for the Ramanathapuram District comprising the local areas forming the panchayat unions specified below, namely:

Name of the panchayat unions:

1. Ramanathapuram
2. Tirupullani
3. Mandapam
4. Tiruvadanai
5. R.S. Mangalam
6. Paramakudi
7. Bogalur
8. Nainarkoil
9. Mudukulathar
10. Kadaladi
11. Kamuthi

(G.O. Ms. No. 88, Rural Development (C-1) Department, dated 13th April 1995)

7.1.21 Constitution of District Panchayat for Pasumpon Muthuramalinga Thevar District*

In exercise of the powers conferred by sub-section (1) of Section 24 of the Tamil Nadu Panchayats Act, 1994 (Tamil Nadu Act 21 of 1994), the Governor of Tamil Nadu hereby constitutes with effect on and from the 14th April 1995, a district panchayat for the Pasumpon Muthuramanlinga Thevar District comprising the local areas forming the panchayat unions specified below, namely:

Name of the panchayat unions:

1. Sivagangai
2. Kalayarkoil
3. Manamadurai
4. Thirupuvanam
5. Ilayangudi
6. Devakottai
7. Kannangudi
8. Sakkottai
9. Kallal
10. Thirupathur
11. Singampuneri
12. A. Pudur

(G.O. Ms. No. 90, Rural Development (C-1) Department, dated 13th April 1995)

(*The name of the district has since been changed as Sivagangai)

7.1.22 Constitution of District Panchayat for Kamarajar District*

In exercise of the powers conferred by sub-section (1) of Section 24 of the Tamil Nadu Panchayat Act, 1994 (Tamil Nadu Act 21 of 1994), the Governor of Tamil Nadu hereby constitutes with effect on and from the 14th April 1995, a district panchayat for the Kamarajar District comprising the local areas forming the panchayat unions specified below, namely:

Name of the panchayat unions:

1. Aruppukottai
2. Kariapatti
3. Tiruuchili
4. Narikudi
5. Virudhunagar
6. Sattur
7. Sivakasi
8. Vembakottai
9. Srivilliputhur
10. Watrap
11. Rajapalavam

(G.O. Ms. No. 92, Rural Development (C-1) Department, dated 13th April 1995)

(*The name of the district has since been changed as Virudhunagar)

7.1.23 Constitution of District Panchayat for Tirunelveli-Kattabomman District*

In exercise of the powers conferred by sub-section (1) of Section 24 of the Tamil Nadu Panchayats Act, 1994 (Tamil Nadu Act 21 of 1994), the Governor of Tamil Nadu hereby constitutes with effect on and from the 14th April 1995, a district panchayat for the Tirunelveli-Kattabomman District comprising the local areas forming the panchayat unions specified below, namely:

Name of the panchayat unions:

1. Palayamkottai
2. Manur
3. Sankarankoil
4. Kuruvikulam
5. Melaneelithanallur
6. Cheranmadevi
7. Ambasamudram
8. Kadayam
9. Pappakudi
10. Nanguneri
11. Kalakadu
12. Valliyur
13. Radhapuram
14. Tenkasi
15. Kadayanallur
16. Alangulam
17. Keelapavoor
18. Shencottai
19. Vasudevanallur

(G.O. Ms. No. 94, Rural Development (C-1) Department, dated 13th April 1995)

(*The name of the district has since been changed as Tirunelveli)

7.1.24 Constitution of District Panchayat for Chidambaranar District*

In exercise of the powers conferred by sub-section (1) of Section 24 of the Tamil Nadu Panchayats Act, 1994 (Tamil Nadu Act 21 of 1994), the Governor of Tamil Nadu hereby constitutes with effect on and from the 14th April 1995, a district panchayat for the Chidambaranar District comprising the local areas forming the panchayat unions specified below, namely:

Name of the panchayat unions:

1. Tuticorin	7. Sathankulam
2. Srivaikundam	8. Kovilpatti
3. Karunkulam	9. Kayathar
4. Tiruchendur	10. Vilathikulam
5. Alwarthirunagari	11. Pudur
6. Udangudi	12. Ottapidaram

(G.O. Ms. No. 96, Rural Development (C-1) Department, dated 13th April 1995)

(*The name of the district has since been changed as Thoothukudi)

7.1.25 Constitution of District Panchayat for Kanniyakumari District

In exercise of the powers conferred by sub-section (1) of Section 24 of the Tamil Nadu Panchayats Act, 1994 (Tamil Nadu Act 21 of 1994), the Governor of Tamil Nadu hereby constitutes with effect on and from the 14th April 1995, a district panchayat for the Kanniyakumari District comprising the local areas forming the panchayat unions specified below, namely:

Name of the panchayat unions:

1. Agastheeswaram	6. Kurunthancode
2. Rajakkamangalam	7. Melpuram
3. Thovalai	8. Munchira
4. Thackalai	9. Killiyur
5. Tiruvattar	

(G.O. Ms. No. 98, Rural Development (C-1) Department, dated 13th April 1995)

7.2 ELECTED REPRESENTATIVES

7.2.1 Disclosure of Assets and Liabilities by Chairman, Vice-Chairman and Members of District Panchayat

1. Short title—These rules may be called the Tamil Nadu Panchayats (Disclosure of Assets and Liabilities by Chairman/Vice-Chairman and Members of District Panchayat) Rules, 1999.

2. Definition—In these rules, unless the context otherwise requires, Member of the Family means person related whether by blood or marriage to the chairman, vice-chairman and members of district panchayat or his wife or her husband and wholly dependant on such chairman, vice-chairman and member

3. Periodical disclosure of assets of chairman, vice-chairman and members of district panchayat—The chairman, vice-chairman and every member of a district panchayat shall

(a) if he is elected after the date of coming into force of these rules, within a period of thirty days, after such election; and

(b) thereafter, at intervals of every twelve months ending with the 31st day of March, furnish in duplicate to the district panchayat in the Form appended to these rules a return of

(i) all properties owned, acquired or inherited by him or his family members including their liabilities; and

(ii) all properties held on lease or mortgage either in his own name or in the name of his family members, including their liabilities together with details of the means by which, or the sources from which such property was acquired or inherited.

4. Returns to be placed at the meeting and to be public document—(1) After the receipt of the return specified in Rule 3 the secretary shall, cause it to be placed at the meeting of the district panchayat and send a copy to the Inspector.

(2) Such return shall be deemed to be a public document and the secretary, with the permission of the district panchayat, may, subject to such condition including payment of fees specified in Rule 5 give to any person on demand a copy of such return.

5. Fee for furnishing return—The fee for furnishing a copy of any return or part thereof shall be ten rupees or the amount to be fixed by the Government from time-to-time.

(G.O. Ms. No. 182, Rural Development (C4), 30th August 1999)

APPENDIX

Form

(See Rule 3)

Returns of Assets and Liabilities of the Chairman, Vice-Chairman or Member of the ________________ District Panchayat as on the ______________________________

Name of the____________________________

Date of election:

Part I – Assets and Liabilities of the ____________________________________

1. Immovable Property

(a)	*Land*	*Owned*		*Wet*	*Dry*	*Irrigated dry*
	Extent: Date of acquisition: Value of acquisition: Leased in: Extent: Date of acquisition: Value of acquisition:					
(b)	*Building* Plinth Area: Date of acquisition: Value of acquisition	*Owned*	*Terraced*	*Tiled*	*Thatched*	*Purpose for which the building is used: commercial or residential*
	Plinth Area: Date of acquisition: Value of acquisition:	*Leased in*	*Terraced*	*Tiled*	*Thatched*	*Purpose for which the buildings is used commercial (or) residential*

2. Business interests:
   (a) Shares
   (b) Stock
   (c) Scrip
   (d) Partnership
   (e) Debentures and securities
3. Other interest:
   Bank Account
4. Jewellery:
   (*i*) Gold
   (*ii*) Precious stones
   (*iii*) Silver Ware
5. Movables (including motor vehicles)

6. Details of Trusts with which he has any connection
7. Remarks, if any, of the ____________________
   (Explain the nature of acquisition of properties)
8. Liabilities

Part II – Assets and Liabilities of his family members

Name of the Family member ____________________

1. **Immovable Property**

(a)	*Land*	*Owned*		*Wet*	*Dry*	*Irrigated dry*
	Extent: Date of acquisition: Value of acquisition: Leased in: Extent: Date of acquisition: Value of acquisition:					
(b)	*Building* Plinth Area: Date of acquisition: Value of acquisition	*Owned*	*Terraced*	*Tiled*	*Thatched*	*Purpose for which the building is used: commercial or residential*
	Plinth Area: Date of acquisition: Value of acquisition:	*Leased in*	*Terraced*	*Tiled*	*Thatched*	*Purpose for which the buildings is used commercial (or) residential*

2. Business interests:
   (i) Shares
   (ii) Stock
   (iii) Scrip
   (iv) Partnership
   (v) Debentures and securities
3. Other interest:
   Bank Account
4. Jewellery:
   (*i*) Gold
   (*ii*) Precious stones
   (*iii*) Silver Ware
5. Movables (including motor vehicles)
6. Details of Trusts with which he has any connection
7. Remarks, if any, of the ____________________
   (Explain the nature of acquisition of properties)
8. Liabilities

DECLARATION

I _________________________ declare that to the best of my knowledge and belief and the information furnished in the above return is true and complete.

Place:
Date:

Signature

7.2.2 Travelling Allowance to Members of District Panchayats

1. Short title—These rules may be called the Tamil Nadu District Panchayats (Payment of Travelling Allowance to Members) Rules, 1997.

2. Definition—In these rules:

(1) "Act" means the Tamil Nadu Panchayats Act, 1994 (Tamil Nadu Act 21 of 1994), and

(2) all other words and expressions used in these rules but not defined therein shall have the meanings respectively assigned to them in the Act.

(a) Every member who attends a meeting of the district panchayat shall be entitled to travelling allowance, daily allowance and sitting fees as may be notified by the Government from time-to-time.

Note— The word 'member' in this notification shall include the chairman and the vice-chairman of the district panchayat.

(b) Elected members of the district panchayat need not produce certificates that they travelled by the class by which travelling allowance is claimed. Such certificates need not be insisted on in passing the claim.

(c) The above rates of travelling allowance, mileage and daily allowance will apply to elected members when they are deputed on an enquiry of inspection either as single person or in a committee.

(d) (1) When any elected member of the district panchayat claims travelling allowance or daily allowance for journeys or halts made for any business connected with a meeting of the district panchayat, the claim shall be preferred to the Chief Executive Officer in the form specified in that behalf by him.

(2) Claim for travelling and daily allowance shall be preferred by an elected member within a period of two months from the date of completion of journey for which the claim is preferred.

(3) Other members shall draw their travelling and daily allowances from the sources from which they draw their pay, in the usual course.

(4) In preferring the claim against the Government, a certificate to the effect that a member himself has not claimed or drawn any travelling or daily allowance from any other source for the same period shall be furnished by him in the bill.

(e) (1) The claim for travelling and daily allowances of elected members shall after scrutiny and countersignature by the Chief Executive Officer or any person authorized by him in this behalf be drawn by him and disbursed to the members.

(2) Before countersigning the travelling allowance bills of members of the State Legislature and the Members of Parliament, the Chief Executive Officer or any person authorized by him in this behalf should ascertain from the Legislative Assembly Secretariat, whether the members concerned have been paid any allowances for the same journeys and period for which travelling allowance is claimed in their bills and the Legislative Assembly Secretariat shall, after satisfying itself that no such payment has been made, furnish a certificate of non-payment when such bills are referred to it.

(G.O.Ms.No.177, Rural Development (C-1) Department, dated 9th June 1997)

7.3 POWER AND FUNCTIONS

7.3.1 Submission of Annual Reports

1. Short title—These rules may be called the Tamil Nadu District Panchayats (Submission of Annual Reports) Rules, 1999.

2. Definition—In these rules, unless the contest otherwise requires, "Act" means the Tamil Nadu Panchayats Act, 1994 (Tamil Nadu Act 21 of 1994).

3. Submission of annual return—Every district panchayat shall prepare and furnish in the format specified in Appendix A an annual report consisting of the following particulars, namely:

(i) Name of the district panchayat area, population, demographic features, village panchayats and panchayat unions in the district;

(ii) Composition of district panchayat and its committees, functioning of the district panchayat and committee including important resolutions passed;

(iii) Sectoral planning and district planning undertaken under sub-section (3) of Section 240 of the Act;

(iv) Powers and functions exercised under Sections 163 and 164 of the Act, nature of advice tendered by district panchayat to Government and panchayats;

(v) Exercise of powers and responsibilities entrusted under Section 257 of the Act and other powers exercised under the Act;

(vi) Details of schemes executed by district panchayat for the Government and Government of India and for any other agency including its aim specifically and poverty alleviation rural development and other programmes, and schemes implemented in any of the subjects assigned under Section 257 of the Act;

(vii) Statement of income and expenditure of district panchayat during the year, funds received as per State Finance Commission, devolution from State Government, grants received from the government and Government of India, Scheme funds received for the development programmes—their sources, use and applications during the year schemes implemented under Government of India, Finance Commission grants;

(viii) Audit of accounts, audit certificate including observation made;

(ix) District panchayats interaction with district administration, District Collector, District Rural Development Agency, Lead banks, Co-operatives, panchayat unions, village panchayats and development departments;

(x) Studies, consultation undertaken and reports prepared for the development and welfare schemes of the districts;

(xi) Analysis of past performance, current status and future of the district in the overall economic development of the State.

4. Particulars of elected member—Every district panchayat shall furnish particulars of its elected members as specified in Appendix B.

5. Income and expenditure statement—Every district panchayat shall furnish income and expenditure statement as specified in Appendix C.

6. Activities—Every district panchayat shall furnish its activities taken during the year reported upon as specified in Appendix D.

7. Preparation of annual report—District panchayat shall prepare the annual report referred to under Rule 3 for the previous financial year before the 30th September in the succeeding financial year with audit certificate and statement as required by the Director of Local Fund Audit. The district panchayat shall approve the annual report before the 30th of October in the succeeding financial year. After approval of annual report the same shall be signed and sealed by the Chairman and Secretary respectively.

8. Submission of annual report to Government—Every district panchayat shall send 500 copies of annual reports in Tamil and English to Government before the thirtieth day of November. Two sets of annual reports shall also be sent to District Collector/Inspector and two sets of annual reports shall be transmitted to the Director of Rural Development before thirtieth of November in the succeeding financial year. The Director of Rural Development shall forward the annual reports of the district panchayats with his views thereon before the thirty-first of December in the succeeding financial year to Government. After scrutiny, the Government shall lay all such reports within reasonable times with their comments thereon the Table of the legislature as provided in sub-section (2) of Section 165 of the Act.

(G.O. Ms. No.23, Rural Development (C4) Department dated 1st February 1999)

APPENDIX A

(See Rule 3)

Annual Report on District Panchayat for the year_______________(Year to be mentioned)

1. Name of the district
2. Total geographical area of the district
3. Population of district
   Male____________ Female __________
   SC______ST_____ BC/MBC________Total
4. Number of panchayat unions/taluks
5. Number of villages
6. Number of village panchayats
7. Name of panchayat unions
8. Composition of district panchayat (Details to given in Annexure I):
   (1) Total number of members in the district panchayat
   (2) ST/SC/ST (W)/SC (W)/Women/General
   (3) Name of the chairman
   (4) Name of the vice-chairman
   (5) Whether any casual vacancy for any post occurred during the period under report
   (6) Action taken to fill it up
   (7) Number of meetings held
   Ordinary
   Urgent
   Special
   (8) Whether the meetings have been conducted regularly (sixty days shall not lapse between two meetings).
   (9) Follow up action taken on the resolution of the district panchayats.
   (10) Number of standing committees according to subjects.
   (11) Number of members of each committee
   (12) Function of each committee.
   (13) Brief on the proceedings of each of the Committees__________
   (14) Details of sectoral programmes enumerated in Schedule IV of the Act being implemented by the district panchayat along with staff and financial outlay during the year_________
   (15) Details of the State Sector Schemes (other than mentioned in column (13) if any, being implemented by district panchayat.
   (16) Details of entrustment of powers in respect of 29 items to the district panchayat (relevant Government orders to be indicated) and action taken in pursuance of entrustment (separate report to be annexed).
   (17) Personnel
   (a) transferred to district panchayat from each of the departments;
   (b) personnel working on deputation basis.
   (18) Role of district rural development agency and district panchayat in the district development efforts.
   (19) Role of MPs and MLAs in district panchayat (Minutes of the meetings to be scrutinized to examine their role).
   (20) Methodology for the preparation of annual plan for the district (A simple copy of the plan prepared by the district panchayat for the current or preceding year to be attached).
   (21) Budget estimates:
   (i) Whether the Budget has been prepared by the district panchayat and duly passed in its meeting?
   (ii) Has the Inspector scrutinized the Budget and returned with comments if any?
   (iii) Has the Budget finally been passed by the district panchayat in its meeting duly incorporating the suggestion and remarks of the Inspector?
   (22) Duties of Secretary (Job Chart to be attached)
   (23) Duties of other officers of the district panchayat (Job Chart to be enclosed).
   (24) Powers of Chairman (Functional distribution of powers to be enclosed).
   (25) Party-wise affiliation of the district panchayat members.
   (26) Number of elected representatives trained so far.
   (27) Number of officials trained so far.
   (28) General powers of the district panchayat (Copy of the order to be attached).
   (29) Statement of income and expenditure of district panchayat during the year_____
   (i) Details of receipts and expenditure to be furnished separately as Annexure.
   (30) (a) Financial Devolution as per State Finance Commission Report (Otherwise).
   (b) The Devolution of Tenth Finance Commission Grant to district panchayat.

(31) Amount of grants devolved to the ________ district panchayat (Rs. in lakhs) ________ in each year__________

(32) District panchayat fund (Details to be furnished):
(a) What is the percentage of expenditure from district panchayat funds of the district panchayat:
(i) for maintenance
(ii) on capital items
(iii) any other items

(33) Can district panchayat raise loans? If any, provide details.

(34) Management of common property resources of the district panchayat (Give details).

(35) Mechanism for supervision and control of the Government over the district panchayat (Furnish rules and Government orders).

(36) Composition of District Planning Committee and role of the Chairman, district panchayat.

(37) Functions of District Planning Committee (copy of the order to be enclosed).

(38) Maps, statistics, district profile, etc., to be attached.

(39) Activities performed by district panchayat during the year (____________)

(40) Particulars of different departments operating at the district level where district panchayat has interactions (example Electricity Board, Banks, Public Works Department, Highways, Forest, etc.)

(41) Particulars of different departments which are functioning under the direct control of district panchayat.

(42) Organizational chart of all administrative units with staffing pattern functioning at the district panchayat.

(43) Annual administration reports (attach copies for two years).

(44) Role and involvement of district panchayat in the implementation of various Rural Development and Poverty Alleviation Programmes.

(45) Interaction between district panchayat with District Rural Development Agencies (DRDAs).

(46) District level plan aggregation activities undertaken for last two years.

(47) Any other items (Please specify and furnish details).

APPENDIX B
(See Rule 4)

Sl. No.	*Name*	*Sex*	*Age*	*Caste*	*Education*	*Occupation*	*Size of holding*	*Monthly income*

APPENDIX C
(See Rule 5)

Income and Expenditure of District Panchayat

Sl. No.	*Source of income*	*Year*	*Year*	*Sl. No.*	*Source of expenditure*	*Year*	*Year*

APPENDIX D

(See Rule 6)

Activities of the District Panchayat (Year)

Sl. No.	*Activity*	*Total value of works*	*Value of contribution obtained from panchayat fund*	*People's contribution*

Secretary,

________________________District Panchayat.

Place:

Date:

Seal of the District Panchayat

7.3.2 Preparation and Submission of Administration Report of District Panchayat

1. Short title—These rules may be called the Tamil Nadu Panchayats (Preparation and Submission of Administration Reports of Panchayat Union Councils and District Panchayats) Rules, 1999.

2. Definition—In these rules, unless the context otherwise requires, "Act" means the Tamil Nadu Panchayats Act, 1994 (Tamil Nadu Act 21 of 1994).

3. Preparation of consolidated administration report—The Commissioner of every panchayat union council shall, as soon as may be not later than 30th June every year, prepare a consolidated report on the administration of the panchayat union council and on the administration of all village panchayats in the panchayat union during the preceding year in two parts, namely (a) embodying the particulars specified in Appendix A; and (b) the annual account indicating income and expenditure of the panchayat union during the year in Appendix B.

4. Prescribed date for submission of report—Once the Administration Report along with audit report is ready, their copies shall be supplied to the members of the panchayat union council in advance before they meet to consider the report. Ten copies of the report together with a copy of the resolution of the panchayat union council shall be submitted to the district panchayat not later than the 30th September of the year following that to which the report relates. The report and the resolution of the council thereon shall be kept in places accessible to the public, one such copy being affixed to the notice board of the office of the panchayat union council.

5. Prescribed date for submission of general report on the administration by district panchayat—The date before which the district panchayat shall submit the general report on the administration of panchayat union councils and village panchayats to the district panchayat to the Government, with a copy of the Inspector referred to in sub-section (3) of Section 99 of the Tamil Nadu Panchayats Act, 1994 (Tamil Nadu Act 21 of 1994) shall be the 30th October of the year following that to which the report relates.

6. Publishing the general report on the administration—The general report and the resolution of the district panchayat shall be published in the district gazette and be kept in places accessible to the public in the district, copies being affixed in the notice board of the office of the district panchayat and Inspector.

(G.O. Ms. No. 247, Rural Development (C-4) Department, dated 3rd December 1999)

APPENDIX A

(See Rule 3)

Consolidated Report on the Administration of the _____________ Panchayat Union Council and Village Panchayats in the said Panchayat Union in the _______________ District Panchayat for the year _____________

I. Constitution and Management

1. **Jurisdiction**
   (i) The area of the panchayat union as on 31st March of the year to which the report relates in square kilometres.
   (ii) Changes in the jurisdiction of the panchayat union during the year under report, if any.
   (iii) Total number of wards.
   (iv) Number and names of village panchayat coming with in the panchayat union.
   (v) Details of population (as per latest available census figures), (a) Male, (b) Female, (c) Total, (d) Density of population per square metre, (e) Schedule Caste/Schedule Tribe population, (f) Percentage of women population in total population, (g) Percentage of Schedule Caste/Schedule Tribe population in total population.
2. **Personnel**
   (i) The council, break up details of members and (a) Number of Schedule Caste and Schedule Tribe members including women, (b) Number of other women members, (c) Others, (d) Vacancy, if any (e) Total number of members items (a)+(b)+(c)+(d).
   (ii) Changes, if any, in the total strength.
   (iii) Number of seats fell vacant (with ward members and category of reservation) and date from which they were vacant.
   (iv) Was election of members ordinary or casual, held during the year and if so date of election?
   (v) Whether elections have been held and seats filled up within six months from the date of vacancy?
   (vi) Date of first meeting after the ordinary election.
3. **Holders of Different Offices**
   (i) Chairman and vice-chairman: Briefly state on each of them mainly on the following:
   (a) Name and party affiliation,
   (b) Date of election and ward he represents,
   (c) Date of taking oath and date of first meeting after ordinary election,
   (d) Removal of chairman, if any, and
   (e) No-confidence motion, if any, moved.
   (ii) Panchayat Union Commissioner, Block Development Officer (Panchayats), Deputy Block Development Officer Extension Officers: Indicate names, date of joining etc. on each of them.
4. **Election**—(i) Ordinary election, (ii) Casual Elections, and (iii) Election disputes. Provide brief on the elected members and election disputes, if any.
5. **Panchayat union council meeting**—Provide details of meeting conducted, ordinary, urgent special with dates and subjects decided, attendance of members at meetings—average percentage of attendance; and number of meetings adjourned if any for want of quorum with dates (ii) Total number of subjects (a) Taken up in agenda, (b) Number disposed of, (c) Number of items adjourned once or more with reasons therefor, and (d) number of items on which action needs to be initiated, number disposed of and number pending.
6. **Committees**—Details of statutory committees and other committees formed, meeting held, with summary of working of the committees. Furnish details on Joint Committees, if any and the work done by them.
7. **Establishment**—What is the sanctioned strength? What is the cost of establishment? Expenditure incurred on plaints and suits and on law charges. Location of the panchayat union office. Was the building repaired during the year and if so the expenditure incurred? Are the prescribed forms and registers maintained?

8. **Roads, bridges, ferries and buildings**

(a) Roads (i) Provide details on road density and facilities of (a) National Highway, (b) State Highways, (c) Major district roads, (d) Other district roads, (e) Panchayat union roads, and (f) Village panchayat roads.

Furnish the following information on panchayat union roads:

(a) Cement concrete	No ...length
(b) B.T.	No ...length
(c) Metalled	No ...length
(d) Gravelled	No....length
(e Earthen	No....length
Total	No....length

(ii) Bus route roads—No.... length, Number of hamlets covered by route buses and town buses, (iii) the expenditure on the maintenance of panchayat union roads, with comparative figures for the last three years, (iv) whether a programme has been drawn up for block-topping of metalled roads and unmetalled roads, (v) was any road transferred to the control of State Government and if so the length? was any road taken over from village panchayats and if so, the number and length, (vi) Any encroachments of roads and the condition of roads, (vii) Details of gangmazdoors and road inspectors employed and expenditure incurred on them.

(b) Bridges—(i) Details of capital works such as bridges, causeway and culverts incurred in the year. Percentage of such expenditure to the total amount spent on roads, (ii) Number of bridges, culverts, causeways etc. improved, repaired and the expenditure incurred during the year, (iii) amount spent on (a) new works, (b) repairs.

(c) Ferries—What is the total receipt and charges, the rate of charges, the method of collection and the convenience offered?

(d) Panchayat union buildings and other assets—(i) The building and other assets that are maintained by the panchayat union; (ii) Any work of improvement and maintenance like white washing, colour washing, painting carried out and the expenditure thereon; (iii) Whether any maintenance grant received under any scheme, and give details; (iv) Was any new asset created or new building completed and if so under which scheme?

9. **Choultries, rest sheds, bus shelters and water sheds**—(i) Number of choultries, rest sheds, bus shelters and water sheds maintained; the receipt and charges therefrom; (ii) Endowments if any for choultries and water shed and their condition; (iii) Cost of free feeding, if any and number of persons fed.

10. **Tools**—Plant machinery and stores: (i) Total ordinary expenditure on tools, plants, and stores; (ii) Percentage of such expenditure on communication; capital expenditure on tools plants and machinery or vehicle; and expenditure on repair charges, Petrol, Oil and Lubricant charges and their maintenance.

11. **Lighting**—(i) Number of street lights installed, under different categories. Expenditure incurred on new installation and cost of maintenance of existing street lights.

12. **Medical**—(i) Number of PHCs, rural dispensaries and other public medical institutions in union area, the average population served by each institution; (ii) Number of medical officers and other paramedical and contingent staff of panchayat union, (iii) Number of private medical institutions, hospitals, dispensaries and practitioners in the panchayat union area.

13. **Health service**—(i) Number of patients treated for minor ailments by the rural dispensary and the expenditure per patient, expenditure on doctors, non-medical staff and medicines. (ii) Is there any maternity ward, or inpatient facility available and if so the number treated as inpatients and deliveries in the maternity ward, (iii) Accommodation equipment etc. details may be given.

14. **Maternity relief and family welfare**—(i) Number of maternity and child welfare centres functioning. Do they workout to one centre for every 10,000 population. Do they have own building and facilities. Number of panchayat union staff employed for these centres and the expenditure incurred by the panchayat union. (ii) Family welfare: (a) What is the birth rate, death rate, net population growth rate, and infant mortality rate, maternity mortality rate in the panchayat union area. (b) Number of vasectomy and sterlisation done in the union area.

15. **Endemic and epidemic diseases**—(i) The steps taken on the preventive measures to control diseases affecting pregnant women, mother and children, and on communicable diseases. (ii) Value of medicines, vaccines and other materials supplied to the public health staff for prevention of diseases.
16. **Sanitation**—(a) Number of houses and percentage of houses having house flush out toilets and school toilets. What is the general sanitary condition in the panchayat union? Name the villages where all houses have toilets. (b) Food adulteration: (i) Steps taken to control food adulteration by means of licensing of hotels, sweet meat shop etc. (ii) Whether the food adulteration act has been extended to the union area? (iii) Whether the conditions of licence enforced?(c) Dangerous and offensive trades: (i) What are all the trades identified and number of licences issued trade-wise, amount collected by way of fees village panchayat-wise, and furnish other details. (ii) Indicate details an industrial pollution affection the environments and if so what steps taken by the union to prevent such pollution.
17. **Water supply**—(i) Total number of habitation having 300 population and above and of which how many have piped water supply and 40 litres per capita water supply. (ii) Total number of habitation having bore well pumps, hand pumps. (iii) Number of water supply installations available in the union (hand pumps, power pumps, Ground Level Reservoir, Over Head Tank etc.). (iv) Number of houses having water supply connections and water charges collected by village panchayats during the year.
18. **Fairs and festivals**—Notified fairs and festivals controlled by the panchayat union, dates of such festivals, estimated number of persons visiting the festivals, special arrangements made for the health and comfort of such persons, the expenditure incurred for such arrangements and the receipt by way of auction and issuing licences to shops in the fair and other receipts.
19. **Veterinary service and dairy development**—(i) Number of veterinary dispensaries functioning with location, number of animals treated. (ii) Artificial insemination centres and sub-centres functioning. (iii) Is the veterinary relief adequate? (iv) Number of milch animals in the panchayat union dairy co-operative and furnish information on the same.
20. **Eradication of untouchability**—(i) Protection of Civil Rights Act, 1955, State the steps taken to eradicate untouchability in the union, with special reference to service of tea in tea stalls and meals in hotels; and (ii) Number of prosecution filed under the Protection of Civil Rights Act and the result of prosecution?
21. **Markets**—(i) Panchayat union and village panchayat markets, location, periodicity, receipt and charges from the markets, improvements carried in the year and the development needed for better services and income; (ii) Private markets, number, licence fee realised, enforcement of licence conditions; (iii) Factories and industries located in the panchayat union; (iv) Industrial units run by the panchayat union, production, sales, expenditure, and profit loss, may be furnished.
22. **Social forestry**—(i) Number and variety of trees available in panchayat union roads and tanks, (ii) What is the auction amount fetched by way of leasing the enjoyment of the usufructs of such trees for the last three years, (iii) Steps taken to plant more trees on vacant road sides and tank beds, (iv) Whether forest department has been permitted to raise social forestry in tanks and if so the name of tank, extent covered, (v) Number of prosecutions launched for illicit tree cuttings.
23. **Land encroachment**—(i) Road side stalls. Are those obstructing traffic flow? What is the receipt by way of collection of fees from such stalls? (ii) Encroachments: (a) Number of encroachments existing, licensed and pending; (b) Number of encroachment found to be objectionable on inspection by Commissioner; and (c) Number of encroachments reported by Village Administrative Officer and action taken to remove such encroachments.
24. **Land utilisation and irrigation**—Extent of land cultivated: (i) Extent of land (a) Wet (b) Dry. (ii) Net cultivated area (a) Wet (b) Dry, (iii) Gross cultivated area (a) Wet (b) Dry. (iv) Source of irrigation (a) Wells (b) Tanks (c) Channels (Length in kilometre) (d) others. (v) Number of tanks vested with panchayat union and village panchayats. (vi) Number improved or desilted during the year, and

expenditure incurred. Execution of Kudimaramath. Amount of excess Kudimaramath grant sanctioned by Government. Number of sources taken up for Kudimaramath, number completed and area covered, amount of Kudimaramath fees levied by panchayats.

25. **Financial position**—(1) Income: (i) Land revenue, (ii) Rate of local cess surcharge, (iii) Rate of local irrigation fees. (2) The opening and closing balances and the extent of the total receipts and expenditure during the year. (3) Balance pertaining to remunerative enterprises government grants and loans due by the union. (4) Ways and means position during the year. (5) (i) Receipt and expenditure on all accounts, and (ii) Receipts and expenditure under general account ordinary.
26. **Capital expenditure**—(a) Total expenditure on capital works: (i) on development works entrusted, (ii) other items, (iii) government grant received on the development works and contribution if any paid from panchayat union funds, and (iv) expenditure incurred from loans.
27. **Debt**—Debt at the beginning of the year, incurred during the year, repaid during the year and balance at the close of the year. Total interest paid on debt on account of the arrears of previous year and for the year under reports.
28. **Investment**—Details of amount invested, year of investment, nature of securities, interest, date of maturity etc.
29. **Audit**—Inspection remarks of Assistant Director of Local Fund Account.
30. Furnish details of assets and liabilities.
31. Visit of distinguished persons notable activities of the panchayat union council during the year.

APPENDIX B

(See Rule 3)

Income and Expenditure of Panchayat Union

Sl. No.	*Source of Income*	*Amount Rs.*	*Sl. No.*	*Head of Account for expenditure*	*Year*	*Amount Rs.*
(1)	(2)	(3)	(4)	(5)	(6)	(7)

7.3.3 Duties and Responsibilities of District Panchayat

(1) Sections 163, 164, 165 and 166 of the Tamil Nadu Panchayats Act, 1994 specify the functions, powers and duties etc., of district panchayats.

(2) The district panchayat, as envisaged in Section 163 of the Tamil Nadu Panchayats Act, 1994 has an advisory role and the Government direct that it should function as a forum for discussing the progress of various development schemes in the rural areas of the district, in a manner similar to the District Development Council.

(3) The Government also direct that

(i) the staff of district panchayats be treated as Government Servants on deputation and be paid only from Government funds;

(ii) the appointing authority for such Officers shall have the power of disciplinary control over such Officers; and

(iii) the accounts of the district panchayats be audited by the Local Fund Audit Department and that the accounts of the district panchayats, pending further orders, be maintained in the same formats as the District Rural Development Agency. The financial instructions applicable to District Rural Development Agency shall apply to the district panchayats also.

(4) The District Collector has been notified as the Inspector of Panchayats in respect of district panchayats as reiterated in Letter No.46669/C1/96-2, dated 30.1.97. The Collector shall exercise powers under Section 202 of the Tamil Nadu Panchayats Act, 1994.

(G.O.Ms.No.176, Rural Development (C4) Department, dated 9th June 1997)

7.4 PROCEDURE

7.4.1 District Panchayats Conduct of Meetings and Subjects for Discussion

1. Short title—These rules may be called the Tamil Nadu District Panchayats (Procedure in Regard to Transaction of Business, Conduct of Meeting and Subject for Discussion at the Meeting) Rules, 1997.

2. Definition—In these rules the context unless and otherwise requires:

(a) "Act" means the Tamil Nadu Panchayats Act, 1994 (Tamil Nadu Act 21 of 1994); and

(b) All other words and expressions used in these rules but not defined therein shall have the meanings respectively assigned to them in the Act.

3. Procedure in regard to transaction of business and conduct of meeting of district panchayat: The District Panchayat shall meet at the place specified by the chairman of the district panchayat (hereinafter referred to as "the Chairman") upon such days and at such times as it may be arranged and also at other times as often as a meeting shall be called by the chairman:

Provided that not more than sixty days shall elapse between one meeting of the district panchayat and the another meeting.

4. (1) No meeting shall be held unless notice of the day and time when the meeting is to be held and of the business to be transacted thereat has been given at least ten clear days before the day of the meeting.

(2) In cases of urgency, the chairman may convene a meeting on giving shorter notice then that specified in sub-rule (1).

(3) The agenda for the meeting shall be approved by the chairman, any member who wishes to have any subject included in the agenda or move any resolution shall intimate his intention by notice in writing to the chairman and such notice shall contain a copy of the subject or resolution which he wishes to include or move. Subjects or resolutions contained in notices received twenty clear days before the date of meeting shall ordinarily be considered for inclusion in the agenda for that meeting. The chairman shall decide on the admissibility of the subject or resolution and shall disallow any subject or resolution, if it in his opinion contravenes the provisions of Tamil Nadu Panchayats Act, 1994 (Tamil Nadu Act 21 of 1994) or the Rules made thereunder and his decision thereon shall be final. Any subject or resolution admitted by the chairman shall be included in the notices for the meeting. On any subject or resolution included in the agenda, the chairman shall have the right of recording his views in a note and such note shall be circulated to the members or placed before the district panchayat at the time of the consideration of such subject or resolution by the district panchayat:

Provided that a supplemental agenda may be brought by the chairman before the district panchayat for consideration at ordinary meetings with the consent of the majority of members present at the meeting who are entitled to vote.

5. The chairman of the district panchayat or in his absence, the vice chairman shall preside over the meeting of the district panchayat. In the absence of both the chairman and vice-chairman, a member chosen by the members present at the meeting shall preside over the meeting.

6. No business shall be transacted at a meeting unless there be present at least one-third of the number of members then on the district panchayat.

7. If within half-an hour after the time appointed for a meeting a quorum is not present the meeting shall stand adjourned.

8. All matters at a meeting of the district panchayat shall be decided by a majority of votes of members present and voting. In the case of equality of votes, the chairman of the district panchayat, or in his absence the person presiding, will have a second or casting vote.

9. The minutes of the proceedings of each meeting of the district panchayat shall be drawn up and entered in a Minutes book to be kept for that purpose and shall be signed by the chairman or in his absence by the member presiding thereat. A copy of the proceedings of the meeting containing a fair summary of views expressed by the members present shall also be drawn up and a copy of the same published on the notice board of the office of the district panchayat.

10. The Chief Executive Officer or any person authorized by him in this behalf shall have the custody of the proceedings and records

of the district panchayat and may grant copies of any such proceedings and records on payment of such fees as the Government may, by order, fix from time-to-time. Copies shall be certified by the chairman or any officer authorized by him in this behalf.

11. Subject for discussion in the district panchayats:

(1) In respect of district panchayats, it will not be possible to discuss all matters relating to all executive departments of the Government at every meeting. At the same time, it has to be ensured that not too much time is allowed to elapse between two sessions at which the subjects relating to any particular department are brought up for discussion at the district panchayat, with reference to these considerations, the subjects to be brought up before the district panchayat can be grouped under the following three heads:

(i) **Production Programmes** (which will include all programmes relating to Agriculture, Animal Husbandry, Industries and connected matters like Irrigation, Electricity, Co-operatives etc.).

(ii) **Welfare Services Programmes** (which will include Social Welfare, Health, Education, Noon Meal centres, Adi Drivida and Backward class welfare and all works other than those connected with production).

(iii) **Development Programmes** (which will include roads, water supply, infrastructure, buildings and other development programmes).

(2) It should be possible to earmark each meeting of the district panchayat for the discussion of one set of programmes as illustrated below:
I session – Discussion on Production Programmes
II session – Discussion on Welfare Programmes
III session – Discussion on Development Programmes
and so on.

(3) All the District Level Officers, whose subjects are being discussed at the meeting of district panchayat shall attend the meeting and assist in the discussions relating to known subjects. There shall be no absentees for the district panchayat council meeting except with the prior permission of the chairman.

Note 1—The term 'District Level Officer' shall refer to the senior most officer of the Government department whose jurisdiction is coterminus with the District:
Provided that where there are two or more officers of equal ranking a particular department all of such will attend the district panchayat council meeting.

Note 2—The word 'department' will include autonomous bodies like Tamil Nadu Electricity Board and Tamil Nadu Water Supply and Drainage Board but shall not include public sector undertakings.

Note 3—(i) The Chief Executive Officer of the district panchayat shall call for reports from the department on the progress of implementation of schemes and programmes at the district level including details regarding budgets and allocation and such other details as may be necessary to facilitate a detailed discussion on the activities of that department.
(ii) On receipt of the requisition from the Chief Executive Officer the district level officer or officers shall send to the Chief Executive officer in the manner and format required the details called for to facilitate a detailed discussion of the activities of that department.
(iii) The Chief Executive Officer should submit to the Government and Director of Rural Development a copy of the proceedings of each Meeting immediately after the Meeting is over. The returns thus secured will be consolidated for the whole state and placed before the cabinet if necessary.

(G.O. Ms. No. 175, Rural Development (C-1) Department, dated 9th June 1997)

7.4.2 Guidelines for District Panchayat Meeting

Section 90 of the Tamil Nadu Panchayats Act, 1994 stipulate that:

"Every panchayat shall meet at such times and places and shall subject to the provisions of Section 89, observe such rules as procedure in regard to transaction of business at its meetings (including the quorum at meetings) as may be prescribed:

Provided that not more than sixty days shall elapse between any two meetings of the panchayat".

The word 'panchayat' refers to all the 3 tiers of panchayat.

Meeting of elected bodies, including district panchayat may be conducted as per above provisions of the Act.

(DRD's Lr.No.Rc.79384/96/PCA-3, dated 27th January 1997)

7.4.3 Moving of Resolutions at Meetings of District Panchayats

1. Short title—These rules may be called the Tamil

Nadu Panchayats (Moving of Resolutions at Meetings of District Panchayats) Rules, 1999.

2. **Admission of resolution**—(1) A member in whose name a resolution appears on the list of business shall, when called on to move the resolution, shall move the resolution or if he is absent or proposes to withdraw or is unwilling to move the resolution or has ceased to be a member before the meeting, any member present at the meeting may move such resolution. If no member moves such resolution, it shall be considered to have been withdrawn.

(2) Every resolution which has been moved shall be seconded; otherwise it shall not be discussed.

3. **Mode of discussion**—(1) No speech, except with the permission of the chairman, shall exceed five minutes in duration:

Provided that the person, who has moved the resolution, when moving the same, may speak for not more than ten minutes.

(2) The discussion of a resolution shall be strictly limited to the subject moved.

(3) When an amendment to any resolution is moved, the chairman shall, before taking the consent of the district panchayat thereon, State or read to the district panchayat the terms of the original motion and of the amendment proposed.

(4) Ordinarily, the chairman shall put the amendments to vote in the order in which they have been moved and lastly the original motion if all the amendments are lost. But it shall be his discretion in any case to put to vote the original motion and the amendments in such order as he thinks fit.

4. **Amendment to a resolution**—(1) When a resolution is under discussion, any member may, subject to Rules 3 and 6, move an amendment to such resolution.

(2) Every amendment, which has been moved, shall be seconded; otherwise it shall not be discussed.

5. **Withdrawal of a resolution**—(1) A member who has moved a resolution or an amendment thereto shall not withdraw the same except by leave of the district panchayats.

(2) No discussion shall be permitted on motion for leave to withdraw except with the permission of the chairman.

6. **Division of resolution into points for voting**—When any resolution involving several points has been discussed, it shall be the discretion of the chairman to divide the subject in to points and put each of such points separately to vote.

(G.O. Ms. No. 272 Rural Development (C-4) Department dated 28th December 1999)

7.4.4 Interpellation of Chairman of District Panchayat

1. **Short title**—These rules may be called the Tamil Nadu Panchayats (Interpellation of Chairman of District Panchayat, by the Members) Rules, 1998.

2. **Restrictions on questions**—No question shall be asked or answered at a meeting as to any matter not connected with the administration of the district panchayat and no question shall be asked except as to matters of fact and the answer shall be confined to a statement of facts. Except as thus provided, any question may be asked by any member, subject to the conditions and restrictions specified in these rules.

3. **Intimation as to questions**—A member who wishes to ask a question shall intimate his intention in writing to the chairman by giving at prior notice of not less than ten clear days and such notice shall contain a copy of the question he wishes to ask.

4. **Admissible questions**—In order that a question may be admissible, it must satisfy the following conditions, namely:

(i) it shall be related to the administration of the district panchayat and it shall be based on facts;

(ii) it shall not relate to any name or statement not strictly necessary to make the question intelligible;

(iii) if a question contains a statement, the member asking it shall make himself responsible for the accuracy of the statement;

(iv) it shall not contain arguments, inferences, ironical, satirical expressions or defamatory statements;

(v) it shall not ask for an expression of opinion or the solution of an abstract legal question or of a hypothetical proposition;

(vi) it shall not be asked as to the character or conduct of any person except in his official or public capacity;

(vii) it shall be short and brief and shall not be of excessive in length; and

(viii) a question once fully answered may not be asked again.

5. **Decision as to the Questions**—The chairman shall decide on admissibility of a question and either or disallow it before allow the date fixed for the next meeting for which it may be within the time specified under Rule 3. He may disallow any

question, if in his opinion, it is an abuse of the right of questioning or where in his opinion it cannot be answered consistently in the public interest, and shall disallow any question which in his opinion, contravenes any of these rules; and in such case the question shall not be entered in the proceedings of the district panchayat.

6. Entry of questions into the agenda—Questions allowed by the chairman, shall be entered in the agenda and the chairman shall answer every question so entered, if not previously withdrawn by the member putting it, in the order in which it stands in the paper, before any business is entered upon at the meeting. The answer shall be confined to a statement of facts only:

Provided that the chairman may, at his discretion, on the ground of public interest, answer a question on the agenda, even though the question may have been withdrawn.

7. Supplementary questions—Any member may put a supplementary question for the purpose of seeking further answers and clarification regarding which an answer has been given:

Provided that the chairman, shall disallow any supplementary question if, in his opinion, it infringes the rules as to the subject matter of question and does not confirm to the conditions specified under Rule 4:

Provided further that the chairman may decline to answer a supplementary question without notice, in which case it may be put only in the form of a fresh question at a subsequent meeting.

8. Bar of discussion on answered questions—No discussion shall be permitted in respect of any question or of any answer given to a question, asked under these rules.

9. Minutes—The question asked and the answer given it to shall be entered in the minutes of the district panchayat.

10. Moving a resolution—The procedure prescribed in 1 to 9 of these rules for raising question shall be followed to move a resolution in the district panchayat.

11. Questions from the first part of business—Questions shall form the first part of business to be transacted in the district panchayat followed by subjects or agenda for discussion and the resolution moved by the members shall be the last item for discussion.

(G.O. Ms. No. 145, Rural Development (C-1) Department, dated 14th July 1998)

7.5 STANDING COMMITTEES

7.5.1 Constitution and Functions of Standing Committees

1. Short title—These rules may be called Tamil Nadu Panchayats (Constitution and Functions of Standing Committees of District Panchayat) Rules, 2001.

2. Definition—In these rules unless the context otherwise requires "Act" means the Tamil Nadu Panchayats Act, 1994 (Tamil Nadu Act 21 of 1994).

3. Constitution of standing committees—(1) Every district panchayat shall constitute the following standing committees as provided in Section 97(1) (a) of the Act:

(i) Food and agriculture
(ii) Industries and labour
(iii) Public works
(iv) Education
(v) Health and welfare including prohibition

4. Members of the committee

(a) The district panchayat shall elect members of each standing committee from among the elected members of the district panchayat and the strength of each standing committee shall not exceed seven members and two members shall be persons other than the members of the district panchayat nominated by the district panchayat from out of persons representing Non-Government Organisations, Community Based Organisation, Social Workers and experts in the subjects related to the standing committee who can contribute the transaction of business.

(b) The chairman of the district panchayat shall be the *ex-officio* member of all the standing committees.

(c) The district panchayat shall also nominate the officers at district level of the Government departments related to the subjects of the standing committee as members of the standing committee without voting rights to assist the committee in the function allotted to it.

5. President of the committee—The president of each standing committee shall be selected by the members of the respective committee. The President of the Health and Welfare Committee shall be from among the women members of the district panchayat.

6. Food and agriculture standing committee—(1) The committee shall organise district level workshop and seminars on issues connected to agricultural production and productivity or changing crop pattern, soil and water conservation, mixed farming integrated area development, increase employment generation through value addition to agricultural produce in rural areas. Integrated farming, water conservation and irrigation management shall also be looked into by the committee.

(2) The committee shall also monitor and assist in the implementation of programmes relating to Agriculture and Agricultural extension, Animal Husbandry, Horticulture, Sericulture, Floriculture, Pisciculture, Dairy Development, Poultry Development, Area Development programmes like Drought Prone Area Development, Integrated Watershed Development, Wasteland Development Programme, Social Forestry, Soil Conservation and Water Management.

(3) The committee shall also monitor, inspect and offer suggestions on the implementation of the various development programmes of the Government departments attached to the committee. All the district level departmental officers included in the committee by the district panchayat shall assist, advise and offer technical guidance to the members of the committee in their work.

7. Industries and labour standing committee—(1) The standing committee on industries and labour shall identify the growth centres for small scale industries and activity cluster for self-employment under poverty alleviation programme based on local resources and potentials. The committee shall engage experts and organise workshop and seminars for preparing potential linked plan for small scale industrial activities and establishment of growth centres for industries.

(2) All the schemes of Khadi, village and cottage industries shall be monitored and inspected by the committee.

(3) The committee shall co-ordinate in the identification of cluster activities and preparation and approval of project formulations for Self Help Groups under S.G.S.Y in co-ordination with the district level committee on S.G.S.Y.

8. Public works standing committee—(1) The standing committee may inspect all the public works executed in the district by the Rural Development Department, Public Works Department, Highways, TWAD, Agricultural Engineering and Irrigation Departments and other line departments after giving due notice to the department concerned and make recommendation on the action that should be taken on quality and timely completion of work throughout the district.

(2) The committee shall identify the requirements of infrastructures for roads, bridges, irrigation tanks, drinking water supply, power distribution system etc. and give recommendation for inclusion of such works in the departmental plans through the district panchayat. The committee shall specially suggest works benefiting more than one panchayat union and a large number of village panchayats.

9. Education standing committee—(1) The committee shall monitor the functioning of all the schools in the district. It shall identify the gaps in the infrastructural requirements like school buildings; drinking water and toilet facilities, etc. and recommend to the concerned departments for inclusion in the plans of the department.

(2) The committee shall fix the benchmark on key indicators like literacy level, drop-outs, enrolment level, standard and quality of teaching and fix goals to ensure overall literacy level improvement with the needed infrastructure.

(3) The committee shall conduct awareness campaigns, seminars and workshops on improvement of education at all levels including adult literacy and measures to reinduct drop-outs in the schools to continue their education.

(4) The committee shall monitor the implementation of various programmes implemented to promote education including DPEP or any other externally aided projects.

10. Health and welfare standing committee including prohibition—(1) The committee shall visit all the public health and medical institutions in the district and suggest measures for improving their functioning to the concerned departments through the district panchayat.

(2) The committee shall identify areas where additional public health and medical facilities and infrastructures like buildings are required and recommend to the Government through the district panchayat concerned.

(3) The committee may arrange seminars, workshops and campaigns on public health, nutrition and rural sanitation, immunization campaigns to create awareness of the Government programmes for the rural public.

(4) The committee shall monitor the schemes benefiting welfare of women, children, physically handicapped, destitute, widows, old age people, bonded labourers, scheduled castes and scheduled tribes and other socially disadvantaged group.

(5) It may organise special campaigns, seminars and workshops to create awareness among the

above people on the Government schemes of social security programmes to enable them to avail the facilities.

(6) The committee shall co-ordinate at district level on eradication of child labour, prohibition of liquor, prevention of female infanticide, anti-dowry movement, widows remarriage, eradication of untouchability etc. All the poverty alleviation programmes of the Government of India and the Government of Tamil Nadu like self employment programmes and social sector programmes shall be monitored by the committee.

11. Preparation of the plan—(1) Every standing committee shall prepare the perspective 5 year and annual sectoral development plan for the area of the district panchayat in consultation with the village panchayat plan and plan of panchayat union council.

(2) Such plan may incorporate all necessary requirements on the infrastructures development wherever necessary.

(3) The standing committees can also make a special project plans indicating the benchmark and setting the goals for achieving it in the prescribed time frame either under routine scheme or under special scheme.

(4) The standing committee may seek the assistance and involve social workers, experts, non-government organizations, community based organisations or institutions and arrange special workshops, inter-actions, seminars, resource survey and awareness campaign for preparing the comprehensive sectoral plans.

(5) All the plans prepared by the standing committee shall be placed before the district panchayat and only after due approval it may be forwarded to the district planning committee or Government departments.

(6) The standing committee shall co-ordinate the implementation of the sectoral plans on their respective subjects.

12. Interface with NGOs/CBOs—Each committee shall identify the Non-Government Organisations/Community Based Organisations who are performing outstandingly in the area related to the committee and promote their active involvement through organizing workshops, seminar etc., in the development activities in co-ordination with Panchayati Raj Institutions, Government Departments and community.

13. Inspection—Every standing committee may visit and inspect such units, branches, centre, establishment or institution implementing programmes on the subjects assigned to them. The president of the committee shall intimate in writing to the head of such units, branches, centre, establishment, institution as the case may be, three days in advance, clearly indicating the date, time and purpose of visit or inspection. The Secretary of the district panchayat shall arrange to get the detailed notes from the Head of the unit, branch, centre, establishment, institution atleast 5 days in advance and circulate the same to the members of the committee.

14. Notice and agenda for committee—The president of the standing committee shall fix the date, time and venue of the meeting of the committee and circulate the agenda for discussion atleast three days in advance. The meeting shall generally take place in the district panchayat office.

15. Periodicity of meeting—Every committee shall meet once in two months.

16. Approval of district panchayat—Every observation, suggestion or recommendation of each standing committee shall be placed in the next meeting of the district panchayat for approval.

17. Rights of the Secretary of district panchayat—(1) The Secretary of the district panchayat shall have the right to attend the meeting of all the standing committees.

(2) The Secretary shall ensure that all the governmental departmental officers attached to the standing committees attend the meeting of the committee without fail.

(3) The administrative and secretarial support to the committee shall be arranged by the Secretary of the district panchayat.

7.5.2 Election of Members of Standing Committees

1. Short title—These rules may be called the Standing Committees of the District Panchayat (Election of Members) Rules, 1998.

2. Definition—In these rules, unless the context otherwise requires:

(a) "Committees" means the standing committees of district panchayat;

(b) "Chairman" means chairman of district panchayat;

(c) "President" means the president of the meeting.

3. Holding of election of members—The Election of members to the Standing Committees shall be held in the office of the district panchayat and shall be from among the elected members of the district panchayat at a meeting specially convened for the purpose.

4. Convening of meeting

(a) The meeting for the election of members to the committee shall be convened by the chairman within thirty days of the occurrence of a casual vacancy:

Provided that where the chairman fails to convene the meeting, the Inspector shall convene the same.

(b) Notice of the day and hour of the meeting shall be given to all the elected members and to the Inspector under acknowledgement not less than seven clear days previous to the date of the meeting.

(c) The Inspector shall depute an observer not below the rank of Assistant Director of Rural Development or Revenue Divisional Officer to be present at this meeting in order to ensure that the election is conducted in a free and fair manner.

5. Presiding over the meeting—The meeting shall be presided over by the chairman or in his absence by the vice-chairman, or in the absence of both the chairman and the vice-chairman, by a member not intending to contest as a candidate at the election and chosen by the members present at the meeting to preside for the occasion. Such a person shall be the president of the meeting.

6. Nominations

(a) Every candidate for election shall file a nomination in the Form I appended to these rules. It shall be proposed by a member. There is no need for a seconder. No proposer shall propose more than the number of candidates to be elected.

(b) The president of the meeting shall record the names of members so proposed in the minutes of the meeting after ascertaining in writing their willingness to serve in the committees. He shall read out the names of the candidates proposed to the hearing of the members present at the meeting.

7. Procedure in contested and uncontested election

(a) If the number of contesting candidates is more than the number of seats to be filled, a poll shall be taken.

(b) If the number of contesting candidates is equal to the number of seats to be filled, the president shall forthwith declare all such candidates to be duly elected to the committee.

(c) If the number of contesting candidates is less than the number of seats to be filled, the president of the meeting shall forthwith declare all the contesting candidates to be duly elected and arrange for the conduct of election in respect of the remaining seats at the next meeting, which shall be convened within fifteen days.

8. Provision of voting compartment—For conducting the poll, the president shall provide in the place where the meeting is held, a voting compartment in which the members can record their votes screened from observation. The president shall also place a ballot box for the receipt of ballot papers in the view of the president of the meeting and the members. The ballot box shall be so made that the ballot papers can be introduced therein but cannot be withdrawn therefrom without the box being unlocked or opened.

9. Ballot box to be shown empty—The president shall immediately before the votes are taken, show the ballot box to be empty to such members as may be present so that they may see that it is empty and shall then lock it up and the place a seal upon it in such a manner as to prevent its being opened without breaking such seal.

10. Ballot paper—Every member wishing to vote shall be supplied with a ballot paper of uniform size and same colour in the Form II appended to these rules on which the names of all the candidates shall be legibly written or typewritten or cyclostyled in Tamil, and signed by the president before being handed over to the members.

11. Procedure for voting—Every member shall, on receiving the ballot paper proceed to the voting compartment and record his vote by putting a cross mark (x) on the ballot paper against the name of the candidate for whom be wishes to vote by using the seal supplied by the president. He shall, before leaving the voting compartment, fold up the ballot paper so as to conceal the cross mark and put the ballot paper so folded up into the ballot box in the presence of the president.

12. Voting by illiterate, blind, etc., persons—

(a) If owing to illiteracy or blindness or other physical infirmity, a member is unable to read the ballot paper and make a cross mark thereon and seeks assistance for doing so, the president shall record the vote in the ballot paper in accordance with the wishes of the member and fold it up so as to conceal the vote.

(b) The member shall then himself or with the assistance of the president of the meeting insert the ballot paper into the ballot box.

(c) While acting under this rule, the president shall observe as much secrecy as is feasible and shall keep a brief record of each such instance but shall not indicate therein the manner in which any vote has been given.

13. Recording of votes—After the voting by members is over, the president shall open the ballot box in the presence of the members present, take out the ballot papers therefrom and record the number of votes obtained by each candidate in a statement.

14. Invalidation of ballot papers—A ballot paper shall be treated as invalid on which:

(a) there is no cross mark; or

(b) if votes are given on it in favour of more candidates than the number of candidates to be elected; or

(c) a cross mark and some other mark are put opposite the name of the same candidate; or

(d) any mark is made by which the member may afterwards be identified; or

(e) if it is uncertain to which candidate the mark is intended to apply; or

(f) the mark has been made by any seal other than the one provided for this purpose.

15. Declaration of result of election—After the completion of the counting of votes, the president shall forthwith declare the candidate to whom; the largest number of valid votes has been given, to be duly elected.

16. Procedure in case of equality of votes—If after the counting of the votes is completed, candidates are found to have secured equal number of votes and the addition of one vote will entitle one of these candidates to be declared elected, the president shall forthwith decide between these candidates by lot, and proceed as if the candidates on whom the lot falls had received an additional vote and declare him elected.

17. Reporting of the result of the election—Immediately after the counting, the president of the meeting shall:

(a) prepare a record of the proceeding of the meeting in the minutes book, read out the minutes aloud, sign it, attesting with his initials every correction made therein; and also permit any member present at the meeting to affix his signature to such record if he expresses his desire to do so.

(b) send a report of the result of the election to the Inspector and to such other officer or authority as may be specified by the Government by general or special order;

(c) publish on the notice board of the office of the district panchayat, a notification signed by him stating the names of the persons elected as members to the committee; and

(d) the observer of the election shall separately send a detailed report to the Inspector within twenty-four hours as to whether the election was conducted in a free and fair manner:

Provided that where the government are satisfied based on the report of the Inspector that the election has not been conducted in a free and fair manner, the Government may cancel the result of the election and order a fresh election.

18. Disposal of ballot papers

(a) The president shall make up the ballot papers into a separate packet, seal the packet and note thereon a description of its contents, the election to which it relates and the date thereof.

(b) These packets shall not be opened and their contents shall not be inspected or produced except under the order of a competent court.

(c) The packets shall be retained in safe custody in the office of the district panchayat for a year and shall then, unless otherwise directed by the orders of a competent court, be destroyed.

19. Election of Chairman to each committee—The procedure prescribed for the election of members to the committee shall apply to the election of the Chairman to each committee.

(G.O. Ms. No. 151, Rural Development (C-1) Department, dated 20th July 1998)

APPENDIX
Form I
[See Rule 6(a)]

Nomination Paper for Election of Members to the Standing Committees

I, ____________________________ and elected member from hereby nominate Thiru/Tmt/Selvi

_________________________ a member elected from ___________ ward of the above district panchayat as a candidate for election as a member of the Standing Committee for.

Signature of the Proposer

Declaration of the Candidate

I ____________________________ a member elected from ______________________ ward of the ______________________________ district panchayat hereby give my consent to this nomination.

Signature of the Candidate

Form II
(See Rule 10)
Ballot Paper

DISTRICT PANCHAYAT

Date of election ____________

Name of the candidates duly nominated for election as members of the Standing Committee for __________________________

1.
2.
3.
4.

President of the meeting

7.5.3 Election of Members of Appointment Committee

1. Short title—These rules may be called the Appointment Committee of the District Panchayat (Election of Members) Rules, 1999.

2. Definitions—In these rules unless the context otherwise requires

(a) "committee" means the appointment committee of the district panchayat;

(b) "president" means the president of the meeting.

3. Constitution of the Committee—There shall be an appointment committee for every district panchayat which shall be comprised the chairman of the district panchayat concerned, the Secretary and one member elected annually by the district panchayat concerned, the chairman of the district panchayat shall be chairman of the Committee.

4. Holding of election of member—The Election of Member to the Committee shall be held in the office of the district panchayat concerned and shall be from among the elected members of such district panchayat at a meeting specially convened for the purpose.

5. Convening of meeting

(a) The meeting for the election of a member to the Committee shall be convened by the chairman of the district panchayat concerned with in thirty days of the occurrence of a casual vacancy:

Provided that where the chairman of the district panchayat concerned fails to convene the meeting, the Inspector shall convene the same.

(b) Notice of the day and hour of the meeting shall be given to all the elected members and to the Inspector under acknowledgement at atleast seven clear days prior to the date of the meeting,

(c) The Inspector shall depute an Observer in the rank of an Assistant Director of Rural Development Department or Revenue Divisional Officer to be present at this meeting in order to ensure that the election is conducted in a free and fair manner.

6. Presiding over the meeting—The meeting shall be presided over by the chairman or, in the absence of the chairman by the vice-chairman of the district panchayat concerned or in the absence of both the chairman and the vice-chairman of the district panchayat concerned, by a member not intending to contest as a candidate at the election and chosen by the members present at the meeting to preside over the meeting such a person shall be styled as the president.

7. Nominations—(a) Every candidate for election shall be nominated in Form I appended to these rules below by a member as a proposer. There is no need for a seconder. No proposer shall sign more than one nomination.

(b) The president shall record the names of the members so proposed in the minutes of the meeting after ascertaining in writing their willingness to serve in the committee for a period of one year from the date of election. He shall readout the names of the candidates proposed to the hearing of the members present at the meeting.

8. Procedure in contested and uncontested election—If the number of contesting candidates is mote than one, a poll shall be taken.

(a) If there is only one contesting candidate, the president shall forthwith declare the candidate to be duly elected to the committee.

(b) If no candidates are forthcoming then the president shall arrange for the conduct of election at the next meeting, which shall be convened within fifteen days.

9. Provision of voting compartment—For conducting a poll, the president shall provide in the place where, the meeting is held, a voting compartment in which the members can record their votes, screened from observation. The president shall also place a ballot box for the receipt of ballot papers in view of the president and the members. The ballot box shall be so constructed that the ballot papers cannot be withdrawn there from without the box being unlocked or opened.

10. Ballot box to be shown empty—The president of the meeting shall immediately before the votes are taken, show the ballot box empty to such members as may be present so that they may see that it is empty and shall then lock it up and place a seal upon it in such a manner so as to prevent it being opened without breaking such seal.

11. Ballot paper—Every member wishing to vote shall be supplied with a ballot paper of uniform size in the Form II appended to these rules, and of same colour on which the names of all the candidates shall be legibly written or typewritten or cyclostyled in Tamil and signed by the president before being handed over to the members.

12. Procedure for voting—Every member shall on receiving the ballot paper proceed to the voting compartment and record his vote by putting a cross mark on the ballot paper against the name of the candidate for whom he wishes to vote, by using the seal supplied by the president. He shall, before leaving the voting compartment, fold up the ballot paper so as to conceal the cross mark and put the ballot paper so folded up into the ballot box in the presence of the president.

13. Voting by illiterate blind or disabled person—(a) If owing to illiteracy or blindness or other physical infirmity, a member is unable to read the ballot paper and make a cross mark thereon and seeks for assistance for doing so, the president shall record the vote in the ballot paper in accordance with the wishes of such member and fold it up so as to conceal the vote.

(b) The member shall then, himself or with the assistance of the president insert the ballot paper into the ballot box.

(c) While acting under this rule, the president shall observe as much secrecy as is feasible and shall keep a brief record of each such instance but shall not indicate there in the manner in which any vote has been given.

14. Recording of votes—After the voting by members is over, the president shall open the ballot box in the presence of the members present take out the ballot papers therefrom, record the number of votes obtained by each candidate in a statement.

15. Invalidation of ballot papers—A ballot paper shall be treated as invalid, on which

(a) there is no cross mark; or

(b) votes are given on it in favour of more candidates than one; or

(c) a cross mark and some other mark are put opposite the name of the same candidate; or

(d) any mark is made by which the member may after wards be identified; or

(e) it is uncertain as to which candidate the mark is intended to apply; or

(f) the mark has been made by any seal other than the one provided for this purpose.

16. Declaration of result of election—After the completion of the counting of votes, the president shall forthwith declare the candidate to whom the largest number of valid votes has been given, to be duly elected.

17. Procedure in case of equality of votes—After the counting of the vote is completed, and in the event of there being an equality of votes between any two or more candidates and the addition of one vote will entitle one of these candidates to be declared elected, the president shall forthwith decide between these candidates by lot and proceed as if the candidates on whom the lot falls had received an additional vote and declare him elected.

18. Reporting of the result of the election—After completion of the voting and immediately after the counting, the president shall

(a) prepare a record of the proceeding of the meeting in the minutes book, read out the minutes aloud, sign it, attesting with his initials every correction made therein; and also permit any member present at the meeting to affix his signature to such record if he expresses his desire to do so;

(b) send a report of the result of the election to the Inspector and to such other Officer or authority as may be specified by the Government in this regard, by general or special order;

(c) publish on the notice board of the Office of the district panchayat, a notification signed by him stating the name of the person elected as member of the committee; and

(d) the observer of the election shall separately send a detailed report to the Inspector with in twenty four hours as to whether the election was conducted in a free and fair manner:

Provided that where the Government is satisfied, based on the report of the Inspector that the election has not been conducted in a free and fair manner, they may cancel the result of the election and order a fresh election.

19. Disposal of ballot papers—(a) The president shall then make up the ballot papers into a separate packet, seal up the packet and note thereon a description of its content, the election to which it relates and the date thereof.

(b) The packet shall not be opened and its contents inspected or produced except under the order of a competent court.

(c) The packet shall be retained in safe custody in the Office of the district panchayat for a year and shall then unless otherwise directed by the orders of a competent Court, be destroyed.

(G.O.Ms.No.207, Rural Development (C4) Department, dated 30th September 1999)

Form I
[See Rule 7(a)]

Nomination Paper for Election of Members to the Committee

I,______________an elected member from ward of (the name of the District Panchayat_________________) District Panchayat hereby nominate Thiru/Thirumathi/Selvi___________a member elected from ward of the above said District Panchayat as a candidate for election as a member of the Appointment Committee of the above said District Panchayat.

Signature of the Proposer

Declaration of the Candidate

I,_________________a member elected from ward of the said District Panchayat hereby give a consent to this nomination.

Signature of the Candidate

Form II

(See Rule 11)

Ballaot Paper

____________District Panchayat.

Date of election____________

Name of candidates duly nominated for election as members of the Appointment Committee:

1.

2.

3.

President of the Meeting

(G.O.Ms.No.212, Rural Development (C4) Department, dated 5th October 1999)

7.6 ADMINISTRATION

7.6.1 Location of District Panchayat Office

The Special Officers of the district panchayats are requested to identify a suitable location for creating office complex for the district panchayat. Pending creation of a separate complex, the Special Officer may locate the "Office of the District Panchayat" in a suitable Government building if available at the District Headquarters or locate the Office in a rented premises. The Special Officer may determine the rent for the hired building as per norms and debit the expenditure to the District Panchayat (General) Fund. Until a separate Office premises is located the "Office of the district panchayat may function from the premises of the District Rural Development Agency with a District sign board".

(G.O.Ms.No.100, Rural Development (C-1) Department, dated 13th April 1995)

7.6.2 Permission to Purchase Ambassador Car and Sanction of Post of Driver for the Car of District Panchayat

The Government accord sanction for the purchase of one Ambassador Car and creation of post of a Driver in the scale of pay of Rs. 975-25-1150-30-1660 to all the district panchayats in lieu of the Jeep already sanctioned to the district panchayat.

(G.O.Ms. No. 256, Rural Development (C-1) Department, dated 13th December 1996)

7.6.3 Claim of Taxi Charges – Refused

The Government rejected the proposals of the chairman of district panchayat; Perambalur claiming Taxi charges till the Car, is sanctioned to the district panchayat and for claiming Taxi charges during the period when his vehicle went out of repair.

(Govt. Lr. No. 47013/C1/Rural Development Department, dated 1st July 1999)

7.6.4 Implementation of Schemes, Functions and Staff

The Government issued revised orders in the implementation of schemes by the District Panchayat and the District Rural Development Agency as follows:

(1) The schemes mentioned in the G.O. cited shall be continued to be implemented by the District Rural Development Agency and funds for such schemes need not be transferred from the District Rural Development Agency and the district panchayat.

(2) The staff, Annexure 1 of the G.O. shall continue to work in the District Rural Development Agency.

(3) In order to enable the district panchayat to discharge its function, the following minimum staff shall be transferred from the District Rural Development Agency to work in the district panchayat.

(a) Any one of the Assistant Project Officer

(b) One Assistant

(c) One Junior Assistant or Assistant Technical Inspector

(d) One Steno or Typist

(e) Two Office Assistants.

(G.O.Ms.No.15, Rural Development (C-1) Department, dated 17th January 1997)

G.O. Ms. No. 100, Rural Development Department, dated 13th April 1995)

7.7 ESTABLISHMENT

7.7.1 Staffing Pattern of District Panchayat

Notifications have been published in the Extraordinary issues of Tamil Nadu Government Gazette dated 13.4.1995 constituting district panchayats with effect from 14.4.1995 in each District except Madras District and appointing the Collectors as Special Officers for their respective Districts. Consequent upon the creation of the district panchayats, the following orders are issued on the Organisational arrangements, activities entrusted to the district panchayats and the funds of the district panchayats.

1. Organisational set up

2. Sanction is hereby accorded for the creation of posts of one Chief Executive Officer and one Deputy Chief Executive Officer for each district panchayat. The scale of pay of the Chief Executive Officer shall be either in the senior scale of I.A.S. or in the cadre of Joint Director of Rural Development in Rs. 3700-125-4700-150-5000. The scale of pay of the Deputy Chief Executive Officer shall be in the cadre of Divisional Development Officer/Assistant Project Officer in Rs. 2200-75-2800-100-4000. Until further orders, the Additional Collectors (Development)/ Project Officers of District Rural Development Agency are placed in full additional charge of the post of Chief Executive Officer. No additional charge allowance shall be paid for this purpose.

3.The post of Assistant Project Officer (R) in the District Rural Development Agency is transferred to the control of the district panchayat, and designated as the Deputy Chief Executive Officer sanctioned in para 1 above. The incumbent presently holding the post of Assistant Project Officer (R) wherever such post exists is transferred along with the post and appointed as the Deputy Chief Executive Officer until further orders. The three posts of Additional Personal Assistant (Panchayat Development) to the Collector wherever they exist are also transferred to the district panchayats.

4.Until a full fledged organisational structure emerges for a district panchayat, orders are hereby issued for the temporary sanction of some posts to each district panchayat an indicated in the annexure to this order. Orders are also hereby issued for the temporary transfer of these posts from the District Rural Development Agencies and the Panchayat Development Wing of the Collectorates to the district panchayats as indicated in the Annexure. The posts transferred from District Rural Development Agencies and Panchayat Development Wing of the Collectorates shall constitute a reduction in the sanctioned strength of each District Rural Development Agency and the Panchayat Development Wing of the Collectorates as the case may be. The Collectors and the project Officers/District Rural Development Agencies are requested to ensure as far as possible, the transfer of the individuals holding the posts to the district panchayats along with the posts.

5. The Accounts Officers of the District Rural Development Agency shall also hold additional charge of the post of Accounts Officer of the District Panchayat until further orders. No additional charge allowance shall be paid for this purpose.

(G.O.Ms. No. 100, Rural Development (C1) Department, dated 13th April 1995)

ANNEXURE
Staff Sanctioned for District Panchayats

Category	*No. of posts sanctioned for each District Panchayat*	*Total requirement for all District Panchayats*	*No. of posts diverted from*		*Remarks*
1. Chief Executive Officer	1	22	–	–	New sanctioned held as additional charge by Project Officer/DRDA

(*Contd.*)

(*Contd.*)

Category	*No. of posts sanctioned for each District Panchayat*	*Total requirement for all District Panchayats*	*No. of posts diverted from*		*Remarks*
2. Deputy Chief Executive Officer	1	22	19 [APO (R)]	3 Addl. PA (PD)	Existing posts of APO(R) and Add I.P.A.(PD) to the Collector are transferred
3. Assistant Director (Agrl.)	1	22	22 [APO (FM)]	–	Existing posts of APO(FM) transferred
4. Assistant Director (Animal Husbandry)	1	22	22 [APO (AH)]	–	Existing post of APO(AH) transferred
5. Accounts Officer	1	22	–	–	New sanction held as additional charge by Accounts Officer, DRDA
6. Superintendent/ Accountant	2	44	44	–	At the rate of two from each DRDA
7. Assistant Statistical Inspector	2	44	44	–	At the rate of two from each DRDA
8. Assistants	5	110	44	66	At the rate of two from each DRDA and three from each Collectorate (P.D. Wing)
9. Junior Assistants	2	14	22	22	At the rate of one from each DRDA in the Collectorate
10. Steno–Typists	1	22	22	1	At the rate of one from each DRDA
11. Typists	2	44	22	22	At the rate of one from each DRDA and the Collectorate
12. Record Clerks	1	22	–	22	At the rate of one from each Collectorate
13. Office Assistants	4	88	88	–	At the rate of four from each DRDA

7.7.2 Status of Staff of District Panchayat

All the Government Servants transferred to the district panchayats by virtue of the transfer of posts shall continue to be Government Servants subject to the disciplinary control as per the orders in force. The Chief Executive Officer shall be the head of Office for the purpose of day to day administration. Other than the posts indicated in the annexure, either the Special Officer, or the Chief Executive Officer shall not create any new posts for the district panchayats without specific sanction of the Government.

This order issues with the concurrence of Finance Department *vide* its U.O.No.1615/FS/P/95/dated 31.3.95.

(G.O. Ms. No. 100 (C1) Rural Development, dated 13th April 1995)

7.8 AUDIT AND ACCOUNTS

7.8.1 Sanction of Grants

The following grants are sanctioned to the District Panchayat to function in a separate Office with all the required infrastructures for the separate Office.

(1) Out of the funds of Rs. One crore released as 10th Finance Commission Grant of the Government of India during 1996-97, the district panchayats can incur expenditure not exceeding Rs. 15 lakhs for setting up of an Office and for other capital expenditure like the following:

(a) Vehicle — Jeep
(b) Telephone — (1) District Panchayat Office
(2) Chairman Room in District Panchayat Office
(3) Residence of Chairman of District Panchayat (Direct Line Telephone)
(i) Furniture and fittings required for the Meeting Hall of the District Panchayat
(ii) Other items required for the District Panchayat Office

(4) Wherever there are District Board Buildings the district panchayat shall function in that building only. If there are no District Board Buildings, the district panchayat can function in rented building.

(5) District panchayat can open an account in any Nationalised Bank for transaction.

(G.O. Ms. No. 228, Rural Development (C-1) Department, dated 15th October 1996)

7.8.2 Procedure for Expenditure of Surplus Funds

For the sanction of works from the surplus funds from district panchayat, the authorities for sanction with financial limit shall be as follows:

Authority

(1) Individual works costing upto Rs. 10 lakhs District Panchayat-Inspector.
(2) Individual works costing Rs. 10 lakhs to Rs. 25 lakhs—District Collector.
(3) Individual works costing Rs. 25 lakhs to Rs. 1 crore—Director of Rural Development.
(4) Individual works costing more than Rs. 1 crore—Government.

The following conditions shall be observed while sending proposals for sanction of works for surplus funds from district panchayats.

(1) For the individual capital works selected for execution under surplus funds sanction of district panchayat shall be obtained.

(2) Before sending proposals for sanction of works, the District shall ensure sufficient funds are reserved for day to day administration.

(G.O. Ms. No. 189, Rural Development Department, dated 3rd October 1998)

7.8.3 Expenditure for the Office

In G.O. Ms. No. 228, Rural Development Department, dated 15.10.96, the purpose for which expenditure could be incurred has been clearly specified. I am, therefore, directed to inform that repairs and renovation works to the existing Government Buildings other than District Board Building should not be undertaken from the allocation of Rs. 15 lakhs for the purpose of occupation by the District Panchayat Office.

(Govt. Lr. No. 39560/C1/96-1, Rural Development Department, dated 7th November 1996)

7.9 CONTROLLING AUTHORITIES

7.9.1 Procedure for Conduct of Annual Inspection

The Government have notified the following officers as inspecting officers of district panchayats in the order cited.

(a) Joint Director of Rural Development.
(b) Additional Director of Rural Development.
(c) District Collectors.

(d) Any other officer not below the rank of a Joint Director, Rural Development nominated by the government.

(e) Inspector of Panchayats

The annual inspection of district panchayat has to be completed before 31st December of every year. The format for taking the inspection is enclosed.

The Commissioner of Rural Development shall initiate action to draw up a programme of annual inspection of all the district panchayats in the state in the month of April every year allocating the district, to the District Collectors, Joint Director (Project Officers), Additional Directors of Rural Development. The Commissioner of Rural Development is also authorised to take up annual inspection of any one of the district panchayats in the state.

The programme of annual inspection of district panchayats drawn up by the Commissioner of Rural Development will be communicated to all the district panchayats and to the inspecting officers in the month of April itself. The inspecting officers shall take up inspection of the district panchayats and complete before 31st December. The inspection reports shall be submitted to the Government and to the Commissioner of Rural Development simultaneously.

If any serious irregularities are noticed during inspection of district panchayat, the inspecting officer shall send a special report to the Collector, the Commissioner of Rural Development and the Government for immediate follow up action.

The Secretary, District Panchayat shall be responsible for the production of all the records and registers for the annual inspection. He shall also submit replies to the inspection notes within thirty days of its receipt after getting approval of the replies in the meeting of the district panchayat.

District Panchayat Office (Office Annual Inspection Notes)

1. Section I General
2. Section II Office Procedure
3. Section III Accounts Maintenance
4. Section IV Section
   District Panchayat Fund
   District Panchayat Meeting Details

District Panchayat Office

Office Annual Inspection Notes

Section I: General

1. Name of Office
2. Date of Inspection
3. Period of Inspection
4. Name and Designation of the Inspecting Officer
5. Officers who worked during the period of Inspection and their periods of service
6. Name of the Collector who inspected last and date of such Inspection

Section II: Office Administration

1. (a) Office Location:
   (b) Whether Inspection Notes of last year were sent, replies obtained and review made? Whether defects pointed out have been rectified?

Office Procedure

2. Distribution Register
   (a) Is Distribution Register maintained? Is it daily closed and the signature of Deputy BDO obtained?
   (b) Are all current numbers, periodicals and enclosures are numbered and entered in the register?
   (c) Are all currents not disposed so far, taken over to the new Distribution Register from April 1?
   (d) Is Distribution Register verified and checked every month by the Secretary District Panchayat?
3. Personal Register

Sl. No.	*Name*	*Section*	*Period of service*	*Subjects dealt with in the section*

4. Is there delay in taking initial action? If so point out such cases.

Section No.	File No.	Date of receipt of Tapal	Date of action	Delay

5. Is there delay in taking further action? If so point out such cases.

Section	File No.	Date of last action	Date of next action	Delay

6. Is there delay in handing over closed files to record?

Section	File No.	Date of closure	Date of Handing over to Record	Delay

7. Is Reminder Diary maintained properly?
8. Verify a few closed files to find out whether there are any premature disposals?
9. Has Secretary, District Panchayat and Deputy BDO has prepared Schedule for check of Registers and are they adhering to it? Is there any delay in submission for check?

Section	Deputy Block Development Officer		Secretary District Panchayat	
	Month	Date of check	Month	Date of check

10. Are the comments during check instructive?
11. Are all the defects pointed out rectified?
12. Has Deputy BDO checked the P.R. with the pending currents? Has any current been neglected in taking further action?
13. Are Title Heads for subjects given in the P.R. correct and suitable?
14. Is there any unnecessary and unsuitable correspondence that can be avoided?
15. While rejecting complaint petitions, whether reasons are recorded correctly and orders of the Officer obtained?

4. Periodical Register

1. Is consolidated periodical register maintained?
2. Are all the periodicals are entered in the periodical register of the Clerk?

Section	Weekly	Monthly	Quarterly	Half yearly	Year

3. Is monthly calendar of periodicals prepared by the Deputy BDO and are despatch watched?
4. Are all the periodicals entered in the previous years registers carried over to the current Register and certificate given?
5. Is Calendar of periodicals to be sent every month prepared in advance and affixed in the first page of the Register? Is there delay in despatch of periodical? If so point out a few defects.
6. Has action been taken to reduce the number of periodicals or to arrange its periodicity?
7. Is the register checked along with Personal Register?

5. Stock Files

1. Is the subject on which stock files are to be maintained fixed? Are they maintained accordingly?
(Subject-wise Stock Files to be maintained)

Section	Stock File	Subjects

2. Has Index been prepared for all the Stock files?
3. Are obsolete and cancelled orders weeded out from the stock file?
4. If amendments are issued are such amendments carried out in the original reference in the Stock File.
5. Has the Secretary, district panchayat checked the Stock Files?

(a) Are all Stock Files neatly arranged and stitched?

5. (a) Fair Copy Register

1. Is the Fair Copy Register maintained in the prescribed format?
2. Is the registers checked daily by the Secretary district panchayat?
3. Is there any delay in F.C.? If so point out a few cases.

(b) Computer – Use of Computer

1. Are the following particulars consolidated and entered in the computer?
2. Basic particulars
3. Scheme-wise list of works sanctioned and their progress.
4. Village Panchayat Annual Plan and other local bodies and other Government departments? Consolidated and District level Annual Plan prepared?

Sl. No. of F.C. Register	*Date of receipt*	*Date of typing*	*Delay*

6. Attendance Register

1. Is the Attendance Register submitted to the Secretary for daily check?
2. Is Late Attendance Register maintained and whether time of arrival and signing the register noted? Has Casual Leave or Earned Leave deducted for late attendance?
3. Is Casual Leave Register maintained in the prescribed format?
4. Are entries of leave taken properly entered?
5. Has additional Casual Leave taken regularised according to leave availed?

7. Establishament

(a) Is the Register of Service Register maintained correctly? Are Service Registers opened for all employees as per Fundamental Rules?

(b) Are all Service Registers verified and Certificate given as per Fundamental Rules and Service Rules?

(c) Total No. of Service
  (i) Registers to be maintained.
  (ii) No. of Service Registers shown for checking?
  (iii) Reasons for not showing the Register.

(d) Has the signature of the employee obtained once in five years in taken of having verified the entries.

(e) Are the nominations for the following schemes obtained and filed?
  (1) G.P.F.
  (2) Gratuity
  (3) Family Benefit Fund
  (4) Special Provident Fund

(f) Are any other defects noticed in the maintenance of Service Register? (Example) Is immovable property statement obtained and filed? Omission of entries of passing of Test, General Educational Qualification and some verification etc.

2. Increment
   (a) Is the Register of Increment maintained in the prescribed form and entries made quarter-wise?
   (b) Is there delay in sanction of increment?
3. Probation register
   (a) Is the register maintained to water declaration of completion of probation?
   (b) Is the registers checked along with the check of P.R.
   (c) Is there delay in declaration of probation?
4. (a) List out the names and Designation of Officers due for retirement next year?

Sl. No.	*Name and Designation*	*Date of superannuation*

   (b) Are there delays in the sanction of pension according to G.O.No.837 (Finance) dated 6.9.80 to any retired/heirs of deceased panchayat union and other employees?
   (c) Have any persons retired during the period of inspection?
   (d) Have they been given the following terminal benefits?
      (i) Pension
      (ii) G.P.F.

(iii) Encashment of leave
(iv) Leave on private affairs.

8. Suspension

(a) Is any Head of Office or subordinate been suspended?
Furnish date of suspension and stage of disciplinary action for each case of suspension
(b) Are currents opened on the due dates and registered as fresh current in the Personal Register?
(c) Is the Register checked periodically?

9. Stamp Account

(a) Is Stamp Account maintained properly?
(b) Stamp Register.
Is the Deputy BDO verifying the stock and stamps every day with the stock as per Account?
(c) When preparing the monthly indent for purchase of stamps? Is the stock of stamps on hand verified by the Secretary district panchayat?
(d) Verify stock and stamps on hand and give remarks.

10. Local and Outstation Despatch Register

1. Is the Register maintained properly?
2. Is the Register checked by the Deputy BDO and the Secretarydistrict panchayat in the prescribed time?
   (a) Is suspension ordered on public interest?
   (b) Has urgent action been taken to finalise the Disciplinary action taken against the persons under suspension?
   (d) Have they been given subsistence allowance as per F.R.53? Has any review been made?
   (e) Has action been taken to revise the subsistence allowance in over six month cases?

11. Disciplinary Action

(a) How many disciplinary actions were initiated during the period of Inspection? Furnish details.
(b) Has action taken to dispose of disciplinary action?
(c) For how many persons, punishments were inflicted? Have entries of punishment made in the Service Register? Furnish details.

12. Office Order Book

(a) Is Office Order Book maintained?
(b) Have obsolete Government Orders weeded out?

13. Call Book

(a) Is the 'Call Book' Register maintained in the prescribed form?

14. Arrear List

(a) Is monthly arrear list prepared by the Clerks and consolidated arrear list prepared every month as per G.O. No. 100 P & AR, dated 24.2.78?
(b) Is the consolidated arrear list checked usefully?
(c) Have instructions been given to dispose of files pending for more than six months?
(d) Furnish list of over six months file, scheme-wise.

Section	*Over six months*	*Over one year*	*Total*

15. Office Library

(a) Is a Library Register maintained? Have the Stock of Books verified every half year and certificate given?
(b) Are there any books taken from the Library by the Clerks and not returned for a very long time?
(c) Is the cost of missing book recovered from the person responsible and deleted from the Stock Register?

16. Record

(a) Is there a separate record room available?
(b) Is destruction of records have been arranged in order?

(c) Is destruction list prepared? If so has it been approved by Secretary of district panchayat?
(d) Any files are converted to R.Dis., it should be kept in R.Dis. bundle?
(e) If R.Dis and D.Dis. files are not to be kept permanently, it should be decided and ordered by the Secretary of district panchayat? Do any files move in this category?
(f) After destruction of files the list of destruction have been attested by the district panchayat Secretary
(g) Is destruction list maintained in concerned register?
(h) Is record issued register maintained properly?
(i) Are move any files issued from record and not returned for more than 3 months, and action to be taken to get back the file (after the completion of 3 months period).

17. Diary

(a) Is Diary of the district panchayat Secretary sent to the district panchayat in time.

18. Register of Special Letters

(a) Is Special Register maintained?
(b) Is it checked by the district panchayat Secretary daily?
(c) Have replies to any letters not sent in time? If so it should be shown in the prescribed statement given below?

Register No.	*Section Clerk*	*File No.*	*Date of receipt*	*Date of last action taken*	*Delay*

19. Record Sheet

(a) Is individual record sheet maintained and entries made upto date?

20. Vehicle

(a) Register No./Date of purchase.
(b) Whether the log book has been maintained upto date?
(c) Whether the details of fuel utilized and the fuel used per 1 litre for one km. entered in log book?
(d) Whether Fuel Register is maintained?
(e) Whether Expenditure Register is maintained properly?
(f) Whether the vehicle met with an accident? Whether Register for Accident is maintained?
(g) Whether Register for condemned items are maintained? Whether action has been taken for disposing them by auctioning?
(h) Whether log book Part II is maintained properly?
(i) Whether vehicle Stock Register is maintained?
(j) Whether quarterly verification takes place?
(k) Whether ceiling for expenditure for a quarter is violated?
(l) Whether ratification orders is received for excess expenditure?
(m) Whether fuel is utilized above the ceiling?
(n) Whether the vehicle is sent for service every month?
(o) Whether the vehicle is taken out of district?
(p) Whether the vehicle has been utilized by other Officers?
If so particulars on action taken to recover the expenditure?
(q) Whether register for tools and plants is maintained?
(r) Whether the vehicle has been sent for carrying out repairs in private firm without the permission of DMV?
(s) Whether tyre/battery has been purchased from private firms?
(t) During the service inspection whether the battery purchased newly? Furnish details.
(u) Whether Tour Programme is being sent to district panchayat president every month?
(v) Whether 'C' Form is renewed and maintained safely?
(w) Whether periodical inspection done to the vehicle? If the vehicle is condemned furnish orders of condemnation and action taken to purchase spare vehicle?

21. Tools and Plants

(a) Is sufficient tools and plants available?
(b) Stock Register for Tools have been checked and certificate given every year? If stock entries have not been made properly it should brought to the notice and should be taken necessary action.

22. Stationery

(a) Whether Stationery Register is maintained properly?
(b) Whether the stock is verified every half-year?

23. Office Building

(a) Whether District Panchayat Office is situated in own building and the building has necessary space?
(b) Whether maintenance of building has been made? If so mention last date of maintenance?
(c) Whether the building is built in the Government land?

Section III: Maintenance of Funds (Government Funds)

1. Verify whether the following registers are maintained properly and give remarks.
   (a) Bill Passed Registers (TNTC 70)
   (b) Pay Bill Register [TNTC 32-4(D)]
   (c) T.A. Bill Register (Allotment and expenditure to be noted)
   (d) Acquittance Register for T.A. Bills
   (e) Advance Recoverable Register
   (f) (1) Register for Festival Advance
   (2) Register for Uniform clothes
   (3) Register for Handloom clothes
   (4) Register for Khadi clothes
   (5) Register for Marriage Advance
   (6) Register for Cycle Advance.
   (g) Register for Last Pay Certificate
   (h) Cash Book
   (i) FBF, SPF Registers.

2. Permanent Advance Register

(a) Whether the Permanent Advance Register is maintained correctly?
(b) Whether the advance on hand is verified with vouchers?
Closing Balance on the date of inspection
Rs. Vouchers.
(c) Is any advance drawn against the norms and expenditure made?
(d) For the expenses are made above Rs. 500/- One rupee Revenue stamp should be pasted on sub-vouchers. Sub-vouchers should be attested after cancellation.
(e) Are all adjustments made in Red Ink?

3. Contingent Expenditure Register

(a) Whether Contingent Expenditure Register is maintained?
(b) Whether the expenditure entered it is in order?
(c) If any deposits are paid? If should be entered in the concerned head of account?
Whether included in the budget estimate?

4. Register for Security Deposit

(a) Whether the Security Register is maintained in prescribed proforma?
(b) Whether Bonds on Security are entered properly should be verified and attested by the Secretary, district panchayat.
(c) At the time of audit whether the Security Register and Bonds are verified?

5. Maintenance of Accounts

(a) Are all receipts kept safely in the double lock cash chest?
(b) Is double lock cash chest fixed on the wall?
(c) If receipts are kept in the cash chest for Rupees one thousand above, it has to be remitted to concerned Account.
(*vide* G.O.453, Fin. & Treasury Accounts, dated 7.6.83)
(d) Is everyday cash balance verified frequently/surprisingly by the Secretary, district panchayat?
(e) At the time of inspection, cash balance shall be verified physically by the inspecting Officer? and recorded in the notes?
(f) If Cashier post is not sanctioned to the Office, who will disburse the cash? Is deposit received from him and accounted for?

Section IV: District Panchayat Fund

1. Are separate Scheme Accounts maintained in the bank/post office for General Fund in the Treasury?
2. Whether Bank/Treasury balances are reconciled with district panchayat Accounts?
3. Whether the release of grants to panchayat unions, village panchayats and departments have been reconciled (or) not. If it is not taken to Account, give reasons.
4. Has Utilisation Certificate obtained from the concerned department and the local bodies?

6. Scheme-wise Particulars

Department	*Scheme*	*Amount given*	*Amount utilized*	*Balance*

(a) Is action taken to get back the balance?

7. Audit

Previous audit taken by Accountant General for which period?

Year-wise pending audit objection details

No. Settled

No. Pending

Is final reply prepared and sent to Accountant General?

Local Fund Audit Objections

Last date of audit

Pending (year-wise)

Settlement

Balance

Is final reply prepared and sent to L.F. Account?

8. Field Inspection

(a) Pending works

Name of Scheme	*Balance*	*Current*	*Total*	*Inspected*		
				Previous month	*Current month*	*Upto the month*

(b) Completion of work

(c) Are any irregularities noticed at the time of inspection and action taken to rectify them?

(d) Works executed through other Departments.

Inspection of works						
Sl. No.	*Name of Scheme*	*Balance*	*Current*	*Total*	*Completed*	*Balance*

9. Are Scheme and Saving Funds invested in Deposit Account. If so give details.

Details of District Panchayat

1. Details of district panchayat inauguration. Give details.
2. Details of district panchayat members.

	General		*SC/ST*		*Total*	
	Male	*Female*	*Male*	*Female*	*Male*	*Female*
President						
Vice-President						
Members						

3. Is Agenda and meeting notice given to every Councillor?
4. If at the time of Council Meeting are any subjects added or rejected by Chairman/Secretary.
5. Is Agenda served to Members in time? If not furnish reasons?
6. If Attendance Register maintained?
7. If meeting adjourned for want of quorum?
8. If there any subject taken for discussion in the meeting?
9. Are there any subjects not included in agenda of ordinary meeting?
10. Are meeting subjects postponed for any particular reason?
11. If it is so, the same subject is included for discussion in next meeting.
12. Is administration report prepared and sent to the Collectors approval by the district panchayat? What are the remarks of the Collector?
13. Are all Standing Committees formed?
    (a) Are all the resolutions of the Committee placed before district panchayat meeting?
    (b) Is a register maintained for disbursement of T.A. to the members?
    (c) Is follow up action taken on the resolution of district panchayat?
14. Is Annual Plan approved?
15. Is the list of other department works placed before the district panchayat?

District Panchayat Fund

1. District Panchayat Fund – Cash Book
   (a) Is Cash Book maintained properly and account closed upto the end of the last month?
   (b) Is abstract of the monthly account prepared and necessary attestation obtained from the Secretary of district panchayat.

(c) Are the Accounts reconciled with Bank/Treasury Pass Book?
(d) Is reconciliation register maintained properly and all the accounts are reconciled correctly?
(e) Is monthly statement of Accounts sent to L.F. Department in time.
(f) When was the last annual account sent?
(g) Is daily cash balance report sent?
(h) Is miscellaneous demand register maintained?
(i) Upto which year audit is taken?
   1. Total No. of objections
   2. No. settled
   3. Balance.

Annual District Development Plan

Is Annual Development Plan prepared consolidating the plans prepared by village panchayats and panchayat unions and sent to District Planning Committee in time. If it is not sent in time to District Planning Committee give reasons.

Duties of Secretary of District Panchayat

Is the relation between district panchayat Chairman and district panchayat Secretary cordial?
Works executed for district panchayat.
Participation for district panchayat meeting and in the discussion on subjects.
Administrative capacity.
General

7.10 MISCELLANEOUS

7.10.1 Awarding of Prizes to the Best Performing District Panchayats

The State Finance Commission recommended that the Awards may be given to the Presidents and Officers of local bodies to encourage their functioning and also for strengthening their institution from out of the incentive fund of the Government. The Government passed the following orders in this regard.

(a) 3 Village Panchayats in a District, 3 Panchayat Unions in a District level, 3 District Panchayats, 3 Panchayat Unions and 3 Village Panchayats at State level shall be selected every year and they can be awarded prizes as per Annexure I of this order.
(b) For awarding of prizes as per Annexure I, and for conduct of functions at District and State Level an amount of Rs. 10 lakhs is provided. (District level functions at the rate of Rs. 25,000/-, for 28 Districts Rs. 7 lakhs and for the State level function Rs. 3 lakhs). Moreover for giving Medals to the selected local bodies sanction is accorded for a sum of Rs. 3.54 lakhs.
(c) For selection of Village Panchayats and Panchayat Unions of District level, a Committee shall be constituted with the following Members.

President—District Collector

Members

(1) Additional Collector (Development)/Project Officer, District Rural Development Agency.
(2) One MLA nominated by the District Collector.
(3) One Social Worker nominated by the District Collector.
(4) One NGO working for the Welfare of Women and Children selected by the President and Members of the District Level Committee.
(5) The respective Assistant Director (Panchayats) of the Districts.

(d) For selection of the best village panchayats, panchayat unions and district panchayat at State Level Committee shall be constituted with following members.

Chairman—Secretary, Rural Development Department

Members

(1) Director of Rural Development.
(2) One Social Worker nominated by Government.
(3) One NGO working for the Welfare of local bodies nominated by Government.
(4) One MLA nominated by Government.

(e) The following Time-table shall be observed in the selection and awarding of best panchayats as per Annexure II.

The District Collectors and the Director of Rural Development are requested to take action to form the District Level and the State Level Committees.

The total expenditure involved in this programme, Rs. 1,95,54,000/- (Rupees One Crore Ninety Five Lakhs and Fifty Four thousand only) shall be sanctioned from equalisation and incentive grant sanctioned by the State Government.

ANNEXURE I

DETAILS OF PRIZES

Awarding of Prizes to 3 Best Village Panchayats at District Level

1st Prize	Rs. 1.00 lakhs
2nd Prize	Rs. 0.50 lakhs
3rd Prize	Rs. 0.25 lakhs
Rs. 1.75 lakhs × 28	Rs. 49.00 lakhs

Awarding of Prizes to 3 Best Panchayat Unions at District Level

1st Prize	Rs. 2.00 lakhs
2nd Prize	Rs. 1.00 lakhs
3rd Prize	Rs. 0.50 lakhs
Rs. 3.50 lakhs × 28	Rs. 98.00 lakhs

Awarding of Prizes to 3 Best District Panchayats at State Level

1st Prize	Rs. 10.00 lakhs
2nd Prize	Rs. 5.00 lakhs
3rd Prize	Rs. 3.00 lakhs
	Rs. 18.00 lakhs

Awarding of Prizes to 3 Best Panchayat Unions at State Level

1st Prize	Rs. 6.00 lakhs
2nd Prize	Rs. 3.00 lakhs
3rd Prize	Rs. 2.00 lakhs
	Rs. 11.00 lakhs

Awarding of Prizes to 3 Best Panchayats at District Level

1st Prize	Rs. 3.00 lakhs
2nd Prize	Rs. 2.00 lakhs
3rd Prize	Rs. 1.00 lakhs
	Rs. 6.00 lakhs
Total	Rs. 182.00 lakhs

ANNEXURE II

Time Schedule for Giving Awards to Local Bodies

	Last Date
District Level	
Receipt of Application	May
Scrutiny of Application and Selection of Local Bodies	July
Awarding of Prize	August
State Level	
Receipt of application at State level	August
Scrutiny of Application and Selection of Local Bodies	September
Awarding of Prize	October

(G.O. Ms. No. 97, Rural Development Department, dated 1st June 1999)

7.10.2 Guidelines for Selection of Best District Panchayat

In order to select the best district panchayat in a financial year, the following two stages of selection process may be adopted (a) Identification of eligible district panchayat for selection, (b) Selection of best district panchayat by awarding marks for performance under various items. Only those district panchayat which cross the ferries in (a) shall be evaluated for selection of best District Panchayat as per the questionnaires in (b).

The district panchayat which comes under one or more of the categories noted below cannot be taken for consideration as best district panchayat.

(1) District panchayat whose chairman or vice-chairman has been removed under Section 209 of the Tamil Nadu Panchayats Act, 1994 or against whose such action is pending consideration.

(2) District panchayat where serious financial irregularities are noticed during inspection or audit.

(3) After eliminating all the in eligible district panchayat, the other district panchayat may be evaluated by awarding marks for their performance. The district panchayats after evaluation may be selected and given rank as I, II, or III on the basis of marks awarded to them. If all the district panchayats obtain equal marks, the selection committee may scrutinize the registers maintained in the district panchayat and select one. In case, the selection committee is not able to select one district panchayat from among the district panchayats which have obtained equal marks. Such stage may be noted by the Committee.

Guidelines for Selection of Performing District Panchayat

Total marks: 100
For each question: 5 marks

Sl. No.	*Item*	*5 marks*	*3 ½ marks*	*2 marks*	*No marks*
1.	Whether District Panchayat meetings are conducted at regular interval	Conducted 12 or more than 12 meetings	Conducted 6-12 meetings	Conducted 3-5 meetings	Conducted less than 3 meetings
2.	Percentage of attendance in District Panchayat Meeting	100%	75-99%	50-74%	Less than 50%
3.	Percentage of attendance of women members in District Panchayat Meeting	100%	75-99%	50-74%	Less than 50%
4.	Whether the resolutions are passed based on agenda served to the members and passed based on detailed discussion with the members	Yes	–	–	No
5.	Whether District Panchayat Standing Committees have been constituted and they are functioning regularly	All the Standing Committees have been constituted and they are functioning regularly	All the Standing Committees have been constituted. But only three committees are functioning	All the Standing Committees have been constituted. But only 2 committees are functioning	Standing Committees have been constituted. But not functioning
6.	Whether Annual Plan of District Panchayat is prepared based on the proforma and regulations	Yes	–	–	No
7.	Whether Budget of District Panchayat is prepared and approved in time	Yes	–	–	No
8.	Whether works are approved in time	Yes	–	–	No
9.	Average cost of estimate of works taken by the District Panchayat	More than Rs. 10 lakhs	Rs. 5 lakhs to Rs. 10 lakhs	Rs. 2.5 lakhs to Rs. 5 lakhs	Less than Rs. 2.5 lakhs
10.	Whether the amount allotted for work is spent properly, Average percentage	100%	75-99%	50-74%	Less than 50%

Sl. No.	Item	5 marks	3 ½ marks	2 marks	No marks
11.	Works taken by the District Panchayat under Namakku Naame Thittam	More number of works in all 28 districts	Next number of works	Next number of works	–
12.	Whether District Panchayat Statistics have been consolidated and published	Yes	All the statistics have been consolidated, but not released	Only part of statistics have been consolidated but not published	No
13.	Whether Administration Report of District Panchayat is placed to Tamil Nadu State Legislative Assembly as per Section 165 of Tamil Nadu Panchayats Act, 1994	Yes	–	–	No
14.	Participation of Chairman and Members of District Panchayat in the Campaign of Anna Marumalarchi Thittam	All have participated	Only the Chairman has participated	Only members have participated	Not participated
15.	Whether schemes taken up under Section 164(d) of Tamil Nadu Panchayat Act, 1994 is inspected by District Panchayat properly	Excellent	Good	Satisfactory	No
16.	Allegations against Functions and meetings of District Panchayat	No	–	–	Yes
17.	Whether District Panchayat prepared Annual Plan and Five Year Plan for the District	Yes	Prepared only Five Year Plan	Prepared Annual Plan only	No
18.	Whether the District Panchayat has advised to the Government on classification of Fairs and Festivals, classification of roads under Section 163 of Tamil Nadu Panchayats Act, 1994	Yes on four subjects	Yes on two subjects	Yes on one subject	No
19.	Whether the District Panchayat Accounts have been audited in time	Yes	–	–	No
20.	Whether all the schemes and works have been completed in time	Yes all the times	Yes more than 75%	Yes 50%-74%	Less than 50

(G.O. Ms. No. 27, Rural Development (C1) Department, dated 5th February 2000).

PART VIII

RULES AND INSTRUCTIONS RELATING TO DISTRICT PLANNING COMMITTEE

8.1 CONSTITUTION OF DISTRICT PLANNING COMMITTEE

8.1.1 Constitution of District Planning Committee in 28 Districts

In exercise of the powers conferred by sub-section (1) of Section 241 of the Tamil Nadu Panchayats Act, 1994 (Tamil Nadu Act 21 of 1994), the Governor of Tamil Nadu hereby constitutes a District Planning Committee to the following districts, namely:

1. Kancheepuram
2. Tiruvallur
3. Vellore
4. Cuddalore
5. Vilupuram
6. Salem
7. Erode
8. Coimbatore
9. Dindigul
10. Madurai
11. Tiruchirappalli
12. Karur
13. Perambalur
14. Tirunelveli
15. Ramanathapuram
16. Virudhunagar
17. Thoothukudi
18. Kanniyakumari
19. Dharmapuri
20. Nagapattinam
21. Sivagangai
22. Thanjavur
23. The Nilgiris
24. Pudukkottai
25. Theni
26. Thiruvarur
27. Namakkal
28. Tirunvannamalai

(G.O. Ms. No. 327, Rural Development (C-1) Department, dated 14th November 1997)

8.1.2 Notification of Members of District Planning Committee

Under sub-clause (iv) of clause (a) of sub-section (2) of Section 241 of the Tamil Nadu Panchayats Act, 1994 (Tamil Nadu Act 21 of 1994) as amended by the Tamil Nadu Panchayats (Sixth Amendment) Ordinance, 2000, the Governor of Tamil Nadu hereby specifies the number of persons to be elected as members of the District Planning Committee of the district specified in column (1) of the Table, from among the members of the respective district panchayats, town panchayats and councillors of the Municipal Corporations and the Municipal Councils in the respective district as specified in the corresponding entries in columns (2) and (3) respectively thereof:

The Table

Name of the district	*Members to be elected from District Panchayats*	*Members to be elected from town Panchayats and councillors of the municipal corporations and municipal councils*
(1)	(2)	(3)
Thiruvallur	4	4
Kancheepuram	5	3
Vellore	5	3
Thiruvannamalai	7	1
Cuddalore	6	2
Villupuram	7	1
Dharmapuri	7	1
Salem	6	6
Namakkal	4	4
Erode	4	4
Coimbatore	5	7
The Nilgiris	2	6
Perambalur	7	1
Thiruchirapalli	7	5
Karur	5	3
Thanjavur	5	3
Nagapattinam	6	2
Thiruvarur	6	2
Pudukottai	7	1
Dindugal	5	3
Madurai	6	6
Theni	4	4
Ramanathapuram	6	2
Sivagangai	6	2
Virudhu Nagar	5	3
Tirunelveli	6	6
Thoothukudi	5	3
Kanniyakumari	2	6

(G.O. Ms. No. 21, Rural Development (C-4) Department dated 1st February 2000)

8.1.3 Election of Members to the District Planning Committee

1. Short title—These rules may be called the Tamil Nadu Local Bodies (Election of Members to the District Planning Committee) Rules, 1999.

2. Definition—(1) In these rules, unless the context otherwise requires:

(i) "Act" means the Tamil Nadu Panchayats Act, 1994 (Tamil Nadu Act 21 of 1994);

(ii) "ballot box" includes any box, bag or other receptacle used for the insertion of ballot paper by voters;

(iii) "candidate" means a person who has been or claims to have been duly nominated as a candidate at the election of members to the committee;

(iv) "casual vacancy" means a vacancy occurring otherwise than by efflux of time and "casual election" means an election held to fill a casual vacancy;

(v) "committee" means the District Planning Committee in a district;

(vi) "contesting candidate" means a candidate whose nomination has been duly accepted under sub-rule (5) of Rule 16, and who has not withdrawn his nomination;

(vii) "election Court" means the Court of the District Judge under whose jurisdiction the local bodies fall;

(viii) "form" means a form appended to these rules;

(ix) "Local Bodies" means the District Panchayat, Town Panchayats, Municipal Council and Municipal Corporations in a district;

(x) "marked copy of the voters list" means a copy of the voters list set apart for the purpose of marking the name of voters to whom a ballot paper is issued at the election of members to the committee;

(xi) "ordinary vacancy" means a vacancy occurring by efflux of time and "ordinary election" means an election held to fill an ordinary vacancy.

(xii) "polling officer" means the officer appointed under sub-rule (2) of Rule 19 of these rules, to assist the Presiding Officer in the performance of his duties;

(xiii) "polling station" means a place fixed under sub-rule (1) of Rule 19 of these rules for taking poll at the election of members to the Committee;

(xiv) "presiding officer" means an officer appointed under sub-rule (2) of Rule 19 of these rules for taking poll at the polling station;

(xv) "public holiday" means any day which is a public holiday for purposes of Section 25 of the Negotiable Instruments Act, 1881 (Central Act XXVI of 1881);

(xvi) "rural segment" means the rural area comprising the district panchayat in a district;

(xvii) "urban segment" means the urban area comprising the entire Town Panchayats, Municipal Councils and Municipal Corporation in a district;

(xviii) "voter" means a member is relation to a district panchayat or Town Panchayat or a Councillor in relation to a Municipal Council or Municipal Corporation, whose name is entered in the voters list of the district concerned for the time being in force;

(xix) "voters list" means the list containing the names of the voters.

(2) Words and expression used but not defined in these rules shall have the meanings respectively assigned to them in the Act. In the absence of such meaning, the Tamil Nadu General Clauses Act, 1891 (Act I of 1891) shall apply for the interpretation of these rules, as it applies for the interpretation of a Tamil Nadu Act.

3. Powers and Functions of the State Election Commission—(1) The preparation of voters list and the conduct of election of members to the Committee shall be under the superintendence and control of the Tamil Nadu State Election Commission (hereinafter called as the State Election Commission) and for this purpose it shall have power to give such directions as it may deem necessary to any officer or employee of the Government engaged, appointed, or empowered under these rules, for the purpose.

(2) The State Election Commission may subject to its control and revision, delegate its power to such officers as it may deem necessary.

(3) All such officers, and the police personnel posted for election duty shall be deemed to be on deputation to the State Election Commission for the period commencing on and from the date of preparation of voters list till its completion and from the date of notification calling for such election and ending with the date of completion of such election and shall during that period subject to the control, superintendence of the State Election Commission.

4. State Election Officer—The Director of Rural Development, Director of Town Panchayats and Commissioner of the Municipal Administration shall be the State Election Officers who shall co-ordinate and supervise the preparation and publication of the voters list and also the conduct of election of members to the Committee in respect of the district panchayat, Town Panchayats and Municipal Councils and Corporations respectively.

5. District Election Officer—The District Collector shall be the District Election Officer who shall co-ordinate and supervise the preparation and publication of the voters list also the conduct of election of members to the Committee. He shall report the vacancies within a week to the State Election Commission. He shall also perform such other functions as may be entrusted to him by the State Election Commission.

6. Registration Officer—The District Collector shall be the Registration Officer for the purposes of preparing and publishing the voters list.

7. Returning Officer—An officer not below the rank of Joint Director or District Revenue Officer nominated by the State Election Commission shall be the Returning Officer for the conduct of election of members to the committee.

8. General duties of the Returning Officer—Subject to the Superintendence, direction and control of the State Election Commission and under the supervision and guidance of the District Election Officer, the Returning Officer shall be responsible for the proper conduct of election of members to the Committee in the manner provided in these rules and any other orders issued by the State Election Commission.

9. Assistant Returning Officer—(1) The Returning Officer may appoint as many Assistant Returning Officers as required for each section of a segment to assist the Returning Officer in the performances of all or any of his duties and functions:

Provided that every such person shall be an officer of the Government not below the rank of Assistant Director or Deputy Collector.

(2) Every Assistant Returning Officer shall, subject to the control of the Returning Officer, be competent to perform all or any of the duties of the function of the Returning Officer.

10. Preparation and publication of voters list—(1) The Registration Officer shall prepare the voters list in Form 1 containing the names of all members of the district panchayat, Town Panchayat and Councillors of the Municipal Corporations and the Municipal Councils in the District concerned.

(2) The voters list shall be prepared as follows:

(a) There shall be only one voters list for a district.

(b) All members or councillors of the respective local bodies who are holding office as such shall be included in the voters list.

(c) There shall be segment and section in the voters list showing the names of local bodies as specified below:

Part A – Rural Segment
Section 1 – District Panchayat
Part B – Urban Segment
Section 2 – Municipal Corporations
Section 3 – Municipal Councils
Section 4 – Town Panchayats

(d) Serial number of voters shall be given consecutively.

(e) The names of local bodies shall appear first and then the names of members or councillors, as the case may be, appear below that local body ward-wise.

(f) The names of voters shall be arranged in the order of serial number of ward or division to which they are elected.

(g) The State Election Commission shall decide matters relating to number of copies of the list to be printed, custody and supply of voters list to the local bodies and to the candidates and fixing of sale price to the public.

(3) The voters list shall be prepared before conducting every ordinary or casual election.

(4) The voters list shall be published along with a notice in Form 2 on a date which shall not be less than thirty days prior to the issue of notification referred to in sub-rule (1) of Rule 11 in the notice board of the Offices of the Registration Officer and the Returning Officer and in the office of the local bodies. In the case of additions, deletions and corrections of names, if any, after such publication, the Registration Officer shall cause necessary amendments to the voters list:

Provided that no such amendment shall be caused, after the last date of making nomination for the election of members to the Committee.

(5) Two copies of the voters list as amended and updated from time-to-time, shall be in the custody of the Registration Officer for a period of six years from the date of its final publication or till a new consolidated list is published, whichever is earlier.

11. Notification of Programme of Election—(1) For the purpose of filling up of ordinary and causal vacancies in the committee, the State Election Commission shall, in consultation with the Government, publish a notification, calling upon the voters to elect members to the committee on such date or dates as may be specified therein.

(2) The notification referred to in sub-rule (1) shall specify

(a) the date on which the notice of election shall be published in the offices of the local bodies.

(b) the last date for making nominations which shall be the third day after the publication of notice of election referred to in clause (a) or, if that day is a public holiday, the next working day and the hours between which the nominations may be made which shall be 11.00 a.m. and 3.00 p.m. on each day the time and date for scrutiny of the nominations which shall be 11.00 a.m. of the day immediately following the last date for making nominations or, if that day is a public holiday, the next working day, the hour and date upto which the withdrawal of nominations maybe made which shall be 3.00 p.m. of the second day after the date for scrutiny of nominations or, if that day is a public holiday, the next working day.

(c) The date on which the votes of voters shall be taken if there is a poll which shall be a date not earlier than the seventh day after the last date for the withdrawal of nominations and the polling hours during which the poll shall be open which shall not be less than 5 hours between 10.00 a.m. and 3.30 p.m.

(d) The date before which the election shall be completed.

(e) The date on which the first meeting of the newly elected members of the committee shall be held for the transaction of business.

(3) The notification referred to in sub-rule (1) shall be published in the Tamil Nadu Government Gazette and the respective District Gazette and also in the offices of the local bodies.

(4) The casual vacancy shall be filled up within a period of three months from the date of its occurrence:

Provided that no causal vacancy shall be filled in cases where the expiry of the tenure of the Committee is due within three months.

12. Notice of election—In pursuance of the notification of the State Election Commission under sub-rule (1) of Rule 11, the Returning Officer shall published on the date specified by the Election Commission in the offices of the local bodies, a notice of election in Form 3.

(2) The notice of election under sub-rule (1) shall contain the following particulars, namely:

(i) segment or segments for which election to be held and the number of members to be elected for each segment.

(ii) the dates on which the place at which and the hours between which the nomination papers shall be presented.

(iii) the person or persons by whom the nomination papers shall be received.

(iv) the date and the hours and the place at which the nomination papers shall be taken up for scrutiny.

(v) the last date on which and hours upto which the nomination papers shall be withdrawn.

(vi) the date on which and hours and the place at which the votes of the voters shall be taken, if there is a poll.

(vii) the date on which and the hours and place at which the Returning Officer shall commence the counting of votes.

(viii) the date before which the election shall be completed.

(ix) the date on which the first meeting of the elected members of the Committee shall be held for the transaction of business.

(3) The notice of election shall be published in the notice board of the offices of the Returning Officer and local bodies.

13. Presentation of nomination paper—(1) The nomination of every candidate shall be made by means of nomination paper in Form 4 which may be obtained from the officers specified in the notice of election on any working day during office hours.

(2) On the date or dates specified in the election notice for the presentation of nomination papers, any candidates who intends to contest the election of members to the Committee shall, either in person, or by his proposer deliver to the Returning Officer at the place and during the hours specified in that behalf, a nomination paper duly filled and signed by the candidates and by a proposer who shall also be a voter of the same section to which the candidate belongs:

Provided that a proposer shall not sign more number of nomination papers than the number of members to be elected from the section to which he belongs:

Provided further that a candidate may also sign as a proposer to as many candidates of the same section, as there are vacancies to be filled up less one number.

(3) On the presentation of a nomination paper, the Returning Officer shall satisfy himself that the names and roll numbers of the candidate and his proposer as entered in the nomination paper are the same as those entered in the list:

Provided that the Returning Officer may over look any inaccurate description or clerical mistake or printing error in regard to the names and numbers of the candidates and proposer in the list.

14. Receipt of nominations—(1) The Returning Officer shall, on receiving nomination paper inform the person presenting the same the date, time and place fixed for the scrutiny of nomination and shall enter on the nomination paper its serial number which shall be separate for candidate from each segment and shall sign there on recording the date on which and the hour at which the nomination paper has been presented to him.

(2) After closing of the time fixed for receiving the nomination paper, on each day, the Returning Officer shall publish in the notice board of his office, a notice in Form 5 containing the details of all the nomination papers presented to him on that day.

(3) On the last day, after the expiry of the hour fixed for receipt of nomination papers, the Returning Officer shall publish in the notice board of his office a consolidated list of nomination papers received by him in Form 6 together with the information regarding the date, time and place fixed for the scrutiny of nomination.

(a) If a candidate considers that his name is incorrectly spelt or he is otherwise incorrectly shown in his nomination paper, he may at any time before the list of contesting candidates is prepared, furnish in writing to the Returning Officer the proper form and spelling of his name and the Returning Officer shall on being satisfied as to the genuineness of the request make necessary correction or alteration in the list of nomination in Form 6 and adopt that form and spelling in the list of contesting candidates.

15. Scrutiny of nomination—(1) On the date and hour notified the Returning Officer shall take up the scrutiny of nominations segment-wise at such place fixed for scrutiny. The candidate and his proposer shall be allowed to attend the office at the time of such scrutiny. The Returning Officer shall give them all reasonable facilities for perusal of the nomination papers of all the candidates which have been entered in the list of nomination in Form 6.

(2) If any candidate or his proposer objects to any nomination, he shall do so in writing.

(3) The Returning Officer shall, then, examine the nomination papers and decide section-wise of each segment all objections which may be raised to any nomination and may either on such objection or on his own motion after such enquiry as he thinks necessary reject any nomination on anyone of the grounds:

(a) that there has been a failure to comply with any of the provisions in these rules; or

(b) that the signature of the candidate or the proposer on the nomination paper is not genuine.

(4) The Returning Officer shall not reject any nomination paper on the ground of any defect which is not of a substantial character.

(5) The Returning Officer shall endorse on each nomination paper his decision accepting or rejecting the same. If the nomination paper is rejected he shall record in writing a brief statement of the reasons for such rejection and furnish a copy of the same to the candidate concerned, if any application in this behalf has been made to him.

(6) Immediately after the scrutiny of all the nomination papers, the Returning Officer shall prepare a list of validity nominated candidates in Form 7 and publish a copy thereof in the notice board of his office. The list of validly nominated candidates shall be drawn up in the order of Tamil alphabet.

16. Withdrawal of candidates and preparation of list of contesting candidates—(1) Any candidate may withdraw his nomination by giving a notice in Form 8 written by him and delivered to the Returning Officer before the time fixed for that purpose. The notice may be delivered either by such candidate in person or by his proposer who has been authorized in this behalf in writing by such candidate.

(2) On receipt of such notice, the Returning Officer shall note thereon the date and time at which it was delivered to him.

(3) No person who has given a notice of withdrawal of his nomination under sub-rule (1) shall be allowed to withdraw his notice again.

(4) At the close of that date and time fixed for the withdrawal of nominations the Returning Officer shall, on being satisfied as to the genuineness of the notice of the withdrawal and identity of the person delivering it under sub-rule (1) publish in his office a notice showing the list of candidates who have withdrawn their nominations in Form 9.

(5) Immediately after the expiry of the period within which the nomination may be withdrawn under sub-rule (1) the Returning Officer shall prepare in Form 10 a list of contesting candidates in Tamil alphabetical order, which shall be published in the notice board of his office.

17. Procedure in contested and uncontested elections—(1) If the number of contesting candidates is equal or less than the number of vacancies to be filled up in a segment, the Returning Officer shall immediately after the publication of the list of contesting candidates, declare such candidates as duly elected and publish the same in Form 11 in the notice board of his office.

(2) If the number of contesting candidates is more than the number of vacancies to be filled up in a segment, then the Returning Officer shall arrange for a poll to be taken for that segment.

18. Ballot papers—(1) Every ballot paper for election of members to the committee from the rural segment and the urban segment shall be in Form 12 and in Form 13 respectively. The names of the contesting candidates shall be provided on the ballot papers in the same order in which the names appear in Form 10. The size of the ballot paper and other matters regarding thereto shall be decided by the State Election Commission.

(2) Both the ballot papers and the counterfoils shall be serially numbered and shall be stamped on their reverse by such distinguishing mark and in such manner as may be directed by the State Election Commission

19. Provision of polling station appointment of Presiding Officers and Polling Officers—(1) The Returning Officer shall for the purpose of conducting poll, provide one polling station for each section of a segment at the District Head Quarters. At each polling station there shall be set up two number of voting compartment in which voters record their votes screened from observation of others.

(2) The Returning Officer shall appoint for each polling station one Presiding Officer and not more than three polling officers to assist the Presiding Officer.

20. Appointment of polling agents—(1) Each contesting candidate may appoint one polling agent and one relief polling agent to act as the polling agent of such candidate at each polling station.

(2) Every such appointment shall be made in Form 14 and shall be handed over to the polling agent for production at the polling station.

(3) Each contesting candidate or his polling agent shall have a right to be present at the polling station provided for taking the poll.

(4) Where any Act or thing is required or authorised by these rules to be done in the presence of the polling agent, the non attendance of any such agent at the time and place appointed for the purpose shall not invalidate the act or thing done, if the act or thing is otherwise done fully in accordance with these rules.

21. Identification of voters—The Commissioners of Municipal Corporation and Municipal Councils, the executive officers of the Town Panchayats and the Chief Executive Officer of the district panchayat shall issue a certificate of identity to each councillor, member, as the case may be, of the respective local bodies in Form 15 duly signed in ink with official seal. The voter shall produce this identification certificate before he is permitted to receive the ballot paper and vote.

22. Marked copy of voters list—There shall be two marked copy of voters list for each polling station.

23. Procedure for voting—(1) The Presiding Officer shall immediately before the commencement of the poll, show the ballot box empty to such contesting candidates or their polling agents present and shall then seal it using a metal wire in such a way that the ballot paper can only be inserted but could not be withdrawn from it.

(2) As soon as a voter enters into the polling station the Polling Officer concerned shall verify the identity of the voter on the basis of the identification certificate issued under Rule 21. After establishing the identity of the voter correctly and before any ballot paper is delivered to a voter, the Presiding Officer shall affix his signature in full on back of that ballot paper and affix the distinguishing mark of the polling station. The serial number and other particulars of the voter shall be noted in the counterfoil and the voter shall be required to sign it. The entry relating to the voter in the marked copy of the list shall be underlined.

(3) The voter, on receiving the ballot paper shall forthwith proceed to one of the voting

compartments which is vacant and then with the aid of the instrument supplied for the purpose make a mark on the ballot paper against the name(s) of the candidate or candidates for whom he intends to vote. He shall then fold the ballot paper so as to ensure secrecy of voting and then insert the folded ballot into the ballot box kept for the purpose.

(4) Every voter shall vote without undue delay and shall leave the polling station as soon as he had voted shall not insert anything except ballot paper in the ballot box.

(5) If the Presiding Officer is satisfied that owing to old age, blindness, illiteracy or other physical infirmity a voter is unable to read the names of the candidates or to make mark or marks thereon without assistance, the Presiding Officer shall permit the voter to take with him a companion of not less than 18 years of age to the voting compartment for recording his vote on the ballot paper on his behalf and in accordance with his wishes. The Presiding Officer shall keep a record of all such cases under this rule in his diary.

(6) Any voter whom the Presiding Officer considers that he is causing obstruction disobeying the direction of the Presiding Officer or adopting unfair and unreasonable measures so as to delay the poll or waste the ballot paper, the Presiding Officer shall have power, to direct such voter to leave the polling station after taking back the ballot paper, if any, with such a voter.

24. Spoilt and returned ballot papers—(1) A voter who has inadvertently dealt with his ballot paper in such a manner that it cannot be used as a valid ballot paper, may return it to the Presiding Officer, who if satisfied of the inadvertence, may issue another ballot paper and the ballot paper so returned shall be marked "Spoilt-Returned" and mentioned in the diary.

(2) If a voter after obtaining a ballot paper decides not to use it, he shall return it to the Presiding Officer and the ballot paper so returned shall be marked "Returned Cancelled" by the Presiding Officer.

(3) If a voter, to whom a ballot paper has been issued, refuses after warning given by the Presiding Officer to observe the procedure as laid down in Rule 23, the ballot paper issued to him shall whether he has recorded his vote thereon or not, be taken back from him by the Presiding Officer. After the ballot paper has been taken back, the Presiding Officer shall record on its back the words "Cancelled Voting procedure violated".

(4) All such ballot papers specified in sub-rules (1), (2) and (3) shall be signed by the Presiding Officer below those words and kept in separate covers.

25. Closing of poll—(1) The Presiding Officer shall close the polling station at the hour fixed in that behalf under clause (c) of sub-rule (2) of Rule 11 of these rules and shall not thereafter admit any voter into the polling station:

Provided that all voters present at the polling station before it was closed, shall be allowed to cast their votes.

(2) If any question arises as to whether a voter was present at the polling station before it was closed, it shall be decided by the Presiding Officer whose decision shall be final.

(3) The Presiding Officer of each polling station shall, after the close of the poll, close the slit of the ballot box and seal the slit and also allow any candidate or his polling agent present to affix his seal. The ballot boxes shall thereafter be sealed and secured. The last serial number of the ballot paper shall be announced to the candidates or his polling agent present.

(4) The Presiding Officer, shall then make up the following into separate packets and seal them with the seal supplied and allow the candidates or polling agents to affix their own seal, if they so desire:

(i) The marked copy of the voters list;
(ii) The unused ballot papers and spoilt returned and cancelled ballot papers; and
(iii) Any other papers directed by the State Election Commission.

(5) The Presiding Officer shall, at the close of poll prepare a ballot paper account in Form 16 and close his diary.

(6) The Presiding Officer shall then deliver the ballot boxes (used and unused), the ballot paper account, the Presiding Officer Diary, sealed packers referred to in sub-rule (4) and all other polling materials to the Returning Officer who shall arrange to receive them and grant a receipt for the same.

26. Arrangements for counting and appointment of counting staff—(1) There shall be one counting centre at the District Headquarters with one counting table for each section of a segment with necessary furniture and other seating arrangements at such scale as the Returning Officer considers necessary with reference to the counting of votes and for accommodating counting staff and the candidates.

(2) The Returning Officer or the Assistant Returning Officer shall appoint as many counting

teams as may be determined by the State Election Commission for counting the votes polled for each section of a segment. Each team shall consist of one counting Supervisor and two counting Assistants. The Returning Officer shall arrange to give training to the counting staff.

27. Admission to the place fixed for counting—(1) The counting of votes shall take place on the day at the place and hour appoint in that behalf. The votes shall be counted by or under the supervision and direction of the Returning Officer. Each contesting candidate and his counting agent shall have a right to be present at the time of counting. The counting agent shall be appointed in writing by the candidate in Form 17. No person shall be allowed to be present except the following:

(i) the counting Supervisors and counting Assistants;

(ii) public servants on duty in connection with the election; and

(iii) such person as may be authorized by the State Election Commission.

(2) No person who has been employed by or on behalf of any candidate for any purpose whatsoever connected with the election shall be appointed to assist in counting the votes.

28. Opening of ballot boxes—Before any ballot box is opened at a counting table the Returning Officer shall satisfy himself that none of the ballot boxes has in fact, been tampered with. Then at the hour appointed for the counting of votes, the ballot boxes shall be opened one by one in the presence of the candidates or their agent, votes polled taken out and put in a big tray. After taking out all the votes polled the ballot box shall be shown empty to those present. The Returning Officer shall, then, verify the ballot paper account submitted by the Presiding Officer under sub-rule (5) of Rule 25.

29. Counting of votes—The vote polled by each candidate shall be counted form each polled valid ballot paper using a counting sheet in Form 18. When a first valid polled ballot paper is taken up for counting votes, the name of the candidate against whom vote has been marked, shall be read out by one of the counting Assistants and the second counting Assistant shall forthwith enter "1" below the name of that candidate in the column intended for him. Likewise reading and entering of votes marked in that ballot paper shall be completed fully before the next ballot paper is taken up. When the second valid polled ballot paper is taken up and the name of the same candidate is read out for the second time, the second counting Assistant shall enter "2" below the number "1". If less number of votes than the required of votes are marked, then, a 'dash' (–) shall be entered below the name of the candidate who has not secured any vote. In such manner each valid polled ballot paper shall be counted and entries shall be made accordingly. The Returning Officer shall then make the entries relating thereto in a result sheet in Form 17.

30. Fresh poll in the case of destruction of polling materials—(1) If at the election of members to the Committee:

(a) any polling material used at a polling station or at a place appointed for counting of votes is unlawfully taken out of the custody of the Presiding Officer or the Returning Officer or is accidentally or intentionally destroyed, or lost or is damaged or tampered with to such an extent that the result of the poll at that polling station cannot be ascertained; or

(b) any such error or irregularity in procedure as is likely to vitiate the poll is committed at a polling station; the Returning Officer shall forthwith report the matter to the State Election Commission through the District Election Officer.

(2) Thereupon the State Election Commission shall after taking all material circumstances into account, if satisfied:

(a) that a fresh poll is necessary, declare the poll at the polling station to be void, appoint a day and fix the hours for taking a fresh poll at that polling station and notify the day so appointed and hours so fixed in such a manner as it may deem fit besides intimating the contesting candidates; or

(b) that the result of the poll at the polling station shall not in any way affect the result of the election or that the error or irregularity in procedure is not material, issue such directions to the Returning Officer to continue the poll and complete the election.

(3) The provisions of these rules or orders made thereunder shall apply to every such poll as they apply to the original poll.

31. Rejection of ballot paper—(1) A ballot paper shall be rejected:

(a) if no vote is recorded thereon; or

(b) if votes are given in favour of more candidates than the number of candidates to be elected; or

(c) if it bears any mark or writing by which the voter can be identified; or

(d) if the mark indicating the votes thereon is placed in such manner as it makes it doubtful to which candidate the vote has been given; or

(e) if it is a spurious ballot paper; or

(f) if it is so damaged or mutilated that its identity as a genuine ballot paper can not be established; or

(g) if it bears a serial number, or is of a design, different from the serial numbers or design, as the case may be, of the ballot papers authorized for use at that polling station; or

(h) if it does not bear both the distinguishing mark or the signature of the Presiding Officer which it should have borne under the provisions of sub-rule (2) of Rule 23; or

(i) if it is not the relevant ballot paper; and

(j) if all votes are marked in an area outside the area intended for making votes:

Provided that where the Returning Officer is satisfied that any such defect as is mentioned in clause (g) or clause (h) has been caused by any mistake or failure on the part of the Presiding Officer, the ballot paper shall not be rejected merely on the ground of such defect:

Provided further that a ballot paper shall not be rejected merely on the ground that the mark indicating the vote is not distinct or made more than once, if the intention that the vote shall be for a particular candidate clearly appears from the way the paper is marked.

(2) All ballot paper rejected under sub-rule (1) shall be made into separate bundle.

(3) The decision of the Returning Officer under this rule shall be final, subject only to the decision of the Election Court on an election petition.

32. Declaration of result of Election and Publication—(1) As soon as the counting of votes is completed, the Returning Officer shall draw a list of contesting candidates arranged in descending order of votes secured by them. He shall, then, declare as many candidates from the top of the list as there are vacancies to be filled up, as duly elected.

In the event of there being an equality of votes between any two candidates, and the addition of one vote to anyone of such candidate will entitle him to be declared duly elected, the Returning Officer shall draw a lot in the presence of such candidates, and the candidate, whose name is first drawn shall be deemed to have secured one additional vote and shall be declared elected. The Returning Officer shall, then complete the result sheet in Form 17, declare the results in Form 19 and then send a Return of election in Form 21 to the District Election Officer, State Election Officer and the State Election Commission.

(2) Any contesting candidate on application be permitted to take a copy or an extract of the result sheet in Form 19.

(3) As soon as the signed copy of the Return of election in Form 21 referred to in sub-rule (1) is received, the State Election Commission shall publish the same in the Tamil Nadu Government Gazette and the District Election Officer shall arrange to publish the same in the District Gazette and also in the notice board of the offices of the local bodies in a consolidated form.

33. Disposal of ballot papers and election records—(1) The Returning Officer shall, after declaring the result, retain in his custody or cause to be deposited in the custody of the officer as may be specified by the State Election Commission, the following polling materials and records:

(a) sealed packet containing nominations and other records received upto the publication of valid list of contesting candidates;

(b) sealed packets of the ballot papers, whether counted rejected, cancelled or unused, spoilt and returned; and

(c) marked copy of the voters list.

(2) The materials referred to under sub-rule (1) shall be put into a steel box duly sealed and kept in safe custody of the Returning Officer or the officer specified by the State Election Commission under sub-rule (1) for a period of one year and shall thereafter, unless otherwise directed by the Election Court, they shall be destroyed.

34. Duration of the term of the committee—The terms of the Committee shall be co-terminus with the term of the local bodies.

35. Removal of difficulties—(1) The State Election Commission may issue such general or special direction as may, in its opinion is necessary for the purpose of giving effect to these rules or for holding the election under the Act.

(2) If any difficulty arises in giving effect to the provisions of these rules, or in holding the election, the State Election Commission as occasion may require, may, by order do anything which appears to it necessary for the purpose of removing the difficulty.

36. Savings—Notwithstanding anything contained in these rules all orders, directions, issued by the Government, State Election Commission or State Election Officer, for the preparation of voters list and for conduct of election under these rules, shall unless repugnant to these rules, be deemed to have been issued or made under these rules.

(G.O. Ms. No. 245, Rural Development (C-4) 2nd December 1999)

FORM 1

[See Rule 10(1)]

Voter List for the Election of Members to the District Planning Committee from the Rural and Urban Segments

Name of the District

Names of Members and Councillors of the District Panchayat, Municipal Corporation, Municipal Councils and Town Panchayats, as the case may be.

Part A – Rural Segment
Section 1 – District Panchayat

Part B – Urban Segment

Section 2 – Municipal Corporation
Section 3 – Municipal Councils
Section 4 – Town Panchayats

Section 1____________________District Panchayat

Sl. No.	*Name of the Member*	*Ward No. to which elected*
(1)	(2)	(3)
1.		
2.		
3.		
4.		

Section 2____________________Municipal Corporation

Sl. No.	*Name of the Member*	*Ward No. to which elected*
(1)	(2)	(3)
1.		
2.		
3.		
60.		

Section 3____________________Municipal Council

Sl. No.	*Name of the Member*	*Ward No. to which elected*
(1)	(2)	(3)
1.		
2.		
3.		
60.		

Section 4____________________Town Panchayat

Sl. No.	*Name of the Member*	*Ward No. to which elected*
(1)	(2)	(3)
1.		
2.		
3.		
16.		
30.		

Electoral Registration Officer and Collector________________________________District

FORM 2
Notice of Publication of Voters List
[See Rule 10(4)]

Notice is hereby given that the Vofer list relating the election of members to the District Planning Committee from member of District Panchayats/Town Panchayats from Councillors of Municipal Corporation/Municipal Council________________has been prepared in accordance with the Tamil Nadu Panchayat Local Bodies (Election of Members to the District Planning Committee) Rules, 1999 by adopting latest list of members of the local bodies and is published this day the________(date)__________(month)_________(year) for the general information of the electors.

Registration Officer and
Collector,__________District.

2. In the event of a Poll, the Poll will be held at the Polling Station located in the office of the Collector________floor No./Room No.

FORM 3
Notice of Election
[See Rule 12 (1)]

Election of members of the District Planning Committee__________________District.

Notice is hereby given that:

1. Elections are to be held to elect Member or Members to the District Planning Committee__________(District) as

The Table

Segment	*Name of Members to be elected*
(a) Rural segment containing the member of the District Panchayat	....
(b) Urban segment containing the member of the Town Panchayat and the Councillors of the Municipal Corporation, Municipal Council	....

2. Nomination papers may be delivered by a candidate or his proposer to the Returning Officer/Assistant Returning Officer at (place)_________________between 11.00 a.m. and 3.00 p.m. on any day (other than a public holiday) from______________to______________at________________(place of receipt).
3. Forms of nomination papers will be available in the Office and the Offices of the local Bodies and the Office of the Assistance Returning Officer from this date on all working days.
4. The nomination papers will be taken up for scrutiny at 11.00 a.m. on_________at_________(time) at ________(place)
5. Notice of withdrawal of candidature shall be delivered by a candidate or his proposer who has been specifically

authorizes in this behalf in wiring by the candidate to the Returning Officer/Assistant Returning Officer upto 3.00 p.m. on________________at____________________(place).

6. In the event of the election being contested, the poll shall be taken on _______________between___________a.m. and _______________p.m. at the polling station located in the office of the Collector_______________(place)
7. The counting of votes shall commence at_______________a.m. on_________at_____________(place)
8. The election shall be completed before_______________(date).
9. The newly elected members shall enter into office with effect from a date notified by the Government in this behalf and hold office upto the date of expiry of the term of office or the local body to which such members are elected as members.

Returning Officer and Collector

Place_______________
Date_______________

FORM 5
Notice of Nomination for Rural/Urban Segment
[See Rule 14(2)]

Election of Members to the District Planning Committee_______________(District)

Notice is hereby given that the following nomination in respect of the above election has been received upto the prescribed hours on the day_______________(date).

Serial Number of Nomination	*Name of the Candidate*	*Name of Father/Husband*	*Name Local Body to which belongs*
(1)	(2)	(3)	(4)
Sex	*Voter list number of the candidate*	*Name of the proposer*	*Voter list number of the proposer*
(5)	(6)	(7)	(8)

Returning Officer/Assistant Returning Officer

Place_______________
Date_______________

FORM 6
List of Nominations Received for Rural/Urban Segment
[See Rules 14(3), 14(4) and 14 (5)]

Election of Members to the District Planning Committee___________(Name of the District)

List of nomination received for the election of members to the District Planning Committee_______________(Name of the District)

Serial Number	*Name of the Candidate*	*Father's/Husband's Name*	*Name of local body to which belongs*	*Sex*
(1)	(2)	(3)	(4)	(5)

Note: The nomination papers will be taken up for scrutiny at 11.00 a.m._____at________(place)

Retuning Officer/Assistant Returning Officer

FORM 7
List of Validly Nominated Candidates for Rural/Urban Segment
[See Rule 15 (6)]

Election of Members to the District Planning Committee

List of nomination received for the election of member/members from Rural/Urban Segment.

Serial Number	Name of the Candidate	Father's/Husband's Name	Name of local body to which belongs	Sex
(1)	(2)	(3)	(4)	(5)

Returning Officer/Assistant Returning Officer

FORM 8
Notice of Withdrawal
[See Rule 16(1)]

Election of Members to the District Planning Committee____________from the Rural/Urban Segment

To
The Returning Officer and
the Collector,
____

I____________a candidate nominated at the above election from the Rural/Urban segment do hereby give notice that I withdraw my candidate.

I hereby authorize Thiru/Tmt/Selvi____________who has proposed my candidature to present this notice or withdrawal?

Signature of Candidate

Place____________
Date____________

The notice was delivered to me at my office at____________(hour) on ____________(date) by____________the____________candidate/the proposer.

Date____________

Returning Officer/Assistant Returning Officer

RECEIPT FOR NOTICE OF WITHDRAWAL
(To be handed over to the person delivering the notice)

The notice of withdrawal of candidature by Thiru/Tmt/Selvi____________a candidate at the election of members from the Rural/Urban segment of the District Planning Committee____________(Name of the District) was delivered to me by the____________at my office at____________(hour) on____________(date).

Returning Officer/Assistant Returning Officer

Note: * Here insert one of the following alternatives as may be appropriate:
(1) Candidate; or
(2) Candidate's proposer who has been authorized in writing by the candidate to deliver it.

FORM 9
List Showing Notices of Withdrawal of Nominations
[See Rule 16(4)]

Election of members to the District Planning Committee____________(name of the District) from the Rural/Urban Segment.

Notice is hereby given that the following candidate/candidates at the above election has/have withdrawn his candidature/their candidature today.

Name of the candidate	Name of local body to which he belongs	Remarks
(1)	(2)	(3)

Returning Officer/Assistant Returning Officer

Place____________
Date____________

FORM 10
List of Contesting Candidates
[See Rules 16(5) and 18]

Election of Members to the District Planning Committee__________(Name of the District____________)
List of contesting candidates for election of members from the Rural/Urban segment

Serial Number	*Name of candidate*	*Sex*	*Ward No. and name of the Local body to which he belongs*	*Address of the candidate*
(1)	(2)	(3)	(4)	(5)

Note: The poll will be taken on_______between_________a.m. and__________p.m. at the polling station located ______

Returning Officer/Assistant Returning Officer

Place____________
Date____________

FORM 11
Declaration of the Result of Election
[See Rule 17 (1)]

Election of members to the District Planning Committee____________(Name of the District)

DECLARATION

In pursuance of the provisions contained in sub-rule (1) of Rule 17 of the Local Bodies (Election of Members to the District Planning Committee) Rules, 1999.

I declare that

Thiru/Tmt/Selvi____________________________

Who is an elected member from Division/Ward No. __________of the_________(Name of local body) has been duly elected as member from the Rural/Urban segment to the District Planning Committee__________(Name of the District) this day___________(day).

Returning Officer,
District Planning Committee Members Election

Place____________
Date____________

FORM 12
Ballot Paper for Rural Segment
[See Rule 18 (1)]

Election of Members to the District Planning Committee
Counter foil
Election Roll Part A—Rural Segment Section 1 Sl. No.
Signature of the Elector
Foil
Election of members to the District Planning Committee

Sl. No.	*Name of the Candidate*	*Ward No. of the District Panchayat*	*Space for making vote*
1.			
2.			
3.			
4.			
etc.			

FORM 13
Ballot Paper for the Urban Segment
[See Rule 18 (1)]

Election of Members to the District Planning Committee
Counter foil
Electoral Roll Part B—Urban Segment
Section__________________Serial No.____________

Signature of the Elector.

Foil
Election of Members to the District Planning Committee

Serial Number	*Name of the candidate*	*Ward/Division No.*	*Space for making vote*
1.			
2.			
3.			
4.			
etc.			

FORM 14
Appointment of Polling Agent
[See Rule 20 (2)]

Election of Members to the District Planning Committee

I______________________________________a candidate in the above election do hereby appoint Thiru______________________of______________________as Polling Agent to attend the Polling Station of Section ____________________________________or Rural/Urban Segment.

Date____________ **Signature of Candidate**

I agree to act as such polling agent

Place____________

Date_____________ **Signature of Polling Agent**

Declaration of polling agent to be signed before the Presiding Officer.

I hereby declare that at the above election I will not do anything forbidden by the relevant Section 58 of the Tamil Nadu Panchayats Act, 1994 which I have read/has been read over to me.

Signature of Polling Agent

Date____________
Signed before me

Date_____________ **Signature of Presiding Officer**

(To be handed over to the polling agent for production at the polling station)

Section 58 of the Tamil Nadu Panchayats Act, 1994

"Every officer, clerk, agent or other person performing any duty in connection with the recording or counting of votes at an election who except for some purpose authorized by law, communicates to any person any information showing directly or indirectly for which candidate any voter has voted, and every person, who by any improper means procures any such information, shall be punished with imprisonment which may extend to six months or with fine, or with both."

FORM 15
Certificate of Identity
[See Rule 21]

This is to certify that the person whose name is specified below is an elected member from Division/Ward No.________________of the local body specified against him.

Name of the Member Division/Ward No.
Name of the local body
Chief Executive Officer/Commissioner/Executive Authority

____

Local Body.
Place____________

Date____________

FORM 16
[See Rule 25 (5)]

Election of Members to the District Planning Committee___________(Name of the District)

Part –1
Ballot Paper Account

Serial Number	*Particulars*	*Rural segment/Urban segment*	
		Total Number	
		From	*To*
(1)	(2)	(3)	(4)

1. Ballot papers received (No.)
2. Ballot paper unused (i.e. not issued to voters)
   (a) With the signature of Presiding Officer
   (b) Without the signature of Presiding Officer
   Total (a+ b)
3. *Ballot papers used at the Polling Station (1–2 = 3)
4. *Ballot papers used at the Polling Station but NOT INSERTED INTO THE BALLOT BOX
   (a) Ballot papers cancelled for violation of voting procedure
   (b) Ballot papers cancelled for other reasons
5. *Ballot papers to be found in the ballot box (3–4 = 5)
   (*Serial numbers need not be given)
   * (Strike out whichever is not applicable)

Signature of the Presiding Officer

FORM 17
Appointment of Counting Agents
[See Rule 27 (1)]

Election of Members to the District Committee

To
The Returning Officer

I______________________A candidate at the above election do hereby appoint the following as my counting agent to attend the counting of votes at______________________

Name of the Counting agent	*Address of the Counting agent*
(1)	(2)

Date____________ **Signature of Candidate**

I agree to act as such counting agent

Place____________

Date____________

Declaration of counting agent to be signed before the Returning Officer. **Signature of Counting Agent.**

Agent ________

I hereby declare that at the above election I will not do anything forbidden by the relevant Section 58 of the Act, which I have read/has been read over to me.

Signature of Counting Agent

Date____________

Signed before me
Signature of Returning Officer

Date____________

(To be handed over to the counting agent for production at the counting centre)

Section 58 of the Tamil Nadu Panchayats Act, 1994

"Every officer, clerk, agent or other person performing any duty in connection with the recording or counting of votes at an election who except for some purpose authorized by law, communicates to any person any information showing directly or indirectly for which candidate any voter has voted, and every person, who by any improper means procures any such information, shall be punished with imprisonment which may extend to six months or with fine, or with both."

FORM 18
Counting Sheet
[See Rule 28]

Election of Members to the District Planning Committee____________(Name of the District) Urban/Rural segment
Serial No. of Polled Valid Ballot Paper

Serial No. of Polled Valid Ballot Paper	*Name of candidates who secured vote in the polled valid ballot paper noted in col. (1)*					*Votes marked*	*Total (Column 2 to 6+7)*
	Name of the candidate	*Name of the candidate*	*Name of the candidate*	*Name of the candidate*	*Name of the candidate*		
(1)	(2)	(3)	(4)	(5)	(6)	(7)	(8)
1.							
2.							
3.							
4.							
5.							
...							
...							
300							
Total							

Item 1 Value of valid votes counted including partially marked votes (i.e. as per Column 8)
Item 2 Value of rejected votes (*i.e.* Number of rejected votes × Number of members to be elected)
Item 3 Total value of the votes counted and rejected (i.e. Items 1+2 above)
Item 4 Total value of the number of votes polled (i.e. Number of votes × Number of members to be elected)
Item 5 shall be tallied with Item 4.

FORM 19
Result Sheet
[See Rule 32 (1)]

Election of Member/Members to the District Planning Committee__________(Name of the District) from Rural/ Urban segment.

Serial Number	*Name of the Candidate*	*Votes Secured*
(1)	(2)	(3)
1.		
2.		
3.		

Total votes secured
Value of votes not marked fully

Total

Item 1 Value of valid counted including votes not marked fully
Item 2 Number of rejected votes
Item 3 Value of rejected votes
Item 4 Total value of votes counted and rejected (i.e. Item 1+Item 3)
Item 5 Total value of the number of votes polled (i.e. number of votes × number of members to be elected
(Item 4 shall be tallied with Item 5)

Returning Officer

Place:
Date:
Counting Supervisor

FORM 20
Declaration of the Result of Election
[See Rule 32 (1)]

Election of members to the District Planning Committee__________(Name of the District)

DECLARATION

In pursuance of the provisions contained in sub-rule (1) of Rule 32 of the Local Bodies (Election of Members to the District Planning Committee) Rules, 1999.

I declare that
Thiru/Tmt/Selvi____________________

____

Who is an elected member from Division/Ward No.__________of the__________(Name of local body) has been duly elected as member from the Rural/Urban segment to the District Planning Committee__________Name of District) this day__________date.

Returning Officer
District Planning Committee Members Election

Place__________
Date__________

FORM 21
Return of Election
[See Rule 32(1)]

Election of members to the District Planning Committee__________(Name of the District) from the Rural/Urban segment.

Serial Number	*Name of the Candidate*	*Number of valid votes polled*	*Remarks*
(1)	(2)	(3)	(4)
1.			
2.			
3.			

I declare that the following candidate has/candidates have been duly elected to the segment specified against his/their name or names.

Name of the candidate	*Ward No. and name of Local Body from which elected*	*Rural/Urban segment from which elected*
(1)	(2)	(3)
1.		
2.		
3.		

Place_____________

Date_____________

Returning Officer

8.2 PROCEDURE

8.2.1 Conduct of meeting of District Planning Committee

1. Short title—These rules may be called the Tamil Nadu District Planning Committee Conduct of Meetings, Quorum and Procedure in regard to Transaction of Business Rules, 1999.

2. Definition—In these rules unless the context otherwise requires:

(i) "Act" means the Tamil Nadu Panchayats Act, 1994 (Tamil Nadu Act 21 of 1994);

(ii) "Committee" means District Planning Committee;

(iii) "Urban local bodies" means the town panchayats, municipal councils and municipal corporation as defined in the explanation to Section 241 of the Act;

(iv) All other words and expressions used in these rules but not defined therein shall have the meanings respectively assigned to them in the Act.

3. Period of Membership in the Committee—Elected representative of the panchayats, Urban local bodies, Members of House of People, Members of the Council of States, Members of the Tamil Nadu Legislative Assembly shall cease to be the member of the Committee the moment they cease to be representative of the respective panchayats, urban local bodies, House of people, Council of States, the Tamil Nadu Legislative Assembly. This shall also apply for the post of vice-chairman of the Committee.

4. Procedure for convening and conduct of meeting—(1) The meeting shall be conducted at the place specified by the chairperson.

(2) No meeting shall be held on any day declared by the Government as holiday and other local holidays declared by the Collector of the district concerned.

(3) The Committee shall meet atleast once in three months for the transaction of business on such days at such time as it may arrange and also at such other times as often as a meeting shall be convened by the Chairperson.

5. Notice of the meeting—No meeting shall be held unless notice of the day and time when the meeting is to be held and of the business to be transacted there at, has been given not less than ten clear days prior to the day of the meeting.

6. Agenda—The agenda for the meeting shall be prepared within the limits of the functions mentioned in sub-sections (6) and (7) of Section 241 of the Act by the Secretary and approved by the Chairperson.

7. Service of meeting notice and agenda—Notice of the meeting with the agenda shall be served on all the members of the Committee following the procedure specified below:

(a) by giving or tendering notice of the meeting to the member concerned in person; or

(b) in case personal service could not be effected by tendering it to an adult member of the Committee member's family; or

(c) if no adult member of his family is available for such service it shall be sent by registered post with acknowledgement due; or

(d) if no adult member of his family is available for such service by affixing it on the conspicuous place of his last known residence or business place of member in the presence of Village Administrative Officer of that village.

(e) The copies of the notice of the meeting with agenda of the Committee may be supplied to the local press representatives.

8. Attendance of the meeting—The members attending the meeting of the Committee shall sign in an attendance register kept for the purpose.

9. Quorum—(1) No business shall be transacted at a meeting unless there be present not less than one-fifth of the number of members of the committee throughout the duration of the meeting.

(2) If within half an hour after the time appointed for a meeting a quorum is not present, the meeting shall be adjourned to a date and time to be specified by the Chairperson.

10. Adjournment of the meeting for other reasons—The Chairperson while transacting the business at the meeting can adjourn any meeting *sine die* for valid reasons.

11. Minutes of the proceedings—At each meeting of the Committee, minutes shall be drawn up and entered in a book kept for that purpose.

12. Custody of records—The Secretary of the Committee shall have the custody of proceedings and records of the Committee.

13. Official members without voting right—All District Officers of Government departments and Government bodies as specified by the Government by order from time-to-time shall be the special invitees of the Committee without voting right. They cannot be counted for the purpose of the quorum.

(G.O.Ms.No.100, Rural Development (C4) Department, dated 8th June 1999).

PART IX

RIGHT TO INFORMATION ACT

9.1 RIGHT TO INFORMATION ACT

9.1.1 Right to Information Act—Contents

THE TAMIL NADU RIGHT TO INFORMATION ACT, 1997 (ACT NO. XXIV OF 1997)

The following Act of the Tamil Nadu Legislative Assembly received the assent of the Governor on the 4th May 1997 and is hereby published for general information:

An Act to make provision for securing the right to information in the State of Tamil Nadu and for matters relating thereto.

WHEREAS it is necessary that every Governmental action should, be transparent to the public.

AND WHEREAS to achieve this object, every citizen should be able to get information from the Government.

Be it enacted by the Legislative Assembly of the State of Tamil Nadu in the forty-eighth year of the Republic of India as follows:

1. **Short title and commencement**—(1) This Act may be called the Tamil Nadu Right to Information Act, 1997.

(2) It shall come into force at once.

2. **Definitions**—In this Act, unless the context otherwise requires:

(1) "Competent authority" means any authority, officer not below the rank of Deputy Collector or an Officer of an equivalent grade and above empowered by the Government by notification, to be the competent authority for the purpose of this Act;

(2) "Government" means the State Government;

(3) "information" includes copy of any document relating to the affairs of the State or any local or other authorities constituted under any Act for the time being in force or a statutory authority or a company, corporation or a co-operative society or any organisation owned or controlled by the Government.

3. **Right of access to information.**—(1) Every person *bona fide* requiring information may have access to such information in accordance with the procedure specified under this Act.

(2) Notwithstanding anything contained in sub-section (1), no person shall be given information relating to:

(a) information relating to defence security;

(b) information whose disclosure will prejudice the security integrity and sovereignty of the Nation and the State;

(c) information whose disclosure would harm the conduct of international relations or affairs;

(d) information received in confidence from foreign, Governments, foreign courts or international organisations;

(e) information whose disclosure would harm the frankness and candour of internal discussion, including:

(i) proceedings of Cabinet and Cabinet committees;

(ii) internal opinion, advice, recommendations, consultation and deliberation;

(iii) projections and assumptions relating to internal policy analysis; analysis of alternative policy options and information relating to rejected policy options;

(iv) confidential communications between departments, public bodies and regulatory bodies;

(f) information relating to confidential communications between Ministers and the Governor;

(g) information whose disclosure would prejudice the administration of justice, including fair trial and the enforcement or proper administration of the law;

(h) information whose disclosure would prejudice legal proceedings or the proceedings of any tribunal, public inquiry or other formal investigation (whether actual or likely) or whose disclosure has been or is likely to be addressed in the context of such proceedings;

(i) information covered by legal professional privilege;

(j) information whose disclosure would prejudice the prevention, investigation or detection of crime, the apprehension of offenders;

(k) information whose disclosure would harm public safety or public order;

(l) information whose disclosure would endanger the life or physical safety of any person, or identify the source of information or assistance given in confidence for law enforcement or security purposes;

(m) information whose disclosure would increase the likelihood of damage to the environment; or rare or endangered species and their habitats;

(n) information whose disclosure would harm the ability of the Government to manage the economy, prejudice the conduct of official market operations, or could lead to improper gain or advantage to any person;

(o) information whose disclosure would prejudice the assessment or collection of tax, duties, or assist tax avoidance or evasion;

(p) information including commercial confidences, trade secrets or intellectual property whose unwarranted disclosure would harm the competitive position of a third party;

(q) information whose disclosure could lead to improper gain or advantage or would prejudice:
 (i) the competitive position of a department or other public body or authority;
 (ii) negotiations or the effective conduct of personnel management or commercial or contractual activities;

(r) information held in consequence of having been supplied in confidence by a person who:
 (i) gave the information under a statutory guarantee that its confidentiality would be protected; or
 (ii) was not under any legal obligation, whether actual or implied, to supply it, and has not consented to its disclosure.

(s) information whose disclosure is prohibited under any enactment, regulation or international agreement;

(t) information whose release would constitute a breach of Parliament/Legislative Assembly/ Council Privilege;

(u) the documents referred in Sections 123 and 124 of the Indian Evidence Act, 1872 (Central Act 1 of 1872);

(v) any matter which is likely to:
 (i) help the commission of offence;
 (ii) help or facilitate escape from legal custody or affect prison security; or
 (iii) impede the process of investigation or apprehension or prosecution of offenders.

(3)(a) Any person who wants to have access to the information may make an application in the manner prescribed to the competent authority in such form with such particulars, as may be prescribed.

(b) Where an application is made under clause (a) and the information is not available with the competent authority but is available with another department or authority, the competent authority may transfer the application to the competent, authority with whom such information is available and inform the applicant accordingly. The competent authority to whom such application is transferred, shall furnish the information within thirty working days from the date of receipt of the application from the competent authority from whom it has been referred or received.

(c) Where an application is so transferred to a department or authority, the head of that department or authority shall be deemed to be a competent authority.

(d) (i) Upon the receipt of an application requesting for an information, the competent authority shall consider it and pass orders thereon either granting or refusing the request, as soon as practicable and in any case, within thirty working days from the date of receipt of application.

(ii) In other cases, the competent authority shall take all reasonable steps to inform the applicant of its decision on the request as soon as practicable.

(4)(a) If in the opinion of the competent authority any information, if disclosed, is likely to cause breach of the peace or cause violence, or disharmony among the section of the people on the basis of religion, language, caste, creed, community or if it is prejudicial to public interest, the competent authority shall refuse to give information.

(b) Any application made under clause (a) shall be rejected, for reasons to be recorded in writing, if in the opinion of the competent authority:

(i) any such information sought falls in any one or more categories of items listed under Section 3(2), or

(ii) the disclosure of the information sought would be prejudicial to the maintenance of public order, or maintenance of essential services and supplies.

4. Appeal—(1) Any person aggrieved by an order of the competent authority or any person who has not received any order from the competent authority within thirty working days may appeal to the Government or to such other authority as any be notified by the Government, subject to such rules as may be prescribed.

(2) The decision of the Government or such other authority as may be prescribed shall be final.

(3) No order adversely affecting any person shall be passed except after giving that person a reasonable opportunity of being heard.

5. Protection of action taken in good faith—No suit, prosecution or other legal proceeding shall lie against any authority or person for anything done in good faith or intended to be done in pursuance of this Act or the rules made thereunder.

6. Power to remove difficulties—If any difficulty arises in giving effect to the provisions of this Act, the Government may, by an order published in the Tamil Nadu Government Gazette, make such provisions not inconsistent with the provisions of this Act and appear to them to be necessary or expedient for removing the difficulty:

Provided that no such order shall be made after the expiry of two years from the date of commencement of this Act.

7. Power to make rules—(1) The Government may make rules for carrying out the purposes of this Act.

(2)(a) All rules made under this Act shall be published in the Tamil Nadu Government Gazette and unless they are expressed to come into force on a particular day, shall come into force on the day on which they are so published.

(b) All notifications issued under this Act shall, unless they are expressed to come into force on a particular day, come into force on the day on which they are published.

(3) Every rule made or notification issued under this Act shall, as soon as possible, after it is made or issued, be placed on the table of the Legislative Assembly, and if, before the expiry of the session in which it is so placed or the next session, the Assembly makes any modification to any such rule or notification or the Assembly decides that the rule or the notifications should not be made or issued, the rule or notification shall, thereafter, have effect only in such modified form or be of no effect, as the case may be, so, however, that any such modification or annulment shall be without prejudice to the validity of anything previously done under that rule or notification.

9.1.2 Right to Information Rules 1997

[G.O. Rt.No. 1757, Public (S.C.), dated 6th May, 1998]

No. SRO A-26(a)/98.—In exercise of the powers conferred by sub-section (1) of Section 7 of the Tamil Nadu Right to Information Act, 1997 (Tamil Nadu Act XXIV of 1997), the Governor of Tamil Nadu makes the following rules:

Rules

1. Short title—These rules may be called the Tamil Nadu Right to Information Rules, 1997.

2. Definitions—In these rules, unless the context otherwise requires,–

(1) "Act" means the Tamil Nadu Right to Information Act, 1997 (Tamil Nadu Act XXIV of 1997).

(2) "appellate authority" means the authority specified in sub-section (1) of Section 4 of the Act.

3. Right of access to information—Any person who wants to have access to any information under the Act may make an application to the competent authority in the Form annexed to these rules by post or in person. The Competent Authority shall consider the application as provided for in sub-sections (3) and (4) of Section 3 of the Act.

4. Appeal—(1) Any person aggrieved by an order of the competent authority may prefer an appeal to the appellate authority within two months from the date receipt of the order of the competent authority along with a copy of such order. Any person who has not received any order from the competent authority within thirty working days from the date of his application may prefer an appeal to the appellate authority within two months from the date of completion of thirty working days from the date of his application.

(2) Every appeal shall specify:

(a) the name and address of the appellant and the particulars regarding the competent authority;

(b) the date of receipt of order, if any, of the competent authority appealed against;

(c) the grounds of appeal;

(d) the relief which the applicant claims.

(3) (a) On receipt of appeal, the appellate authority shall, as soon as possible, examine and ensure that the appeal has been preferred within the prescribed time limit.

(b) In the proceedings before the appellate authority the appellant shall be given an opportunity of making representation.

(c) Every order of the appellate authority shall be communicated to the appellant concerned and also the competent authority against whose order the appeal was preferred.

ANNEXURE

[1]Form

(See Rule 3)

To

____

(The Competent Authority to be specified)

(1)	Full Name of the Applicant	
(2)	Address	
(3)	Particulars of the information required	
	(i)	Nature of information required
	(ii)	Name of the Office or Department to which the information relates
	(iii)	Subject matter of information
	(iv)	The year and place or area to which the information relates
	(v)	Purpose for which the information is required

Place:

Date: **Signature of the Applicant**

DECLARATION

I, ____________________________(Name of the appellant), son of/daughter of/wife of______________aged______________years hereby declare that the particulars furnished in the appeal are to the best of my knowledge and belief, true and correct and that I have not suppressed any material fact.

Place__________

Date__________ **Signature of the Appellant**

To

The *____________________________ Department.
Secretariat, Chennai–600009/Such other authority.

1. Substituted by G.O. Ms. No. 1040, Public (Establishment I and LEG), dated 3rd August, 1999, Published in Tamil Nadu Government Gazette Part III—Section 1(a), dated 18th August, 1999, Issue No.32, page 191.

* Name of the Department to be filled up.

9.1.3 Tamil Nadu Right to Information Rules, 1997 – Amendments – Issued

In exercise of the powers conferred by sub-section (1) of Section 7 of the Tamil Nadu Right to Information Act, 1997 (Tamil Nadu Act 24 of 1997), the Governor of Tamil Nadu here by makes the following amendments to the Tamil Nadu Right to Information Rules, 1997.

Amendments

In the said rules:

(1) in Rule 2, in clause (2), for the expression "sub-section (1) of Section 4" the expression "sub-section (1) of section 4 of the Act" shall be substituted;

(2) in the Annexure, for the Form, the following Form shall be substituted, namely:

FORM

(See Rule 3)

To

____

(The Competent Authority to be specified)

(1) Full name of the applicant :

(2) Address :

(3) Particulars of information required :

(i) Nature of information required :

(ii) Name of the office or department to which the information relates :

(iii) Subject matter of information :

(iv) The year and place or area to which the information relates :

(v) Purpose for which the information is required :

Place______________

Date______________

Signature of the Applicant

(G.O.Ms.No.1040, Public (Establishment. I & IEG) Department dated 3.8.1999)

9.1.4 Right to Information Act 1997, obtaining of Information from Officers

In exercise of power conferred under sub-section (1) of Section 2 of Tamil Nadu Right to Information Act, 1997 (Tamil Nadu Act 24 of 1997), the Governor of Tamil Nadu hereby empowers the Officers notified in column 3 against the organisation or institutions mentioned in column 2 to be the competent authorities within their respective jurisdiction for the purpose of the Act.

Sl. No.	*Institution or Organisation*	*Competent authority*
(1)	(2)	(3)
1.	Village Panchayat and Panchayat Union Council	P.A. to the Collector (PD)
2.	District Panchayat	Secretary, District Panchayat
3.	District Planning Committee	Secretary, District Planning Committee
4.	District Rural Development Agency	Project Officer, District Rural Development Agency
5.	Directorate of Rural Development	Director of Rural Development
6.	Rural Development Department	Deputy Secretary/Joint Secretary (OP) Rural Development Department
7.	Rural Extension and Training Centres	Principal, Rural Extension and Training Centres
8.	Tamil Nadu Water Supply and Drainage Board, Divisional Level/Taluk Level	Superintending Engineer, Tamil Nadu Water Supply and Drainage Board
9.	Tamil Nadu Water Supply and Drainage Board, Regional Office	Chief Engineer, Tamil Nadu Water Supply and Drainage Board
10.	Tamil Nadu Water Supply and Drainage Board, Head Office	Managing Director, Tamil Nadu Water Supply and Drainage Board

(G.O. Ms. No. 171, Rural Development (OPM) Department, dated 10th August 1998)

9.1.5 The National RTI Act, 2005 [Act No. 22 of 2005] [15th June, 2005]

An Act to provide for setting out the practical regime of right to information for citizens to secure access to information under the control of public authorities, in order to promote transparency and accountability in the working of every public authority, the constitution of a Central Information Commission and State Information Commissions and for matters connected therewith or incidental thereto.

Whereas the Constitution of India has established democratic Republic;

And whereas democracy requires an informed citizenry and transparency of information which are vital to its functioning and also to contain corruption and to hold Governments and their instrumentalities accountable to the governed;

And whereas revelation of information in actual practice is likely to conflict with other public interests including efficient operations of the Governments, optimum use of limited fiscal resources and the preservation of confidentiality of sensitive information;

And whereas it is necessary to harmonise these conflicting interests while preserving the paramountcy of the democratic ideal;

Now, therefore, it is expedient to provide for furnishing certain information to citizens who desire to have it.

Be it enacted by Parliament in the Fifty-sixth Year of the Republic of India as follows:—

CHAPTER I
PRELIMINARY

1. Short title, extent and commencement—(1) This Act may be called the Right to Information Act, 2005.

(2) It extends to the whole of India except the State of Jammu and Kashmir.

(3) The provisions of sub-section (1) of Section 4, sub-sections (1) and (2) of Section 5, Sections 12, 13, 15,16, 24, 27 and 28 shall come into force at once, and the remaining provisions of this Act shall come into force on the one hundred and twentieth day of its enactment.

2. Definitions—In this Act, unless the context otherwise requires,—

(*a*) "appropriate Government" means in relation to a public authority which is established, constituted, owned, controlled or substantially financed by funds provided directly or indirectly—
  (*i*) by the Central Government or the Union territory administration, the Central Government;
  (*ii*) by the State Government, the State Government;

(*b*) "Central Information Commission" means the Central Information Commission constituted under sub-section (1) of Section 12;

(*c*) "Central Public Information Officer" means the Central Public Information Officer designated under sub-section (1) and includes a Central Assistant Public Information Officer designated as such under sub-section (2) of Section 5;

(*d*) "Chief Information Commissioner" and "Information Commissioner" mean the Chief Information Commissioner and Information Commissioner appointed under sub-section (3) of Section 12;

(*e*) "competent authority" means—
  (*i*) the Speaker in the case of the House of the People or the Legislative Assembly of a State or a Union territory having such Assembly and the Chairman in the case of the Council of States or Legislative Council of a State;
  (*ii*) the Chief Justice of India in the case of the Supreme Court;
  (*iii*) the Chief Justice of the High Court in the case of a High Court;
  (*iv*) the President or the Governor, as the case may be, in the case of other authorities established or constituted by or under the Constitution;
  (*v*) the administrator appointed under Article 239 of the Constitution;

(*f*) "information" means any material in any form, including records, documents, memos, e-mails, opinions, advices, press releases, circulars, orders, logbooks, contracts, reports, papers, samples, models, data material held in any electronic form and information relating to any private body which can be accessed by a public authority under any other law for the time being in force;

(*g*) "prescribed" means prescribed by rules made under this Act by the appropriate Government or the competent authority, as the case may be;

(*h*) "public authority" means any authority or body or institution of self-government established or constituted—
   (*a*) by or under the Constitution;
   (*b*) by any other law made by Parliament;
   (*c*) by any other law made by State Legislature;
   (*d*) by notification issued or order made by the appropriate Government, and includes any—
      (*i*) body owned, controlled or substantially financed;
      (*ii*) non-Government organisation substantially financed, directly or indirectly by funds provided by the appropriate Government;

(*i*) "record" includes—
   (*a*) any document, manuscript and file;
   (*b*) any microfilm, microfiche and facsimile copy of a document;
   (*c*) any reproduction of image or images embodied in such microfilm (whether enlarged or not); and
   (*d*) any other material produced by a computer or any other device;

(*j*) "right to information" means the right to information accessible under this Act which is held by or under the control of any public authority and includes the right to—
   (*i*) inspection of work, documents, records;
   (*ii*) taking notes, extracts or certified copies of documents or records;
   (*iii*) taking certified samples of material;
   (*iv*) obtaining information in the form of diskettes, floppies, tapes, video cassettes or in any other electronic mode or through printouts where such information is stored in a computer or in any other device;

(*k*) "State Information Commission" means the State Information Commission constituted under sub-section (1) of Section 15;

(*l*) "State Chief Information Commissioner" and "State Information Commissioner" mean the State Chief Information Commissioner and the State Information Commissioner appointed under sub-section (3) of Section 15;

(*m*) "State Public Information Officer" means the State Public Information Officer designated under sub-section (1) and includes a State Assistant Public Information Officer designated as such under sub-section (2) of Section 5;

(*n*) "third party" means a person other than the citizen making a request for information and includes a public authority.

CHAPTER II
RIGHT TO INFORMATION AND OBLIGATIONS OF PUBLIC AUTHORITIES

3. Right to information—Subject to the provisions of this Act, all citizens shall have the right to information.

4. (1) Every public authority shall—
   (*a*) maintain all its records duly catalogued and indexed in a manner and the form which facilitates the right to information under this Act and ensure that all records that are appropriate to be computerised are, within a reasonable time and subject to availability of resources, computerised and connected through a network all over the country on different systems so that access to such records is facilitated;
   (*b*) publish within one hundred and twenty days from the enactment of this Act,—
      (*i*) the particulars of its organisation, functions and duties;
      (*ii*) the powers and duties of its officers and employees;
      (*iii*) the procedure followed in the decision-making process, including channels of supervision and accountability;
      (*iv*) the norms set by it for the discharge of its functions;
      (*v*) the rules, regulations, instructions, manuals and records, held by it or under its control or used by its employees for discharging its functions;
      (*vi*) a statement of the categories of documents that are held by it or under its control;
      (*vii*) the particulars of any arrangement that exists for consultation with, or representation by, the members of the public in relation to the formulation of its policy or implementation thereof;
      (*viii*) a statement of the boards, councils, committees and other bodies consisting of two or more persons constituted as its part or for the purpose of its advice, and as to whether meetings of those boards,

councils, committees and other bodies are open to the public, or the minutes of such meetings are accessible for public;

(*ix*) a directory of its officers and employees;

(*x*) the monthly remuneration received by each of its officers and employees, including the system of compensation as provided in its regulations;

(*xi*) the budget allocated to each of its agency, indicating the particulars of all plans, proposed expenditures and reports on disbursements made;

(*xii*) the manner of execution of subsidy programmes, including the amounts allocated and the details of beneficiaries of such programmes;

(*xiii*) particulars of recipients of concessions, permits or authorisations granted by it;

(*xiv*) details in respect of the information, available to or held by it, reduced in an electronic form;

(*xv*) the particulars of facilities available to citizens for obtaining information, including the working hours of a library or reading room, if maintained for public use;

(*xvi*) the names, designations and other particulars of the Public Information Officers;

(*xvii*) such other information as may be prescribed; and thereafter update these publications every year;

(*c*) publish all relevant facts while formulating important policies or announcing the decisions which affect public;

(*d*) provide reasons for its administrative or quasi-judicial decisions to affected persons.

(2) It shall be a constant endeavour of every public authority to take steps in accordance with the requirements of clause (*b*) of sub-section (1) to provide as much information *suo motu* to the public at regular intervals through various means of communications, including internet, so that the public have minimum resort to the use of this Act to obtain information.

(3) For the purposes of sub-section (1), every information shall be disseminated widely and in such form and manner which is easily accessible to the public.

(4) All materials shall be disseminated taking into consideration the cost effectiveness, local language and the most effective method of communication in that local area and the information should be easily accessible, to the extent possible in electronic format with the Central Public Information Officer or State Public Information Officer, as the case may be, available free or at such cost of the medium or the print cost price as may be prescribed.

Explanation.—For the purposes of sub-sections (3) and (4), "disseminated" means making known or communicated the information to the public through notice boards, newspapers, public announcements, media broadcasts, the internet or any other means, including inspection of offices of any public authority.

5. Designation of Public Information Officers—(1) Every public authority shall, within one hundred days of the enactment of this Act, designate as many officers as the Central Public Information Officers or State Public Information Officers, as the case may be, in all administrative units or offices under it as may be necessary to provide information to persons requesting for the information under this Act.

(2) Without prejudice to the provisions of sub-section (1), every public authority shall designate an officer, within one hundred days of the enactment of this Act, at each sub-divisional level or other sub-district level as a Central Assistant Public Information Officer or a State Assistant Public Information Officer, as the case may be, to receive the applications for information or appeals under this Act for forwarding the same forthwith to the Central Public Information Officer or the State Public Information Officer or senior officer specified under sub-section (1) of Section 19 or the Central Information Commission or the State Information Commission, as the case may be:

Provided that where an application for information or appeal is given to a Central Assistant Public Information Officer or a State Assistant Public Information Officer, as the case may be, a period of five days shall be added in computing the period for response specified under sub-section (1) of Section 7.

(3) Every Central Public Information Officer or State Public Information Officer, as the case may be, shall deal with requests from persons seeking information and render reasonable assistance to the persons seeking such information.

(4) The Central Public Information Officer or State Public Information Officer, as the case may be, may seek the assistance of any other officer as he or she

considers it necessary for the proper discharge of his or her duties.

(5) Any officer, whose assistance has been sought under sub-section (4), shall render all assistance to the Central Public Information Officer or State Public Information Officer, as the case may be, seeking his or her assistance and for the purposes of any contravention of the provisions of this Act, such other officer shall be treated as a Central Public Information Officer or State Public Information Officer, as the case may be.

6. Request for obtaining information—(1) A person, who desires to obtain any information under this Act, shall make a request in writing or through electronic means in English or Hindi or in the official language of the area in which the application is being made, accompanying such fee as may be prescribed, to—

(*a*) the Central Public Information Officer or State Public Information Officer, as the case may be, of the concerned public authority;

(*b*) the Central Assistant Public Information Officer or State Assistant Public Information Officer, as the case may be,

specifying the particulars of the information sought by him or her:

Provided that where such request cannot be made in writing, the Central Public Information Officer or State Public Information Officer, as the case may be, shall render all reasonable assistance to the person making the request orally to reduce the same in writing.

(2) An applicant making request for information shall not be required to give any reason for requesting the information or any other personal details except those that may be necessary for contacting him.

(3) Where an application is made to a public authority requesting for an information,—

(*i*) which is held by another public authority; or

(*ii*) the subject matter of which is more closely connected with the functions of another public authority,

the public authority, to which such application is made, shall transfer the application or such part of it as may be appropriate to that other public authority and inform the applicant immediately about such transfer:

Provided that the transfer of an application pursuant to this sub-section shall be made as soon as practicable but in no case later than five days from the date of receipt of the application.

7. Disposal of request—(1) Subject to the proviso to sub-section (2) of Section 5 or the proviso to sub-section (3) of Section 6, the Central Public Information Officer or State Public Information Officer, as the case may be, on receipt of a request under-section 6 shall, as expeditiously as possible, and in any case within thirty days of the receipt of the request, either provide the information on payment of such fee as may be prescribed or reject the request for any of the reasons specified in Sections 8 and 9:

Provided that where the information sought for concerns the life or liberty of a person, the same shall be provided within forty-eight hours of the receipt of the request.

(2) If the Central Public Information Officer or State Public Information Officer, as the case may be, fails to give decision on the request for information within the period specified under sub-section (1), the Central Public Information Officer or State Public Information Officer, as the case may be, shall be deemed to have refused the request.

(3) Where a decision is taken to provide the information on payment of any further fee representing the cost of providing the information, the Central Public Information Officer or State Public Information Officer, as the case may be, shall send an intimation to the person making the request, giving—

(*a*) the details of further fees representing the cost of providing the information as determined by him, together with the calculations made to arrive at the amount in accordance with fee prescribed under sub-section (1), requesting him to deposit that fees, and the period intervening between the despatch of the said intimation and payment of fees shall be excluded for the purpose of calculating the period of thirty days referred to in that sub-section;

(*b*) information concerning his or her right with respect to review the decision as to the amount of fees charged or the form of access provided, including the particulars of the appellate authority, time limit, process and any other forms.

(4) Where access to the record or a part thereof is required to be provided under this Act and the person to whom access is to be provided is sensorily disabled, the Central Public Information Officer or State Public Information Officer, as the case may be, shall provide assistance to enable access to the

information, including providing such assistance as may be appropriate for the inspection.

(5) Where access to information is to be provided in the printed or in any electronic format, the applicant shall, subject to the provisions of sub-section (6), pay such fee as may be prescribed:

Provided that the fee prescribed under sub-section (1) of Section 6 and sub-sections (1) and (5) of Section 7 shall be reasonable and no such fee shall be charged from the persons who are of below poverty line as may be determined by the appropriate Government.

(6) Notwithstanding anything contained in sub-section (5), the person making request for the information shall be provided the information free of charge where a public authority fails to comply with the time limits specified in sub-section (1).

(7) Before taking any decision under sub-section (1), the Central Public Information Officer or State Public Information Officer, as the case may be, shall take into consideration the representation made by a third party under Section 11.

(8) Where a request has been rejected under sub-section (1), the Central Public Information Officer or State Public Information Officer, as the case may be, shall communicate to the person making the request—

(*i*) the reasons for such rejection;

(*ii*) the period within which an appeal against such rejection may be preferred; and

(*iii*) the particulars of the appellate authority.

(9) An information shall ordinarily be provided in the form in which it is sought unless it would disproportionately divert the resources of the public authority or would be detrimental to the safety or preservation of the record in question.

8. Exemption from disclosure of information— (1) Notwithstanding anything contained in this Act, there shall be no obligation to give any citizen—

(*a*) information, disclosure of which would prejudicially affect the sovereignty and integrity of India, the security, strategic, scientific or economic interests of the State, relation with foreign State or lead to incitement of an offence;

(*b*) information which has been expressly forbidden to be published by any court of law or tribunal or the disclosure of which may constitute contempt of court;

(*c*) information, the disclosure of which would cause a breach of privilege of Parliament or the State Legislature;

(*d*) information including commercial confidence, trade secrets or intellectual property, the disclosure of which would harm the competitive position of a third party, unless the competent authority is satisfied that larger public interest warrants the disclosure of such information;

(*e*) information available to a person in his fiduciary relationship, unless the competent authority is satisfied that the larger public interest warrants the disclosure of such information;

(*f*) information received in confidence from foreign Government;

(*g*) information, the disclosure of which would endanger the life or physical safety of any person or identify the source of information or assistance given in confidence for law enforcement or security purposes;

(*h*) information which would impede the process of investigation or apprehension or prosecution of offenders;

(*i*) cabinet papers including records of deliberations of the Council of Ministers, Secretaries and other officers:

Provided that the decisions of Council of Ministers, the reasons thereof, and the material on the basis of which the decisions were taken shall be made public after the decision has been taken, and the matter is complete, or over:

Provided further that those matters which come under the exemptions specified in this section shall not be disclosed;

(*j*) information which relates to personal information the disclosure of which has no relationship to any public activity or interest, or which would cause unwarranted invasion of the privacy of the individual unless the Central Public Information Officer or the State Public Information Officer or the appellate authority, as the case may be, is satisfied that the larger public interest justifies the disclosure of such information:

Provided that the information which cannot be denied to the Parliament or a State Legislature shall not be denied to any person.

(2) Notwithstanding anything in the Official Secrets Act, 1923 (19 of 1923) nor any of the exemptions permissible in accordance with sub-section (1), a public authority may allow access to information, if public interest in disclosure outweighs the harm to the protected interests.

(3) Subject to the provisions of clauses (*a*), (*c*) and (*i*) of sub-section (1), any information relating to any occurrence, event or matter which has taken place, occurred or happened twenty years before the date on which any request is made under secton 6 shall be provided to any person making a request under that section:

Provided that where any question arises as to the date from which the said period of twenty years has to be computed, the decision of the Central Government shall be final, subject to the usual appeals provided for in this Act.

9. Grounds for rejection to access in certain cases—Without prejudice to the provisions of Section 8, a Central Public Information Officer or a State Public Information Officer, as the case may be, may reject a request for information where such a request for providing access would involve an infringement of copyright subsisting in a person other than the State.

10. Severability—(1) Where a request for access to information is rejected on the ground that it is in relation to information which is exempt from disclosure, then, notwithstanding anything contained in this Act, access may be provided to that part of the record which does not contain any information which is exempt from disclosure under this Act and which can reasonably be severed from any part that contains exempt information.

(2) Where access is granted to a part of the record under sub-section (1), the Central Public Information Officer or State Public Information Officer, as the case may be, shall give a notice to the applicant, informing—

(*a*) that only part of the record requested, after severance of the record containing information which is exempt from disclosure, is being provided;

(*b*) the reasons for the decision, including any findings on any material question of fact, referring to the material on which those findings were based;

(*c*) the name and designation of the person giving the decision;

(*d*) the details of the fees calculated by him or her and the amount of fee which the applicant is required to deposit; and

(*e*) his or her rights with respect to review of the decision regarding non-disclosure of part of the information, the amount of fee charged or the form of access provided, including the particulars of the senior officer specified under sub-section (1) of Section 19 or the Central Information Commission or the State Information Commission, as the case may be, time limit, process and any other form of access.

11. Third party information—(1) Where a Central Public Information Officer or a State Public Information Officer, as the case may be, intends to disclose any information or record, or part thereof on a request made under this Act, which relates to or has been supplied by a third party and has been treated as confidential by that third party, the Central Public Information Officer or State Public Information Officer, as the case may be, shall, within five days from the receipt of the request, give a written notice to such third party of the request and of the fact that the Central Public Information Officer or State Public Information Officer, as the case may be, intends to disclose the information or record, or part thereof, and invite the third party to make a submission in writing or orally, regarding whether the information should be disclosed, and such submission of the third party shall be kept in view while taking a decision about disclosure of information:

Provided that except in the case of trade or commercial secrets protected by law, disclosure may be allowed if the public interest in disclosure outweighs in importance any possible harm or injury to the interests of such third party.

(2) Where a notice is served by the Central Public Information Officer or State Public Information Officer, as the case may be, under sub-section (1) to a third party in respect of any information or record or part thereof, the third party shall, within ten days from the date of receipt of such notice, be given the opportunity to make representation against the proposed disclosure.

(3) Notwithstanding anything contained in Section 7, the Central Public Information Officer or State Public Information Officer, as the case may be, shall, within forty days after receipt of the request under Section 6, if the third party has been given an opportunity to make representation under sub-section (2), make a decision as to whether or not to disclose the information or record or part thereof and give in writing the notice of his decision to the third party.

(4) A notice given under sub-section (3) shall include a statement that the third party to whom the notice is given is entitled to prefer an appeal under Section 19 against the decision.

CHAPTER III
THE CENTRAL INFORMATION COMMISSION

12. Constitution of Central Information Commission—(1) The Central Government shall, by notification in the Official Gazette, constitute a body to be known as the Central Information Commission to exercise the powers conferred on, and to perform the functions assigned to, it under this Act.

(2) The Central Information Commission shall consist of—

(*a*) the Chief Information Commissioner; and

(*b*) such number of Central Information Commissioners, not exceeding ten, as may be deemed necessary.

(3) The Chief Information Commissioner and Information Commissioners shall be appointed by the President on the recommendation of a committee consisting of—

(*i*) the Prime Minister, who shall be the Chairperson of the committee;

(*ii*) the Leader of Opposition in the Lok Sabha; and

(*iii*) a Union Cabinet Minister to be nominated by the Prime Minister.

Explanation.—For the purposes of removal of doubts, it is hereby declared that where the Leader of Opposition in the House of the People has not been recognised as such, the Leader of the single largest group in opposition of the Government in the House of the People shall be deemed to be the Leader of Opposition.

(4) The general superintendence, direction and management of the affairs of the Central Information Commission shall vest in the Chief Information Commissioner who shall be assisted by the Information Commissioners and may exercise all such powers and do all such acts and things which may be exercised or done by the Central Information Commission autonomously without being subjected to directions by any other authority under this Act.

(5) The Chief Information Commissioner and Information Commissioners shall be persons of eminence in public life with wide knowledge and experience in law, science and technology, social service, management, journalism, mass media or administration and governance.

(6) The Chief Information Commissioner or an Information Commissioner shall not be a Member of Parliament or Member of the Legislature of any State or Union territory, as the case may be, or hold any other office of profit or connected with any political party or carrying on any business or pursuing any profession.

(7) The headquarters of the Central Information Commission shall be at Delhi and the Central Information Commission may, with the previous approval of the Central Government, establish offices at other places in India.

13. Term of office and conditions of service—(1) The Chief Information Commissioner shall hold office for a term of five years from the date on which he enters upon his office and shall not be eligible for reappointment:

Provided that no Chief Information Commissioner shall hold office as such after he has attained the age of sixty-five years.

(2) Every Information Commissioner shall hold office for a term of five years from the date on which he enters upon his office or till he attains the age of sixty-five years, whichever is earlier, and shall not be eligible for reappointment as such Information Commissioner:

Provided that every Information Commissioner shall, on vacating his office under this sub-section be eligible for appointment as the Chief Information Commissioner in the manner specified in sub-section (3) of Section 12:

Provided further that where the Information Commissioner is appointed as the Chief Information Commissioner, his term of office shall not be more than five years in aggregate as the Information Commissioner and the Chief Information Commissioner.

(3) The Chief Information Commissioner or an Information Commissioner shall before he enters upon his office make and subscribe before the President or some other person appointed by him in that behalf, an oath or affirmation according to the form set out for the purpose in the First Schedule.

(4) The Chief Information Commissioner or an Information Commissioner may, at any time, by writing under his hand addressed to the President, resign from his office:

Provided that the Chief Information Commissioner or an Information Commissioner may be removed in the manner specified under Section 14.

(5) The salaries and allowances payable to and other terms and conditions of service of

(*a*) the Chief Information Commissioner shall be the same as that of the Chief Election Commissioner;

(*b*) an Information Commissioner shall be the same as that of an Election Commissioner:

Provided that if the Chief Information Commissioner or an Information Commissioner, at the time of his appointment is, in receipt of a pension, other than a disability or wound pension, in respect of any previous service under the Government of India or under the Government of a State, his salary in respect of the service as the Chief Information Commissioner or an Information Commissioner shall be reduced by the amount of that pension including any portion of pension which was commuted and pension equivalent of other forms of retirement benefits excluding pension equivalent of retirement gratuity:

Provided further that if the Chief Information Commissioner or an Information Commissioner if, at the time of his appointment is, in receipt of retirement benefits in respect of any previous service rendered in a Corporation established by or under any Central Act or State Act or a Government company owned or controlled by the Central Government or the State Government, his salary in respect of the service as the Chief Information Commissioner or an Information Commissioner shall be reduced by the amount of pension equivalent to the retirement benefits:

Provided also that the salaries, allowances and other conditions of service of the Chief Information Commissioner and the Information Commissioners shall not be varied to their disadvantage after their appointment.

(6) The Central Government shall provide the Chief Information Commissioner and the Information Commissioners with such officers and employees as may be necessary for the efficient performance of their functions under this Act, and the salaries and allowances payable to and the terms and conditions of service of the officers and other employees appointed for the purpose of this Act shall be such as may be prescribed.

14. Removal of Chief Information Commissioner or Information Commissioner

(1) Subject to the provisions of sub-section (3), the Chief Information Commissioner or any Information Commissioner shall be removed from his office only by order of the President on the ground of proved misbehaviour or incapacity after the Supreme Court, on a reference made to it by the President, has, on inquiry, reported that the Chief Information Commissioner or any Information Commissioner, as the case may be, ought on such ground be removed.

(2) The President may suspend from office, and if deem necessary prohibit also from attending the office during inquiry, the Chief Information Commissioner or Information Commissioner in respect of whom a reference has been made to the Supreme Court under sub-section (1) until the President has passed orders on receipt of the report of the Supreme Court on such reference.

(3) Notwithstanding anything contained in sub-section (1), the President may by order remove from office the Chief Information Commissioner or any Information Commissioner if the Chief Information Commissioner or a Information Commissioner, as the case may be—

(*a*) is adjudged an insolvent; or

(*b*) has been convicted of an offence which, in the opinion of the President, involves moral turpitude; or

(*c*) engages during his term of office in any paid employment outside the duties of his office; or

(*d*) is, in the opinion of the President, unfit to continue in office by reason of infirmity of mind or body; or

(*e*) has acquired such financial or other interest as is likely to affect prejudicially his functions as the Chief Information Commissioner or a Information Commissioner.

(4) If the Chief Information Commissioner or a Information Commissioner in any way, concerned or interested in any contract or agreement made by or on behalf of the Government of India or participates in any way in the profit thereof or in any benefit or emolument arising therefrom otherwise than as a member and in common with the other members of an incorporated company, he shall, for the purposes of sub section (1), be deemed to be guilty of misbehaviour.

CHAPTER IV
THE STATE INFORMATION COMMISSION

15. Constitution of State Information Commission— (1) Every State Government shall, by notification in the Official Gazette, constitute a body to be known as the__________(name of the State) Information Commission to exercise the powers conferred on, and to perform the functions assigned to, it under this Act.

(2) The State Information Commission shall consist of—

(*a*) the State Chief Information Commissioner, and

(*b*) such number of State Information Commissioners, not exceeding ten, as may be deemed necessary.

(3) The State Chief Information Commissioner and the State Information Commissioners shall be appointed by the Governor on the recommendation of a committee consisting of—

(*i*) the Chief Minister, who shall be the Chairperson of the committee;

(*ii*) the Leader of Opposition in the Legislative Assembly; and

(*iii*) a Cabinet Minister to be nominated by the Chief Minister.

Explanation.—For the purposes of removal of doubts, it is hereby declared that where the Leader of Opposition in the Legislative Assembly has not been recognised as such, the Leader of the single largest group in opposition of the Government in the Legislative Assembly shall be deemed to be the Leader of Opposition.

(4) The general superintendence, direction and management of the affairs of the State Information Commission shall vest in the State Chief Information Commissioner who shall be assisted by the State Information Commissioners and may exercise all such powers and do all such acts and things which may be exercised or done by the State Information Commission autonomously without being subjected to directions by any other authority under this Act.

(5) The State Chief Information Commissioner and the State Information Commissioners shall be persons of eminence in public life with wide knowledge and experience in law, science and technology, social service, management, journalism, mass media or administration and governance.

(6) The State Chief Information Commissioner or a State Information Commissioner shall not be a Member of Parliament or Member of the Legislature of any State or Union territory, as the case may be, or hold any other office of profit or connected with any political party or carrying on any business or pursuing any profession.

(7) The headquarters of the State Information Commission shall be at such place in the State as the State Government may, by notification in the Official Gazette, specify and the State Information Commission may, with the previous approval of the State Government, establish offices at other places in the State.

16. Term of office and conditions of service—(1) The State Chief Information Commissioner shall hold office for a term of five years from the date on which he enters upon his office and shall not be eligible for reappointment:

Provided that no State Chief Information Commissioner shall hold office as such after he has attained the age of sixty-five years.

(2) Every State Information Commissioner shall hold office for a term of five years from the date on which he enters upon his office or till he attains the age of sixty-five years, whichever is earlier, and shall not be eligible for reappointment as such State Information Commissioner:

Provided that every State Information Commissioner shall, on vacating his office under this sub-section, be eligible for appointment as the State Chief Information Commissioner in the manner specified in sub-section (3) of Section 15:

Provided further that where the State Information Commissioner is appointed as the State Chief Information Commissioner, his term of office shall not be more than five years in aggregate as the State Information Commissioner and the State Chief Information Commissioner.

(3) The State Chief Information Commissioner or a State Information Commissioner, shall before he enters upon his office make and subscribe before the Governor or some other person appointed by him in that behalf, an oath or affirmation according to the form set out for the purpose in the First Schedule.

(4) The State Chief Information Commissioner or a State Information Commissioner may, at any time, by writing under his hand addressed to the Governor, resign from his office:

Provided that the State Chief Information Commissioner or a State Information Commissioner may be removed in the manner specified under Section 17.

(5) The salaries and allowances payable to and other terms and conditions of service of—

(*a*) the State Chief Information Commissioner shall be the same as that of an Election Commissioner;

(*b*) the State Information Commissioner shall be the same as that of the Chief Secretary to the State Government:

Provided that if the State Chief Information Commissioner or a State Information Commissioner, at the time of his appointment is, in receipt of a pension, other than a disability or wound pension, in respect of any previous service under the Government of India or under the Government of a State, his salary in respect of the service as the State

Chief Information Commissioner or a State Information Commissioner shall be reduced by the amount of that pension including any portion of pension which was commuted and pension equivalent of other forms of retirement benefits excluding pension equivalent of retirement gratuity:

Provided further that where the State Chief Information Commissioner or a State Information Commissioner if, at the time of his appointment is, in receipt of retirement benefits in respect of any previous service rendered in a Corporation established by or under any Central Act or State Act or a Government company owned or controlled by the Central Government or the State Government, his salary in respect of the service as the State Chief Information Commissioner or the State Information Commissioner shall be reduced by the amount of pension equivalent to the retirement benefits:

Provided also that the salaries, allowances and other conditions of service of the State Chief Information Commissioner and the State Information Commissioners shall not be varied to their disadvantage after their appointment.

(6) The State Government shall provide the State Chief Information Commissioner and the State Information Commissioners with such officers and employees as may be necessary for the efficient performance of their functions under this Act, and the salaries and allowances payable to and the terms and conditions of service of the officers and other employees appointed for the purpose of this Act shall be such as may be prescribed.

17. Removal of State Chief Information Commissioner or State Information Commissioner—(1) Subject to the provisions of sub-section (3), the State Chief Information Commissioner or a State Information Commissioner shall be removed from his office only by order of the Governor on the ground of proved misbehaviour or incapacity after the Supreme Court, on a reference made to it by the Governor, has on inquiry, reported that the State Chief Information Commissioner or a State Information Commissioner, as the case may be, ought on such ground be removed.

(2) The Governor may suspend from office, and if deem necessary prohibit also from attending the office during inquiry, the State Chief Information Commissioner or a State Information Commissioner in respect of whom a reference has been made to the Supreme Court under sub-section (1) until the Governor has passed orders on receipt of the report of the Supreme Court on such reference.

(3) Notwithstanding anything contained in sub-section (1), the Governor may by order remove from office the State Chief Information Commissioner or a State Information Commissioner if a State Chief Information Commissioner or a State Information Commissioner, as the case may be—

(*a*) is adjudged an insolvent; or

(*b*) has been convicted of an offence which, in the opinion of the Governor, involves moral turpitude; or

(*c*) engages during his term of office in any paid employment outside the duties of his office; or

(*d*) is, in the opinion of the Governor, unfit to continue in office by reason of infirmity of mind or body; or

(*e*) has acquired such financial or other interest as is likely to affect prejudicially his functions as the State Chief Information Commissioner or a State Information Commissioner.

(4) If the State Chief Information Commissioner or a State Information Commissioner in any way, concerned or interested in any contract or agreement made by or on behalf of the Government of the State or participates in any way in the profit thereof or in any benefit or emoluments arising therefrom otherwise than as a member and in common with the other members of an incorporated company, he shall, for the purposes of sub-section (1), be deemed to be guilty of misbehaviour.

CHAPTER V
POWERS AND FUNCTIONS OF THE INFORMATION COMMISSIONS, APPEAL AND PENALTIES

18. Powers and functions of Information Commissions—(1) Subject to the provisions of this Act, it shall be the duty of the Central Information Commission or State Information Commission, as the case may be, to receive and inquire into a complaint from any person—

(*a*) who has been unable to submit a request to a Central Public Information Officer or State Public Information Officer, as the case may be, either by reason that no such officer has been appointed under this Act, or because the Central Assistant Public Information Officer or State Assistant Public Information Officer, as the case may be, has refused to accept his or her application for information or appeal under this Act for forwarding the same to the Central Public Information Officer or State Public Information Officer or senior officer specified in sub-section (1) of Section 19 or the Central Information Commission or the State Information Commission, as the case may be;

(*b*) who has been refused access to any information requested under this Act;

(*c*) who has not been given a response to a request for information or access to information within the time limit specified under this Act;

(*d*) who has been required to pay an amount of fee which he or she considers unreasonable;

(*e*) who believes that he or she has been given incomplete, misleading or false information under this Act; and

(*f*) in respect of any other matter relating to requesting or obtaining access to records under this Act.

(2) Where the Central Information Commission or State Information Commission, as the case may be, is satisfied that there are reasonable grounds to inquire into the matter, it may initiate an inquiry in respect thereof.

(3) The Central Information Commission or State Information Commission, as the case may be, shall, while inquiring into any matter under this Section, have the same powers as are vested in a civil court while trying a suit under the Code of Civil Procedure, 1908, in respect of the following matters, namely—

(*a*) summoning and enforcing the attendance of persons and compel them to give oral or written evidence on oath and to produce the documents or things;

(*b*) requiring the discovery and inspection of documents;

(*c*) receiving evidence on affidavit;

(*d*) requisitioning any public record or copies thereof from any court or office;

(*e*) issuing summons for examination of witnesses or documents; and

(*f*) any other matter which may be prescribed.

(4) Notwithstanding anything inconsistent contained in any other Act of Parliament or State Legislature, as the case may be, the Central Information Commission or the State Information Commission, as the case may be, may, during the inquiry of any complaint under this Act, examine any record to which this Act applies which is under the control of the public authority, and no such record may be withheld from it on any grounds.

19. Appeal—(1) Any person who, does not receive a decision within the time specified in sub-section (1) or clause (a) of sub-section (3) of Section 7, or is aggrieved by a decision of the Central Public Information Officer or State Public Information Officer, as the case may be, may within thirty days from the expiry of such period or from the receipt of such a decision prefer an appeal to such officer who is senior in rank to the Central Public Information Officer or State Public Information Officer as the case may be, in each public authority:

Provided that such officer may admit the appeal after the expiry of the period of thirty days if he or she is satisfied that the appellant was prevented by sufficient cause from filing the appeal in time.

(2) Where an appeal is preferred against an order made by a Central Public Information Officer or a State Public Information Officer, as the case may be, under Section 11 to disclose third party information, the appeal by the concerned third party shall be made within thirty days from the date of the order.

(3) A second appeal against the decision under sub-section (1) shall lie within ninety days from the date on which the decision should have been made or was actually received, with the Central Information Commission or the State Information Commission:

Provided that the Central Information Commission or the State Information Commission, as the case may be, may admit the appeal after the expiry of the period of ninety days if it is satisfied that the appellant was prevented by sufficient cause from filing the appeal in time.

(4) If the decision of the Central Public Information Officer or State Public Information Officer, as the case may be, against which an appeal is preferred relates to information of a third party, the Central Information Commission or State Information Commission, as the case may be, shall give a reasonable opportunity of being heard to that third party.

(5) In any appeal proceedings, the onus to prove that a denial of a request was justified shall be on the Central Public Information Officer or State Public Information Officer, as the case may be, who denied the request.

(6) An appeal under sub-section (1) or sub-section (2) shall be disposed of within thirty days of the receipt of the appeal or within such extended period not exceeding a total of forty-five days from the date

of filing thereof, as the case may be, for reasons to be recorded in writing.

(7) The decision of the Central Information Commission or State Information Commission, as the case may be, shall be binding.

(8) In its decision, the Central Information Commission or State Information Commission, as the case may be, has the power to—

(*a*) require the public authority to take any such steps as may be necessary to secure compliance with the provisions of this Act, including—

(*i*) by providing access to information, if so requested, in a particular form;

(*ii*) by appointing a Central Public Information Officer or State Public Information Officer, as the case may be;

(*iii*) by publishing certain information or categories of information;

(*iv*) by making necessary changes to its practices in relation to the maintenance, management and destruction of records;

(*v*) by enhancing the provision of training on the right to information for its officials;

(*vi*) by providing it with an annual report in compliance with clause (b) of sub-section (1) of Section 4;

(*b*) require the public authority to compensate the complainant for any loss or other detriment suffered;

(*c*) impose any of the penalties provided under this Act;

(*d*) reject the application.

(9) The Central Information Commission or State Information Commission, as the case may be, shall give notice of its decision, including any right of appeal, to the complainant and the public authority.

(10) The Central Information Commission or State Information Commission, as the case may be, shall decide the appeal in accordance with such procedure as may be prescribed.

20. Penalties—(1) Where the Central Information Commission or the State Information Commission, as the case may be, at the time of deciding any complaint or appeal is of the opinion that the Central Public Information Officer or the State Public Information Officer, as the case may be, has, without any reasonable cause, refused to receive an application for information or has not furnished information within the time specified under sub-section (1) of Section 7 or malafidely denied the request for information or knowingly given incorrect, incomplete or misleading information or destroyed information which was the subject of the request or obstructed in any manner in furnishing the information, it shall impose a penalty of two hundred and fifty rupees each day till application is received or information is furnished, so however, the total amount of such penalty shall not exceed twenty-five thousand rupees:

Provided that the Central Public Information Officer or the State Public Information Officer, as the case may be, shall be given a reasonable opportunity of being heard before any penalty is imposed on him:

Provided further that the burden of proving that he acted reasonably and diligently shall be on the Central Public Information Officer or the State Public Information Officer, as the case may be.

(2) Where the Central Information Commission or the State Information Commission, as the case may be, at the time of deciding any complaint or appeal is of the opinion that the Central Public Information Officer or the State Public Information Officer, as the case may be, has, without any reasonable cause and persistently, failed to receive an application for information or has not furnished information within the time specified under sub-section (1) of Section 7 or malafidely denied the request for information or knowingly given incorrect, incomplete or misleading information or destroyed information which was the subject of the request or obstructed in any manner in furnishing the information, it shall recommend for disciplinary action against the Central Public Information Officer or the State Public Information Officer, as the case may be, under the service rules applicable to him.

CHAPTER VI
MISCELLANEOUS

21. Protection of action taken in good faith—No suit, prosecution or other legal proceeding shall lie against any person for anything which is in good faith done or intended to be done under this Act or any rule made thereunder.

22. Act to have overriding effect—The provisions of this Act shall have effect notwithstanding anything inconsistent therewith contained in the Official Secrets Act, 1923, and any other law for the time being in force or in any instrument having effect by virtue of any law other than this Act.

23. Bar of jurisdiction of courts—No court shall entertain any suit, application or other proceeding in respect of any order made under this Act and no such order shall be called in question otherwise than by way of an appeal under this Act.

24. Act not to apply to certain organizations—(1) Nothing contained in this Act shall apply to the intelligence and security organisations specified in the Second Schedule, being organisations established by the Central Government or any information furnished by such organisations to that Government:

Provided that the information pertaining to the allegations of corruption and human rights violations shall not be excluded under this sub-section:

Provided further that in the case of information sought for is in respect of allegations of violation of human rights, the information shall only be provided after the approval of the Central Information Commission, and notwithstanding anything contained in Section 7, such information shall be provided within forty-five days from the date of the receipt of request.

(2) The Central Government may, by notification in the Official Gazette, amend the Schedule by including therein any other intelligence or security organisation established by that Government or omitting therefrom any organisation already specified therein and on the publication of such notification, such organisation shall be deemed to be included in or, as the case may be, omitted from the Schedule.

(3) Every notification issued under sub-section (2) shall be laid before each House of Parliament.

(4) Nothing contained in this Act shall apply to such intelligence and security organisation being organisations established by the State Government, as that Government may, from time to time, by notification in the Official Gazette, specify:

Provided that the information pertaining to the allegations of corruption and human rights violations shall not be excluded under this sub-section:

Provided further that in the case of information sought for is in respect of allegations of violation of human rights, the information shall only be provided after the approval of the State Information Commission and, notwithstanding anything contained in Section 7, such information shall be provided within forty-five days from the date of the receipt of request.

(5) Every notification issued under sub-section (4) shall be laid before the State Legislature.

25. Monitoring and Reporting—(1) The Central Information Commission or State Information Commission, as the case may be, shall, as soon as practicable after the end of each year, prepare a report on the implementation of the provisions of this Act during that year and forward a copy thereof to the appropriate Government.

(2) Each Ministry or Department shall, in relation to the public authorities within their jurisdiction, collect and provide such information to the Central Information Commission or State Information Commission, as the case may be, as is required to prepare the report under this section and comply with the requirements concerning the furnishing of that information and keeping of records for the purposes of this section.

(3) Each report shall state in respect of the year to which the report relates—

(*a*) the number of requests made to each public authority;

(*b*) the number of decisions where applicants were not entitled to access to the documents pursuant to the requests, the provisions of this Act under which these decisions were made and the number of times such provisions were invoked;

(*c*) the number of appeals referred to the Central Information Commission or State Information Commission, as the case may be, for review, the nature of the appeals and the outcome of the appeals;

(*d*) particulars of any disciplinary action taken against any officer in respect of the administration of this Act;

(*e*) the amount of charges collected by each public authority under this Act;

(*f*) any facts which indicate an effort by the public authorities to administer and implement the spirit and intention of this Act;

(*g*) recommendations for reform, including recommendations in respect of the particular public authorities, for the development, improvement, modernisation, reform or amendment to this Act or other legislation or common law or any other matter relevant for operationalising the right to access information.

(4) The Central Government or the State Government, as the case may be, may, as soon as

practicable after the end of each year, cause a copy of the report of the Central Information Commission or the State Information Commission, as the case may be, referred to in sub-section (1) to be laid before each House of Parliament or, as the case may be, before each House of the State Legislature, where there are two Houses, and where there is one House of the State Legislature before that House.

(5) If it appears to the Central Information Commission or State Information Commission, as the case may be, that the practice of a public authority in relation to the exercise of its functions under this Act does not conform with the provisions or spirit of this Act, it may give to the authority a recommendation specifying the steps which ought in its opinion to be taken for promoting such conformity.

26. Appropriate Government to prepare programmes—(1) The appropriate Government may, to the extent of availability of financial and other resources—

(*a*) develop and organise educational programmes to advance the understanding of the public, in particular of disadvantaged communities as to how to exercise the rights contemplated under this Act;

(*b*) encourage public authorities to participate in the development and organisation of programmes referred to in clause (a) and to undertake such programmes themselves;

(*c*) promote timely and effective dissemination of accurate information by public authorities about their activities; and

(*d*) train Central Public Information Officers or State Public Information Officers, as the case may be, of public authorities and produce relevant training materials for use by the public authorities themselves.

(2) The appropriate Government shall, within eighteen months from the commencement of this Act, compile in its official language a guide containing such information, in an easily comprehensible form and manner, as may reasonably be required by a person who wishes to exercise any right specified in this Act.

(3) The appropriate Government shall, if necessary, update and publish the guidelines referred to in sub-section (2) at regular intervals which shall, in particular and without prejudice to the generality of sub-section (2), include—

(*a*) the objects of this Act;

(*b*) the postal and street address, the phone and fax number and, if available, electronic mail address of the Central Public Information Officer or State Public Information Officer, as the case may be, of every public authority appointed under sub-section (1) of Section 5;

(*c*) the manner and the form in which request for access to an information shall be made to a Central Public Information Officer or State Public Information Officer, as the case may be;

(*d*) the assistance available from and the duties of the Central Public Information Officer or State Public Information Officer, as the case may be, of a public authority under this Act;

(*e*) the assistance available from the Central Information Commission or State Information Commission, as the case may be;

(*f*) all remedies in law available regarding an act or failure to act in respect of a right or duty conferred or imposed by this Act including the manner of filing an appeal to the Commission;

(*g*) the provisions providing for the voluntary disclosure of categories of records in accordance with Section 4;

(*h*) the notices regarding fees to be paid in relation to requests for access to an information; and

(*i*) any additional regulations or circulars made or issued in relation to obtaining access to an information in accordance with this Act.

(4) The appropriate Government must, if necessary, update and publish the guidelines at regular intervals.

27. Power to make rules by appropriate Government—(1) The appropriate Government may, by notification in the Official Gazette, make rules to carry out the provisions of this Act.

(2) In particular, and without prejudice to the generality of the foregoing power, such rules may provide for all or any of the following matters, namely—

(*a*) the cost of the medium or print cost price of the materials to be disseminated under sub-section (4) of Section 4;

(*b*) the fee payable under sub-section (1) of Section 6;

(*c*) the fee payable under sub-sections (1) and (5) of Section 7;

(*d*) the salaries and allowances payable to and the terms and conditions of service of the officers and other employees under sub-section (6) of Section 13 and sub-section (6) of Section 16;

(*e*) the procedure to be adopted by the Central Information Commission or State Information Commission, as the case may be, in deciding the appeals under sub-section (10) of Section 19; and

(*f*) any other matter which is required to be, or may be, prescribed.

28. Power to make rules by competent authority—(1) The competent authority may, by notification in the Official Gazette, make rules to carry out the provisions of this Act.

(2) In particular, and without prejudice to the generality of the foregoing power, such rules may provide for all or any of the following matters, namely—

(*i*) the cost of the medium or print cost price of the materials to be disseminated under sub-section (4) of Section 4;

(*ii*) the fee payable under sub-section (1) of Section 6;

(*iii*) the fee payable under sub-section (1) of Section 7; and

(*iv*) any other matter which is required to be, or may be, prescribed.

29. Laying of rules—(1) Every rule made by the Central Government under this Act shall be laid, as soon as may be after it is made, before each House of Parliament, while it is in session, for a total period of thirty days which may be comprised in one session or in two or more successive sessions, and if, before the expiry of the session immediately following the session or the successive sessions aforesaid, both Houses agree in making any modification in the rule or both Houses agree that the rule should not be made, the rule shall thereafter have effect only in such modified form or be of no effect, as the case may be; so, however, that any such modification or annulment shall be without prejudice to the validity of anything previously done under that rule.

(2) Every rule made under this Act by a State Government shall be laid, as soon as may be after it is notified, before the State Legislature.

30. Power to remove difficulties—(1) If any difficulty arises in giving effect to the provisions of this Act, the Central Government may, by order published in the Official Gazette, make such provisions not inconsistent with the provisions of this Act as appear to it to be necessary or expedient for removal of the difficulty:

Provided that no such order shall be made after the expiry of a period of two years from the date of the commencement of this Act.

(2) Every order made under this section shall, as soon as may be after it is made, be laid before each House of Parliament.

31. Repeal—The Freedom of Information Act, 2002 (5 of 2003) is hereby repealed.

THE FIRST SCHEDULE

[See Sections 13(3) and 16(3)]

Form of oath or affirmation to be made by the Chief Information Commissioner/the Information Commissioner/the State Chief Information Commissioner/the State Information Commissioner

"I, __________, having been appointed Chief Information Commissioner/Information Commissioner/State Chief Information Commissioner/State Information Commissioner swear in the name of God solemnly affirm that I will bear true faith and allegiance to the Constitution of India as by law established, that I will uphold the sovereignty and integrity of India, that I will duly and faithfully and to the best of my ability, knowledge and judgment perform the duties of my office without fear or favour, affection or ill-will and that I will uphold the Constitution and the laws.".

THE SECOND SCHEDULE

[See Section 24]

Intelligence and security organisation established by the Central Government

1. Intelligence Bureau.
2. Research and Analysis Wing of the Cabinet Secretariat.
3. Directorate of Revenue Intelligence.
4. Central Economic Intelligence Bureau.
5. Directorate of Enforcement.
6. Narcotics Control Bureau.
7. Aviation Research Centre.
8. Special Frontier Force.
9. Border Security Force.
10. Central Reserve Police Force.
11. Indo-Tibetan Border Police.
12. Central Industrial Security Force.
13. National Security Guards.
14. Assam Rifles.
15. Special Service Bureau
16. Special Branch (CID), Andaman and Nicobar.

17. The Crime Branch-C.I.D.-CB, Dadra and Nagar Haveli.
18. Special Branch, Lakshadweep Police.

9.1.6 Provision of a Transparent, Clean and Efficient Administration

"The Government pledges to adopt all means necessary to provide a transparent, clean and efficient administration in the State. The concept of "file closing week" will be implemented to ensure expeditious clearing of files within 9 days. E-governance will be employed to facilitate citizen-government interface".

1. Certain provisions are already in existence in the Secretariat Office Manual defining the duties and responsibilities of Assistant Officers/Section Officers/Under Secretary/Deputy Secretary/Joint Secretary relating to checking of delays and arrears (Both internal and external arrears). Similar provisions for checking the delays and arrears were available in the Tamil Nadu Government Office Manual also. As per the instructions contained in Paragraph 306 (1) of Secretariat Office Manual, the papers received should normally be submitted to officers within a period of five-days from the date of their receipts. But specific period has not been prescribed for the closure of such papers. However, in a G.O.Ms.No.89, Personnel and Administrative Reforms (A) Department, dated 13.5.99, certain time limit has been prescribed for the disposal of Petitions received in Government Offices as indicated below:

(a) One week for giving acknowledgement to the petitioners.
(b) 30 days for giving final reply for which time has not been statutorily prescribed.
(c) 90 days for giving final reply in other cases.

2. Considering the development in the electronic communication system, the Government feels that it is necessary to prescribe certain procedures for making the Public aware of the transparent and speedy disposal of the petitions received in the Government Offices.

3. The Government accordingly, direct that each office having direct dealings with the Public should take speedy action to publish the rules and regulations on welfare schemes so as to enable the Public to be aware of these schemes. They should also take immediate action on the grievance petitions received from the Public/Government Officials as detailed below:

(a) The petition should be disposed of within a period of 90 (ninety) days at any cost.
(b) File closing weeks be conducted on every Monday (or on the next working day if Monday is holiday) just like Public Grievances Day observed by District Collectors. The result of action taken on each petition should be intimated to the petitioner.
(c) Secretaries to Government are requested to critically review the pending cases and issue suitable instructions to the authority concerned.
(d) Necessary entries should also be made in the Computer Network then and there updating the action taken.

4. Necessary amendment to Secretariat Office Manual and Tamil Nadu Government office Manual will be issued separately.

(G.O. Ms. No. 104 dated 15.6.2001 of Personnel and Administrative Reforms Department).

PART X

TAMIL NADU TRANSPARENCY IN TENDERS ACT, 1998

10.1 TAMIL NADU TRANSPARENCY IN TENDERS ACT, 1998

10.1.1 Tamil Nadu Transparency in Tenders Act, 1998

1. Short title, extent and commencement—(1) This Act may be called the Tamil Nadu Transparency in Tenders Act, 1998.

(2) It extends to the whole of the State of Tamil Nadu.

(3) It shall come into force on such date as the Government may, by notification, appoint.

2. Definition—In this Act, unless the context otherwise requires:

(a) 'Construction' means all works associated with the construction, reconstruction, demolition, repair or renovation of a building, structure or any other related works;

(b) 'Goods' means raw materials, products, equipment and other objects of every kind and description and includes electricity;

(c) 'Government' means the State Government;

(d) 'Procurement' means acquisition by any means by purchase of goods or services and also of construction;

(e) 'Procuring entity' means the entity specified in the Schedule to this Act;

(f) 'Tender' means the formal offer made in pursuance of an invitation by the procuring entity;

(g) 'Tender Bulletin' means the bulletin published for each district or State, containing details of invitation and acceptance of tender;

(h) 'Tender Bulletin Officer' means any officer appointed by the government to publish the district or State Tender Bulletin;

(i) 'Tender Document' means a set of papers containing schedule of works, rates, requirement of goods or services technical specifications, procedure and criteria as may be prescribed for evaluation and comparison of tenders and such other particulars as may be prescribed.

3. Prohibition or Procurement except by tender—(1) No procurement shall be made by the procuring entity except by tender.

(2) The provisions of Sections 9 and 10 shall not apply to any procurement made by a procuring entity, in the normal course, if it is for carrying on business of selling and buying goods:

Provided that in case of procurement by the procuring entities on behalf of and for sale to Government or Government organisations for any Government programme, such procurement shall be only by tender.

4. Regulation of tenders—No tender shall be invited or accepted by any authority after the commencement of this Act, except in accordance with the procedure specified in this Act and the rules made thereunder.

5. Appointment of bulletin officer—The government may, by notification appoint

(a) an officer of the Government not below the rank of a Deputy Secretary to Government as State Tender Bulletin Officer;

(b) an officer not below the rank of a Deputy Collector as District Tender Bulletin Officer for every district.

6. Functions of bulletin officer—(1) On receipt of intimation relating to details of notice of invitation of Tender, from the Tender Inviting Authority, information relating to acceptance of tender together with a comparative analysis and reasons for acceptance of tenders from the Tender Accepting Authority, the State or as the case may be, the District Tender Bulletin Officer shall, publish the same in the State or District Tender Bulletin, as the case may be within such time as may be prescribed:

Provided that, if the procurement covers more than one district, the invitation and acceptance of tenders shall be published in the State Tender

Bulletin and also in the District Tender Bulletin of such districts.

(2) The Tender Bulletin shall be made available for sale in the office of the Tender Bulletin Officer and at such other places as may be specified by him.

7. Appointment of tender inviting authority and tender accepting authority—(1) The Government or the procuring entity, may, by order, appoint an officer under its control as Tender Inviting Authority for carrying out the functions assigned to it under this Act.

(2) The Government or the procuring entity, may, by order, appoint an officer or a committee consisting such number of officers as may be prescribed as Tender Accepting Authority for carrying out the functions assigned to it under this Act.

(3) Not withstanding anything contained in sub-sections (a) and (b):

(a) where the Government is the Tender Accepting Authority, Tamil Nadu Government Business Rules shall be followed for tender acceptance ensuring adherence to the other provisions of this Act.

(b) where a multi-member Tender Accepting Authority is discharging its functions under other Acts, such Multi-member Authority shall be deemed to be Tender Accepting Authority under this Act.

8. Opening of tender—The Tender Accepting Authority or any other officer authorised by it, shall open the tenders in the presence of tenderers present and who have submitted tenders in such time and in such place as may be specified in the tender document.

9. Functions of tender inviting authority—(1) The Tender Inviting Authority shall invite tenders in the form of a notice containing such particulars as may be prescribed.

(2) The Tender Inviting Authority shall communicate the notice inviting tenders to the Bulletin Officers according to the value of the procurement and within such time as may be prescribed, so as to publish the same in the appropriate Tender Bulletin.

(3) The Tender Inviting Authority shall also publish the notice inviting tenders in Indian Trade Journal and in daily newspapers having wide circulation depending upon the value of the procurement prescribed.

(4) The Tender Inviting Authority shall supply the schedule of rates and tender documents in such manner and in such places as may be prescribed to every intending tenderer who has applied for such document.

10. Evaluation and acceptance of tender—(1) The Tender Accepting Authority shall cause an objective evaluation of the tender taking into consideration the schedule of rates as mentioned in the tender document and the prevailing market rate for procurement and comparison of the tenders in accordance with the procedure and criteria specified in the tender document.

(2) After evaluation and comparison of tenders as specified in sub-section (1), the Tender Accepting Authority shall accept the lowest tender ascertained on the basis of objective and quantifiable factors specified in the tender document and giving relative weights among them.

(3) Notwithstanding anything contained in sub-section (2), if the Tender Accepting Authority decides that the prices of the lowest tender is higher with reference to the prevailing market rate or the schedule of rates, he may negotiate for a reduction of price with that tenderer.

(4) If at any time before the acceptance of tender, the Tender Accepting Authority receives information that a tenderer who has submitted tender has been banned by any procuring entity, he shall not accept the tender of that tenderer even if it may be the lowest tender.

(5) In case where two or more tenderer quoted the same price, the Tender Accepting Authority shall split the procurement among such tenderers taking into consideration the experience and credentials of such tenderers. Where such splitting is not possible or could not be done equally, he shall record reasons for the same.

(6) If the Tender Accepting Authority proposes to accept the tender as per the provisions of this section, he shall pass orders accepting the tender together with reasons for such acceptance.

(7) The Tender Accepting Authority shall intimate the information regarding the name and address of the tenderer whose tender has been accepted along with the reasons for rejection of other tenders to the appropriate Tender Bulletin Officers.

11. Appeal—(1) Any tenderer aggrieved by the order passed by the Tender Accepting Authority under Section 10 may appeal to the Government within ten days from the date of receipt of order and the Government shall dispose the appeal within fifteen days from the date of receipt.

(2) In disposing of an appeal under sub-section (1), the Government may, after giving the party an opportunity of making his representations, pass such order thereon as they may deem fit.

(3) The order of the Government on such appeal shall be final.

(4) The Government may, pending the exercise of their powers under this section pass such interlocutory orders as they may deem fit.

12. Right to reject tender—(1) After negotiation with the tenderer and before passing the order accepting a tender as under sub-section (6) of Section 10, if the Tender Accepting Authority decides that the price quoted by such tenderer is higher by the percentage as may be prescribed over the schedule of rates or prevailing market price, he shall reject the tender.

(2) The Tender Accepting Authority before passing the order accepting a tender may also reject all the tenders for reasons such as changes in the scope of procurement, new technologies or substantial design changes, lack of anticipated financial resources, court orders, accidents or calamities and other unforeseen circumstances.

13. Power to obtain information—Notwithstanding anything contained in this Act or in any other law for the time being in force, the government may with a view to ensuring transparency in tender process, by order in writing, call for any information relating to transparency from the Tender Inviting Authority or from the Tender Accepting Authority on any matter in tender processing and the said authority shall furnish the same to the Government.

14. Power of Government to call for records—The Government may at any time, with a view to ensuring transparency in tender, process, require any authority:

(a) to produce records relating to invitation and acceptance of tenders;

(b) to furnish the tender document, estimate, statement, accounts or statistics relating to such tenders; and

(c) to furnish any report.

15. Procedure to be followed in certain cases—The provisions of this Act to the extent they are not consistent with the procedure prescribed in the Projects funded by International Agreements or by International Financial Agencies shall not apply.

16. Provisions of this Act not to apply in certain cases—The provisions of Sections 9 and 10 shall not apply to procurement

(a) during natural calamities and emergencies declared by the Government;

(b) available from a single source only from a supplier or cases in which a particular supplier or contractor has exclusive rights in respect of the goods or services or construction and no reasonable alternative or substitute exists or where the procuring entity having procured goods, equipment technology from a supplier or contractor determines that additional supplies must be procured from that specific supplier or contractor for reasons of standardisation and compatibility with the existing goods, equipment or technology:
Provided that a committee of three experts consisting one technical representatives of the procuring entity, one technical representative of a State or Central Government Organisation dealing with similar procurement and one representative from a reputed Academic or Research Institution or Non-commercial Institution having expertise in such line, declares it as single source procurement;

(c) from certain departments of Government, public sector undertakings, statutory boards and such other institutions only in respect of goods manufactured or services provided by them for a period not exceeding two years from the date of commencement of this Act;

(d) of low value and local purchase as may be prescribed;

(e) from the rate contract of Director General of Supplies and Disposals and Association of State Road Transport Undertakings; and

(f) by spot purchase of cotton by Spinning Mills, Oil seeds and Oils by Tamil Nadu Agro Industries Corporation or Tamil Nadu Co-operative Oil Seeds Grower's Federation Limited, animals from shandies, Sugarcane by Sugar Mills, Paddy by Direct purchase centres of the Tamil Nadu Civil Supplies Corporation, Clothing by Co-optex from registered Primary Weaver Co-operative, Milk by Tamil Nadu Co-operative Milk Producer Federation from Districts and Primary Milk Co-operative Societies, Palm Oil by Tamil Nadu Civil Supplies Corporation from Tamil Nadu Co-operative Oil Seeds Growers' Federation for Noon Meal scheme, Clothing by Government Departments, Public Sector Undertakings and statutory departments form Co-optex and similar organisations and materials as may be notified by Government.

17. Central Act XLV of 1860 Officers deemed to be public servants—Every Officer acting under or in pursuance of, the provisions of this Act or rule or order or notification made thereunder, shall be deemed to be public servant within the meaning of Section 21 of the Indian Penal Code.

18. Indemnity—No suit or other legal proceeding shall lie against the Government or any officer or authority of the Government in respect of anything which is in good faith done or intended to be done.

19. Bar of Jurisdiction—Save as otherwise provided in this Act no order passed or proceeding taken by any officer or authority under this Act shall be called in question in any court and no injunction shall be granted by any court in respect of any action taken or to be taken by such officer or authority in pursuance of any power conferred by or under this Act.

20. Act to override other laws—The provision of this Act shall have effect notwithstanding anything inconsistent therewith contained in any other law for the time being in force or any custom or usage or agreement or decree or order of a Court or a Tribunal or other authority.

21. Power to remove difficulties—If any difficulty arises in giving effect to the provisions of this Act, the government may, by an order published in the Tamil Nadu Government Gazette, make such provision, not inconsistent with the provisions of this Act as appear to them to be necessary or expedient for removing the difficulty:

Provided that no such order shall be made after the expiry of a period of two years from the date of commencement of this Act.

22. Power to make rules—(1) The Government make rules for carrying out the purposes of this Act.

(2) (a) All rules made under this Act shall be published in the Tamil Nadu Government Gazette and unless they are expressed to come into force on a particular day, shall come into force on the date on which they are so published.

(b) All notifications issued under this Act shall, unless they are expressed to come into force on a particular day, come into force on the day on which they are published.

(3) Every rule made or notification or order issued under this Act shall as soon as possible, after it is made or issued, be placed on the table of the Legislative Assembly, and if, before the expiry of the session in which it is so placed or the next session, the Assembly makes any modification in any such rule or notification or order, or the Assembly decides that the rule or notification or order should not be made or issued, the rule or notification or order shall thereafter have effect only in such modified form or to be of no effect as the case may be, so, however, that any such modification or annulment shall be without prejudice to the validity of anything previously done under that rule or notification or order.

23. Savings—All the existing rules, regulations, departmental codes, manuals, orders shall so far as they are not inconsistent with the provisions of this Act and the rules made thereunder, continue in force.

(G.O. Ms. No. 445, Finance Department, dated 26th September, 2000)

THE SCHEDULE
[See Section 2 (c)]
Procuring Entity

1. Government Departments
2. Public sector undertaking of the government
3. Statutory boards formed by the government
4. Local bodies in the state
5. Co-operative institutions in the state
6. Universities
7. Societies formed by the government

10.1.2 Tamil Nadu Transparency in Tenders Act, 1998, Date of Coming into Force of the Act

In exercise of the powers conferred by sub-section (3) of Section 1 of the Tamil Nadu Transparency in Tenders Act, 1998 (Tamil Nadu Act 43 of 1998) the Governor of Tamil Nadu hereby appoints the first day of October 2000 as the date on which the said Act shall come into force.

10.1.3 Tamil Nadu Transparency in Tenders Rules, 2000

CHAPTER I
PRELIMINARY

1. Short title and commencement

(a) These rules may be called the Tamil Nadu Transparency in Tenders Rules, 2000.

(b) They shall come into force on the date 1st October, 2000.

2. **Definitions**—In these rules, unless there is anything repugnant in the subject or context,

(a) "act" means the Tamil Nadu Transparency in Tenders Act, 1998 (Tamil Nadu Act 43 of 1998);

(b) "supply and installation contract" means a contract under which the tenderer is required to supply, erect, test and commission the equipment at the place specified by the procuring entity;

(c) "fixed rate contract" means a contract where a set of rates and terms and conditions are fixed for the supply of unit quantities of goods or certain standardized services;

(d) "pre-qualification" means the process by which the tenderers are first screened for their capability and resources to implement the contract before they are permitted to offer their tenders;

(e) "two-cover system" means a procedure under which the tenderers are required to simultaneously submit two separate sealed covers, one containing the Earnest Money Deposit and the details of their capability to undertake the tender which will be opened first and the second cover containing the price quotation which will be opened only if the tenderer is found qualified to execute the tender;

(f) "earnest money deposit" means the amount required to be remitted by a tenderer along with his tender indicating his willingness to implement the contract; and

(g) "piece-work contract" and "lump sum contract" shall have the same meaning as in the Tamil Nadu Public Works Department Code.

CHAPTER II
GENERAL

3. **Categories of procurement**—(1) For the purposes of the application of these rules, procurement is categorized as follows, namely

(i) Construction; and

(ii) Supply of goods and services.

(2) While the provision of these rules shall apply in general to each of the categories of procurement in sub-rule (1), where a specific provision has been made in the rules regarding any specific category, that specific provision shall prevail as against any general provision in so far as that category of procurement is concerned.

4. **Methods of tendering**—(1) Procurement of different categories shall be effected by the following methods of tendering, namely

(i) Piece-work contract;

(ii) Lump sum contract;

(iii) Turn-key contract;

(iv) Multi-stage contracting including pre-qualification and two cover system; and

(v) Fixed rate contract.

(2) The tender inviting authority shall decide the method of tendering to be followed in each case having regard to the category, size and complexity of the procurement.

(3) While the provisions of these rules shall apply to each of the methods of procurement indicated in sub-rule (1) generally where a specific provision has been made in these rules regarding a particular method of tendering such specific provision shall prevail as against any general provision in so far as that particular method of tendering is concerned.

CHAPTER III
PUBLICITY

5. **Publication of tender bulletin**—(1) The District Tender Bulletin shall be published by the District Bulletin Officer atleast once in every week.

(2) The State Tender Bulletin shall be published by the State Tender Bulletin Officer at least once in every week.

(3) The Tender Bulletin Office shall cause to be published all notices inviting tenders and intimations of acceptance of tenders received upto twenty four hours prior to the actual publication of the bulletin.

(4) In case a notice inviting tender or information relating to acceptance of the tender needs to be published urgently, then the Secretary to Government of the concerned administrative department in the case of the State Tender Bulletin or the District Collector in the case of the District Tender Bulletin can for reasons to be recorded in writing, direct the

respective tender bulletin officers to publish an extraordinary issue of the tender bulletin.

6. Distribution of tender bulletins—(1) The Tender Bulletin Officer shall make the tender bulletin available at any office of a Government department, local authority, statutory board, public sector undertaking, local body, university or co-operative institution.

(2) The Tender Bulletin Officer shall make available adequate copies of the tender bulletin at the office of the Tender Inviting Authority whose notice inviting tenders and intimation of tender acceptance finds place in the bulletin.

(3) Any person or institution can be enrolled as a regular subscriber to the tender bulletin on payment of a fixed fee annually, half-yearly or quarterly as the case may be.

7. Tender bulletin to contain information only—(1) The tender bulletin shall contain only information of the notice inviting tenders and the orders accepting a tender and does not in itself create a legal right or liability.

(2) A notice inviting tender will not be invalidated merely on the grounds that the notice although published in newspapers has not been published in one or the other of the District Tender Bulletins or State Tender Bulletins or when published in the State Tender Bulletin could not be published in a District Tender Bulletin or *vice versa*.

8. Information to be published in the district tender bulletin—Subject to the provisions of Rule 10, notice inviting tenders and decisions on tenders in all cases where the value of the procurement exceeds rupees five lakhs or below rupees twenty five lakhs shall be published in the District Tender Bulletin of the district where the headquarters of the Tender Inviting Authority is located and in the district where the work is to be executed or goods and services supplied.

9. Information to be published in the state tender bulletin—The notice inviting tenders and decisions on tenders shall be published in the State Tender Bulletin in cases where

(a) the value of procurement exceeds rupees twenty five lakhs.

(b) the Tender Inviting Authority is a Secretary to Government, or a head of a Government department, or Local Authority or the Chief Executive of a Public Sector Undertaking, Statutory Board, Apex Co-operative Institution, University or State Level Society formed by the Government.

(c) in any other case, where the Tender Inviting Authority deems it fit.

10. Details to be mentioned in notice inviting tenders—The Notice Inviting Tenders shall contain the following details, namely

(a) The name and address of the procuring entity and the designation and address of the Tender Inviting Authority;

(b) Name of the scheme, project or programme for which the procurement is to be effected;

(c) The date upto which and places from where the tender documents can be obtained;

(d) The amount of earnest money deposit payable;

(e) The last date and time for receipt of tenders;

(f) The date, time and place for opening of tenders received; and

(g) Any other information the Tender Inviting Authority considers relevant.

11. Publication of notice inviting tenders in newspapers—(1) The Tender Inviting Authority shall have the notice inviting tenders published in the Indian Trade Journal in all cases where the value of procurement exceeds rupees ten crores.

(2) The number, editions and language of the newspapers in which the notices inviting tenders shall be published will be based on the value of procurement.

(3) In cases where publication of Tender Notices is to be done only in Newspapers with circulation within the District, the Information and Public Relations Officer attached to the District Collectorate shall be the competent authority to release the advertisement and in all other cases the competent authority to release the advertisement shall be the Director of Information and Public Relations, Chennai.

(4) The notice inviting tender shall be given due publicity in Newspapers and also on notice boards in the District Offices. For tenders above rupees fifty lakhs Director of Information and Public Relations will publish the Notice Inviting Tenders as per instructions of the tendering department. For other tenders, Director of Information and Public Relations will publish keeping in mind the request of the department. There should not be any additional insertion and no publication of Notice Inviting Tenders in newspapers not requested by the tendering departments for tenders above rupees fifty lakhs.

12. Sending notice inviting tenders to all possible tenderers—The Tender Inviting Authority may if he considers necessary, send the Notice Inviting Tenders to all possible tenderers including registered contractor, past supplier, any potential supplier and any other well known company or firm directly.

CHAPTER IV
NOTICE INVITING TENDERS AND TENDER DOCUMENTS

13. Technical specifications contained in the tender documents—(1) The technical specifications contained in the tender documents shall include a detailed description of what is proposed to be procured.

(2) Unbiased technical specifications shall be prepared by observing the following safeguard, namely

(a) Use of brand names and catalogue numbers shall be avoided and where it becomes unavoidable, along with the brand name the expression "or equivalent" shall be added;

(b) Wherever possible the appropriate Indian Standard with the number shall be incorporated;

(c) In the case of construction tenders, detailed estimates shall be prepared by the competent technical authorities based on the schedule of rates and standard date as revised from time-to-time provided that for large and prestigious projects, the Government shall permit any procuring entity to engage a qualified private architect or consultant to prepare the design and estimates; and

(d) In case alternative designs or materials are permitted, the conditions for their acceptability and the method of their evaluation shall be clearly stated.

14. Commercial conditions—(1) The tender documents shall require all tenderers without exception to pay an earnest money deposit ordinarily not exceeding one per cent of the value of the procurement by means of a demand draft, bankers, cheque, specified small savings instruments or where the procuring entity deems fit, irrevocable bank guarantee in a prescribed form. The tender document shall clearly state that any tender submitted without the earnest money deposit in the approved form be summarily rejected provideu that any category of tenderers specifically exempted by the Government from the payment of earnest money deposit will not be required to make such a deposit.

(2) The tender documents shall specify the period for which the tenderer should hold the prices offered in the tender valid:

Provided that the initial period of validity shall not be less than ninety days.

(3) The tender documents shall require that as a guarantee of the tenderer's performance of the contract, a security deposit be taken from the successful tenderer subject to the conditions that

(a) the amount of the deposit not exceeding five per cent of the value of the orders placed; and

(b) the deposit being in the form of demand draft or bankers cheque or specified small savings instruments or where the procuring entity deems fit, irrevocable bank guarantee in a prescribed form.

(4) The tender documents shall clearly indicate the payment terms conforming to the following requirements:

(a) Payment shall ordinarily be effected only on completion of delivery against the orders placed, subject to the exceptions specified in the tender documents.

(b) Mobilization advances may be paid in the case of construction or supply and installation contracts of a large and complex nature, for a value exceeding rupees one crore provided that such mobilization advance shall not ordinarily exceed ten per cent of the value of the contract, shall be secured against irrevocable bank guarantee and shall be recovered in the subsequent bills payable along with interest as per specific terms set in the tender documents provided that in case of mobilisation advance for plant machinery and equipment, they are also hypothecated to the Governor of Tamil Nadu in addition to other requirements.

(c) Percentage of payment to be withheld for the effective performance of the contract, provided that withheld amount do not exceed ten per cent of the total value of contract;

(d) Payment terms for imports shall be based on standard terms of international trade and the payment may be effected through irrevocable letters of credit drawn on banks;

(5) The tender documents shall clearly indicate whether any variations in the commercial terms prescribed in the documents will be permitted and if so to what extent such variations would be considered.

(6) The tender documents and the contract shall include a clause for payment of liquidated damages

and penalty payable by the tenderer in the event of non-fulfilment of any or whole of the contract.

(7) The tender documents shall clearly indicate the terms on which the tenders will be enquired to quote their price which should be inclusive of all costs of delivery at the final destination such as transportation, payment of duties and taxes leviable, insurance and any incidental services and giving the break up thereof.

(8) The tender documents shall include a price adjustment clause to reflect any changes either upward or downward in major cost components such as labour, equipment, material and fuel, based on a prescribed formula in the case of large contracts where the period of execution is likely to exceed eighteen months.

(9) The tender documents shall indicate the quantity proposed to be procured in the tender, and the tender accepting authority shall be ordinarily permitted to vary the quantity finally ordered only to the extent of twenty five per cent either way of the requirement indicted in the tender documents.

15. Tender documents to clearly specify evaluation criteria—(1) The tender documents shall clearly indicate the criteria in addition to price which are to be adopted for evaluating the tenders and how such criteria will be quantified or evaluated.

(2) The qualification criteria in terms of the required experience, available manufacturing and construction capacity, technical and other manpower and financial status shall be clearly stated in the tender documents.

16. Supply of tender documents—(1) The Tender Inviting Authority shall make available the tender documents from the date of publication of the tender.

(2) The Tender Inviting Authority shall ensure that the tender documents are made available to any person who is willing to remit the cost of the document provided that in the cases where the procuring entity as a system of registration of contractors, the tender documents will be supplied only to registered contractors in the appropriate class.

(3) The Tender documents shall be made available at the following officers, namely:

(a) the office of the Tender Inviting Authority.
(b) any other office or place indicted by the procuring entity.

(4) The Tender Inviting Authority shall send by registered post or courier the tender documents to any prospective tenderer who makes a request for the documents on payment of cost along with postal charges at the risk and responsibility of the prospective tenderer.

17. Clarification to tender documents—(1) At any time after the issue of the tender documents and before the opening of the tender, the Tender Inviting Authority may make any changes, modifications or amendments to the tender documents and shall send intimation of such change to all those who have purchased the original tender documents.

(2) In case any one tenderer asks for a clarification to the tender documents before 48 hours of the opening of the Tender, the Tender Inviting Authority shall ensure that a reply is sent and copies of the reply to the clarification sought will be communicated to all those who have purchased the tender document without identifying the source of the query.

CHAPTER V
RECEIPT OF TENDERS AND TENDER OPENING

18. Place and time for receipt of tenders—(1) The Tender Inviting Authority shall ensure that adequate arrangements are made for the proper receipt and safe custody of the tenders at the place indicated for the receipt of tenders.

(2) The Tender Inviting Authority shall take all measures to ensure that no intending tenderer is hindered in submitting his tender.

(3) The Tender Inviting Authority shall permit the submission of tenders by post or courier, provided that the Tender Inviting Authority shall not be responsible for any delay in transit in such cases.

(4) The Tender Inviting Authority shall not accept any tenders submitted by facsimile (Fax) or by electronic mail.

(5) The Tender Inviting Authority may extend the last date and time for receiving tenders after giving adequate notice to all intending tenders in cases where

(a) the publication of the tender notice has been delayed;
(b) the communication of changes, in the tender documents to the prospective tenderers under sub-rule (1) of Rule 17 took time;
(c) any of the tenderers requested clarifications communication of which took time to all the tenderers; and
(d) any other reasonable grounds exist, for such extension which shall be recorded in writing by the Tender Inviting Authority.

19. Marking of covers in which the tender is submitted—The tenderer shall be responsible for properly superscribing and sealing the cover in which the tender is submitted and the Tender Inviting Authority shall not be responsible for accidental opening of the covers that are not properly superscribed and sealed as required in the tender documents before the time appointed for tender opening.

20. Minimum time for submission of tenders—(1) The Tender Inviting Authority shall ensure that adequate time is provided for the submission of tenders and a minimum time is allowed between date of publication of the Notice Inviting Tenders in the relevant Tender Bulletin or in the newspapers whichever is later and the last date for submission of tenders. This minimum period shall be as follows:

(a) for tenders upto rupees two crores in value, fifteen days; and
(b) for tenders in excess of rupees two crores in value, thirty days.

(2) Any reduction in the time stipulated as per sub-rule (1) has to be specifically authorized by an authority superior to the Tender Inviting Authority for reasons to be recorded in writing.

21. Opening of tenders—(1) All the tenders received by the Tender Accepting Authority shall be opened at the time specified in the Notice Inviting Tenders and in cases where an extension of time for the submission of tenders had been given subsequent to the original Notice Inviting Tenders in accordance with sub-rule (5) of Rule 18 at the time so specified subsequently.

(2) The time specified for the opening of tenders shall be immediately after the closing time specified for the receipt of tenders allowing a reasonable period, not exceeding one hour, for the transportation of the tenders received to the place they are to be opened in the presence of the tenderers who choose to be present.

(3) The tenders will be opened in the presence of the tenderers or one representative of the tenderer who chooses to be present.

22. Procedure to be followed at tender opening—The following procedure shall be followed at the tender opening.

(1) All the envelopes received containing tenders shall be counted.

(2) All the tenders received in time shall be opened.

(3) Any tender received subsequently shall not be opened and shall be returned unopened to the tenderer.

(4) On opening the tender, the members of the Tender Scrutiny Committee shall initial the main bid including the prices and any corrections.

(5) A record of the corrections noticed at the time of the bid opening shall be maintained.

(6) The name of the tenderers and the quoted prices should be read out aloud.

(7) The fact whether earnest money deposit has been submitted and other documents required produced may be indicated, but this shall be merely an examination of the documents and not an evaluation.

(8) Minutes of the tender opening shall be recorded. The signatures of the tenderers present shall be obtained unless any of the tenderers or his representative refuses to sign the minutes.

23. Changes and alterations not to be permitted after tender opening—No changes, amendments which materially alter the tendered prices shall be permitted after the opening of the tender, except as per the procedure prescribed in sub-section (3) of Section 10 of the Act.

24. Tender scrutiny committee—(1) A Tender Scrutiny Committee may be constituted to scrutinize the tender documents, supervise opening of tenders, to carry out the preliminary examination and detailed evaluation of the tenders received and to prepare an evolution report for the consideration of the Tender Accepting Authority.

(2) The constitution of a Tender Scrutiny Committee will be obligatory in all cases where the value of the procurement exceeds limit as may be specified.

CHAPTER VI
TENDER EVALUATION

25. Tender evaluation to be in accordance with evaluation criteria—The Tender Accepting Authority shall cause the evaluation of tenders to be carried out strictly in accordance with the evaluation criteria indicted in the tender documents.

26. Time taken for evaluation and extension of tender validity—(1) The evaluation of tenders and awards of contract shall be completed, as far as may be practicable, within the period for which the tenders are held valid.

(2) The Tender Accepting Authority shall seek extension of the validity of tenders for the completion of evaluations.

(3) In case the evaluation of tenders and award of contract is not completed within extended validity period all the tenders shall be deemed to

have become invalid and fresh tenders may be called for.

27. Process of tender evaluation to be confidential until the award of the contract is notified—(1) Subject to the provision of Sections 12 and 13 of the Act, the Tender Inviting Authority shall ensure the confidentiality of the process of tender evaluation until orders on the tenders are passed.

(2) The Tender Accepting Authority shall cause the information on orders passed on the tenders published in the Tender Bulletin.

(3) Tenderers shall not make attempts to establish unsolicited and unauthorised contact with the Tender Accepting Authority. Tender Inviting Authority or Tender Scrutiny Committee after the opening of the Tender and prior to the notification of the Award and any attempt by any tenderer to bring to bear extraneous pressures on the Tender Accepting Authority shall be sufficient reason to disqualify the tenderer.

(4) Notwithstanding anything contained in sub-rule (3), the Tender Inviting Authority or the Tender Accepting Authority may seek *bonafide* clarifications from tenders relating to the tenders submitted by them during the evaluation of tenders.

28. Initial examination to determine substantial responsiveness—(1) The Tender Inviting Authority shall cause an initial examination of the tenders submitted to be carried out in order to determine their substantial responsiveness.

(2) The initial examination shall consider the following factors, namely

(*a*) Whether the tenderer meets the eligibility criteria laid down in the tender documents;

(*b*) Whether the crucial documents have been duly signed;

(*c*) Whether the requisite earnest money deposit has been furnished;

(*d*) Whether the tender is substantially responsive to the technical specifications, commercial conditions set out in the biding documents including the testing of samples where required

(3) Tenders which on initial examination are found not to be substantially responsive under any of the clauses under sub-rule (2) may be rejected by the Tender Accepting Authority.

29. Determination of the lowest evaluated price—(1) Out of the tenders found to be substantially responsive after the initial examination the tenderer who has bid the lowest evaluated price in accordance with the evaluation criteria or the tenderer scoring the highest on the evaluation criteria specified as the case may be shall be determined.

(2) In determining the lowest evaluated price, the following factors shall be considered, namely

(*a*) the quoted price shall be corrected for arithmetical errors;

(*b*) in cases of discrepancy between the prices quoted in words and in figures, lower of the two shall be considered;

(*c*) adjustments to the price quoted shall be made for deviations in the commercial conditions such as the delivery schedules and minor variations in the payment terms which are quantifiable but deemed to be non-material in the context of the particular tender;

(*d*) the evaluation shall include all central duties such as customs duty and central excise duty as a part of the price, but shall exclude sales tax if the bidders are from other States and Tamil Nadu;

(*e*) in the case of purchase of equipment, the operation and maintenance and spare part costs for appropriate periods as may be specified in bid documents may be quantified, where practicable and considered.

(3) In order to secure the best possible procurement price, negotiations with tenderer determined as per clauses (1) and (2) above are permissible subject to provisions in Section 10 of the Act.

30. Preparation of evaluation report and award of tenders—(1) The Tender Scrutiny Committee or the officer evaluating the tender shall prepare detailed evaluation report which shall be considered by the Tender Accepting Authority before taking a final decision of the tender.

(2) The evaluation report shall be prepared in the standardized format as may be prescribed.

(3) As soon as the tenderer qualified to perform the contract is identified, in accordance with Section 10(6) of the Act. The Tender Accepting Authority shall pass order accepting the tender and communicate the order of acceptance to the successful tenderer. The Tender Accepting Authority will also send to the Tender Bulletin Officer a statement of evaluation of the tenders with a comparative statement of tender received and decision thereon for publication in the Tender Bulletin.

(4) Within such reasonable time as may be indicated in the tender documents, the tenderer whose tender has been accepted will be required to execute the contract agreement in the prescribed format.

(5) In case the successful tenderer fails to execute necessary agreements as prescribed within the period specified, then his Earnest Money Deposit shall be forfeited and his tender held as a non-responsive.

CHAPTER VII
EVALUATION AND AWARD OF TENDERS IN SPECIAL CASES

31. Procurement in special cases—In the case of purchase of goods where the quantity offered at the lowest price is less than the total quantity required, the Tender Accepting Authority may, after placing orders with the lowest evaluated tenderer for the entire quantity offered by such tenderer subject to his ability to supply, adopt either both of the following procedures to procure the balance quantity:

1. Negotiate with the next lowest tenderer in strict ascending order of evaluated price and require them to match the price offered by the lowest evaluated tenderer and place orders until the entire quantity required is ordered; or

2. Require all the other eligible tenderers who participated in the tender and offered a price higher than that offered by the lowest evaluated tenderer, to submit sealed offers of the quantity they would be willing to supply at the price quoted by the lowest evaluated tenderer, and thereafter place order for the remaining required quantity with all those who match the lowest evaluated price such that those who bid lower prices in the original tender get a higher priority for supply.

3. In case the bidders other than lowest evaluated bidder fail to agree to accept the lowest price or the total quantity offered by them at the price quoted by the tenderer with lowest evaluated price is less than the required quantity the Tender Accepting Authority may place orders for remaining required quantity at different rates with different suppliers in the ascending order of evaluated price until the entire quantity at different rates with different suppliers in the ascending order of evaluated price until the entire quantity required is covered:

Provided that, where different quantities have to be procured at more than one price from one or more tender, the Tenders Accepting Authority may decide not to procure beyond a price considered economical although the entire quantity originally stated to be required in the tender documents is not ordered.

4. In cases where the Tender Accepting Authority such as Tamil Nadu Electricity Board, Tamil Nadu Civil Supplies Corporation, Project Director, Integrated Child Development Scheme (ICDS) is of the view that the commodity to be purchased is so vital nature and the failure in supply would affect the public interest and that it is necessary to have more than one supplier, the Authority may place orders on the tenderer quoting the lowest evaluated price for not less than 60 per cent of the quantity covered in the tender at the price quoted by him and place orders for the remaining quantity on the tenderers quoting the next lowest evaluated prices at the lowest evaluated price and shall specify this is the tender documents.

32. Pre-qualification procedure—(1) The Tender Inviting Authority shall for reasons to be recorded in writing provide for pre-qualification of tenderers on the basis of:

(a) experience and past performance in the execution of similar contracts;
(b) capabilities of the tenderer with respect to personnel, equipment and construction or manufacturing facilities; and
(c) financial status and capacity.

(2) Only the bids of pre-qualified bidders shall be considered for evaluation.

33. Low value procurement—For the purposes of clause (d) of Section 16 of the Act, "low value procurement" means any procurement which is less than rupees two lakhs in value.

(G.O. Ms. No. 446, Finance Department, dated 26th September 2000)

10.1.4 State Tender Bulletin Officer/District Tender Bulletin Officers

Notification

In exercise of the powers conferred by clauses (a) and (b) of Section 5 of the Tamil Nadu Transparency in Tenders Act, 1998 (Tamil Nadu Act 43 of 1998), the Governor of Tamil Nadu hereby appoints the Joint Director (Information), Information and Tourism Department as State Tender Bulletin Officer and the District Public Relation Officer attached to the Collector of every District as District Tender Bulletin Officer for the respective districts.

(G.O. Ms. No.447, Finance Department, dated 26th September, 2000).

INDEX